lonely planet

Bali & Lombok

Paul Greenway
James Lyon
Tony Wheeler

[Handwritten annotations:]

Cantik = beautiful
indah = interesting
mengingan kan = to wish for
ingin tahu = to wonder
Membali = to buy
Memberikan = to give
melihat = to see
sampai = to come to
minggu lagu = yesterday

Ngukan = kata = word
Sibuk = busy
Sici = holy
tampan = handsome smart

LONELY PLANET PUBLICATIONS
Melbourne • Oakland • London • Paris

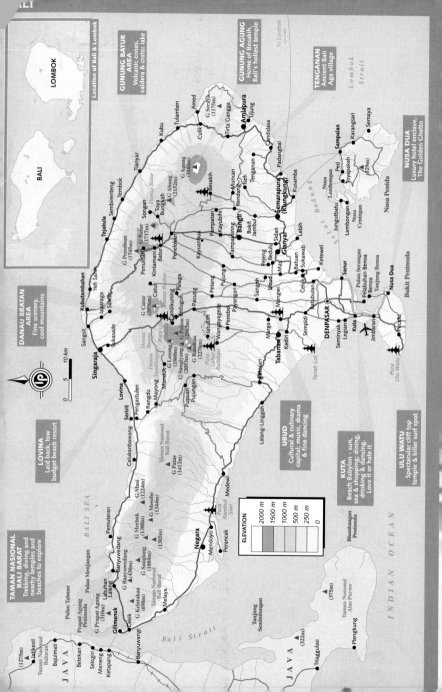

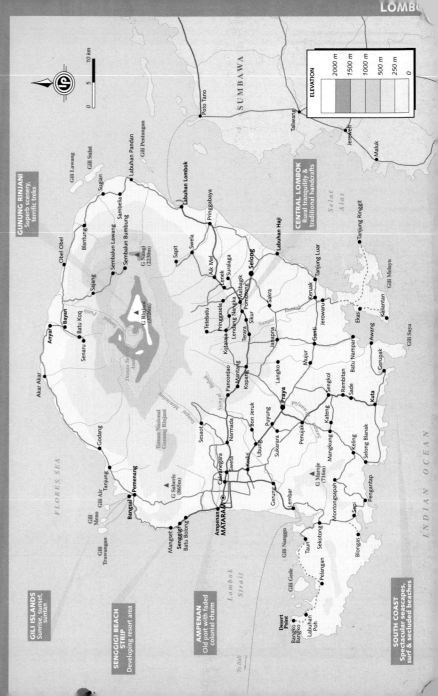

LOMBOK

Bali & Lombok
7th edition – February 1999
First published – January 1984

Published by
Lonely Planet Publications Pty Ltd A.C.N. 005 607 983
192 Burwood Rd, Hawthorn, Victoria 3122, Australia

Lonely Planet Offices
Australia PO Box 617, Hawthorn, Victoria 3122
USA 150 Linden St, Oakland, CA 94607
UK 10a Spring Place, London NW5 3BH
France 1 rue du Dahomey, 75011 Paris

Photographs
All of the images in this guide are available for licensing from
Lonely Planet Images.
email: lpi@lonelyplanet.com.au

Front cover photograph
Two enduring symbols of Bali – the lotus flower and stone carvings;
Richard I'Anson (Lonely Planet Images).

ISBN 0 86442 606 2

Printed by The Bookmaker Pty Ltd
Printed in China

Contents – Text

Contents – Maps

MAP LEGEND – SEE BACK PAGE

The Authors

Paul Greenway

Gratefully plucked from the blandness and security of the Australian Public Service, Paul has contributed to many Lonely Planet guides, including *Indonesia*, *Mongolia*, *Iran* and *Madagascar & Comoros*. During the rare times that he is not travelling (or writing, reading and dreaming about it), Paul relaxes to tuneless heavy metal music, eats and breathes Australian Rules football and will do anything (like going to Mongolia) to avoid settling down.

James Lyon

A sceptic by nature and a social scientist by training, James worked as an editor at Lonely Planet's Melbourne office before he 'jumped the fence' to become a researcher and writer. He's worked on Lonely Planet's *Mexico*, *Maldives*, *California* and *South America* guides, but still finds Bali the most exotic place on earth. His best experiences of Bali and Lombok include temple festivals, Balinese feasts, trekking on Rinjani, taking photos at sunrise and getting lost on back roads. He also likes Balinese gardens, gamelan music, street-stall snacks and Bintang beer.

Tony Wheeler

Tony was born in England, but grew up in Pakistan, the West Indies and the United States. He returned to England to do a degree in engineering and worked as an automotive engineer before returning to univesity to complete an MBA. It was around this time that he met Maureen, and in 1972 they set off on an overland trip through Asia to get travel out of their systems. Instead, they established Lonely Planet in Australia and built it into a travel publishing success. Tony and Maureen still travel for several months each year.

FROM THE AUTHOR

Paul Greenway Thanks to the many travellers and people in Bali who helped with information and directions, or, at least, a smile. The tourist offices in Denpasar, Kuta and Mataram were especially helpful. I am also grateful to Anne-Marie van Dam, my 'Dutch connection', who loves Indonesia as much as I do; Graeme Fay, at the Australian Consulate in Denpasar; and the unknown people at Bali Online. At Lonely Planet, thanks to Sue Galley and Kristin Odijk for sending me to Bali; the previous author, James Lyon, for creating the opportunity for me to go there; Peter Turner, for the information about trekking on Gunung Rinjani; and the long-suffering editors, cartographers and designers who had to battle with my manuscript and maps.

Acknowledgements

THANKS

Many thanks to the travellers who used the last edition and wrote to us with helpful hints, useful advice and interesting anecdotes:

Doris Abe, M Adamick, R Adams, K Adler, Freddy Agustian, M Albinson, Christina Almtun, Gil Alvarez, Dean Anderson, Geoff Anderson, D Aslanis, Beck & John Auderton, Anna Barbeau, Georgina Barnes, Chris Bater, Karin Baysen, H&M Berger, Brett Bigham, Michele Bindi, Roger Blairs, Lindsay Blake, Joe Bogacz, Doug Boleyn, Iain Booth, Melanie Borchers & Silvia, Harry Bos, David Boyall, Rudy Broers, Michael Browne, Kars JH Bruins, Judy Burgess, Stanley Burnton, Anthony Byrnes, Craig & Cathy Caddell, Ann Campion, Delgis Canahuate, Flavio Capozza, Tim Chambers, Bob Charlton, Ted Chi, Barry Chin, Jim Christopherson, Alison Cilliers, Peter Clark, Sandie Codron, Michael J Condran, Jason Cook, Jonathan Copeland, Inna Costantini, Michael L Cox, Todd Daniels, Sue Davis, D&E Dekort-Mesalles, Peter Deleuran, Buffy Dolling, Annick Donkers, Jo Donovan, John Dow, Mildred AJ Dumpel, K Dwelle, Hans Dieter Eisele, Barry & Helen Elswood, Sarah Emmort, Birgit Ensslin, Morten Erbs, Richard Essex, Tracy Ewen, Roger Fan, Elizabeth Faust, George & Susan Fesus, Michael Folk, Grant Four, Frederic Frantz, Dominique Fung, Erika Gagnon, Bill Galager, A Le Gale, Mike Galvin, Diana Gardener, Alan Garner, Lynn Garrett, Peter Giaschi, Francine Gignoro, Philippe Gignoro-Simmonds, Boyd Gilchrist, Jenny Gilder, Monique van Gils, Helen Godfrey, Mike Godfrey, J Goldman, Nick Goodyer, Gary & Carolyn Gracie, Chester Gudzowski, Rebecca Haagsma, Russell Hall, Svend Erik Hansen, Peter Hapmann, Nigel Hartnup, Gilbert Hascoet, J Hedmark, Arie Heij, Kristien Van den Hente, RB Hodgson, Christine Holbert, Paul Holt, M Hormel, Chris Howard, Marten Hubbeling, Betty Hughes, Helena Hultbring, Bruce Ingram, Torben Isager, John Ivanac, Wendy Jackson, Jenny Jacoby, Margaret Jensen, K Jensen, Peter Jensen, Iago Jones, Gregory Jones, Ron Jordon, Sharon Josef, JP Boxberger, Andreas Furre Kamphaung, Robert & Caro Kay, G Kechagioglou, Jo Kessel, Dana Kizlaitis, Nick Konier, Rianne van de Laar, Marc Lampo, I Wayne Landuh, Sigrid Langker, D Larsen, Heidi Larsen, Bridget Page Leary, Judith Leshner, Charlotte Lesson, Pauline Lewis, Cynthia Linggar, Ron Lister, Ian Loarden, Ellen Loomer, Fabrizio Loschi, Ante Lundberg, J Macfarlane, Dee Mahan, Patti Mailman, Mary Makena, John Marshall, J Mascall & Kids, Bruce Mattinson, Karsten Matzen, Roland Mayer, Sonia McBeath, Malcolm McComas, Dudley McFadden, Rhoda McKenzie, G McNeal, Dr Terrance Micnsek, Melanie Miles, Justine Millard, Ronald Mioch, Moura Modiman, Hassan Molla, David Morgan, Jane M S, Geoff Muirden, Ken Murray, N Myerson, Jerome Nhan, Russell O'Shea & Family, Shane O'Sullivan, Nicolai Oswald, Urska Pajer, A Parissi, Nick Park, Simone & Aris Petratos, Mervi Peurala, Richard Phillips, Mike Pifko, PooleAssociatesLtd, Alison & Simon Porges, H&W Prajogo, Sally Purbrick, Jemma Purdey, JR Purey-Cust, Adi Putra, Bob Radley, Stuart Rathbone, Bernt Ringvold, S Risto, Mark Robinson, R Robinson, Nia Roderick, David Rowan, Danny Sadler, Mie Saltoft, Adam Shapiro, Jamar Shaw, Loren Siebert, Ms RA Sierp, Ralph Simmonds, John Sims, Pettina Slade, Hans G Smaal, Lisa Smith, Annette Solyst, Nichola Stead, Sean Stevens, Karina Stockman, L Stopforth, Frode Storsker, Raden Supardi, Mike Tainton, Eriko Tanimoto, Santos Te, F&M Thebaud, Alice Thomas, C Tiligada, Mark Townson, Jim Trotter, David Troup, Harry Vandervoot, Lue Vang, Van Rees Vellinga, Norman Wake, Joachim Weber, Tony Weston, Terry White, Julie White, Christine Whitehead, Mort Winski, Grace Wong, Kia Bossom Wood, Helen Woodward, Ian Woolfenden, R Yates, Peter Yendell, Klaas De Young, Suellen Zim.

This Book

This edition of *Bali & Lombok* is the result of the work of several authors over a number of years. Tony Wheeler first covered the islands as part of his pioneering *South-East Asia on a shoestring* in the mid-70s. He then expanded and improved the coverage, in concert with Mary Coverton, to create the 1st edition of this title in 1984. Alan Samagalski updated both Bali and Lombok for the 2nd edition, Tony returned for the 3rd edition and James Lyon assisted him for the 4th. James covered both islands for the 5th and 6th editions. This 7th edition was updated by Paul Greenway

Thanks to Michael Slovsky for information that appears in the Bali and Lombok Arts sections, as well as access to the crafts in his Ishka shops in Melbourne. Thanks also to Kirk Wilcox for the original Bali surfing section, and to Haji Radiah of Lendang Nangka for assistance with the Sasak language section. The 200km bicycle tour of Bali is based on Hunt Kooiker's now out of print *Bali by Bicycle* book.

From the Publisher

This book was edited by Pete Cruttenden and mapped and laid out by Maree Styles in LP's Melbourne office. Tony Davidson and Mic Looby assisted Pete with editing and proofing, and Paul Piaia pitched in with the maps. Thanks to Jenny Bowman for her fab illustrations, Quentin Frayne for his work on the Language chapter, Margie Jung for the gorgeous cover, Tim Uden for his layout assistance and Kristin Odijk and Adam McCrow for their care and attention.

Foreword

ABOUT LONELY PLANET GUIDEBOOKS

The story begins with a classic travel adventure: Tony and Maureen Wheeler's 1972 journey across Europe and Asia to Australia. Useful information about the overland trail did not exist at that time, so Tony and Maureen published the first Lonely Planet guidebook to meet a growing need.

From a kitchen table, then from a tiny office in Melbourne (Australia), Lonely Planet has become the largest independent travel publisher in the world, an international company with offices in Melbourne, Oakland (USA), London (UK) and Paris (France).

Today Lonely Planet guidebooks cover the globe. There is an ever-growing list of books and there's information in a variety of forms and media. Some things haven't changed. The main aim is still to help make it possible for adventurous travellers to get out there – to explore and better understand the world.

At Lonely Planet we believe travellers can make a positive contribution to the countries they visit – if they respect their host communities and spend their money wisely. Since 1986 a percentage of the income from each book has been donated to aid projects and human rights campaigns.

Updates Lonely Planet thoroughly updates each guidebook as often as possible. This usually means there are around two years between editions, although for more unusual or more stable destinations the gap can be longer. Check the imprint page (following the colour map at the beginning of the book) for publication dates.

Between editions up-to-date information is available in two free newsletters – the paper *Planet Talk* and email *Comet* (to subscribe, contact any Lonely Planet office) – and on our Web site at www.lonelyplanet.com. The *Upgrades* section of the Web site covers a number of important and volatile destinations and is regularly updated by Lonely Planet authors. *Scoop* covers news and current affairs relevant to travellers. And, lastly, the *Thorn Tree* bulletin board, and *Postcards* section of the site carry unverified, but fascinating, reports from travellers.

Correspondence The process of creating new editions begins with the letters, postcards and emails received from travellers. This correspondence often includes suggestions, criticisms and comments about the current editions. Interesting excerpts are immediately passed on via newsletters and the Web site, and everything goes to our authors to be verified when they're researching on the road. We're keen to get more feedback from organisations or individuals who represent communities visited by travellers.

> Lonely Planet gathers information for everyone who's curious about the planet – and especially for those who explore it first-hand. Through guidebooks, phrasebooks, activity guides, maps, literature, newsletters, image library, TV series and Web site we act as an information exchange for a worldwide community of travellers.

Research Authors aim to gather sufficient practical information to enable travellers to make informed choices and to make the mechanics of a journey run smoothly. They also research historical and cultural background to help enrich the travel experience and allow travellers to understand and respond appropriately to cultural and environmental issues.

Authors don't stay in every hotel because that would mean spending a couple of months in each medium-sized city and, no, they don't eat at every restaurant because that would mean stretching belts beyond capacity. They do visit hotels and restaurants to check standards and prices, but feedback based on readers' direct experiences can be very helpful.

Many of our authors work undercover, others aren't so secretive. None of them accept freebies in exchange for positive write-ups. And none of our guidebooks contain any advertising.

Production Authors submit their raw manuscripts and maps to offices in Australia, USA, UK or France. Editors and cartographers – all experienced travellers themselves – then begin the process of assembling the pieces. When the book finally hits the shops some things are already out of date, we start getting feedback from readers, and the process begins again....

WARNING & REQUEST

Things change – prices go up, schedules change, good places go bad and bad places go bankrupt – nothing stays the same. So, if you find things better or worse, recently opened or long since closed, please tell us and help make the next edition even more accurate and useful. We genuinely value all the feedback we receive. Julie Young coordinates a well-travelled team that reads and acknowledges every letter, postcard and email and ensures that every morsel of information finds its way to the appropriate authors, editors and cartographers for verification.

Everyone who writes to us will find their name in the next edition of the appropriate guidebook. They will also receive the latest issue of *Planet Talk*, our quarterly printed newsletter, or *Comet*, our monthly email newsletter. Subscriptions to both newsletters are free. The very best contributions will be rewarded with a free guidebook.

Excerpts from your correspondence may appear in new editions of Lonely Planet guidebooks, the Lonely Planet Web site, *Planet Talk* or *Comet*, so please let us know if you *don't* want your letter published or your name acknowledged.

Send all correspondence to the Lonely Planet office closest to you:

Australia: PO Box 617, Hawthorn, Victoria 3122
UK: 10A Spring Place, London NW5 3BH
USA: 150 Linden St, Oakland CA 94607
France: 1 rue du Dahomey, Paris 75011

Or email us at: talk2us@lonelyplanet.com

For news, views and updates see our Web site: www.lonelyplanet.com

HOW TO USE A LONELY PLANET GUIDEBOOK

The best way to use a Lonely Planet guidebook is any way you choose. At Lonely Planet we believe the most memorable travel experiences are often those that are unexpected, and the finest discoveries are those you make yourself. Guidebooks are not intended to be used as if they provide a detailed set of infallible instructions!

Contents All Lonely Planet guidebooks follow the same format. The Facts about the Country chapters or sections give background information ranging from history to weather. Facts for the Visitor gives practical information on issues like visas and health. Getting There & Away gives a brief starting point for researching travel to and from the destination. Getting Around gives an overview of the transport options when you arrive.

The peculiar demands of each destination determine how subsequent chapters are broken up, but some things remain constant. We always start with background, then proceed to sights, places to stay, places to eat, entertainment, getting there and away, and getting around information – in that order.

Heading Hierarchy Lonely Planet headings are used in a strict hierarchical structure that can be visualised as a set of Russian dolls. Each heading (and its following text) is encompassed by any preceding heading that is higher on the hierarchical ladder.

Entry Points We do not assume guidebooks will be read from beginning to end, but that people will dip into them. The traditional entry points are the list of contents and the index. In addition, however, there is a complete list of maps and an index map illustrating map coverage.

There's also a colour map that shows highlights. These highlights are dealt with in greater detail in the Facts for the Visitor chapter, along with planning questions and suggested itineraries. Each chapter covering a geographical region begins with a locator map and another list of highlights. Once you find something of interest in a list of highlights, turn to the index.

Maps Maps play a crucial role in Lonely Planet guidebooks and include a huge amount of information. A legend is printed on the back page. We seek to have complete consistency between maps and text, and to have every important place in the text captured on a map. Map key numbers usually start in the top left corner.

Although inclusion in a guidebook usually implies a recommendation, we cannot list every good place. Exclusion does not necessarily imply criticism. In fact there are a number of reasons why we might exclude a place – sometimes it is simply inappropriate to encourage an influx of travellers.

Introduction

Say Bali, and most westerners think of paradise and tourism. Bali offers plenty of both and much more. The image of Bali as a tropical paradise dates back to western visitors in the 1920s, and this image has been cultivated by the international tourist industry rather than by the Balinese, who do not even have a word for paradise in their language. Nevertheless, Bali is a good candidate for paradise – so picturesque it could be a painted backdrop, with rice paddies tripping down hillsides like giant steps, volcanoes soaring up through the clouds, lush tropical jungle, long sandy beaches and warm blue water. But Bali's landscape is more than a backdrop; it is imbued with spiritual significance, and forms a part of the rich cultural life of the Balinese, whose natural grace fits the image of how people should live in paradise.

There's no denying that Bali has become a mass tourism destination, and perhaps this is a disappointment to some visitors who not only expect a paradise, but expect it to be untouched by the rest of the world. It's still a great place for a tropical island holiday if that's what you want – lots of people do. There's reasonably priced accommodation at every standard, wonderful food, entertainment, nightlife and lots of shopping. But if you want something more, Bali is a place which really rewards an extra effort to go beyond the tourist experience. Those who complain about the number of tourists are often those who stay only in tourist areas, while a few kilometres away are villages which rarely see a tourist at all, and where people live in traditional houses and continue a timeless round of religious rituals and rice cultivation.

In fact, the Balinese seem to cope with tourism better than the tourists. Bali has a long history of absorbing – and profiting from – foreign influences. Six centuries ago,

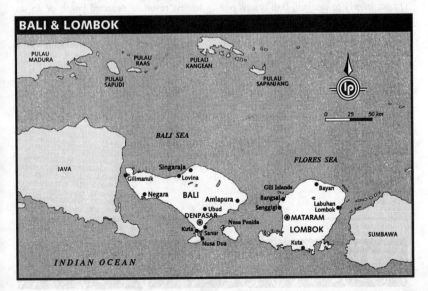

BALI & LOMBOK

as Islam swept across the islands of South-East Asia, the last great Hindu dynasty on Java retreated to Bali with an entire entourage of scholars, artists and intelligentsia.

Bali's fertility and the extraordinary productivity of its agriculture permitted the further development of this cultural heritage, with distinctive movements in art, architecture, music and dance; a culture with a vitality which has hardly faltered to this day. Festivals, ceremonies, temple processions, dances and other activities take place almost continuously on Bali – they're easy to enjoy, but so complex that you would need a lifetime to really understand them. It's the great strength of Bali's culture that makes it so much more than a tropical paradise stereotype.

The paradise image also sells Bali short because it denies the reality of Bali as a place in the real world – a rapidly developing province in a fast growing nation in one of the most dynamic regions on earth. Some visitors are still surprised to find that the Balinese are not isolated innocents, but sophisticated, well informed people who drive cars, watch TV and like making money. Thanks largely to tourism, Bali is now one of the wealthiest regions of Indonesia, and the Balinese have a high standard of education and an international perspective which will put them at the forefront of dramatic changes in their country. The rich cultural traditions of Bali are confronting a fast changing future – it may be frightening, but it's also exciting for any visitor with an interest in the developing world.

The island of Lombok, just to the east, is less developed, but also changing fast. It has as much natural beauty as Bali, although far fewer tourists. Its beaches are better, its great volcano is larger and more spectacular, and it has a greater variety of landscapes – parts of Lombok drip with water, while pockets are chronically dry, parched and cracked. The culture is rich, but not as colourful or as accessible as on Bali. Its indigenous people, the Sasaks, are predominantly Muslim, although elements of ancient animist beliefs survive, and Balinese and Bugis communities add to the diversity. There are fewer facilities for tourists, and tourism seems less intrusive on Lombok, but this is set to change.

If you're more into outdoor activities, you'll find both islands offer world class surfing and diving, challenging treks and great possibilities for bicycle touring. Whether your idea of paradise is a luxury tourist resort, a deserted beach or an unspoiled rural landscape, you still have a good chance to find it on Bali or Lombok. A combination of the two makes for a great travel experience.

BALI

Facts about Bali

HISTORY

There are few traces of Stone Age people on Bali, although it's certain that the island was populated very early in prehistoric times – fossilised human remains from neighbouring Java have been dated to as early as 250,000 years ago. The earliest human artefacts found on Bali are stone tools and earthenware vessels dug up near Cekik (west Bali), estimated to be 3000 years old. Other artefacts indicate that the Bronze Age began on Bali before 300 BC.

Little is known of Bali during the period when Indian traders brought Hinduism to the Indonesian archipelago. The earliest written records are inscriptions on a stone pillar near Sanur (south Bali), dating from around the 9th century AD, and by that time Bali had already developed many similarities to the island you find today. Rice, for example, was grown with the help of a complex irrigation system, probably very like that employed now. The Balinese had also already begun to develop the cultural and artistic activities which have made the island so interesting to visitors to the present day.

Hindu Influence

The Hindu state of Java began to spread its influence into Bali during the reign of King Airlangga (1019-42). At the age of 16, when his uncle lost the throne, Airlangga fled into the forests of west Java. He gradually gained support, won back the kingdom once ruled by his uncle and went on to become one of Java's greatest kings. Airlangga's mother had moved to Bali and remarried shortly after his birth, so when he gained the throne there was an immediate link between Java and Bali. At this time the courtly Javanese language known as Kawi came into use among the royalty of Bali, and the rock-cut memorials seen at Gunung Kawi, near Tampaksiring, are a clear architectural link between Bali and 11th century Java.

After Airlangga's death, Bali retained its semi-independent status until Kertanagara became king of the Singasari dynasty on Java two centuries later. Kertanagara conquered Bali in 1284, but the period of his greatest power lasted a mere eight years, when he was murdered and his kingdom collapsed. However, the great Majapahit dynasty was founded by his son, Vijaya (or Wiiaya). With Java in turmoil, Bali regained its autonomy, and the Pejeng dynasty, centred near modern day Ubud, rose to great power. In 1343, the legendary Majapahit chief minister, Gajah Mada, defeated the Pejeng king Dalem Bedaulu and brought Bali back under Javanese influence.

Although Gajah Mada brought much of the Indonesian archipelago under Majapahit control, this was the furthest extent of their power. On Bali, the 'capital' was moved to Gelgel, near modern Semarapura (Klungkung in east Bali), around the late 14th century and for the next two centuries this was the base for the 'king of Bali', the Dewa Agung. As Islam spread into Java, the Majapahit kingdom collapsed into disputing sultanates. The Gelgel dynasty on Bali, under Dalem Batur Enggong, extended its power eastwards to the neighbouring island of Lombok and even westwards across the strait to Java.

As the Majapahit kingdom fell apart, many of its intelligentsia, including the priest Nirartha, moved to Bali (for details see the Ulu Watu section in the South Bali chapter and Tanah Lot in the West Bali chapter). Nirartha is credited with introducing many of the complexities of Balinese religion to the island. Artists, dancers, musicians and actors also fled to Bali at this time and the island experienced an explosion of cultural activity. The final great exodus to Bali took place in 1478.

The Portuguese

The great Italian explorer Marco Polo was believed to have stopped at the Indonesian archipelago as early as 1292, but the Portuguese were the first Europeans to establish themselves in the region. Vasco da Gama arrived seeking domination of the valuable spice trade in the 'spice islands' of the Moluccas (now Maluku) in 1512, but did not venture as far as Bali. The Spanish and English tried to wrest control of the Moluccas away from the Portuguese, but it was the Dutch who eventually laid the foundations of the Indonesian state.

The Dutch

The first Europeans to set foot on Bali itself were Dutch seamen in 1597. Setting a tradition that has prevailed to the present day, they fell in love with the island and when Cornelius de Houtman, the ship's captain, prepared to set sail from the island, several of his crew refused to come with him. At that time, Balinese prosperity and artistic activity, at least among the royalty, was at a peak, and the king who befriended de Houtman had 200 wives and a chariot pulled by two white buffaloes, not to mention a retinue of 50 dwarfs whose bodies had been bent to resemble kris (traditional dagger) handles! By the early 1600s, the Dutch had established trade treaties with Javanese princes and controlled much of the spice trade, but they were interested in profit, not culture, and barely gave Bali a second glance.

In 1710, the 'capital' of the Gelgel kingdom was shifted to nearby Klungkung (now called Semarapura), but local discontent was growing, lesser rulers were breaking away, and the Dutch began to move in using the old policy of divide and conquer. In 1846, the Dutch used Balinese salvage claims over shipwrecks as a pretext to land military forces in north Bali.

In 1894, the Dutch chose to support the Sasaks of Lombok in a rebellion against their Balinese rajah. The rajah capitulated to the Dutch demands, only to be overruled by his younger princes who defeated the Dutch forces in a surprise attack. Dutch anger was roused, a larger and more heavily armed force was dispatched and the Balinese overrun. Balinese power on Lombok finally

came to an end – the crown prince was killed and the old rajah was sent into exile.

With the north of Bali long under Dutch control and Lombok now gone, the south was never going to last long. Once again it was disputes over the ransacking of wrecked ships that gave the Dutch the excuse they needed to move in. In 1904, after a Chinese ship was wrecked off Sanur, Dutch demands that the rajah of Badung pay 3000 silver dollars in damages were rejected, and in 1906 Dutch warships appeared at Sanur.

The Dutch forces landed despite Balinese opposition, and four days later had marched 5km to the outskirts of Denpasar. On 20 September 1906, the Dutch mounted a naval bombardment on Denpasar and then began their final assault. The three princes of Badung realised that they were outnumbered and outgunned, and that defeat was inevitable. Surrender and exile, however, was the worst imaginable outcome so they decided to take the honourable path of a suicidal *puputan* – a fight to the death. First the palaces were burned, and then dressed in their finest jewellery and waving ceremonial golden krises, the rajah led the royalty and priests out to face the Dutch with their modern weapons.

The Dutch begged the Balinese to surrender rather than make their hopeless stand, but their pleas went unheeded and wave after wave of the Balinese nobility marched forward to their death. In all, nearly 4000 Balinese died. The Dutch then marched east towards Tabanan and took the rajah of Tabanan prisoner, but he also committed suicide rather than face the disgrace of exile.

The kingdoms of Karangasem and Gianyar had already capitulated to the Dutch and were allowed to retain some of their powers, but other kingdoms were defeated and their rulers exiled. Finally, the rajah of Klungkung followed the lead of Badung, and once more the Dutch faced a puputan. With this last obstacle disposed of, all of Bali was under Dutch control and became part of the Dutch East Indies. There was little development of an exploitative plantation economy on Bali, and the common people noticed very little difference between rule by the Dutch and the rajahs.

WWII

Dutch rule over Bali was short-lived, however, for Indonesia quickly fell to the Japanese after the bombing of Pearl Harbor. In 1942, the Japanese invaded Bali at Sanur in south Bali, but the Balinese could offer no resistance. The Japanese established headquarters in Denpasar and Singaraja, and were initially welcomed as Asian liberators of European colonialism, but it soon became evident that the Japanese were more despotic and intrusive than the Dutch. By the time the Japanese surrendered and left Bali in August 1945, the islanders were suffering extreme poverty, but the Japanese presence did foster several paramilitary, nationalist and anti-colonial organisations which were ready to fight the returning Dutch.

Founder of the modern Indonesian state, Ahmed Soekarno.

Independence

On 17 August 1945, just after the conclusion end of WWII, the Indonesian leader Ahmed Soekarno proclaimed the nation's independence, but it took four years to convince the Dutch that they were not going to get their great colony back. In a virtual repeat of the puputan nearly 50 years earlier, a Balinese resistance group called Tentara Keamanan Rakyat (People's Security Force) was wiped out in the battle of Marga on 20 November 1946. This event is recognised in a museum at Margarana in west Bali (see the Marga section in the West Bali chapter), and Bali's airport is named after the leader of the Balinese group, Ngurah Rai. In 1949, the Dutch finally recognised Indonesia's independence.

Independence was not an easy path for Indonesia to follow at first, and Soekarno, an inspirational leader during the conflict with the Dutch, proved less adept at governing the nation in peacetime. An ill-advised 'confrontation' with Malaysia in 1963 was just one event that sapped the country's energy. To Soekarno, Britain's involvement in the Malaysia federation translated into a threat of western imperialism on his doorstep. His decision to embark on the confrontation led to military action between the Indonesian forces and 50,000 British, Australian and New Zealand soldiers along the border between Kalimantan and Malaysia. This 'confrontation' was never a serious threat to the survival of Malaysia, but the military expense caused severe economic problems for Indonesia.

1965 Coup & Backlash

On 30 September 1965, an attempted coup – blamed on the Communist Party (PKI) – led to Soekarno's downfall. General Mohamed Soeharto emerged as the leading figure in the armed forces, displaying great military and political skill in suppressing the coup.

The PKI was outlawed and a wave of anti-Communist reprisals followed, which escalated into a wholesale massacre of suspected Communists throughout the Indonesian archipelago.

On Bali, the events had an added local significance as the main national political organisations, the Nationalist Party (PNI)

Western Visitors in the 1930s

Modern tourism started on Bali in the late 1960s, but the island had an earlier, and in many ways much more intriguing, tourist boom in the 30s. A prime source of inspiration for these between-the-wars visitors was Gregor Krause's book *The Island of Bali*, published in 1920. Krause had worked in Bangli as a doctor between 1912 and 1914, and his photographs of an uninhibited lifestyle in a lush, tropical environment aroused western interest on Bali.

By the early 30s, about 100 tourists a month were visiting the island and the first concerns were already being raised about whether Balinese culture could withstand such a massive onslaught! Visitors included some talented and very interesting individuals, who played a great part in creating the image of Bali which persists today and aided the rejuvenation of many dormant or stultified Balinese arts. Furthermore, they ensured their own immortality with the numerous books they wrote about their experiences on the island (see the Books section in the Bali Facts for the Visitor chapter for details).

Miguel Covarrubias (1904-57) The book *Island of Bali* by this Mexican artist is still the classic introduction to the island and its culture. Covarrubias visited Bali twice in the early 30s and, like many visitors at that time, Walter Spies was his introduction to the island and its people. The book contains many illustrations and paintings by Covarrubias, and photographs by his wife Rose. He was also involved in theatre design and printmaking.

Walter Spies (1895-1942) Spies was the father figure for the cast of 30s visitors, and in many ways played the largest part in interpreting Bali for them and establishing the image of Bali which prevails today. The son of a wealthy diplomat, Spies was born in Moscow in 1895 and raised there during the final years of Tsarist rule. At the age of 15 he was sent away to school in Dresden, but returned to his family just as WWI broke out. Twice in his life Spies was imprisoned due to his nationality: firstly near Moscow and then in a small town in the Ural mountains.

As the upheavals of the revolution swept Russia, Spies returned to his family in Moscow, before escaping from the country in disguise. In 1919 he was in Dresden, and then moved to Berlin where he joined a circle of artists, musicians and filmmakers. In 1923 Spies abruptly left Europe for Java in what was then the Dutch East Indies. He first visited Bali in 1925 and two years later moved there permanently.

Befriended by the important Sukawati family, he built a house at the confluence of two rivers at Campuan, west of Ubud. His home soon became the prime gathering point for the most famous visitors of the 30s and Spies, who involved himself in every aspect of Balinese art and culture, was an important influence on its great renaissance.

In 1932 he became curator of the museum in Denpasar, and with Rudolf Bonnet and Cokorda Gede Agung Sukawati, their Balinese patron, he founded the Pita Maha artists' cooperative in 1936. He co-authored *Dance & Drama in Bali*, which was published in 1938, and he re-created that most Balinese of dances, the Kecak, for a visiting German film crew. Despite his comfortable life in Ubud, he moved to the remote village of Iseh in eastern Bali in 1937.

In 1938 things suddenly went very wrong for Spies when a puritan clampdown in Holland spread to the Dutch colony and he was arrested for homosexual activities with minors. Spies was imprisoned in Denpasar, and then moved to Java where he was held in jail in Surabaya for eight months. He was no sooner released than WWII began and, when the Germans

Western Visitors in the 1930s

invaded Holland in 1940, he was arrested again – this time as an enemy alien. Spies was held in Sumatra until the Pacific War began. On 18 January 1942 Spies, along with other prisoners of war, was shipped out of Sumatra bound for Ceylon (now Sri Lanka). The next day the ship was bombed by Japanese aircraft and sank near the island of Nias. Spies drowned.

Spies' paintings were a curious mixture of Rousseau and surrealism, and the Rousseau influence is mirrored in many Balinese paintings today. However, if Spies was merely a talented artist, his memory would be a much fainter one today. To his ability as a painter must be added his consuming interest in all aspects of Balinese art, culture and life, as well as his role as a window to Bali for other western visitors and as a vital force in the encouragement and growth of Balinese art. Last, but far from least, he was a colourful and fascinating character, clearly in love with life and in headlong pursuit of all it could offer.

Colin McPhee (1900-65) A chance hearing of a record of gamelan music compelled US musician Colin McPhee to join the stream of talented 30s visitors. His book, *A House in Bali*, was not published until 1944, long after his departure from the island, but it remains one of the best written of the Bali accounts, and his tales of music and house building are often highly amusing. After WWII, McPhee taught music at UCLA and played an important role in introducing Balinese music to the west, and encouraging gamelan orchestras to visit the USA.

Rudolf Bonnet (1895-1978) Bonnet was a Dutch artist who, along with Walter Spies, played a major role in the development of Balinese art in the mid-30s. Bonnet arrived on Bali in 1929, two years after Spies, and immediately contacted him. In 1936 he was one of the principal forces behind the foundation of the Pita Maha artists' cooperative, and his influence on Balinese art to this day is very clear. Where Spies' work was often mystical, Bonnet's work concentrated on the human form and everyday Balinese life. To this day the numerous classical Balinese paintings with their themes of markets, cockfights and other aspects of day-to-day existence are indebted to Bonnet.

Bonnet was imprisoned in Sulawesi by the Japanese during WWII and returned to Bali in the 50s to plan the Museum Puri Lukisan in Ubud. He left the island, but returned in 1973 to help establish the museum's permanent collection. He died in 1978 on a brief return visit to Holland. Bonnet's ashes were returned to his beloved Bali to be scattered at the 1979 cremation of Balinese patron Cokorda Gede Agung Sukawati.

K'tut Tantri A woman of many aliases, K'tut Tantri was named Vannine Walker, or perhaps it was Muriel Pearson, when she breezed in from Hollywood in 1932. She was born on the Isle of Man and grew up there and in Scotland before working as a journalist in Hollywood. The film *Bali, The Last Paradise* had served as the inspiration to send her to Bali, where she dyed her red hair black (only demons have red hair) and was befriended by the prince of the kingdom of Bangli.

She teamed up with Robert Koke to open the first hotel at Kuta Beach (the Kuta Beach Hotel) in 1936. Later she fell out with the Kokes and established her own hotel. She stayed on when war swept into the archipelago, was imprisoned by the Japanese, survived long periods of solitary confinement during the war and then worked for the Indonesian Republicans in their postwar struggle against the Dutch. As Surabaya Sue she broadcast from Surabaya in support of their cause. Her book *Revolt in Paradise* (written as K'tut Tantri) was published in 1960.

Western Visitors in the 1930s

Robert & Louise Koke In 1936, Americans Robert Koke and Louise Garret arrived on Bali as part of a long trip through South-East Asia. They fell in love with the island and Kuta Beach, and soon established the Kuta Beach Hotel, at first in partnership with K'tut Tantri, although their accounts of the hotel differ widely.

While the Dutch insisted that the hotel was nothing more than a few 'dirty native huts', it was an instant hit and Bali's 30s tourist boom ensured that it was always full. The rooms were a series of individual thatched-roof cottages, remarkably like the cottage-style hotels which are still popular on Bali today. Robert Koke, who learned to surf in Hawaii, can also claim the honour of introducing surfing to Bali.

The Koke's success continued until the Japanese entry into WWII. The pair made a last-minute escape from Bali and when Robert Koke visited Bali just after the war, only traces of the hotel's foundations remained. Robert Koke retired from a long career with the CIA in the 70s, and in 1987 Louise Koke's long-forgotten story of their hotel was published as *Our Hotel in Bali*, illustrated with her incisive sketches and her husband's excellent photographs.

Other Western Visitors Numerous other western personages made pilgrimages to Bali in the 30s; Charlie Chaplin and Nöel Coward were the equivalents of today's rock star visitors, adding a touch of glamour to Bali as a destination.

Others played their part in chronicling the period, such as writers Hickman Powell, whose book *The Last Paradise* was published in 1930, and German author Vicki Baum, whose book *A Tale from Bali*, a fictionalised account of the *puputan* (fight to the death) of 1906, is still in print.

Colin McPhee's wife Jane Belo does not even make a fleeting appearance in her husband's book *A House in Bali*, but she was a talented anthropologist who also played a key role in interpreting Bali in the 30s. Margaret Mead also visited and wrote about Bali at this time, as did American dancer Katherine Mershon.

and PKI, crystallised existing differences between traditionalists who wanted to maintain the old caste system, and radicals who saw the caste system as repressive and who were urging land reform. After the failed coup, religious traditionalists on Bali led the witch-hunt for the 'godless Communists'. Some of the killings were particularly brutal, with numerous people being rounded up and clubbed to death by fanatical mobs. The Chinese community was particularly victimised. Eventually the military stepped in to control the anti-Communist purge, but no-one on Bali was untouched by the killings, estimated at between 50,000 and 100,000 out of a population of about two million.

Soeharto & the New Order

Following the failed coup and its aftermath, Soeharto established himself as president and took control of the government, while Soekarno disappeared from the limelight. Under Soeharto's 'New Order' government, Indonesia looked to the west in foreign policy, and western-educated economists set about balancing budgets, controlling inflation and attracting foreign investment.

Politically, Soeharto ensured that the Golkar party, with strong support from the army (Angkatan Bersenjata Republika Indonesia – or ABRI), became the dominant political force. Under the banner of 'guided democracy', other political parties were banned or crippled by the disqualification of

After more than 30 years in power, General Mohamed Soeharto was toppled in 1998.

candidates and the disenfranchisement of voters. Regular elections maintained the appearance of a national democracy, but until recently, Golkar won every election easily.

On Bali, economic growth has been achieved by a huge expansion in the tourist industry, which has transformed the southern part of the island. While there have been dramatic improvements in infrastructure – particularly roads, telecommunications, electricity and water supply – the downside has been the displacement of local populations and disruption of many traditional communities.

Indonesia Today

In early 1997, South-East Asia began to suffer a severe economic crisis (see the Economy entry in this chapter). A year later, 76-year-old Soeharto was re-elected unopposed to a seventh five-year presidential term, much to the anguish of anti-Soeharto and pro-democracy activists. Soeharto then appointed his protege, the 61-year-old Dr Bacharuddin Jusuf Habibie, as the Vice-President.

To help deal with the continuing economic crisis, Soeharto grudgingly agreed in May 1998 to the International Monetary Fund's demand to increase the government-subsidised price of electricity and petrol, resulting in immediate increases in the cost of most public transport. The price of rice and other food staples also increased, and the Indonesian-Chinese community, which owns many shops, bore the brunt of riots which broke out across Java, Sumatra and Kalimantan. Many students were killed during clashes with police, causing a seemingly unstoppable momentum of protests and looting across Java, which left about 1100 dead and seriously damaged the central business district of Jakarta. None of this strife spilled over to Bali, although ferries from Java were temporarily cancelled by officials to ensure that Javanese protesters did not start troubles on Bali.

To the surprise of many, Soeharto resigned on 21 May 1998 after 32 years in power, and handed the presidency to Habibie. Habibie soon made a few encouraging moves, such as releasing political prisoners and promising democratic elections before the end of 1999,

Dr Bacharuddin Jusuf Habibie has assumed the Indonesian presidency at a time of enormous economic and social turmoil.

but most Indonesians remain unsatisfied because Habibie is deemed to be a Soeharto crony, and Soeharto has yet to be stripped of his enormous fortune or tried for corruption. While the economic crisis continues, Habibie's presidency remains tenuous.

GEOGRAPHY

Bali is a small island, midway along the string of islands which makes up the Indonesian archipelago. It's adjacent to Java, the most heavily populated island, and immediately west of the chain of smaller islands comprising Nusa Tenggara. Bali has an area of 5620 sq km, measuring approximately 140km by 80km.

South and north of the central mountains are Bali's agricultural lands. The southern region is a wide, gently sloping area where most of Bali's abundant rice crop is grown. This south-central region is the island's true rice basket. The northern coastal strip is narrower, rising rapidly into the foothills of the central range. It receives less rain, but coffee, copra and rice are grown here, and cattle are also raised.

Bali also has some arid and lightly populated regions. These include the western mountain region and its northern slopes down to the sea – an area virtually unpopulated and reputed to be the last home of the Balinese tiger. The eastern and northeastern slopes of Gunung Agung are also dry, as are the Bukit Peninsula and Nusa Penida islands, which cannot support intensive wet-rice agriculture.

GEOLOGY

Bali is dramatically mountainous – the central mountain chain which runs the whole length of the island includes several peaks approaching or over 2000m. Gunung Agung, known as the 'mother mountain', is 3142m high.

Bali is volcanically active and extremely fertile. The two go hand-in-hand because eruptions contribute to the land's exceptional fertility, and high mountains provide the dependable rainfall which irrigates Bali's complex and amazingly beautiful patchwork of rice terraces. Of course, the volcanoes are a hazard as well – Bali has often had disastrous eruptions and no doubt will again in the future. The massive eruption of Gunung Agung mountain in 1963 killed thousands, devastated vast areas of the island and forced many Balinese to accept resettlement in other parts of Indonesia (see the boxed text 'The 1963 Eruption' in the East Bali chapter).

The central mountain chain reaches its highest point in the east. Balinese mythology relates that the Hindu holy mountain, Mahameru, was set down on Bali, but split into two parts – Gunung Agung and Gunung Batur. These two holy mountains are both active volcanoes. The other major mountains are Batukau ('stone coconut shell') at 2276m, and Abang at 2152m. Apart from the volcanic central range, there are the limestone plateaus which form the Bukit Peninsula, in the extreme south of Bali, and the island of Nusa Penida.

CLIMATE

Just 8° south of the equator, Bali has a tropical climate which is hot all year. The average temperature hovers around 30°C (mid-80s°F) year-round, but the humidity can make the heat feel very oppressive. Direct sun feels incredibly hot, especially in the middle of the day when you'd be crazy if you didn't stay in the shade. There are dry and wet seasons – dry from April to September and wet from October to March – but it can rain at any time of year and even during the wet season rain is likely to pass quickly. In general, the best months are April to September, when the humidity is lower and the rain is light and infrequent.

Overall, the climate is gently tropical, but there are marked variations across the island: around the coast, sea breezes temper the heat, and as you move inland you also move up, so the altitude works to keep things cool. In fact, at times it can get very chilly up in the highlands, and a warm sweater or light jacket can be a good idea in mountain villages like Kintamani and Candikuning. The northern slopes of Gunung

Batur always seem to be wet and misty, while a few kilometres away, the east coast is nearly always dry and sunny.

Air-conditioning is not really needed on Bali. A cool breeze always seems to spring up in the evening, and the open bamboo windows, so common in Balinese architecture, make the most of the lightest breeze.

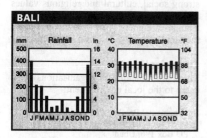

ECOLOGY & ENVIRONMENT

For hundreds of years, Bali has sustained a substantial population with intensive wet rice cultivation, supported by an elaborate irrigation system which makes careful use of all the surface water. The rice paddies are a complete ecological system, home for much more than just rice. In the early morning you'll often see the duck herders leading their flocks out for a day's paddle around a flooded paddy, and at night young boys head out with lights to trap tasty frogs and eels. Other crops are often grown on the levees between the fields, or planted as a rotation crop after several rice harvests.

It's tempting to paint a picture of an ecologically sustainable island paradise, but it hasn't always been perfect. The periodic volcanic eruptions, which spread essential fertilising ash over much of the island, also cause death and destruction. Droughts, insect plagues and rats have, at various times in Bali's history, ravaged the rice crops and led to famine. The population has been kept at sustainable levels by high infant mortality and short life expectancy. On the other hand, deforestation is hardly an issue on Bali because most of the tropical rainforests

were cleared long ago to make way for rice cultivation.

To increase agricultural output, new high-yield varieties of rice were introduced (see the Economy section later in this chapter), but these resulted in new problems with insect, viral and fungal pests, and a greater need for irrigated water.

The demand for high productivity, combined with ecological sustainability, has created an ongoing environmental management task.

There is very little manufacturing industry, so industrial pollution is not a big problem, but the tourism industry, although dependent on an attractive environment, does have its adverse effects.

Tourism

In 1997, 1,230,316 foreigners flew *directly* to Bali (and countless more tourists travelled to Bali from other islands in Indonesia) – an increase of more than 7000% since 1969. About 22% of tourists came from Australia, and 20% from Japan.

Not surprisingly, the unrestrained development of tourism throughout Bali has caused irreparable damage to the environment.

Land Use The most obvious example is the building explosion in the south, where urban sprawl and hotels built on prime agricultural land means that rice and other staple foods cannot be grown. Native flora has been destroyed, causing erosion; this is most evident around Ubud where many hotels are sited on the hill tops. The handful of golf courses also use an enormous amount of important land.

Water Supply When you put together air-conditioning, cleaning, showers, swimming pools and gardens, each top-end hotel on Bali uses a staggering 570L of fresh water per day per guest. This water is often piped from the central mountains, and sometimes re-directed from sources for rice paddies. In Nusa Dua, some village wells have dried up because the big hotels dig theirs much deeper, lowering the water table.

Coastal & Marine Environment Surfing, diving and snorkelling are very popular on Bali, but continually damage reefs and marine life. Other serious problems are untreated sewage flowing into the ocean, and drainage of pesticides into water sources, such as the golf course near Danau Batur lake. Candidasa is a classic example of how coral reefs have been destroyed to help make cement, so the beaches have eroded – and hoteliers wonder why tourists are deserting the place. Mangroves help maintain the coastal tides and stop erosion, but are often destroyed; and the extension of the airport into the sea caused massive coastal erosion.

Traffic & Pollution The cheap rental of cars and motorbikes is placing an enormous strain on the narrow roads, and causing immense air and noise pollution. A high standard of living for locals also means many more motorbikes on the roads. Rubbish, including a lot of non-biodegradable plastic, is collected to maintain the appearance of cleanliness, but it's often buried haphazardly, dumped on the few pieces of vacant land or burnt with a billowing stench.

Local Economy Tourists with large wads of cash cause rampant inflation among the local economy; for example, villagers often cannot compete with hotels when buying vegetables at the market. Shops often import food, because less land and fewer workers are now available to grow food. Tourism may create a small middle and upper class, but poor farmers often become hawkers, masseurs or taxi drivers because their land has been commandeered for tourist projects.

The Good News There is *some* good news, however. Tourists interested in culture do promote local traditions; dancing, art and music continue, if only for the tourist industry. A few tourist ventures have ploughed profits back into local community and environmental projects. A vast amount of west Bali has been allocated as a national park to conserve the environment, and stop urban development.

Balinese can also be proud of the fact that prostitution and drug use is very limited among locals, unlike some countries such as the Philippines and Thailand. There is little or none of the obvious resentment against tourists that can be experienced in the Caribbean. The Balinese still have strong social, cultural and religious values and traditions despite everything, and crime against foreigners is very low considering the temptations.

Organisations

There are a handful of organisations dedicated to the local environment:

Environmental Bamboo Foundation
(☎ 974027, fax 974029)
PO Box 196, Ubud
Indonesia International Rural and Agriculture Development Foundation
(☎ 261204, fax 701098, email lodge@denpasar.wasantara.net.id)
PO Box 3704, Denpasar 8001. This outfit is about 'raising the prosperity of Indonesians through improved education and relevant agribusiness systems', and it runs an eco-tourism resort near Jimbaran.
Wisnu Foundation
(☎/fax 424758, email greenbali@denpasar.wasantara.net.id)
Jl Muding Indah 1/1, Kerobakan, Denpasar. This nonprofit organisation, established a few years ago by Balinese, is supported by donations and grants.

FLORA & FAUNA

Nearly all of the island is cultivated, and only in the Taman Nasional Bali Barat national park in west Bali are there traces of Bali's earliest plant life. The island is geologically young and virtually all its living things have migrated from elsewhere, so there's really no such thing as 'native' plants and animals. This is not hard to imagine in the heavily populated and extravagantly fertile south of Bali, where the orderly rice terraces are so intensively cultivated as to look more like a work of sculpture than a natural landscape.

Flora

Trees Like most things on Bali, trees have a spiritual and religious significance, and you will often see them decorated with scarves and black-and-white check cloths. The *waringin* (banyan) is the holiest Balinese tree and no important temple is complete without a stately one growing within its precincts. The banyan is an extensive shady tree with an exotic feature: creepers which drop from its branches take root to propagate a new tree. Thus the banyan is said to be 'never-dying' since new offshoots can always take root. The shady frangipani trees with their beautiful and sweet-smelling white flowers are almost as common in temples as the banyan.

Bali has monsoonal rather than tropical rainforest, so it lacks the valuable rainforest hardwoods that require rain all year. The forestry departments are experimenting with new varieties in plantations around the Taman Nasional Bali Barat, but at the moment nearly all the wood used for carving is imported from Sumatra and Kalimantan.

A number of plants have great practical and economic significance. Bamboo *(tiing)* is grown in several varieties, and is used for everything from *sate* sticks and string to rafters and gamelan resonators. The various types of palm provide coconuts, sugar, fuel and fibre.

Flowers & Gardens Balinese gardens are a delight. The soil and climate can support a huge range of plants, and the Balinese love of beauty and the abundance of cheap labour means that every space can be landscaped. The style is generally informal, with curved paths, a rich variety of plants and usually a water feature.

You can find almost every type of flower on Bali, but some are seasonal and others are restricted to the cooler mountain areas. Many of the flowers will be familiar to visitors – hibiscus, bougainvillea, poinsettia, oleander, jasmine, water lily and aster are commonly seen in the southern tourist areas, while roses, begonias and hydrangeas are found mainly in the mountains. Less familiar flowers includes: Javanese ixora (called *soka* or *angsoka*), with round clusters of bright red-orange flowers; *champak* (or *cempaka*), a very fragrant member of the magnolia family; flamboyant, the flower of the royal poinciana flame tree; *manori* (or *maduri*), which has a number of traditional uses; and water convolvulus (or *kangkung*), the leaves of which are commonly used as a green vegetable. There are literally thousands of types of orchid.

Flowers can be seen everywhere – in gardens or just by the roadside. Flower fanciers should make a trip to the Danau Bratan area for the botanical gardens and the Candikuning flower market. A visit to the plant nurseries along the road between Denpasar and Sanur is also worthwhile.

Fauna

Domestic Animals Bali is thick with domestic animals, including ones that wake you up in the morning and others that bark all night. Chickens and roosters are kept both for food purposes and as pets. Cockfighting is a popular male activity and a man's fighting bird is a prize possession (see the boxed text 'Cockfights' later in this section). Balinese pigs are related to wild boar, and look gross with their sway backs and sagging stomachs. They inhabit the family compound, cleaning up all the garbage and eventually end up spit-roasted at a feast – they taste a lot better than they look.

Balinese cattle, by contrast, are delicate and graceful animals which seem more akin to deer than cows. Although the Balinese are Hindus, they do not generally treat cattle as holy animals, yet cows are rarely eaten or milked. They are, however, used to plough rice paddies and fields, and there is a major export market for Balinese cattle to Hong Kong and other parts of Asia.

Ducks are another everyday Balinese domestic animal and a regular dish at feasts. Many families keep a flock of ducks which are brought out of the family compound and led to a convenient pond or flooded rice paddy to feed during the day. The morning and evening parade of ducks is a familiar sight throughout the island and is one of Bali's many delights.

Wildlife Bali has plenty of lizards and the small ones (onomatopoeically called a *cecak*) that hang around light fittings in the evening, waiting for an unwary insect, are a familiar sight. Although fairly large lizards, geckos are often heard but rarely seen. The loud and regularly repeated two-part cry 'geck-oh' is a nightly background noise, and it is considered lucky if you hear the lizard call seven times.

Bats are quite common and not only in well known haunts like the Bat Cave (Goa Lawah) near Kusamba in east Bali. They materialise at sunset to start their nocturnal hunt. The little chipmunk-like Balinese squirrels are occasionally seen in the wild, although more often in cages.

Bali's only wilderness area, Taman Nasional Bali Barat (see the National Parks entry later in this section), has a number of wild species, including grey and black monkeys (which you will also see around the hills in central Bali), *muncak* or mouse deer, squirrels and iguanas. Bali used to have tigers and, although there are periodic rumours of sightings in the remote northwest of the island, nobody has proof of seeing one for a long time.

Marine Life There is a rich variety of coral, seaweed, fish and other marine life in the coastal waters. Much of it can be appreciated by snorkellers, but the larger marine animals are only likely to be seen while diving (see the Diving section in the Bali Facts for the Visitor chapter). Turtles are endangered, but can still be seen wild in the waters around Nusa Penida. Cavorting dolphins are an attraction at sunrise off Lovina, on the northern coast.

Birds There are more than 300 species of bird on Bali, although only one is endemic to the island – the highly endangered Bali starling (see the boxed text of the same name in the West Bali chapter). Other birds have adapted to Bali's intensively cultivated

landscape, and can be seen in or near many of the tourist areas.

Cruelty to Animals
Cockfighting is a long-standing and popular activity among Balinese men, although it is not a highly conspicuous feature of Balinese life.

Bull races are a regular and traditional event in north and west Bali, and are sometimes promoted as a tourist attraction. The animals do not seem to be severely mistreated and they probably fare no worse than racehorses in most western countries.

Cockfights

Cockfights are a regular feature of temple ceremonies – a combination of gambling, excitement, sport and blood sacrifice all rolled into one. Men keep fighting cocks as prized pets. Carefully groomed and cared for, they are lovingly prepared for their brief moment of glory or defeat. On quiet afternoons the men will often meet in the *banjars* to compare their roosters, spar them against one another and line up the odds for the next big bout.

You'll often see the roosters by the roadside in their bell-shaped cane baskets – they're placed there to be entertained by passing activity. When the festivals take place, the cocks are matched one against another, a lethally sharp metal spur tied to one leg and then, after being pushed against each other a few times to stir up the blood, they're released and the feathers fly. It's usually over in a flash – a slash of the spur and one rooster is down and dying. Occasionally a rooster turns and flees, but in that case both roosters are put in a covered basket where they can't avoid fighting. After the bout, the successful betters collect their pay-offs and the winning owner takes home the dead rooster for his cooking pot.

Green Sea Turtles

Green sea turtles are found in the waters around Bali and throughout Indonesia. Tragically, about 30,000 are killed every year for meat (used in ceremonies) and shells (for jewellery, combs and other trinkets), and Bali is the site of the most intensive slaughter of the species in the world. The turtles are also constantly threatened by waters polluted by plastic bags, sewage and oil leaks.

The environmental group Greenpeace has long campaigned to protect Indonesia's sea turtles. It appeals to travellers not to eat turtle meat or buy any turtle products, including shells, stuffed turtles and turtle-leather goods. In any case, it is illegal to export any products made of green sea turtles from Indonesia. In many countries, including Australia, the UK, the USA and other EU countries, it is illegal to import turtle products without a permit.

Endangered Species

Thankfully, some efforts are being made to help protect rare and endangered species of wildlife on Bali, such as the Bali starling and green sea turtles. The Indonesian Gibbon Foundation (☎ 0361-724655) also helps protect species of endangered monkeys on Bali and the rest of Indonesia. The Taman Burung Bali Bird Park and the Taman Kupu-Kupu Bali (Butterfly Park) are major tourist attractions, but do boast active captive-breeding programs.

National Parks

The only national park on Bali is the Taman Nasional Bali Barat. It covers most of the western end of Bali, a substantial area of coastal mangrove and the adjacent marine area. The management of the park is to be integrated with a conservation and environment plan for the whole island. For more information, see the West Bali chapter.

GOVERNMENT & POLITICS

Indonesian government is centralised and hierarchical, and the important strategic decisions regarding Bali's development are made by the central government in Jakarta. Executive power rests with the president of the republic. Under the national government there are 27 *propinsi* (provinces), of which Bali is one. Indonesia has 1000 members of the People's Consultative Assembly, comprising 400 elected representatives (but very few from Bali) and 100 officers from the armed forces.

The provincial government does not have the same sort of autonomy as a state does in a federal system, such as the USA, Australia or Germany. It acts more as a delegate of the central government, and is responsible for implementing national policy in the province. The governor of a province is appointed by the president for a five year term from a short list of candidates nominated by the provincial house of representatives, the Dewan Perwakilan Rakyat Daerah. Representatives to the provincial house are elected by popular vote every five years.

Within Bali there are eight *kabupaten*, or districts, which have their origins in the precolonial rajahs' kingdoms, and were the basis of the Dutch administrative districts which were known as regencies. Denpasar

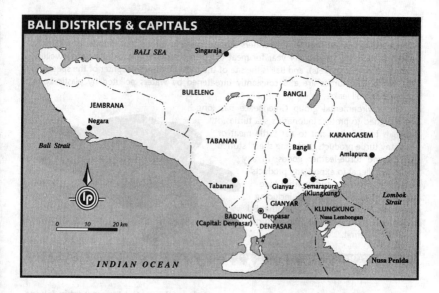

BALI DISTRICTS & CAPITALS

BALI SEA

Singaraja

JEMBRANA

BULELENG

BANGLI

Negara

Bali Strait

TABANAN

KARANGASEM

Bangli

Amlapura

Tabanan

Gianyar Semarapura
(Klungkung)

Lombok Strait

GIANYAR

KLUNGKUNG

BADUNG Denpasar Nusa Lembongan
(Capital: Denpasar) DENPASAR

0   10   20 km

INDIAN OCEAN

Nusa Penida

was part of the Badung district until 1992, when the city, together with Sanur and Tanjung Benoa, became a separate *kabupaten kota* or city district. Badung's administration is still mostly in Denpasar.

Each kabupaten is headed by a government official known as a *bupati*. The districts are then further divided into 51 subdistricts headed by a *camat*; then subdivided further into an official *desa* or village (612 at last count), administered by a *perbekel*; and still further into an enormous number (about 3500) of *banjar* and *dusun*, which are the local divisions of a village.

ECONOMY

Bali's economy is basically agrarian: the vast majority of the Balinese are peasants who work in the fields, and agriculture contributes about 40% of Bali's total economic output, although a much smaller proportion of its export income. Coffee, copra and cattle are major agricultural exports – most of the rice goes to feed Bali's own population. Economically, Bali is a poor island, but it is growing at a fast rate. Typically, a

policeman earns about 250,000 rp per month, and an average public servant about 400,000 rp per month.

Tourism

Tourism accounts for about one third of the economy – not only in the provision of accommodation, meals and services to visitors, but also in providing a market for all those arts and crafts. The clothing industry has enjoyed spectacular growth from making beachwear for tourists – it now accounts for around half the value of Balinese exports. Handcrafts are also exported directly, as well as being sold to tourists, and Balinese woodcarvings are sold as souvenirs from the Cook Islands to the Caribbean.

Even in respect of controversial tourism projects, there is a national belief that Bali must enable its tourist potential to be developed in the national interest. Despite this, there has been vocal opposition on Bali to some recent tourist developments, and to some extent this parallels discontent and opposition at a national level – see the earlier Ecology & Environment section.

The tourism industry in Indonesia started to nose-dive in mid-1997, and has yet to fully recover. The fall started with the well publicised forest fires in the Indonesian provinces of Kalimantan and Irian Jaya, thousands of kilometres away. Tourist workers on Bali hoped the very low value of the rupiah would prompt a rush of tourists looking for a cheap holiday, but many still avoided Bali because of the riots and political instability, primarily in Java, in early 1998. There were no fires or riots on Bali, but tourists stayed away in droves, or at least kept within the security blanket of the tourist centres.

Fishing

Although the Balinese are an island people, their unusual tendency to focus on the mountains rather than the sea is reflected in the relatively small output of the fishing industry. Most exported fish are sardines, but there is some export of tuna and processed fish products.

Seaweed is a growing industry, and provides a valuable source of income to many poor coastal communities. For information on this industry, see the boxed text 'Sea Grass of Lembongan' in the Nusa Penida chapter.

Pancasila

Since it was first expounded by Indonesian leader Ahmed Soekarno in 1945, the Pancasila (Five Principles) have remained the philosophical backbone of the Indonesian state. It was meant by Soekarno to provide a broad philosophical base on which a united Indonesian state could be formed. All over Indonesia you'll see the Indonesian coat of arms with its symbolic incorporation of the Pancasila hung on the walls of government offices and the homes of village heads, on the covers of student textbooks or immortalised on great stone tablets. These principles are:

Faith in God – symbolised by the star. This is perhaps the most important and contentious principle. As interpreted by Soekarno and the Javanese syncretists who have ruled Indonesia since independence, this can mean any god – Allah, Vishnu, Buddha, Christ etc. For many Muslims, however, it means belief in the only true God, Allah, but the government goes to great lengths to suppress both Islamic extremism and calls for an Islamic state in multi-ethnic and multi-religious Indonesia.

Humanity – symbolised by the chain. This represents the unbroken unity of humankind, and Indonesia takes its place among this family of nations.

Nationalism – symbolised by the head of the buffalo. All ethnic groups in Indonesia must unite.

Representative Government – symbolised by the banyan tree. As distinct from the western brand of parliamentary democracy, Soekarno envisaged a form of Indonesian democracy based on the village system of deliberation *(permusyawaratan)* among representatives to achieve consensus *(mufakat)*. The western system of 'majority rules' is considered a means by which 51% potentially oppresses the other 49%.

Social Justice – symbolised by the sprays of rice and cotton. A just and prosperous society gives adequate supplies of food and clothing for all – these are the basic requirements of social justice.

Rice, Rice, Rice

The process of growing rice starts with the bare, dry and harvested fields. The remaining rice stalks are burnt off and the field is then liberally soaked and repeatedly ploughed. Nowadays this may be done with a mechanical, petrol-powered cultivator, but often two bullocks or cattle pulling a wooden plough are still used. Once the field is reduced to the required muddy consistency, a small corner of the field is walled off and the seedling rice is planted there. The rice is grown to a reasonable size and then lifted and replanted, shoot by shoot, in the larger field. After that it's easy street for a while as the rice steadily matures.

The walls of the fields have to be kept in working order and the fields weeded, but generally this is a time to practise the gamelan, watch the dancers, do a little woodcarving or just pass the time. Finally, harvest time rolls around and the whole village turns out for a period of solid hard work. Planting the rice is strictly a male occupation but everybody takes part in harvesting it.

New introduced varieties have led to changes in traditional practices and customs. Because the new rice falls easily from the stalk, it cannot be carried to the village after harvesting and it must be threshed in the fields. The husking is often now done by small mechanical mills, rather than by women pounding it in wooden troughs. A number of songs, rituals and festivals associated with old ways of harvesting and milling rice are dying out, and everyone agrees that the new rice doesn't taste as good as *padi Bali*. Small areas of padi Bali are still planted and harvested in traditional ways to placate the rice goddess Dewi Sri, and there are still temples and offerings to her in every rice field.

Rice

Although the Balinese grow various crops, rice is by far the most important. There can be few places where people have played such a large part in changing the natural landscape, yet at the same time making it so beautiful. The terraces trip down hillsides like steps for a giant, in shades of gold, brown and green as delicately selected as an artist's palette.

There are three words for rice in Indonesian – *padi* is the growing rice plant (hence padi or paddy fields); *beras* is the uncooked grain; and *nasi* is cooked rice, as in *nasi goreng* and *nasi putih*.

The intricate organisation necessary for growing rice is a large factor in the strength of Bali's community life. The rice growers' association, known as a *subak*, has to carefully plan the use of irrigation water. The Balinese use irrigation so successfully that they are reputed to be some of the best rice growers in the world, managing two harvests a year, although there are no distinct times for planting and harvesting the rice.

Rice production on Bali has increased substantially with the widespread adoption of new high-yield varieties of rice in place of the traditional rice, *padi Bali*. The best known of these, IR36, was introduced in 1969. The new rice varieties can be harvested sooner (four months after planting instead of five for the traditional variety) and are resistant to many diseases.

New strains now account for more than 90% of the rice planted on Bali, but there have been problems. IR36 requires the use of more pesticides, and over-use of these chemicals has resulted in ecological changes such as the depletion of frog and eel populations, which depend on the insects for survival.

Economic Crisis of 1997-8

In early 1997, most countries in South-East Asia were beginning to feel the effects of a severe down-turn in their economies. For

Indonesia, with the largest workforce in the region, the result was devastating. Indonesia had to seek rescue packages from the International Monetary Fund totalling about US$40 billion, but this didn't stop numerous bankruptcies, widespread unemployment and the rupiah plummeting to about 20% of its previous value, to more than 12,000 rp to $US1 in mid-1998.

The current minimum wage (which is about 200,000 rp per month) does not adequately cover the costs of a family's basic food needs, and by the end of 1998 an estimated 48% of the population of Indonesia will be living below the poverty line. The dire economic situation was exacerbated by the forest fires in Kalimantan and Irian Jaya which devastated the logging industry, and the fires and riots which seriously affected the vital tourist industry throughout the country.

POPULATION & PEOPLE

Bali is a densely populated island, with an estimated 2.9 million people in 1995 – about 520 people per sq km. The population is almost all Indonesian; 95% are of Balinese Hindu religion and could be described as ethnic Balinese. Most of the other residents are from other parts of Indonesia – particularly

---

The Continuing Harvest

A legend relates how a group of Balinese farmers promised to sacrifice a pig if their harvest was good. As the bountiful harvest time approached, no pig could be found and it was reluctantly decided that a child should be sacrificed.

Then one of the farmers had an idea: they had promised the sacrifice after the harvest. If there was always new rice growing, then the harvest would always be about to take place and no sacrifice would be necessary. Since then, the Balinese have always planted one field of rice before harvesting another.

Java, but also Sumatra and Nusa Tenggara; the tourist industry is a magnet for people seeking jobs and business opportunities. Quite a few Balinese have moved to more lightly populated islands as part of the *transmigrasi* (transmigration) programme.

The Balinese people are predominantly of the 'Malay' race – descendants of the groups which travelled south-east from China in the migrations of around 3000 BC. Before that, Bali may have been populated by people related to Australian Aborigines, who appear to have mixed at least a little with the group which displaced them. Other ethnic strands may have come from India, Polynesia and Melanesia, and a diverse range of physical features from all those groups can be seen in Bali's current population.

What defines the Balinese people is cultural rather than racial, and the Balinese culture embraces both the minority Bali Aga groups, whose Hindu traditions predate the arrival of the Majapahit court from Java in the 15th century, and the vast majority of Balinese whose culture is a legacy of that influx.

Caste System

The caste system derives from Hindu traditions on Java dating back to about 1350, although it is not nearly as strict as the system in India. On Bali, caste determines roles in religious rituals and the form of language to be used in every social situation.

Most aspects of Balinese culture have proved to be adaptable – as Bali becomes more and more a part of Indonesia and the rest of the world – but the question of caste is problematic. There were pressures on and within the caste system even before the Dutch arrived, and the colonial period entrenched a caste structure which suited the Dutch interests more than those of the Balinese. During the 1960s, the Communists opposed the caste system as a feudal relic; a view shared by liberals and intellectuals, at least until the massacres of suspected Communists in 1965-6.

Despite the persistence of honorific titles, the practical importance of one's caste is diminishing, as status becomes more a matter of education, economic success and community influence.

The importance of caste differences in language is mitigated by the use of 'polite' forms of Balinese language, or by using the national Indonesian language (Bahasa Indonesia), itself a sign of some status. In a traditional village, however, caste is still very much a part of life, and caste concepts are still absolutely essential to religious practices.

About 90% of Bali's ethnic population belongs to the common *sudra* (also known as *wong kesamen*) caste, and the rest belong to the *triwangsa* caste (which means 'three people'), also known as *wong menak*. The triwangsa is divided into three sub-castes, listed in order of importance:

Brahmana are high priests, with titles of Ida Bagus (male) and Ida Ayu (female);

Ksatriyasa (or Satriana) are merchants, with titles of Cokodor (males) and Ana Ayung (females);

Wesia (or Gusti) are the main caste of the nobility, with titles of Gusti Ngura or Dewa Gede (male), and Gusti Ayu or Dewa Ayu (female).

Minority Groups

Ethnic minorities on Bali include some communities of the indigenous Bali Aga people, a small Chinese contingent in the larger towns, and a few thousand Indian and Arab merchants in Denpasar, plus a number of more or less permanent western visitors, many of them women married to Balinese men.

In general terms, the island is a model of religious tolerance, with two Christian villages (one Catholic, one Protestant), some Chinese temples, a Buddhist monastery and Javanese and other Muslim communities, particularly around the ports of Gilimanuk, Singaraja and Padangbai. Some Muslims have upset some Balinese by building mosques, insisting on Islamic regulations (such as not eating pork, and keeping dogs) and not being part of temple and village ceremonies.

Population Growth

Population control continues to be a priority of the Indonesian government, and the family planning slogan *dua anak cukup* (two children is enough) remains a recurring theme in roadside posters. It seems to be quite successful, as many young families are limiting themselves to two children (or sometimes maybe three), but certainly not the seven or nine children common two or three generations ago. The success of the programme can be measured in the decline of the birth rate to around 11.8 live births per 1000 population, one of the lowest in the country.

EDUCATION

In Indonesia, education begins with six years of primary school (Sekolah Dasar or SD), then three years of junior high school (Sekolah Menengah Pertama or SMP) and three years of senior high school (Sekolah Menengah Atas or SMA), which leads to university. More than 90% of children on Bali complete primary school, but only about 25% completes secondary school. Schooling is not free and, although government schools do not charge much, many of the poorest families send children to work rather than to school. For the wealthy, expensive private schools offer higher standards at all levels. Literacy on Bali is higher than the national average of around 77%. Going to university

Rotary Sight Restoration Project

On Bali, blind men cannot work, while women who have white eyes caused by disease are regarded as 'evil', and often shunned from Balinese society. But most eye problems among the Balinese are simply cataracts, which can be cured with quick, cheap operations.

The Rotary Sight Restoration Project, supported by the Australian branch of the international organisation Rotary, was established on Bali in 1991. Since that time, the project has significantly improved the lives of 10,000 Balinese by providing free eye treatment.

is expensive and only a minority can afford it. There are universities in Denpasar, Singaraja and a campus on Bukit Peninsula.

ARTS

Music, dance and drama are closely related on Bali, with Balinese dance the most obvious example of the three elements working together. For a full discussion of Balinese dance, see the section of the same name in the Ubud & Around chapter later in this book.

Gamelan

Balinese music is based around an ensemble known as a gamelan, which can comprise from four to as many as 50 or more instruments. It is derived from Javanese gamelan, although the playing style is quite different. Gamelan music is almost completely percussion – apart from the simple *suling* flute and the two stringed *rebab*, there are virtually no wind or string instruments. Unlike many forms of Asian music, the Balinese gamelan is accessible to ears attuned to western music. Although it sounds strange at first with its noisy, jangly percussion (there are none of the soothing passages found in some western music), it's exciting and enjoyable.

The main instruments of the gamelan are the xylophone-like *gangsa*, which have bronze bars above bamboo resonators. The player hits the keys with their hammer in one hand, while their other hand moves close behind to dampen the sound from each key just after it is struck. Although the gangsa make up the majority of the instruments and it is their sound which is most prevalent, the actual tempo and nature of the music is controlled by the two *kendang* drums – one male and one female.

Other instruments are the deep *trompong* drums, the small *kempli* gong and the small *cengceng* cymbals used in faster pieces. On Bali, a gamelan orchestra is also called a *gong*. A *gong gede* is the traditional form – *gede* means large or big, and the gong gede comprises the complete traditional orchestra, with between 35 and 40 musicians. The *gong*

kebyar is the modern, popular form of gong, and usually has up to 25 instruments. There are even more ancient forms of the gamelan, such as the *gamelan selunding* still occasionally played in Bali Aga villages like Tenganan in east Bali.

A village's gamelan is usually organised through a banjar, which owns the instruments and stores them in the *bale gong*. The musician's club is known as a *seksa*, and the members meet to practise in the *bale banjar* (a large pavilion for meeting, debate, gamelan practise etc). Gamelan playing is traditionally a male occupation, but a gamelan for women has been established in Ubud. The pieces are learned by heart and passed down from father to son – there is little musical notation or recording of individual pieces.

The gamelan is also played on Java and Javanese gamelan music is held to be more 'formal' and 'classical' than Balinese. A perhaps more telling point is that Javanese gamelan music is rarely heard, apart from at special performances, whereas on Bali you seem to hear gamelans playing everywhere you go. Gamelan music, in both Balinese and Javanese styles, is available on cassette tapes and the occasional CD. Look in the music shops and bigger department stores in the Kuta region.

For information on buying gamelan instruments, see the boxed text 'Buying Arts & Crafts' in the following Facts for the Visitor chapter.

Architecture

For the Balinese, architecture has a cosmic significance that is much more important than the physical materials, the construction or the decoration.

A village, a temple, a family compound, an individual structure and even a single part of the structure must all conform to the Balinese concept of cosmic order. They consist of three parts which represent the three worlds of the cosmos – the world of gods (swah), the world of humans (bhwah) and the world of demons (bhur).

They also represent a three part division

Intricate wooden carvings are an integral part of Balinese architecture, particularly at temples where they can cover every available space.

of a person: the head *(utama)*, the body *(madia)* and the legs *(nista)*.

The units of measurement used in traditional buildings are based on the anatomical dimensions of the head of the household, ensuring harmony between the dwelling and those that live in it. Traditionally, the designer of the building is a combination architect-priest called an *undagi*.

A basic element of Balinese architecture is the *bale*, a rectangular, open-sided pavilion with a steeply pitched roof of palm thatch. A family compound will have a number of bale for eating, sleeping and working. The focus of a community *(banjar)* is a large pavilion, the *bale banjar*, used for meetings, debates, gamelan practice etc.

Large, modern buildings like restaurants and the lobby areas of new hotels are often modelled on the bale, and they can be airy, spacious and handsomely proportioned. Beyond a certain size traditional materials cannot be used; concrete is substituted for timber, and sometimes the roof is tiled rather than thatched.

Other elements of modern Balinese architecture are derived from traditional temple design, particularly the decorative carving frequently seen in fancier modern buildings like banks and hotels. Some see this trend as a natural and appropriate development of Balinese style, while others regard the use of traditional features in modern buildings as pure kitsch. Buildings with these features are sometimes described as Baliesque, or Bali Rococo if the decoration is excessive.

Visitors may be disappointed by Balinese palaces *(puri)*, which are neither large nor imposing. These are the traditional residences of the Balinese aristocracy, although now they may be used as hotels or as a regular family compound.

A Balinese palace would never be built more than one storey high – a Balinese noble could not possibly use a ground-floor room if the feet of people on an upper floor were walking above.

Temple Architecture See the 'Balinese Temples' section on the facing page for a discussion of religious architecture and its significance, information on temple festivals, and a list and map of Bali's major temples.

Painting & Carving

Traditionally, painting, carving and other decorative arts were employed only for the adornment of temples and the making of ritual offerings and festival trappings. It was not until the arrival of western artists in the 1930s that paintings and sculptures were seen as artistic creations in their own right, and the range of themes, techniques and styles expanded enormously. Tourism has created a huge market for arts and crafts, and there are many excellent examples showing the Balinese flair for decoration, colour and creativity. For more information, see the 'Balinese Arts & Crafts' colour section following this chapter.

For details on temple sculpture, see the section 'Balinese Temples' on the facing page.

continued on page 44

BALINESE TEMPLES

The number of temples on Bali is simply astonishing – they're everywhere. In fact, since every village has several and every home has at least a simple house-temple, there are actually more temples than homes. The word for temple on Bali is *pura*, which is a Sanskrit word literally meaning 'a space surrounded by a wall'. Like a traditional Balinese home, a temple is walled in, so the shrines you see in rice fields or at magical spots such as by old trees are not real temples. You'll find simple shrines or thrones at all sorts of unusual places. They often overlook crossroads, intersections or even dangerous curves in the road. They either protect passers-by, or give the gods a ringside view of the accidents!

Like so much else of Balinese religion, the temples, although nominally Hindu, owe much to the pre-Majapahit era. Throughout most of the year the temples are quiet and empty, but at festival times they are colourful and active, elaborately decorated, with offerings being made, traditional dances performed, gamelan music ringing out and all manner of activities taking place from cockfights to gambling.

All temples are oriented mountains-sea, not north-south. *Kaja*, the direction towards the mountains, is the most important direction, so at this end of the temple the holiest shrines are found. The direction towards the sea is *kelod*. The sunrise, or *kangin*, is the second most important direction, so on this side you find the secondary shrines. Kaja may be towards a particular mountain – Pura Besakih in east Bali is pointed directly towards Gunung Agung – or it may just be the mountains in general, which run east-west along the length of Bali.

Temple Types

There are three basic temple types which almost every village will have. The most important is the *pura puseh* (temple of origin), which is dedicated to the village founders and is at the kaja end of the village. In the middle of the village is the *pura desa* for the spirits that protect the village community in its day-to-day life. At the kelod end of the village is the *pura dalem* (temple of the dead). The graveyard is also here, and the temple will often include representations of Durga, the terrible side of Shiva's wife Parvati. Both Shiva and Parvati have a creative and destructive side, and it's their destructive powers that are honoured in the pura dalem.

Other temples include those dedicated to the spirits of irrigated agriculture. Rice growing is so important on Bali, and the division of water for irrigation purposes is handled with such care, that these *pura subak* or *pura ulun suwi* can be of considerable importance. Other temples may also honour dry-field agriculture, as well as the flooded rice paddies.

In addition to these 'local' temples, Bali also has a lesser number of great temples. Each family worships its ancestors in the family temple, the clan worships in its clan temple and the village in the pura puseh. Above these come the temples of royalty or state temples, and in many cases a kingdom would have three of these – a main state temple in the heartland of the state (like Pura Taman Ayun in Mengwi in west Bali), then a mountain temple (like Pura Besakih) and a sea temple (like Pura Luhur Ulu Watu in south Bali).

Every house on Bali has its house temple which is at the kaja-kangin corner of the courtyard. There will be shrines to the Hindu 'trinity' of Brahma, Shiva and Vishnu; to *taksu*, the divine intermediary; and to *tugu*, the lord of the ground.

Left: Perched on the slopes of Gunung Agung, Pura Besakih is Bali's most important temple complex, containing 23 separate but related temples. The site has been used for religious purposes since prehistoric times, with some temple foundations dating back at least 2000 years.

RICHARD I'ANSON

Temple Architecture

While Balinese houses are often attractive places (due in large part to their beautiful gardens), they've never been lavished with the architectural detail reserved for temples. Indeed, many of the decorative features and sculpture most associated with Balinese buildings are traditionally found only in temples.

Temples are designed to set rules and formulae. A temple compound contains a number of *gedongs* (shrines) of varying sizes made from solid brick and stone, but always heavily decorated with carvings. The entrance to larger temples is through a sculptured tower split down the middle *(candi bentar)*, and the entrance to the inner courtyard is through a carved door in another tower, also heavily carved. Also see the boxed text 'Typical Temple Design' on the following pages.

Right: Ubud is justly famous as a centre of Balinese crafts and dance, but it also has a huge range of temples, with many displaying intricately carved stone decoration.

SARA-JANE CLELAND

Typical Temple Design

There is a great deal of variation in temple design, but the small two-courtyard temple illustrated has all the basic elements. Larger temples may have more courtyards and more shrines, and similar small temples may have the less important buildings and shrines arranged in a different pattern.

1 Candi Bentar This is the temple gateway; it's an intricately sculptured tower which looks as if it has been split down the centre and then moved apart.

2 Kulkul Tower This is the warning drum tower from which a wooden split drum (known as a *kulkul*) is sounded to announce events at the temple or warn of danger.

3 Bales These are pavilions, generally open sided, for temporary use or for storage. They may include a *bale gong* (3A), where the gamelan orchestra plays during festivals, or a *paon* (3B), used as a temporary kitchen to prepare offerings for temple ceremonies. A particularly large bale used as a stage for dances or cockfights is known as a *wantilan* (3C).

4 Kori Agung or Paduraksa The gateway to the inner courtyard is an intricately sculptured stone tower (like the candi bentar), but you gain entry through a doorway reached by steps in the middle of the tower. The door is normally kept closed except during festivals.

5 Raksa or Dwarapala These are the statues of fierce guardian figures who protect the doorway and keep out evil spirits. Above the doorway there will be the equally fierce face of a *bhoma*, with hands outstretched to keep back unwanted spirits.

6 Aling Aling If Raksa and the bhoma slip up and an evil spirit does manage to slither through the entrance, the aling aling, a low wall directly behind the entrance, should keep them at bay since evil spirits find it notoriously difficult to make right-angle turns.

7 Side Gate For most of the year, when no ceremony is in process, entry to the inner courtyard is made through this side gate which is always open. Presumably, evil spirits don't think of getting in this way.

8 Small Shrines or Gedongs These usually include shrines to Ngrurah Alit and Ngrurah Gede, who organise things and ensure that the correct offerings are made.

9 Padmasana This is the stone throne for the sun god Surya, and is situated at the most auspicious kaja-kangin corner. The throne rests on the 'world turtle', or *badawang*, which is held by two snake-like *nagas* (mythological serpents).

10 Meru These are multi-roofed Balinese shrines. Usually there will be an 11 roofed meru (11A) to Sanghyang Widi, the supreme Balinese deity, and a three roofed meru (11B) to the holy mountain Gunung Agung.

Typical Temple Design

12 Small Shrines or Gedongs More small shrines will be found at the kaja (mountain) end of the courtyard. Typically these include a shrine like a single-roofed meru to Gunung Batur (another of Bali's sacred mountains); a shrine known as the Maospait dedicated to the original Majapahit settlers who brought the Hindu religion to Bali; and a shrine to the *taksu* who acts as an interpreter for the gods. Trance dancers are said to be mouthpieces for the taksu or it may use a medium to convey the gods' wishes.

13 Bale Piasan These are open pavilions used for the display of temple offerings. There may be several of these bales.

14 Gedong Pesimpangan This is a stone building dedicated to the village founder or a local deity.

15 Paruman or Pepelik This open pavilion in the centre of the inner courtyard is where the gods are supposed to assemble to watch the ceremonies of a temple festival.

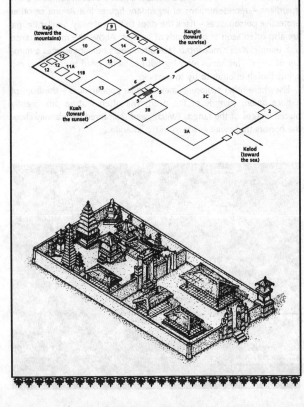

Temple Sculpture & Decoration

Architecture and sculpture are inextricably bound together – a temple gateway is not just put up, every square centimetre of it is intricately carved and a diminishing series of demon faces is placed above it as protection. Even then, it's not complete without a couple of stone statues to act as guardians.

The level of decoration does vary. In small or less important temples, the sculpture may be limited or even nonexistent. In other temples, particularly some of the exuberantly detailed temples of northern Bali, the sculpture may be almost overwhelming in its intricacy and interest. Sometimes a temple is built with minimal decoration, in the hope that some sculpture can be added when more money is available. Sculpture also deteriorates fairly rapidly, and is restored or replaced as resources permit – it's not uncommon to see a temple with old carvings that are barely discernible, next to new work which has just been finished.

Sculpture often appears in a number of set places in temples. Door guardians – representations of legendary figures like Arjuna or other protective personalities – flank the steps to the gateway. Similar figures are also often seen at both ends of bridges. Above the main entrance to a temple, Kala's monstrous face often peers out, sometimes a number of times – his hands reaching out beside his head to catch any evil spirits foolish enough to try to sneak in.

Elsewhere other sculptures make regular appearances – the front of a *pura dalem* (temple of the dead) will often feature prominently placed images of the rangda (witch), and sculptured panels may show the horrors that await evildoers in the afterlife.

PAUL BEINSSEN

Left: The demon Kumba Karna is a *rakshasa* (demon of noble character) and so is suitable as a guardian of temple portals.

Top Left: A Bali Aga woman attends to a home temple at the village of Tenganan in east Bali.

Top Right: Worshippers carry offerings of food, fruit and flowers during a festival at Bali's holiest temple, Pura Besakih, in east Bali.

Bottom: A festival scene from Pura Besakih.

RICHARD I'ANSON

SARA-JANE CLELAND

SARA-JANE CLELAND

Top: Pura Besakih, Bali's principal temple, with it's spectacular setting on the slopes of Gunung Agung.

Middle: Dedictaed to Dewi Danu, the goddess of the waters, the scenic Pura Ulun Danu Bratan sits on the shore of Danau Bratan, near Candikuning in central Bali.

Bottom: Pura Gurung Labuh, a beautiful and tranquil temple near the Campuan bridge, west of Ubud in Bali.

PAUL BEINSSEN

Top: Like most Balinese towns, Ubud is dotted with shrines in its gardens, fields and streets. This shrine appears in an Ubud garden.

Bottom left & right: Intricate woodcarvings are are a common adornment on Balinese temples.

GREGORY ADAMS

GREGORY ADAMS

SARA-JANE CLELAND

SARA-JANE CLELAND

RICHARD I'ANSON

ADAM MCCROW

RICHARD I'ANSON

RICHARD I'ANSON

Top left, middle & right: Examples of temple statuary from across Bali.

Middle left & right: Detail of temple doors.

Bottom: Statues for sale at the village of Batubulan in south Bali.

Major Temples

Directional Temples Certain special temples on Bali are of such importance that they are deemed to be owned by the whole island rather than by individual villages or local community organisations. There are nine *kahyangan jagat*, or directional temples, spread across the island:

Temple	Location	Region
Pura Besakih	Besakih	east Bali
Pura Ulun Danu	Batur	central mountains
Sambu	Gunung Agung	east Bali
Pura Lempuyang	near Tirta Gangga	east Bali
Pura Goa Lawah	near Padangbai	east Bali
Pura Masceti	near Gianyar	east Bali
Pura Luhur Ulu Watu	Ulu Watu	south Bali
Pura Luhur Batukau	Gunung Batukau	central mountains
Pura Ulun Danu Bratan	Candikuning (Danau Bratan)	central mountains

Most of these temples are well known, easily accessible and familiar objectives for many tourist groups, but some are rarely seen by visitors to Bali.

Pura Masceti, on the coast south of Gianyar, is easily reached but infrequently visited. It takes a stiff walk to reach remote Pura Lempuyang at the eastern end of the island.

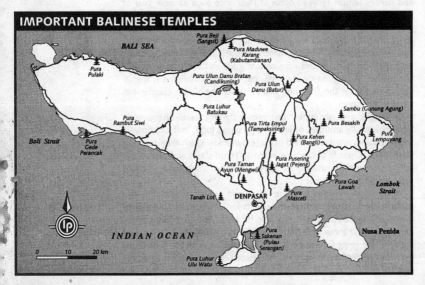

IMPORTANT BALINESE TEMPLES

BALI SEA

Pura Beji (Sangsit)

Pura Maduwe Karang (Kabutambanan)

Pura Pulaki

Puru Ulun Danu Bratan (Candikuning)

Pura Ulun Danu (Batur)

Pura Luhur Batukau

Sambu (Gunung Agung)

Pura Rambut Siwi

Pura Tirta Empul (Tampaksiring)

Pura Besakih

Pura Kehen (Bangli)

Pura Lempuyang

Bali Strait

Pura Gede Perancak

Pura Taman Ayun (Mengwi)

Pura Pusering Jagat (Pejeng)

Pura Goa Lawah

Lombok Strait

Tanah Lot

DENPASAR

Pura Masceti

Nusa Penida

INDIAN OCEAN

Pura Sakenan (Pulau Serangan)

Pura Luhur Ulu Watu

0   10   20 km

World Sanctuaries Bali boasts six *sad-kahyangan*, or world sanctuaries. It's not so easy to list the six 'world sanctuaries' as there is considerable dispute as to which ones make the grade. Usually the six are drawn from the list of nine directional temples, but other important temples like Pura Pusering Jagat, with its enormous bronze drum at Pejeng, near Ubud, or Pura Kehen in Bangli (east Bali) may also creep on to some lists.

Other Important Temples There are numerous other important temples around the island apart from the world sanctuaries and directional temples. They include:

Pura Maduwe Karang – an agricultural temple on the north coast famous for its spirited bas reliefs, including one of a bicycle rider.
Pura Rambut Siwi – a beautiful coastal temple towards the western end of the island.
Pura Taman Ayun – the large and imposing state temple at Mengwi, northwest of Denpasar.
Pura Tirta Empul – the beautiful temple at Tampaksiring, with springs and bathing pools at the source of Sungai Pakerisan, to the north of Ubud.
Tanah Lot – the enormously popular sunset temple perched on a rock just off the coast west of Denpasar.

Temple Festivals

For much of the year Balinese temples are deserted, but every now and then they come alive with days of frenetic activity and nights of drama and dance. Temple festivals occur at least once each Balinese year of 210 days. The annual 'temple birthday' is known as an *odalan*. Since most villages have at least three temples, you're assured of at least five or six annual festivals in every village. But that's only the start – there can be special festival days common throughout the islands, festivals for certain temples, festivals for certain gods and festivals because it just seemed like a good idea to have one. The Public Holidays & Special Events section in the following Bali Facts for the Visitor chapter has more information.

While the men slaughter their prized fighting birds, the women bring beautifully arranged offerings of prepared food, fruit and flowers to the temple, artistically piled in huge pyramids which they carry on their heads. Outside the temple, *warungs* (food stalls) and other stalls selling toys and trinkets are set up. In the outer courtyard a gamelan provides further amusement.

While all this activity is going on in and around the temple, the *pemangkus* (temple guardians and priests for temple rituals) suggest to the gods that they should come down for a visit and enjoy the goings-on. That's what those little thrones are for in the temple shrines – they are symbolic seats for the gods to occupy during festivals. Sometimes small images known as *pratimas* are placed on the thrones, to represent the gods.

At some festivals, the images and thrones of the deities are taken out of the temple and ceremonially carried down to the sea (or just to a suitable expanse of water if the sea is too distant) for a ceremonial bath. Gamelans follow the merry procession and provide a suitable musical accompaniment.

Back in the temple women dance the stately Pendet, an offering dance for the gods, and all night long there's activity, music and dancing. It's just like a country fair, complete with food stands, amusements, games, stalls, gambling, noise, colour and confusion.

Finally, as dawn approaches, the entertainment fades away, the women perform the last Pendet, the pemangkus suggest to the gods that maybe it's time they made their weary way back to heaven and the people wend their weary way back to their homes.

Temple Etiquette

Foreigners can enter temple complexes, except perhaps during a major festival, but only practising Hindus are allowed to enter the actual temples themselves. You don't have to go barefoot as in many Buddhist shrines, but you are expected to be appropriately dressed. Normally, you have to wear a sarong, but you're often excused if you are wearing long trousers or a skirt. Many temples rent sarongs for about 1000 rp, but you can buy one yourself for about 10,000 rp. You'll soon recoup the cost if you visit many temples, and you're certain of being politely dressed even at temples where no sarongs are for rent. Often, you also need a scarf or *selandong* to tie around your waist, but if you need one, they can also be rented outside temples.

Priests should be shown respect, particularly at festivals. They are the most important people at the temple and should, therefore, be on the highest plane. Don't put yourself higher than them by, for example, climbing up on a wall to take photographs.

There will usually be a sign outside temple entrances warning you to be well dressed and respectful, and also requesting that women do not enter the temple while menstruating. Menstruating women are believed to be 'ritually unclean', and the same prohibition applies to people with open wounds, women who have recently given birth and those who are recently bereaved.

continued from page 34

Wayang Kulit

The shadow puppet plays known as *wayang kulit* are popular not only on Bali, but throughout the whole archipelago. The plays are far more than mere entertainment, however, for the puppets are believed to have great spiritual power and the *dalang*, the puppet master and storyteller, is an almost mystical figure. He has to be a person of considerable skill and even greater endurance. He not only has to manipulate the puppets and tell the story, but he must also conduct the small gamelan orchestra, the *gender wayang*, and beat time with his chanting – having long run out of hands to do things with, he performs the latter task with a horn held with his toes!

The dalang's mystical powers come into play because the wayang kulit, like so much of Balinese drama, is another phase of the eternal struggle between good and evil. The endurance factor comes in because a wayang kulit performance can last six or more hours and the performances always seem to start so late that the drama is only finally resolved as the sun peeps up over the horizon.

The intricate lace figures of shadow puppets are made of buffalo hide carefully cut with a sharp, chisel-like stylus and then painted. The figures are completely traditional – there is no deviation from the standard list of characters and their standardised appearance, so there's no mistaking who is who.

Although wayang kulit performances normally are held at night, there are sometimes daytime temple performances, where the figures are manipulated without a screen.

At night-time performances, the dalang sits behind a screen on which the shadows of the puppets are cast, usually by an oil lamp which gives a far more romantic flickering light than modern electric lighting would do. Traditionally, women and children sit together in front of the screen, while the men sit behind the screen with the dalang and his assistants.

The characters are arrayed to the right and

Wayang kulit performances remain a vital part of village social life, providing a forum for the latest news and gossip, as well as passing a rich oral tradition on to the next generation.

left of the puppet master – goodies to the right, baddies to the left. The characters include nobles, who speak in the high Javanese language Kawi, and common clowns, who speak in everyday Balinese. The dalang also has to be a linguist! When the four clowns (Delem and Sangut are the bad ones, Twalen and his son Merdah are the good ones) are on screen, the performance becomes something of a Punch and Judy show, with much rushing back and forth, clouts on the head and comic insults.

The noble characters are altogether more refined – they include the terrible Durga and the noble Bima. Wayang kulit stories are chiefly derived from the great Hindu epics, the *Mahabharata* and the *Ramayana*.

For details on buying wayang kulit puppets, see the boxed text 'Buying Arts & Crafts' in the following Facts for the Visitor chapter.

Artists in Postwar Bali

Bali's postwar visitors have never matched that brilliant period of the 1930s when the island seemed to be packed with talented western residents, all busy painting, composing or scribbling down their unique experiences. The war brought the artistic renaissance of the 30s to a juddering halt and it was not until the 50s that a new artistic impetus arrived, an impetus which has to some extent been waylaid by the spawning of 'mass art' by mass tourism since the 70s.

While the visitors of the 30s ranged from artists and anthropologists to musicians and writers, more recent noted visitors have almost all been artists. Plenty of rock stars have been short-term visitors and the book, *A House in Bali,* has been recreated thousands of times with Australian or European holiday homes, but there have been no writers to hold the faintest candle to the earlier chroniclers.

Arie Smit (1916) – Dutch painter Smit was working as an artist in the colonial topographical service in Batavia (modern day Jakarta) when the Pacific War began. Captured by the Japanese, he was taken first to Singapore and then to Thailand, where he survived the infamous labour camps building the railway up to the Burmese border crossing the 'Bridge on the River Kwai'.

Smit returned to Indonesia after the war and taught art in Bandung before moving to Bali to live as an artist from 1956. Smit's paintings have been exhibited in Bali and elsewhere in South-East Asia, but his name will go down in the history books as the inspiration for the Young Artists' movement. Smit still lives in Ubud.

Theo Meier (1908-82) – A Swiss artist, Meier first visited Bali in 1936 and lived in Sanur before WWII. Much of his pre-war work was lost when the Japanese destroyed his studio, but he returned to Bali after the war and lived for some time in Iseh in the house that fellow artist Walter Spies had established just before the war. In 1957 he moved to Chiang Mai in Thailand, where he lived until his death in 1982, though he was a frequent visitor to Bali.

Adrien Jean Le Mayeur de Merpes (1880-1958) – The life of this Belgian-born artist is documented in the boxed text 'The Artist from Belgium' in the Sanur section of the South Bali chapter.

Donald Friend (1915-89) – This peripatetic Australian artist travelled to Bali in 1966 and, with occasional interruptions, spent most of his time there until he returned to Australia in 1980. He produced some of his finest work on Bali.

Antonio Blanco (1926) – Manila-born Spanish artist Blanco married a Balinese woman and moved to Bali in the late 50s. His house, near the river confluence in Campuan, Ubud, is where he paints and lives the life of a colourful (and comfortable) artist. Visitors who pay to enter his fine home often get a chance to hear his views on life, the universe and everything.

Han Snel (1925) – Dutch artist Snel was a conscript soldier sent to recapture the Dutch East Indies after WWII. He deserted, took Indonesian citizenship and has lived on Bali since the 50s, running one of Ubud's finest hotels with his Balinese wife.

The Family Compound

Although many modern Balinese houses, particularly in Denpasar or the larger towns, are arranged much like houses in the west, there are still a great number of traditional Balinese homes. In Ubud, for example, nearly every house will follow the same traditional walled design.

Like houses in ancient Rome, the Balinese house looks inward; the outside is simply a high wall. Inside there will be a garden and a separate small building, or *bale*, for each function. There will be one building for cooking, one building for washing and the toilet, and separate buildings for each 'bedroom'. What there won't be is a 'living room' because in Bali's mild tropical climate you live outside – the 'living room' and 'dining room' will be open verandah areas, looking out into the garden. The whole complex is oriented on the *kaja-kelod* axis, between the mountains and the sea.

Analogous to the human body, there's a head (the family temple with its ancestral shrine), arms (the sleeping and living areas), legs and feet (the kitchen and rice storage building), and even an anus (the garbage pit). There may be an area outside the house compound where fruit trees are grown or a pig may be kept. Usually the house is entered through a gateway backed by a small wall known as the *aling aling*. It serves a practical and a spiritual purpose, both preventing passers-by from seeing in and stopping evil spirits from entering. Evil spirits cannot easily turn corners so the aling aling stops them from simply scooting straight in through the gate!

1 **Sanggah Kemulan**
   Family Temple
2 **Uma Metan**
   Sleeping pavilion for the family head
3 **Tuga**
   Shrine
4 **Pengidjeng**
   Shrine
5 **Bale Tiang Sanga**
   Guest pavilion

6 **Natar**
   Courtyard with frangipani or hibiscus shade tree
7 **Bale Sikepat**
   Sleeping pavilion for relatives
8 **Fruit trees and coconut palms**
9 **Vegetable garden**
10 **Bale Sekenam**
   Working and sleeping pavilion
11 **Paon**
   Kitchen

12 **Lumbung**
   Rice barn
13 **Rice-threshing area**
14 **Aling Aling**
   Screen wall
15 **Lawang**
   Gate
16 **Apit Lawang**
   Gate shrines

JAMES LYON

The open-sided pavilion, or *bale*, is the basic unit of Balinese architecture.

The Family Compound

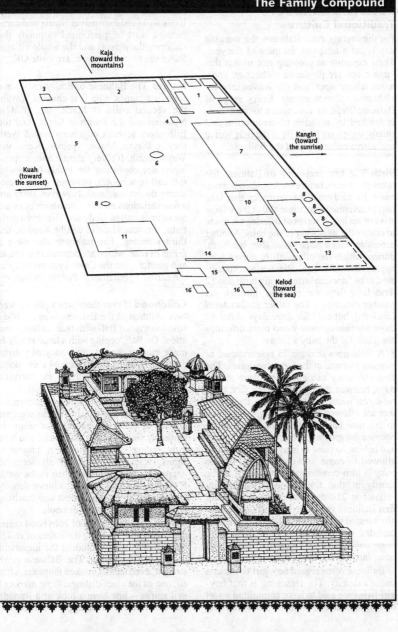

Kaja
(toward the mountains)

Kangin
(toward
the sunrise)

Kuah
(toward
the sunset)

Kelod
(toward
the sea)

SOCIETY & CONDUCT
Traditional Culture

For the average rural Balinese, the working day is not a long one for most of the year. Their expertise at growing rice means that large crops are produced without an enormous labour input, and this leaves time for elaborate cultural events. Every stage of Balinese life, from conception to cremation, is marked by a series of ceremonies and rituals, which are the basis of the rich, varied and active cultural life of the Balinese.

Birth The first ceremony of Balinese life takes place even before birth – when women reach the third month of pregnancy they take part in ceremonies at home and at the village river or spring. A series of offerings is made to ensure the wellbeing of the baby. Another ceremony takes place soon after the birth, during which the afterbirth is buried with appropriate offerings. Women are considered to be 'unclean' after giving birth and 12 days later they are 'purified' through yet another ceremony. The father is also *sebel* (unclean), but only for three days. After 42 days, another ceremony and more offerings are made for the baby's future.

A child goes through 13 celebrations, or *manusa yadnya*, in the formative years. The first ceremony or *oton* takes place at 105 days, halfway through the baby's first Balinese year when, for the first time, the baby's feet are allowed to touch the ground. Prior to this time babies are carried continuously because the ground is believed to be impure, and babies, so close to heaven, should not be allowed to come into contact with it. The baby is also ceremonially welcomed to the family at this time. Another ceremony follows at 210 days, at the end of his/her first Balinese year, when the baby is spiritually blessed to the ancestral temple. The first birthday is celebrated in grand style, with huge and expensive feasts for family and other members of the community.

Balinese often regard boy-girl twins as a major calamity. The reasoning is that boy-girl twins are said to have committed a sort of spiritual incest while in the womb and

that this is dangerous for the whole village. Extensive (and expensive) rituals and ceremonies must be performed to purify the children, the parents and the whole village. Same sex twins, however, are quite OK.

Names The Balinese basically only have four first names. The first child is Wayan, the second child is Made, the third is Nyoman and the fourth is Ketut. And the fifth, sixth, seventh, eighth and ninth? Well, they're Wayan, Made, Nyoman, Ketut and Wayan again. It's very simple and, surprisingly, not confusing for locals (except at roll call in school?), although many westerners do get confused. However, there are a few variations on this – first-born boys are sometimes called Gede and first-born girls Putu; the second child can be Kardek, the third Komang. The Balinese also have a series of titles which are dependent on caste and gender – see the Caste Systems entry in the earlier Population & People section.

Childhood If ever there was a people who love children, it the Balinese – as anybody who has visited Bali with their children can attest. On Bali, coping with a large family is made much easier by the policy of putting younger children in the care of older ones. One child always seems to be carrying another one around on his or her hip.

Despite the fact that Balinese children are almost immediately part of a separate society of children, they always seem remarkably well behaved. Of course, you hear kids crying occasionally, but tantrums, fights, screams and shouts all seem to happen far less frequently than in the west. It's been said that parents achieve this by treating children with respect and teaching them good behaviour by example.

After the ceremonies of babyhood come the ceremonies marking the stages of childhood and puberty, including the important tooth-filing ceremony. The Balinese prize straight, even teeth. Crooked fangs are, after all, one of the chief distinguishing marks of evil spirits – just have a look at a Rangda mask! A priest files the upper front teeth to

Foreign Affairs

A 'holiday romance' in the heady and exotic environment of tropical Bali has become the stuff of legends. Sweet-talking Balinese 'gigolos' and love-struck women caught in their flattery are part of the mythology of the tourist in Bali. Although a great number of tourists do have an affair with a Balinese or other Indonesian person during their holiday, they are just as likely to have a romance with a fellow traveller as with a local.

Many Balinese people supplement poor wages or survive solely on the tips and gifts that grateful tourists bestow upon them. Undoubtedly some Balinese people are unable to see beyond dollar signs in their interactions with tourists. This may be more prevalent during the current economic crisis. There are also Balinese 'culture brokers', guides who become the bridge between the tourist domain and the rest of Bali. This may involve inviting tourists to their homes (and their beds), taking them to family ceremonies and enriching their experience in every way. Some relationships between Balinese people and tourists inevitably develop into serious love affairs, marriage and even migration.

Mary and Agus met in a gateway in Legian in 1979. He was a waiter from west Bali and she thought she was passing through on the way to India. Their initial 'holiday romance' lasted for three months, the duration of a visa in those days, and developed into a long-distance love affair. Mary and her young son travelled to Bali three times, Agus spent six months in Melbourne and, when his visa expired, they all went to Thailand and India in a vain attempt to avoid separation. Three months of poverty and confusion in Calcutta confirmed that they should formalise their relationship and seek a permanent place to stay together. After 14 months' separation, while they waited for Agus' fiance visa to Australia, Mary returned to Bali and they married in Agus' village in west Bali in 1982. In 1983 they had a civil ceremony in Melbourne in their back garden with the friends and family who had been so supportive over the years. They have three children between them and have run their Balinese restaurant in West Melbourne for 10 years. They all have regular visits back to Bali to stay with the family and Agus' mother has visited Melbourne twice.

Many 'holiday romances' develop into long-term relationships. Lovers are often forced by time, distance and finances to make commitments to migration in order to continue seeing each other. Plenty of these affairs do end in bitterness and heartbreak, and certainly a number of mixed marriages have ended in divorce. There is no crystal ball to foretell the future.

People on holiday may seek a sexual relationship to complete the experience. Others may find themselves attracted to a local and return time and time again in pursuit of love. It is difficult to operate in the gulf between 'first' and 'third' world existence when neither party has any real understanding of the other's world. But life is an adventure. If we are mindful of 'safe sex', part of that protective behaviour should involve recognising our own needs and having realistic expectations of the people we meet along the way.

❀❀❀❀❀❀❀❀❀❀❀❀❀❀❀❀❀❀❀❀❀❀❀❀❀❀❀❀❀❀❀❀❀❀❀❀

produce an aesthetically pleasing straight line. Today the filing is often only symbolic – one pass of the file.

Marriage Every Balinese expects to marry and raise a family, and marriage takes place at a comparatively young age. Marriages are not, in general, arranged as they are in many other Asian communities, although strict rules apply to marriages between the castes.

There are two basic forms of marriage on Bali. The respectable form, in which the family of the man visits the family of the woman and politely proposes that the marriage take place, is mapadik. The Balinese, however, like their fun and often prefer marriage by elopement *(ngorod)* as the more exciting option.

Of course, the Balinese are also practical so nobody is too surprised when the young man spirits away his bride-to-be, even if she loudly protests about being kidnapped. The couple go into hiding and somehow the girl's parents, no matter how assiduously they search, never manage to find her.

Eventually the couple re-emerge, announce that it is too late to stop them now, the marriage is officially recognised and everybody has had a lot of fun and games. Marriage by elopement has another advantage: apart from being exciting and mildly heroic, it's cheaper.

Men & Women Social life on Bali is relatively free and easy and, although Balinese women are not kept cloistered, the roles of the sexes are strictly delineated. There are certain tasks clearly to be handled by

Jamu

Throughout Indonesia, you will often see women walking in the street with huge baskets strapped to their backs, full of bottles of strange looking liquids.

These women, known as *gendong* from the Bahasa Indonesia word for 'carry on the back', sell *jamu* – a drink enjoyed by many Indonesians. Jamu is a tonic believed to revitalise the drinker, cure numerous ailments – such as stress, headaches and rheumatism – and improve fertility.

Jamu consists of herbs and all sorts of minerals – among other things – but the exact ingredients and recipes are kept secret, only passed from one generation of gendong to another. If you want to try a jamu, a blend will be created especially for you, but for best results you will need to take a course of jamu over a long period of time.

women, and others which are reserved for men. Running the household is very much the women's task. In the morning women sweep and clean, and put out the offerings for the gods.

Every household has a shrine or godthrone where offerings must be placed, and areas on the ground, such as at the compound entrance, where offerings for the demons are derisively cast. While women are busy attending to these tasks, the men of the household are likely to be looking after the fighting cocks and any other pets.

Marketing is also a female job, although at large markets cattle selling is definitely a male job. The traditional position of women as preparers of food – and as the buyers and sellers – places them in a good position to take part in the tourist industry. A successful Balinese restaurant or shop is much more likely to have been established by a local woman than a man. In agriculture there's also a division of labour based on sex roles: although everybody turns out in the fields at harvest time, planting the rice is purely a male activity.

In Balinese leisure activities the roles are also gender based. Both men and women dance, but usually only men play in the gamelan. The artistic skills are almost completely left to men, although today you do see some women painters, sculptors and woodcarvers.

Community Life The Balinese have an amazingly active and organised village life – you simply cannot be a faceless nonentity on Bali. You can't help but get to know your neighbours as your life is so entwined and interrelated with theirs. Or at least it still is in the small villages that comprise so much of Bali. Even in the big towns, the banjar ensures that a strong community spirit continues.

The plans of the village *(desa)* generally follow a similar pattern. In the centre, usually at the crossroads of the two major streets, there will be the open meeting space known as the *alun alun*. It's actually more than just a meeting space, because you will also find temples, the town market or even the former prince's home.

The *kulkul* (warning drum) tower will be here and quite likely a big banyan tree. For example, in Ubud, the palace, banyan tree (with its kulkul drums) and temple are all in the centre of town – near the *bemo* stop and the market.

Although village control by the desa authorities is not as strict as it once was, there is still detailed and careful organisation of land ownership because of the necessary interrelation of water supply to the rice fields. Each individual rice field is known as a *sawah* and each farmer who owns even one sawah must be a member of their local *subak* (rice growers' association). The rice paddies must have a steady supply of water and it is the subak's job to ensure that the water gets to everybody.

The head of the local subak will often be the farmer whose rice paddies are at the bottom of the hill, for he will make quite certain that the water gets all the way down to his fields, passing through everybody else's on the way!

Of course, the subak has far more to do than share out the water and ensure that the water channels, dykes and so forth are in good order. Each subak will have its small temple out among the rice fields, where offerings to the spirits of agriculture are made and regular meetings held for the subak members. Like every temple on Bali there are regular festivals and ceremonies to observe. Even individual sawahs may have small altars.

Each desa is further subdivided into banjars, which each male adult joins when he marries. It is the banjar which organises village festivals, marriage ceremonies and even cremations.

Throughout the island you'll see the open-sided bale banjars – they're nearly as common as temples. They serve a multitude of purposes, from a local meeting place to a storage room for the banjar's musical equipment and dance costumes.

Gamelan orchestras are organised at the banjar level and a glance in a bale banjar at any time might reveal a gamelan practice, a meeting, food being prepared for a feast, and even a group of men getting their roosters together in preparation for the next round of cockfights.

Death & Cremation There are ceremonies for every stage of Balinese life, but often the last ceremony – the cremation or *pitra yadna* – is the biggest. A Balinese cremation can be an amazing, spectacular, colourful, noisy and exciting event. In fact, it often takes so long to organise a cremation that years have passed since the death; during that time the body is temporarily buried.

Of course an auspicious day must be chosen for the cremation and, since a big cremation can be a very expensive business, many less wealthy people may take the opportunity of joining in at a larger cremation and sending their dead on their way at the same time. Brahmanas, however, must be cremated immediately.

A cremation ceremony is a fine opportunity to observe the incredible energy the Balinese put into creating real works of art which are totally ephemeral. A lot more than a body gets burnt at the cremation. The body is carried from the burial ground (or from the deceased's home if it's an 'immediate' cremation) to the cremation ground in a high, multi-tiered tower made of bamboo, paper, string, tinsel, silk, cloth, mirrors, flowers and anything else bright and colourful they can think of.

The tower is carried on the shoulders of a group of men, the size of the group depending on the importance of the deceased and hence the size of the tower (although in modern times the size of the towers has been limited by the presence of overhead power lines). The funeral of a former rajah or high priest may require hundreds of men to tote the tower.

Along the way to the cremation ground certain precautions must be taken to ensure that the deceased's spirit does not find its way back home; for instance, getting the spirits confused about their whereabouts, by shaking the tower, running it around in circles, spinning it around, throwing water at it, generally making the trip to the cremation ground anything but a stately and funereal crawl.

Meanwhile, there's likely to be a priest halfway up the tower, hanging on grimly as it sways back and forth, and doing his best to soak bystanders with holy water. A gamelan sprints along behind, providing a suitably exciting musical accompaniment to the procession.

At the cremation ground the body is transferred to a funeral sarcophagus – this should be in the shape of a bull for a Brahmana, a winged lion for a Ksatriyasa, and a sort of elephant-fish for a Sudra. Almost anybody from the higher castes will use a bull – a black bull for Brahmanas or a white bull for priests. Finally, up it all goes in flames – funeral tower, sarcophagus, body, the lot. The eldest son does his duty by poking through the ashes to ensure that there are no bits of body left unburnt.

And where does your soul go after cremation? Why, to a heaven which is just like Bali!

Avoiding Offence

All sorts of behaviour is often tolerated in tourist areas, especially Kuta, but it may still be insensitive and disrespectful. In other parts of the island – particularly the more traditional rural villages and religious sites – visitors should be aware and respectful of local sensibilities, and dress and act appropriately.

Dress In much of Asia, including Bali and particularly (Islamic) Lombok, shorts are not considered polite attire for men or women. Similarly, sleeveless singlet tops are not considered respectable – you're supposed to cover your knees, shoulders and armpits. At Kuta, and the other beach resorts on Bali and Lombok, shorts and singlets have become a part of everyday life, however, and in any case tourists are considered a little strange and their clothing habits are expected to be somewhat eccentric.

Many women go topless on Bali's tourist beaches, but bring a bikini top for less touristy beaches and definitely if you're going to Lombok. Women are better off dressing modestly – revealing tops are just asking for trouble. Short pants are marginally acceptable if they are the baggy type which almost reach the knees.

In temples and government offices, you're expected to be 'properly' dressed, and shorts and singlets don't fulfil that expectation. Thongs (flip-flops) are acceptable in temples if you're otherwise well dressed, but not for government offices. If you want to renew a visa, or even get a local driving licence, ask yourself how you'd dress in a similar situation back home.

It is customary to take off your shoes before entering someone's house. Always remove your footwear before entering a mosque.

Behaviour People within many Asian cultures resent being touched on the head – the head is regarded as the abode of the soul and is therefore sacred.

When handing over or receiving things, it's polite to use the right hand – the left hand is used as a substitute for toilet paper. To show great respect to a high-ranking or elderly person, give something to them using both hands.

Talking to someone with your hands on your hips is impolite and is considered a sign of contempt, anger or aggressiveness – it's the same stance taken by characters in traditional dance and operas to signal these feelings to the audience.

Handshaking is customary for both men and women on introduction and greeting.

The correct way to beckon to someone is with the hand extended and a downward waving motion of all the fingers (except the thumb). The western method of beckoning, with the index finger crooked upward, won't be understood and is considered very rude.

Temple Etiquette See the 'Balinese Temples' section earlier in this chapter for tips on appropriate behaviour at temples and temple complexes.

Small Talk Balinese are sociable and like to chat, and much small talk involves asking questions. The stock questions (in Bahasa Indonesia) are:

Where are you from?	*Dari mana?*
Where are you going?	*Mau ke mana?*
What's your name?	*Siapa nama?*
How long have you been in Indonesia?	*Sudah berapa lama di Indonesia?*
Are you married?	*Sudah kawin?*
What's your religion?	*Apakah beragama?*
Where are you staying?	*Tinggal di mana?*
How many times have you been to Bali?	*Berapa kali sudah ke Bali?*

If you're not comfortable telling a stranger where you're staying, give some vague reply like 'in a cheap *losmen* at the other end of town. I can't remember the exact name, but it's run by a guy called Wayan'.

The question about marriage should be treated very carefully. Indonesians find it absurd that anyone would not want to be married, and being divorced is a great shame. Your social relations will go more smoothly if you say you are 'already married' *(sudah kawin)* or 'not yet married' *(belum kawin)*.

If you are over 30 years in age, it's better to be 'married' or else people will assume there must be some serious defect in your personality. If you really can't handle being 'married', you could say your spouse is dead, which is considered less of a tragedy than being divorced. If you are a woman who does not want a lot of attention from local guys, it is easier to be 'married' than single.

Be careful about the religion question. Many Indonesians presume that westerners are Christian. If you are an atheist you'll be better off not telling them; in Indonesia the logic is that Communists are atheists, and therefore if you are an atheist you must be a Communist.

In all cases, try not to get annoyed by the questions and ask some of your own to show a polite interest in the other person. This is a great way to deflect attention from your personal business and learn something about the local people.

For detailed information on Bahasa Bali, Bahasa Indonesia and Sasak langauges, see the Language chapter at the end of this book.

RELIGION
Islam

The Religion section in the Facts about Lombok chapter has a summary about Islam, the religion of Balinese minority groups from Java, Sulawesi and Lombok.

Hinduism

The Balinese are nominally Hindus, but Balinese Hinduism is a world away from that practised in India. At one time, Hinduism was the predominant religion in Indonesia (as evidenced by the many remarkable Hindu monuments on Java), but it died out with the spread of Islam through the archipelago. The final great Hindu kingdom, that of the Majapahits, virtually evacuated to Bali, taking not only their religion and its rituals, but also their art, literature, music and culture.

It's a mistake, however, to think that this was purely an exotic seed being implanted on virgin soil. The Balinese probably already had strong religious beliefs and an active cultural life. The new influences were simply overlaid on the existing practices – hence the peculiar Balinese interpretation of Hinduism. Of course there are small enclaves of other religions on Bali, particularly the Muslims whose mosques are often seen at ports and fishing villages around the coast, and also Christians.

You can't get away from religion on Bali: there are temples in every village; shrines in every field; and offerings being made at every corner. Balinese also feel that their religion should be an enjoyable thing, for mortals as well as the gods. It's summed up well in their attitude to offerings – you make up a lot of fancy food for offerings, but once the gods have eaten the 'essence' of the food, you've got enough 'substance' left over for a fine feast.

Basically, the Balinese worship the same

gods as the Hindus of India – the trinity of Brahma, Shiva and Vishnu – although the Balinese have a supreme god, Sanghyang Widi. This basic threesome is always alluded to, but never seen, on Bali – a vacant shrine or empty throne tells all.

Other, secondary Hindu gods may occasionally appear, such as Ganesh, Shiva's elephant-headed son, but a great many other purely Balinese gods, spirits and entities have far more everyday reality. The Rangda may bear a close relation to Durga, the terrible side of Shiva's wife Parvati, but it's certain that nobody in India has seen a Barong.

The interpretation of the Hindu pantheon as being many manifestations of a single god makes the religion consistent with the first of the five national principles of Pancasila: a belief in one God (see the boxed text 'Pancasila' under Government & Politics in this chapter).

To the Balinese, spirits are everywhere; it's a reminder that animism is the basis of much of Balinese religion. The offerings put out every morning are there to pay homage to the good spirits and to placate the bad ones – the Balinese take no chances! And if the offerings thrown on the ground are immediately consumed by dogs? Well, so it goes, everybody is suspicious of dogs anyway.

Temples

For a discussion of religious architecture and its significance, information on temple festivals, and a list and map of Bali's major temples, see the Balinese Temples section earlier in this chapter.

LANGUAGE

The indigenous language, Bahasa Bali, is a spoken language with various forms based on traditional caste distinctions. The average traveller need not worry about Balinese, however. It's interesting to consider and fun to pick up a few words, but for practical travelling purposes, and to communicate with Balinese, it's wiser to put your efforts into learning Bahasa Indonesia.

Bahasa Indonesia is the national language, used in the education system and for all legal and administrative purposes. It is becoming more and more widely used, partly because of its importance in official use, partly because of the number of non-Balinese now living and working on Bali, and also because it's a polite form of language which avoids the intricacies of the caste system.

For the visitor who wants to pick up enough to get by in the common language, Indonesian is very easy to learn. In fact, it is rated as one of the simplest languages in the world, as there are no tenses, plurals or genders and often one word can convey the meaning of a whole sentence.

Furthermore, it is an easy language to pronounce; there are no tonal complications, and it uses the same Roman alphabet as English – unlike most other languages in Asia (with the exception of Malay, on which Bahasa Indonesia is based). It can also be a delightfully poetic language – *hari* is 'day' and *mata* is 'eye', therefore *matahari* is the 'eye of the day', ie 'the sun'.

English is common in the tourist areas, and is usually spoken very well. Many Balinese in the tourist industry also have a smattering (or more) of German, Japanese, French and/or Italian.

A few older people speak Dutch and are often keen to practice it. The Balinese facility for learning and speaking foreign languages is very impressive. Nevertheless, if you want to travel in remote areas, and communicate with people who aren't in the tourist business, it's a good idea to learn some Bahasa Indonesia.

Written Indonesian can be idiosyncratic, however, and there are often inconsistent spellings of place names. Compound names are written as one word or two – Airsanih or Air Sanih; Padangbai or Padang Bai etc. Words starting with 'Ker' sometimes lose the 'e', as in Kerobokan/Krobokan.

In addition, some Dutch variant spellings remain in common use. These tend to occur in business names, with 'tj' instead of the modern 'j' (as in Tjampuhan/Campuan), and 'oe' instead of 'u' (as in Soekarno/Sukarno).

Phrasebooks & Audio Packs

The most useful language for travellers to Bali and Lombok is Bahasa Indonesia, and a good phrasebook is a wise investment, particularly if you plan to go off the beaten track. Lonely Planet's *Indonesian phrasebook* is a concise and handy introduction to this language.

If you want to learn enough Indonesian for your trip, taught within the context of a story, try Lonely Planet's *Indonesian audio pack*. Available at a few bookshops on Bali is the *Bali Pockset Dictionary* (25,000 rp), which lists grammar and vocabulary in English, Indonesian and low, polite and high level Balinese.

For detailed information on Bahasa Bali, Bahasa Indonesia and Sasak (spoken on Lombok), see the Language chapter at the back of this book.

BALINESE
ARTS & CRAFTS

BERNARD NAPTHINE

The richness of Bali's arts and crafts has its origins in the fertility of the land and the extraordinary productivity of its agriculture. Food in abundance can be produced with a small input of labour, allowing plenty of time for cultural activities.

Every Balinese is an artist and craftsperson and, until the tourist invasion, painting or carving was simply an everyday part of life. Bali had no art galleries or craft shops in those days – what was produced went into temples or was used for festivals. It's a different story now, with hundreds, even thousands, of galleries and craft shops in every possible place a tourist might pass. The real problem with Balinese art and craft today is that there is simply too much of it.

You can't turn around without tripping over more carvings, and in the galleries there are so many paintings that they're stacked up in piles on the floor. Unfortunately, much of this work is rubbish, churned out quickly for people who want a cheap souvenir. There is still much beautiful work produced, but you have to sort through a lot of junk to find it.

Part of the problem is that Balinese art has always been something that is produced today, deteriorates tomorrow, is worn out the next day and thrown away the day after. As a result, very little you see will be old, and even less antique.

Indeed, it's the everyday, disposable crafts which are probably the most surprising on Bali. Even the simplest activities are carried out with care, precision and the Balinese artistic flair. Just glance at those little offering trays placed on the ground for the spirits every morning – each one a throwaway work of art. Look at the temple offerings, the artistically stacked pyramids of fruit or other beautifully decorated foods. Look for the *lamaks*, long woven palm leaf strips used as decorations in festivals and celebrations, or the stylised female figures known as *cili*, which are representations of Dewi Sri. See the intricately carved coconut-shell wall hangings, or simply marvel at the care and energy that goes into constructing huge funeral towers and exotic sarcophagi, all of which will soon go up in flames.

To understand the crafts of Bali it's important to know the crafts of Java, as the cultural and trading relationship between the two islands has always been strong. The ceremonial dagger (kris), so important in a Balinese family, will often have been made on Java. Most of the sarongs that are worn for important ceremonies are made in central Java, except for the *ikat* sarongs from Gianyar. Similarly, Java is the main supplier of puppets and metalwork items, including sacred images.

In many ways, Bali is a showroom for all the crafts of Indonesia. A typical tourist shop will sell puppets and batiks from Java, ikat

Title page: A trance dancer, surrounded by smoke and incense, seeks spirits to enter her body.

Box: A carved guardian defends the entrance to an Ubud temple.

garments from Sumba, Sumbawa and Flores, and textiles and woodcarvings from Bali, Lombok and Kalimantan.

Buying Arts & Crafts

For information on buying sculpture, paintings, woodcarvings, gamelan instruments and wayang kulit puppets, see the boxed text 'Shopping for Arts & Crafts' in the following Facts for the Visitor chapter.

Right: Detail of a carved stone temple wall in Ubud.

BERNARD NAPTHINE

PAINTING

Of the various art forms popular on Bali, painting is probably the one most influenced by western ideas and western demand. Prior to the arrival of western artists after WWI, painting was, like other Balinese art, primarily for temple and palace decoration. The influence of western artists not only expanded it beyond these limited horizons, it also showed the way to whole new subject areas and, possibly most important of all, gave the artists new materials to work with.

Balinese paintings have been classified into several groups or styles, but there is some overlap between them and there are some artists whose work does not really fit into any of the main styles. The best place to see fine examples of every style is the Neka Museum in Ubud.

First, there are the classical, or Kamasan, paintings, named for the village of Kamasan near Semarapura (Klungkung) – these are also called *wayang* style. The Ubud style of painting developed in the 1930s with the influence of the Pita Maha artists' cooperative. The similar Batuan style started at the same time in a nearby village. The postwar Young Artists' style developed in the 1960s, influenced by Dutch artist Arie Smit, who is still an Ubud resident. Finally, the modern or 'academic' style can be loosely defined as anything which doesn't fall into the main Balinese categories – it shows influences of everything from the Post-Impressionists to Rothko.

BERNARD NAPTHINE

Left: An example of the Young Artists' school of painting, Neka Museum, Ubud.

Classical Painting

Until the arrival of the western artists in the 1920s and 1930s, Balinese painting was strictly limited to three basic kinds – *langse*, *iders-iders* and calendars. Langse are large rectangular decorative hangings used in palaces or temples. Iders-iders are scroll paintings hung along the eaves of temples. The style can be traced back to 9th century Javanese sculpture – the 14th century temple complex at Panataran in eastern Java has relief sculptures which display the wayang figures, rich floral designs and flame-and-mountain motifs characteristic of classical Balinese painting.

Balinese calendars are still used to set dates and predict the future, although today most of them are painted for tourists. There are two types – the simpler yellow-coloured calendars from Bedulu, near Ubud, and the more complex classical calendars from Semarapura and Kamasan. The style has also been adapted to create large versions of the zodiacal and lunar calendar, especially the 210 day *wuku* calendar which still regulates the timing of Balinese festivals.

The old langse paintings were prized by local rulers and presented as gifts between rival royal households. The paintings also helped fulfil the important function of imparting ethical values and customs *(adat)* to the ordinary people, in much the same way as traditional dance and *wayang kulit* puppetry.

In fact, it is from the wayang tradition that Kamasan painting takes its essential characteristics – the stylisation of human figures shown either in profile or three-quarters view, their symbolic gestures, and the depiction of divine and heroic characters as refined, and of evil ones as vulgar and crude. The paintings were generally in a narrative sequence, rather like a comic strip, with a series of panels telling a story. The definitive example of this style is the painted ceilings of the Kertha Gosa (Hall of Justice) in Semarapura.

Bottom left: A royal court scene from one of the 267 panels lining the roof of the Kertha Gosa at Semarapura (Klungkung) in east Bali.

Bottom right: From the same ceiling, a salutory lesson for would-be criminals, as sinners are punished for their acts.

GREGORY ADAMS

GREGORY ADAMS

Classical paintings may still show action in comic-strip style, and commonly depict scenes from ancient Hindu epics, the *Ramayana* and *Mahabharata*. Other themes are the *Kakawins* poems, written in the archaic Javanese language of Kawi, and indigenous Balinese folklore with its pre-Hindu/Buddhist beliefs in demonic spirit forces.

Traditionally, the style is essentially linear, with the skill of the artist apparent in the overall composition and sensitivity of the line work. The colouring was of secondary importance and left to apprentices, usually the artist's children. Natural colours were made from soot, clay, pig's bones and other such ingredients, and artists were strictly limited to a set list of shades. Today, paints are all modern oils and acrylics, but the style still uses a limited range of colours. A final burnishing gives an aged look even to the new paints, and these pictures are known as *lukisan antik* (antique paintings).

The Pita Maha

Walter Spies and Rudolf Bonnet were the western artists who turned Balinese artists around in the 1930s (see the boxed text 'Western Visitors in the 1930s' in the Facts about Bali chapter). At that time painting was in a serious decline: painting styles had become stagnant, and since few commissions were forthcoming from palaces and temples, painting was virtually dying out as an art form.

Bonnet and Spies, with their patron Cokorda Gede Agung Sukawati, formed the Pita Maha (literally, 'great vitality'), to encourage painting as an art form and find a market for the best paintings. The group had more than 100 members at its peak in the 1930s.

The changes Bonnet and Spies inspired were revolutionary – suddenly Balinese artists started painting single scenes instead of narrative tales and using everyday life rather than romantic legends as their themes. Paintings influenced by the Pita Maha asso-

BERNARD NAPTHINE

Left: An example of the modern Balinese style of painting from the Contemporary Art Hall at the Neka Museum in Ubud.

ciation typically depict a scene from everyday life – harvesting rice, bartering in the market, watching a cockfight, presenting offerings at a temple or preparing a cremation. These paintings came to be known as the 'Ubud style'.

Batuan is a noted painting centre which came under the influence of the Pita Maha at an early stage, but retained many features of classical painting. Batuan painters also started to depict scenes from daily life, but included many scenes in each painting – a market, a dance, a rice harvest and other scenes might all appear in a single work. The Batuan style is also noted for its inclusion of some very modern elements, such as sea scenes with the odd windsurfer.

Not only the themes changed, the actual way of painting also altered. More modern paint and materials were used and the stiff formal poses of old gave way to realistic three-dimensional representations. Even more importantly, pictures were painted for their own sake – not as something to cover a space in a palace or temple.

In one way, however, the style remained unchanged – Balinese paintings were packed with detail, every spare corner of the picture was filled in. A painted Balinese forest has branches and leaves reaching out to fill every tiny space and is inhabited by a whole zoo of creatures. You can see fine examples of these new styles at the Museum Puri Lukisan in Ubud and, of course, in all the galleries and art shops.

The new artistic enthusiasm was short-lived, however, for WWII interrupted and later in the 1950s and 1960s Indonesia was wracked by internal turmoil and confusion. The new styles degenerated into stale copies of the few original spirits, with one exception: the development of the Young Artists' style.

Bottom: A scene from the *Arja* opera rendered in the detailed style typical of the Ubud region.

GREGORY ADAMS

The Young Artists

Dutch painter Arie Smit survived imprisonment by the Japanese during WWII and arrived on Bali in 1956. One day while painting in Penestanan, just outside Ubud, he noticed a young boy drawing in the dirt and wondered what he would produce if he had proper equipment to paint with. The story is regularly told of how the lad's father would not allow him to take up painting until Smit offered to fund somebody else to watch the family's flock of ducks.

Other 'young artists' from Penestanan soon joined that first pupil, I Nyoman Cakra, but Arie Smit did not actively teach them. He simply provided the equipment and the encouragement, and unleashed what was clearly a strong natural talent. An engaging new naive style quickly developed, as typically Balinese rural scenes were painted in brilliant technicolour.

The style quickly caught on and is today one of the staples of Balinese tourist art. Of course, not all the artists are young boys anymore, and the style is also known as work by 'peasant painters'. I Nyoman Cakra, the original Young Artist, still lives in Penestanan, still paints and cheerfully admits that he owes it all to Smit.

Other Styles

There are some other variants of the main Ubud and Young Artists' styles. The depiction of forests, flowers, butterflies, birds and other naturalistic themes, sometimes called Pengosekan style, became popular in the 1960s, but can probably be traced back to Rousseau, who was a significant influence on Walter Spies. An interesting development of this is the depiction of underwater scenes, with colourful fish, coral gardens and some largely imaginary sea creatures. Somewhere between Pengosekan and Ubud styles are the miniature landscape paintings which are a popular commercial offering.

Though many of the Pita Maha artists turned to the hitherto unexplored themes of daily life, the new techniques were also used to depict some traditional subjects. There were some radically new versions of Rangda, Barong, Hanoman, the *Ramayana* characters, and other figures from Balinese and Hindu mythology. Scenes from folk tales and stories also appeared, in many cases featuring dancers, nymphs and love stories with an understated erotic appeal.

Academic Painting

A small but growing number of Balinese artists receive formal art training, often in schools in Yogya or overseas. Others are influenced by western or Asian artists who visit and work on Bali for various periods. Basically, any painting that does not depict a recognisably Balinese subject or does not follow one of the well established Bali styles can be called 'academic', and is very likely to be the work of someone who has had formal art training.

GREGORY ADAMS

Left: Detailed natural scenes (such as this piece featuring sulphur-crested cockatoos) have proven popular with buyers and artists alike in Ubud in recent times.

WOODCARVING

Like painting, woodcarving has undergone a major transformation over the past 50 years, from being a decorative craft to something done for its own sake. Prior to this change in attitude, woodcarving was chiefly architectural decoration – on carved doors or columns, for example – or of figures such as garudas or demons with a protective or symbolic nature. There were also decorative carvings on minor functional objects, such as bottle stoppers, and the carved wooden masks used in Balinese dance and theatre. Yet, as with painting, it was the same demand from outside that inspired new carving subjects and styles. It was also some of the same western artists who served as the inspiration.

Bottom left: Beautifully crafted Javanese *wayang golek* puppets featuring beaten metal adornments and human hair in the traditional *sanggul* style.

Bottom right: Intricate detail and bright colours are a feature of carvings from the villages of Tegallalang and Pujung just north of Ubud.

As with the new painting styles, Ubud was a centre for the revolution in woodcarving. Some carvers started producing highly stylised and elongated figures, and the wood was sometimes left with its natural finish rather than being painted. Others carved delightful animal figures, some totally realistic, some complete caricatures. More styles and trends developed: whole tree trunks carved into ghostly, intertwined 'totem poles'; and curiously exaggerated and distorted figures.

GREGORY ADAMS

GREGORY ADAMS

GREGORY ADAMS

GREGORY ADAMS

Any visitor to Bali is likely to be exposed to woodcarving in all its forms, whether it be the traditional ornate carved double doors seen in houses and losmen, the carved figures of gods carried in processions and seen in temples, or the myriad carved items in craft shops.

Almost all carving is of local woods, including *belalu*, a quick-growing light wood, and the stronger fruit timbers such as jackfruit wood. Ebony from Sulawesi has been used for the last 30 years or so. Sandalwood, with its delightful fragrance, is expensive, soft and used for some small, very detailed pieces.

Woodcarving is a craft practised throughout Bali. Tegallalang and Jati, on the road from Ubud to Batur, are noted woodcarving centres. Many workshops line the road east of Peliatan, near Ubud, to Goa Gajah. The route from Mas, through Peliatan, Petulu and up the scenic slope to Pujung is also a centre for family-based workshops; listen for the tapping sound of the carvers' mallets.

An attempt to separate traditional and foreign influences is difficult. The Balinese are keen observers of the outside world and have always incorporated and adapted foreign themes in their work. Balinese carvings of religious figures may be based on Hindu mythology, but are very different from the same figures made in India.

Carving, however, suffers from similar problems to painting in that there's an overwhelming emphasis on what sells, with the successful subjects mimicked by every carver on the block. Still, there's always something interesting to see, the technical skill is high and the Balinese sense of humour often shines through – a frog clutches a large leaf as an umbrella, or a weird demon on the side of a wooden bell clasps his hands over his ears.

Top left: Javanese *wayang golek* puppets are common items in craft shops across Bali.

Top right: A woodcarving of a bumblebee dancer from the modern Oleg Tambuliligan dance.

Mask Carving

Mask making is a specialised form of woodcarving, and only experts carve the masks used in so many of Bali's theatre and dance performances. A particularly high level of skill is needed to create the 30 or 40 masks used in the Topeng dance. The mask maker must know the movements that each Topeng performer uses so that the character can be shown by the mask.

Other Balinese masks, such as the Barong and Rangda, are brightly painted and decorated with real hair, enormous teeth and bulging eyes.

Mas is recognised as the mask-carving centre of Bali. The small village of Puaya, near Sukawati, also specialises in mask making. The Museum Negeri Propinsi Bali in Denpasar has an extensive mask collection and is a good place to visit to get an idea of styles before buying anything from the craft shops.

Top left: Raksana demon masks ready for use in a Barong performace at Batubulan village in south Bali.

Bottom left: Hanoman warrior monkeys await procession at Semarapura (Klungkung) in east Bali.

Right: A ceremonial mask for sale in Ubud.

GREGORY ADAMS

GREGORY ADAMS

BERNARD NAPTHINE

JEWELLERY

Bali, along with Thailand and Mexico, is a major producer of world fashion jewellery and variations on the same designs are common to all three centres. The Balinese work is nearly always handmade, – rarely involving casting techniques – and uses imported silver. Balinese silver, mined near Singaraja, is alsso used for filigree and other traditional silver work.

GREGORY ADAMS

Left: A bride adorned in traditional handbeaten gold jewellery.

FABRICS & WEAVING

Weaving is a popular craft and the standard woven Balinese sarong is an attractive workaday item. The sarong is not only a comfortable article of clothing, but can serve as a sheet, towel and a multitude of other uses – and you will certainly need one if you intend to visit any temples.

The more elegant fabrics, like *endek* and *songket*, are necessary for special occasions – it is a religious obligation to look one's best at a temple ceremony. Dress for these occasions is a simple shirt or blouse, a sarong and a *kain;* a separate length of cloth wound tightly around the hips, over the sarong.

For more formal occasions, the blouse is replaced by a length of songket wrapped around a woman's chest. These chest cloths are called *kamben*. The styles of wearing the sarong are different for men and women.

Batik

Traditional batik sarongs are handmade in central Java. The dyeing process has been adapted by the Balinese to produce brightly coloured and patterned fabrics for clothing etc, although batik is not an indigenous Balinese technique.

Watch out for 'batik' fabric which has actually been screen printed in factories. The colours will be washed out compared to the rich colour of real batik cloth, and the pattern is often only on one side (in true batik cloth, the dye penetrates to colour both sides).

Right: Bolts of batik cloth for sale display the bright hues brought by the Balinese to this style of traditional Javanese weaving.

RICHARD I'ANSON

Ikat

In various places in Indonesia you'll find material woven by the complex *ikat* process, where the pattern is dyed into the threads *before* the material is woven. Ikat usually involves pre-dyeing either the warp threads, those stretched on the loom, or the weft threads, those which are woven across the warp. The usual Balinese technique, in which the weft threads are pre-dyed, is known as *endek*. The resulting pattern is geometric and slightly wavy, like a badly tuned TV. Its beauty depends on the complexity of the pattern and the harmonious blending of colours. Typically the pattern is made in colours of similar tone – blues and greens; reds and browns; or yellows, reds and orange. Ikat sarongs and kain are not everyday wear, but they are not for strictly formal occasions either.

Gringsing

In the Bali Aga village of Tenganan, in eastern Bali, a double *ikat* process is used in which both the warp *and* weft are pre-dyed. Called *gringsing* (or geringsing), this complex and extremely time-consuming process is practised nowhere else in Indonesia. Typical colours are red, brown, yellow and deep purple. The dyes used are obtained from natural sources, and some of the colours can take years of mixing and ageing. The dyes also weaken the cotton fabric, so old examples of gringsing are extremely rare.

Bottom: The traditional *ikat* method of weaving in which pre-dyed threads are woven on a handloom.

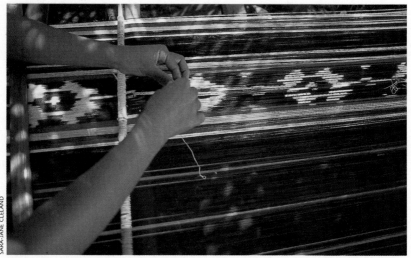

SARA-JANE CLELAND

Songket

A more elaborate material, for ceremonial and other important uses, *songket* cloth has gold or silver threads woven into the tapestry-like material, and motifs include birds, butterflies, leaves and flowers. Songket material is used for kamben, kain, and sarongs worn exclusively for ceremonial occasions.

Prada

Another technique for producing very decorative fabrics for special occasions, *prada* involves the application of gold leaf, or gold or silver paint or thread to the surface of a finished material. Motifs are similar to those used in songket. The result is not washable, so prada is reserved for kain, which are worn over the top of a sarong.

JAMES LYON

RICHARD I'ANSON

Top right: An example of the *songket* method of *ikat* weaving, which employs metallic threads of silver and gold.

Bottom right: Bolts of *ikat* cloth, employing animals and patterned motifs, for sale at a village market.

KRIS

Often with an ornate, jewel-studded handle and sinister-looking wavy blade, the kris is the traditional and ceremonial dagger of Bali and Indonesia. Although a Balinese-made kris is slightly larger and more elaborate than one from Java, they are almost exactly the same shape. A kris can be the most important of family heirlooms, a symbol of prestige and honour. It is supposed to have great spiritual power, and an important kris is thought to send out magical energy waves requiring great care in its handling and use. Even making a kris requires careful preparation, as does anything on Bali which involves working with the forces of magic.

Bottom left: The wavy-bladed Kris dagger is said to rattle in its scabbard to warn its owner of impending danger.

Bottom right: Atypically, a young woman holds a kris during a *pandanus* leaf fight at the Bali Aga village of Tenganan Dauh Tukad in east Bali.

SARA-JANE CLELAND

GREGORY ADAMS

LOMBOK ARTS & CRAFTS

See the colour section in the Facts about Lombok chapter later in this book.

Facts for the Visitor

SUGGESTED ITINERARIES

If you're based in south Bali, you can see most of the island on day trips and be back in your hotel every night. You can take organised tours (see the Bali Getting Around chapter for more information); alternatively, you can rent a vehicle, or a charter a vehicle and driver, to visit the sights independently. It's more difficult and time consuming on public transport – because it's slow and services become infrequent in the afternoon – but it's certainly a cheaper and more interesting way to get around. If you're travelling independently, your itinerary will depend on your interests, time and energy.

Short Trips

Here are some trips that can be done in less than a day from the main tourist areas, especially if you rent or charter a vehicle.

Bukit Peninsula Check out the luxury enclave at Nusa Dua – bluff your way into a bar in one of the five star hotels for a free inspection and an expensive drink. Go to Tanjung Benoa for water sports and lunch at a beachside restaurant. Then visit the clifftop temple at Ulu Watu, stop at Jimbaran for a swim at the beautiful beach and finish with a seafood dinner as the sun goes down.

Ubud Area If you come on a day trip, stop for lunch in one of Ubud's excellent restaurants, and visit at least one of the museums. There's an almost unbroken stretch of villages selling handcrafts between Denpasar and Ubud. Other attractions include the temple at Mengwi, Goa Gajah cave, and the impressive Gunung Kawi.

East Bali A most pleasant trips is a circuit from Rendang, around the slopes of Agung to Amlapura, then following the coast back to south Bali via Candidasa. You can also do the trip via Bangli, taking the scenic back road from there to Rendang. Other detours

are to Besakih; the southern road through Sidemen and Iseh; around the eastern peninsula; and to Tenganan or Padangbai. Other possible stops include Putung, Tirta Gangga, and Semarapura (Klungkung).

Inner West In a day trip west of Denpasar with your own transport, you can visit the temple at Mengwi, Sangeh Monkey Forest, the memorial at Marga, Subak museum at Tabanan, and finish with sunset, and a meal or drink, at Tanah Lot.

Gunung Batur There are several interesting routes to Batur from south Bali, and each has its own attractions. You can get there via: (a) Bedulu and Tampaksiring; (b) Tegallalang, through several craft villages along scenic roads; (c) Gianyar and Bangli; or (d) Semarapura, Rendang and Besakih.

North Bali The usual circuit to the north coast is via Gunung Batur one way and Danau Bratan the other. It's possible in a single day with your own transport, but start early. On the north coast, explore Singaraja, Lovina, Banjar and Yeh Sanih. On the way to/from Danau Bratan, stop at Gitgit waterfalls; and see the temple and botanical gardens at Danau Bratan. If time permits, the Munduk-Seririt road is very scenic.

Longer Trips

Most of the trips previously mentioned can be combined, and/or extended to several days, or even weeks, if you want to explore in depth. There's at least basic accommodation in or near most of the places mentioned, and if you want western comforts, you'll find quite a few mid-range and top-end hotels in out-of-the-way locations, as well as in all the main tourist areas.

Around the Coast Roads run all the way around the coast of Bali, except in the far south where they are mainly inland routes.

Bali Highlights

Beaches

- **Jimbaran (south Bali)** A wonderful place for seafood, seabreezes and sunsets.
- **Kuta Region (south Bali)** The surf can be rough and crowded, and the beach is more scruffy further north.
- **Mushroom Bay (Nusa Lembongan)** It's pretty and isolated – except when the day trippers come by yacht from Bali.
- **Sanur (south Bali)** There's plenty of beachside restaurants and bars, and a lovely walkway.
- **Siyut (east Bali)** It's isolated, so you need your own transport.

Museums

- **Museum Negeri Propinsi Bali (Denpasar)** It has good exhibits and is easy to reach, but has complicated opening hours.
- **Museum Puri Lukisan (Ubud)** A fabulous collection of art in a pretty setting.
- **Museum Seni Lukis Klasik (east Bali)** A private collection of art and crafts, on a main road near Semarapura (Klungkung).
- **Semara Pura (Semarapura)** A palace converted to a museum of Balinese history.

Outdoor Activities

- **Diving** The diving among coral reefs is excellent; diving centres are all over Bali.
- **Rafting** Rafting for novices is great fun, and there's heaps of operators in south Bali.
- **Surfing** There are plenty of surf breaks in south Bali; most are easy to reach.
- **Walking** There are many easy walks to pretty villages and across rice fields near Ubud, Putung, Tirta Gangga, the lakes in central Bali and Pelaga.

Scenery

- **Bukit Jambal (east Bali)** There are several restaurants and a good stopoff on the way to/from Pura Besakih.

There are many places to stop for the night – or longer – and a round-the-island trip can be done entirely on public transport (and it's also quite feasible by bicycle – see the Bali Getting Around chapter). Allow at least five days, or even longer if you plan to stop for relaxing, sightseeing, snorkelling or whatever. Going anti-clockwise, you could visit Semarapura; Padangbai; Candidasa; Tirta Gangga; Amed; Tulamben; Yeh Sanih; Singaraja; Lovina; Gilimanuk (Taman Nasional Bali Barat national park); Medewi; and several places around Tabanan.

East Bali This area can be covered in one day, but it's well worth spending more time here, especially if you are into hiking, diving or snorkelling. You could spend two to three days in Padangbai, Candidasa, Tirta Gangga, stay one of the hotels in or around Sidemen, rent a bungalow along the coast between Amed and Selang, and/or Tulamben – allow plenty of time to move between each town by public bemo. Attractions include beautiful scenery, diving, traditional villages, some important temples and a climb up Gunung Agung.

West Bali While you can see most of the sights in the inner west in a day trip, it's worth spending a few days in the west, or heading west while criss-crossing from

Bali Highlights

- **Gunung Agung (east Bali)** The views from Bali's highest point are superb, but it's often clouded over.
- **Penelokan (central mountains)** The views of Danau Batur and Gunung Batur are awesome, but hawkers can be annoying.
- **Rendang-Amlapura (east Bali)** On the southern slopes of Gunung Agung, this road goes through pretty villages and rice fields.
- **Sidemen (east Bali)** There are stunning views along the Duda-Semarapur road.

Temples & Monuments
- **Gunung Kawi (Tampaksiring)** It has incredible shrines cut into rocky hills, amid a lush valley.
- **Pura Besakih (east Bali)** Bali's Mother Temple, on the slopes of Gunung Agung, is fairly touristy, with plenty of hawkers.
- **Pura Luhur Ulu Watu (south Bali)** A cliff-top temple, it's perfect at sunset.
- **Pura Rambut Siwi (west Bali)** A remote temple, on a cliff overlooking a pretty beach, this temple sees few tourists.
- **Tanah Lot (south Bali)** Another stunning cliff-top temple, but it's unbelievably busy, especially during sunsets.

Villages
- **Kusamba (east Bali)** A pretty fishing village, with traditional boats and saltmakers.
- **Munduk (central mountains)** A remote village with many examples of a Dutch colonial past, plus great hiking nearby.
- **Teganan (east Bali)** An original Bali Aga village, with plenty of handcrafts to buy.
- **Tejakula (east Bali)** Famous for its baths, it rarely sees tourists.
- **Tirta Gangga (east Bali)** Delightfully clustered around a water palace, there's great hiking nearby.

north to south. From Tabanan, go north to Danau Bratan and across to Munduk, then down to the coast to Lovina. Stay at Lovina, then head back to Seririt and south across the mountains via Pupuan. There are three routes south of Pupuan – they're all scenic, but it's best to take the westernmost one. You can stay at Medewi or Negara.

Heading west again, the Christian villages of Palasari and Belimbingsari make an interesting detour. At Gilimanuk, you can arrange a trek in the national park. You can return via the north coast, with side trips to Pulau Menjangan. Back to south Bali, try the scenic Seririt-Pupuan-Antosari-Tabanan road, or return via Danau Batur.

Central Mountains Many people stay only a single night in Toya Bungkah and climb Gunung Batur for the sunrise, but it's worth allowing lots of time to trek around the various volcanic features. You could easily spend two or three days here, then go down to the north coast, staying in Singaraja or Lovina. You can take the main road south of Singaraja via the Gitgit waterfalls to Danau Bratan, or the more scenic route via Munduk. Allow some more time if you want to hike around Munduk, or enjoy the water sports on Danau Bratan. Another possible detour is to Jatuluih and the sacred temple on the southern slopes of Gunung Batukau.

PLANNING
When to Go

The best time to visit Bali and Lombok, in terms of the weather, is during the cooler dry season, from April to October. The rest of the year is more humid, more cloudy, and has more rainstorms, but you can still enjoy a holiday.

There are also distinct tourist seasons which affect the picture. The European summer holidays bring the biggest crowds; July, August and early September are busy. Accommodation can be very tight in these months and prices are higher. From Christmas until the end of January, airfares to and from Australia are higher and flights can be booked solid. The school holidays in early April, late June-early July and late September also see more Australians, but most of them are on package tours to resort areas in south Bali. Many Indonesians visit Bali around Christmas and during some Indonesian holidays. Outside these times Bali has surprisingly few tourists and there are empty rooms and restaurants everywhere.

Balinese festivals, holidays and special celebrations occur all the time, and most of them are not scheduled according to western calendars, so don't worry too much about timing your visit to coincide with local events (although you may wish to refer to the Public Holidays & Special Events section later in this chapter).

What Kind of Trip?

The basic choice is between independent travel or a package tour. There's no reason why you can't take your kids either – see the Travelling with Children section later in this chapter.

Independent Travel Bali and Lombok are easy to get around as an independent traveller. There are many transport options, from cheap public buses and bemos to air-conditioned rental cars, and the extensive network of tourist shuttle buses makes it easy. Distances are short and everywhere is accessible by some means, even if you have to walk. Most tourist accommodation is in a few main resort areas, but there are inexpensive places to stay all over the island (although not so many on Lombok). Some people are nervous about flying into a strange place with no confirmed reservations or definite itinerary, but it's quite OK on Bali, and even on Lombok.

If you're here for the sun, sea, and beach scene, go to Kuta, Sanur, Lovina or any of the quiet coastal places. If you want to see Balinese art and culture, and enjoy good food and rural walks, stay in or near Ubud. For surfing, diving or trekking, see the relevant sections later in this chapter. To see a bit of everything, refer to the Suggested Itineraries section earlier in this chapter.

Package Holidays Pre-paid holiday packages, which include return airfares and a week or so worth of accommodation, are popular and often very good value – in fact, sometimes a package tour costs less than a standard excursion airfare. It works as the fare which is built into the package is substantially lower than the excursion airfare. However, you have to book and pay for at least a substantial proportion of your package holiday in advance; flight times are often inflexible and difficult to change; and a package holiday is only good value if you're travelling as a couple or family.

If you're only going to Bali for a short holiday, and you really want to stay in a hotel with air-con and a swimming pool, then a package tour can be a good deal. If you want to stay for longer than a couple of weeks, and you're quite happy to stay in cheaper hotels, the cost advantage of a package tour diminishes – the extra cost of the normal airfare is offset by the saving in accommodation. You may be able to do a bit of both, with a week of package holiday followed by a week or more of independent travel – ask your travel agent about the possibilities.

There are other catches with package holidays. One is that you get stung savagely for drinks, tours, meals and other extras at the hotel, and this can add a lot to the cost of a trip you thought you had already paid for.

Everything from a Legong dance to your laundry will cost more if you get it through the hotel, which will add up to 21% tax and service to every item on the bill. Also, you may not see much of Bali. The high cost of tours and a lack of information about alternative accommodation can keep you at your hotel, within the comfortable boundaries of the restaurant, pool, bar, beach and your air-conditioned room.

If you're in a hotel in the golden ghetto of Nusa Dua, or somewhere by itself on the coast, it's very difficult to get out of its expensive clutches. If you stay in Sanur, Candidasa, Ubud or, especially, Kuta, there are dozens of restaurants, tour agents, craft shops and bars that will give you much better value for money than the equivalent services in a package-tour hotel.

Maps

Visitors will find maps in this guidebook more than adequate, but if you're spending a long time on Bali, or driving, trekking or surfing, you may want to buy a more detailed map. Most maps are available in your home country, but some can only be found on Bali; the Bookshops section later in this chapter mentions the best places to find maps. Because Bali is so humid, paper gets damp and soggy; bring some adhesive plastic film and cover the whole map with it.

The free tourist maps of Bali are pretty good, but they're normally only available at the airport and upmarket travel agencies – rarely at tourist offices. Here is a rundown of the best maps available:

- Bali Pathfinder has a good map which includes the provincial capitals, Ubud and south Bali, but has nothing for Sanur, Nusa Dua or Kuta. It costs 12,500 rp; is mainly available in Ubud; and is very hard to re-fold.
- Nelles' full-colour *Bali* map (1:180,000) is excellent for topography and roads, although the maps of Kuta, Denpasar and Ubud aren't particularly good.
- Periplus Travel Maps has a decent contour map (1:250,000), with a detailed section on south Bali, plus maps of the main towns areas. Roads and other features are not 100% accurate, however. It is easy to buy on Bali.

- The map published by Putri is available on Bali for 15,000 rp. It has good, colourful maps of provincial capitals, Nusa Dua and Ubud, but not Kuta and Sanur.
- The provincial maps published by PT Karya Pembina Swajaya, and available at the Gramedia Bookshop in Denpasar, are detailed and the best for trekking. They cost about 7400 rp each.
- Travel Treasure Maps has a colourful annotated map of Bali, with detailed sketch maps of the main tourist areas and handy snippets of information. It has French, Italian and Spanish versions and is available on Bali for 15,000 rp.

What to Bring

'Bring as little as possible' is the golden rule of good travelling. It's better to leave something behind and get a replacement when you're there than bring too much and have to lug unwanted items around. Also, you can buy just about anything you need (and heaps that you don't need) on Bali.

You should bring little more than lightweight clothes – short-sleeved shirts or blouses, T-shirts and light pants. A light sweater is a good idea for cool evenings, particularly if you're going up into the mountains; Kintamani, Candikuning and other towns in the central mountains can actually get quite cold. You'll also need more protective clothes if you're going to travel by motorbike. A hat and sunglasses are important protection from tropical sun. An umbrella will help protect you against short, sharp rain showers at any time of the year.

Men should bring at least one pair of long pants and a collared shirt, and women a long skirt or dress, for occasions when they may have to look respectable, such as visiting temples. Bring some shoes and socks too. You never know if you'll be invited to a special event or have to deal with officialdom. (See the Avoiding Offence section in the preceding Facts about Bali chapter for more information.)

TOURIST OFFICES
Local Tourist Offices

The main tourist office for the Bali province is in Renon, Denpasar, but the staff tend to spend more time implementing policy than providing information. There are also tourist offices in each provincial capital. While staff are usually friendly, they normally offer little more than a few brochures and basic maps. The best tourist offices are in Denpasar (on Jl Surapati), Kuta and Ubud.

Tourist Offices Abroad

Indonesian Tourist Promotion Offices (ITPO) abroad can supply brochures and information about Indonesia. Useful publications include *Travel Planner*, *Tourist Map of Indonesia* and the *Calendar of Events* for the whole country. Garuda Airlines offices overseas can also often provide the same sort of information. There are ITPO offices at:

Australia
(☎ 02-9233 3630, fax 9233 3629)
Level 10, 5 Elizabeth St,
Sydney, NSW 2000
Germany
(☎ 069-233677/8, fax 230840)
Wiessenhuttenstrasse 17 D.6000, Frankfurt am Main 1
Indonesia
(☎ 021-570 4879)
9th floor, Bank Pacific Bldg, Jl Sendirman 8, Central Jakarta
Japan
(☎ 03-3585 3588, fax 3582 1397)
2nd floor, Sankaido Bldg, 1-9-13 Akasaka, Minatoku, Tokyo 107
Singapore
(☎ 534 2837, fax 533 4287)
Ocean Bldg, 10 Collyer Quay 15-07, Singapore 0104
UK
(☎ 0171-493 0030, fax 493 1747)
3-4 Hanover St, London W1R 9HH
USA
(☎ 213-387-2078, fax 380-4876)
3457 Wilshire Blvd, Los Angeles, CA 90010

VISAS & DOCUMENTS
Passport

Your passport absolutely, positively *must* be valid for at least six months from the date of your arrival. Some travellers have been caught out by this, and are normally sent home on the next available flight.

Visas

Visitors from Australia, Japan, Malaysia, New Zealand, the UK, the USA, Canada and most of western Europe don't need a visa to enter Indonesia at the usual ports of entry, which includes Denpasar. You will be issued with a tourist card on arrival (valid for 60 days), as long as you (a) have a ticket out of Indonesia or enough money to fund your trip and departure (although these conditions are less enforced at the international airport on Bali); and (b) a passport valid for at least six months after your arrival. Keep the tourist card with your passport as you'll have to hand it back when you leave the country. Remember it's valid for 60 days, not two months – some travellers have been fined for overstaying by only a day or so.

For citizens of countries not on the visa-free list, a visa can be obtained from any Indonesian embassy or consulate.

Social & Business Visas If you have a good reason for staying longer (eg study or family reasons), you can apply for a 'social & cultural visa'. You will need an application form from an Indonesian embassy or consulate, and possibly a letter of introduction or promise of sponsorship from someone in Indonesia. It's initially valid for one month, but it can be extended for one month at a time at an immigration office within Indonesia for a maximum of six months – if you can find a local sponsor. There are high application fees (eg A$100 in Australia), and high extension fees within Indonesia too.

For a business visitor's visa, you will need evidence that you are performing a necessary task in Indonesia – your employer should arrange this. It's sometimes easier, and even cheaper, to leave the country every two months and get a new tourist card than to get a visa and update it every month.

Extensions It's not possible to extend a 60 day tourist card, unless there's a medical emergency or you have to answer legal charges. If you want to spend more time in Indonesia you have to leave the country and then re-enter – expats living in Bali do this all the time through Singapore.

Immigration Offices

There are two main immigration offices *(kantor imigrasi)*. The office in Denpasar (☎ 227828), just up the street from the main post office in Renon, is open Monday to Thursday, from 8 am to 2 pm, and until 11 am on Friday and noon on Saturday. The other (☎ 751038) is at the international airport. If you have to apply for changes to your visa, make sure you're neatly dressed.

Onward Tickets

Officially, an onward/return ticket is a requirement for a tourist card (and normal visa), but these days you are rarely asked to show this anywhere in Indonesia. If you arrive by air on Bali, you will be assumed to be on a package tour (whether you are or not), so onward/return tickets are rarely requested. If you look scruffy or broke, you may be asked to present a ticket or evidence of sufficient funds to support yourself during your stay – US$1000 in cash or travellers cheques (or the equivalent in other currencies) should be sufficient. A credit card in lieu of cash or travellers cheques may not satisfy these requirements.

Travel Insurance

A travel insurance policy to cover theft, loss and medical problems is essential.

Some companies offer a range of medical-expense options; the higher ones are chiefly for countries such as the USA, which have extremely high medical costs. There is a wide variety of policies available, so check the small print.

Some policies also specifically exclude 'dangerous activities', which can include scuba diving, renting a local motorbike on Bali and Lombok, and even trekking. Be aware that a locally acquired motorbike licence is not valid under some policies.

You may prefer a policy which pays doctors or hospitals directly rather than you having to pay on the spot and claim later. If you have to claim later make sure you keep all documentation. Some policies ask you to call back (reverse charges) to a centre in your home country, or a nearby country, where an immediate assessment of your problems is made. Check that the policy covers ambulances and an emergency flight home.

Driving Licence & Permits

If you plan to drive a car or motorbike, you *must* have an International Driving Permit. If you want to rent a motorbike, also make sure that your International Driving Permit is endorsed for motorbikes. (Refer to the Bali Getting Around chapter for details about local licences on Bali.) If you have a normal driving licence, then an International Driving Permit is easy to obtain from your national motoring organisation.

Hostel Cards

There are few hostels on Bali. They are not particularly good value and no cheaper than the usual basic accommodation.

Student, Youth & Senior Citizens' Cards

The International Student Identity Card can get you a discount on domestic flights (a maximum age limit of 26 applies). There are virtually no discounts or special deals for senior citizens.

Photocopies

All your important documents (passport data page and visa page, credit cards, travel insurance policy, driving licence, air/bus/train tickets etc) should be photocopied before you leave home. Leave one copy with someone at home and keep another with you, separate from the originals.

EMBASSIES
Indonesian Embassies & Consulates

Australia
  Embassy:
  (☎ 02-6273 3222)
  8 Darwin Ave, Yarralumla, ACT 2600
  Consulates:
  Adelaide, Darwin, Melbourne, Perth and Sydney

Canada
  Embassy:
  (☎ 613-231 0186)
  55 Parkdale Ave, Ottawa, Ontario K1Y 1E5
  Consulates:
  Toronto and Vancouver
France
  Embassy:
  (☎ 01 45 03 07 60)
  47-49 Rue Cortambert 75116, Paris
  Consulate:
  Marseille
Germany
  Embassy:
  (☎ 0228-382990)
  2 Bernakasteler Strasse,
  53175 Bonn
  Consulates:
  Berlin, Bremen, Dusseldorf, Hamburg,
  Hannover, Kiel, Munich and Stuttgart
Malaysia
  Embassy:
  (☎ 03-984 2011)
  233 Jl Tun Razak, Kuala Lumpur
  Consulate:
  (☎ 04-282 4686)
  467 Jl Burma, Penang
  Consulate:
  (☎ 082-241734)
  5A Pisang Rd, Kuching, Sarawak
  Consulate:
  (☎ 088-219110)
  Jl Kemajuan, Karamunsing, Kota Kinabalu,
  Sabah
  Consulate:
  (☎ 089-772052)
  Jl Apas, Tawau, Sabah
Netherlands
  Embassy:
  (☎ 070-310 8100)
  8 Tobias Asserlaan, 2517 KC Den Haag
New Zealand
  Embassy:
  (☎ 04-475 8697)
  70 Glen Rd, Kelburn, Wellington
Papua New Guinea
  Embassy:
  (☎ 253116)
  1+2/410, Kiroki St, Sir John Guise Drive,
  Waigani, Port Moresby
Philippines
  Embassy:
  (☎ 02-285 5061/7)
  185 Salcedo St, Legaspi Village, Makati,
  Manila
  Consulate:
  Davao

Singapore
  Embassy:
  (☎ 737 7422)
  7 Chatsworth Rd
Thailand
  Embassy:
  (☎ 02-252 3135)
  600-02 Phetburi Rd, Bangkok
UK
  Embassy:
  (☎ 0171-499 7661)
  38 Grosvenor Square, London W1X 9AD
USA
  Embassy:
  (☎ 202-775 5200)
  2020 Massachusetts Ave NW, Washington DC
  20036
  Consulates:
  Chicago, Honolulu, Houston, Los Angeles,
  New York and San Francisco

Embassies & Consulates in Indonesia

With the growing number of foreign visitors
to Bali, the extent of diplomatic representa-
tion is increasing. However, most of the
foreign representatives on Bali are consular
agents (or honorary consuls) who can't offer
the same services as a full consulate or
embassy. The embassies are all in Jakarta,
the national capital, and for many nationali-
ties this means a long trek there if your
passport is stolen. There are also a few consulates in Surabaya.

Your Own Embassy As a tourist, it's important to realise what your own embassy (ie
the embassy of the country of which you are
a citizen) can and can't do.

Generally speaking, it won't help much
in emergencies if the trouble you're in is remotely your own fault. Remember that you
are bound by the laws of the country you
are in. Your embassy will not be sympa-
thetic if you end up in jail after committing
a crime locally, even if such actions are
legal in your own country.

In genuine emergencies you might get
some assistance, but only if other channels
have been exhausted. For example, if you
need to get home urgently, a free ticket
home is exceedingly unlikely – the embassy
would expect you to have insurance. If you

have all your money and documents stolen, it might assist with getting a new passport, but a loan for onward travel is out of the question. Embassies used to keep letters for travellers or have a small reading room with home newspapers, but these days the mail holding service has been stopped and even newspapers tend to be out of date.

Bali Only Australia and Japan (which together make up nearly half of all visitors) have proper consular facilities. Most places are open Sunday to Thursday, from about 8 am to noon and 1 to 4 pm; and will be closed on Indonesian and their own national holidays. Many of the consulates listed below have pager systems for emergency calls. All telephone area codes are ☎ 0361.

Australia
(☎ 235092/3, ☎ 234139 ext 3311 for emergencies, fax 231990, email ausconbali @denpasar.wasantara.net.id)
Jl Mochammad Yamin 4, Renon, Denpasar.
Responsible for all Commonwealth citizens and, at a pinch, Irish citizens.
France
(☎/fax 285485)
Jl Bypass Ngurah Rai, Sanur
Germany
(☎ 288535, fax 288826)
Jl Pantai Karang 17, Sanur
Netherlands
(☎ 751517 during business hours,
☎ 753174 for emergencies, fax 752777)
Jl Raya Kuta 599, Kuta
USA
(☎ 233605 during business hours, ☎ 234139 ext 3575 for emergencies, fax 222426)
Jl Hayam Wuruk 188, Renon, Denpasar

Jakarta Indonesia is a big country, and is important in the Asian region. Most nations have an embassy in Jakarta (area code ☎ 021), including:

Australia
(☎ 522 7111)
Jl Rasuna Said, Kav 15-16
Brunei
(☎ 571 2180)
8th Floor, Wisma BCA,
Jl Sudirman, Kav 22-23

Canada
(☎ 525 0709)
5th Floor, Wisma Metropolitan I,
Jl Sudirman, Kav 29
France
(☎ 314 2807)
Jl Thamrin 20
Germany
(☎ 384 9547)
Jl Raden Saleh 54-56
Malaysia
(☎ 522 4947)
Jl Rasuna Said, Kav X/6 No 1
Myanmar (Burma)
(☎ 314 0440)
Jl H Augus Salim 109
Netherlands
(☎ 511515)
Jl Rasuna Said, Kav S-3,
Kuningan
New Zealand
(☎ 330680)
Jl Diponegoro 41
Papua New Guinea
(☎ 725 1218)
6th Floor, Panin Bank Centre,
Jl Sudirman No 1
Philippines
(☎ 310 0302)
Jl Imam Bonjol 6-8
Thailand
(☎ 390 4055)
Jl Imam Bonjol 74
UK
Embassy:
(☎ 330904)
Jl Thamrin 75
Consulate-General:
(☎ 390 7484/7)
19th floor, Deustche Bank Bldg,
Jl Imam Bonjol
USA
(☎ 360360)
Jl Merdeka Selatan 5

CUSTOMS

Indonesia has the usual list of prohibited imports, including drugs, weapons and anything remotely pornographic. In addition, TV sets, radio receivers, fresh fruit, printed matter containing Chinese characters and Chinese medicines are prohibited.

Each adult can bring in 200 cigarettes (or 50 cigars or 100g of tobacco), a 'reasonable amount' of perfume and 2L of alcohol.

Photographic equipment (both still and video cameras), computers, typewriters and tape recorders must be declared to customs on entry, and you must take them with you when you leave. Customs officials rarely worry about how much gear tourists bring into Indonesia, however, especially on Bali.

There is no restriction on the import of foreign currency, but the export of rupiah is currently limited to 50,000 rp. Surfers with more than two or three boards may be charged an unofficial 'fee'. If you've nothing to declare, customs clearance is quick and painless.

Indonesia is a signatory to the Convention on International Trade in Endangered Species (CITES) and as such bans the import and export of products made from endangered species. In particular, it is forbidden to export any product made from green sea turtles or turtle shells. In the interests of conservation, as well as conformity to customs laws, please don't buy turtle shell products. There may also be some ivory artefacts for sale on Bali, and the import and export of these is also banned in most countries.

It's also forbidden to export antiquities, ancient artefacts or other cultural treasures, so if someone tries to sell you an 'ancient' bronze statue, remind them of this law and they may decide it's not so old after all!

MONEY

The economic crisis which started in early 1997 hit Indonesia very hard indeed (see the Economy section in the Facts about Bali chapter), and has affected prices, and the pricing structure, on Bali. The good news for the visitor is that Bali, and Indonesia in general, is currently extremely good value – about three times cheaper than it was only six months before. Because the rupiah is so unstable, most mid-range hotels, all top-end hotels and restaurants, some tourist attractions, some car rental agencies and most tour companies list their prices in US dollars. However, in most cases you can still pay in rupiah (although the exchange rate used is, not surprisingly, more advantageous for the vendor than the tourist).

Currency

Indonesia's unit of currency is the rupiah (rp). There are coins worth 50, 100, 500 and 1000 rp. Notes come in denominations of 100, 500, 1000, 5000, 10,000, 20,000 and 50,000 rp. There is another series of new notes and coins for the higher denominations, which even confuse locals at times.

Exchange Rates

The Bank of Indonesia (BoI) has an official exchange rate, but it is not legally set – it's a more-or-less free market rate. There's no black market. The following table lists the exchange rates for cash at the BoI; bear in mind that you'll get better rates from moneychangers at tourist centres.

Country	Unit		Rupiah
Australia	A$1	=	4766
Canada	C$1	=	4875
euro	€1	=	9153
France	FF1	=	1963
Germany	DM1	=	4646
Italy	1000 lira	=	4701
Japan	¥100	=	6577
Netherlands	Gl1	=	4126
New Zealand	NZ$1	=	4024
UK	UK£1	=	12,829
USA	US$1	=	7536

Exchanging Money

Changing money on Bali is very easy. The rates offered for travellers cheques are sometimes up to 5% less than cash, and small amounts (ie under US$100 or the equivalent) sometimes get a slightly lower rate. Rates offered by banks and moneychangers fluctuate every day (sometimes several times a day), and vary between places. So, if you can, look around for the best rate, and change enough in competitive places like Kuta to last while you travel to more remote areas. Remember that banks enjoy many public holidays, and that all moneychangers close around Nyepi (see the Public Holidays & Special Events section later in this chapter).

If you're out in the sticks, it can be hard to change big notes – breaking a 10,000 rp note in an out-of-the-way location can be a major hassle. Away from the major centres notes tend to stay in circulation much longer and can get very tatty – when they get too dog-eared, people won't accept them. If you are using public transport, get as much small change as you can by changing larger notes at hotels, restaurants and large shops.

Banks Most major banks have branches in the main tourist centres (particularly Kuta, Sanur and Ubud) and the provincial capitals. Smaller towns may not have banks at all. Even if they do, and they change money, the exchange rates may be woeful. Banking hours are generally from 8 am to 2 pm Monday to Friday, and until about 11 am on Saturday.

It is worth noting that a few banks at the time of research were close to bankruptcy because of the economic crisis, so it is unclear which banks will be operating in the future.

Moneychangers Exchange rates offered by moneychangers are normally better than the banks in the main tourist areas, but this is not always true where tourists are less frequent. Moneychangers are always quicker and stay open a lot longer, however. If a moneychanger won't change as much as you want, just change the rest at a different place later.

The exchange rates are advertised on boards along the footpaths or on windows outside the shops – but look around because rates do vary enormously. In or around up-market hotels and modern shopping centres, the rates are often absurdly low – about 20% lower than somewhere around the corner. Moneychangers with better rates often charge a small commission, but most claim that they charge 'no commission'. Always ask about any commission before the exchange, and watch out for scams (see the Dangers & Annoyances section later in this chapter).

ATMs Automatic Teller Machines (ATMs) are starting to appear on Bali, but they are primarily for customers (normally Indonesians) with an account at that particular bank. A few larger banks accept major in-

ternational credit cards, but some don't always work. If the ATM is closed or not working, it's best to go to the bank during business hours, and obtain a cash advance over the counter.

Kuta has the most ATMs on Bali, and the ATM at the domestic terminal takes Visa, MasterCard, Cirrus and Alto cards. The exchange rates used by the banks for ATM transactions will, naturally, be more advantageous to them than to you, but unlike a cash advance you shouldn't be charged a commission.

Credit Cards Visa, MasterCard and American Express are accepted by most of the bigger businesses that cater to tourists. You sign for the amount in rupiah and the bill is converted into your domestic currency. You should always check the exchange rate when you receive your account back home – not surprisingly, the rate will favour the bank.

You can also get cash advances on major credit cards over the counter, or at an ATM. Normally, Bank BDI, Bank BCA, Bank Panir, Bank Danamon, Bank BII, Bank Bali, Bank Duta and Lippo Bank accept Visa, and often Cirrus. Bank Bali, Bank BDI, Bank BCA and Lippo Bank also take MasterCard. The less common BNDI Bank takes Diners Club.

Cash advances over the counter (but not normally at ATMs) do attract a commission, so shop around if you can. For example, Bank Danamon charges 15,000 rp for any advance under a million rupiah, or 20,000 rp for more than a million. Bank BII applies a one-off charge of 10,000 rp for a transaction of any amount.

American Express The main American Express office (☎ 773334, fax 773306) is at the Galleria shopping centre at Nusa Dua, and there is another branch (☎ 286060) at the Grand Bali Beach Hotel, Sanur. Neither will change Amex travellers cheques, but customers can collect mail at either branch.

International Transfers Having money sent to you on Bali can take some time, so don't wait until you're desperate. The Bank

Ekspor-Impor (Exim for short) is one of the best for inward money transfers from abroad. It can take up to one week, and is paid in rupiah. Some overseas banks can transfer funds via the 'Swift' system to Bank Exim branches on Bali and Lombok, which takes around 24 hours. Amex also has a money transfer service called MoneyGram, which is expensive, but quick and reliable. A cash advance on your credit card will be quicker, easier and cheaper than having money sent.

Giro Dutch nationals can use the very convenient *giro* system. If you have an account at Postbank, you can buy 'post cheques' in rupiah, similar to travellers cheques. These can be changed at any post office in Indonesia with giro facilities – look for the sign *kantor pos dan giro* – if you show your giro 'guarantee card' and passport. With the 'guarantee card', Dutch nationals can also obtain money from ATMs that accept the Cirrus credit card.

Security

Bring most of your money in travellers cheques for security and convenience, although cash normally gets a better exchange rate. Carrying a credit card for major purchases, and as an emergency backup, is a good idea.

US dollars are the most negotiable currency, particularly in more remote areas. British, Canadian, German, Dutch, French, Japanese and Australian cash and travellers cheques are negotiable at competitive rates in tourist areas, and can be changed in most major towns. Travellers cheques (but not cash) in New Zealand dollars and Italian lira are sometimes hard to change anywhere. It is always prudent to change as much as you can (and want to carry) in tourist areas, before heading into more remote regions.

Costs

On Bali, you can spend as much as you want – there are hotels where a double can be US$500 or more a night, where lunch can cost more than US$75 per person, and a helicopter can be arranged for you if you're desperate to see Bali *fast*. At the other extreme, you can find decent budget singles/doubles for as little as 10,000/15,000 rp and enjoy a filling meal from a *warung* (food stall) for about 3500 rp.

In general, travellers who don't need air-con and hot water will discover they can get good rooms almost anywhere on Bali for under 40,000 rp. Indeed, sometimes as little as 25,000 rp will get you a fine 'economy' room in a mid-range hotel. You can have an excellent meal for 15,000 rp, including a large bottle of beer, at most tourist restaurants. You don't even have to get into the really rock-bottom warungs to eat for under 5000 rp, excluding alcohol.

Transport is equally affordable – remember that Bali and Lombok are small islands. Public minibuses, buses and bemos are the local form of public transport and they're very cheap. With the current favourable exchange rate, hiring your own car or motorbike is now very attractive: a motorbike costs around 17,500 rp a day; a small Suzuki jeep is about 60,000 rp; and a chartered car or bemo, with driver, will be about 80,000 rp. However, these prices will certainly increase with inflation, and the costs will depend on the exchange rate when you get there.

Entry Charges Nearly every temple, or place of tourist interest, has an entry charge of about 1000/500 rp for adults/children – occasionally less, sometimes more. If there is no fixed charge and a donation is requested, anything from 1000 to 5000 rp is usually acceptable, but you may be pressured into 'donating' a lot more – a common scam. Parking for cars and motorbikes is usually extra, and you are often charged more for a camera or video and about 1000 rp to rent a sarong and/or sash if you visit a temple.

Government-run tourist attractions also charge an insurance premium of 50 to 100 rp on top of the admission price. This supposedly covers you against accident or injury while you're there, or maybe it just covers the management against you suing them. It won't add greatly to your peace of mind, but it's only a few rupiah and you have to pay it anyway.

Tipping

Tipping a set percentage is not expected on Bali or Lombok, but restaurant workers are poorly paid; if the service is good, it's appropriate to leave about 1000 rp or the small change. The expensive hotels slap a 21% tax and service charge on top of their bills, and the service component is distributed among hotel staff.

Bargaining

Many everyday purchases on Bali require bargaining. This particularly applies to clothing and arts and crafts. Meals in restaurants are generally fixed in price, as is all transport where you buy a ticket. Accommodation has a set price, but this is often negotiable; when the supply of rooms exceeds demand, or if you are staying at that hotel for several days, hotels will often bend their prices. This particularly applies in places like Kuta, Lovina, Ubud and Candidasa where there's lots of competition. On the other hand, many *losmen* (small hotels) will charge more than their usual price if they have to pay a commission to a taxi driver, or if they think you look so tired or disoriented that you won't make it to the place next door.

There's always going to be someone who will boast about how they got something cheaper than you did. *Don't go around feeling that you're being ripped off all the time.* Remember, there is no such thing as a 'right price': when the seller and buyer are happy with the price, it's then 'right'. For handcrafts

How to Haggle

In an everyday bargaining situation the first step is to establish a starting price – *always* ask the seller for their price rather than make an initial offer. Then ask if that is the 'best price' and you may get an immediate reduction. To bargain effectively you should know, before you start, approximately how much the vendor will accept. At the very least you should have an idea of what you consider is a fair price for the article, and not just try to get it for less than the first asking price.

Your 'first price' should be a worthwhile notch below what you're willing to pay, but not so low as to be ludicrous. A silly offer suggests that the customer hasn't any idea of what the price should be, and is therefore a target for some serious overcharging. Of course, lots of people have bought things they didn't want because their paltry first offer was accepted.

As a rule of thumb your first price could be anything from one-third to two-thirds of the asking price – assuming that the asking price is not completely crazy. Then, with offer and counter offer, you move closer to an acceptable price – the seller asks 25,000 rp for the painting, you offer 15,000 rp and so on until eventually you compromise at 20,000 rp (22,000 rp if they're a better bargainer, 18,000 rp if you are). Along the way you can plead end-of-trip poverty or claim that Ketut down the road is likely to be even cheaper. The seller is likely to point out the exceptional quality of the item and plead poverty too. An aura of only mild interest helps – if you don't get to an acceptable price you're quite entitled to walk away. On the other hand, if you're obviously desperate or pressed for time, and there's not much competition, vendors will not be in a hurry to drop their price.

Remember it's not a matter of life or death. Bargaining should be an enjoyable part of shopping on Bali, so maintain your sense of humour. When you name a price, you're committed – you have to buy if your offer is accepted. The best buy is said to be at the 'morning price'. The seller feels that making a sale to the first customer will ensure good sales for the rest of the day, so is more likely to lower the price for an early-morning customer.

and clothes, quality is more important than price – when you get that treasure home, you won't be worried that you might have got it for a few thousand rupiah less, but you will be disappointed if it falls apart.

If you are accompanied by a local (driver, guide, friend or whatever) on a shopping spree (as opposed to buying one or two items), you may find it harder to bargain the price down. Even if your companion is not on a commission for taking you to the place, he/she will tend to feel very uncomfortable seeing a fellow local being 'beaten down' by a foreigner. It reflects on both the guide and the shopkeeper, and each loses face. The advantages of finding things more easily and quickly is often outweighed by this local loyalty.

Taxes

In some parts of Bali (including Ubud and Kuta) and Lombok (including Gili Islands), you must pay a 10% tourist tax, to 'help with the development of the district', or something similar. This is often already included, or not payable at all, for rooms in the budget range, and it may or may not be included in the room rate offered at mid-range hotels – so ask if tax is included. Restaurants in these areas will normally add 10% to your bill. Almost all top-end hotels and restaurants throughout both Bali and Lombok will add taxes and service charges of up to 21% to your bill.

POST & COMMUNICATIONS

Bali is one of the best places in Indonesia and South-East Asia to send and receive mail, and to communicate by email – if you have the expertise and the recipient has the technology.

Postal Rates

Sending postcards and normal-sized letters (ie under 20gm) by airmail costs 1000 rp to Australia and New Zealand; 1400 rp to Europe; and 1500 rp to the USA and Canada. Delivery takes seven to 10 days, but if you want the 'express service' (ie delivery in five to seven days) the cost is 2500 rp to Australia, and 3000 rp to the rest of the world.

For anything over 20g, the charge is based on weight. Sending large parcels is quite expensive, but at least you can get them properly wrapped and sealed.

Sending Mail

Every substantial town has a post office *(kantor pos)* open from about 8 am to 3 pm, Monday to Friday. In the larger cities and some tourist centres, the main post offices are often open longer hours for basic postal services – until 8 pm during the week, and until noon or later on weekends. In small towns, and dotted around the tourist centres, there are also postal agencies called *warpostels* or *warparpostels*. They provide normal postal and telephone services – often for slightly higher rates – and are sometimes open extended hours.

Receiving Mail

There are poste restante services at the various post offices around Bali. Your mail should be available during normal working hours. The Denpasar post office is inconveniently located, so you're better off having mail sent to you via the post offices at Kuta, Ubud or Singaraja. Mail should be addressed to you with your surname underlined and in capital letters, then 'Kantor Pos', the name of the town, and then 'Bali, Indonesia'. You can also have mail sent to your hotel, or to American Express offices if you are a customer.

Telephone

The telecommunications service within Indonesia is provided by Telkom, a government monopoly. All of Indonesia is covered by a domestic satellite telecommunications network. Two companies provide international connections – dial ☎ 001 for Indosat and ☎ 008 for Satelindo. It's usually possible to get on to the international operator or get an international connection within a minute.

Telephone Area Codes The country code for Indonesia is ☎ 62. Bali has six telephone area codes. They relate to the boundaries of each district, but are listed here according to the relevant chapters in the book.

South Bali
- ☎ 0361: Berewa, Bukit Peninsula, Canggu, Denpasar, Jimbaran, Kuta, Legian, Seminyak, Nusa Dua, Pelabuhan Benoa, Sanur, Sidakarya, Tanjung Benoa, Tuban

Ubud & Around
- ☎ 0361: Batuan, Batubulan, Bedulu, Bona, Celuk, Kutri, Mas, Pejeng, Singapadu, Sukawati, Tampaksiring, Ubud

East Bali
- ☎ 0361: Gianyar
- ☎ 0363: Amlapura, Buitan (Balina), Candidasa, Padangbai, Tirta Gangga
- ☎ 0366: Bangli, Besakih, Manggis, Mendira, Putung, Semarapura (Klungkung), Sidemen

West Bali
- ☎ 0361: Dukuh, Lalang-Linggah, Mengwi, Penatahan, Tabanan, Tanah Lot, Wanasari
- ☎ 0362: Pemuteran, Pulaki
- ☎ 0365: Belayu, Cekik, Gilimanuk, Medewi, Negara, Perancak

Central Mountains
- ☎ 0361: Pelaga, Petang
- ☎ 0362: Munduk, Pancasari
- ☎ 0366: Buahan, Kedisan, Kintamani, Penelokan, Toya Bungkah
- ☎ 0368: Bedugul, Candikuning, Pacung

North Bali
- ☎ 0362: Banjar, Celukanbawang, Gitgit, Jagaraga, Kubutambahan, Lovina, Sangsit, Sawan, Seririt, Singaraja, Yeh Sanih

Telephone Numbers Periodically, the telephone numbers in an area will change. If you dial an old number you should get a recorded message telling you how to convert it to a new number – don't hang up too quickly because the message is repeated in English after the Indonesian version.

Phone books can be a little hard to find, but the local directory assistance operators (☎ 108) are very helpful and some of them speak English. If you call directory assistance and have to spell out a name you want, try to use the Alpha, Bravo, Charlie system of saying the letters, otherwise just use simple, common English words to help the operators identify the letters.

Useful Telephone Numbers The listed numbers work throughout Bali and Lombok.

They are listed in the Bali telephone book (if you can find one) and in the *Bali Post* newspaper, but in Indonesian:

Directory assistance, local	☎ 108
Directory assistance, long distance	☎ 106
Directory assistance, international	☎ 102
Operator assisted local calls	☎ 100
Operator assisted international calls	☎ 101
Ambulance	☎ 118
Fire Brigade	☎ 113
Police	☎ 110

Telephone Offices A *kantor telekomunikasi* (telecommunications office), usually called a *wartel* (a contraction of 'warung telekomunikasi'), can be operated by either Telkom or a private business. From these you can make local, long-distance *(interlokal)* and international calls.

The official charge for international calls is the same from anywhere on Bali (except from hotels), but conditions do vary. In the few areas that still don't have a computerised, automatic exchange, there is a three minute minimum and increments of one minute thereafter. When you book the call, you may be asked how long you want to talk for, and will be cut off as soon as the time you requested is up. In areas with modern exchanges you dial the call yourself, and the cost increases in *pulsa* – a unit of time which varies according to the destination. The number of pulsa is shown on a display on the front of the phone. This display also shows the price, sometimes including the 10% tax, sometimes not.

You're supposed to get discounts of 25 to 50% for calls in the evenings and on Sunday, but very few private wartels actually discount the price. The official Telkom price of a one minute call (including the 10% tax) is 6215 rp to Australia and New Zealand, 6875 rp to USA and Canada, and 7865 rp to Europe.

You can usually make reverse-charge (collect) calls, but most private wartels charge for this. A few wartels will let you receive an incoming call, so you can make a quick call, give the wartel's number and have the overseas party call you back for an extra fee.

Private wartels can be found all over the island – often in a hotel or with a money-changing business. They provide a pretty good service, but charge slightly higher prices than Telkom offices.

Public Telephones There are several types of public phones, some of which can be used for international calls. A few old phones still take 50 or 100 rp coins, while some hotels and shops have modern phones where a local call costs 200 rp for one minute. (Some take two larger 100 rp coins; some, the smaller gold ones.)

With Home Country Direct Dial telephones, one button gets you through to your home country operator and you pay with a credit card or reverse the charges. These can be found in Kuta, Ubud, Denpasar and Sanur.

Mobile Telephones Some mobile telephones from your home country will operate in Indonesia – check with your mobile telephone company. One reader from Europe was charged 450 rp per minute for a local call, and only 5500 rp per minute to Europe.

Indonesian Telephone Cards A few public phones, called *telepon kartu*, take local Telkom phone cards, but a high proportion of them are out of service. The most likely place to find a working card phone is in a well supervised location, such as the airport, the lobby of a big hotel or outside a wartel.

You can buy Telkom telephone cards *(kartu telepon)* at wartels, bookshops and money-changers. If you pay the proper price for a card, an international call from a card phone costs about the same per minute as a call from a wartel. It may even be cheaper if you call on Sunday, or any other off-peak time, and can't get a discount from the wartel. However, overcharging for telephone cards is common, and they will cost foreigners about 30,000 rp for 100 units and 50,000 rp for 200 units.

Foreign Telephone Cards Some foreign telephone companies issue cards that enable you to call your home country from overseas

and have the cost billed to your home phone account. You must arrange this before you leave home. You can use the facility from most public and private phones (fancy hotels will charge a fee) by ringing a special number to access your home country operator, and quoting your card number and a personal identification number. Your phone company will give you a list of the access codes for foreign countries and a schedule of prices. This facility is convenient, but not necessarily cheap, and it doesn't always work from card phones.

Fax
Fax services are available at most wartels. At some of them you can arrange to receive a fax, and or even have it delivered to a specified address, for a fee. The cost of sending an international fax is timed at the same rate as an international telephone call, although sometimes there's a set charge per page.

Email & Internet Access
Like many places throughout the world, Bali is now firmly on the Internet. There are Internet centres, where you can send and receive messages and surf the Net, in Ubud, Kuta/Legian, Sanur, Nusa Dua and Lovina. The cost is expensive by Indonesian standards, but is affordable for most visitors because of the low value of the rupiah. Access to personal accounts and surfing the Net can be frustratingly slow. Try to use somewhere which does not have a high charge for the 'first 15 minutes', because you may use this time just to access your account, or find just one Web site. There are several Internet Service Providers, all based in Jakarta.

INTERNET RESOURCES
The World Wide Web is a rich resource for travellers. You can research your trip, hunt down bargain air fares, book hotels, check on weather conditions or chat with locals and other travellers about the best places to visit (or avoid!).

One place to start your web explorations

Bali on the Net

There is a staggering amount of information on the Internet about Bali. You can get background information and book tours, hotels and rental cars – but always remember that you are more likely to get better value by booking these after you arrive, rather than on the Net.

A good place to start surfing the Net is Lonely Planet's award-winning site (www.lonely planet.com/dest/sea/bali.htm) from where there are numerous links to other sites. It is also worth checking out the following:

Web Site	Address	Comments
Access Bali Online	www.baliwww.com	useful details about festivals, and links to sites about diving and culture
ARMA	www.nusantara.com/arma	for a sneak preview of what is at the ARMA art museum in Ubud
Bali Online	www.indo.com	excellent site with very useful information about festivals, culture and so on
Bali Paradise Online	www.bali-paradise.com	good for accommodation bookings, travel, business, diving and festivals
Bali Travel Forum	www.balivillas.com/bali	mainly a commercial site, but also has heaps of interesting reports from other travellers
Bali Travel Web	www.baliweb.com	produced in Bali, this site has excellent information about surfing and accommodation, among other things
Indonesian Observer	www.indoexchange.com/ indonesian-observer	current affairs about Indonesia by the English-language daily newspaper from Jakarta
Indo Surf & Lingo	www.peg.apc.org/ ~indosurf~	the best place to 'surf' the Net about surfing
Internet Travellers Information Service	www.isitnet.com/english/ asia/indonesia/ indonesiatop.htm	set up by volunteers, it has detailed, but not always up-to-date, information for travellers, by travellers
Open World Resort Guides	www.openworld.co.uk/ cityguides/bali	the place to check out the top notch resorts, with maps and local attractions too

is the Lonely Planet Web site (www.lonely planet.com). Here you'll find succinct summaries on travelling to most places on earth, postcards from other travellers and the Thorn Tree bulletin board, where you can ask questions before you go or dispense advice when you get back.

You can also find travel news and updates to many of our guidebooks, while `the sub-WWWay section can link you to the most useful travel resources elsewhere on the Web.

BOOKS

It is striking how much has been published about Bali in the western world, and how little of it has been written by Balinese – it says a lot about the western fascination with Bali. The few articles in English by Balinese are quite recent, and are academic rather than popular titles. Various Indonesian academic journals regularly have articles about aspects of Bali – its geography, economy, history and so on – but they are not very accessible to a general audience.

Prices of books on Bali are disappointingly high – they are either imported from overseas and very expensive, or printed in Indonesia but blatantly priced for tourists.

Oxford University Press publishes a number of good paperback titles on Bali as part of the *Oxford in Asia* series. Another publisher of interest is KITLV in Leiden, the Netherlands. Its *Bibliography of Bali* lists over 70,000 publications on Bali.

The Indonesian publisher, Java Books, distributes titles on Balinese culture, architecture, crafts etc. The distributor on Bali is PT Wira Mandala Pustaka (☎ 751197, email mndlbali@indo.net.id), Jl Kuta Permai IV, 6, Kuta.

Most books are published in different editions by different publishers in different countries. As a result, a book might be a hardcover rarity in one country, while it's readily available in paperback in another. Fortunately, bookshops and libraries search by title or author, so your local bookshop or library is best placed to advise you on the availability of the following recommendations.

Lonely Planet

If you're also planning to visit other parts of Indonesia, you can buy other Lonely Planet guidebooks: *Java* is a detailed but compact guide to Bali's large and powerful neighbour; *Indonesia* covers the entire archipelago; while *Indonesia's Eastern Islands* covers the islands from Lombok to Timor.

There are also guidebooks to *South-East Asia*; *Malaysia, Singapore & Brunei*; and *Papua New Guinea*; as well as the *Singapore* city guide. Our *Indonesian phrasebook* is a concise and handy introduction to Bahasa Indonesia. You can pick up these guidebooks at major bookshops in Kuta, Denpasar and Ubud (see the Bookshops entry a little later in this section).

Serious divers and snorkellers could consider buying *Diving and Snorkelling Guide* *to Bali and the Komodo Region*, part of Lonely Planet's new series of diving and snorkelling guides. This colourful and informative book details 31 spectacular diving and snorkelling sites around Bali, Lombok and other nearby islands.

Guidebooks

There are a number of travel guides to Bali, although many are long on background reading and colour photos, but short on up-to-date travel information and useful maps. Some tourist offices hand out mildly interesting booklets in English and Indonesian about their particular districts; the booklets for Badung (ie mainly Denpasar) and Buleleng (ie north Bali) districts are particularly detailed.

Guides about diving, surfing and language are listed under the relevant sections later in the chapter.

The Essential Guide to Living & Shopping in Bali. Although written by the Bali International Women's Association with the expat in mind, it is still useful for anyone staying on Bali for a while. It is available at major bookshops, especially in Ubud, and costs 55,000 rp.

Have You Been in Bali? This small and pricey (30,000 rp) booklet has some interesting tidbits about Balinese culture and traditions. It is mainly available in Ubud.

Art & Culture

Naturally enough, there's lot to check out here, including:

The Art & Culture of Bali by Urs Ramseyer. For information on Bali's complex and colourful artistic and cultural heritage, this expensive tome is one of the best around.

Artists on Bali by Ruud Spruit. This well illustrated description of the work of six European artists on Bali follows their influence on Balinese styles.

Balinese Architecture – Towards an Encyclopaedia by Made Wijaya. Unusual, large and expensive, it looks like a scrap book, but is full of information about traditional, colonial and contemporary Balinese buildings, with illustrations of interesting examples and features. It is available on Bali.

Balinese Music by Michael Tenzer. This is the

most up-to-date and readable treatment of all types of music throughout Bali.

Balinese Paintings by Anak Agung Made Djelantik. This concise and handy overview of the field was written by a Balinese.

Balinese Textiles by Brigitta Hauser, Marie-Louise Nabholz-Kartaschoff & Urs Ramseyer. This large and lavishly illustrated guide details the various styles of weaving and their significance.

Dance & Drama in Bali by Beryl de Zoete & Walter Spies. Published in 1938, this excellent book draws from Spies' deep appreciation and understanding of Bali's arts and culture.

Island of Bali by Miguel Covarrubias. Covarrubias was a Mexican artist, and this 1937 book (which is still widely available) is a very worthwhile investment for anybody with a real interest in Bali. It's readable yet learned, incredibly detailed yet always interesting. The closing speculation that tourism may spoil Bali is thought-provoking, but it's also a real pleasure to discover how some aspects of Bali are still exactly the way Covarrubias describes them.

Masks of Bali by Judy Slattim. Anyone interested in this fascinating aspect of Balinese culture should look for this handy book.

Perceptions of Paradise: Images of Bali in the Arts. The Neka Museum in Ubud publishes this substantial, well produced and beautifully illustrated book on Balinese art. An economical and useful introduction to Balinese painting can be found in *The Development of Painting in Bali*, also published by the Neka Museum. It covers the various schools of painting and has short biographies of well known artists, including many of the western artists who have worked on Bali.

Woodcarvings of Bali by Fred Eiseman. This refined artform on Bali is well covered in this book.

Early Western Visitors

Western visitors to Bali in the 1930s (refer to the boxed text of the same name in the Facts about Bali chapter) were a cultured and varied lot, many of whom had an irresistible urge to put their experiences down on paper. Fortunately, many of those classic early accounts have been republished, although they are rarely available on Bali.

A House in Bali by Colin McPhee. This is a wonderful account of a musician's lengthy stays on Bali to study gamelan music. He's an amazingly incisive and delightfully humorous author, and the book is superbly written. Like many other western visitors in the 1930s, his book was not published till much later – in this case, 1944.

A Tale from Bali by Vicki Baum. Baum was another visitor who came under the spell of Walter Spies. Her historical novel is based around the events of the 1906 *puputan* (suicidal battle) which brought the island under Dutch control.

Bali by Gregor Krause. A German doctor who worked for the Dutch government in Bangli in 1912, Krause was also a talented photographer, whose images of Bali – first published in Germany (1920) in two volumes – were an instant success. A selection of his pioneering photographs and text have recently been republished as *Bali 1912*, which is a book of great interest, but poor design.

The Last Paradise by Hickman Powell. Published in 1930, this was one of the first signs of the explosion of western accounts which followed. The book is very readable, but at times it gets quite cloyingly over-romantic – everything is just 'too beautiful' and 'too noble'.

Our Hotel in Bali by Louise Koke. This is a readable account of the original Kuta Beach Hotel, which she and her husband ran from the mid-1930s until WWII. The book was written during the war, but not published until 1987. It's a long way from the pre-war Kuta to the Kuta of today.

Revolt in Paradise by K'tut Tantri. Through the eyes of a western woman, this book tells of life on the island during the 1930s, and in the midst of the post-WWII Indonesian revolution. Besides her Balinese name, she has also been known as Vannine Walker, Muriel Pearson and a number of other pseudonyms.

Walter Spies & Balinese Art by Hans Rhodius & John Darling. Spies was the keystone of the pre-war Bali foreign set, and his colourful, multi-dimensional and ultimately tragic life is well documented in this intriguing account of his work and influence on Balinese art.

History & Anthropology

For a deeper understanding of Bali's past, try the following titles:

Bali in the 19th Century by Ide Anak Agung Gede. Covering the early colonial period and the ritual capitulation of the Balinese nobility, this tome is more interesting than many others because the author is of Balinese nobility.

Balinese Character – a Photographic Analysis by Margaret Mead & Gregory Bateson. Penned by two of the many prominent anthropologists who have worked on Bali, their study, written in 1942, has been heavily discussed and criticised. For example, a passivity which they observed in children, and explained in cultural terms, was more probably attributable to malnutrition.

The Balinese People – A Reinvestigation of Character by GD Jensen & LK Suryani. This is a critique of the Mead-Bateson book, *Balinese Character – a Photographic Analysis.*

The Interpretation of Cultures by Clifford Geertz. Written by a noted American anthropologist, this book includes three essays on Bali.

Monumental Bali by AJ Bernet Kempers. For descriptions of the ancient sites of Bali, with text which puts them in historical and cultural context, it is hard to go past this well written and illustrated book – it could turn a casual tourist into a Balinese temple buff. It also contains a detailed bibliography.

General

For a more multi-disciplinary approach, try:

A Little Bit of One O'Clock by William Ingram. Available on Bali (70,000 rp), this paperback relates an American's life with a Balinese family, and explains a lot of culture and tradition in a readable way.

Bali – A Paradise Created by Adrian Vickers. Vickers traces Balinese history and development by concentrating on the island's image in the west. His idea is that the impression is a manufactured one, the result of a conscious decision to create an image of an ideal island paradise.

Bali – Sekala & Niskala; Vol I: Essays on Religion, Ritual & Art and *Bali – Sekala & Niskala; Vol II: Essays on Society Tradition & Craft* by Fred Eiseman. These attractive anthologies of essays cover many aspects of Balinese life.

Bali High – Paradise from the Air by Leonard Leuras & Rio Helmi. This collection of photographs taken from a helicopter offers some surprising new perspectives and angles. Some of the most interesting shots are actually not of Bali at all, but of neighbouring Lombok.

Bali Style by Rio Helmi & Barbara Walker. This superbly illustrated book covers architecture, landscaping and decoration on contemporary Bali.

Bali, The Ultimate Island by Leonard Leuras & R Ian Lloyd. This is the ultimate coffee-table book on Bali. It's a heavyweight volume with superb photographs, both old and new, together with interesting text.

The Balinese by Hugh Mabbett. This is another readable collection of anecdotes, observations and impressions of Bali and its people. If you develop a real interest in Kuta, read Mabbet's *In Praise of Kuta*, which you might find in some Kuta bookshops. It recounts Kuta's early history and its frenetic modern development.

Balinese Gardens by William Warren & Invernizzi Tettoni. This is a handsome and expensive coverage of the wonders of Balinese gardens and landscapes.

Birds of Bali by Victor Mason & Frank Jarvis. Written by the man who conducts bird-watching walks around Ubud, the book is enhanced by lovely watercolour illustrations.

The Butterflies of Bali by Victor Mason. This novel – actually written by the expert in birds on Bali – is a good read, and is available in Ubud (it has very little to do with butterflies, however).

Flowers of Bali & Fruits of Bali by Fred & Margaret Wiseman. For some lighter reading, these nicely illustrated books will tell you what you're admiring or eating.

Food of Bali by Heinz von Holzen, Lothar Arsana & Wendy Hutton. This mouth-watering book not only explains the cultural context of Balinese food, but also describes ingredients and techniques, and has recipes for over 70 delicious dishes which you can try at home.

On the Edge of a Dream: Magic and Madness in Bali by Michael Weise. Through the story of several westerners trying to find the 'real Bali', and to 'find themselves', Weise makes some insightful comments about the effects of tourism on the island. The book is available on Bali.

Stranger in Paradise by Made Wijaya. Regarded as a local classic, it tells the story of a western man's life on Bali in the late 1970s, when foreigners were rare. It is available on Bali.

Bookshops

Although the number of decent bookshops on Bali is not huge, they all have an interesting selections of books and maps, as well as local and international newspapers and magazines and Lonely Planet guides. The best bookshops on the island are: Gramedia Book Shop in Denpasar; M-Media, Kuta; and Ganesha and Ary's bookshops in Ubud.

If you just want something easy to read on the beach, numerous bookshops and book exchanges in the tourist centres sell second-hand novels in most of the major European languages, and many budget hotels also sell used books.

NEWSPAPERS & MAGAZINES

Indonesian readers can enjoy the daily *Bali Post*. Two English-language dailies are published in Jakarta, and available on Bali – *Jakarta Post* (1800 rp) and the *Indonesian Observer* (2150 rp), which is better. Current issues can be bought from a few shops in Kuta/Legian, Sanur and Ubud, but mostly from guys who hang around the streets and charge considerably more.

Current editions of *Time* (6200 rp) and *Newsweek* (4500 rp), and recent copies of the *International Herald Tribune* (about 5000 rp), are also available in the tourist areas. Recent Australian, US and European newspapers are available only one or two days after publication date, mainly from guys around the streets. Due to the current exchange rates, however, the rupiah prices for these imported newspapers are comparatively high.

Several tourist-oriented magazines and newspapers are available on Bali – and all are free.

Bali Advertiser (☎/fax 0361-755392, email baliads @denpasar.wasantara.net.id) is a thin publication of classified ads, mainly for the expat community. It is useful if you're looking for house rentals, work, or discounted travel or accommodation.

Bali Echo is a glossy magazine that comes out every two months. It always has some interesting articles and excellent photos, but is hard to find – try an airline office in Sanur or the Denpasar Tourist Office.

Bali Kini, published by the Indonesian Tourist Promotion Office, is another superb publication, with wonderful articles and great photos – try to find some previous editions to read. It is available from the two tourist offices in Denpasar, and in Kuta.

Bali News, subtitled the 'Pulse of Paradise' (1500 rp) has been resurrected temporarily. It is a readable collection of foreign, Indonesian and Balinese news, sport, entertainment and information, but is extremely hard to find – look for it at bookshops and supermarkets in Kuta.

Bali Plus is worth picking up, although it's full of ads and unashamedly caters almost exclusively to people staying in south Bali.

Bali Tourist Guide is another monthly, with some text in Japanese. It is full of ads and has a lot of information about other parts of Indonesia, but there are some decent articles about Bali.

This Month in Bali, printed in English and Japanese, is often only available at the international airport, and is worth picking up as soon as you arrive.

RADIO & TV
Radio

The government radio station, Radio Republic Indonesia (RRI), broadcasts 24 hours a day, and has an English-language news service twice daily. There are several other stations on Bali. Radio Menara (105.8FM) and Radio Plus Bali (106.5FM) feature western music, with Indonesian-speaking DJs. Most other radio programmes are broadcast from Java, via repeater stations on Bali – try 99.5FM for western rock and rap music.

Bali FM (100.9FM) is a tourist oriented radio station which broadcasts in English and Indonesian over most of southern Bali. It plays some contemporary rock and lots of oldies, and has a regular news service. Occasionally it will broadcast an emergency message for a tourist who needs to be contacted urgently.

Short-wave broadcasts, such as Voice of America and the BBC World Service, can be picked up on Bali, although Radio Australia is now very difficult to receive, as a result of government cuts to its funding.

TV

Several public and private television stations broadcast a range of foreign movies, mostly with Indonesian subtitles, plus bizarre Indonesian quiz shows, soap operas from all over the world (with Indonesian subtitles), and sports – mainly basketball from the US and football from Europe. There are also English-language news services on TVRI at 7.30 pm; on SCTV at 8 am; and on RCTI at 8.30 am. The daily *Jakarta Post* includes a list of programmes for each

The Terror of TV

TV may pose a much greater threat to Balinese culture than mass tourism. It's not so much that the content of the TV programmes threaten to undermine traditional beliefs – but when you see an entire warung full of people watching a sitcom from Mexico or a quiz show from Egypt, with Indonesian subtitles, you wonder if there will ever be enough time for attending to the business of the community, let alone practising traditional dances or playing the gamelan.

channel (but at Jakarta time). International networks like CNN, ESPN and TV Australia are popular in mid-range, upwardly mobile tourist hotels.

VIDEO SYSTEMS

The various countries of the world cannot agree on a single TV broadcasting standard. Indonesia subscribes to the PAL broadcasting standard, the same as Australia, New Zealand, the UK and most of Europe. Competing systems include SECAM (France, former Soviet republics, Egypt) and NTSC (Canada, Japan, Taiwan, Latin America and the USA).

PHOTOGRAPHY & VIDEO

Bali is one of the most photogenic places on earth, so take plenty of film, and always make sure you're ready to photograph or film the unexpected.

Film & Equipment

Fortunately, a good variety of film is widely available at reasonable prices. In the tourist centres of south Bali, a roll of Kodak 24 or 36 print film costs about 17,000 or 19,000 rp – prices for Konica and Fuji are a little cheaper. A roll of Kodachrome 36 slide film costs about 35,000 rp, without processing. It pays to shop around if you want to buy a lot of film, or if you have special requirements

– and always check the expiry date before handing over your cash.

Developing and printing is also widely available, very cheap and reasonably good quality. You can get colour print film done in a few hours (some places even claim to develop in less than '23 minutes') at one of the innumerable photographic shops in the tourist centres and major towns. A roll of 24/36 print film costs about 25,200/34,800 rp to develop, but prices do vary, so shop around. There are also special deals around for double prints (about 800 rp each) and enlargements. Slide film takes two or three days to develop, and costs more.

Photography

Shoot early in the day – between 10 am and 3 pm the sun is intense and straight overhead, so you're likely to get a bluish, washed-out look to your pictures. In the late afternoon, the sky is often overcast or hazy, and it's hard to get really clear, sharp images – and the sun can often set very quickly. If you do shoot in the middle of the day, a skylight filter will cut out some of the haze. When the sun is low in the sky, a lens hood can help reduce problems with reflection or direct sunlight on the lens.

Those picturesque, green rice fields come up best if backlit by the sun. For the oh-so-popular sunset shots at Kuta, Lovina and Tanah Lot, set your exposure on the sky without the sun making an appearance – then shoot at the sun.

It's surprisingly dark in the shade of the trees, so you might find it difficult to take photos of lush gorges or monkey forests without a flash. Faster film (400 ASA) can be useful.

Video

Properly used, a video camera can give a fascinating record of your holiday. As well as videoing the obvious things – sunsets and spectacular views – remember to record some of the ordinary everyday details of life in the country. Often the most interesting things occur when you're actually intent on filming something else. Remember too that, unlike still photography, video 'flows', so, for example, you can shoot scenes of countryside rolling past the train window, to give an overall impression that isn't possible with ordinary photos.

Video cameras these days have amazingly sensitive microphones, and you might be surprised how much sound will be picked up. This can also be a problem if there is a lot of ambient noise – filming by the side of a busy road might seem OK when you do it, but viewing it back home might simply give you a deafening cacophony of traffic noise. One good rule to follow for beginners is to try to film in long takes, and don't move the camera around too much. Otherwise, your video could well make your viewers seasick! If your camera has a stabiliser, you can use it to obtain good footage while travelling on various means of transport, even on bumpy roads. And remember, you're on holiday – don't let the video take over your life and turn your trip into a Cecil B de Mille production.

Blank video tapes are available in some of the bigger stores in Denpasar and the main tourist areas. They're not particularly cheap and the range is limited, so it would probably be better to bring plenty of tapes with you. Bring them in sealed packages – customs authorities can insist on viewing tapes they suspect may contain prohibited material like pornography, although it's pretty unlikely. Bring spare parts and batteries.

Restrictions & Entry Charges

Military installations are not widespread on Bali, but you should be aware that these are sensitive subjects – if in doubt, ask before you shoot. You are welcome to take photos of ceremonies in the villages and temples, but please be discreet. Also ask before taking photos inside a mosque or a Hindu temple (rather than just the surrounds of the temple which most people can visit and photograph without needing to ask). Most tourist attractions charge a few more rupiahs for using a still or video camera.

Photographing People

Photograph with discretion and manners. It's always polite to ask first, and if they say no, then don't. A gesture, smile and nod are all that is usually necessary. Often people will ask you to take their photo, and you more-or-less have to – the problem is getting them in a natural pose. And don't be surprised if you're asked to be in a few holiday snaps taken by 'domestic' (ie Indonesian) tourists. If you promise to send someone a copy of a photo, get their address and do so.

There's one place where you must not take photographs at all – public bathing places. Just because the Balinese bathe in streams, rivers, lakes or other open places doesn't mean they don't think of them as private places. Balinese simply do not 'see' one another when they're bathing, and to intrude with a camera is like sneaking up to someone's bathroom window and pointing your camera through.

TIME

Bali, Lombok and the islands of Nusa Tenggara to the east are all on Central Indonesian Standard Time (Waktu Indonesian Tengah or WIT), which is eight hours ahead of GMT/UTC or two hours behind Australian Eastern Standard Time. Java is another hour behind Bali/Lombok.

Not allowing for variations due to daylight-saving time in foreign countries, when it's noon on Bali and Lombok, it's 11 pm the previous day in New York and 8 pm in Los Angeles, 4 am in London, 5 am in Paris and Amsterdam, noon in Perth, 1 pm in Tokyo, and 2 pm in Sydney and Melbourne.

As Bali is close to the equator, days and nights are approximately equal in length. The sun pops up over the horizon at about 6 am and drops down in the west at about 6 pm. The sunsets are often orange-fire spectaculars, but don't expect to enjoy a pleasant twilight – it gets dark almost immediately.

'Bali time' is an expression which refers to the Balinese reluctance to be obsessed by punctuality. It is equivalent to *jam karet*, the 'rubber time' found in other parts of Indonesia, but is even more elastic. Many Balinese in the tourist industry and other sectors of the economy are now learning about deadlines, and punch-card clocks are now a common sight near staff entrances.

ELECTRICITY

Electricity is usually 220-240V AC on Bali. In some smaller villages it's still 110V (if they have electricity at all), so check first. Wall plugs are the standard round variety with two pins used in Europe. Electricity is usually fairly reliable and blackouts are not common, although the electricity grid is always running at its maximum capacity. In many small towns, and even in parts of larger towns, electricity is a recent innovation – if you travel around a lot you're likely to stay in the odd losmen where lighting is provided with oil lamps.

Even where there is electricity, the lighting can be very dim. Lots of losmen seem to have light bulbs of such low wattage that you can almost see the electricity crawling around the filaments. Street lighting can also be a problem – there often isn't any. If stumbling back to your losmen down dark alleys in Kuta, or through the rice paddies in Ubud, doesn't appeal, a strong torch (flashlight) can be very useful.

WEIGHTS & MEASURES

Indonesia follows the metric system. For people accustomed to the imperial system, there is a conversion table at the back of this book.

LAUNDRY

All the fancier hotels advertise laundry services, and charge quite steeply for them. The cheaper places don't advertise the fact, but will normally wash and iron your clothes for a pretty reasonable price. The family-run laundry services in the back streets of the tourist centres are the cheapest: in Kuta, for example, a shirt, jeans or skirt costs as little as 750 rp to wash and iron. Allow 24 hours, or a bit longer if it's been raining.

TOILETS

You'll still encounter Asian-style toilets in cheaper losmen around Bali (particularly in

the far west) and Lombok. These toilets have two footrests and a hole in the ground – you squat down and aim. In most places catering for tourists, the western-style, sit-down toilets are the norm. If you need a public toilet in a tourist centre, go to a bar or restaurant. At many tourist attractions on Bali (but not on Lombok), there are public toilets which cost about 300 rp per visit. Elsewhere, you may have to find somewhere private and discreet, which is not always easy on Bali.

Apart from places that cater to the tourist trade, you won't find toilet paper in any hotel or restaurant toilet, so bring your own, or learn to wash yourself with water (left hand only). If there is a bin next to the toilet, it's for toilet paper – the sewerage system may not be able to cope with toilet paper, so please use the bin. To locate a toilet ask for the *kamar mandi* (bathroom), *kamar kecil* (little room) or WC (pronounced 'waysay').

HEALTH

Travel health depends on your predeparture preparations, your daily health care while travelling and how you handle any medical problem that does develop. While the potential dangers can seem quite frightening, in reality few travellers experience more than an upset stomach on Bali or Lombok. The greatest risk is accidental injury, particularly from traffic accidents.

Predeparture Planning

Immunisations For some countries no immunisations are necessary, but the further off the beaten track you go the more necessary it is to take precautions. Be aware that there is often a greater risk of disease with children and in pregnancy.

Plan ahead for getting your vaccinations: some of them require more than one injection, while some vaccinations should not be given together. Note that some vaccinations should not be given during pregnancy, or to people with allergies – discuss with your doctor. It is recommended you seek medical advice at least six weeks before travel.

There are no health entry requirements for Indonesia, but if you have been to Africa or

Medical Kit Check List

Consider taking a basic medical kit including:

☐ **Aspirin** or **paracetamol** (acetaminophen in the US) – for pain or fever.

☐ **Antihistamine** (such as Benadryl) – a decongestant for colds and allergies, it also eases the itch from insect bites or stings and helps to prevent motion sickness. Antihistamines may cause sedation and interact with alcohol, so care should be taken when using them; take one you know and have used before, if possible.

☐ **Antibiotics** – useful if you're travelling well off the beaten track, but they must be prescribed; carry the prescription with you.

☐ **Lomotil** or **Imodium** – to treat diarrhoea; prochlorperazine (eg Stemetil) or metaclopramide (eg Maxalon) is good for nausea and vomiting.

☐ **Rehydration mixture** – to treat severe diarrhoea; which is particularly important when travelling with children.

☐ **Antiseptic**, such as povidone-iodine (eg Betadine) – for cuts and grazes.

☐ **Multivitamins** – especially useful for long trips when dietary vitamin intake may be inadequate.

☐ **Calamine lotion** or **aluminium sulphate spray** (eg Stingose) – to ease irritation from bites or stings.

☐ **Bandages** and **Band-aids**

☐ **Scissors, tweezers** and a **thermometer** – (note that mercury thermometers are prohibited by airlines).

☐ **Cold and flu tablets** and **throat lozenges** – Pseudoephedrine hydrochloride (Sudafed) may be useful when flying with a cold to avoid ear damage.

☐ **Insect repellent, sunscreen, Chapstick** and **water purification tablets**

☐ **A couple of syringes** – in case you need injections in a country with medical hygiene problems. Ask your doctor for a note explaining why they have been prescribed.

South America in the previous six days, you may need a vaccination for yellow fever. Other vaccinations are highly recommended. Record all vaccinations on an International Certificate of Vaccination, available from your doctor or national health department. (For more information on the diseases themselves, see the individual disease entries later in this section.)

Discuss your personal requirements with your doctor, but vaccinations you should consider for this trip include:

Hepatitis A Hepatitis A vaccine (eg Avaxim, Havrix 1440 or VAQTA) provides long-term immunity (possibly more than 10 years) after an initial injection and a booster at six to 12 months. Alternatively, an injection of gamma globulin can provide short-term protection against hepatitis A – two to six months, depending on the dose given. It is not a vaccine, but is ready-made antibody collected from blood donations. It is reasonably effective and, unlike the vaccine, it is protective immediately, but because it is a blood product, there are current concerns about its long-term safety. Hepatitis A vaccine is also available in a combined form, Twinrix, with hepatitis B vaccine. Three injections over a six month period are required, the first two providing substantial protection against hepatitis A.

Typhoid Vaccination against typhoid may be required if you are travelling for more than a couple of weeks in most parts of Asia, Africa, Central and South America and Central and Eastern Europe. It is now available either as an injection or as capsules to be taken orally.

Diphtheria & Tetanus Vaccinations for these two diseases are usually combined and are recommended for everyone. After an initial course of three injections (usually given in childhood), boosters are necessary every 10 years.

Hepatitis B Travellers who should consider vaccination against hepatitis B include those on a long trip, as well as those visiting countries where there are high levels of hepatitis B infection, where blood transfusions may not be adequately screened or where sexual contact or needle sharing is a possibility. Vaccination involves three injections, with a booster at 12 months. More rapid courses are available if necessary.

Polio Everyone should keep up to date with this vaccination, which is normally given in childhood. A booster every 10 years will maintain immunity.

Rabies Vaccination should be considered by those who will spend a month or longer in a country where rabies is common, especially if they are cycling, handling animals, caving or travelling to remote areas, and for children (who may not report a bite). Pre-travel rabies vaccination involves having three injections over 21 to 28 days. If someone who has been vaccinated is bitten or scratched by an animal, they will require two booster injections of vaccine; those not vaccinated require more.

Japanese B Encephalitis Consider vaccination against this disease if you're spending a month or longer in a high risk area (including parts of Asia), making repeated trips to a risk area or visiting during an epidemic. It involves three injections over 30 days.

Tuberculosis The risk of TB to travellers is usually very low, unless you will be living with or closely associated with local people in high risk areas such as Asia, Africa and some parts of the Americas and Pacific. Vaccination against TB (BCG) is recommended for children living on Bali or Lombok for three months or more.

Malaria Medication
Antimalarial drugs do not prevent you from being infected but kill the malaria parasites during a stage in their development and significantly reduce the risk of becoming very ill or dying.

Expert advice on medication should be sought, as there are many factors to consider including the area to be visited, the risk of exposure to malaria-carrying mosquitoes, the side effects of medication, your medical history and whether you are a child or adult or pregnant. Travellers to isolated areas in high risk countries may like to carry a treatment dose of medication for use if symptoms occur.

Health Insurance
Ensure that you have adequate health insurance. See the Travel Insurance entry under Visas & Documents earlier in this chapter for details.

Travel Health Guides
If you are planning to be away or travelling in remote areas for a long period of time, you may like to consider taking a more detailed health guide.

CDC's Complete Guide to Healthy Travel, Open Road Publishing, 1997. This has the recommendations for international travel from the US Centers for Disease Control & Prevention.

Staying Healthy in Asia, Africa & Latin America, Dirk Schroeder, Moon Publications. Probably the best all-round guide to carry; it's detailed and well organised.

Travellers' Health, Dr Richard Dawood, Oxford University Press. Comprehensive, easy to read, authoritative and highly recommended, although it's rather large to lug around.

Where There is No Doctor, David Werner, Macmillan. A very detailed guide intended for someone, such as a Peace Corps worker, going to work in an underdeveloped country.

Travel with Children, Maureen Wheeler, Lonely Planet Publications. Includes advice on travel health for younger children.

Web Sites There are also a number of excellent travel health sites on the Internet. From the Lonely Planet Web site there are links at www.lonelyplanet.com/weblinks/wlprep.htm#heal to the World Health Organization and the US Centers for Diseases Control & Prevention.

Other Preparations Make sure that you are healthy before you start travelling. If you require a particular medication, bring an adequate supply, as it may not be available locally. Take part of the packaging showing the generic name, rather than the brand, as this will make getting replacements easier. It's a good idea to have a legible prescription or letter from your doctor to show that you legally use the medication to avoid any problems.

Ensure your teeth are healthy before you travel; it's not hard to find a dentist *(dokter gigi)* on Bali and Lombok, but it's not really how you want to spend your holiday. If you wear glasses, take a spare pair and your prescription. You can get new spectacles made up quickly, cheaply and competently in the tourist centres.

Basic Rules
Food There is an old colonial adage which says: 'If you can cook it, boil it or peel it you can eat it ... otherwise forget it'. Vegetables and fruit should be washed with purified water or peeled where possible – many tourist

Nutrition

If your food is poor or limited in availability, if you're travelling hard and fast and therefore missing meals, or if you simply lose your appetite, you can soon start to lose weight and place your health at risk.

Make sure your diet is well balanced. Cooked eggs, tofu, beans, lentils and nuts are all safe ways to get protein. Fruit you can peel (bananas, oranges or mandarins for example) is usually safe (melons can harbour bacteria in their flesh and are best avoided) and a good source of vitamins. Try to eat plenty of grains (including rice) and bread. Remember that although food is generally safer if it is cooked well, overcooked food loses much of its nutritional value. If your diet isn't well balanced or if your food intake is insufficient, it's a good idea to take vitamin and iron pills.

Make sure you drink enough – don't rely on feeling thirsty to indicate when you should drink. Not needing to urinate or small amounts of very dark yellow urine is a danger sign. Always carry a water bottle with you on long trips. Excessive sweating can lead to loss of salt and therefore muscle cramping. Salt tablets are not a good idea as a preventative, but in places where salt is not used much adding salt to food can help.

restaurants on Bali and Lombok wash all their vegetables, and advertise the fact.

Beware of ice cream which is sold in the street or anywhere it might have been melted and refrozen, but frozen ice cream with name brands, and kept in a freezer, is fine.

Shellfish such as mussels, oysters and clams should be avoided as well as under-cooked meat, particularly in the form of mince. Steaming does not make shellfish safe for eating.

If a place looks clean and well run and the vendor also looks clean and healthy, then the food is probably safe. In general, places that are packed with travellers or locals will be fine, while empty restaurants are question-able. The food in busy restaurants is cooked and eaten quite quickly with little standing around and is probably not reheated.

Water The number-one rule is *be careful of the water* and especially ice. If you don't know for certain that the water is safe, then assume the worst. That said, if you have travelled elsewhere in Asia, and think you have built up an immunity to a few water-borne germs, you should have no problems drinking tap water on Bali (remember that

glasses you drink from have been washed in tap water).

If you don't want to risk tap water, bottled water and soft drinks are generally fine, and readily available. Only use water from containers with a serrated seal – not tops or corks. Take care with fruit juice, particular-ly if water may have been added.

Milk should be treated with suspicion as it is often unpasteurised, although boiled milk is fine if it is kept hygienically. Tea or coffee should also be OK, since the water should have been boiled.

Water Purification The simplest way of pu-rifying water is to boil it thoroughly. Vigorous boiling should be satisfactory; however, at high altitude water boils at a lower tempera-ture, so germs are less likely to be killed. Boil it for longer in these environments.

Consider purchasing a water filter for a long trip. There are two main kinds of filter. Total filters take out all parasites, bacteria and viruses, and make water safe to drink. They are often quite expensive, but they can be more cost effective than buying bottled water. Simple filters (which can be as simple as a nylon mesh bag) remove dirt and larger foreign bodies from the water so that chemical solutions work much more effectively; if water is dirty, chemical solutions may not work at all. It's very important when buying a filter to read the specifications, so that you know exactly what it removes from the water and what it doesn't. Simple filtering will not remove all dangerous organisms, so if you cannot boil water it should be treated chemically.

Chlorine tablets will kill many pathogens, but not some parasites like giardia and amoebic cysts. Iodine is more effective in purifying water and is available in tablet form. Follow the directions carefully and remember that too much iodine can be harmful.

Medical Problems & Treatment

Self-diagnosis and treatment can be risky, so you should always seek medical help. Although we do give drug dosages in this section, they are for emergency use only. Correct diagnosis is vital.

Antibiotics should ideally be administered only under medical supervision. Take only the recommended dose at the prescribed intervals and use the whole course, even if the illness seems to be cured earlier.

Everyday Health

Normal body temperature is 37°C or 98.6°F; more than 2°C (4°F) higher indicates a high fever. The normal adult pulse rate is 60 to 100 per minute (children 80 to 100, babies 100 to 140). As a general rule the pulse increases about 20 beats per minute for each °C (2°F) rise in fever.

Respiration (breathing) rate is also an indicator of illness. Count the number of breaths per minute: between 12 and 20 is normal for adults and older children (up to 30 for younger children, 40 for babies). People with a high fever or serious respiratory illness breathe more quickly than normal. More than 40 shallow breaths a minute may indicate pneumonia.

Stop immediately if there are any serious reactions and don't use the antibiotic at all if you are unsure that you have the correct one. Some people are allergic to commonly prescribed antibiotics such as penicillin or sulpha drugs; carry this information (eg on a bracelet) when travelling.

Hospitals

There are several decent public hospitals in Denpasar, and a few around Bali, mainly in the district capitals. There are also private medical clinics – mainly for tourists – in Nusa Dua, Tanjung Benoa, Kuta/Legian and Ubud. In more remote areas, facilities are basic; generally a small public hospital, doctor's surgery or community health care centre (called a *puskesmas*).

Specialist facilities for neurosurgery and heart surgery are nonexistent, and the range of available drugs (including painkillers) is limited. Your hotel should be able to recommend a local English-speaking doctor, or you could call one of the upmarket hotels and ask them. Travel insurance policies often have an emergency assistance phone number, which might be able to recommend a doctor or clinic, or use its contacts to find one in a remote area.

Health care is not free on Bali, and you will get certainly more prompt attention if you can pay cash up front for treatment, drugs, surgical equipment, drinking water, food and so on. As an example, the Legian Medical Clinic in Kuta charges 50,000 rp for a consultation, and considerably more for a visit to a hotel. Try to get receipts and paperwork so you can claim it all later on your travel insurance.

In hospitals on Bali, services such as meals, washing and clean clothing, are normally provided by the patient's family. If you are unfortunate enough to be on your own in a Bali hospital, contact your consulate – you need help.

Pharmacies

There are plenty of pharmacies (drugstores) – *apotik* or *apotek* – in the tourist centres, and usually a few in the major towns, often located near the main hospital or a doctor's surgery. Always double-check the expiry date before you buy any medicines.

Environmental Hazards

Heat Exhaustion Dehydration and salt deficiency can cause heat exhaustion. Take time to acclimatise to high temperatures, drink sufficient liquids and don't do anything too physically demanding.

Salt deficiency is characterised by fatigue, lethargy, headaches, giddiness and muscle cramps. Salt tablets may help, but adding extra salt to your food is better. Anhidrotic heat exhaustion – caused by an inability to sweat – is quite rare. It's most likely to strike people who have been in a hot climate for some time, rather than newcomers.

Heatstroke This serious, occasionally fatal, condition can occur if the body's heat-regulating mechanism breaks down and the body temperature rises to dangerous levels. Long, continuous periods of exposure to high temperatures and insufficient fluids can leave you vulnerable to heatstroke.

The symptoms are feeling unwell, not sweating very much (or at all) and a high body temperature (39°C to 41°C or 102°F to 106°F). Where sweating has ceased the skin becomes flushed and red. Severe, throbbing headaches and lack of coordination will also occur, and the sufferer may be confused or aggressive. Eventually the victim will become delirious or convulse. Hospitalisation is essential, but in the interim get victims out of the sun, remove their clothing, cover them with a wet sheet or towel and then fan continually. Give fluids if they are conscious.

Jet Lag This is experienced when a person travels by air across more than three time zones (each time zone usually represents a one hour time difference). It occurs because many of the functions of the human body (such as temperature, pulse rate and emptying of the bladder and bowels) are regulated by internal 24 hour cycles. When we travel long distances rapidly, our bodies take time to adjust to the 'new time' of our destination, and we may experience disorientation, fatigue, insomnia, anxiety, impaired concentration and loss of appetite. These effects will usually be gone within three days of arrival, but to minimise the impact of jet lag:

- Rest for a couple of days prior to departure.
- Try to select flight schedules that minimise sleep deprivation; arriving late in the day means you can go to sleep soon after you arrive. For very long flights, try to organise a stopover.
- Avoid excessive eating (which bloats the stomach) and alcohol (which causes dehydration) during the flight. Instead, drink plenty of noncarbonated, nonalcoholic drinks such as fruit juice or water.
- Avoid smoking.
- Make yourself comfortable by wearing loose-fitting clothes and perhaps bringing an eye mask and ear plugs to help you sleep.
- Try to sleep at the appropriate time for the time zone you are travelling to.

Motion Sickness Eating lightly before and during a trip will reduce the chances of motion sickness. If you are prone to motion sickness try to find a place that minimises movement – near the wing on aircraft, close to midships on boats, near the centre on buses. Fresh air usually helps; reading and cigarette smoke don't. Commercial motion-sickness preparations, which can cause drowsiness, have to be taken before the trip commences. Peppermint (including mint-flavoured sweets) and ginger (available in capsule form) and are natural preventatives.

Prickly Heat Prickly heat is an itchy rash caused by excessive perspiration trapped under the skin. It usually strikes people who have just arrived in a hot climate. Keeping cool, bathing often, drying the skin and using a mild talcum or prickly heat powder or resorting to air-conditioning may help.

Sunburn On Bali and Lombok, you can get sunburnt very quickly, even through cloud, and especially while rafting, trekking, swimming, surfing, snorkelling and diving. Use a maximum strength sunblock (readily available on both islands); protect your eyes with good quality sunglasses, particularly if you are near water or sand; and take extra care with areas that don't normally see sun, like your feet. A broad-rimmed hat provides good protection, but you should also put sunblock on your nose, lips and ears. Even good sunblocks wash off with heavy sweating and swimming, so reapply every two or three hours. For surfers, a helmet protects your head against the sun as well as coral. Calamine lotion or aloe vera provide some relief from mild sunburn.

Infectious Diseases

Diarrhoea The infamous 'Bali Belly', or travellers' diarrhoea, affects a few visitors, but it's usually not a serious health risk, it doesn't last long and with a little care you can generally avoid it completely. Most 'Bali Bellies' are usually just a stomach rebelling against something new and different, rather than something unhealthy. Simple things like a change of water, food or climate can all cause a mild bout of diarrhoea, but a few rushed toilet trips with no other symptoms is not indicative of a major problem.

Dehydration is the main danger with any diarrhoea, particularly in children and the elderly, as dehydration can occur quickly. Under all circumstances *fluid replacement* (at least equal to the volume being lost) is the most important thing to remember. Weak black tea with a little sugar, soda water, or soft drinks allowed to go flat and diluted 50% with clean water are all good. With severe diarrhoea a rehydrating solution is preferable to replace minerals and salts lost. Commercially available oral rehydration salts (ORS) are very useful; add them to boiled or bottled water. In an emergency you can make up a solution of six teaspoons of sugar and a half teaspoon of salt to a litre of boiled or bottled water. You need to drink at least the same volume of fluid that you are losing in bowel movements and vomiting. Urine is the best guide to the adequacy of replacement – if you have small amounts of concentrated urine, you need to drink more. Keep drinking small amounts often. Stick to a bland diet as you recover.

Loperamide or diphenoxylate can be used to bring relief from the symptoms, although they do not actually cure the problem. Only use these drugs if you do not have access to toilets eg if you *must* travel. For children under 12 years these preparations are not recommended. Do not use these drugs if the person has a high fever or is severely dehydrated.

In certain situations antibiotics may be required: diarrhoea with blood or mucus (dysentery), any diarrhoea with fever, profuse watery diarrhoea, persistent diarrhoea not improving after 48 hours and severe diarrhoea. These suggest a more serious cause of diarrhoea and in these situations gut-paralysing drugs should be avoided.

In these situations, a stool test may be necessary to diagnose what bug is causing your diarrhoea, so you should seek medical help urgently. Where this is not possible the recommended drugs for bacterial diarrhoea (the most likely cause of severe diarrhoea in travellers) are norfloxacin 400mg twice daily for three days or ciprofloxacin 500mg twice daily for five days. These are not recommended for children or pregnant women. The drug of choice for children would be co-trimoxazole (Bactrim, Septrin or Resprim) with the dosage dependent on weight. A five day course is given. Ampicillin or amoxycillin may be given in pregnancy, but medical care is necessary.

Two other causes of persistent diarrhoea in travellers are giardiasis and amoebic dysentery.

Giardiasis is caused by a common parasite, *Giardia lamblia*. Symptoms include stomach cramps, nausea, a bloated stomach, watery, foul-smelling diarrhoea and frequent gas. Giardiasis can appear several weeks after you have been exposed to the parasite. The symptoms may disappear for a few days and then return; this can go on for several weeks.

Amoebic dysentery, caused by the protozoan *Entamoeba histolytica*, is characterised by a gradual onset of low-grade diarrhoea, often with blood and mucus. Cramping abdominal pain and vomiting are less likely than in other types of diarrhoea, and fever may not be present. It will persist until treated and can recur and cause some other health problems.

You should seek medical advice if you think you have giardiasis or amoebic dysentery, but where this is not possible, Tinidazole (Fasigyn) or metronidazole (Flagyl) are the recommended drugs. Treatment is a 2g single dose of Fasigyn or 250mg of Flagyl three times daily for five to 10 days.

Fungal Infections Fungal infections occur more commonly in hot weather and are usually found on the scalp, between the toes or fingers, in the groin and on the body (ringworm). You get ringworm (which is a fungal infection, not a worm) from infected animals or other people. Moisture encourages these infections.

To prevent fungal infections wear loose, comfortable clothes, avoid artificial fibres, wash frequently and dry carefully. If you do get an infection, wash the infected area at least daily with a disinfectant or medicated soap and water, and rinse and dry well. Apply an antifungal cream or powder like tolnaftate. Try to expose the infected area to air or sunlight as much as possible and wash all towels and underwear in hot water, change them often and let them dry in the sun.

Hepatitis Hepatitis is a general term for inflammation of the liver. It is a common disease worldwide. The symptoms are fever, chills, headache, fatigue, feelings of weakness and aches and pains, followed by loss of appetite, nausea, vomiting, abdominal pain, dark urine, light-coloured faeces, jaundiced (yellow) skin and the whites of the eyes may turn yellow.

Hepatitis A is transmitted by contaminated food and drinking water. The disease poses a real threat to travellers. You should seek medical advice, but there is not much you can do apart from resting, drinking lots of fluids, eating lightly and avoiding fatty foods. People who have had hepatitis should avoid alcohol for some time after the illness, as the liver needs time to recover.

Hepatitis E is transmitted in the same way, it can be very serious in pregnant women.

There are almost 300 million chronic carriers of **Hepatitis B** in the world. It is spread through contact with infected blood, blood products or body fluids, for example through sexual contact, unsterilised needles and blood transfusions, or contact with blood via small breaks in the skin. Other risk situations include having a shave, tattoo, or having your body pierced with contaminated equipment. The symptoms of type B may be more severe and may lead to long term problems. **Hepatitis D** is spread in the same way, but the risk is mainly in shared needles. **Hepatitis C** can lead to chronic liver disease. The virus is spread by contact with blood usually via contaminated transfusions or shared needles. Avoiding these is the only means of prevention.

HIV & AIDS Infection with the Human Immunodeficiency Virus (HIV) may develop into Acquired Immune Deficiency Syndrome (AIDS), which is a fatal disease. HIV is a major problem in many countries of Asia; and Bali has one of the highest rates of HIV infection in Indonesia. Official HIV figures in Indonesia are unrealistically low – it's widely believed the real figures are much higher and are set to increase significantly unless the promotion of safe sex and hospital procedures are improved. The primary risk for most travellers is contact with workers in the sex industry and other travellers (in Indonesia the spread of HIV is primarily through heterosexual activity). Apart from abstinence, the most effective prevention is to practise safe sex using condoms.

Any exposure to blood, blood products or body fluids may put the individual at risk. The disease is often transmitted through sexual contact or dirty needles – vaccinations, acupuncture, tattooing and body piercing can be potentially as dangerous as intravenous drug use. HIV/AIDS can also be spread through infected blood transfusions; some developing countries cannot afford to screen blood used for transfusions.

If you do need an injection, ask to see the

syringe unwrapped in front of you, or take a needle and syringe pack with you.

Fear of HIV infection should never preclude treatment for serious medical conditions.

Intestinal Worms These parasites are most common in rural, tropical areas. The different worms have different ways of infecting people. Some may be ingested on food including undercooked meat and some enter through your skin. Infestations may not show up for some time, and although they are generally not serious, if left untreated some can cause severe health problems later. Consider having a stool test when you return home to check for these and determine the appropriate treatment.

Schistosomiasis Also known as bilharzia, this disease is carried in water by tiny worms. They infect certain varieties of freshwater snails found in rivers, streams, lakes and particularly behind dams. The worms multiply and are eventually discharged into the water.

The worm enters through the skin and attaches itself to your intestines or bladder. The first symptom may be a tingling and sometimes a light rash around the area where it entered. Weeks later a high fever may develop. A general feeling of being unwell may be the first symptom, or there may be no symptoms. Once the disease is established abdominal pain and blood in the urine are other signs. The infection often causes no symptoms until the disease is well established (several months to years after exposure) and damage to internal organs irreversible.

Avoiding swimming or bathing in fresh water where bilharzia is present, is the main method of preventing the disease. According to the US Center for Diseases Control & Prevention, bilharzia is found in more remote parts of Indonesia (such as Kalimantan and Irian Jaya), but there is currently no risk on Bali or Lombok.

Sexually Transmitted Diseases Gonorrhoea, herpes and syphilis are among these diseases; sores, blisters or rashes around the genitals, discharges or pain when urinating are common symptoms. In some STDs, such as wart virus or chlamydia, symptoms may be less marked or not observed at all especially in women. Syphilis symptoms eventually disappear completely but the disease continues and can cause severe problems in later years.

While abstinence from sexual contact is the only 100% effective prevention, using condoms is also effective. The treatment of gonorrhoea and syphilis is with antibiotics. The different sexually transmitted diseases each require specific antibiotics. There is no cure for herpes or AIDS.

Typhoid Typhoid fever is a dangerous gut infection caused by contaminated water and food. Medical help must be sought.

In its early stages sufferers may feel they have a bad cold or flu on the way, as early symptoms are a headache, body aches and a fever which rises a little each day until it is around 40°C (104°F) or higher. The victim's pulse is often slow relative to the degree of fever present – unlike a normal fever where the pulse increases. There may also be vomiting, abdominal pain, diarrhoea or constipation.

In the second week the high fever and slow pulse continue and a few pink spots may appear on the body; trembling, delirium, weakness, weight loss and dehydration may occur. Complications such as pneumonia, perforated bowel or meningitis may occur.

Insect-Borne Diseases

Filariasis, Lyme disease and typhus are all insect-borne diseases, but they do not pose a great risk to travellers. For more information on them see Less Common Diseases at the end of the health section.

Malaria This serious and potentially fatal disease is spread by mosquito bites. During and just after the wet season, there is a very low risk of malaria in north Bali, and a slightly higher risk in far west Bali, particularly in and around Gilimanuk. So, if you are staying in budget accommodation anywhere outside of south Bali, or trekking in north or west Bali during, or just after, the rainy season, it is prudent to undertake a course of antimalarial drugs. However, it is not currently considered necessary to take antimalarial drugs if you are sticking to the tourist centres in south Bali, regardless of the season – but confirm this with your doctor prior to departure.

If you are travelling to endemic areas, eg to Lombok or further afield in Indonesia, it is extremely important to avoid mosquito bites and to take tablets to prevent this disease. Symptoms range from fever, chills and sweating, headache, diarrhoea and abdominal pains to a vague feeling of ill-health. Seek medical help immediately if malaria is suspected. Without treatment malaria can rapidly become more serious and can be fatal.

If medical care is not available, malaria tablets can be used for treatment. You need to use a malaria tablet which is different from the one you were taking when you contracted malaria. The standard treatment dose of mefloquine is two 250mg tablets and a further two six hours later. For Fansidar, it's a single dose of three tablets. If you were previously taking mefloquine and cannot obtain Fansidar, then other alternatives are Malarone (atovaquone-proguanil; four tablets once daily for three days), halofantrine (three doses of two 250mg tablets every six hours) or quinine sulphate (600mg every six hours). There is a greater risk of side effects with these dosages than in normal use if used with mefloquine, so medical advice is preferable. Be aware also that halofantrine is no longer recommended by the WHO as emergency standby treatment, because of side effects, and should only be used if no other drugs are available.

If you intend to go scuba diving, seek your doctor's advice before using mefloquine, because it may make symptoms of decompression sickness harder to diagnose.

Travellers are advised to prevent mosquito bites at all times. The main messages are:

- wear light coloured clothing
- wear long pants and long sleeved shirts
- use mosquito repellents (available on Bali and Lombok) containing the compound DEET on exposed areas (prolonged overuse of DEET may be harmful, especially to children, but its

use is considered preferable to being bitten by disease-transmitting mosquitoes)
- avoid highly scented perfumes or aftershave
- use a mosquito net impregnated with mosquito repellent (permethrin) – these are widely available on both islands
- impregnating clothes with permethrin effectively deters mosquitoes and other insects

Dengue Fever This viral disease is transmitted by mosquitoes and occurs mainly in tropical and subtropical areas of the world. Dengue fever has been responsible for many recent deaths in Sumatra, Java (including Jakarta and Bandung), Nusa Tenggara and Sulawesi – but it is not currently a risk on Bali and Lombok. It is particularly prevalent during the wet season (about October to March).

Signs and symptoms of dengue fever include a sudden onset of high fever, headache, joint and muscle pains (hence its old name, 'breakbone fever'), and nausea and vomiting. A rash of small red spots appears three to four days after the onset of fever. Dengue is commonly mistaken for other infectious diseases, including influenza.

You should seek medical attention if you think you may be infected. Infection can be diagnosed by a blood test. There is no specific treatment for dengue.

Japanese B Encephalitis This viral infection of the brain is transmitted by mosquitoes. Most cases occur in rural areas as the virus exists in pigs and wading birds. Symptoms include fever, headache and alteration in consciousness. Hospitalisation is needed for correct diagnosis and treatment. There is a high mortality rate among those who have symptoms; of those that survive many are intellectually disabled. While extremely rare on Bali and Lombok, there have been instances during the rainy season. Consider the vaccination if you spend a month or longer on Bali or Lombok, especially during the wet season.

Cuts, Bites & Stings

Rabies is passed through animal bites – see Less Common Diseases later in this section for details of this disease.

Bedbugs & Lice Bedbugs live in various places, but particularly in dirty mattresses and bedding, evidenced by spots of blood on bedclothes or on the wall. Bedbugs leave itchy bites in neat rows. Calamine lotion or Stingose spray may help.

All lice cause itching and discomfort. They make themselves at home in your hair (head lice), your clothing (body lice) or in your pubic hair (crabs). You catch lice through direct contact with infected people or by sharing combs, clothing and the like. Powder or shampoo treatment will kill the lice and infected clothing should then be washed in very hot, soapy water and left in the sun to dry.

Insect Bites & Stings Bee and wasp stings are usually painful rather than dangerous. However in people who are allergic to them severe breathing difficulties may occur and require urgent medical care. Calamine lotion or a sting relief will ease discomfort, and ice packs will reduce the pain and swelling. There are some spiders with dangerous bites but antivenenes are usually available. There are various fish and other sea creatures which can sting or bite dangerously or which are dangerous to eat. Local advice is the best suggestion.

Cuts & Scratches Wash well and treat any cut with an antiseptic such as povidone-iodine. Where possible avoid bandages and Band-Aids, which can keep wounds wet. Some surfers get cut on coral, as do divers who (needlessly) walk on or touch coral. Coral cuts are notoriously slow to heal and if they are not adequately cleaned, small pieces of coral can become embedded in the wound. Avoid walking on coral cuts by wearing shoes when walking on reefs, and clean any cut thoroughly with hydrogen peroxide if available. A good dressing is a Chinese preparation called Tieh Ta Yao Gin which may sting a little, but will dry and heal coral cuts in the warm tropical climate.

Jellyfish Some jellyfish can be found in waters off the coast of Bali, and particularly between the Gili Islands and the mainland of Lombok, but their sting is painful rather than potentially fatal. Dousing in vinegar will deactivate any stingers which have not 'fired'. Calamine lotion, antihistamines and analgesics may reduce the reaction and relieve the pain. Local advice is the best way of avoiding contact with these sea creatures.

Leeches & Ticks Leeches may be present in damp rainforest conditions; they attach themselves to your skin to suck your blood. Trekkers often get them on their legs or in their boots. Salt or a lighted cigarette end will make them fall off. Do not pull them off, as the bite is then more likely to become infected. Clean and apply pressure if the point of attachment is bleeding. An insect repellent may keep them away.

You should always check all over your body if you have been walking through a potentially tick-infested area as ticks can cause skin infections and other more serious diseases. If a tick is found attached, press down around the tick's head with tweezers, grab the head and gently pull upwards. Avoid pulling the rear of the body as this may squeeze the tick's gut contents through the attached mouth parts into the skin, increasing the risk of infection and disease. Smearing chemicals on the tick will not make it let go and is not recommended.

Snakes Indonesia has several poisonous snakes, the most famous being the cobra *(ular sendok)*. All sea snakes are poisonous and are readily identified by their flat tails.

To minimise your chances of being bitten always wear boots, socks and long trousers when walking through undergrowth where snakes may be present. Don't put your hands into holes and crevices, and be careful when collecting firewood.

Snake bites do not cause instantaneous death and antivenenes are usually available. Immediately wrap the bitten limb tightly, as you would for a sprained ankle, and then attach a splint to immobilise it. Keep the victim still and seek medical help, if possible with the dead snake for identification.

Don't attempt to catch the snake if there is a possibility of being bitten again. Tourniquets and sucking out the poison are now comprehensively discredited.

However, the closest that most visitors to Bali and Lombok will ever get (or want to get) to a nasty poisonous snake is a cage at a reptile park.

Less Common Diseases

The following diseases pose a small risk to travellers, and so are only mentioned in passing. Seek medical advice if you think you may have any of these diseases.

Cholera This is the worst of the watery diarrhoeas and medical help should be sought. Outbreaks of cholera are generally widely reported, so you can avoid such problem areas. *Fluid replacement is the most vital treatment* – the risk of dehydration is severe as you may lose up to 20L a day. If there is a delay in getting to hospital then begin taking tetracycline. The adult dose is 250mg four times daily. It is not recommended for children under nine years nor for pregnant women. Tetracycline may help shorten the illness, but adequate fluids are required to save lives.

Filariasis This is a mosquito-transmitted parasitic infection found in many parts of Africa, Asia, Central and South America and the Pacific. Symptoms include fever, pain and swelling of the lymph glands; inflammation of lymph drainage areas; swelling of a limb or the scrotum; skin rashes; and blindness. Treatment is available to eliminate the parasites from the body, but some of the damage already caused may not be reversible. Medical advice should be obtained promptly if the infection is suspected.

Lyme Disease Lyme disease is an infection transmitted by ticks, and can be acquired throughout North America, Europe and Asia. The illness usually begins with a spreading rash at the site of the tick bite and is accompanied by fever, headache, extreme fatigue, aching joints and muscles and mild neck stiffness. If untreated, these symptoms usually resolve over several weeks but over subsequent weeks or months disorders of the nervous system, heart and joints may develop. Treatment works best early in the illness. Medical help should be sought.

Rabies Rabies is a fatal viral infection found in many countries, including Indonesia. Many animals can be infected (such as dogs, cats, bats and monkeys) and it is their saliva which is infectious. Any bite, scratch or even lick from a warm-blooded, furry animal should be cleaned immediately and thoroughly. Scrub with soap and running water, and then apply alcohol or iodine solution. Medical help should be sought promptly to receive a course of injections to prevent the onset of symptoms and death.

Despite the thousands of mangy stray dogs all over Bali, there is no current risk of rabies on the island, but serious outbreaks of rabies have been reported in more distant islands of Nusa Tenggara (but not on Lombok).

Tetanus Tetanus is caused by a germ which lives in soil and in the faeces of horses and other animals. It enters the body via breaks in the skin. The first symptom may be discomfort in swallowing, or stiffening of the jaw and neck; this is followed by painful convulsions of the jaw and whole body. The disease can be fatal. It can be prevented by vaccination.

Tuberculosis (TB) TB is a bacterial infection usually transmitted from person to person by coughing but may be transmitted through consumption of unpasteurised milk. Milk that has been boiled is safe to drink, and the souring of milk to make yoghurt or cheese also kills the bacilli. Travellers are usually not at great risk as close household contact with the infected person is usually required before the disease is passed on.

Typhus Typhus is spread by ticks, mites or lice. It begins with fever, chills, headache and muscle pains followed a few days later by a body rash. There is often a large painful sore at the site of the bite and nearby lymph nodes are swollen and painful. Typhus can be treated under medical supervision. Seek local advice on areas where ticks pose a danger and always check your skin (including hair) carefully for ticks after walking in a danger area such as a tropical forest. A strong insect repellent can help, and serious walkers in tick areas should consider having their boots and trousers impregnated with benzyl benzoate and dibutylphthalate.

Women's Health

Tampons and pads are widely available in supermarkets in the tourist areas on Bali. If you're travelling to more remote parts of Bali, or anywhere on Lombok, take a supply with you.

Gynaecological Problems Antibiotic use, synthetic underwear, sweating and contraceptive pills can lead to fungal vaginal infections, especially when travelling in tropical climates. Fungal infections are characterised by a rash, itch and discharge and can be treated with a vinegar or lemon-juice douche, or with yoghurt. Nystatin, miconazole or clotrimazole pessaries or vaginal cream are the usual treatment. Maintaining good personal hygiene and wearing loose-fitting clothes and cotton underwear may help prevent these infections.

Sexually transmitted diseases are a major cause of vaginal problems. Symptoms include a smelly discharge, painful intercourse and sometimes a burning sensation while urinating. Medical attention should be sought and male sexual partners must also be treated. Remember that in addition to these diseases HIV or hepatitis B may also be acquired during exposure. Besides abstinence, the best thing is to practise safe sex using condoms.

Pregnancy It is not advisable to travel to some places while pregnant as some vaccinations normally used to prevent serious diseases are not advisable in pregnancy eg yellow fever. In addition, some diseases are much more serious for the mother (and may

increase the risk of a stillborn child) in pregnancy eg malaria.

Most miscarriages occur during the first three months of pregnancy. Miscarriage is not uncommon, and can occasionally lead to severe bleeding. The last three months should also be spent within reasonable distance of good medical care. A baby born as early as 24 weeks stands a chance of survival, but only in a good modern hospital. Pregnant women should avoid all unnecessary medication, but vaccinations and malarial prophylactics should still be taken where needed. Additional care should be taken to prevent illness and particular attention should be paid to diet and nutrition. Alcohol and nicotine, for example, should be avoided.

WOMEN TRAVELLERS

I felt perfectly safe in Bali, being a female alone. I was a bit anxious to start with, but that soon disappeared. I would recommend it to other women travellers, no problems.

Julie White, UK

Kuta Cowboys

In tourist areas of Bali, and to a lesser extent on Lombok, you'll encounter young men who are keen to spend time with visiting women. Commonly called Kuta cowboys, beach boys, bad boys, guides or gigolos, these guys can be super cool, with long hair, lean bodies, tight jeans and lots of tattoos. They play a mean guitar and they're good on the dance floor. While they don't usually work a straight sex-for-money deal, the visiting woman pays for the meals, drinks and accommodation, and commonly buys the guy presents.

It's not uncommon for them to form long-term relationships, with the guy hopeful of finding a new and better life with his partner in Europe, Japan, Australia or the USA. One female reader wrote that 'the main young male occupation in Lovina is finding and living off foreign girlfriends'.

While most of these guys around Bali are genuinely friendly and quite charming, some are predatory con-artists who practise elaborate deceits, or downright theft, to get a woman's money. Many of them now come from outside Bali, and have a long succession of foreign lovers. Be sceptical about what they tell you, particularly if it comes down to them needing money. Always insist on using condoms.

Hassles & Precautions

Some local (and foreign) men will try their luck with female tourists. If you don't appreciate this sort of attention, never respond to come-ons or rude comments. Completely ignoring them is always best – a haughty attitude can work wonders. A husband (which equals any male partner) and/or children confer respectability. Even an imaginary husband can be used as a deterrent – he may arrive at any moment.

Some women have written to complain about low levels of assault, or intended assault, from local men as well as drunken foreign men. This occurs mostly in some areas of the tourist centres – for example, on the beach and outside nightclubs in the wee hours at Kuta.

Late at night in the tourist centres, single women should take a taxi (and sit in the back seat). However, on the whole, Bali and Lombok are safer for women than most areas of the world and, with the usual care and caution, women can feel secure travelling alone.

GAY & LESBIAN TRAVELLERS

Although you will often see friends of the same sex holding hands, this does not indicate homosexuality. Paradoxically, a male and female holding hands is regarded as quite improper in most of Indonesia, although it's becoming more common among young heterosexual couples on Bali.

Gay travellers will experience few problems on Bali. Hotels are generally happy to rent a room with a double bed to any couple, and there are several active gay bars and nightclubs in the Kuta region.

Homosexual behaviour is not illegal; the age of consent for sexual activity is 16 years. Immigration officials may restrict entry to people who reveal HIV positive status. Gay men in Indonesia are referred to

Waria

Indonesia, and particularly Java, has a long tradition of female impersonators, often working as entertainers, hostesses or prostitutes. They may be transsexual, but are mostly transvestite. They were customarily known as *banci*, but the term *waria* is now more polite and acceptable – it's a combination of the words *wanita* (female) and *pria* (male).

as *homo*, or more recently *gay*, and are quite distinct from the female impersonators called *waria* (see the boxed text of the same name).

Gay Balinese experience difficulties not so much because of their sexual preferences, but because they are expected to become parents and participate in the family and community life which is so important in Balinese culture. For this reason, many gays feel compelled to leave Bali and live in other parts of Indonesia. Paradoxically, many gays from other parts of the country come to live on Bali, as it is more tolerant, and also because it offers opportunities to meet foreign partners.

Entertainment

In the Kuta/Legian/Seminyak area, there are a few specific gay bars and nightclubs, but owners do seem to regularly change their attitude towards gay customers. According to several readers, Goa 2001 Pub Restaurant and Cafe Luna (both in Legian) have not recently been kind to gays.

More welcoming are: the popular Hulu Cafe (with drag shows every Wednesday, Friday and Sunday nights); G-Land on Jl Dhyana Pura, Seminyak; Ulu Cafe, at Bali Padma Hotel, Legian (currently on Sunday only); La Lucciola, Seminyak; Raja's 1 in Legian, and Raja's 2 at Kuta Square (both are restaurants); and Gado Gado and Double Six, both in Seminyak (and popular with everyone).

Web Sites

One of the best Web sites to check out is Utopia Asia (www.utopia-asia.com). The Hulu Cafe, mentioned above, also has an interesting Web site (www.ozemail.com.au/~hulucafe).

DISABLED TRAVELLERS

Bali and Lombok are difficult destinations for those with limited mobility. While some of the airlines flying to Bali have a good reputation for accommodating people with disabilities, the airport in Denpasar is not well set up. Passengers must often walk across the tarmac to their planes, and access them by steps. Contact the airlines, and ask them if they provide skychairs, and what arrangements can be made for disembarking and boarding at Denpasar.

The bemos, minibuses and buses which provide public transport all over the islands are certainly not made for very large, tall or physically disabled people, nor for wheelchairs. The minibuses used by tourist shuttle bus and tour companies are similar. Upmarket hotels often have steps, but nothing for wheelchairs, while the cheaper places usually have more accessible bungalows on ground level. Out on the street, the footpaths, where they exist at all, tend to be narrow, uneven, potholed and frequently obstructed.

The only hotels likely to be set up at all for disabled travellers are the big international chains like the Hyatt (at Nusa Dua and Sanur), Sheraton (Nusa Dua, Senggigi and Kuta) and the Hilton (Nusa Dua). If you're keen to see Bali, your best bet is to contact these corporations in your home city and ask them what facilities they have for disabled guests in their Bali hotels.

Bali (and to a lesser extent, Lombok) is an enormously rewarding destination for unsighted people or those with limited vision. Balinese music is heard everywhere, and the languages are fascinating to listen to. The smells of incense, spices, tropical fruit and flowers pervade the island, and are as exotic as you could wish for. With a sighted companion, most places should be reasonably accessible.

SENIOR TRAVELLERS

If you have trouble climbing stairs or walking on rough ground, you will find it difficult to get around Bali and Lombok. However, as in many Asian cultures, older people are treated with great respect. Senior travellers are probably better off staying in better hotels, and travelling on organised tours.

Take all the medication, equipment and prescriptions that you need, and don't expect anything special from the hospitals on the islands. There are no special deals for senior travellers on Bali or Lombok, but they are inexpensive destinations so this is not a real problem.

TRAVEL WITH CHILDREN

Travelling with children *(anak-anak)* anywhere requires energy and organisation, but on Bali the problems are somewhat lessened by the Balinese affection for children. They believe that children come straight from God, and the younger they are, the closer they are to God. To the Balinese, children are considered part of the community and everyone, not just the parents, has a responsibility towards them. If a young child cries, the Balinese get most upset and insist on finding a parent and handing the child over with a reproachful look. Sometimes they despair of uncaring western parents, and the child will be whisked off to a place where it can be cuddled, cosseted and fed. In tourist areas this is less likely, but it's still common in a more traditional environment. A toddler may even get too much attention!

Children are a social asset when you travel on Bali, and people will display great interest in any western child they meet. You will have to learn their ages and sex in Bahasa Indonesia – *bulan* means month, *tahun* (year), *laki-laki* (boy) and *perempuan* (girl). You should also make polite enquiries about their children, present or absent.

For more information, get hold of *Travel with Children* by Lonely Planet's Maureen Wheeler. She, and her husband Tony, have travelled all around the world with their children – and survived to tell the tale.

Accommodation

A package tour in a hotel with a swimming pool, air-con and a beachfront location is fun for kids, very convenient and provides a good break for the parents, but you won't see much of Bali unless you make a real effort to get out. A beachfront place in Sanur, Lovina or Candidasa, or a place with a pool in Ubud, would be the best choices for a package holiday with kids. The Kuta-Legian area has very heavy traffic and the surf can be rough, although it does have the only fast-food joints, video arcades and cinemas on the island. At most mid-range and upmarket hotels it's likely there will be other kids to play with.

If you travel independently, you can stay in losmen or budget hotels, in smaller, quieter areas with minimal traffic and few tourists. The facilities aren't as good, but you can get perfectly acceptable accommodation and good clean food for a lot less than the cost of a package-tour hotel. You will have much closer contact with the Balinese, and your children will be secure with the losmen owner's family watching over them.

Most places, at whatever price level, have a 'family plan' which means that children up to about 12 years old can share a room with their parents free of charge. The catch is that hotels charge for extra beds – between 5000 rp in a losmen and US$30 in an expensive hotel. If you need more space, just rent a separate room for the kids. You can usually negotiate a cheaper price for the second room (single room rate is a common deal). One reader suggested bringing some blow-up air mattresses for the kids from home, and placing them on the floor of the one family room – hotels rarely charge extra for this.

Very few hotels offer special programmes or supervised activities for kids, although most of them can arrange a baby-sitter.

Food

The same rules apply as for adults – kids should drink only clean water, eat only well cooked food or fruit that you have peeled yourself. If you're travelling with a young baby, breast feeding is much easier than bottles. For older babies, mashed bananas, eggs, peelable fruit and *bubur* (rice cooked to a mush in chicken stock) are all generally available. In tourist areas, restaurants serve yoghurt, pancakes, bread, fruit juices, ice cream and milk shakes, and supermarkets sell jars of western baby food and packaged UHT milk and fruit juice. Bottled drinking water is available everywhere. Bring plastic bowls, plates, cups and spoons for do-it-yourself meals.

Health

If your child develops stomach trouble, it may be no more than 'Baby Bali Belly'. If there is no pain or stomach cramps, put the child on a light, bland diet and make sure the fluid intake is kept high. The major danger is dehydration, so it's a good idea to carry an electrolyte mixture with you for such cases. Ask your doctor to recommend a kaolin mixture for your child; Pepto-Bismol is very good. If the child has a fever, the stools contain blood or mucus, or diarrhoea persists for more than two days, you should continue the fluid replacement treatment and find a doctor quickly.

Bali is officially in a malarial zone, but the risk in most tourist areas is so slight that it is probably not worth a child taking anti-malarial drugs (but confirm this with your own doctor before you go). In any case, the first defence against malaria is to protect your child from mosquito bites. If you're going to Lombok, however, a course of antimalarials is definitely required – refer to the Health section earlier in this chapter.

Never let your child run around in bare feet, as worms and other parasites can enter through the feet. Any cut or scratch should be washed immediately and treated with Betadine. Head lice are common on both islands; lice shampoo will get rid of them.

Tropical sun is a very real hazard. Use a total sunblock (SPF 15+) on all exposed skin, whenever they are out, and reapply it every few hours, especially if they have been swimming. Hats, shirts and shorts should always be worn in the sun. The lightweight Lycra T-shirts which kids can wear while swimming are excellent. If your child does get sunburnt, apply Caladryl.

Dangers

The main danger is traffic, so try to stay in less busy areas. If your children can't look after themselves in the water then they must be supervised – don't expect local people to act as lifesavers. Steep stairways and unfenced drops are other common hazards.

Other Problems

On Bali, and especially on Lombok, things are not always set up for children with the sorts of facilities, safeguards and services which western parents regard as basic. Here, children are part of a small community and they share the same furniture, food, transport and entertainment as everyone else. Not many restaurants provide a highchair; many places with great views have nothing to stop your kids falling over the edge; shops often have breakable things at kiddie height; and violent videos are sometimes shown in circumstances and at volumes where they can't be ignored.

Hotel and restaurant staff are usually very willing to help and improvise, so always ask if you need something for your children. The situation is improving as more young kids come to Bali and more parents make their wishes known.

What to Bring

Apart from those items already mentioned in the earlier Health section, bring some infant analgesic (like Panadol for kids), anti-lice shampoo, a medicine measure and a thermometer.

You can take disposable nappies (diapers) with you, but they're widely available on Bali (less so on Lombok). Cloth nappies are more environmentally friendly, and not too much trouble – just rinse them in the bath with the hand-held shower head, soak them in a plastic bucket (always available) and wash them in the bucket when you can.

A folding stroller isn't much use because there are few paved footpaths which are wide and smooth enough. A papoose or a backpack carrier, is a much more useful way to move around with children.

Some equipment, such as snorkelling gear and boogie boards, can be rented easily in the tourist centres. A simple camera, or a couple of the throwaway ones, will help your child feel like a real tourist. A pair of binoculars can make looking at things more fun, and bring a few books for older children, and a scrap book for their cuttings and drawings.

Baby-Sitting & Child Care

Most expensive hotels advertise a baby-sitter service (sometimes written in 'Indoglish' as a 'baby sister'). The price is proportional to the cost of the hotel and can be quite expensive by local standards. It's fine for a few hours in the evening, but the baby-sitter may not be willing or experienced enough to entertain and supervise active kids for a whole afternoon. In small, family-style losmen, you'll always find someone to look after your children – often the owners' daughters, sisters or nieces; and they will be much more comfortable looking after your child in their own family compound or village. Generally speaking, most Balinese over the age of 14 will be responsible child minders.

For more regular child care, you'll need a *pembantu*, which roughly translates as a nanny. Ask around to find a good one. They generally prefer to look after kids at their own place rather than yours – about 15,000 rp for two children for one day is a reasonable fee.

Activities

Many of the things which adults want to do on Bali and Lombok will not interest their children. Have days when you do what they want, to offset the times you drag them to shops or temples. Encourage them to learn about the islands so they can understand and enjoy more of what they see.

Water play is always fun – you can often use a hotel pool, even if you're not staying there. If your kids can swim a little, they can have a lot of fun with a mask and snorkel. Chartering a boat for a few hours sailing and snorkelling is good value. Hiring paddle boards is OK for a while, but can get pretty expensive. You can buy a model *prahu* (small boat) and try sailing it on a quiet beach. Colourful kites are sold in many shops and market stalls; get some string at a supermarket. For some more tips about where to take the kids, refer to the Activities section later in this chapter.

In Ubud, there are a number of craft courses like woodcarving and batik. Older children may like to see some Balinese dances – the Kecak dance is probably the most entertaining for kids. Some restaurants have video movies for kids in the early evening; the ones shown later in the evening are inevitably loud and violent. TV stations often show cartoons in the afternoon, in English with Indonesian sub-titles.

USEFUL ORGANISATIONS

A few useful organisations are mentioned in the relevant text throughout the book, but the following may be of interest:

Bali International Women's Association
  (☎/fax 774451) PO Box 3552, Denpasar. BIWA was established by expats to 'foster friendship and mutual understanding'.
Hash House Harriers
  This running club has events in south Bali. Contact the Beggar's Bush Pub in Ubud; Kalimantan Bar & Restaurant in Sanur; and Lips bar in Kuta. A male-dominated group, with the accent more on drinking than running, this is definitely not everyone's cup of tea.
Rotary Club
  (☎ 0361-758635, fax 757125, email adrian@denpasar.wasantara.net.id) PO Box 48, Nusa Dua. This international organisation has a few branches around Bali and Lombok.

DANGERS & ANNOYANCES

If anyone is worried about travelling on Bali because of the problems caused by the economic crisis then there is no need to fret – it's safer than a Saturday night out in London!

Michelle Walder, UK

Theft

Violent crime is relatively uncommon, but there is some bag snatching, pickpocketing and thieving from losmen rooms and parked cars in the tourist centres. Don't leave anything on the back seat of a rented vehicle – the ubiquitous *jimny* jeeps are only ever rented by comparatively wealthy foreigners.

Snatchers sometimes work in pairs from a motorcycle – they pull up next to someone in a busy area, the guy on the back grabs the bag and slashes the strap, the guy on the front hits the throttle and they're gone within half a second. Money belts, or bum bags, worn *outside* the clothes are particularly vulnerable. Always carry money belts inside your clothes; and bags over your neck (not shoulder). Put all your money in your money belt *before* you leave the bank or moneychanger office.

Pickpockets on bemos are also prevalent. The usual routine is for somebody to start a conversation to distract you, while an accomplice steals your wallet or purse. Bemos are always tightly packed, and a painting, large parcel, basket or the like can serve as a cover. The thieves can be very cunning, charming and skilful – so be careful.

Losmen rooms are often not that secure. Don't leave valuables in your room, and beware of people who wander in and out of losmen; always keep your room locked if you're not actually in it. Thieves often enter through open-air bathrooms, so fasten the bathroom door. Keep your valuables at more than an arm's length from any unsecured window. Many foolish people lose things by simply leaving them on the beach while they go swimming. You can leave airline tickets or other valuables in the safe deposit boxes which are found at many moneychangers, banks and hotels.

Some years ago there were mugging incidents down some of Kuta's less frequented *gangs* (alleys) at night, but that activity rapidly diminished after Kuta *banjars* (local village groups) organised vigilante groups to patrol after dark.

Rip-Offs & Scams

Bali has such a relaxed atmosphere, and the people are so friendly, that you may not be on the lookout for scams. It's hard to say when an 'accepted' practice like overcharging becomes an unacceptable rip-off, but be warned that there are some people on Bali (but not always Balinese) who will engage in a practised deceit in order to get money from a visitor. Here is a rundown on the most common scams.

Can I fix your car? A friendly local discovers a 'serious problem' with your car or motorbike. Coincidentally, he has a brother/cousin/friend nearby who can help, and before you know it they've put some oil in the sump, or changed the wheel, and are demanding an outrageous sum for their trouble. The con relies on creating a sense of urgency, so beware of anyone who tries to rush you into something without mentioning a price.

Want to visit my village? A Balinese guy takes a foreign friend to see 'his' poor village (although it may not be his village). The visitor is shocked by the poor circumstances of the Balinese guy, who concocts a hard-luck story about a sick mother who can't pay for an operation, a brother who needs money for his education or an important religious ceremony that his family can't afford. Visitors have been persuaded to hand over large sums of money on such a pretext. A healthy scepticism is your best defence.

Anyone for a game of cards? This one is used all over the world. Friendly locals will somehow convince a visitor that easy money can be made in a card game. They're taken to some obscure place, and do well at first. Then, after a few drinks and a spell of bad luck, the visitor has suddenly accumulated large debts. Gambling is illegal in Indonesia, so the victim has no recourse to the law.

Have I got a deal for you! Although not always a genuine scam, high pressure sales of holiday 'timeshares' have trapped some visitors, who sign up while caught in the euphoria of Bali and then regret it later. Don't add more credence to the sales pitch just because a westerner is involved. Claims that you have won 'a great prize' are all just part of the spiel.

Want to change some money? In the Kuta region especially, many travellers are being shortchanged by moneychangers, who use sleight of hand and deliberately misuse the calculator. Always count your money at least twice in front of the moneychanger, and don't let him touch the money again after you've finally counted it. Try to change even amounts, eg US$100, which are easier to convert to rupiah, or bring your own pocket calculator.

Hawkers, Pedlars & Touts

A few hours in Kuta, and I was ready to loose it with the next person who persisted in trying to sell me a fake watch/painting/hair braiding. The Balinese are quick to point out (with some superiority) that these people are from Java – another planet as far as the Balinese are concerned.

Linda Stopforth & Ray Yates, New Zealand

Many visitors regard the persistent attentions of people trying to sell things in the major tourist centres on Bali as *the* number one annoyance. (It is less of a problem on Lombok.) These activities are officially restricted in certain areas, like the waterside at Kuta Beach, or the environs of just about any decent hotel or restaurant, but elsewhere, visitors are frequently, and often constantly, hassled to buy things.

Some hawkers display a superb grasp of sales techniques in several languages (often with a wide range of Australian, English and American slang), and have a persistence that's as impressive as it is infuriating. Some of Bali's most successful tourist businesses are run by people who started by selling postcards to tourists.

The best way to deal with hawkers is to completely ignore them from the first instance. Eye contact is crucial – don't make any! Even a polite *tidak* ('no') seems to encourage them. Never ask the price or comment on the quality unless you're interested in buying, or you want to spend half an hour haggling. It may seem very rude to ignore people who smile and greet you so cheerfully, but you might have to be a lot ruder to get rid of a hawker after you've spent a few minutes politely discussing his/her watches, rings and prices. In many Asian cultures, it is impolite to say 'no' anyway – it's better form to firmly change the subject to anything other than what is for sale.

Unfortunately, as times get tough (and it is during the current economic crisis), and tourists get more wary, some hawkers have become aggressive, and even violent, which is a good reason not to get involved if you don't want to buy something. On the other hand, many hawkers are genuinely friendly and helpful people. Don't let their commercial imperatives get to you – they are just trying to make a living.

Begging

You may be approached by the occasional beggar on the streets of Kuta – typically a woman with a young child. Begging has no place in traditional Balinese society, so it's likely that most of the beggars come from elsewhere.

Children often ask for sweets, pens, cigarettes etc; please do not encourage this. If you want to contribute to a kid's education, with pens, books or whatever, give them to the teacher or parent.

Traffic

Apart from the dangers of actually driving on Bali (see the Bali Getting Around chapter), the traffic in most tourist areas is often annoying, and frequently dangerous to pedestrians. Footpaths can be rough, even unusable, so you often have to walk on the roadway.

Those zebra stripes across the road are mainly decorative – never expect traffic to stop because you think you're on a pedestrian crossing.

Traffic Accidents

A few years ago, some hotels provided free motorbike rental to anyone (with or without a licence, or experience) as part of a package holiday. Following pressure from foreign consulates on Bali, which were fed up repatriating tourists on wheelchairs, crutches or in coffins, this is no longer the case.

It is still very easy for anyone to rent a motorbike, however, but only those with experience should do so – the traffic on Bali (less so on Lombok) is very heavy, especially in south Bali; many roads throughout both islands are narrow, windy and potholed; and large trucks, bemos and buses regularly ply the roads, with little regard for tiny motorbikes driven by foreigners. Refer to the Bali Getting Around chapter for more tips about motorbike safety.

Swimming

The beaches at Kuta and Legian are subject to heavy surf and strong currents – always swim between the flags. Most other beaches are protected by coral reefs, but be careful when swimming over coral (and you should never walk on it at all). It can be very sharp and coral cuts can easily become infected (see the earlier Health section).

Swimming while under the influence of any intoxicant is always a dangerous business. Trained lifeguards only operate at Kuta-Legian, Nusa Dua, Sanur and (sometimes) Senggigi.

Drugs

The old image of floating sky-high over Bali has faded considerably. There are some government posters around suggesting that 'you don't need drugs to experience the magic of Bali' – and even the posters have faded. Neither marijuana nor magic mushrooms (or any other drug) is part of traditional Balinese culture.

You may be offered dope on the street, particularly in the Kuta region, but you're very unlikely to get a good deal. Tablets purported to be Ecstasy are sold on the street and at some nightclubs, but they could contain just about anything. In all cases, entrapment by police and informers is a real possibility.

The authorities take a dim view of recreational drug use, and losmen owners can be quick to turn you in. It is an offence not to report someone whom you know to be using drugs, and there are not many places on Bali where you could light up a joint without someone getting a whiff of it. Fortunately, the number of westerners in jail for drug offences on Bali is now quite small. It's not that the police or the courts are becoming lenient – they're not; it's just that the whole scene is way out of fashion.

Bali's famed magic mushrooms *(oong)* come out during the wet season. They are usually mixed with food, such as an omelette, or in a drink – if a barman offers you an 'umbrella cocktail' you may get more than you thought. The mushrooms contain psilocybin, which is a powerful hallucinogen, but the

Those Damn Dogs

If there's one thing wrong with Bali it has to be those horrible, mangy, flea-bitten, grovelling, dirty, noisy, disgusting dogs (*anjing* in Indonesian; *asu* in high Balinese; *cicing* in low Balinese). If you prefer, use asu when you're referring to dogs in a positive way, cicing in a negative way. Dogs are rarely referred to as asu!

Just why does Bali have so many dogs? Well, they're scavengers, garbage clearers and simply accepted as part of the picture. It's widely (and probably correctly!) thought that demons inhabit them, which is why you often see them gobbling down the offerings put out for the bad spirits.

A popular theory is that they were created simply to keep things in balance – with everything on Bali so beautiful and picturesque the dogs were put there to provide a contrast. Ubud is particularly well endowed with cicing – terrible, apocalyptic dogs that howl all night long like it's the end of the world.

There may have been some decline in the dog population over the last few years, although there has been no mass extermination campaign. Whenever the subject was raised, locals made knowing comments about people who allegedly caught the dogs to eat them. Interestingly, these people always come from another part of Bali – nobody *here* eats dogs. With the current outbreak of rabies in the nearby Nusa Tenggara islands, and the subsequent slaughter of stray dogs, the future may be bleak from some of the homeless mutts on Bali.

❀❀❀❀❀❀❀❀❀❀❀❀❀❀❀❀❀❀❀

dosage in a mushroom omelette is pretty inexact and the effect is very variable. Psilocybin may give you a stratospheric high, but it may also result in paranoid or psychotic reactions which can be extremely unpleasant. One place where you may be offered oong is on the Gili Islands, off the coast of Lombok, probably because there are no police on any of the islands.

One drug that is very popular among visitors is alcohol. There are lots of bars and pubs around, and an awful lot of beer bottles being recycled (or so we hope). The local firewater, *arak*, is distilled from rice wine and can be very strong. Overdosing on this stuff has probably caused more foreigners to freak out than all the other drugs on Bali combined. Nicotine is also worth mentioning – those sweet smelling clove cigarettes *(kretek)* may be tempting, but they are high in tar and nicotine and very addictive.

LEGAL MATTERS

Gambling is illegal (although carried out in some rural areas), as is pornography. The Indonesian government takes the smuggling, using and selling of drugs very, *very* seriously. Once you've been caught, and put in jail, there is little that your consulate on Bali (if you have one) can do. You may have to wait up to six months in jail before you even go to trial. It is also an offence for a visitor with a tourist card to engage in paid work or stay in the country for more than 60 days.

Generally, you're unlikely to have any encounters with the police unless you drive a rented car or motorbike (see the Bali Getting Around chapter). Drinking and driving is not clever, and an accident under the influence of alcohol or any drug may invalidate your car/motorbike insurance, and possibly even your travel insurance policy. Some governments (including the Australian government) have laws making it illegal for their citizens to engage in child prostitution or other paedophiliac activities anywhere in the world.

If you have to report a crime or have other business at a police station, expect a lengthy and bureaucratic encounter. You should dress as respectably as possible, bring a fluent Indonesian-speaking friend for interpretation and moral support, arrive early and be very polite. It is always a good idea to contact your consulate first: they are used to foreigners getting into trouble, and have useful contacts and can recommend

English-speaking lawyers. Some underpaid police officers may ask for a bribe, and you may be forced to oblige if you want any quick or decent assistance. There are police stations in all district capitals.

BUSINESS HOURS

Government office hours on Bali/Lombok are roughly Monday to Thursday from 7.30 am to 3.15 pm, and Friday until 11 am, but they are not completely standardised. Post offices may open on Saturday until 1 pm, and postal agencies will often keep longer hours.

Most commercial businesses are open Monday to Friday from 8 am to 4 pm, and also on Saturday morning, often closing for an hour or so at lunch time. Banking hours are generally from 8 am to 2 pm Monday to Friday, and until about 11 am on Saturday.

Moneychangers, travel agents and shops catering to tourists keep longer hours and are normally open every day.

PUBLIC HOLIDAYS & SPECIAL EVENTS

Apart from the usual western calendar, the Balinese also use two local calendars.

Wuku Calendar

The *wuku* calendar is used to determine festival dates. The calendar uses 10 different types of weeks between one and 10 days long, which all run simultaneously. The intersection of the various weeks determines auspicious days. The seven day and five day weeks are of particular importance. A full year is made up of 30 individually named seven day weeks.

Galungan, which celebrates the death of a legendary tyrant called Mayadenawa, is one of Bali's major festivals. During this 10 day period all the gods, including the supreme deity Sanghyang Widi, come down to earth for the festivities. *Barongs* (mythical lion-dog creatures) prance from temple to temple and village to village, and locals rejoice with feasts and visits to families. You'll notice the bamboo poles called *penjor*, which line the village streets, laden with gifts to the gods. The celebrations culminate with the

Kuningan festival, when the Balinese say thanks and goodbye to the gods.

Every village on Bali will celebrate Galungan and Kuningan in grand style. Particularly colourful festivals are held at the temple on Pulau Serangan, just off south Bali, and all around Ubud. Forthcoming dates are:

Year	Galungan	Kuningan
1999	9 June	19 June
2000	5 January	15 January
2000	3 August	13 August
2001	1 March	11 March

Saka Calendar

The Hindu *saka* (or *caka*) calendar is a lunar cycle that more closely follows the western calendar in terms of the length of the year (eg in 1998, the saka year was 1920). Nyepi is the major festival of the saka year – it's the last day of the year, that is the day after the new moon of the ninth month.

Certain major temples celebrate their festivals by the saka calendar. This makes the actual date difficult to determine from our calendar, since the lunar saka calendar does not follow a fixed number of days like the wuku calendar.

The full moons which fall around the end of September to the beginning of October, or from early to mid-April, are often times for important temple festivals and *odalan* processions.

Before or after you arrive on Bali, find out about local festivals and other special events. Bali has about 20,000 temples, and each is celebrated every 210 days, so you'll probably come across several odalan processions and festivals during your trip. Foreigners are welcome to watch and take photographs, but please be discreet and unobtrusive, and dress conservatively.

Public Holidays

The following holidays are celebrated throughout Indonesia:

Tahun Baru Masehi
(New Year's Day)   1 January
Ramadan   May/June

Nyepi

The major festival for the Hindu Balinese is Nyepi, usually held around the end of March or early April. It celebrates the end of the old year and the start of the new one, according to the saka calendar, and usually coincides with the end of the rainy season. Visitors are welcome to help celebrate, but the lack of public transport can cause interruptions to travel plans.

The Ceremonies

During the day before Nyepi, ceremonies known as *pratima* are held at town squares and sports grounds at different times throughout the island (so with a guide and vehicle you may be able to witness several). Later that afternoon, at about 4 pm, the villagers, all dressed up in traditional garb, gather somewhere central, such as the market. While men play instruments, locals offer gifts of food and flowers to the *ogoh-ogoh*, a huge monster doll. Then the *ngrupuk* march starts, where young men lift the ogoh-ogoh by poles, and walk around the village (or immediate suburban area) two or three times, passing major buildings and important temples. This is followed by prayers and speeches. When it gets dark, evil spirits are noisily chased away with anything that makes enough noise. With flaming torches and bonfires, the ogoh-ogoh is then burnt, and much drinking and revelry ensues. The best place to see this is Denpasar.

For the Visitor

The day of Nyepi (which officially lasts for 24 hours from 6 am) is one of complete and utter inactivity, so when the evil spirits descend they decide that Bali is uninhabited and leave the island alone for another year. With very few exceptions, *everything* all over Bali will close or stop during Nyepi: all road, air and sea transport ceases; all shops, bars and restaurants close; and no-one (including foreigners) is allowed to leave the environs of their hotel – police patrols will strictly enforce this. Only the international airport, special airport buses and taxis, and hospitals will function during this 24 hour period. Stock up on snacks, or stay at a hotel with a restaurant, which should provide simple meals for guests. Government offices, banks and many shops also close the day before Nyepi, and some shops remain closed the day after.

For visitors, Nyepi is a day for catching up on sleep, writing letters or washing. Others may wish to plan a side-trip to Lombok (which is predominantly Muslim, and won't close for the day), but you will miss out on the festivities prior to Nyepi. While some may resent this interruption to their travel plans, the Balinese ask that you respect their customs for this short time.

Nyepi (Hindu New Year)	March-April	Hari Proklamasi Kemerdekaan (Indonesian Independence Day)	17 August
Hari Paskah (Good Friday)	March-April		
Hari Waicak (Buddha's birth, enlightenment and death)	April-May	Isra Miraj Nabi Muhammed (ascension of the Prophet Muhammed)	Oct/November
Idul Adha (Muslim festival)	April-May	Hari Natal (Christmas Day)	25 December
Muharram (the Islamic New Year)	April-May		
Ascension of Christ	April-May		
Maulud Nabi Muhammed or Hari Natal (birthday of the Prophet Muhammed)	July		

The Muslim population on Bali and Lombok observes Islamic festivals and holidays, including Ramadan. See the Lombok Facts for the Visitor chapter for more information.

Special Events

Try to beg, borrow or steal the annual *Calendar of Events* booklet. It is published by the Indonesian tourism department and lists every temple ceremony and village festival on Bali for the current (western) year.

Before you leave home, check out the Web sites listed earlier in this chapter, or try an Indonesian Tourist Promotion Office (listed under Tourist Offices Abroad earlier in this chapter). After you arrive, you can pick one up from the tourist offices in Denpasar (both of them), or in Kuta.

Most of the larger, more popular and more interesting special events held throughout Bali are detailed in the relevant text, and are listed by town. Others include:

Lovina and Singaraja
   Special bull races are held nearby on 17 August and 31 March, plus other occasions.
Marga
   An independence ceremony is held on 20 November every year.
Pabean, near Denpasar
   Purification ceremonies are held irregularly.

Bali Arts Festival

The annual Bali Arts Festival is based at the arts centre in Denpasar, and lasts for about one month over June and July. It's a great time to be on Bali, and the festival is an easy way to see an enormous amount and variety of traditional dances, music and crafts from all over the island. The productions of the Ramayana and Mahabharata ballets are grand, and the opening ceremony and parade in Denpasar is particularly colourful.

Details about events and times are available at tourist offices in the tourist centres of south Bali, or check the Web sites listed in the boxed text 'Bali on the Net' earlier in this chapter. You can easily take a day trip to Denpasar from Kuta, Ubud, Sanur and Nusa Dua.

Pulau Serangan
   The Pemendakan grand festival is irregularly held on this island in south Bali.
Pura Besakih
   All sorts of festival and ceremonies are held (see the East Bali chapter).
Pura Jagatnatha, Denpasar
   Moon festivals are held during every full and new moon.

SURFING

Thanks to Kirk Willcox, former editor of the Australian surfing magazine Tracks, *who compiled much of the following surfing information.*

In recent years, the number of surfers on Bali has increased enormously, and good breaks can get very crowded. Many Balinese have taken to surfing (main ski), and the grace of traditional dancing is said to influence their style. The surfing competitions on Bali are a major local event. Facilities for surfers have improved, and surf shops in Kuta will sell just about everything you need.

Charter yachts take groups of surfers for day trips around various local reefs, or for one week 'surfaris' to great breaks on east Java (Grajagan, aka G-Land), Nusa Lembongan, Lombok and Sumbawa, some of which just can't be reached by land. You'll see them advertised in the surfing press, and at numerous agents in Kuta. Yacht charter prices are about US$200 per person per week, including food and transport. It is a bit cramped, and the seas are rough at times, but it's great fun.

Agencies

Surf shops and tour agencies on Bali come and go. The biggest and best are located in the Kuta region: Tubes Bar, on Poppies Gang II, is a long-running and popular centre for anything to do with surfing. There are several other surf shops and tour agencies within 100m of Tubes, and a few huge surf shops along Jl Legian.

If you have access to the Internet, it is worth, ahem, 'surfing' the Net (or buying a surfing magazine) to check out which foreign surfing agencies operate tours to Bali. Some include:

Surf Express
  (☎ 02-9262 3355)
  Level 4, 2 Barrack St, Sydney, NSW 2000, Australia
Surf Travel Company
  (☎ 02-9527 4722)
  25 Cronulla Plaza, Cronulla Beach, NSW 2230, Australia
Waterways
  (☎ 818-376-0341, 800-928-375)
  Suite #1, 15145 Califa St, Van Nuys, CA 91411, USA

Books & Charts

Indo Surf & Lingo by Peter Neely tells surfers where and when to find good waves around Bali. (Neely also runs an informative Web site – www.peg.apc.org/~indosurf~) The book also has some tips on surfing around other nearby islands, and a language guide with Indonesian translations of useful words like 'big', 'wave' and 'tube'. It has good information and a good attitude, and is available at surf shops in the Kuta region. The tide table from Tubes Bar is an essential adjunct; the ones often pinned up on the walls of hotel foyers in Kuta are usually out of date.

Equipment

A small board is usually adequate for the smaller breaks, but a few extra inches on your usual board length won't go astray. For the bigger waves – eight foot and upwards – you will need a gun. For a surfer of average height and build, a board around the seven foot mark is perfect.

You can bring a couple of boards, but if you have more than two or three, customs officials may object, suggesting that you intend to sell them. They sometimes ask for a 'fee' of about 50,000 rp per extra board, although it's not clear whether this is an official charge or not.

To get your boards to Bali in reasonable condition, you need a good board cover. Bali-bound airlines are used to carrying boards, but fins still get broken off. Bring a soft roof rack to secure your boards to a car,

taxi or bemo – if you simply tie your boards to the top of a rented car, without a roof rack, the local police may want to fine you. Long hikes with your board are difficult unless you have a board-strap – add some foam padding to the shoulder. Take a good pair of running shoes for walking down steep, rocky paths on cliff faces. Before booking any long-distance buses, find out if they will accept surfboards – some don't, or will charge extra.

Wax is available locally, but take your own anyway if you use it – in the tepid water and the hot sun a sticky wax is best. Board repairs and materials are readily available in Kuta, but it's always advisable to have your own, especially if you're going to more remote spots. You can carry resin in a well sealed container, but don't carry hardener or acetone on a plane.

To protect your feet take a pair of wetsuit booties or reef boots. A wetsuit vest is also very handy for chilly, windy overcast days, and it also protects your back and chest from sunburn, and from being ground into the reefs. If you are a real tube maniac and will drive into anything no matter what the consequences, you are advised to take a short-sleeved spring-suit. A Lycra swim-shirt (a 'rashie' to Australians) is good protection against chills and sunburn.

Bring Betadine or surgical spirit, and cotton buds to put it on your cuts each night. Also bring a needle and pointy tweezers to remove sea urchin spines. Adhesive bandages that won't come off in the water are also necessary – Elastoplast is excellent. The pharmacies on Bali are fairly well stocked, but it's easier to take your own.

A surfing helmet is a good idea, not just for protection from the reefs, but also to keep the sun off while you wait in the lineup. And it will probably give you better protection in a motorbike accident than the helmets that come with rented bikes.

Surviving Surfing

Wear a shirt when surfing and take ample supplies of a good sunblock, or you will miss out on good surf because you're too burnt to move. Riding a motorbike with a surfboard can be deadly, although you can rent bikes with board brackets on the side, which some surfers think are safer. Renting a car between a few surfers is just as cheap, and a lot better. Brush up on basic mouth-to-mouth resuscitation – you might be called upon to use it, especially around the beach breaks of Kuta where people often get into trouble.

If you write yourself off severely while surfing, or on the way to surf, head to the top hotels which have access to the best doctors. The medical centres at Kuta, Tanjung Benoa and Nusa Dua are modern and well equipped, and handy to the surfing areas around Bukit Peninsula. Go for the more expensive private surgeries, be prepared to pay cash up front and be glad you took out travel insurance. If it's serious, get the next plane home.

Where to Surf

The swells come from the Indian Ocean, so the surf is on the south side of the island, and strangely, on the north-west coast of Nusa Lembongan where the swell funnels into the strait between there and the Bali coast.

In the dry season (around April to September), the west coast has the best breaks, with the trade winds coming in from the south-east; this is also when Nusa Lembongan works best. In the wet season (October to March), surf the eastern side of the island, from Nusa Dua around to Padangbai. If there's a north wind – or no wind at all – there are also a couple of breaks on the southern coast of Bukit Peninsula. There are lots of places to stay around Kuta, but nothing affordable near the breaks on Bukit Peninsula, so you'll need some transport.

The most well known breaks are listed in this section, but there are other places which you can find. As you learn more about the weather and the ocean conditions you'll know where to look. No-one is giving away any 'secret spots'. Most of the main surf breaks are shown on the South Bali map at the start of that chapter.

Kuta & Legian For your first plunge into the warm Indian Ocean, try the beach breaks

at **Kuta Beach**; on full tide go out near the lifesaving club at the south end of the beach road. At low tide, try the tubes around **Halfway Kuta**, probably the best place on Bali for beginners to practise. Start at the beach breaks if you are a bit rusty. The sand here is fine and packed hard, so it can hurt when you hit it. Treat even these breaks with respect. They provide zippering left and right barrels over shallow banks and can be quite a lot of fun. Some days you won't feel like travelling all over the island looking for surf and you will be content with little sessions out here.

Further north, **Legian Beach** breaks can be pretty powerful, with lefts and rights on the sand bars off Jl Melasti and Jl Padma. (At Kuta and Legian you will encounter most of the local Balinese surfers. Over the years their surfing standard has improved enormously and because of this, and also because it is their island, treat them with respect. By and large, they're usually quite amenable in the water, although some surfers have found their holidays cut short by a falling out with the locals. Give them the benefit of the doubt on a wave, and avoid getting into fights.)

Further north again, there are more beach breaks off Seminyak, such as the **Oberoi** near the hotel of the same name. This is the trendy end of Kuta-Legian and the beach scene can be fun, but the sea is fickle and can have dangerous rip tides – take a friend and take good care.

For more serious stuff, go to the reefs south of the beach breaks, about 1km out to sea. **Kuta Reef**, a vast stretch of coral, provides a variety of waves. You can paddle out in around 20 minutes, but the easiest way is by outrigger. You will be dropped out there and brought back in for a fee. The main break is a classic left-hander, best at mid to high tide with a five to six foot swell, when it peels across the reef and has a beautiful inside tube section; the first part is a good workable wave. Over seven feet it tends to double up and section.

The reef is well suited for backhand surfing. It's not surfable at dead low tide, but you can get out there not long after the tide turns. The boys on the boats can advise you if necessary. It gets very crowded here, but if conditions are good there's another, shorter left, 50m further south along the reef, which usually has fewer surfers. This wave is more of a peak and provides a short, intense ride. On bigger days, check out breaks on the outer part of the reef, 150m further out.

South of Kuta Reef there are some good breaks around the end of the airport runway. Offshore from Hotel Patra Jasa Bali is a reef break called **Airport Lefts**, with a workable wave at mid to high tide. Further south, **Airport Rights** has three right-handers that can be a bit fickle, and are shallow and dangerous at low tide – they're best for good surfers at mid to high tide with a strong swell. Get there by outrigger from Kuta.

Ulu Watu When Kuta Reef is five to six feet, Ulu Watu, the most famous surfing break on Bali, will be six to eight feet with bigger sets. Kuta and Legian sit on a huge bay – Ulu is way out on the southern extremity of the bay, and consequently picks up more swell than Kuta. It's about a half-hour journey from downtown Kuta by private transport; some surf shops near Tubes Bar have handy shuttle bus services for 25,000 rp per person return.

Just before the temple, a sign points to Suluban surf beach. You can't drive right in by car – get a ride on a motorbike from the road or walk about 3km. In any case you have to walk the last few hundred metres, so a board-strap and small backpack are useful.

A concrete stairway leads into the Ulu Gorge and in front of you is a sight you will never forget, especially if a decent swell is running. The thatched warungs are set on one side of the gorge, above the cave; one warung is right on the edge of the cliff. The Ulu Watu bay stretches out in front of you. In the shade you can eat, drink, rest, even stay overnight.

It is one of the best set ups for surfers in the world and everything is carried in by the Balinese. Local boys will wax your board, get drinks for you and carry the board down into the cave, one of the only ways out to the waves.

Ulu Watu has about seven different breaks. If it's your first trip here, sit for a while in the shade and survey the situation. See where other surfers are sitting in the line up and watch where they flick off. **The Corner** is straight in front of you to the right. It's a fast-breaking, hollow left that holds about six foot. The reef shelf under this break is extremely shallow so try to avoid falling head first. At high tide, **The Peak** starts to work. This is good from five to eight feet, with bigger waves occasionally right on the Peak itself. You can take off from this inside part or further down the line. A great wave. At low tide, if the swell isn't huge, go further south to **The Racetrack**, a whole series of bowls.

At low tide when the swell is bigger, **Outside Corner** starts operating, further out from The Racetrack. This is a tremendous break and on a good day you can surf one wave for hundreds of metres. The wall here on a 10 foot wave jacks up with a big drop and bottom turn, then the bowl section. After this it becomes a big workable face. You can usually only get tubed in the first section. When surfing this break you need a board with length, otherwise you won't be getting down the face of any of the amazing waves.

Another left runs off the cliff which forms the southern flank of the bay. It breaks outside this in bigger swells, and once it's seven foot, a left-hander pitches right out in front of a temple on the southern extremity. Out behind The Peak, when it's big, is a bombora appropriately called **The Bommie**. This is another big left-hander and it doesn't start operating until the swell is about 10 foot. On a normal five to eight foot day there are also breaks south of The Peak. One is a very fast left, and also very hollow, usually only ridden by goofy-footers because of its speed.

Observe where other surfers paddle out and follow them. If you are in doubt, ask someone. It is better having some knowledge than none at all. Climb down into the cave and paddle out from there. When it's bigger you will be swept to your right. Don't panic, it is an easy matter to paddle around the whitewater from down along the cliff. Coming back in you have to aim for the cave. When it's bigger, come from the southern side of the cave as the current runs to the north. If you miss the cave, paddle out again and repeat the procedure. If you get into trouble ask for help from a fellow surfer.

Padang Padang Just Padang for short, this super shallow, left-hand reef break is just north of Ulu towards Kuta. There are a number of ways to get there. If you are at Ulu you can simply walk along a narrow cliff track and climb down to the beach. Again, check this place carefully before venturing out. A rough but driveable road goes to a car park with a warung, a short walk from the beach. It's a very demanding break that only works over about six feet from mid to high tide – a great place to watch from the cliff top.

If you can't surf tubes, backhand or forehand, don't go out. **Padang** is a tube. After a ledgey take-off, you power along the bottom before pulling up into the barrel. So far so good, now for the tricky part. The last section turns inside out like a washing machine on fast forward. You have to drive high through this section, all the time while in the tube. Don't worry if you fail to negotiate this trap, plenty of other surfers have been caught too. After this the wave fills up and you flick off. Not a wave for the faint-hearted and definitely not a wave to surf when there's a crowd.

Bingin North of Padang and accessible by road, this once secret spot can now get crowded. It's best at mid-tide with a six foot swell. The outside reef, **Impossibles**, has fast tube sections, but don't stay on for too long.

Balangan At the end of a rough road north of Bingin, Balangan is an alternative when the tide is too high or the crowds are too big. It's a fast left over a shallow reef, which is unsurfable at low tide. It can work

on swells less than four feet, and doesn't get deadly until the swell hits about 10 feet.

Canggu North of Kuta/Legian/Seminyak, on the northern extremity of the bay, Canggu has a nice white beach, a warung, a very expensive hotel, and a few surfers. There are right and left breaks over a 'soft' rock ledge – well, it's softer than coral. Five to six foot is an optimum size for Canggu. There's a good right-hander that you can really hook into, which works on full tide, and what Peter Neely calls 'a sucky left ledge that tubes like Ulu but without the coral cuts', which works from mid-tide. A driveable track goes right to the beach – get there early, before the crowds and the wind.

Balian There are a few breaks near the mouth of Sungai Balian (Balian River) in west Bali – look for the Taman Rekreasi Indah Soka recreation park, along the main road, just west of Lalang Linggah. You'll be charged a few hundred rupiah to get in; park at the beach end of the track. There are a few warungs. The breaks are mainly lefts, and they work best at mid to high tide.

Medewi Further along the southern coast of west Bali is a softer left called **Medewi** – it's a point break which can give a long ride right into the river mouth. This wave has a big drop, which fills up then runs into a workable inside section. It's worth surfing if you feel like something different, but to catch it you need to get up early in the morning because it gets blown out as the wind picks up. It works best at mid to high tide with a six foot swell, but depends on the direction. There are several places to stay and eat at Medewi, and it's easily accessible by public transport.

Nusa Lembongan In the Nusa Penida group, this island is separated from the south-east coast of Bali by the Selat Badung (Bandung Strait). You can easily get there by public or shuttle boat from Sanur, and there are plenty of good budget hotels on the island (see the Nusa Penida chapter for details).

The strait is very deep, and generates huge swells which break over the reefs off the north-west coast of Lembongan. **Shipwreck**, clearly visible from the beach, is the most popular break, a classic right which works well at low tide and even better at high tide.

A bit to the south, **Lacerations** is a very fast right breaking over a very shallow reef – hence the name. Still further south is a smaller, more user-friendly left-hander called **Playground**.

There's also a break off **Nusa Ceningan**, the middle island of the group, but it's very exposed and only surfable when it's too small for the other breaks. Remember that Lembongan is best with an easterly wind, like Kuta and Ulu Watu, so it's dry-season surfing.

Nusa Dua During the wet season you surf on the east side of the island, where there are some very fine reef breaks. The reef off the expensive resort area of Nusa Dua has very consistent swells. There's nowhere cheap to stay in Nusa Dua, but there is at nearby Tanjung Benoa. The main break is 1km off the beach to the south of Nusa Dua – go past the golf course, and look for the small hand-written sign that tells you where to park. There's a warung, and some boats to take you out. There are lefts and rights which work well on a small swell at low to mid-tide. On bigger days take a longer board and go further out, where powerful peaking waves offer long rides, fat tubes and lots of variety. Further north, in front of the Club Med, is a tubing, fast right reef break called **Sri Lanka**, which works best at mid-tide and can handle swells from six to 10 feet.

Sanur Sanur reef has a hollow wave with excellent barrels. It's fickle, and doesn't even start till you get a six foot swell, but anything over eight feet will be world class, and anything over 10 feet will be brown-board-shorts material. There are other reefs further offshore and most of them are surfable. **Hyatt Reef**, over 2km from shore, has a shifty right peak which can give a great ride at full tide.

Closer in, opposite the Sanur Beach market, **Tanjung Sari** gives long left rides at low tide with a big swell, while **Tanjung Right** can be a very speedy wall on a big swell. The classic right is off the Grand Bali Beach Hotel. A couple of kilometres north, **Padang Galak** is a beach break at high tide on a small to medium swell, but it can be very dirty.

Ketewel & Lebih These two beaches are north-east of Sanur, but access is from the main Gianyar road. They're both right-hand beach breaks, which are dodgy at low tide and close out over six feet. There are probably other breaks along this coast all the way to Padangbai, but there needs to be a big swell to make them work.

South Coast The extreme south coast, around the end of Bukit Peninsula, can be surfed any time of the year providing there is a northerly wind, or no wind at all – get there very early to avoid onshore winds. The peninsula is fringed with reefs and gets big swells, but access is a problem. There are a few roads, but the shoreline is all cliffs. If you want to explore it, charter a boat on a day with no wind and a small swell.

Nyang Nyang is a right-hand reef break, reached by a steep track down the cliff. **Green Ball** is another right, which works well on a small to medium swell, ie when it's almost flat everywhere else. Take the road to the Bali Cliffs Resort, fork left just before you get there and take the steps down the cliff. The south coast has few facilities and tricky currents, and it would be a bad place to get into trouble – be very careful on the cliff tracks and in the water.

DIVING & SNORKELLING

With its warm water, extensive coral reefs and abundant marine life, Bali offers some superb diving and snorkelling possibilities. Scuba diving offers more demanding possibilities than snorkelling, although obviously it is more expensive; often requires transport, by land or water, to get to the best sites; and you need to be qualified unless you go on a training course. A number of operators conduct diving trips for visitors, and there are also package tours specifically for scuba divers. Diving may not be as good during the wet season (October to March), as storms tend to reduce visibility – although Pulau Menjangan and Nusa Penida can still be good.

Diving Tours

If you want to do a package diving tour, find a reputable operator near where you live by contacting your local dive club or buying a scuba diving magazine. These days, the best way to get current, reliable information is to surf the Internet; an incredible amount of information about diving on Bali is now available.

Alternatively, contact one of the Bali-based dive operations listed here and throughout this book, and ask them to recommend a package-tour operator in your area.

If you're a keen diver travelling independently, it might be a good idea to book your diving trips in advance (particularly easy on the Internet), to ensure you get a good guide who speaks your language, and to allow them time to make up a group with a similar level of experience. Most divers don't bother, however, and easily arrange a trip the same (or next) day by contacting a diving agency when they are on Bali.

When booking a tour, let the diving company know what areas interest you most, and what your level of experience is. Ensure you bring your scuba certification, even if you just want to do the occasional dive. The international safety code does not enable operators to let you dive without recognised certification. Most of the main qualifications are recognised, including PADI, NAUI, BSAC, CMAS, FAUI and SSI.

Warning Some readers have complained about diving crews rifling through, and even stealing, possessions left on the boat while diving. It is best to leave your valuables at your hotel, or at the diving agency, rather than on the boat.

Equipment

All the equipment you need is available on Bali, but you may not be able to get exactly what you want in the size you need, and the quality is variable – some operators use equipment right to the end of its service life. The basic equipment to bring is a mask, snorkel and fins – you know they'll fit and they're not too difficult to carry. You may save a little on dive costs, and you can use them when you want to snorkel off the beach.

Your next priority is a thin, full-length wetsuit, which is important for protection against stinging animals and coral abrasions. A thicker one (3mm) would be preferable if you plan frequent diving, deep dives or a night dive – the water can be cold, especially deeper down. You can rent wetsuits from diving agencies on Bali for about US$5 per day. Some small, easy-to-carry things to bring from home include protective gloves, spare straps, silicone lubricant and extra globes for your torch (flashlight). Most operators can rent good quality regulators (about US$5 per day) and BC vests (about US$5), but if you bring your own you'll save money, and it's a good idea if you're planning to dive in more remote locations than Bali, where the rental equipment may not be as good.

A set of all the above equipment will cost around US$15 per day on top of the basic cost of a dive. Tanks and weight belt – as well as lunch, drinking water, transport, guides and insurance – are included in the deal. You are not permitted to take sealed tanks on a plane anyway, and you'd be crazy to carry lead weights.

Diving Courses

There are many operators who are licensed to take out certified divers (ie those with recognised open-water qualifications), but only a few of them have qualified instructors who can train a beginner to this level. If you're not a qualified diver, and you want to try some scuba diving on Bali, you have three options. Firstly, nearly all the operators offer an 'introductory', 'orientation' or 'initial' dive for beginners, usually after some classroom training and shallow-water practice. These courses are reasonably cheap (from around US$50 to US$75 for one dive), but can be nasty. Some of the less professional outfits conduct these 'introductory' dives with unqualified, or even inexperienced, dive masters and minimal back-up, in sometimes difficult conditions, as low as 20m. Experienced divers are horrified by this practice, and there are a quite

a few scary stories. Novices would be well advised to stick with well known and reputable operators, and ensure that the people actually conducting the dive (not the ones who sign you up, or the owners of the company) are properly qualified instructors.

Secondly, some of the larger hotels and diving agencies offer four or five-day 'resort courses' which certify you for basic

Considerations for Responsible Diving

The popularity of diving is placing immense pressure on many sites. Please consider the following tips when diving and help preserve the ecology and beauty of reefs:

- Do not use anchors on the reef, and take care not to ground boats on coral. Encourage dive operators and regulatory bodies to establish permanent moorings at popular dive sites.
- Avoid touching living marine organisms with your body or dragging equipment across the reef. Polyps can be damaged by even the gentlest contact. Never stand on corals, even if they look solid and robust. If you must hold on to the reef, only touch exposed rock or dead coral.
- Be conscious of your fins. Even without contact the surge from heavy fin strokes near the reef can damage delicate organisms. When treading water in shallow reef areas, take care not to kick up clouds of sand. Settling sand can easily smother the delicate organisms of the reef.
- Practise and maintain proper buoyancy control. Major damage can be done by divers descending too fast and colliding with the reef. Make sure you are correctly weighted and that your weight belt is positioned so that you stay horizontal. If you have not dived for a while, have a practice dive in a pool before taking to the reef. Be aware that buoyancy can change over the period of an extended trip: initially you may breathe harder and need more weight; a few days later you may breathe more easily and need less weight.
- Take great care in underwater caves. Spend as little time within them as possible as your air bubbles may be caught within the roof and thereby leave previously submerged organisms high and dry. Taking turns to inspect the interior of a small cave will lessen the chances of damaging contact.
- Resist the temptation to collect or buy corals or shells. Aside from the ecological damage, taking home marine souvenirs depletes the beauty of a site and spoils the enjoyment of others. The same goes for marine archaeological sites (mainly shipwrecks). Respect their integrity; some sites are even protected from looting by law.
- Ensure that you take home all your rubbish and any litter you may find as well. Plastics in particular are a serious threat to marine life. Turtles can mistake plastic for jellyfish and eat it.
- Resist the temptation to feed fish. You may disturb their normal eating habits, encourage aggressive behaviour or feed them food that is detrimental to their health. Minimise your disturbance of marine animals. In particular, do not ride on the backs of turtles as this causes them great anxiety.

dives in the location where you do the course. A resort course will give you a better standard of training than just an introductory dive, but it doesn't make you a qualified diver. These courses cost about US$300, which is about the same cost as a full course on Bali, and you may have to be a guest at an expensive hotel to start with.

Lastly, if you are serious about diving, the best option is to enrol in a full open-water diving course which will give you an internationally recognised qualification. A four day open-water course, to CMAS or PADI standards, with a qualified instructor, manual, dive table and certificate, will cost from about US$275. Experienced divers can also upgrade their skills with advanced open-water courses in night diving, wreck diving, deep diving and so on, from around US$120 to US$150 per day, depending on the course and the operator.

Diving Operations on Bali

Dive operators in the southern tourist centres can arrange trips to the main dive sites anywhere around the island, and all major diving areas and tourist centres have dive operators. The cost depends on the number of people in the group and the distance to the dive site. For a group of six divers on a local trip, count on US$40 to US$60 for two dives. A trip to remote areas like Pulau Menjangan from south Bali will cost considerably more.

Another option is to get yourself to an area near where you want to dive, and contact a local dive operation. This gives you a chance to do some sightseeing on the way, and will be cheaper because you're not paying extra to transport you and your equipment. It also permits a much more comfortable schedule. To travel from Sanur to Pulau Menjangan, do two dives and drive back means a long day, and will require a very early start.

At the time of research, some operators were discounting their fees, often up to 50%. In places where the competition is considerable (Kuta, Sanur, Tanjung Benoa, Lovina, and Candidasa) you can shop around and negotiate prices, especially if you are using the operator for more than one dive.

There are many dive operations on Bali and the number is growing. The following is a partial list of the more established and reputable operators based in south Bali (area code ☎ 361), although some also have other offices around the island. Other reputable local diving operators are also mentioned in the regional chapters. You can pick up brochures (and sometimes price lists) of the various diving operators from most travel agencies and hotels in the tourist centres.

Bali Marine Sports
(☎ 289308, fax 287872)
Jl Ngurah Rai, Blanjong, Sanur
Barrakuda Diving Service
(☎/fax 722839)
Jl Pendidikan, Sidakarya, Denpasar. Barrakuda offers all levels of dive courses with qualified instructors.
Baruna Water Sports
(☎ 753820, fax 753809)
Jl Ngurah Rai 300B, Denpasar. Baruna has branches all over Bali, but several travellers have recently complained about poor service.
Dive & Dives
(☎ 288052, fax 289309)
Jl Ngurah Rai 23, Sanur. This well regarded PADI operation is slightly more expensive than some, but worth using.
Mimpi Dive Centre
(☎ 701070, fax 701074)
Kawasan Bukit Permai, Jimbaran. This more upmarket, quality outfit has several branches, and resorts, around Bali.
Surya Water Sports
(☎/fax 287956)
Jl Karang Sari 1, Betngandang, Sanur. This operation has been recommended by several divers, and usually allows nondivers to accompany their diving friends free of charge.

Dive Sites

Some of Bali's main dive sites are listed in this section, roughly in order of their accessibility from south Bali. For more details on local diving operators, accommodation, food and getting to these places, see the entries in the relevant chapters.

Nusa Dua The beach is nice and gently sloping, but for the best diving, take a boat out to the reef. There's a drop-off, and colourful corals are seen between 3m and 20m.

Sanur Very accessible by boat from the main tourist beach, Sanur's reef is colourful and has lots of tropical fish which can be seen at depths of less than 12m.

Padangbai This beautiful bay is becoming more popular with tourists – you can dive from the beach, or get an outrigger canoe to the best sites, especially the **Blue Lagoon**, with lots of fish and colder water than south Bali.

Candidasa There are quite a few dive sites on the reefs and islands around Candidasa, and it's a comfortable base for diving trips to the east coast. The fish life here is particularly rich and varied, and is said to include sharks. The currents on this coast are strong and unpredictable – it's recommended for experienced divers only. The **Canyon** at Tepekong is a particularly challenging dive.

Tulamben The big diving attraction is the wreck of the **USAT** *Liberty*, which is spectacular but eerie, encrusted with marine flora and inhabited by thousands of tropical fish. It's close to the shore and can easily be appreciated by snorkellers, but divers will find it even more interesting – depths are less than 30m. There's also the **Tulamben Wall**, a 60m drop-off into Lombok Strait. The wreck is a very popular dive, so to avoid other groups you can stay at Tulamben, where there are several dive operations and hotels, and dive early or late in the day.

Amed Amed has a very isolated black sand beach. You dive from the beach (actually at Cemeluk, near Amed), which slopes gently then drops off to about 35m, with a spectacular wall. There are lots of fish, and a great variety of coral. Several diving sites, operators and hotels have now been established along this remote north-east peninsula.

Lovina The beaches west of Singaraja has an extensive coral reef, with pools of very calm water. You can dive or snorkel from a boat, but you don't have to go deep to enjoy the area – it's a good spot for beginners.

Pulau Menjangan 'Deer Island' is in the Taman Nasional Bali Barat national park, accessible by boat from Labuhan Lalang. It has superb, unspoilt coral (partly because of the absence of human development in the area), lots of sponges and fish, great visibility and a spectacular drop-off. It's regarded as the best diving on Bali. Transport to the remote location, and boat rental, can make this a more expensive dive, but it's worth it. There are dive operators in Lovina and around Pemuteran.

Nusa Penida There are dive sites all around Nusa Penida and Nusa Lembongan. At Lembongan you enter from the white sand beach which slopes gently out to the reef, where diving is from five to 20m down.

Dives around Penida are more demanding, with big swells, strong and fickle currents, and cold water. There are some impressive underwater grottoes in the area, and the amount of large marine life, including manta rays, sharks and turtles, is impressive. There are no dive operators on Penida or Lembongan, so you will need to organise the trip from mainland Bali (ie Tanjung Benoa, Candidasa or Sanur), an hour or so away by boat. Choose a good operator who knows the area well.

Snorkelling

If you just want to do a little snorkelling, there's a pretty good coral reef off Nusa Dua, Sanur and along the Lovina Beach strip on the north coast. There's also good snorkelling on the reefs off Padangbai (boats will take you out) and at Tulamben, Amed and various points along the north-east coast. Most areas with coral and tourists will have a place that rents masks, snorkels and fins for 5000 to 7500 rp per day, but check the condition of the equipment before you take it away.

TREKKING

Bali is not usually thought of as a trekking destination, but so many people climb Gunung Batur to see the sunrise that it can get crowded up there some mornings. There are numerous other possibilities for treks in the Batur area, around the volcanoes near Bedugul and in the Taman Nasional Bali Barat national park in west Bali. Probably the biggest challenge is a climb of Gunung Agung (3142m).

Bali does not offer remote 'wilderness treks'; it's simply too densely populated. For the most part, you make day trips from the closest village, often leaving before dawn to avoid the clouds which usually blanket the peaks by mid-morning – you won't need a tent, sleeping bag or stove. However, waterproof clothing and a sweater at least are essential for trekking in the central mountains. Treks in the national park must be accompanied by a guide, which can be arranged at the park offices at Cekik or Labuhan Lalang. There are many guides, with varying degrees of competence, who will gladly show you the way up Gunung Batur or Gunung Agung.

Walking is a good way to explore the backblocks. You can walk from village to village on small tracks and between the rice paddies, eating in warungs and staying in losmen in the larger villages – there's usually somewhere to stay, or someone to put you up. You can flag down a bemo if you do find yourself stuck and it's not too late in the day (not many bemos operate after 5 pm). Despite the enormous number of tourists on Bali, it's relatively easy to find places where tourists are a rarity. Of course, you may have to be content with a pretty basic standard of food and accommodation.

Several agencies that offer rafting and other adventure activities are discovering the financial benefits of also offering hiking trips. These invariably follow some ricefields for a couple of hours, and visit a 'traditional village'. These hikes are expensive at about US$45 per person for two hours; you are better off arranging something with a local guide or agency in Ubud, Tirta Gangga, or around Gunung Batur.

You can easily go on short hikes, without guides, around Tirta Gangga; to villages near Ubud; between and around Tamblingan, Buyan and Bratan lakes; around Pelaga and Petang; near Padangbai; around Munduk; and up and down Lemapura and Seraya mountains. Details are in the relevant chapters.

RAFTING

Rafting has become popular, and is usually done as a day trip from Kuta, Sanur, Nusa Dua or Ubud. Operators pick you up from

Considerations for Responsible Trekking

The increasing popularity of trekking on Bali is placing enormous pressure on the local environment. Please consider the following tips when trekking and help preserve the ecology and beauty of wilderness areas:

- Carry out all your inorganic waste (metal, foil, plastic etc). Make an effort to carry out rubbish left by others.
- Avoid buying water in plastic bottles. Use the water purification methods mentioned in the Health section earlier in this chapter.
- Dispose of human waste at least 100m from any watercourse. Dig a small hole, and bury any toilet paper.
- Do not use soap or shampoo, or wash cooking utensils, within 100m of any watercourse.
- Stick to existing tracks to avoid erosion, and damage to flora.
- Do not engage in, or encourage, any hunting.
- Do not feed any wildlife, or pick any wildflowers.
- Always follow social and cultural considerations when interacting with the local community.

your hotel, take you to the put-in point, provide all the equipment and guides, and return you to your hotel a few hours later. The best time is during the wet season (October to March), or just after; by the middle of the dry season (April to September), the best rapids may just be a dribble.

Most operators use the Sungai Ayung (Ayung River), near Ubud, where there are between 19 and 25 Class II (ie exciting but safe) rapids. During the rare bits of calm water, you can admire the stunning gorges and rice paddies from the boat. Other outfits plunge down Sungai Telagawaja in east Bali, which never seems to dry up; or Sungai Unda, which starts from Gunung Agung and flows through Semarapura, and has many rapids, from Class II to Class IV.

You should bring with you shorts, shirt, sandshoes (sneakers) and sunscreen. Afterwards, you will need a change of clothes and a towel (although this may be supplied). The operator should provide plastic bags for cameras. Prices include all transport, equipment and insurance, and a hot shower and lunch afterwards. You can book any trip directly, or through a travel agent or hotel in the tourist centres. Many companies now offer rafting trips. Like scuba diving, however, it is worth paying more for a reputable operator, with reliable equipment and experienced guides, such as the following (all telephone area codes are ☎ 0361).

Ayung River Rafting
  (☎ 238759, fax 224236)
  This Balinese company runs trips down the Ayung for US$63 per person.

Bali Adventure Tours
  (☎ 721480, fax 721481, email baliadventuretours@bali-paradise.com)
  This heavily advertised outfit offers trips down the Ayung from US$49 (with no lunch) to US$70. It has other deals, including a visit to its nearby Elephant Safari Park, for US$97.

Activities on Bali

Activity	Location	Cost
Bird Watching	around Ubud	US$33
Boat Trips	Padangbai, Pemuteran, Sanur	varied prices
Bungee Jumping	Gianyar, Kuta-Legian	about US$45
Cruises	Lovina, Nusa Penida, Nusa Lembongan, Pemuteran, Tanjung Benoa, Tulamben	varied prices
Cycling Tours	Gunung Batur, Ubud	from 35,000 rp for a half-day
Dolphin Tours	Lovina	from 15,000 rp per person
Elephant Rides	near Ubud	US$53
Fishing	Kuta, Sanur, Tanjung Benoa	about US$100 per person, per day
Golf	Danau Bratan, Sanur, Tanah Lot, Nusa Dua	*very* expensive
Horse Riding	Legian, Pemuteran, Tanah Lot, Yeh Gangga	about US$15 to US$30 per hour
Kayaking	near Ubud, Danau Tamblingan	from US$59
Mountain Biking	near Ubud, Gunung	varied prices
Paragliding	Ulu Watu	US$69
Theme Parks	Sanur, near Ubud	varied prices
Water Sports	Danau Bratan, Kuta-Legian, Lovina, Sanur, Tanjung Benoa	from US$20 per hour

Bali Safari Whitewater Rafting
(☎ 221315, fax 221316)
This agency ventures down the Telagawaja for US$65.
Sobek
(☎ 287059, fax 289448)
This well established agency runs trips on the Ayung for about US$68.
Under River Rafting
(☎ 227444, fax 245963)
This outfit prefers to plunge down the Sungai Unda, and costs US$65.

OTHER ACTIVITIES

There is a plethora of other activities available on Bali, including the adventurous (rafting), relaxing (golf), crazy (bungee-jumping) or a little weird (camel safaris). Most operators will charge US dollars and lots of them, but you can pay in rupiah. You can pick up brochures, and book, at most travel agencies in the tourist centres.

Bali is small and easy to get around, so you can enjoy breakfast at your Kuta hotel, then go horse riding near Ubud, para-sailing at Tanjung Benoa or kayaking on Danau Tamblingan, and be back in time for the start of the evening happy hour. You may want to (or have to) ration your time and money according to your specific interests. The boxed text 'Activities on Bali' will give you some idea of what activities are available, where they are located and the approximate cost (at the time of research). Details about the more popular and interesting activities can be found in the relevant chapters.

COURSES

If you have the time, you will probably appreciate Bali more if you join a cultural, language or cooking class. For current information about what courses are available in each tourist centre, look for ads at your hotel and local restaurants and bars; ask friends and hotel staff; and check out the locally produced tourist newspapers and magazines. More details about each course can be found in the relevant chapters.

Balinese Art, Dance, Music & Culture
In Denpasar, the BLTCC and several large outfits run courses in dance, music and art.

There's free courses for foreigners in Nusa Dua. In and near Ubud, several places run courses in batiks and music.
Cooking Classes
Short courses are available in Denpasar, Ubud, Sanur and Lovina.
Language
In Denpasar, the Indonesia Australia Language Foundation (IALF) and Bali Language Training & Cultural Centre (BLTCC) run courses. In Ubud, there are several courses available. In Australia, several larger universities offer three week to two-month language courses in Bali; look for ads in the major newspapers.
Meditation & Spiritual Interests
For the Balinese, everything on the island is imbued with spiritual significance, and this ambience is an attraction for spiritually inclined foreigners. Meditation courses are held in Ubud. Meditation is also possible at Bali's only Buddhist monastery in Banjar.

WORK

Quite a lot of foreigners own businesses on Bali, mostly hotels, restaurants and tour agencies. Many more are engaged in business concerns, such as buying and exporting clothing, handcrafts or furniture. Some of them are doing so legally, with the appropriate work or business visa. These visas are difficult to obtain, however, requiring sponsorship from an employer, or evidence of a business which brings investment to Indonesia; and you must get a business visa before you arrive. With the 60 day tourist card, you are not officially allowed to work, and you'll have to leave the country every 60 days. Even if you do get work, payment is often in rupiah, which doesn't convert into a lot of foreign currency these days.

Australian universities, and the Australian Department of Foreign Affairs & Trade, sometimes administer student exchange programmes. Anyone seeking long-term paid or volunteer work in Indonesia may want to contact one of the following agencies:

Global Volunteers
(☎ 612-482-0915, fax 482-1074)
375 E Little Canada Rd, St Paul, MA 55117-1628, USA. This organisation arranges professional and paid volunteer work for US citizens.

Lisle Fellowship Inc
(☎ 313-847-7126, fax 419-530-7719,
www.lisle.utoledo.edu)
433 West Sterns Rd, Temperance, MI 48182-
9568, USA. A nonprofit intercultural education
organisation arranges community programmes
on Bali for any nationality, although there are
costs for the 'volunteers'.

Overseas Service Bureau (OSB)
(☎ 03-9279 1788, fax 9419 4280)
PO Box 350, Fitzroy, Vic 3065. The OSB organises professional contracts for Australians.

Volunteer Service Abroad
(☎ 04-472 5759, fax 472 5052)
PO Box 12-246, Wellington 1, New Zealand.
This group organises professional contracts for
New Zealanders.

ACCOMMODATION

Finding a place to stay on Bali is no problem.
In fact, at the bottom end of the market, accommodation on Bali is probably one of the
best value places in the world. Outside the
peak tourist season, 10,000/15,000 rp can get
you an acceptable single/double in many
budget places, and 25,000/40,000 rp can
often get you something very pleasant in the
middle range.

The places to stay listed in this book are
intended to give you a feel for the various
types of accommodation available, and the
going price for a room of a certain standard,
so you can make an informed choice which
meets your own needs. In areas with lots
of accommodation it's impossible to list
every place, but there's always a good cross
section, including the cheapest, the most expensive, and anything that is unusual, special
or interesting. In particular, we try to include
out-of-the-way places that might otherwise
be missed.

The tourist business on Bali is so competitive that places of a similar standard
usually cost about the same price, give or
take a couple of thousand rupiah. Places
which are highly recommended in guidebooks tend to be full when you arrive, and
will raise their prices if business booms.
Also, when there is lots of accommodation
at a similar standard and price, it's not fair
to 'recommend' one place when others
down the street are just as good. If a place

listed in this book seems overpriced, discuss
the price with the staff or go elsewhere. If
you find a great place that's not listed, please
write and tell us and we'll check it out for
the next edition.

Some middle and top-end places can now
be booked on the Internet, but you will probably end up paying the full published rates,
and you obviously won't be able to negotiate face to face.

Camping

The only campground on the whole island is
at the headquarters of the Taman Nasional
Bali Barat national park at Cekik in west Bali.
It is only useful if you want to trek, snorkel
or scuba dive in the national park; and you
will have to bring your camping and cooking
equipment.

Even if you're trekking in the central
mountains, or in the national park, you will
rarely find use for a tent – there are usually
shelters of some sort, and most hikes can be
completed in one day anyway.

Hotels

Budget Hotels The cheapest accommodation on Bali is in small places which are
simple, but clean and comfortable. The best
of them are in interesting locations with
friendly, helpful staff who can really make
your stay a pleasure. A losmen is a small
hotel, often family-run, which rarely has
more than about 10 rooms; names usually
include the word 'losmen', 'homestay' or
'inn'. (The word losmen is a corruption of
the Dutch *logement*.) In theory, a *wisma* is a
smaller place, more like a guesthouse, and a
'bungalow' can be a little more expensive,
but in practice just about any cheap, budget-
range place can be called a losmen.

Losmen are often built in the style of a Balinese home – that is, a compound with an
outer wall and separate buildings around an
inner garden. On Bali, you usually live
outside – the 'living room' is an open verandah. It's pleasant sitting out in the garden,
and you're out there with all the other travellers, not locked away inside a room.

There are losmen all over Bali, and they

vary widely in standards and price. In a few places you'll find a room for as low as 10,000/15,000 rp, but generally they're in the 15,000/25,000 rp range. Bigger and better rooms in popular locations can rise to 25,000/40,000 rp, but can still be very good value. Some of the cheap rooms are definitely on the dull and dismal side, but others are attractive, well kept and excellent value for money. A nice garden can be one of the most attractive features, even in very cheap places. The price usually includes a light breakfast (sometimes just tea), and there is usually an attached bathroom with a shower (cold water only), basin and toilet (usually the European style). All but the cheapest rooms will have a fan *(kipas)*, usually a small table-top one. A ceiling fan is considered classier and always costs a little more.

Budget hotels in district capitals like Singaraja, as opposed to tourist centres like nearby Lovina, usually cater to Indonesian businessmen, so they usually have mandis (see the boxed text of the same name in this section) rather than showers, squat-style toilets and are often located along busy roads.

Budget places are identified by a small sign on the street, often hand written. They don't have brochures, but they often have a business card. These are useful for showing a taxi-driver or anyone else if you can't find the place, or giving to other travellers if the place is good. Staff are unlikely to speak much, if any, English outside of the tourist centres.

Some mid-range hotels have cheaper 'economy' rooms, which means you can enjoy the gardens, service and pool of a mid-range hotel, while paying for a budget-priced room. Also, don't be afraid to check out a mid-range hotel, and ask for a discount if you are staying a few days, or if business is quiet. It's amazing what you might get if you negotiate.

Mid-Range Hotels In Denpasar and the tourist centres (Kuta-Legian, Lovina, Candidasa, Ubud and Sanur) there is a good selection of mid-range hotels. At the beaches they're often constructed in Balinese bungalow style. They're often called something or someone's bungalows or cottages – eg Made's Beach Bungalows or Sunset Cottages. There's a pretty clear distinction between the lower mid-range places, which are nice losmen that have gone upmarket, and the upper mid-range places, which were built as cheap package-tour hotels, but will take all the walk-in trade they can get.

The cheaper mid-range places are priced from about 40,000/60,000 rp, and perhaps an extra 10,000 rp more per person if you can fit three people or a family in the room. These prices should include (but sometimes don't) a light breakfast, eg pineapple, banana and mango fruit salad, toast and tea/coffee; tea or coffee on request throughout the day; a ceiling fan; and your own bathroom with shower and toilet. Don't expect air-conditioning or hot water in this price range. There's sometimes a pool, although it can be tiny and grubby.

Upper mid-range hotels normally give their price in US dollars – a sure sign that they are aspiring to the package-tour market. The dollar figure is the 'published rate', on which the package-tour prices are based, and is always negotiable if you walk in, especially during the low season. These places start from US$30/40, and should include colour TV (usually with local programmes only), hot water and air-conditioning. Rooms will cost more if there's a sunken bar in the swimming pool (often unattended, but it looks good on the brochure) and a colour satellite TV, fridge and telephone in your room. At this price level, they start charging extra for breakfast, and have the cheek to charge up to 21% extra for tax and service. A mid-range hotel may have a variety of rooms and prices, with the main difference being air-con and hot water versus a fan and cold water.

Top-End Hotels The top of the top-end on Bali is world class. The biggest concentration of super-luxury five star hotels is at Nusa Dua, but various hotels at Sanur, Kuta, Legian, Lovina and Ubud are not far behind, while some of the very best ones are at secluded, isolated points around the coast or in

The Mandi

Nearly all the places to stay in tourist areas of Bali have western-style showers, but in remote areas you will still encounter the traditional *mandi*. The word 'mandi' simply means 'to bathe' or 'to wash'. Instead of taps and a sink or bath, the mandi is a large tank of cold water beside which you'll find what looks like a plastic saucepan (it used to be half a coconut shell on a stick). Scoop water out of the mandi tank and pour it over yourself, then soap yourself down and repeat the scooping and showering procedure. You *do not* climb in the tank.

In cheaper losmen there is often a hybrid bathroom, with a mandi-style tank of water *and* a shower head. Many people prefer the splash method, and it's a good backup when the water pressure fails. The mandi scoop is also used for flushing the toilet, and for washing one's bottom afterwards. The bathroom is meant to have water splashed around in it, and a mandi can be a lot of fun for kids or couples.

A warning: mandi water is often icy cold – it usually comes from wells way down deep. You will have to get used to cold water because cheap hotels have nothing else. Anyway, you're in the tropics and you will soon forget what hot water feels like.

In rural areas, many villages don't even have mandis, and bathing in a pool, lake, stream or irrigation channel is a regular and social practice.

the countryside. For this guidebook, top end usually means any place where the cheapest room costs from about US$40 a double (ie about two or three stars and up), but most top end places cost at least two or three times this. Remember: you are far more likely to get a good deal on upmarket accommodation by buying a package tour (ie airfare and accommodation) from home,

rather than booking accommodation yourself, or just turning up at the hotel.

Top end hotels usually have more expensive rooms called 'villas', 'bungalows', 'suites' or whatever. If you want a luxurious room, with lots of space and fancy extras, get the best room in a mid-range hotel. If you want a big pool and garden, or access to special sporting facilities, get the cheapest room in a top end hotel. At a five star hotel, the rooms start at around US$180 a double, and far, far more for suites – plus 10% tax, 11% service charge, a high-season supplement (about US$20/30), at least US$10 per head for breakfast, plus ...

The most tasteful of these hotels feature contemporary architecture in a modern but genuine Balinese style which is both distinctive and attractive. A luxury resort hotel on Bali does not look like a clone of one on Majorca or Maui or Mazatlán. Typically the rooms face inwards, to a lush landscaped garden, in a layout that has its origins in a traditional family compound *(pekarangan)*. The hotel lobby is often styled on a *bale banjar*, the meeting hall of a community or village. The rooms and public areas are often decorated with Balinese paintings, woodcarvings and stonework of the highest quality, and commissions for these works can keep whole villages gainfully employed for months.

If your budget won't stretch this far, there is no reason why you can't go into a luxury hotel for a leisurely (but expensive) meal or drink, or, if you are not too scruffy, a bit of a snoop around to see how the other half are 'surviving'.

Accommodation in Remote Areas

Visitors who only go to the tourist areas don't believe this, but there are lots of areas on Bali with no losmen, restaurants or tourist facilities at all. In remote villages, you can often find a place to stay by asking the village chief or headman, the *kepala desa*. It will usually be a case of dossing down in a pavilion in a family compound, so don't expect any privacy.

The price is negotiable, but will cost from

about 5000 to 10,000 rp per person per night. Your hosts may not even ask for payment, and in these cases you should definitely offer some gifts, like cigarettes, bottled water, sweets or fruit. If they give you a meal, it is even more important to make an offer of payment or gifts – maybe bring a bag of rice.

The opportunity to stay in untouristed villages should not be exploited as a cheap accommodation option by impecunious and unethical freeloaders. If you want to stay in such places, make enquiries locally about appropriate gifts and protocol, and be very sensitive to the social environment. It's a very good idea to take a Balinese friend or guide to help facilitate introductions, and to ensure that you make as few cultural faux pas as humanly possible.

FOOD

You will eat well on Bali: the dining possibilities are endless, the prices pleasantly low and the taste and smell will more than satisfy. Ubud is one place where you will enjoy a wide range of Balinese food, but you can also enjoy fresh seafood at Jimbaran; dishes made out of special brown rice in the inner west, especially around Tabanan; and *babi guling* and other pork dishes around Singaraja and east Bali. Also see the 'Balinese Food' colour section in this chapter.

Balinese Food

Although Bali does have its own cuisine, it's not readily adaptable to a restaurant menu. The everyday Balinese diet at home is a couple of meals and a few snacks of cold steamed rice, with some vegetables, some crunchy stuff like nuts or *krupuk* (prawn crackers), and a little chicken, pork or fish. The food is prepared in the morning and people help themselves throughout the day. Balinese haute cuisine is reserved for the elaborate food offerings made to the gods and sumptuous feasts to celebrate important occasions.

The dishes for a traditional Balinese feast require some time to cook, and the elaborate preparations and ritual are a major community exercise. Two of the great feast

dishes, babi guling (spit-roasted suckling pig) and *betutu bebek* (duck roasted in banana leaves), are the only truly Balinese dishes you'll see with any regularity in restaurants, and they usually have to be ordered a day in advance. The best places to look for Balinese specialities are around Denpasar and in Ubud. Upmarket tourist hotels also do elaborate re-creations of a Balinese feast, but the ambience can be more like a suburban barbecue.

Warungs

I think one of my favourite parts of Bali are the food vendors that sell chicken soup. There are always guys pushing carts around, and you can hear them coming as they clang bells and make other noises.

Kara Deringer, Canada

Balinese like to eat snacks throughout the day, and when they're away from home, they go to a food stall (warung), or cart (often called *kaki lima*) parked along the side of the road, which often serve Javanese, Chinese or even Sumatran (ie Padang) food. The most common is *bakso*, a soup with noodles and meatballs. *Nasi campur* is the most authentic Balinese-style dish served in warungs.

An even simpler snack is *nasi jenggo*, white rice with some spicy sauce, wrapped in a banana leaf. Most of the budget tourist restaurants do Chinese-Indonesian style food, with the standard dishes being nasi goreng, nasi campur, *cap cai* and *gado gado*.

The great paradox of eating on Bali is that the cheaper the place, the tastier the food. The really cheap places are for the locals, and they serve the genuine article.

At a street cart, for about 2000 rp you can get a nasi goreng that's out of this world – hot and spicy, with fresh ingredients that are cooked while you wait. Of course you might have to sit on the curb to eat it, and the plate may not be carefully washed. At a tourist restaurant around the corner, a nasi goreng costs from 5000 rp, but it mightn't be freshly cooked and it won't have the same spicy taste.

Fried noodles *(mie goreng)*, satay *(sate)*

and soup *(soto)* are other cheap staples which taste better and cost less at a warung or kaki lima.

Local Dishes

Food in Indonesia is Chinese influenced, although there are a number of purely Indonesian dishes. See the glossary at the back of this book for a description of meals and their local names.

Fruit

It's almost worth making a trip to Bali or Lombok just to sample the tropical fruit. If you've never gone beyond apples, oranges and bananas you've got some rare treats in store when you discover rambutans, mangosteens, salaks or zurzat. For a description of Indonesian fruit, see the glossary at the end of this book.

Foreign Food

There are a growing number of very good restaurants with what can only be described as 'international menus'. They serve excellent meals for a fraction of what you'd pay in Europe, the USA or Australia, and they are usually spacious open-air places with friendly and efficient service. The best ones are in Ubud and in Kuta-Legian-Seminyak.

Many of the upmarket hotels will also have 1st class kitchens, but the cost will not be much less than back home. In many tourist restaurants in the tourist centres you will be lucky to find even Indonesian food, apart from a token nasi goreng, among all the western dishes.

At all tourist restaurants on Bali you can get omelettes, pancakes and jaffles for breakfast. For lunch and dinner, you can find steaks, spaghetti, hamburgers or pizza, and nachos and guacamole dips for starters – and they are usually well made with fresh ingredients.

And for those who can't live without something from their favourite chain of fast-food restaurants, there are McDonald's, Dunkin' Donuts, KFC, Subway, Wendy's and Pizza Hut in Kuta-Legian and/or Denpasar. Most of them are reasonably priced,

but McDonald's costs about the same as you would pay at home.

DRINKS
Nonalcoholic Drinks

Plastic bottles of drinking water are widely available. A 500ml bottle costs about 1000 rp; a 1.5L bottle is around 2000 rp. It's cheapest in supermarkets and local shops, and some brands, like Aqua, are more popular and a little dearer. In Lovina, Ubud and Candidasa, there are one or two environmentally friendly shops where you can refill your plastic bottles with Aqua drinking water for about half the cost of buying another bottle of water with the same brand.

A variety of popular western soft-drink brands are available – usually in small bottles rather than cans. Coca-Cola, 7-Up, Sprite and Fanta are all there. Fruit juice and UHT milk are available in sealed cartons from supermarkets and most small shops. Locally produced coffee is called *kopi* Bali. It is strong, black and thick, and grown around volcanic areas near Kintamani, on the hills around Pupuan in central Bali, and along the north coast, not far from Singaraja.

Alcoholic Drinks

Beer is expensive compared to other things on Bali, but served cold in a bar or restaurant it's still cheaper than in most western countries, and in eastern Indonesia. Some places offer happy hours where a beer, and other drinks, are a few thousand rupiah cheaper for an hour or two after about 6 pm. The most common brands of beer are Bintang, Bali Hai, Anker and San Miguel. Bintang is the best; Bali Hai is not so good, but is often cheaper. Prices for a large bottle (620ml) range enormously, from about 5000 rp during a happy hour in Kuta to about 12,000 rp during the sunset at Tanah Lot.

Imported wine is expensive on Bali, but there are some efforts to produce a local drop. A company called Hatten, with grapes grown near Singaraja, but 'vintaged' in Sanur, provides a drinkable drop of rosé for about 45,000 rp a bottle, or 7000 to 10,000 rp a glass. If you intend to buy a bottle of

BALINESE FOOD

Box: The ubiquitous chilli.

Left: *Mie kuah pangsit* (meatball noodle soup) at a cremation ceremony.

Top right: A typical Balinese market scene.

Bottom right: Preparing *sate ikan* (fish kebabs) in the village of Mas.

Bali is best described as a society of snackers. This results in the sale of a fantastic variety of savoury and sweet foods from *warung* (roadside stalls), usually run by enterprising women. The traditional packaging for this food is *tekor* (banana leaf), which is cheap, flavour-enhancing, leak-proof and disposable. Unfortunately, plastic, a by-product of Indonesia's booming petrochemical industry, has become a popular replacement over the last ten years and consequently an obvious problem in a takeaway/throwaway society like Bali.

Top: Vegetables, fruits, herbs and spices spread out under a covered market.

Bottom left: Vegies on display at a village market.

Bottom right: Baskets of freshly caught fish for sale on the beach.

Cakes & Sweet Food

Many *jaje* (cakes) are used in *banten* (offerings for the gods). They are later eaten by the Balinese, and anyone else lucky enough to be around. Rice, rice flour, fruits, palm sugar, pandan leaf, peanuts, coconut, salt and coconut oil are important ingredients.

The variety of flavours, textures, colours and shapes produced is extraordinary given the simplicity of Balinese kitchens and cooking methods. Nowadays offering cakes are readily available in markets and supermarkets. They are delicious with *kopi Bali* (sweet black Balinese coffee) or *teh sari* (fragrant black tea).

Top left: Bali delights (clockwise from top left): *jaje matahari* (suncakes), *jaje kuping gajah* (elephant ears cake), *dadar* (pandan crepes), *beginsa* (palm sugar offering cakes) and rambutans.

Top right: Common Balinese ingredients (clockwise from top left): tomatoes, snake beans, limes, pepper and chillies.

Right: A vendor of *cendol* (sticky rice, coconut milk and sugar) at Pura Gelgel in Semarapura.

Left: Melon vendors at Ubud's large and frenetic produce market. The market, which operates every third day, is best visited early in the morning when the quality and variety of produce is high.

Bottom: A Padang restaurant displays its range at an Ubud market.

wine during dinner, you may want to bring a corkscrew from home – it is not a common implement in many restaurants.

Local Drinks

For a list of popular Indonesian and Balinese drinks, both alcoholic and nonalcoholic, see the glossary at the end of this book.

ENTERTAINMENT

The best way to find out about current exhibitions, music, dances and films around Bali is to get hold of a copy of the *Bali Echo*, buy a copy of the English-language daily *Jakarta Post*, ask at your hotel, or look for the notices outside the various establishments.

Cinemas

You may find a *bioskop* (cinema) in some larger towns on Bali and Lombok, but the best ones are in Denpasar, Kuta and Mataram (Lombok). Lurid posters advertising the latest offering are highly visible – often they'll be mounted on a truck which cruises through town with a loudspeaker blasting out rave reviews and bites from the soundtrack.

Balinese tastes in movies are varied in that they like blood-and-guts epics from any part of the world – Hong Kong, Hollywood, India or Java. They don't mind a bit of romance or some humour either, but principally it's action, excitement, violence, suspense and passion.

Films are usually played with the original soundtrack, subtitled in Indonesian, so if it's something from the USA, in theory, you'll be able to understand it. In practice, there can be a high level of audience participation as they don't need to hear the words, and you probably don't either in most of the films. Films seem to be losing audiences to TV and video, and bioskop are closing in many towns. This is quite a pity, because the bioskop is a big social scene for young Balinese and there's usually a good atmosphere. Tickets cost from 3500 to 6500 rp.

In the tourist centres, a fair selection of very recent and popular films are shown on video screens in many bars and restaurants.

The sound and picture quality is often pretty bad, however, and they are often sub-titled in Indonesian. The price of drinks and food in any bar or restaurant showing a film will be comparatively high, and you can't possibly converse with anyone while the film is on.

Cultural Performances

Balinese dance performances and shadow puppet plays are popular entertainment for tourists, but of course they're much more than that. For details, see the Arts section in the Facts about Bali chapter, and the Dance section in the Ubud & Around chapter.

SPECTATOR SPORTS

Bali is no different from the rest of Indonesia: football (soccer) is the main sport, while badminton and volleyball are also popular. Many sports involve gambling, which is illegal. Cockfighting (see the boxed text of the same name in the Facts about Bali chapter) is popular, and can be seen in some rural areas. There are bull races near Negara in west Bali.

The Bali International Cricket Club (☎ 0361-289508) plays on Sunday mornings on the soccer field at the Grand Bali Beach Hotel in Sanur. It's a very social game, and anyone might get on the field if a team is short of numbers. The Australian consulate must accept some responsibility for this form of cultural pollution.

SHOPPING

Many people come to Bali to 'shop 'til they drop', and everyone else will probably end up buying quite a few things anyway. The growing number of western-style department stores and shopping centres in Denpasar, Kuta-Legian, Sanur and Nusa Dua sell a large variety of clothing, shoes, leather goods, sports gear and toys. There's a huge range, the service is generally good, and currently prices are excellent because of the low value of the rupiah.

Balinese and Indonesian arts and crafts are the most popular purchases – see the boxed text 'Buying Arts & Crafts' in this section for details. For a full discussion of Balinese arts and crafts, see the colour section of the same name following the Facts about Bali chapter.

Clothing

All sorts of clothing is made locally, and sold in hundreds of small shops in all tourist centres, especially Kuta-Legian. It's mostly pretty casual, but it's not just beachwear – you can get a tailor-made purple leather battle jacket, or just about anything else you want. Leather is popular, and currently cheap.

Music

Because the current level of the rupiah is so low, CDs featuring western artists are now good value. In Kuta-Legian, CDs of western artists cost 80,000 rp; prices are a little higher in other towns. Cassettes cost about 18,000 rp. The costs of cassettes and CDs featuring Balinese and Indonesian artists is generally lower.

Musical Instruments

Great souvenirs are a few of the more unusual musical instruments, eg gongs and gamelans. The Bali Arts & Crafts map in the boxed text 'Buying Arts & Crafts' in this section lists the best places on Bali to buy musical instruments.

Watches

In the tourist centres, particularly Kuta-Legian, you will be accosted regularly by hawkers selling 'copy watches'. For a reasonably plausible imitation of a Rolex, Tag Heuer or other designer watch, they'll start asking around 60,000 rp or more, but they'll eventually come down to about 30,000 rp. The watches actually work quite well, but don't expect a divers' watch to be waterproof. These watches are illegal copies, and officially it's illegal to import them into countries which respect trademark conventions – in practice, you're unlikely to have any problems bringing home one or two for personal use.

Buying Arts & Crafts

Opportunities to buy arts and crafts are abundant on Bali. Below is a list of places to begin (also refer to the Hawkers, Pedlars & Touts section earlier in this chapter).

Sculpture

Balinese stone is surprisingly light and it's not at all out of the realms of possibility to bring a friendly stone demon back with you in your airline baggage. A typical temple door guardian weighs around 10kg. The stone, however, is very fragile so packing must be done carefully if you're going to get it home without damage. Some of the Batubulan workshops will pack figures quickly and expertly, often suspending the piece in the middle of a wooden framework and packing around it with shredded paper. There are also many capable packing and forwarding agents, though the shipping costs will almost certainly be more than the cost of the article. A 50cm tall door guardian, however, can be bought for around US$50 (including packaging) with a little negotiation. It'll scare the hell out of your neighbour's garden gnomes!

Batubulan, on the main highway from Denpasar to Ubud, is a major stone-carving centre. Stone figures, varying in height from 25cm to 2m, line both sides of the street. Stone craftsmen can be seen in action in the many workshops here as well as in an area north of the main road, around Karang.

Much of the local work is made from a soft, grey volcanic stone called *paras*. It's a little like pumice, not particularly strong or dense, and so soft it can be scratched with a finger nail. When newly worked, it can be mistaken for cast cement, but with age and exposure to the elements, the outer surface becomes tougher and darker. A soft sandstone is also used, and sometimes has attractive colouring. Stone carving is Bali's most durable art form, and, though

Buying Arts & Crafts

it is soon covered in moss, mould or lichen, it outlasts woodcarvings and paintings which deteriorate quickly in the hot, humid atmosphere.

Stone sculpture on Bali is still very much for local consumption rather than, as with painting or woodcarving, for visitors to take home. Yet, although it's less affected by foreign influence than other art forms, many modern trends can still be seen and sculptors are happy to work on new and non-traditional themes. Japanese-style stone lanterns are currently popular.

Paintings

There are a relatively small number of creative original painters on Bali today, and an enormous number of imitators who produce copies, or near copies, in well established styles. Many of these imitative works are nevertheless very well executed and attractive pieces. Originality is not considered as important in Balinese art as it is in the west. A painting is esteemed not for being new and unique but for taking a well worn and popular idea and making a good reproduction of it.

One constant factor in Balinese painting is that it is almost always 'planned' – ie, drawn out and refined before any paint is applied. When the actual painting does take place it can often be done in an almost 'colour by number' manner. Indeed, some name artists will simply draw out the design, decide the colours and then employ apprentices to actually apply the paint. This once again leads to the mass production of remarkably similar themes which is so characteristic of Balinese art.

Unfortunately, much of the painting today is churned out for the tourist market and much of that market is extremely undiscriminating about what it buys. Thus the shops are packed full of paintings in the various popular styles – some of them quite good, a few of them really excellent, many of them uniformly alike and uniformly poor in quality. Even worse, many artists have turned to producing paintings purely attuned to tourist tastes and with nothing Balinese about them. It's rare to see anything really new – most painters aim for safety and that means painting what tourists will buy.

If you want to buy wisely then try to learn a little about Balinese painting before making a purchase. Visit the galleries and the Neka and Puri Lukisan museums in Ubud to see some of the best of Balinese art, as well as some of the European influences that have shaped it. Look at some books on Balinese art. An excellent short introduction to the subject is *Balinese Paintings* by AAM Djelantik. *The Development of Painting in Bali* is a handy little booklet published by the Neka Museum which describes the various styles and illustrates them with paintings from the Neka collection.

Finally, and most importantly, simply look at paintings. Once you've visited the two Ubud museums and seen some of the best work and examples of paintings that set the styles, visit other galleries. The Neka Gallery in Padangtegal near Ubud (not to be confused with the Neka Museum where the art is not for sale) and the Agung Rai Gallery in Peliatan are excellent places to view high-quality work and get an idea of prices. There are many other galleries and you'll soon start to appreciate what's good and what isn't. If it looks good and you like it, buy it.

Paintings can be transported in the cardboard tubes from rolls of fabric, as supplied to drapers. Otherwise you can buy plastic tubes from hardware stores. If you do buy a painting, and can handle the additional weight, consider taking a frame back as well. These are often elaborately carved and works of art in themselves, and are very cheap, especially compared to framing costs in the west.

Buying Arts & Crafts

Woodcarvings

There are few fixed prices for carved wooden items. Many factors determine costs, including the type of wood used, the novelty of the item and your powers of negotiation. If your idea is to send items home, packing and shipping costs can easily be more than the cost of the article. The simplest small carving can be found for 2000 rp or even less, while many good pieces can be bought for 50,000 rp, and there's no upper limit. If you're shopping around, you may see the same article vary in price by anything from 10% to 1000%!

Note that items made from harder woods may have an excess of moisture from Bali's tropical climate and the wood may shrink and crack in drier environments. It may be possible to avoid this

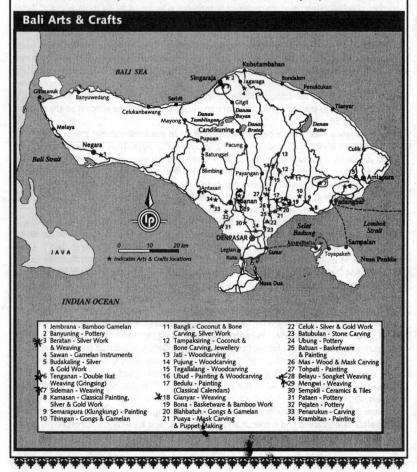

Bali Arts & Crafts

1 Jembrana - Bamboo Gamelan
2 Banyuning - Pottery
3 Beratan - Silver Work & Weaving
4 Sawan - Gamelan Instruments
5 Budakaling - Silver & Gold Work
6 Tenganan - Double Ikat Weaving (Gringsing)
7 Sideman - Weaving
8 Kamasan - Classical Painting, Silver & Gold Work
9 Semarapura (Klungkung) - Painting
10 Tihingan - Gongs & Gamelan
11 Bangli - Coconut & Bone Carving, Silver Work
12 Tampaksiring - Coconut & Bone Carving, Jewellery
13 Jati - Woodcarving
14 Pujung - Woodcarving
15 Tegallalang - Woodcarving
16 Ubud - Painting & Woodcarving
17 Bedulu - Painting (Classical Calendars)
18 Gianyar - Weaving
19 Bona - Basketware & Bamboo Work
20 Blahbatuh - Gongs & Gamelan
21 Puaya - Mask Carving & Puppet Making
22 Celuk - Silver & Gold Work
23 Batubulan - Stone Carving
24 Ubung - Pottery
25 Batuan - Basketware & Painting
26 Mas - Wood & Mask Carving
27 Tohpati - Painting
28 Belayu - Songket Weaving
29 Mengwi - Weaving
30 Sempidi - Ceramics & Tiles
31 Pataen - Pottery
32 Pejaten - Pottery
33 Penarukun - Carving
34 Krambitan - Painting

by placing the carving(s) in a plastic bag at home, and then letting some air in for about one week every month (for a total of three to four months), so the wood can get used to the drier air.

Fabrics & Weaving

Gianyar, in eastern Bali, is a major textile centre with a number of factories where you can watch sarongs being woven; a complete sarong takes about six hours to make. You can buy direct from the factories, although prices can be inflated in the tourist season. Any market will have a good range of textiles, if you know how to bargain.

In the Bali Aga village of Tenganan, in eastern Bali, a double *ikat* process called gringsing is used in which both the warp *and* weft are pre-dyed.

Belayu, a small village in south-western Bali between Mengwi and Marga, is a centre for songket weaving. Songket is also woven near Singaraja.

Ceramics

If you wish to see potters at work, visit the village of Pataen near Tanah Lot. Kapal and Ubung, in northern Denpasar, are also pottery centres. Nearly all local pottery is made from low-fired terracotta. Most styles are very ornate, even for functional items such as vases, flasks, ash trays and lamp bases. Pejaten near Tabanan also has a number of pottery workshops producing small ceramic figures and glazed ornamental roof tiles. Some excellent, contemporary glazed ceramics are produced in Sanur.

Jewellery

Celuk has always been the village associated with silversmithing. The large shops that line the road into Celuk have imposing, bus-sized driveways and slick credit-card facilities. If you want to see the 'real' Celuk, walk about 1km east of the road to visit family workshops. Other silverwork centres include Kamasan, near Semarapura in east Bali, and Beratan, south of Singaraja in north Bali.

Jewellery can be purchased ready-made or made-to-order – there's a wide range of earings, bracelets and rings available, some using gemstones imported from all over the world. Different design influences can be detected from African patterning to the New Age preoccupation with dolphins and healing crystals. Patriot-missile pendants are also available! Prices start at around 2000 rp for silver stud earrings.

You'll find many jewellery workshops in other areas around Ubud. Tampaksiring, northeast of Ubud, has long been a centre for cheaper styles of fashion jewellery. Brightly painted, carved wooden earrings are popular and cheap.

Gamelan

If you are interested in seeing gamelan instruments being made, visit the village of Blahbatuh, on the main road between Denpasar and Gianyar, and ask for Gablar Gamelan.

In northern Bali, Sawan, a small village south-east of Singaraja, is also a centre for the manufacture of gamelan instruments. Jembrana near Negara makes giant gamelan instruments with deep resonating tones.

Wayang Kulit

Wayang Kulit puppets are made in the village of Puaya near Sukawati, south of Ubud, and in Peliatan near Ubud.

Getting There & Away

Most international visitors to Bali will arrive by air, either directly or via Jakarta. For island hoppers, there are frequent ferries between eastern Java and Bali, and between Bali and Lombok, as well as domestic flights between the islands. Lombok is usually visited as a side trip from Bali, by plane, ferry or fast boat – see the Lombok Getting There & Away chapter later in this book.

AIR

Although Jakarta, the national capital, is the gateway airport to Indonesia, there are also many direct international flights to Denpasar. You can also fly to Jakarta first and travel overland through Java to Bali, or transfer to a domestic flight to Denpasar.

Ngurah Rai Airport

The only airport on Bali, Ngurah Rai is just south of Kuta, although it is referred to internationally as just Denpasar. The domestic terminal (☎ 751011, ext 3109) and international terminal (☎ 751011, ext 1454) are a few hundred metres apart.

Arrival procedures at the international airport are fairly painless, although it can take some time for a whole planeload of visitors to clear immigration. Once through customs you're out with the tour operators, touts and taxi drivers. The touts will be working hard to convince you to come and stay at their place in Kuta-Legian, and if you're not sure where you intend to stay they may be worth considering – but you will pay more for accommodation if you get taken there by a tout or a taxi driver. Anyone who helps with your baggage will expect to be paid at least 1000 rp.

Money The rates offered at the exchange counters at the international and domestic terminals are about 10% lower than at moneychangers in the tourist centres; although the counters further away from the customs area have better rates. There is also an ATM for Visa, MasterCard, Cirrus and Alto cards in the domestic terminal.

Taxi From the official counters, just outside the international and domestic terminals, pre-paid airport taxis cost:

Destination	Fare (in rp)
Kuta Beach	10,000
Legian	11,500
Seminyak	12,500
Denpasar	15,000
Jimbaran	17,500
Sanur	17,500
Nusa Dua	17,500
Tanjung Benoa	18,500
Ubud	47,000

It is worth noting that you can only share a pre-paid airport taxi if all passengers are going to the same place; they won't allow passengers to be dropped off along the way.

If you walk across the airport car park, north-east to Jl Raya Tuban, taxis may stop and take you to your destination for the metered rate, which will be cheaper than a pre-paid airport taxi.

Another option is to get a pre-paid taxi from the airport to Bemo Corner in Kuta, and then get a metered taxi or a public bemo to a more distant destination – this should save several thousand rupiah if you're heading to Legian, Sanur or Denpasar. Using a metered taxi *to* the airport will cost about half the pre-paid taxi rates listed here.

Bemo If you are closely watching your budget, keep walking on Jl Raya Tuban, which is on the route for the S1 bemos which loop back to Kuta (about 500 rp) and continue to Denpasar. The bemos are infrequent after 4 pm and don't run at all late at night.

Walking The even more impecunious (and lightly laden) can walk straight up the road to Kuta (about 2.5km), although it's a more pleasant stroll along the beach.

Airlines
International Airlines Most international airlines serving Bali have offices in the Grand Bali Beach Hotel in Sanur Airline offices typically are open Monday to Friday from 8.30 am to 4.30 pm (usually closing for about an hour at lunch time), and also on Saturday morning until about 1 pm.

The telephone and fax numbers for the international airlines are listed here. All have ☎ 0361 telephone area codes.

Air France
 (☎ 288511 ext 1105, fax 287734)
Air New Zealand
 (☎ 756170)
All Nippon Airways (ANA)
 (☎ 761102, fax 761107)
Ansett Australia
 (☎ 289636, fax 289637)

Cathay Pacific Airways
 (☎ 286001, fax 288576 in Sanur, ☎ 753942 at the airport)
Continental Micronesia
 (☎ 287774, fax 287775)
Japan Airlines (JAL)
 (☎ 287577, fax 287460)
KLM – Royal Dutch Airlines
 (☎ 756124/7, fax 753950)
Korean Air
 (☎ 289402, fax 289403)
Lufthansa Airlines
 (☎/fax 287069)
Malaysia Airlines
 (☎ 285071, fax 288716)
Northwest Airlines
 (☎ 287841, fax 287840)
Qantas Airways
 (☎ 288331, fax 287331)
Singapore Airlines
 (☎ 288511 ext 1587)
Thai Airways International
 (☎ 288141, fax 288063)

Indonesian Airlines A few Indonesian airlines now fly to Australia and other parts of Asia. Garuda is the main carrier, but it sometimes cancels flights if they are not full. Be aware that Sempati and Merpati were scaling back services at the time of writing. All of these airline offices have a telephone area code of ☎ 0361.

Bouraq
 (☎ 241397, fax 241390, ☎ 751011 ext 3104 at the airport)
 Jl Sudirman, Blok A47-48, Denpasar. It's open Monday to Saturday from 8 am to 5 pm, although these times do change.
Garuda
 (☎ 225245, fax 226298, ☎ 751026 at the airport, ☎ 227824/5 for bookings and reconfirmations)
 It's open Monday to Friday from 7.30 am to 4.45 pm, and on Saturday from 9 am to 1 pm. The main office is at Jl Melati 61, Denpasar, and there are also sales offices at the Kuta Beach Hotel (☎ 751179); Sanur Beach Hotel, Sanur (☎ 289135); Grand Bali Beach Hotel, Sanur (☎ 288243); Nusa Indah Hotel, Nusa Dua (☎ 771864); and Bali Imperial Hotel, Seminyak (☎ 730681).
Mandala
 (☎ 222751, fax 231659)
 Jl Diponegoro 98, Blok D/23, Denpasar

Air Travel Glossary

Baggage Allowance This will be written on your ticket and usually includes one 20kg item to go in the hold, plus one item of hand luggage.

Bucket Shops These are unbonded travel agencies specialising in discounted airline tickets.

Bumped Just because you have a confirmed seat doesn't mean you're going to get on the plane (see Overbooking).

Cancellation Penalties If you have to cancel or change a discounted ticket, there are often heavy penalties involved; insurance can sometimes be taken out against these penalties. Some airlines impose penalties on regular tickets as well, particularly against 'no-show' passengers.

Check-In Airlines ask you to check in a certain time ahead of the flight departure (usually one to two hours on international flights). If you fail to check in on time and the flight is overbooked, the airline can cancel your booking and give your seat to somebody else.

Confirmation Having a ticket written out with the flight and date you want doesn't mean you have a seat until the agent has checked with the airline that your status is 'OK' or confirmed. Meanwhile you could just be 'on request'.

Courier Fares Businesses often need to send urgent documents or freight securely and quickly. Courier companies hire people to accompany the package through customs and, in return, offer a discount ticket which is sometimes a phenomenal bargain. In effect, what the companies do is ship their freight as your luggage on regular commercial flights. This is a legitimate operation, but there are two shortcomings – the short turnaround time of the ticket (usually not longer than a month) and the limitation on your luggage allowance. You may have to surrender all your allowance and take only carry-on luggage.

Full Fares Airlines traditionally offer 1st class (coded F), business class (coded J) and economy class (coded Y) tickets. These days there are so many promotional and discounted fares available that few passengers pay full economy fare.

ITX An ITX, or 'independent inclusive tour excursion', is often available on tickets to popular holiday destinations. Officially it's a package deal combined with hotel accommodation, but many agents will sell you one of these for the flight only and give you phoney hotel vouchers in the unlikely event that you're challenged at the airport.

Lost Tickets If you lose your airline ticket an airline will usually treat it like a travellers cheque and, after inquiries, issue you with another one. Legally, however, an airline is entitled to treat it like cash and if you lose it then it's gone forever. Take good care of your tickets.

MCO An MCO, or 'miscellaneous charge order', is a voucher that looks like an airline ticket but carries no destination or date. It can be exchanged through any International Association of Travel Agents (IATA) airline for a ticket on a specific flight. It's a useful alternative to an onward ticket in those countries that demand one, and is more flexible than an ordinary ticket if you're unsure of your route.

No-Shows No-shows are passengers who fail to show up for their flight. Full-fare passengers who fail to turn up are sometimes entitled to travel on a later flight. The rest are penalised (see Cancellation Penalties).

On Request This is an unconfirmed booking for a flight.

Air Travel Glossary

Onward Tickets An entry requirement for many countries is that you have a ticket out of the country. If you're unsure of your next move, the easiest solution is to buy the cheapest onward ticket to a neighbouring country or a ticket from a reliable airline which can later be refunded if you do not use it.

Open Jaw Tickets These are return tickets where you fly out to one place but return from another. If available, this can save you backtracking to your arrival point.

Overbooking Airlines hate to fly empty seats and since every flight has some passengers who fail to show up, airlines often book more passengers than they have seats. Usually excess passengers make up for the no-shows, but occasionally somebody gets bumped. Guess who it is most likely to be? The passengers who check in late.

Point-to-Point Tickets These are discount tickets that can be bought on some routes in return for passengers waiving their rights to a stopover.

Promotional Fares These are officially discounted fares, available from travel agencies or direct from the airline.

Reconfirmation At least 72 hours prior to departure time of an onward or return flight, you must contact the airline and 'reconfirm' that you intend to be on the flight. If you don't do this the airline can delete your name from the passenger list and you could lose your seat.

Restrictions Discounted tickets often have various restrictions on them – such as needing to be paid for in advance and incurring a penalty to be altered. Others are restrictions on the minimum and maximum period you must be away, such as a minimum of 14 days or a maximum of one year.

Round-the-World Tickets RTW tickets give you a limited period (usually a year) in which to circumnavigate the globe. You can go anywhere the carrying airlines go, as long as you don't backtrack. The number of stopovers or total number of separate flights is decided before you set off and they usually cost a bit more than a basic return flight.

Stand-by This is a discounted ticket where you only fly if there is a seat free at the last moment. Stand-by fares are usually available only on domestic routes.

Travel Agencies Travel agencies vary widely and you should choose one that suits your needs. Some simply handle tours, while full-services agencies handle everything from tours and tickets to car rental and hotel bookings. If all you want is a ticket at the lowest possible price, then go to an agency specialising in discounted tickets.

Transferred Tickets Airline tickets cannot be transferred from one person to another. Travellers sometimes try to sell the return half of their ticket, but officials can ask you to prove that you are the person named on the ticket. This is less likely to happen on domestic flights, but on an international flight tickets are compared with passports.

Travel Periods Ticket prices vary with the time of year. There is a low (off-peak) season and a high (peak) season, and often a low-shoulder season and a high-shoulder season as well. Usually the fare depends on your outward flight – if you depart in the high season and return in the low season, you pay the high-season fare.

Merpati
> (☎ 261238, fax 231962, ☎ 751011 ext 3107 at the airport)
> Jl Melati 57, Denpasar. It's open every day from 8 am to 7 pm. You can normally make bookings for Merpati at any Garuda office.

Sempati
> (☎ 288511 ext 1587)
> Grand Bali Beach Hotel, Sanur

Buying Tickets

Your plane ticket will probably be the single most expensive item in your budget, and buying it can be an intimidating business. It is always worth putting aside a few hours to research the current state of the market.

Types of Tickets There are plenty of discount tickets which are valid for 12 months, allowing multiple stopovers with open dates. These tickets allow for a great deal of flexibility. APEX (Advance Purchase Excursion) tickets are sold at a discount, but will lock you into a rigid schedule. Such tickets must be purchased two or three weeks ahead of departure, do not permit stopovers and may have minimum and maximum stays, as well as fixed departure and return dates. Unless you really have to return at a certain time, it's best to purchase APEX tickets on a one way basis only. There are stiff cancellation fees if you decide not to use your APEX ticket.

Round-the-World (RTW) tickets usually are offered by an airline, or combination of airlines, and let you take your time (six months to a year) moving from point to point on their routes for the price of one ticket. The main restriction is that you have to keep moving in the same direction. One of the drawbacks is that because you are usually booking individual flights as you go, and can't switch carriers, you can get caught out by flight availabilities, and have to spend less or more time in a place than you want.

Shopping Around Start early: some of the cheapest tickets have to be bought months in advance, and some popular flights sell out early. Talk to other recent travellers – they may help you to avoid some of the same old mistakes. Look at the advertisements in newspapers and magazines, consult reference books and watch for special offers.

An increasingly popular and useful way to get information about current flights and fares, and to even book tickets directly with the airlines or travel agencies, is to surf the Internet. Lonely Planet's Web site (www.lonelyplanet.com) is a good place to look for some useful hints from other travellers, as well find links to sites which provide travel details and costs.

After you have shopped around, phone (or email) a few travel agents. (Airlines can supply information on routes and timetables; however, except at times of inter-airline war, they do not normally supply the cheapest tickets.) Find out the fare, the route, the duration of the journey and any restrictions on the ticket. Then sit back and decide which is best for you.

You may discover that those impossibly cheap flights are 'fully booked, but we have another one that costs a bit more ... ' Or the flight is on an airline notorious for its poor safety standards and leaves you in the world's least favourite airport in the middle of the journey for 14 hours. Or they claim to have only two seats left for that country for the whole of July, which 'we will hold for you for a maximum of two hours ... '. Don't panic – keep looking around.

Please use the fares quoted in this book as a guide only. They are the official fares provided by the airlines at the time of research, but you can often find a travel agency which will discount the official fare. Quoted airfares do not necessarily constitute a recommendation for the carrier.

Bucket Shops If you are travelling from the UK or USA, you will probably find that the cheapest flights are being advertised by obscure bucket shops whose names haven't yet reached the telephone directory. Many such firms are honest and solvent, but there are a few rogues who will take your money and disappear. If you are suspicious about a firm, don't give them all the money at once – leave a deposit of 20% or so and pay the balance when you get the ticket. If they insist on cash in advance, go somewhere else. Once you have the ticket, ring the airline to confirm that you are actually booked on the flight.

Travel Agencies You may decide to pay more than the rock-bottom fare by opting for the safety of a better known travel agent. Firms such as STA Travel (which has offices worldwide), Council Travel in the USA, or Travel CUTS in Canada; are not going to disappear overnight, leaving you clutching a receipt for a nonexistent ticket; they all offer good prices to most destinations.

Precautions Once you have your ticket, write the ticket number down, together with the flight number and other details, and keep the information somewhere separate. If the ticket is lost or stolen, this will help you to obtain a replacement.

It's sensible to buy travel insurance as early as possible. If you buy it the week before you fly, you may find, for example, that you're not covered for delays to your flight caused by industrial action, or cancellation costs should you unexpectedly become sick. Refer to the Travel Insurance entry in the Visas & Documents section of the Bali Facts for the Visitor chapter.

Discounts Some airlines offer discounts of up to 25% to student card holders. Apart from an International Student Identity Card (ISIC), an official-looking letter from your university (or college) is also required by some airlines. Many airlines also require you to be aged 26 or under to qualify for a discount. These discounts are generally only available on ordinary economy-class fares. You wouldn't get one, for instance, on an APEX or an RTW ticket since these are already discounted.

Frequent flyer deals are available on many airlines flying to Bali or the general region. If you fly frequently with a particular airline, you may eventually accumulate enough points to qualify for a free ticket or other goodies. If you fly a lot, contact the airlines for information before buying your ticket.

Travelling with Children Children under two years old travel for 10% of the standard fare (or free, on some airlines), as long as they don't occupy a seat. They don't receive a baggage allowance, however. 'Skycots' should be provided by the airline if requested in advance; these will take a child weighing up to about 10kg. Children from two to 12 years old can usually occupy a seat for half to two-thirds of the full fare and do get baggage allowance. Push chairs can often be taken as hand luggage.

Travellers with Special Needs

If you have special needs of any sort –if you have a broken leg, are a vegetarian, are travelling with a baby or are simply terrified of flying – you should let the airline know as soon as possible so they can make arrangements accordingly.

You should remind them when you reconfirm your booking (at least 72 hours prior to departure) and again when you check in at the airport. It may also be worth ringing round the airlines before you make your booking to find out how they can handle your particular needs.

Airports and airlines can be surprisingly helpful, but they do need advance warning. Most international airports will provide escorts from check-in desk to plane where needed, and there should be ramps, lifts, accessible toilets and phones. Aircraft toilets, however, may present a problem; discuss this with the airline at an early stage and, if necessary, with your doctor.

Departure Tax

The departure tax for all domestic flights from Bali is 11,000 rp, and 30,000 rp for all international flights. Only children under two years of age are exempt.

Australia

There are direct flights to Denpasar on Ansett Australia, Merpati, Garuda or Qantas from Sydney, Melbourne, Adelaide, Perth, Brisbane, Cairns, Darwin and Port Hedland. You can fly directly from each city most days, but sometimes the flight will go via one or two of the other cities.

Fares There are three types of discount fares available between Australia and Bali – Inclusive Tour (IT) fares which are only available when purchased as part of a package tour holiday, excursion fares for 35 days maximum stay, and another which allows you to stay up to one year. There are three seasons. Roughly speaking, the high season is around Christmas, shoulder is the school holidays and the low season is the rest of the year. Flights to or from Australia are very heavily booked in the high and shoulder seasons, so you must plan well ahead.

You'll almost certainly be able to get a better price from one of the more competitive travel agents if you shop around. There are a few conditions with these fares, but agents can sometimes get variations. Check city newspapers for special deals, and don't forget you can often get a package tour, including accommodation, for less than the standard excursion fare. The Flight Centre and STA Travel are major dealers in cheap air fares.

The following is a list of the current 35 day, low-season, one way/return fares to Denpasar in Australian dollars. All airlines have identical prices.

City	Cost	Airline(s)
Adelaide	$729/999	Garuda, Qantas
Brisbane	$729/999	Ansett, Garuda Qantas
Cairns	$729/999	Garuda, Qantas
Darwin	$479/749	Ansett, Garuda Qantas
Melbourne	$729/999	Ansett, Garuda Merpati, Qantas
Perth	$509/779	Garuda, Qantas
Pt Hedland	$428/650	Merpati
Sydney	$729/999	Ansett, Garuda Qantas

Via Nusa Tenggara An interesting and potentially cheaper alternative is the Merpati flight for A$244/396 (low season) one way/return from Darwin to Kupang on the island of Timor. From Kupang, there are regular flights to Bali (A$330/550, low season), or you can island hop by ferry through the Nusa Tenggara archipelago to Bali.

Package Tours To get the Inclusive Tour (IT) fare, you must purchase the airfare as part of a package which includes prepaid accommodation. Formerly, it was a requirement that accommodation was booked for each night of your trip, but you may be able to qualify for an IT fare if you book at least some accommodation, and your trip has a prepaid land content which is more than a specified dollar value. This means that you can get the lower fare, a few cheap nights in a resort hotel and still be able to do some independent travelling staying at cheaper places.

For example, package tours from the eastern coast of Australia, including return airfares, airport transfers and six nights' accommodation, cost from A$999 per person twin share in the low season – the same as the normal airfare alone. Children between two and 12 are usually charged 67% of the adult airfare, and their accommodation is usually charged as an addition to the adult price, although sometimes one or two kids are included in the adult package fare. If you travel as a single, you will usually have to pay a 'single supplement' which offsets any potential savings.

The price of a package varies depending on when you go, how long you stay, and what class of hotel you stay in – these are generally in the Kuta region, Sanur, Ubud or Nusa Dua. Costs vary from one operator to another – even on packages using the same hotels. Sightseeing tours and extensions can be made, but a lot of the tours offered can be obtained far more cheaply on Bali.

New Zealand

Garuda, Qantas and Air New Zealand regularly fly between Auckland or Wellington and Denpasar, often via Melbourne, Brisbane or Sydney. Christmas is the high season; other school holidays are shoulder season; and the rest of the year is the low season. As an example, the Garuda fare from Auckland to Denpasar, via Brisbane, costs about NZ$1375 return. Ask your travel agent about holiday package tours. STA Travel and Flight Centres International are popular agents.

The UK & Ireland

Ticket discounting is a long-established business in the UK and it's wide open – the various agencies advertise their fares and there's nothing under the counter about it at all. Trailfinders in west London produces a lavishly illustrated brochure which includes air fare details. STA Travel also has branches in the UK. Also look for ads in the Sunday papers, in *Exchange & Mart* and the free magazines widely available in London.

Most direct flights from London to Indonesia are with Garuda and Qantas. Garuda is an enthusiastic fare discounter in London, but it only has a couple of flights a week to Denpasar, via Jakarta, and they tend to have quite a few stops on the way. Qantas also has flights every day to Jakarta, via Singapore, and connections to Bali on Garuda. Other airlines fly from London to Jakarta, and/or Denpasar, with stopovers in the capital of their country of origin. Singapore Airlines, Thai Airways, Cathay Pacific, Royal Brunei, Aeroflot, KLM and British Airways do this.

A cheaper option is to fly from London to Singapore on any cheap airline, and make your own way to Bali by sea or land. If you're going on to Australia, it's best to get a through ticket with a stopover in Indonesia. Bali and other Indonesian cities can also be included in round-the-world fares.

There are no direct flights between Indonesia and Ireland. You will probably have to get to a connection in the UK.

Europe

Fares from most other European cities are often usually higher than from London; it may even be cheaper to get to the UK and travel from there. Some national carriers only serve Jakarta, but an add-on fare to

Denpasar with Garuda isn't expensive, and there are frequent connections.

France Air France flies the Paris to Jakarta route, with immediate connections to Bali on Garuda, six times a week. Garuda flies also between Denpasar and Paris, but less regularly. The high season is from July to August. Full one way/return fares in the low season for both airlines start at about 4700/8150 FF.

Germany Lufthansa flies from Frankfurt to Jakarta everyday, with connections to Bali on Garuda, for DM1445/2700 one way/return. Garuda also flies from Frankfurt to Denpasar for about the same price. The high season is around Christmas, and the shoulder season from August to December.

Netherlands KLM flies regularly from Amsterdam to Jakarta, via Singapore, and sometimes directly to Denpasar, via Singapore. Garuda also flies to Denpasar, via Jakarta. The high season is July, August, September and mid-December; the rest of the year is the low season. Airfares vary from Nf1100 to Nf1800 (one way), and are about Nf2500 return, depending on the airline and season. Package tours are available for about the same price. NBBS travel agencies are popular, and provide a free magazine listing all the airfares.

The USA

There are good open tickets which remain valid for six months or one year, but don't lock you into any fixed dates of departure. Most of the cheap tickets to Indonesia (either Jakarta or Denpasar), go via Japan, Korea, Singapore, Taiwan or Hong Kong, and will include the country as a stopover (sometimes you have to stop over).

One example of a full fare (ie before they are discounted by travel agents) is on Northwest Airlines: Los Angeles to Singapore, and then Garuda to Denpasar, for US$895/1625 one way/return; the same deal from New York costs US$1090/1925. An interesting option is on Continental Micronesia, which flies from

Hawaii to Denpasar (US$782/1152), via Guam. Garuda also has flights from Los Angeles to Denpasar (US$895/1625), via Honolulu (US$782/1420).

If you are visiting other parts of Asia, some good deals can be put together. For example, there are cheap tickets between the US west coast and Singapore, with stopovers in Bangkok for little extra, but bookings are high during the high season (summer and Chinese New Year).

The *New York Times, LA Times, Chicago Tribune* and *San Francisco Examiner* all produce weekly travel sections in which you'll find any number of travel agents' ads. Council Travel and STA Travel have offices in major cities nationwide. The magazine *Travel Unlimited* (PO Box 1058, Allston, Mass 02134) publishes details of the cheapest airfares and courier possibilities for destinations all over the world from the USA. And don't forget to check out what's advertised on the Internet.

Canada

Getting discount tickets in Canada is much the same as in the USA – go to the travel agents and shop around until you find a good deal. Again, you'll probably have to fly into Hong Kong or Singapore and carry on from there to Indonesia. Otherwise, fly via the US. Travel CUTS has offices in all major cities. The Toronto *Globe & Mail* and the *Vancouver Sun* carry travel agent's ads. The *Great Expeditions* magazine (PO Box 8000-411, Abbotsford, BC V2S 6HI) is also useful.

Asia

The full fares (one way/return) to Denpasar offered by the Asian airlines are listed here; discounts are possible if you shop around.

Hong Kong
    Cathay Pacific flies daily for US$623/919; Garuda costs the same.
Japan
    JAL flies everyday from Tokyo, via Osaka, for US$914/1737. Garuda flights from Tokyo, Fukoka, Nagoya and Osaka are US$914/1355. An interesting option is on Continental Micronesia, which flies from Tokyo, via Guam, for US$400/800.

Malaysia
    Malaysia Airlines flies from Kuala Lumpur about once a day for US$440 return (no one way fares); and from Johor Bahru on Thursday and Sunday for US$249/391. Garuda offers regular flights from KL for US$274/425.
Philippines
    Garuda has flights departing from Manila for US$534/1014.
Singapore
    Garuda flies via Jakarta for US$274/431. Bouraq also flies via Jakarta or Surabaya for a little less. Look around for very cheap one way Singapore-Jakarta flights (especially on Pakistan Air or Air India); from Jakarta – you can then continue overland or by domestic flight to Bali.
South Korea
    Korean Air currently flies from Seoul to Jakarta for US$1205/2290, with connections to Bali, but this flight may soon be cancelled. Garuda charges US$869/1454 to Denpasar.
Thailand
    Thai Airways flies from Bangkok every day for US$342/490; Garuda flies for US$548/715, via Jakarta.

Other Indonesian Islands

Bali is well connected to most of the Indonesian archipelago. The main carrier is Merpati, although Mandala has daily flights to Yogyakarta; Garuda flies many times a day to Jakarta; Sempati and Bouraq have daily flights to Surabaya and Jakarta; and Bouraq also has irregular flights to Waingapu (Sumba), Maumere (Flores) and Kupang (Timor) in Nusa Tenggara.

The prices, which are almost identical for each airline, have increased considerably in recent years, but the flights are still good value. However, as this book was going to press, the Indonesian government increased all internal air fares by 40%. The current schedules and prices are listed in English in the Indonesian-language daily *Bali Post*. Merpati flies most days from Denpasar to the following destinations (the prices listed below are one way fares):

Java
    Jakarta (642,600 rp), Surabaya (262,200 rp) and Yogyakarta (342,300 rp, via Surabaya)
Lombok
    Mataram (119,000 rp), about 10 times a day

Nusa Tenggara
   Bima (383,600 rp, sometimes via Mataram),
   Maumere (633,400 rp), Kupang (644,000 rp)
   and Dili (779,700 rp)
Maluku
   Ambon (958,300 rp)
Sulawesi
   Manado (1,069,600 rp, via Ujung Pandang)

LAND
Public Bus
Of course, you can't actually travel to or
from Bali on a bus, but plenty of buses do
link Bali with the rest of Indonesia by using
the public ferry (the cost of which is always
included in the bus fare).

Java Many buses from numerous bus companies travel every day between the Ubung
terminal in Denpasar and major cities on
Java, but most travel overnight. Fares vary
between operators, and depend on what sort
of comfort you want – a decent seat, and
even air-con, are worth paying extra for.
From Denpasar, the average fare to Surabaya
(10 to 12 hours) is about 32,000 rp; to Yogyakarta it's about 58,000 rp (15 to 16 hours);
and to Jakarta it's about 90,000 rp (26 to 30
hours). Some companies avoid Denpasar altogether, and travel directly between Java
and Padangbai or Singaraja, via Lovina –
refer to the relevant sections for details.

On Bali, you can buy tickets in advance
at travel agencies in the tourist centres for
a little more than the normal price. Alternatively, you can get them directly from the
bus company offices in Denpasar (see the
Getting There & Away section in the Denpasar chapter); or at the Ubung terminal. If
you just turn up at the Ubung terminal, you
will probably get on a bus within an hour or
so, but it's advisable to book at least one
day ahead. You may even be able to squeeze
on a bus waiting at the ferry terminals at
Ketapang or Gilimanuk, but don't count
on it.

Lombok Plenty of public buses also travel
between Denpasar and Mataram. Refer to
the Lombok Getting There & Away chapter
for details.

Tourist Shuttle Bus
A few companies offer more expensive
tourist shuttle buses for routes between Bali
and Surabaya, Yogyakarta and Jakarta – the
Kuta-based company, Perama, has the most
reputable and extensive service. Before you
buy a ticket on Bali, however, make sure
it is a *direct* shuttle bus service, and not just
a shuttle bus to the Ubung terminal in Denpasar, and then a public bus the rest of the
way to Java. Most shuttle buses leave either
Ubung or Kuta, and cost about 45,000 rp
to Surabaya, 65,000 rp to Yogyakarta, and
100,000 rp to Jakarta.

See the Lombok Getting There & Away
chapter for details about tourist shuttle bus
services between Bali and Lombok.

SEA
Java
Ferries travel between Gilimanuk in west
Bali and Ketapang (Java) every 15 to 30
minutes, 24 hours a day. The actual crossing takes under 30 minutes. The fare is
1000/300 rp for adults/children. A bicycle
costs 1400 rp, a motorbike 2700 rp, and car
or jeep 10,550 rp.

From Ketapang, bemos travel 4km north
to the terminal, where buses leave for
Baluran, Probolingo (for Gunung Bromo),
Surabaya, Yogyakarta and Jakarta. There's
a train station near the ferry port, with trains
to Probolingo, Surabaya and Yogyakarta.
The larger town of Banyuwangi is 8km
south, and has another bus terminal with
transport to destinations in south-east Java.

Lombok
Refer to the Lombok Getting There & Away
chapter later in this book for full details about
sea transport between Bali and Lombok.

Other Indonesian Islands
Four ships from the national shipping line,
Pelni, stop at Pelabuhan Benoa port (Bali) as
part of their regular loops throughout Indonesia: *Tatamailau* links Bali with southern
Sulawesi, Maluku and Irian Jaya; *Dobonso-
lo* with Java, Nusa Tenggara, Maluku and

Irian Jaya; and *Awu* and *Tilongkabila* with Nusa Tenggara and southern Sulawesi.

Pelni prices and schedules were in disarray at the time of research. You can enquire and book at the Pelni office (☎ 721377) at Pelabuhan Benoa (on the coast, south of Denpasar) which is open from 8 am to 4 pm Monday to Friday, and from 8 am to 12.30 pm on Saturday; or at the places listed under Boat in the Getting There & Away section of the Denpasar chapter.

ORGANISED TOURS

For information about the advantages and disadvantages of a package tour holiday, refer to the What Kind of Trip? section in the previous Bali Facts for the Visitor chapter, as well as the Air section earlier in this chapter.

Most international travel agents can arrange straight package tours (ie airfare and accommodation) to Bali, but few offer organised tours around the island because most sights can be easily and cheaply seen on day trips from the tourist centres (see Organised Tours in the Bali Getting Around chapter). There are also specialist tours for those interested in specific activities, such as diving, surfing and trekking (see the Bali Facts for the Visitor chapter), as well as cycling (see the Bali Getting Around chapter).

Java

Several companies in the tourist centres on Bali offer organised tours of one, two or three days to Java to see the magnificent Gunung Bromo and Borobudur Buddhist temple near Yogyakarta, with some sightseeing in west Bali en route (if travelling by bus). Prices range from about US$100 to US$200 per person per day, depending on whether you take a private bus or fly.

The shuttle bus company, Perama, offers interesting two-day trips between Bromo and Lovina, or vice versa, for 100,000 rp per person, all inclusive. Spice Island Cruises (☎ 0361-286283, fax 286284) is one of several companies with upmarket cruises to Nusa Tenggara and Komodo from about US$150 per person per night. All of these trips can be booked at any travel agency on Bali.

Lombok

Refer to the Lombok Getting There & Away chapter for details about organised tours from Bali to Lombok and Nusa Tenggara.

Faces of Bali: An elderly man in Ubud (top); and rice harvesters take a break from working the fields (bottom left & right).

Top: Young boys made up for a dance performance in Ubud, Bali.
Middle left: Girls dressed in traditional clothing for Ubud's Full Moon festival.
Bottom left: Rice harvester in the fields outside Ubud.
Right: Proud owner of a prize-winning fighting cock, Bali.

GREGORY ADAMS

ANDREW BROWNBILL

BERNARD NAPTHINE

PAUL BEINSSEN

Getting Around

The main forms of public transport on Bali are the cheap buses, minibuses and bemos that run on more or less set routes within or between towns. If you want your own transport, you can charter a bemo or rent a car, motorbike or bicycle. Tourist shuttle buses, running between the major tourist centres, are more expensive than public transport but are more comfortable and convenient.

BEMO

The main form of public transport on Bali is the *bemo*, a generic term for any vehicle used as public transport, normally a minibus or van with a row of low seats down each side. The word 'bemo' is a contraction of *becak* (a bicycle rickshaw) and *mobil* (a car), but bemos no longer resemble a motorised rickshaw. Apart from the driver, the bemo sometimes has a young guy (let's call him a 'bemo jockey') who touts for passengers, handles the luggage, collects the fare and makes sure the stereo is working (loudly), but jockeys are being phased out in the more populated areas of Bali.

Warning

See the Dangers & Annoyances section in the Bali Facts for the Visitor chapter for information on pickpocketing on public bemos.

Fares

Most bemos operate on a standard route for a set fare. They normally leave when full, and pick up and drop off people and goods anywhere along the way. Unless you get on at a regular starting point, and get off at a regular finishing point, the fares are likely to be fuzzy. The cost per kilometre is pretty variable, but is cheaper on longer trips. The minimum fare is about 400 rp. The fares listed in this book were correct at the time of research, but are likely to increase by the time you clamber on the bemo.

Bemos are justly famous for overcharging tourists, and finding out the 'correct' fare requires local knowledge and subtlety. The best idea is to find out the correct fare *(harga biasa)* from another passenger, and then hand over the fare while you are still in the bemo, so the driver doesn't scuttle off with your change. The whole business of overcharging tourists is a bit of a game; bemo drivers and jockeys are usually good-humoured about it, but some tourists take it very seriously and have unpleasant arguments over a few hundred rupiah.

Sometimes you will be charged extra (perhaps double the passenger price) if you have a big bag. Make sure you know where you're going, and accept that the bemo normally won't leave until it's full and usually takes a roundabout route to collect/deliver as many passengers as possible. One way to hurry up a departure, and make yourself instantly popular with other frustrated passengers, is to fork out a few extra hundred rupiah and pay for the one or more fares that you seem to be waiting for all day. If you get into an empty bemo, always make it clear that you do not want to charter it. (The word 'charter' is understood by all drivers.)

Terminals & Routes

Every town has at least one terminal for all forms of public transport, *terminal bis*. There are often several in larger towns, according to the direction the bus or bemo is heading; eg Denpasar, the hub of Bali's transport system, has four main bus/bemo terminals, as well as stops for local bemos. Terminals can be confusing, but most bemos and buses are signed and, if in doubt, you will be told where to go by a bemo jockey or driver anyway. The terminals often have offices, sometimes with a notice board showing fares to various destinations – this can be helpful, although the fares are often out of date.

To go from one part of Bali to another, it is often necessary to go via one or more of the terminals in Denpasar, or via a terminal in one of the other larger regional towns. For example, by public bemo from Sanur to Ubud, you go to the Kereneng or Tegal terminals in Denpasar, transfer to the Batubulan terminal, and then take a third bemo to Ubud. This is circuitous and time-consuming, so many visitors prefer the tourist shuttle buses (see the Tourist Shuttle bus entry later in this chapter).

Chartering a Bemo

An excellent way for a group or family to travel anywhere around Bali is by chartered bemo. For example, as an alternative to the Sanur-Ubud trip described earlier, you can, with some negotiating, charter a bemo directly to Ubud from Sanur for around 30,000 rp.

The advantages of chartering a bemo (as opposed to renting a vehicle) are: you don't have to worry about a licence or insurance; the driver can be a real asset, particularly if

you're in Denpasar or one of the larger towns and he speaks some English; and you don't have to worry about the horrific traffic.

Public bemos are licensed to work only on set routes, and they cannot legally be chartered for trips away from their standard route, but you can, for example, easily charter a Denpasar-Ubud public bemo to take you anywhere between Denpasar and Ubud. Even if you only want to charter it one way, the driver will happily pick up passengers on the way back. For a public bemo, just go to a bemo terminal, ask around and bargain long and hard.

Only 'charter bemos' with yellow plates are allowed to carry tourists anywhere around Bali. These sort of bemos have conventional seats, rather than benches down each side, and are often air-conditioned – so they are more expensive than public bemos. It's easy to arrange a charter: just listen for one of the frequent offers of 'transport?' in the streets around the tourist centres; approach a driver yourself; or ask at your hotel – every member of staff has a friend or relative working as a bemo or taxi driver.

A public bemo will cost about 70,000 rp per day, and a 'charter bemo' about 90,000 rp – although this depends greatly on the distance and, more importantly, your negotiating skills. If you are planning to start early, finish late and cover an awful lot of territory, then you will have to pay more. Sometimes you will be given a lower rate if you agree to pay for petrol, but this can be difficult to arrange on a fair basis, so it's better to negotiate a fixed price. Although a driver may reasonably ask for an advance for petrol, never pay the full fare until you have returned. For day trips, you will be expected to buy meals for the driver (nasi campur and water is the standard), particularly if you stop to eat yourself.

Don't bother chartering any bemo that hangs around an obvious tourist spot, like an upmarket hotel, because they will blatantly overcharge and are rarely interested in negotiating. The more savvy drivers will try any trick to increase their rates: eg they will claim you must hire the vehicle for a minimum of five hours; your destination is 'very far' (some drivers genuinely think that 100km is a *long* way); and the 'roads are rough' etc etc.

PUBLIC BUS & MINIBUS

Larger minibuses and full-size buses ply the longer routes, particularly across the northern coastal road, and between Denpasar and Singaraja, and Gilimanuk. They operate out of the same terminals as the bemos. Buses are faster than bemos because they do not make as many stops along the way. A bus is also often slightly cheaper than a bemo if you take it for the full trip (eg Singaraja to Denpasar), but it is more expensive if you want to get off halfway. (On a public bus, the Singaraja to Bedugul route often costs the same as Singaraja to Denpasar because they figure you're taking the place of someone who would make the complete trip.)

TOURIST SHUTTLE BUS

Tourist shuttle buses travel between the main tourist centres on Bali. There are three main routes; and they do not go anywhere west of Tabanan or Bedugul.

Kuta-Legian to Ubud, via Sanur.
Kuta-Legian to Lovina via Ubud and Kintamani or Bedugul.
Kuta-Legian to Lovina, via Ubud, Gianyar, Semarapura (Klungkung), Padangbai, Candidasa, Tirta Gangga, Culik (for Amed), Tulamben, Yeh Sanih and Singaraja.

Shuttle buses are more comfortable and reliable than public transport, but are considerably more expensive. They are generally cheaper than chartering a bemo or hiring a car, but if you're travelling in a group of three to five, chartering a bemo will be cheaper per person than taking a shuttle bus, and will give you more flexibility regarding the departure time and route.

Several shuttle bus companies operate out of Kuta-Legian, but the most reliable and established company, with the widest network, is Perama. The head office is in Kuta (☎ 751551, fax 751170, Jl Legian 39)

and it has offices in all the major towns it travels to. Another decent company is Sympatik (☎ 237506), based in Denpasar. Its network is not as extensive as Perama, but Sympatik is usually not as busy (so there's more room on the bus), and some Sympatik buses are more comfortable.

Always try to book a ticket at least one day before you want to leave. You can book at any of the hundreds of travel agents in the tourist centres, but Perama does offer a 10% discount if you buy another ticket with Perama and show your previous ticket at a Perama office when you book. Shuttle buses will normally pick you up outside the travel agent where you booked or another pre-determined spot – or even from outside your hotel if it's convenient to them.

Fares are set by the shuttle bus companies, and are not negotiable, but fares do vary by up to 20% between companies in busy, competitive places like Kuta, Sanur, Ubud and Lovina. Departure times also vary between companies, so it pays to look around. You may be charged an extra 5000 rp for a surfboard.

CAR & MOTORBIKE
Road Rules & Risks

The first rule is: watch your front – it's your responsibility to avoid anything that gets in front of your vehicle. A car, motorbike or anything else pulling out in front of you, in effect, has the right of way. Often drivers won't even look to see what's coming when they turn left at a junction – they listen for the horn. The second rule is: use your horn to warn anything in front that you're there, especially if you're about to overtake. The third rule is: drive on the left side of the road, although it's often a case of driving on whatever side of the road is available, after avoiding the road works, livestock and other vehicles.

Avoid driving at night or at dusk. Many bicycles, carts and other horse-drawn vehicles do not have proper lights, and street lighting is limited to the main towns. It's terrifying to discover that you're about to run up the back of a mobile noodle stand

Road Distances (km)

	Amed	Bangli	Bedugul	Candidasa	Denpasar	Gilimanuk	Kintamani	Kuta	Lovina	Negara	Nusa Dua	Padangbai	Sanur	Semarapura	Singaraja	Tirtagangga	Ubud
Amed	–																
Bangli	59	–															
Bedugul	144	97	–														
Candidasa	32	52	88	–													
Denpasar	98	47	78	72	–												
Gilimanuk	238	181	148	206	134	–											
Kintamani	108	20	89	71	67	135	–										
Kuta	114	57	57	82	10	144	77	–									
Lovina	89	86	41	139	89	79	70	99	–								
Negara	202	135	104	167	95	33	163	104	107	–							
Nusa Dua	122	81	102	96	24	158	91	14	113	109	–						
Padangbai	45	39	75	13	59	219	58	69	126	154	83	–					
Sanur	105	40	85	79	7	141	78	15	96	102	22	78	–				
Semarapura	37	26	61	27	47	181	46	57	112	124	71	14	52	–			
Singaraja	78	75	30	128	78	90	59	88	11	118	92	115	85	105	–		
Tirtagangga	14	65	101	13	84	212	85	95	112	179	108	26	91	44	142	–	
Ubud	68	29	35	54	23	157	29	33	40	120	47	41	30	29	95	67	–

when there are at least three invisible bicycles that you'll hit if you try to avoid it, and the truck behind you is blaring its horn and about to overtake. Riding at dusk offers the unique sensation of numerous insects, large and small, hitting your face at 60 km/h – at least you won't fall asleep.

Car Rental

Car rental is easy on Bali, and a convenient way to get around, but please consider the drawbacks: (a) you are removed from the people and the countryside; (b) you won't want to stop too long in one place, however appealing, if you're paying 70,000 rp or more per day for the car; (c) driving on Bali is potentially very hazardous, and the consequences of an accident can be serious; and (d) the effects on the environment are obvious and severe.

Big international rental operators have a token presence, but they're very expensive and you'll do far better with local compa-

nies. By far the most popular rental vehicle is the small Suzuki Katana or *jimny* – often white with a multi-coloured streak across the side, and obviously rented and driven by foreigners. They are compact, have good ground clearance and the low gear ratio is very well suited to exploring Bali's back roads, although the bench seats at the back are uncomfortable on a long trip. The main alternative is the Toyota Kijang which seats six, but is still economical and lightweight. Automatic transmission is uncommon on rental cars.

Car rental is very expensive compared with public transport, and can cost as much as, or more than, chartering a bemo with a driver, depending on your negotiation skills. A Suzuki jimny jeep costs from 50,000 to 70,000 rp per day, including insurance and unlimited kilometres, but covers only a small amount of petrol (or none at all). A Toyota Kijang costs from 85,000 rp per day, with unlimited kilometres, but normally excluding insurance and petrol. These costs will vary considerably according to demand, the condition of the vehicle, length of hire and your bargaining talents. If you rent a jimny for a week or more you can expect to pay as little as 40,000 rp per day. Many operators advertise on the Internet, and happily charge US$40 or more per day for a jimny. Do not organise any car rentals on the Net, because you will easily be able to rent exactly the same sort of vehicle after you get to Bali for the rupiah equivalent of about US$8.

Rental and travel agencies at all tourist centres will display signs advertising cars for rent; generally, Kuta is the cheapest place. Always shop around for a good deal, and check out the local newspapers and magazines for the latest prices and special deals. Rental cars have to be returned to the place from where they are rented – you can't do a one way rental, but you can often take them to Lombok. It's a good idea to check a rental car carefully before you drive off. Don't wait until you really need the horn, wipers, lights, spare tyre or registration papers before you find they're not there. It's unusual to find a car that has everything working.

All rental vehicles should have registration plates starting with 'RC' (ie 'rental car'); otherwise they are not legally allowed to be rented. If you drive a vehicle without RC plates and the police stop you, it will be inconvenient at best. You also need an International Driving Permit, which you can get from a motoring organisation at home. Driving without a licence could incur a fine of at least 2,000,000 rp, and a *lot* of bureaucratic hassles.

Taking a Car or Motorbike to Lombok

See the Lombok Getting Around chapter for details about taking a car or motorbike across to Lombok from Bali.

Motorbike Rental

Motorbikes are a popular way of getting around Bali. The environmental impact and the cost are much lower than renting a car, but on a motorbike you still won't meet people the way you do on a bemo, and many things can be missed because you are concentrating on the road. Furthermore, motorbikes are a noisy, unpleasant intrusion in many places on Bali. On the other hand, there are now so many Balinese riding motorbikes that the addition of a few hundred more for tourists will hardly add to the problem.

The major advantage is the enormous flexibility. If you're travelling around on a motorbike, it's easy to stop if you want to, and recommence your journey whenever you choose. If you're travelling in a bemo you may just shoot straight by. Even in a car you'll find that it's harder to stop, more difficult to park, harder to reach some places, and just too damn hot outside the air-conditioned interior.

There is no denying the dangers of riding a motorbike on Bali. Combined with all the normal terrors of riding are narrow roads, unexpected potholes, crazy drivers, children darting out in front of you, dogs and chickens running around, unmarked road works, unlit traffic at night, and 1001 other opportunities for you to do serious harm to yourself. Every year a number of visitors to Bali go home in a wheelchair, on crutches, or in a box. Bali is no place to learn to ride a motorbike.

Finding a Motorbike Motorbikes for rent on Bali are almost all between 90cc and 200cc, with 100cc the usual size. You really don't need anything bigger as the distances are short and the roads are rarely suitable for travelling fast. What's the hurry anyway?

Rental charges vary with the bike and the period of rental: that is, the longer the rental period, the lower the rate; and the bigger or newer the bike, the higher the rate. You can expect to pay from around 17,500 rp for a Honda scooter to 25,000 rp for a Yamaha trailbike. This price usually includes 1L of petrol (you pay the rest) and insurance (often with an excess of about US$100).

The majority of bikes are rented out by

individual owners. There are a few places around Kuta-Legian which seem to specialise in motorbike rental, but generally it is travel agencies, restaurants, losmen or shops with a sign advertising 'motorbike for rent'. You can ask around, or if you have an 'I need a motorbike look', somebody will probably approach you. Kuta-Legian is the easiest and cheapest place to rent a motorbike, but you'll have no trouble finding one in Ubud, Sanur, Candidasa or Lovina. Check the bike over before riding off – there are some pieces of junk around.

Motorbike Licence If your International Driving Permit (IDP) is endorsed for motorbikes you have no problems. If not, you should obtain a local motorbike licence, which is valid for three months on Bali, Lombok and Sumbawa. Some rental agencies don't bother asking foreigners about their IDP, and many readers, who have been stopped on a rented motorbike by police, claim that the police are happy with their standard, non-endorsed IDP. While this is a little risky, a fine is still probably cheaper than getting a local motorbike licence. The situation regarding motorbike licences is very unclear, so discuss it with a reputable motorbike rental agency before you drive anywhere.

The cost of a local motorbike licence is a ridiculous 150,000 rp, so most foreigners don't bother getting one. If you want one, the rental agency/owner will take you to the police station in Denpasar. You pay your money and complete a written test in English with multiple-choice answers – the agency/owner will help you with any tricky questions. The whole process can take as little as 20 minutes if the agency/owner has 'friends' at the police station. Dress properly and bring your passport.

Under no circumstances should you drive a motorbike without an IDP. Your insurance company will disown you if you have an accident, and enforcement is strict. The fine for riding without a permit is a minimum of 2,000,000 rp. Some police may let you off with an 'on-the-spot fine' (see the Police

entry later in this section), but don't count on it. They can impound the motorbike and put you in jail until you pay up.

Other Essentials You must carry the bike's registration papers with you while riding. Make sure the agency/owner gives them to you before you ride off.

Helmets are compulsory and the requirement is enforced in tourist areas, but less so in the countryside. You can even be stopped for not having the chin-strap fastened – a favourite of policemen on the lookout for some extra cash. The standard helmets you get with rental bikes are pretty lightweight. If you value your skull, bring a solid helmet from home (but don't leave it lying around on your bike, because it'll get pinched).

Despite the tropical climate, it's still wise to dress properly for motorcycling. Thongs, shorts and a T-shirt are not going to protect your skin from being ground off as you slide along the pavement. As well as protection against a spill, be prepared for the weather. It can get pretty cold on a cloudy day in the mountains. Coming over the top of Gunung Batur you might wish you were wearing gloves. And when it rains on Bali, it really rains, so be ready for that as well. A poncho is handy, but it's best to get off the road and sit out the storm. Your hands, arms and face can get sunburned quickly when riding, so cover up and use a sunblock.

Insurance

Insurance is not obligatory for cars or motorbikes, but rental agencies or owners require it, so if insurance is not included in your rental price and agreement you will have to pay extra. For a motorbike, insurance can be expensive; and for a car, the cost for a single day can run to 25,000 rp (less per day for longer rentals). Whether it actually does you much good if worst comes to worst is not entirely clear.

A typical policy covers the vehicle for a fixed amount, usually the amount shown in a table for a vehicle of the same type and age, plus a fixed amount for damage to other people or their property, ie 'third party' or 'liability' cover. The main concern seems to be insuring the vehicle – a policy might cover the car for 10,000,000 rp, but provide for only 1,000,000 rp third party cover, and you may be liable for an excess of up to US$250 of any claim and any amount above the sum insured. Your travel insurance may provide some additional protection, although liability for motor accidents is specifically excluded from many policies.

The third party cover might seem inadequate, but if you do cause damage or injury, it's usually enough for your consulate to get you out of jail (see the Accidents entry later in this section).

Ensure that your personal travel insurance covers injuries incurred while driving or motorcycling. Some policies specifically exclude coverage for motorbike riding, or have special conditions.

Fuel

Petrol *(bensin)* is sold by the government-owned Pertamina company, and costs 700 rp per litre. Bali has quite a few petrol (gas) stations, but they often seem to be out of petrol, out of electricity or simply on holiday. In that case look for the little road-side fuel shops that fill your tank from a plastic container with a funnel for about 50 rp over the official price. Petrol pumps usually have a meter which records the litres and a table which shows how much to pay for various amounts, but cheating does occur. Make sure the pump is reset to zero before the attendant starts to put petrol in your vehicle, and check the total amount that goes in before the pump is reset for the next customer. Ensure the amount you are charged is consistent with the capacity of your tank and that the arithmetic is accurate.

Roads

Once you've cleared the southern Bali traffic tangle, the roads are relatively uncrowded. The traffic is heaviest between Denpasar and Kuta and Sanur; as far as Semarapura to the east; to Tabanan in the west; and along the Denpasar-Ubud road. Finding your way around is not difficult: roads are well sign-

posted and maps are easy to find (see the Maps entry in the Planning section of the Bali Facts for the Visitor chapter). Off the main routes, roads often become very pot-holed, but they are usually surfaced – there are few dirt roads on Bali. And always be careful of the infuriating one way streets in major towns, especially Kuta and Ubud.

Accidents

The best advice is: don't have an accident, but remember if you do that it will be considered your fault. The logic behind this is Asian and impeccable: 'I was involved in an accident with you. I belong here, you don't. If you hadn't been here, there would not have been an accident. Therefore it is your fault'.

It is not unusual for a foreign driver to be roughed up by aggrieved locals after an accident, or for them to demand immediate promises of compensation. The incident may be seen as a once-in-a-lifetime chance to get some big money. In these circumstances it is essential to keep a cool head and avoid being pressured into an admission or commitment.

If you are involved in a serious accident (such as one involving death or injury), insist that the police come as soon as possible and have someone you trust contact your consulate. If you concede liability, it could invalidate both your travel insurance policy and the policy you took out when you rented the vehicle. If your vehicle is still going, it may be advisable to drive it straight to the nearest police station, rather than stopping at the scene and risking a violent confrontation. The police are unlikely to take your side, but at least they will ensure that formalities are complied with and excessive reactions are moderated. It is likely that they will impound your vehicle, and they may even detain you in jail until the matter is sorted out. You will be safe there, and any settlement should be official enough to satisfy your insurance company.

With evidence of insurance, your consulate can usually persuade the police that the insurance company will provide restitution, the driver can be released from jail and the details can be sorted later with the insurance company. Without insurance, there will probably have to be some agreement and payment before they let you go.

If it's a minor accident (property damage only), it may be better to negotiate a settlement directly, rather than spend some days hassling with police, lawyers, insurance companies and so on. Try to delay matters a little, so you can recover from the shock, get someone with local knowledge whom you trust to advise you, and perhaps contact your consulate and/or a lawyer.

Police

Police will stop drivers on some very slender pretexts, and it's fair to say that they're not motivated by a desire to enhance road safety. If a cop sees your front wheel half an inch over the faded line at a stop sign, if the chin strap of your helmet isn't fastened, or if you don't observe one of the ever-changing and poorly signposted one way traffic restrictions, you may be waved down. They also do spot checks of licences and vehicle registrations, especially before major holidays.

The cop will want to see your licence and the vehicle's registration papers, and he will tell you what a serious offence you've committed. He may start talking about court appearances, heavy fines and long delays. Stay cool and don't argue. Do not offer him a bribe. Eventually he may suggest that you can pay him some amount of money to deal with the matter. If it's a very large amount, tell him politely that you don't have that much with you. These matters can usually be settled for something between 20,000 and 50,000 rp, although it will be more like 100,000 rp if you don't have an International Driving Permit (IDP). Always make sure you have the correct papers, and don't have too much visible cash in your wallet.

OJEK

Around some major towns, and along roads where bemos rarely or never venture, locals use the unusual form of transport known as an *ojek*. This is where you sit on the back of a motorbike and hang on for dear life, while the driver weaves around trucks and buses. Actually, it's not *that* scary if you use ojeks on quiet country roads, but they are not recommended in the big towns. The fare is negotiable, but about 1000 rp for 5km is fairly standard. They can even carry your luggage, although not securely.

If you hire an ojek for a few hours, the driver may want you to take out insurance against any damage to you in case of accident. He will arrange this, give you the receipt, and charge you extra – about 500 rp per day.

BICYCLE

At times, having a bike on Bali was a bit of a hassle, but all in all it was well worth the experience; a much more intimate means of transport than a bemo.

Eriko Taninoto & Jason Creek, UK

Seeing Bali by pushbike has become very popular in recent years, and the quality of rental bikes has really improved, at least from some outlets. More places are renting bikes and more visitors are bringing bikes with them. Mountain bikes are the most common type, and with their low gear ratios and softer tyres they are much better suited to Bali than 10 speed touring bikes. You can usually bring your pushbike with you in your baggage – some airlines, including Garuda and Qantas, will carry it free.

Bali may not seem like a place for a bicycle tour, with its tropical heat, heavy traffic, frequent rain showers and high mountains. However, the breeze as you ride on the level or downhill really moderates the heat, and once you're out of the congested southern region the traffic is relatively light. The roads are pretty good and frequent roadside food stalls make it easy to duck out of a passing rain shower, and to stock up on 'fuel' (ie food and water). Multi-gear mountain bikes make it possible to get up the higher mountains, but with a bit of negotiating and patience, you can get a public bemo to take you and your bike up the steepest sections.

continued on page 164

BALI BY BICYCLE – A 200KM TOUR

This route is designed to take in the greatest number of points of interest with the minimum use of motorised transport and the maximum amount of level or downhill roads. The tour involves six days riding in a clockwise direction. Evening stops have been planned where there are convenient losmen. The minimum daily distance is about 24km; the maximum is 60km, but 20 to 30km of this distance can usually be covered by bemo. The total distance varies depending on the length of the detours and the bemo legs. There are lots of possible detours, so it can easily evolve into a two week trip. The trip can also be done in an anticlockwise direction.

Day 1 – Kuta to Candikuning *60km (37km by bicycle), riding time seven hours*
Ride north along Jl Legian and continue to Sempidi, on the junction with the Denpasar to Gilimanuk road. At low tide you can do the first 7km north along the beach, turning inland at the Oberoi Hotel and up the main road to Sempidi. From there, go to Mengwi and turn north for about 15km to Luwus. Try to catch a bemo to Bedugul (it's a 700m rise over 16km). You can stay at Bedugul, but there are better places around Candikuning to the north.

Day 2 – Candikuning to Singaraja *30km, three hours*
Before continuing north, have a look at Pura Ulun Danu Bratan, the famous temple in the lake. From the lake, the road goes up and down hills for several kilometres, then there is a steep 1.5km ascent to a 1400m pass and a steep 15km descent to Singaraja. An interesting stop is at Gitgit, where a 15 minute walk through souvenir stalls brings you to a pretty waterfall. You can stay in Singaraja or detour west to the beach strip around Lovina (7 to 13km from Singaraja) – you'll have to backtrack the next day, but at least it's flat.

Day 3 – Singaraja to Penelokan *58km (12km to Kubutambahan, 36km to Penulisan by bemo and the final 10km by bike)*
Ride 12km east of Singaraja to Kubutambahan where there is a turn-off south to Kintamani and Gunung Batur. It's a very steep 36km uphill from to Penulisan, so try to catch a bemo. If cycling, take plenty of water. Penulisan is the highest point on the ride and it's an easy descent (but there's plenty of traffic) from there to Kintamani (4km) or Penelokan (10km). You can make a good detour down the winding road to Danau Batur, and around the lake's north shore to Toya Bungkah where there are many hotels. From Penelokan there

are at least five routes down the slopes of Gunung Batur back to Denpasar. Listed here is the route via Semarapura, with a side trip to the temple at Besakih. Two alternative routes are listed in the following section – they lead either to the Ubud area or Bangli.

Day 4 – Penelokan to Semarapura *31km (excluding Besakih), four hours*

Leaving Penlokan on the main road, ride for about 500m and turn left onto a narrow uphill road (see the Gunung Batur map in the Central Mountains chapter). If you reach a fork in the main road with a sign for Denpasar and Bangli, you've gone too far – turn around and look again. The road traverses small hills as it heads east along the southern rim of the crater, with lovely views of Gunung Batur and the lake. Approximately 4km along the road is a dip with a sign 'Menanga'. Turn right and continue downhill to Rendang with fine views of Gunung Agung all the way. Rendang is the turn-off for Pura Besakih, Bali's mother temple.

From Rendang to Besakih is 6km, mostly uphill. There's a 500m rise in 8km. Consider leaving your bike at the crossroads and taking a bemo both ways, or putting the bike in a bemo going up and having a nice ride down. The stretch from Rendang to Semarapura, a gradual downhill ride of 12km, is one of the most pleasant trips on Bali.

Day 5 – Semarapura to Denpasar *40km, six hours*

The entire road is well surfaced, but traffic is quite heavy. Although there is a total descent of 70m, the road crosses several lush river gorges, resulting in some uphill walking and downhill gliding. Main places of interest along the way are Gianyar (local weaving industry), Batuan (painting and weaving), Celuk (wood-carving and silver-smithing) and Batubulan (stone sculpture).

Day 6 – Denpasar to Kuta (via Sanur) *24km, five hours*

Head east on Jl Gajah Mada, the main street of Denpasar (see the Denpasar map in the Denpasar chapter), and continue for 6km to Sanur. From Sanur the big Jl Bypass runs about 8km to the turn-off south to the Pelabuhan Benoa

CYCLING ROUTES

causeway – a possible detour. The old Sanur to Kuta road runs parallel to the new highway, and is much quieter and more pleasant on a bike. You eventually emerge on the main Kuta to Denpasar road next to a petrol station. You have completed the 200km round trip and are back where you started. Congratulations!

Alternative Routes from Penelokan to Denpasar

On the fourth day of the circle tour, you have a choice of routes from Penelokan back to Denpasar. As alternatives to Semarapura, you can go via either Ubud or Bangli. The Ubud route is:

Penelokan to Ubud (via Tampaksiring) 35km, five hours

About 500m east of Penelokan the road forks. Take the right fork marked 'Denpasar' and 9km later you're in the small junction town of Kayuambua. The road continues for 8km to Tampaksiring, running down verdant volcano slopes past fields of banana, sweet potato and corn, all partially obscured by groves of bamboo. As you approach Tampaksiring, the temple and holy spring of Tirta Empul are on the right. Another 1km down from Tirta Empul is the turn-off to the 11th century rock-face memorials at Gunung Kawi, about 1km east of the main road. Back on the road it's an easy 10km downhill ride to the interesting villages of Bedulu and Pejeng. Turn right at the Bedulu junction and half a kilometre along the road is the Goa Gajah (Elephant Cave). Then it's on to Peliatan and Ubud.

Ubud to Denpasar 26km, four hours

There are several ways down to Kuta from the Ubud area. Heading straight south for 4km, the road passes through Mas, Batuan and Celuk, all known for various crafts. From Batuan to Denpasar (16km) there are many trucks, bemos and cars competing for road space, which makes that part of the trip mentally exhausting.

An interesting alternative is the quieter back road via Sibang. Apart from the early stages, which require some uphill walking, it's an easy descent with little traffic until you are in Denpasar proper. From Denpasar to Kuta you can go via Sanur (described in the Day 6 section of the Bali By Bicycle tour), or the direct route down Jl Iman Bonjol.

Alternatively, you can go via Bangli:

Penelokan to Bangli 20km, three hours

At the fork in the road 500m south of Penelokan, take the road marked 'Bangli' and head south. Bangli has an important temple, and a few places to stay. Continue south from Bangli and you join the Semarapura to Denpasar route about 26km from Denpasar.

continued from page 160

The main advantage of seeing Bali by bicycle is the quality of the experience. By bicycle you can be totally immersed in the environment – you can hear the wind rustling in the rice paddies and the sound of a gamelan orchestra practising, and catch the scent of the flowers. Even in the highly touristed Bali of the late 1990s, cycle tourers on the back roads still experience the unhassled friendliness which seems all but lost on the tourist circuit.

Rental & Purchase

There are plenty of bicycles for rent in Kuta-Legian, Sanur and Ubud, but you cannot always rent them for any long distances. Not that you would want to anyway: many are in poor condition – common problems include worn tyres, chains which break, ineffective brakes, stiff gear changes, terrible seats, no reflectors, no bell and no lights. Because so many foreigners find it very cheap to rent cars and motorbikes, the rental price for bicycles is still about 5000 rp per day. Refer to the earlier Car & Motorbike section for some idea of what to expect on the roads.

Some bike rental places are amenable to special arrangements, such as selling you a bike and then buying it back at the end of your trip. If you want to buy a bicycle, 15 speed mountain bikes are becoming quite common, with the best range in Ubud.

Touring

For touring it is absolutely essential that your bike is in good repair.

Brakes Both the front and rear brakes must be able to stop your bike individually, in case one malfunctions on a steep downhill stretch. Check the brake blocks to see that they are symmetrically positioned and show even wear with plenty of rubber left. They should not rub any part of the rim when you spin the wheel. The real test is whether or not they can hold the bike still when clamped while you push forward with all your strength. If in doubt, buy new brake blocks. Do not go into the central mountains without good brakes.

Wheels & Tyres Turn the bike upside down and spin the wheels. Check the rims carefully for deep rust spots which could cause the wheel to buckle under stress. Look at the rim as it moves by the brake blocks. If the wheel wobbles you will have shimmying problems. Also squeeze the spokes to check for loose or broken ones. Avoid bikes with bald or soft tyres. The shop will pump them up once, but you'll have to do it every day after that.

Bell, Light & Back Reflector A bell and a light are very useful, so make sure both are in working order. The bell should be positioned so it can be used with your hand still gripping the brake. A new back reflector is a good investment if there isn't one on the bike.

Seat Consider buying a new, soft, padded seat, or a tie-on foam seat cover. Have the seat adjusted so that when you are sitting on it you can straighten your leg fully to touch the lower pedal with your heel. If you are very tall, buy an extra long pipe to raise the seat.

Other Accessories A carrier rack over the rear mudguard is ideal for carrying a small bag. One or two elastic shock cords with hooks at each end will secure it. A sturdy steel cable lock is worthwhile. A helmet protects against sunburn as well as concussion.

Lightly oil all moving parts, including the crankshaft and chain. Check to see if all the nuts are securely tightened, especially those to the seat, the brake linkage cables and the brake rims, which tend to vibrate loose. Even the smallest village has some semblance of a bike shop – a flat tyre should cost about 1000 rp to fix. Denpasar has a number of shops selling spare parts and complete bicycles – look along Jl Kartini. For details on a 200km-long bicycle tour through central and east Bali, see the section 'Bali By Bicycle' in this chapter.

HITCHING

You can hitchhike on Bali, but it's not a very useful option for getting around as public transport is so cheap and frequent, and private vehicles are relatively uncommon. If you are standing by the side of the road, waving down vehicles, about the only thing that will stop is a public bus or bemo – for which you will have to pay the normal price.

Bear in mind, also, that hitching is never entirely safe in any country and we don't recommend it. Travellers who decide to hitch should understand that they are taking a small but potentially serious risk. People who do choose to hitch will be safer if they travel in pairs and let someone know where they plan to go.

WALKING

Bali is ideal for some leisurely walking between villages, up mountains and across rice fields. The Trekking section in the earlier Bali Facts for the Visitor chapter has more information.

BOAT

Small boats go to a number of islands around Bali, notably those in the Nusa Penida group. Usually they will pull up to a beach, and you have to wade to and from the boat with your luggage and clamber aboard over the stern. It's difficult with a heavy pack, and you might consider wrapping items like cameras in waterproof bags. You, and your luggage, may also be drenched by spray if the water is rough. Life jackets are not usually provided and safety standards may not satisfy everyone. Details of boat services are given in the relevant chapters.

LOCAL TRANSPORT
Bemos

Bemos cover various local routes in most urban areas, and they're cheap (from about 400 rp), but not quick because they often have to fill up before they go anywhere, and they regularly take detours to collect or drop off passengers.

Dokars

Small pony carts known as a *dokar* provide local transport in some remote areas, and even in central Kuta at night, but they're slow and not particularly cheap. Prices are very negotiable, and depend on demand, number of passengers, your bargaining skills and any nearby competition. A dokar driver will often overcharge tourists as he thinks the tourist will be happy to pay an exorbitant amount for the novelty value. The best idea is to find out what the other passengers are paying.

Taxi

Metered taxis are common in Denpasar and the tourist areas of south Bali. They are a lot less hassle than haggling with bemo drivers, but dearer, of course. You can always find a taxi at the airport, and you will hear them beep their horns at you if you walk anywhere around a tourist centre. Don't get in a taxi if the driver says the meter isn't working – it may suddenly 'fix' itself, but if not, get another taxi. The costs of metered taxis were unclear at the time of research, but are cheap for short trips.

ORGANISED TOURS

Many travellers end up taking one or two organised tours because it can be such a quick, convenient and cheap way to visit a few places, especially where public transport is limited (eg Pura Besakih) or nonexistent (eg Tanah Lot after sunset). All sorts of tours are available from the tourist centres – the posh hotels can arrange expensive day tours for their guests, while tour companies along the main streets in the tourist centres advertise cheaper trips for those on a budget.

There is an extraordinarily wide range of prices, from 45,000 rp to US$60 per person for basically the same sort of tour. The cheaper ones may have less comfortable vehicles, less qualified guides and be less organised, but the savings can be considerable. Higher priced tours may include a buffet lunch, an English-speaking guide and air-conditioning, but generally a higher price is no guarantee of higher quality. Some tours make long stops at craft shops, so you can buy things and earn commissions for the tour operator. Tours are typically in an eight to 12 seat minibus, or jeep which picks you up, and drops you off, at a major hotel or pre-determined place.

Some agencies also arrange more specialised trips, such as diving trips to Pulau Menjangan, or cultural trips to Tenganan village. All tours can be booked at a travel agency or, more usually, at a hotel in a tourist centre. But remember: if you can get together a group of four or more, most tour agencies will arrange a tour to suit you; or you can easily create your own tour by chartering or renting a vehicle. The prices listed here will have inevitably increased by the time you book a tour.

Day Tours

You can take any of the organised tours listed below from Kuta-Legian, Sanur, Nusa Dua, Candidasa or Ubud for about the same price. The Lovina section in the North Bali chapter lists some tours around more remote areas in northern Bali.

Denpasar Tour (four hours)
    Takes in the arts centre, markets, museum and perhaps a temple or two (from 20,000 rp per person).
Sunset Tour (four hours)
    Includes Mengwi, Marga, Alas Kedaton and the sunset at Tanah Lot (from 25,000 rp).
Singaraja-Lovina Tour (eight hours)
    Goes to Mengwi, Bedugul, Gitgit, Singaraja, Lovina, Banjar and Pupuan (from 35,000 rp).
Kintamani-Gunung Batur Tour (eight hours)
    Takes in the craft shops at Celuk, Mas and Batuan, a dance at Batubulan, Tampaksiring and views of Gunung Batur. Alternatively, the tour goes to Goa Gajah, Pejeng, Tampaksiring and Kintamani (from 40,000 rp).
Besakih Tour (eight hours)
    Includes craft shops at Celuk, Mas and Batuan,

Gianyar, Semarapura (Klungkung), Bukit Jambal, Pura Besakih, and return via Bangli or Goa Lawah, near Padangbai (from 40,000 rp). Alternatively, the tour may stop at Tenganan, Tirta Gangga and Candidasa (from about 35,000 rp).
Bedugul Tour (eight hours)
    Includes Sangeh or Alas Kedaton, Mengwi, Bedugul, Candikuning and sunset at Tanah Lot (from 35,000 rp).

Other Tours

Some tour agencies also offer one night/two day organised tours skipping through most of Bali from about 100,000 rp per person. From south Bali, you can get on an organised, all-inclusive tour to the Taman Burung Bali Bird Park, or other attractions such as traditional dances in the evenings. Possible special interest tours for diving, surfing and other activities are discussed in the earlier Bali Facts for the Visitor chapter. The best idea is to visit a few travel agencies, pick up a handful of brochures and spend some time choosing what will suit you best.

Also, some agencies arrange ad hoc trips to see cremation ceremonies and special temple festivals. It may seem in poor taste to boldly advertise for paying visits to a cremation, but good tour companies are sensitive about these occasions, and will ensure that their participants dress and behave appropriately. An organised tour can cost from 20,000 rp to US$14 per person, depending on the agency.

Denpasar

Highlights

- Museum Negeri Propinsi Bali is an interesting museum with a collection of traditional paintings, masks, woodcarvings and dance costumes in buildings representing regional palace styles.

- Pura Jagatnatha is Bali's state temple, and the site of regular festivals featuring wayang kulit shadow puppet plays.

- Taman Wedhi Budaya Arts Centre is an academy and showplace for Balinese culture with nightly Kecak dances, occasional exhibits of traditional and modern art, and the annual Bali Arts Festival.

Denpasar (population about 400,000) is the capital of Bali. It has been the focus of a lot of the island's growth and wealth over the last 25 years, and has much of the bustle and congestion of many fast-growing cities in Asia. There are still tree-lined streets and some pleasant gardens, but the traffic, noise and pollution can make it difficult to enjoy. The main attractions are the museum and the shops and markets, but many visitors find it more comfortable and convenient to stay in Kuta-Legian, Sanur or Ubud, and visit Denpasar as a day trip. Denpasar might not be a tropical paradise, but it's as much a part of 'the real Bali' as the rice paddies and temples around the island.

HISTORY

Denpasar, which means 'next to the market', was an important trading centre, and the seat of local rajahs before the colonial period. The Dutch gained control of northern Bali in the mid-19th century, but their takeover of the south didn't start until 1906. The Dutch attacked at Sanur, and the Balinese retreated to Denpasar. There, under the threat of Dutch artillery, three princes of the kingdom of Badung destroyed their own palaces and made a suicidal last stand – a ritual *puputan* in which the old kingdoms of the south were wiped out.

Singaraja remained the Dutch administrative capital, but a new airport was built in the south. This made Denpasar a strategic asset in WWII, and the Japanese invaded and used it as a springboard to attack Java. After the war, the Dutch moved their headquarters to Denpasar, and in 1958 the city became the official capital of the province of Bali. Formerly a part of Badung district, Denpasar is now a self-governing municipality, which includes Sanur, Pelabuhan Benoa and Pulau Serangan (all of which are covered in the South Bali chapter).

Many of Denpasar's residents are descended from immigrant groups, such as Bugis mercenaries (from Sulawesi) and Chinese, Arab and Indian traders. More recent immigrants, including civil servants, artisans, business people and labourers, come from Java and all over Indonesia, attracted by the opportunities in the growing Balinese capital. Recent immigrants tend to live in detached houses or small apartments, but the Balinese communities still maintain their traditions and family compounds, even as their villages are engulfed by an expanding conurbation.

ORIENTATION

The main road, Jl Gunung Agung, starts at the west side of town. It changes to Jl Gajah Mada in the middle of town, then Jl Surapati and finally Jl Hayam Wuruk. One infuriating aspect of visiting (and driving around) Denpasar is that the names of roads regularly change, often every time they cross another road.

Another problem is the proliferation of one way traffic restrictions, sometimes for only part of a street's length, which often change and are rarely marked on any maps.

DENPASAR

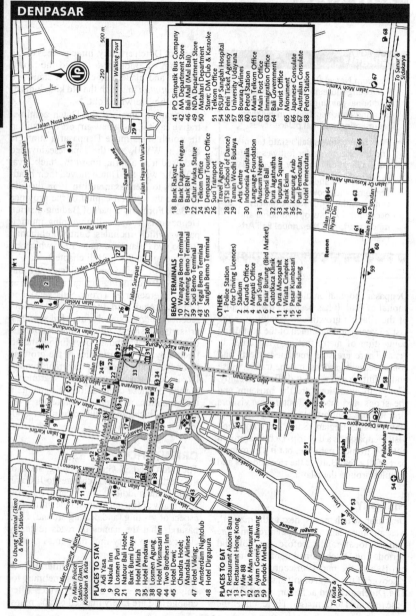

Walking Tour

0   250   500 m

BEMO TERMINALS
10 Wangaya Bemo Terminal
27 Kereneng Bemo Terminal
39 Suci Bemo Terminal
43 Tegal Bemo Terminal
55 Sanglah Bemo Terminal

OTHER
1   Police Station
    (for Driving Licences)
2   Stadium
3   Garuda Office
4   Merpati Office
5   Pasar Burung (Bird Market)
6   Gatotkaca Klinik
11 Pura Maospahit
14 Wisata Cineplex
15 Pasar Kumbasari
16 Pasar Badung
18 Bank Rakyat;
    Bank Dagang Negara
19 Bank BNI
22 Catur Muka Statue
24 Telkom Office
25 Denpasar Tourist Office
26 Suci Transport
    Travel Agency
28 STSI (School of Dance)
29 Taman Wedhi Budaya
    Arts Centre
30 Indonesia Australia
    Language Foundation
31 Museum Negeri
    Propinsi Bali
32 Pura Jagatnatha
33 Puputan Square
34 Bank Exim
36 Kampung Arab
37 Puri Pemecutan;
    Hotel Pemecutan
41 PO Simpatik Bus Company
42 MA Department Store
46 Bali Mall (Mal Bali)
49 NDA Department Store
50 Matahari Department Store;
    DM Club & Karaoke
51 Telkom Office
54 RSUP Sanglah Hospital
56 Pelni Ticket Agency
57 University Udayana
58 Bouraq Airlines
60 Petrol Station
61 Main Telkom Office
62 Main Post Office
63 Immigration Office
64 Government
    Tourist Office
65 Monument
66 Japanese Consulate
67 Australian Consulate
68 Petrol Station

PLACES TO STAY
8   Adi Yasa
9   Nakula Inn
20 Losmen Puri
21 Natour Bali Hotel;
    Bank Bumi Daya
23 Hotel Mirah
35 Hotel Pendawa
38 Losmen Agung
40 Hotel Wismasari Inn
44 Two Brothers Inn
45 Hotel Dewi;
    Chandra Hotel;
    Mandala Airlines
47 Hotel Viking;
    Amsterdam Nightclub
48 Hotel Dirgapura

PLACES TO EAT
12 Restaurant Atoom Baru
13 Restaurant Hong Kong
17 Mie 88
53 Kak Man Restaurant
53 Ayam Goreng Taliwang
59 Pondok Melati

The traffic jams can be intense and parking can be difficult, so avoid driving in Denpasar if you can. If you have rented a vehicle, think about parking it outside of town, or leaving it in Kuta or Sanur, and using taxis, bemos and your feet around Denpasar. The city is pretty flat, so a bicycle would be good – if you could survive the traffic.

In contrast to the rest of Denpasar, the Renon area, south-east of the town centre, is laid out on a grand scale, with wide streets, large car parks and huge landscaped blocks of land. This is the area of government offices, many of which are impressive structures, built with lavish budgets in modern Balinese style.

Maps

The map in this guidebook will be enough for most visitors, although the *Map of Denpasar* provided free by the Denpasar Tourist Office is also useful. If you are crazy enough to drive around Denpasar, you should pick up the *Kodya Denpasar & Kuta* map (6900 rp), available from the Gramedia Book Shop in Denpasar (see the Bookshops entry in the following information section).

INFORMATION
Tourist Offices

The Denpasar Tourist Office (☎ 234569, fax 223602) on Jl Surapati deals with tourism in the Denpasar municipality, which includes Sanur. It offers (free) copies of the valuable *Calendar of Events* booklet, which is relevant for all of Bali; the interesting *Bali Kini* tourist magazine; and the handy *Discover Denpasar* brochure. The office is open Monday to Thursday from 7 am to 2 pm, on Friday until 11 am, and on Saturday until 12.30 pm. If you want information about other places on Bali, go to the other tourist offices in Ubud, Kuta and so on.

Bali's Regional Department of Tourism, Post and Telecommunications (☎ 222387, fax 226313) in Renon is mainly a bureaucratic facility, but if you go to the back of the main building, staff happily hand out a few brochures and maps. It's not worth the trek out to Renon, however, unless you want

to make a complaint. It has the same opening hours as the Denpasar Tourist Office.

Foreign Consulates

The Australian and Japanese consulates can be found in Renon. For a list of other consulates in Bali, and embassies in Jakarta, refer to the Bali Facts for the Visitor chapter.

Money

All major Indonesian banks have offices in Denpasar, and most are located around the corner of Jl Gajah Mada and Jl Arjuna. Bank Exim, on the corner of Jl Hasanudin and Jl Udayana, is one of the best for changing money, and arranging overseas transfers. The rates offered by the moneychangers along the northern end of Jl Diponegoro are better than the banks, but not as good as Kuta. ATMs that accept foreign credit cards can be found at Bank BNI, and at other banks in the immediate vicinity, as well as a building next to the Garuda Airlines office.

Post

The main post office (☎ 223565) has the poste restante service and is inconveniently located in Renon, but is open from 8 am to 8 pm. The post offices in Kuta or Ubud are much more convenient places to send or receive mail.

Telephone

The main Telkom office is also inconveniently located in Renon, but there are *wartels* (telephone offices) all over town. For telephone calls and faxes, the smaller Telkom offices just north of the Denpasar Tourist Office, and along Jl Teuku Umar (further south) are handy. The Denpasar Tourist Office has a Home Country Direct Dial telephone. There are no Internet centres in the city, so you'll have to go to Kuta, Sanur or Ubud.

Travel Agencies

Denpasar is not really set up for tourists. Travel agencies, especially those that congregate around northern Jl Diponegoro, just sell air, boat and bus tickets (refer to the

Getting There & Away section later in this chapter for more details). To book a bungee jump or sunset cruise, contact a travel agent in a tourist centre such as Kuta.

Bookshops

One of the best bookshops on Bali is the Gramedia Book Shop in the basement of the Matahari Department Store on Jl Teuku Umar. It has a large range of expensive souvenir books about Bali in English, French, German and Japanese; and a range of useful maps of Bali, Lombok and Indonesia.

Medical Services

If you must get sick or injured, do it in Denpasar. The city's main hospital, Rumah Sakit Umum Propinsi (RSUP) Sanglah (☎ 227912/5) is open 24 hours, has English-speaking staff, and is regarded by expats as the best on the island.

There are three private medical practices that deal with foreigners: Surya Husadha Clinic (☎ 233786/7) on Jl Pulau Serangan 1-3, just south of RSUP Sanglah; Gatotka-ca Klinik (☎ 223555) on Jl Gatotkaca; and Manuaba Clinic (☎ 426393) on Jl Cokroaminoto.

The ambulance number is ☎ 118. There are plenty of pharmacies around town.

Emergency

The general police emergency number is ☎ 110. For a motorbike licence (see the Bali Getting Around chapter), or to make any general complaint, contact the police station (☎ 228690) on Jl Pattimura. There is no reason to visit the main police station (☎ 424346) along Jl Sangian, about 4km west of Puputan Square.

WALKING TOUR

This walk includes most of the attractions in the middle of town. If you stop at all the sights, it shouldn't take more than two or three hours.

Starting at the Denpasar Tourist Office, head south to the state temple, **Pura Jagatnatha**, and the adjacent **museum**. Opposite the museum is **Puputan Square**, a park which commemorates the heroic but suicidal stand of the rajahs of Badung against the invading Dutch in 1906. A monument depicts a Balinese man, woman and two children in heroic pose, brandishing the weapons which were so ineffective against the Dutch guns. The woman also has jewels in her left hand, as the women of the Badung court reputedly flung their jewellery at the Dutch soldiers to taunt them. The park is popular with locals at lunch time and the early evening.

Back on Jl Surapati, at the intersection with Jl Veteran, is the towering **Catur Muka** statue, which represents Batara Guru, Lord of the Four Directions. The four-faced, eight-armed figure keeps a close eye (or is it eight eyes?) on the traffic swirling around him. From here, take a detour up Jl Veteran to visit the **Pasar Burung** market (see the Shopping section later in this chapter). Behind the market is the interesting **Puri Sutriya** temple, which no-one seems to know, or care, much about.

Head back to Jl Gajah Mada (named after the 14th century Majapahit prime minister) and go west, past banks, shops and restaurants to the bridge over the unattractive Sungai Badung (Badung River). Just before the bridge, on the left, is the **Pasar Badung** (see the Shopping section later in this chapter for information about this market).

At the next main intersection, detour north up Jl Sutomo, and turn left along a small *gang* (lane) leading to the **Pura Maospahit** temple. Established in the 14th century, at the time the Majapahits arrived from Java, the temple was damaged in a 1917 earthquake and has been heavily restored since. The oldest structures are at the back of the temple, but the most interesting features are the large statues of Garuda and the giant Batara Bayu.

Turn back, and continue south along Jl Thamrin to the junction of Jl Hasanudin. On this corner is the **Puri Pemecutan**, a palace destroyed during the 1906 invasion. It has been rebuilt and now operates as a hotel (see Places to Stay later in this chapter), but you can still wander around.

East along Jl Hasanudin, and north up Jl

Sulawesi, just over the river, the mini-district of **Kampung Arab** (see item 36 on the Denpasar map) is named after the many traders of Middle Eastern and Indian descent. You can continue north past Pasar Badung and return to Jl Gajah Mada; or head south down Jl Diponegoro, and back up Jl Sudirman, for some shopping.

MUSEUM NEGERI PROPINSI BALI

Bali's Provincial State Museum (☎ 222680) was built in 1910 by a Dutch official who was concerned about the export of culturally significant artefacts from Bali. It was destroyed in the 1917 earthquake, and revitalised in the 30s by artist Walter Spies.

The museum comprises several buildings and pavilions, including examples of the architecture of both the palace *(puri)* and temple *(pura)*, with features like a split gateway *(candi bentar)* and a warning drum *(kulkul)* tower. The **main building**, to the back as you enter, has a collection of prehistoric pieces downstairs, including stone sarcophagi, and stone and bronze implements. Upstairs are examples of traditional artefacts, including types still in everyday use. Look for the fine wood and cane carrying cases for transporting fighting cocks, and tiny carrying cases for fighting crickets.

The **northern pavilion** is in the style of a Tabanan palace and houses dance costumes and masks, including a sinister *rangda*, a healthy looking *barong* and a towering *barong landung* figure.

The **central pavilion**, with its wide verandah, is like the palace pavilions of the Karangasem kingdom (based in Amlapura) where rajahs held audiences. The exhibits here are related to Balinese religion, and include ceremonial objects, calendars and priests' clothing.

The **southern pavilion** is in the style of a Buleleng palace (from north Bali), and has a varied collection of textiles, including *endek*, double *ikat*, *songket* and *prada* (see the Balinese Arts & Crafts colour section after the Facts About Bali chapter for details).

Tickets cost 750/250 rp for adults/children. The museum has complicated opening hours: from 8 am to 3.45 pm on Sunday, Tuesday, Wednesday and Thursday; it closes a little earlier on Friday and Saturday; and closes completely on Monday. It is reasonably well set up, and most things are labelled in English. You can climb one of the towers inside the grounds for a better view of the whole complex.

PURA JAGATNATHA

Next to the museum, the state temple, Pura Jagatnatha, is dedicated to the supreme god, Sanghyang Widi. Built in 1953, part of its significance is its statement of monotheism. Although Balinese recognise many gods, the belief in one supreme god (which can have many manifestations) brings Balinese Hinduism into conformity with the first principle of Pancasila – the Belief in One God (see the boxed text of the same name in the Facts about Bali chapter).

The shrine, or *padmasana*, is made of white coral, and consists of an empty throne (symbolic of heaven) on top of the cosmic turtle and two *naga* (mythological serpents) which symbolise the foundation of the world. The walls are decorated with carvings of scenes from the *Ramayana* and *Mahabharata*.

Pura Jagatnatha is more frequently used than many Balinese temples – with local people coming every afternoon to pray and make offerings – so it can often be closed to the public. Two major festivals are held here every month, during full moon and new moon, and feature *wayang kulit* (shadow puppet plays). Ask at the Denpasar Tourist Office for exact details, or refer to its *Calendar of Events* booklet.

TAMAN WEDHI BUDAYA

This arts centre (☎ 222776) is a big complex in the eastern part of Denpasar. It was established in 1973 as an academy and showplace for Balinese culture, but it doesn't seem to have much purpose these days. Still, it's a quiet and shaded respite from the maddening traffic, and is worth a look around.

The centre does hold entertaining Kecak

dances (6000 rp) every evening from 6.30 to 7.30 pm, as well as irregular temporary art exhibits. From mid-June to mid-July, the centre hosts the Bali Arts Festival (see the boxed text of the same name in the Bali Facts for the Visitor chapter). You may need to book tickets at the centre for more popular events.

The centre is open Tuesday to Sunday from 8 am to 5 pm; and is free to enter. If you don't fancy the long walk, the Kereneng-Sanur bemo will drop you off at the nearby corner of Jl Hayam Wuruk and Jl Nusa Indah. You can enjoy a meal or drink after the evening dance at the handful of *warungs* opposite the main gate.

COURSES

Denpasar offers a range of courses covering language, cooking, dance and art. Start with the following organisations:

Bali Language Training & Cultural Centre
(☎ 239331) Jl Tukad Pakerisan 80. This agency runs Indonesian language and Balinese art and dance classes. Visitors are welcome to join free dance classes on Saturday afternoon.

Indonesia Australia Language Foundation
(☎ 225243, fax 263509) Jl Kapten Agung 17. This impressive outfit runs two week courses in five different levels of Indonesian language. Prices and conditions are aimed at Australians (although anyone can join): A$700 for the language component, plus A$275 if you want to stay with a family.

Sekolah Tinggi Seni Indonesia (STSI)
(☎ 227316, fax 233100) just off Jl Nusa Indah. This government-run agency offers courses in Balinese and Indonesian music, theatre and dance. Details about courses are listed on the window of the main building, or you can contact it weekdays between 8 am to 2 pm.

Sua Bali Culture & Information Centre
(☎ 98349, fax 921035) PO Box 574, Denpasar. This company teaches Indonesian cooking and language, and Balinese dancing and culture.

PLACES TO STAY

There are plenty of hotels in Denpasar, but the standards are lower, and the prices are higher, than most other places around Bali. Finding somewhere quiet, away from the incessant traffic, is not easy either. It may be wise to pre-book a room during the busier times in July, August, around Christmas and Idul Fitri (the end of Ramadan). Most places include breakfast.

Places to Stay – Budget

Adi Yasa (☎ 222679) is central and friendly, but the cheaper singles/doubles for 12,500/15,000 rp are like a sauna (ie there's no fan) and have a shared bathroom. The newer rooms, for 15,000/20,000 rp, are far nicer, but often full. Just a few metres to the west, *Nakula Inn* (☎ 226446) is better, and worth the few extra rupiah. The large rooms have a private bathroom and ceiling fan, and are located in a cool, shaded setting. They cost 25,000/30,000 rp, plus 5000 rp for breakfast.

Handy to the Tegal bemo terminal is *Two Brothers Inn* (☎ 222704) – look for the sign off Jl Imam Bonjol. This standard losmen is quiet, but also fairly inconvenient, and the staff can be a bit surly. Small rooms, with a shared bathroom, cost 15,000/20,000 rp.

The central *Hotel Mirah* (☎ 240321) is run by a friendly family, and is good value. Clean rooms, with a portable fan and private bathroom, cost 20,000/40,000 rp (more for air-con and TV) and are reasonably quiet despite the location. Another good option is the clean, central and surprisingly quiet *Hotel Wismasari Inn* (☎ 333437). The better rooms at the back cost 30,000 rp; the cheerless rooms inside are 20,000 rp.

As last resorts, try the grubby and noisy *Losmen Puri* for 15,000/20,000 rp; *Losmen Agung* (☎ 483263), with clean but very noisy rooms for 11,000/15,000 rp; or *Hotel Pendawa*, with decent rooms for 25,000 rp – although it's often full.

Places to Stay – Mid-Range

Most mid-range places are on or near busy Jl Diponegoro, and mainly cater to Indonesian business travellers. They are handy to the local shops, but to nothing much else. *Hotel Viking* (☎ 223992) has very noisy 'economy' rooms for 30,000 rp, and better, quieter rooms at the back for 65,000 rp with air-con. A little further south, *Hotel Dirga-*

pura (☎ *226924*) is better value, and more suited to budget travellers. It has dozens of rooms – so there's usually a vacancy – and many are away from the main road. Singles/doubles/triples cost 15,000/20,000/25,000 rp. Among other noisy, mid-range places along Jl Diponegoro are *Hotel Dewi* (☎ *226720*) and *Chandra Hotel* (☎ *226425*).

Hotel Pemecutan (☎ *423491*) is an unusual and atmospheric place in the middle of a palace (see the earlier Walking Tour section) with a pretty garden. It's good value for 50,000/60,000/75,000 rp, with air-con, phone, TV and private bathroom, but ask for a room at the back if you want any sleep. The entrance is on Jl Thamrin, and the reception is a little hard to find.

Places to Stay – Top End
There are no luxury hotels in Denpasar; if you want a top notch place, stay at Kuta, Sanur or Nusa Dua. The government-owned *Natour Bali Hotel* (☎ *225681, fax 235347*) dates from the Dutch days. There are some nice Art Deco details (look at the light fittings in the dining room), but incongruous Balinese decorations have since been added. Prices are still currently quoted in rupiah, so it's not that outrageous at 200,000/217,500 rp, with satellite TV, pool and hot water – but prices are much higher for the 'suite'.

PLACES TO EAT
Most places cater to local people, Indonesian visitors and immigrants, so they offer a good selection of authentic food at reasonable prices. Naturally, the cheapest places are the *warungs* at the bemo/bus terminals, and the markets: Pasar Kumbasari and Pasar Burung. They serve food until 10 pm, after most restaurants in town have closed.

Restaurant Atoom Baru is a typical Asian (as opposed to western) Chinese restaurant. The vast menu has loads of seafood, and other dishes, for 7000 to 12,000 rp. Across the road, the classy *Restaurant Hong Kong* boasts an inordinately wide range of Chinese and Indonesian dishes, but prices are high – from 10,000 to 15,000 rp per dish, and 9500

rp for a large beer (although it is served in an ice-cold glass).

Far better value can be found at *Mie 88*. Although the menu is not extensive, prices are reasonable (from 4500 to 6500 rp), and the beer is cheap (6500 rp for a large one).

There is not much to choose from in Renon, but *Pondok Melati* has good, cheap seafood, although the setting is noisy.

In Sanglah, a number of places along Jl Teuku Umar cater mainly to passing motorists, so if you don't have your own transport, get a bemo. Some, like *Kak Man Restaurant*, serve real Balinese food, as well as standard Indonesian fare. Almost opposite, *Ayam Goreng Taliwag* does Lombok-style food – very *pedas* (spicy). Most of the shopping centres have upstairs *eateries*, which serve cheap Indonesian and Chinese food in air-conditioned comfort.

Fast food addicts may want to visit *McDonald's*, at the NDA Department Store; *KFC* at Matahari's; or *Wendy's* or *Pizza Hut* at the Bali Mall. *Dunkin' Donuts* seems to be everywhere, including NDA's and the Bali Mall.

ENTERTAINMENT
Traditional Performances
Not being a tourist centre, little is on offer here except the evening Kecak dance at the Taman Wedhi Budaya arts centre. The best traditional dancing and music can be seen at places like Ubud.

Bars & Nightclubs
There is not a great choice. Many discos, bars and nightclubs can be found along Jl Diponegoro, such as the *Amsterdam Nightclub*, which features live music later in the week; or around the NDA Department Store, such as *DM Club & Karaoke*. A few of the upmarket restaurants, such as *Restaurant Hong Kong*, also feature the dreaded karaoke machine. It is best to do as the locals do, and go to Kuta-Legian or Sanur.

Cinemas
The younger, more affluent denizens of Denpasar congregate around shopping centres

in the evening, and often later around a local cinema. *Wisata Cineplex* (☎ 423023) has five screens, with recent, western movies subtitled in Bahasa Indonesia. Tickets cost about 6500 rp.

SHOPPING
Souvenirs
Don't spend too long buying souvenirs in Denpasar. The range, quality and price (if you bargain well) will be better elsewhere around Bali, but Denpasar is a good place to buy last-minute mementos before you head home. You'll find some craft shops along Jl Gajah Mada, and more further west, on the corner with Jl Thamrin. Possibilities range from mass-produced schlock to fine-quality arts, crafts and antiques from Bali and other Indonesian islands.

Markets
The pungent Pasar Badung is reputedly the largest and oldest market on Bali. It's very busy in the morning and evening, and is a great place to browse and bargain, except for the unsolicited guides-cum-commission-takers who sometimes attach themselves to you. Most visitors head to the clothing and handicrafts section on the top floor.

Pasar Kumbasari, along the opposite side of the river from Pasar Badung, has handicrafts, fabrics and gold work. Pasar Burung is a bird market with hundreds of caged birds and small animals for sale – although they hardly make practical souvenirs. It's lovely to listen to and very colourful to see, but some visitors may be upset with the cruel conditions. Jl Sulawesi, east of Pasar Badung, has many shops with batik, ikat and other fabrics. There are plenty of gold shops in the area known as Kampung Arab.

Shopping Centres
The western-style shopping centres are quite a recent innovation. The MA Department Store was one of the first, but has since been eclipsed by bigger, newer places such as Matahari, with a wide range of clothes, cosmetics, leather goods, sportswear, toys and baby things; NDA; and the newest and biggest, Bali Mall (Mal Bali). Most places have western fast-food restaurants and an eatery (see the Places to Eat section), and amusement centres for the kids (and the young at heart).

GETTING THERE & AWAY
Denpasar is the hub of road transport on Bali – you'll find buses and minibuses bound for all corners of the island. The Bali Getting There & Away chapter has details of transport by road, air and sea between Bali and other Indonesian islands; and the Lombok Getting There & Away chapter has details of transport between Bali and Lombok.

Air
It is not necessary to come to Denpasar to arrange bookings, tickets or reconfirmation of flights. Most airlines are based in Sanur anyway, and the travel agencies in Kuta, Sanur, Ubud and other tourist centres can provide these services. Airline offices based in Denpasar are listed in the Bali Getting There & Away chapter.

Bemo
Denpasar is *the* hub for bemo transport around Bali. Unfortunately, the city has several confusing terminals, so you'll often have to transfer from one to another. The terminals for transport around Bali are Ubung, Batubulan and Tegal, while the Kereneng, Sanglah, Suci and Wangaya terminals serve specific destinations within, and close to, Denpasar. Most travellers will probably only need to know the terminals which link Kuta and Sanur with other tourist centres, such as Ubud and Padangbai. The touts and drivers at the terminals will assume this and often show you which bemos to catch. Each terminal has regular bemo connections to the other terminals in Denpasar for about 400 to 700 rp.

Bemos and minibuses cover shorter routes between towns, while full-size buses are often used on longer, more heavily travelled routes. Buses tend to be cheaper than smaller vehicles on the same route, but they are less frequent – and the price difference is not worth worrying about. The prices listed here were correct at the time of research, but will probably change by the time you read this. Prices are normally listed at the terminals, and you can always ask other passengers for the current, correct price. You will soon get an idea of what to pay, and whether you are being charged a 'tourist price'.

Ubung North of the town centre, on the road to Gilimanuk, Ubung terminal (☎ 428165) is the terminal for the north and west of Bali.

Destination	Price (rp)
Bedugul (for Danau Bratan)	2100
Gilimanuk (for the ferry to Java)	3900
Kediri (for Tanah Lot)	850
Mengwi	900
Negara	2500
Singaraja (via Pupuan or Bedugul)	3400
Tabanan	1000

Batubulan This is the terminal for eastern and central Bali, although it does also offer a new, useful service (priced for foreigners) directly to Nusa Dua, in the south. The terminal is about 6km north-east of Denpasar.

Destination	Price (rp)
Amlapura	2500
Bangli	1100
Besakih	1700
Candidasa	1900
Gianyar	1000
Kintamani (for Danau Batur)	2500
Nusa Dua	2300
Padangbai (for the Lombok ferry)	1700
Semarapura (Klungkung)	1100
Singaraja	3500
(via Kintamani or Amlapura)	
Tampaksiring	1000
Tirta Gangga	2100
Tulamben	2400
Ubud	1500

Tegal On the road to Kuta, Tegal is the terminal for all of south Bali, except Suwung and Pelabuhan Benoa.

Destination	Price (rp)
Airport	500
Jimbaran	700
Kuta	500
Legian	450
Nusa Dua/Bualu	500
Sanur	500
Ulu Watu	1100

Kereneng East of the town centre, Kereneng has bemos to every other terminal in Denpasar, including Sanglah, as well as to Sanur.

Sanglah From near the main hospital in the south of the city, bemos go to Kereneng, Suwung and Pelabuhan Benoa.

Suci Not really a terminal, but more a roadside stop in the centre of town, bemos link Suci with the other local terminals.

Wangaya From this tiny terminal near the river, bemos go up the middle of Bali – to Pelaga (1300 rp), via Sangeh and Petang; and to Ubung and Kereneng terminals.

Public Bus
The usual route for land travel to Java is from Denpasar to Surabaya, although some buses go as far as Yogyakarta and Jakarta. They usually travel overnight. There are also regular buses from Denpasar to Mataram (Lombok) and further east to Sumbawa, but it's generally better to do this trip in individual stages.

The bus companies have offices along Jl Hasanudin and the top of Jl Diponegoro, such as PO Simpatik (☎ 226907). Other useful ticket agencies are in Hotel Pendawa (see the earlier Places to Stay section) and Suci Transport (☎ 225068). Alternatively, you can book directly at the Ubung bemo/bus terminal, 3km north of the city centre. To Surabaya or even Jakarta, you may get on a bus within an hour of arriving at Ubung, but at busy times you should buy your ticket at least one day ahead. Bus fares include the short ferry trip between Bali and Java, or Lombok.

Tourist Shuttle Bus

None of the shuttle bus companies travel to or from Denpasar, because so few tourists come here, and public transport is frequent and reliable. Shuttle buses do link Kuta, Sanur and Ubud with other tourist centres on Bali, and also go to Java, Lombok and Sumbawa. Refer to those entries elsewhere in this book.

Boat

You can get tickets for the super-fast *Mabua Express* to Lombok from an agency at the Ubung terminal, as well as travel agencies such as Suci Transport. For Pelni boats, buy tickets from Suci Transport (☎ 225068); the Pelni ticket agency (☎ 234680), on Jl Diponegoro; or the Pelni office at Pelabuhan Benoa, on the coast south of the city centre (see the Bali Getting There & Away chapter).

GETTING AROUND
To/From the Airport

Bali's Ngurah Rai airport is just south of Kuta (although it is referred to internationally as just Denpasar). Bemos and taxis are the easiest transport options.

Bemo

The main form of public transport is the bemo, which takes various circuitous routes from and between the domestic bemo terminals. These bemos line up for various destinations at each of the terminals, or you can hail them from anywhere along the main roads – look for the destination sign above the driver's window. The lists in the preceding Getting There & Away section indicate which bemos you will need from one terminal to another. The Tegal-Sanur bemo is handy for Renon, the NDA and Matahari department stores, and Jl Diponegoro; and the Kereneng-Sanur bemo travels along Jl Gajah Mada, past the museum and Denpasar Tourist Office. You can also charter bemos from the various terminals. Prices are negotiable, of course.

Dokar

Despite the traffic, *dokars* (pony carts) are still used in quieter parts of Denpasar. They should cost the same as a bemo, but tourists are always charged more because of the novelty value.

Taxi

Many taxis prowl the streets of Denpasar looking for fares; you will hear them beep at you constantly. Prices are negotiable as few of them have meters. If you want a metered taxi, Praja Bali Taxis (☎ 701111), Airport Taxi (☎ 751011 ext 1611) and Ngurah Rai Taxis (☎ 289090) should use the meter, but the driver will want to charge you a 'tourist price' anyway. Better still, charter a car and driver (as opposed to a taxi) from your hotel. This is worthwhile if visiting places away from the city centre.

Ojek

On some corners, you may be offered a lift on an *ojek* (paying pillion passenger on a motorbike). Driving your own motorbike is hard enough around Denpasar, but being driven around by a local speedster is not a good idea.

AROUND DENPASAR

If you are based in Denpasar, it is easy enough to day trip to anywhere south of the city, and as far as Padangbai, Ubud and Tanah Lot, on any form of public or private transport.

Sidakarya

There is little of interest in this village, about 5km south of Denpasar, unless you stay at the *Bali International Youth Hostel* (☎ 720812) at Jl Mertesari 19 (see the South Bali map in the South Bali chapter). There's a restaurant, and a small pool, but the rooms are not cheap: with a fan, they cost 40,000 rp, or 56,000 rp with air-con. Telephone the hostel to arrange free pick-up from Kuta, Denpasar and the airport. You won't meet a lot of travellers here, however.

South Bali

Highlights

- Kuta is Bali's largest and most notorious beach resort, enjoyed by many for its nightlife, restaurants and shopping; and loathed by others for its crowds, commercialism and rampant development.

- A pleasant mid-range beach resort, Sanur is classier than Kuta and livelier than Nusa Dua. Ideal for families.

- Jimbaran is a beautiful bay where a colourful fishing fleet brings in fresh seafood. It's best enjoyed at a beachfront cafe while the sun sets.

- The cliff-top temple of Pura Luhur Ulu Watu is dedicated to the spirits of the sea, and has intricate carvings depicting Bali's mythological menagerie.

- For surfers, the biggest and best known breaks include Balangan, Bingin, Padang and Ulu Watu – all along the Bukit Peninsula.

❀❀❀❀❀❀❀❀❀❀❀❀❀❀❀❀

The southern part of Bali is the tourist end of the island. Most of the package-tour hotels are found in this area, which has the best beaches and the most places to eat, drink and be entertained. For the Balinese, fishing villages like Kuta, Legian and Jimbaran were not notable places before the tourist boom, although Sanur was known for its sorcerers.

Bukit Peninsula, at Bali's southern extremity, with its poor soils and low rainfall, was even less significant. In Balinese terms, the mountains are always much more auspicious than the sea, but economically the southern coastline is now the most important and dynamic part of the island and the site of its big growth industry – tourism.

HISTORY & TOURISM

Following the bloody defeat of the three princes of the kingdom of Badung in 1906, the Dutch administration was relatively benign, and the south of Bali was little affected until the first western tourists and artists started to arrive. Although Denpasar became the capital of Bali after independence, the phenomenal growth in south Bali is almost entirely a result of the booming tourist industry.

Sanur had the first big hotel on Bali in 1965, but it was such an eyesore that the local *banjar* (community group of representatives) placed subsequent controls on tourist developments.

The growth of mass tourism dates from August 1969 when the Ngurah Rai international airport opened. The first planned tourist resort was conceived in the early 1970s, by 'experts' working for the United Nations and the World Bank. As luxury hotels were built at Nusa Dua, unplanned development raced ahead from Kuta to Legian. Local people made the most of their opportunities, and small-scale, low-budget businesses were set up with the limited local resources.

The most conspicuous recent growth has been around Nusa Dua, but new luxury hotels have also been developed on other parts of Bukit Peninsula, at Jimbaran and along the coast north of Legian. Traditional landholders have been displaced, land speculation is rampant, new coastal roads are planned and the signs of more construction are evident. The number of small hotels, restaurants and shops has also increased as huge numbers of low-budget visitors continue to pour in, attracted by the relative cheapness of a Bali holiday.

Kuta

The Kuta region is overwhelmingly Bali's largest and tackiest tourist beach resort. Most visitors come to the Kuta region sooner or later because it's close to the airport, and has the best range of budget hotels, restaurants and tourist facilities. Some find the area overdeveloped and seedy, but if you have a taste for a busy beach scene, shopping and nightlife, you will probably have a great time – but go somewhere else if you want a quiet, unspoilt, tropical hideaway.

It is fashionable to disparage the Kuta region for its rampant development, low-brow nightlife and crass commercialism, but the cosmopolitan mixture of beach-party he-donism and entrepreneurial energy can be exciting. It's not pretty, but it's not dull either, and the amazing growth is evidence that a lot of people find something to like in Kuta.

The *kelurahan* (local government area) of Kuta extends for nearly 8km along the beach and foreshore. Visitors have a choice of basing themselves, and/or visiting, four different areas:

Kuta has the greatest choice of hotels, restaurants, shops and nightclubs, and the best beach – but the worst traffic and most annoying hawkers.

Legian, to the north, is a slightly quieter version

SOUTH BALI

Tanah Lot · Gaji · To Mengwi & Bedugul · Batubulan · Ketewel
Kayutulang · Ubung · Tohpati
Seseh
Krobokan · DENPASAR · 15 · 14
Canggu · Berewa · 1
See Denpasar Map p168 · Sanur · 13 · Boats to Nusa Lembongan
See Seminyak Map p188 · Abiantimbul · Tegalwangi · 12
Petitenget · 2 · Seminyak · Bali International Youth Hostel
See Kuta-Legian Map p182 · See Sanur Map p204 · 11
Legian · Pesanggaran
0 · 2.5 · 5 km · Kuta Bay · Kuta · Suwung · Pojok
See Tuban Map p189 · Dukuh · Pulau Serangan
Tuban · Pelabuhan Benoa
Ngurah Rai Airport · Teluk Benoa · Selat Badung
Teluk Jimbaran · Jimbaran · Benoa
See Jimbaran Map p213 · Tanjung Benoa
3 · Hotel Villa Koyo · Bualu
4 · Mr Ugly Cafe & Homestay · Nusa Dua · 9
Pantai Suluban · 5 · See Tanjung Benoa & Nusa Dua Map p218
6 · Bukit Peninsula · Kuluh · Under Construction
Pura Luhur Ulu Watu · Pecatu · Bali Cliffs Resort
Ulu Watu · Puri Bali Villas · Pura Mas Suka
7 · 8

SURF BREAKS
1 Canggu
2 Oberoi
3 Balangan
4 Bingin
5 Padang Padang
6 Ulu Watu (Suluban)
7 Nyang Nyang
8 Green Ball
9 Nusa Dua
10 Sri Lanka
11 Hyatt Reef
12 Tanjung Sari
13 Sanur Reef
14 Padang Galak
15 Ketewel

Kuta Beach – Paradise or Purgatory?

The good news is that Kuta is still one of the best beaches on Bali, and watching the spectacular sunset is almost an evening ritual. Kuta has the only surf on the island which breaks over sand instead of coral, and beginning surfers can wipe out without being cut to pieces on the reefs. The accommodation is excellent value, there's a huge choice of places to eat and a growing number of shops with everything from genuine antiques to fake fashion items. Most of the drainage and sewerage problems have been dealt with, and electricity and telephone services are now quite reliable.

Despite the influx of people and influences from all over the world, a traditional Balinese community survives in Kuta. Temples are impressive and well kept, processions and festivals are elaborate, and offerings are made every day.

The bad news is that there are too many people and not enough planning. Jl Legian is a typical narrow island road, yet it carries a near continuous flow of buses, bemos, taxis, cars, trucks and motorbikes. Kuta remains a chaotic mixture of shops, bars, restaurants and hotels on a maze of streets and alleys, often congested with heavy traffic, thick with fumes and painfully noisy.

Kuta is now a beach resort for people who want sun, surf and sand, cheap food and cold beer. Where peacefully stoned freaks once gazed at the sunset, you now have bars where loud-mouthed drunks get plastered every afternoon. Street hawkers who were once persistent but polite, can now be aggressive and even hostile.

of Kuta, with less of everything, including hotels and hawkers.

Seminyak, north of Legian, somehow retains a small town atmosphere, with little traffic and no hawkers, but the beach is scruffy in parts and it's isolated from the 'action' in Kuta.

Tuban, between Kuta and the airport to the south, is newly developed, with mostly good beaches, many upmarket hotels and large shopping centres.

HISTORY

Mads Lange, a Danish copra trader and adventurer, set up at Kuta in about 1839 after an earlier trading venture on Lombok fell victim to local conflicts. Lange established a successful trading enterprise near modern Kuta, and had some success in mediating between local rajahs and the Dutch, who were encroaching from the north. His business soured in the 1850s, and he died suddenly, perhaps from poisoning, as he was about to return to Denmark.

The original Kuta Beach Hotel was started by a Californian couple named Louise and Bob Koke in the 1930s. The guests, mostly from Europe and the USA, were housed in thatched bungalows built in Balinese style. The hotel closed with the Japanese occupation of Bali in 1942, but a modern version opened on the same site in 1959, was rebuilt in 1991 and is now run by the government's hotel chain as Natour Kuta Beach. (The original owners of the hotel wrote a book about their life *Our Hotel in Bali* – see the Books section in the Facts for the Visitor chapter.)

Kuta really began to change in the late 1960s, when it became known as a stop on the hippie trail between Australia and Europe. At first, most visitors stayed in Denpasar and made day trips to Kuta, but more accommodation opened and, by the early 1970s, Kuta had relaxed *losmen* (small, family-run hotels) in pretty gardens, friendly places to eat and a delightfully laid-back atmosphere. Surfers also arrived, enjoying the waves at Kuta and using it as a base to explore the rest of Bali's coastline. Enterprising Indonesians seized opportunities to profit from the tourist trade, often in partnership with foreigners seeking a pretext for staying longer.

Legian, the village to the north, sprang up as an alternative to Kuta in the mid-70s. At first it was a totally separate development, but these days you can't tell where one ends and the other begins. Legian now merges with Seminyak, the next village north. To the south, new developments in Tuban are filling in the area between Kuta and the airport.

Modern Kuta is an international scene; a place where you can order guacamole in an Italian restaurant with local staff speaking English and diners speaking German.

ORIENTATION

The Kuta region is a disorienting place – it's flat, with few landmarks or signs, and the streets and alleys are crooked and often walled on one or both sides so it feels like a maze. The busy Jl Legian runs roughly parallel to the beach from Seminyak in the north through Legian to Kuta. It's a two way street in Legian, but in most of Kuta it's one way going south, except for an infuriating block near Jl Melasti where it's one way going north.

Between Jl Legian and the beach is a tangle of narrow streets, tracks and alleys, with an amazing hodgepodge of tiny hotels, souvenir stalls, *warungs* (food stalls), bars, building construction sites and even a few remaining stands of coconut palms. A small lane or alley is known as a *gang*. Most are unsigned, and too small for cars, although this doesn't stop some drivers trying. The best known lanes are known locally as Poppies Gang I and II – use these as landmarks.

Most of the bigger shops, restaurants and nightspots are along Jl Legian and a few of the main streets which head towards the beach. There are also dozens and dozens of travel agencies, souvenir shops, banks, moneychangers, motorbike and car rental outlets, postal agencies and *wartels* (public telephone offices) – everything a holiday maker could need or want within a few hundred metres walk. No wonder so many

visitors never make it out of the Kuta region – which is a shame, of course, because Bali has so much to offer.

Maps

Surprisingly, very few decent maps of the Kuta region exist, and none of them adequately cover all four areas. The maps in this guidebook will be more than sufficient for most visitors, although the maps of Bali published by Nelles and Travel Treasure (see the Maps entry in the Planning section of the Bali Facts for the Visitor chapter) have reasonable maps of the Kuta region, and of south Bali.

INFORMATION
Tourist Offices

There are three tourist offices. The staff in each are friendly, and happily provide useful information like 'How do I get a bemo to Nusa Dua?', but they can offer very little about hotels and activities, and have few brochures and maps to hand out. Avoid any place which purports to be a 'Tourist Information Centre' – it is a travel agent.

The Badung Tourist Office (π/fax 756176) is responsible for Badung Province (the Kuta region, Nusa Dua and Bukit Peninsula, but not Sanur). It is open daily from 7 am to 6 pm, except Sunday. The Bali Tourist Office (π 754090, fax 758521) is responsible for the whole of the island, but is unhelpful and uninformed, so is not worth trying to find (although it's at the back of the Century Plaza building if you want to check it out). It is open daily from 8 am to 9 pm. The newest office (π 755660) has recently opened directly opposite the Hard Rock Beach Club.

Money

There are many banks around the Kuta region, mainly along Jl Legian and at Kuta Square. However, the numerous moneychangers are faster, more efficient, open longer hours and offer better exchange rates. The rates for moneychangers are advertised on boards on paths or windows outside the shops or offices, but look around because rates do vary enormously. In or near upmarket hotels and modern shopping centres, the rates are absurdly low – about 20% lower than places around the corner. And look out for scams (see the Dangers & Annoyances entry in the earlier Bali Facts for the Visitor chapter).

The only reason to use a real bank is to transfer money or get a cash advance on a credit card. Bank Panir, on Jl Legian, and Bank BCA, on Jl Pantai Kuta, do advances on Visa; Bank Bali and Lippo Bank at Kuta Square work with MasterCard. There are also ATMs for Visa, MasterCard and Cirrus cards at the airport, around Kuta Square (including the ground floor of the Matahari Department Store), and near the corner of Jl Legian and Jl Padma in Legian.

A number of moneychangers and hotels have safety deposit boxes where you can leave airline tickets or other valuables without worrying about them during your stay on Bali. This is a good idea.

Post

The main post office is on a dirt road east of Jl Raya Kuta. It's small, efficient and has an easy, sort-it-yourself poste restante service. It is open Monday to Thursday from 8 am to 2 pm, and until noon on Friday and 1 pm on Saturday. This post office is the best place on Bali to send any large packages back home.

Other postal agencies, which can send but not receive mail, are dotted around the place (and indicated on the relevant maps). There is also a useful postal agency on the ground floor of the Matahari Department Store at Kuta Square, with a fax and poste restante service. Otherwise, if you know where you're staying you can receive mail at your hotel.

Telephone

There are wartels every few hundred metres along Jl Legian, the main roads between Jl Legian and the beach, and along Jl Dhyana Pura in Seminyak. Hours are generally from 7 am to 9 pm, but some are open later. In most places you can make international calls and send faxes, and arrange collect calls for a small fee. You can find Home Country Direct Dial telephones on the ground floor of the Matahari Department Store at Kuta Square, and near the left luggage counter at the international terminal at the airport.

Email & Internet Access

There are three Internet centres in the region, but more are likely to spring up as the demand grows:

Bali@Cyber Cafe & Restaurant
(bi-cafe1@idola.net.id) Based in a breezy, friendly cafe, the costs are reasonable: 6000 rp for the first 15 minutes, and 18,000 rp per hour.
Kambodja
(kambodiana@denpasar.wasantara.net.id) This service, based at a wartel in Kuta Square, is very dear: 15,000 rp for the first 15 minutes, and 10,000 rp for every subsequent 10 minutes.
Legian Cyber Cafe
(cyleg1@idola.net.id) It charges 7500 rp for the first 15 minutes and 12,500 rp for every subsequent 15 minutes; but it's not much of a cafe.

Travel Agencies

Every street and alley in the Kuta region is lined with dozens of travel agencies, and other shops which also act as travel agencies. Most will change money; sell tickets for tourist shuttle buses, traditional dances and organised tours; arrange car and motorbike rental; and book or change airline tickets, but you are better off doing this yourself directly with the airline (most of which are based in Sanur – see the Bali Getting There & Away chapter).

Bookshops

For quality books about Bali, the best bookshop is M-Media, on the 4th floor of the Matahari Department Store at Kuta Square. It also sells maps, and Lonely Planet guidebooks to Asia, Australia and beyond. The few bookshops which sell new and secondhand novels in most European languages, as well as local and international newspapers and magazines, are indicated on the maps in this chapter.

Laundry

The Kuta region is a good place to get some washing done. You can arrange this at your hotel, but it will be cheaper at one of the tiny

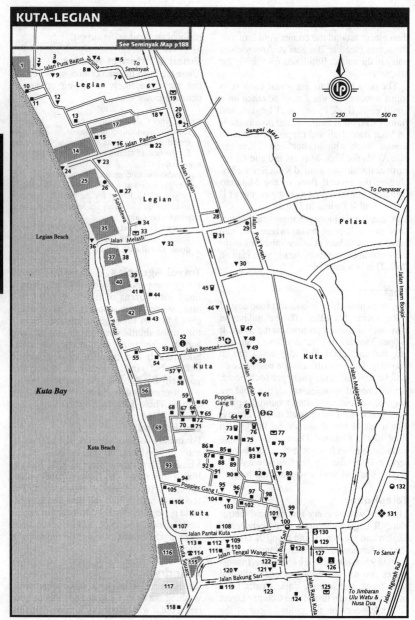

KUTA-LEGIAN

See Seminyak Map p188

To Seminyak

Jalan Pura Bagus Taruna

Legian

Jalan Padma

Jalan Legian

Jl. Sahadewa

Jalan Melasti

Legian

To Denpasar

Legian Beach

Pelasa

Sungai Mati

Jalan Pura Puseh

Kuta

Jalan Benesari

Kuta

Kuta Bay

Kuta Beach

Poppies Gang II

Poppies Gang I

Kuta

Jalan Pantai Kuta

Kuta Square

Jalan Tengal Wangi

Jalan Bakung Sari

Jalan Legian

Jalan Majapahit

Jalan Raya Kuta

Jalan Bumi Sari

Jalan Imam Bonjol

Jalan Nguruh Rai

To Sanur

To Jimbaran
Ulu Watu &
Nusa Dua

0   250   500 m

KUTA-LEGIAN

PLACES TO STAY
1 Hotel Jayakarta
5 Losmen Made Beach Inn;
  Bamboo Palace
8 Baleka Beach Hotel
10 Puri Tantra Beach Bungalows
11 Bali Kelapa Hotel
13 Sinar Indah; Bali Sani Hotel
14 Bali Padma Hotel
15 Garden View Cottages;
  Bank Bali
17 Three Brothers Inn
22 Legian Beach Bungalows
25 Bali Mandira
27 Suri Warthi Beach House
28 Surfers Paradise
34 Sorga Beach Inn
35 Legian Beach Hotel
37 Bali Intan Legian
39 Adus Beach Inn
40 Resort Kul Kul
41 Hotel Camplung Mas
  (Ocean Blue)
42 Hotel Kuta Jaya
43 Sayang Beach Lodging
  & Restaurant
44 Hotel Puri Tanahlot
53 Kuta Bungalows
54 Un's Hotel
55 Komala Indah II & Restaurant
56 Hotel Istana Rama
59 Suka Beach Inn
60 Bali Dwipa;
  Bali Duta Wisata
68 Bounty Hotel
69 Hotel Sahid Bali
70 Poppies Cottages II
71 Bali Sandy Cottages
72 Hotel Barong
74 Ronta Bungalows
  & Warung
75 Jus Edith
78 Sri Kusuma Hotel &
  Bungalows
80 Penginapan Maha Bharata
83 Paradiso Beach Inn
85 Sari Bali Bungalows
86 Sorga Cottages
87 Mimpi Bungalows
88 Suji Bungalow
89 Puri Ayodia Inn
90 Kempu Taman Ayu
91 Rita's House
92 Berlian Inn
93 Hotel Kuta Segara Ceria;
  Kuta Seaview Restaurant
94 Kuta Puri Bungalows;
  Coffee Shop

97 Komala Indah I
102 Poppies Cottages I
104 La Walon Bungalows;
  Masa Inn
105 Sari Yasa Samudra
  Bungalows; Coffee Shop
106 Hotel Aneka Kuta
107 Hard Rock Beach Club &
  Hard Rock Cafe
108 Budi Beach Inn
110 Ida Beach Inn
111 Asana Santhi Homestay
  (Willy I)
112 Kuta Suci Bungalows
113 Yulia Beach Inn
116 Natour Kuta Beach
118 Melasti Bungalows;
  Karthi Inn
119 Hotel Ramayana
124 Bamboo Inn; Zet Inn;
  Jensen's Inn II

PLACES TO EAT
2 Topi Koki Restaurant;
  Bank Bali
4 Rum Jungle Road Bar &
  Restaurant
6 Glory Bar & Restaurant
9 Thai Restaurant, Bar & Bakery
12 Poco Loco
16 Joni Sunken Bar & Restaurant
18 Warung Kopi
23 Rama Garden Restaurant
24 Surya Cafe & Beach Bar
30 Yanie's
32 Orchid Garden Restaurant
36 Karang Mas Cafe
38 Legian Garden Restaurant;
  Restaurant Puri Bali Indah;
  Taman Garden
46 Aroma's Cafe
48 Mama Luccia Italian
  Restaurant
49 Gemini Restaurant
57 Brasil Bali Restaurant
61 Mama's German Restaurant;
  Norm's Sports Bar; Lips
64 Batu Bulong
65 Twice Pub
66 Warung 96; Warung Dewi;
  The Corner Restaurant
67 Warung Nanas; Warung Ziro
79 Bounty II; Game Fantasia
81 Aquarius Bar & Restaurant
84 Mini Restaurant; Expresso
  Bar & Pizzeria
95 Nusa Indah Bar & Restaurant
96 TJs; Bamboo Corner; Bali Asi

98 Poppies Restaurant
99 Sushi Bar Kunti
101 Made's Warung
103 Fat Yogi's
109 Lenny's Seafood; The
  Bookshop
120 Dayu I
121 Bali Aget
123 Agung Cafe; Agung
  Supermarket

BARS & NIGHTCLUBS
31 Peanuts
45 Bounty I
47 001 Club
63 SC (Sari Club)
73 Tubes Bar
76 The Macaroni Club
122 The Pub
128 Casablanca Bar

OTHER
3 Swiss & Austrian Consular
  Agents; Swiss Restaurant
7 Bali@Cyber Cafe
  & Restaurant
19 Postal Agency
20 ATMs
21 The Bookstore
26 Legian Cyber Cafe
29 Bali Bungy
33 Postal Agent
50 Matahari Department Store;
  Timezone; Cinema
51 Legian Medical Clinic;
  Subway Restaurant
52 Bali Tourist Office
58 Adrenalin Park
62 Bank Panir
77 Postal Agency
82 Perama Office
100 Bemo Corner
114 Kambodja Wartel &
  Internet Centre
115 Kuta Square; Matahari
  Department Store;
  McDonalds, Timezone; Banks
117 Kuta Art Market; Artists Cafe
125 Main Post Office
126 Chinese Temple
127 Badung Tourist Office;
  Police Station
129 Public Market
130 Bank BCA
131 Galeal de Wata Shopping
  Centre & KFC
132 Bemos to Nusa Dua;
  Petrol Station

SOUTH BALI

laundries dotted around the various alleys. The current rates are about 750 rp for a shirt, jeans or skirt; 500 rp for shorts or T-shirts; and 400 rp for underwear. Your clothes will be thoroughly cleaned and lovingly ironed within 24 hours – as long as it isn't raining.

Medical Services

Of the several private clinics in the Kuta region, the most accessible and modern is Legian Medical Clinic (☎ 758503). It's open 24 hours a day, and also has an ambulance and dentist service. It charges 50,000 rp for a consultation, or 250,000 rp for an emergency visit to your hotel room. Otherwise, ask your hotel to arrange for a doctor to visit you, or go to the public hospitals in Denpasar.

The newest medical clinic, SOS Natour Clinic (☎ 751361) recently opened directly opposite the Hard Rock Beach Club.

Emergency

The local police station (☎ 751598) is next to the Badung Tourist Office, and there are one or two temporary tourist police posts along Jl Legian. If you have any major problem, or need a local driving licence, go to the main police station on Jl Pattimura in Denpasar.

Dangers & Annoyances

Theft This is not an enormous problem, but visitors do lose things from unlocked hotel rooms or from the beach. Going into the water and leaving valuables on the beach is simply asking for trouble. There are also some snatch thefts, so hang on to your bag and keep your money belt under your clothes – wearing a bumbag over your clothes is not a great idea. Valuable items can be left at your hotel reception, or stored in a security box in a moneychanger's office.

Assaults It is generally safe to walk around the streets in the Kuta region at any time, but there are occasional reports of robberies and assaults on the beaches and around nightclubs late at night, so please be careful. Assaults on women are still rare, but these days the principal threat often comes from drunken foreign men rather than local men. Refer to the Women Travellers and Dangers & Annoyances sections in the Bali Facts for the Visitor chapter for more details.

Water Safety The surf around here can be very dangerous, with a strong current on some tides, especially in Legian. Lifeguards patrol swimming areas of the beaches at Kuta and Legian, which are indicated by red-and-yellow flags. If they say the water is too rough or unsafe to swim in, they mean it. There's also been unsubstantiated reports of sewerage flowing into the sea near Kuta, especially after heavy rain.

Hawkers Touts, hawkers and guides are a major annoyance; and sadly will leave an everlasting impression for many visitors. Beach selling is now restricted to the upper part of the beach, where professionals with licence numbers on their conical hats will importune you to buy anything from a cold drink to a massage or a hair-beading job. Closer to the water, you can lie on the sand in peace – you'll soon find out where the invisible line is.

On the streets and in the restaurants, guys try hard to sell fake fashion watches from boxes which open like jaws as you approach. Local men and women also try to flog caps, jewellery, perfumes and more. You will also be constantly asked 'Transport?' – and, in case you don't understand, the driver will effusively gesticulate the motions of driving a car or motorbike.

ACTIVITIES

There is an absolute plethora of things to do on Bali – most of which are neither typically Balinese nor Indonesian, but great fun nonetheless. From the Kuta region you can easily go surfing, sailing, diving, fishing or rafting anywhere in the southern part of Bali, and be back for the start of a happy hour in the evening. The best idea is to grab a handful of brochures from any travel agent – they will also happily book most activities for you.

Top: Hustle and bustle on Bali's Kuta beach.
Middle: Bali's crashing waves – a magnet for surfers the world over.
Bottom left: Surfboards for hire on Kuta beach, Bali.
Bottom right: A group of Balinese surfers chill out on the beach at Kuta.

Top: Beach procession during a purification ceremony in south Bali.
Bottom left: Sarong seller on Bali's Kuta beach.
Bottom right: Offerings on the beach at Sanur in south Bali.

Refer to the general Activities section in the Bali Facts for the Visitor chapter for an idea of what is on offer around the island.

Surfing

The Kuta-Legian coast has good reef and beach breaks, and the beach break at Kuta is the best place to learn surfing. Beginners can rent surfboards and boogie boards on the beach, or from losmen near the beach, for about 20,000 and 15,000 rp per day respectively, and even get surfing lessons for 50,000 to 65,000 rp per day. A few surf shops along or just off Jl Legian also hire out surfboards and boogie boards, and can arrange repairs, lessons and shuttle buses to nearby surfing spots.

Tubes Bar seems to be one place where surfers hang out and compare waves; it also publishes a tide chart, which is also pinned up at some hotel lobbies and restaurant walls. Otherwise, head to spots around Bukit Peninsula (described in that section later in this chapter), and find out what is happening. The Surfing section in the Bali Facts for the Visitor chapter has more information.

Massage

Many masseurs work on the beaches. The realistic price is about 5000 rp for a half hour massage, or 10,000 rp for one hour, but you will have to bargain hard to get anything near this price. More professional massages in your room, or in a genuine massage establishment, will cost about 40,000 rp per hour.

For the Kids

Adults will also enjoy the slides, pools and water sports at Waterbom Park (☎ 755676 – see the Tuban map). You can enjoy a meal or a drink, or just sit around in the shady gardens – it's easy to spend a whole day here. There are lifeguards and it's well supervised, but children under 12 must be accompanied by an adult. It is open from 8 am to 6 pm, and costs US$12/6 for adults/children. Nearby, you can hurtle around a small track on a go-kart at Le Speed Karts.

The Timezone video arcades, in the two Matahari department stores, have lots of hi-tech games and other amusements, as does Game Fantasia, near the Bounty II bar and restaurant on JL Legian. Taman Festival Bali park, near Sanur, is also a good place to take the young 'uns.

Other Activities

Any of the following local activities can be booked through a travel agency:

Bungee Jumping
The really crazy can try 30 seconds of lunacy with Hackett Bungy Co (☎ 731144) in Legian, Bali Bungy (☎ 752658), or at the appropriately named Adrenalin Park in Kuta. At about US$45 a jump, this is the quickest way to spend your money.

Horse Riding
Two hour rides can be arranged through Loji Garden Hotel (☎ 751672) in Legian for US$60 per person. Puri Pemecutan Stables (☎ 730401), at the Mesari Beach Inn at Seminyak, is better value at US$15 per hour.

Mini-Golf
Sorga Mini Golf on Jl Plawa in Seminyak is apparently struggling for business, so it provides free transport and gives you a free beer on arrival. It is open daily from 10 am to 10 pm.

ORGANISED TOURS

A vast range of tours all around Bali for half a day, full day or even two or three days can be booked through any travel agency or hotel in the Kuta region. These tours are a quick and easy way to see a few sights if your time is limited, if you are not keen about using bemos, or if the bemos are infrequent (such as for the sunset at Tanah Lot or getting to/from Ulu Watu). If you shop around, the cost of an organised tour is not that expensive. The Organised Tours section in the Bali Getting Around chapter lists some available tours, and what they cost.

PLACES TO STAY

Kuta, Legian, Tuban and Seminyak have hundreds of places to stay, so we can't possibly list them all. We have tried to list some (but not all) places that have character, and are convenient and quiet – at a good price. If you disagree, and standards have dropped and/or prices have increased, please let us (and other travellers) know.

The most expensive hotels are along the beachfront, mid-range places are mostly on the bigger roads between Jl Legian and the beach, and the cheapest losmen are along the smaller lanes in between – although this is not always true. Northern parts of Legian, as well as Tuban and Seminyak, have been mostly taken over by mid-range and top-end hotels and resorts, so the best place to find budget accommodation is southern Legian and Kuta.

Most budget places cost from about 15,000/20,000 rp for singles/doubles. They normally have a fan, and a private bathroom with a *mandi* (Indonesian bath with cold water) or (cold) shower, and a European-style toilet. It is often worth paying more, about 40,000/50,000 rp, to stay in the cheapest 'standard' or 'economy' rooms at a mid-range place, so you can also enjoy the spacious gardens and swimming pool. Mid-range hotels usually have swimming pools, and offer rooms with a fan or air-con, and usually hot water. Top-end places have all the trimmings, some of which – like the telephone, TV and room service – you may never use.

Beware of throwaway words like 'beach', 'seaview', 'cottage', 'bungalows' and 'inn' when it comes to hotel names. Places with 'beach' in their name may not be anywhere near the beach and a featureless, three storey hotel block may rejoice in the name 'cottages'. Note that any hotel north of Jl Pantai Kuta and south of Jl Melasti is going to be separated from the beach by a busy, main road, even if the hotel is described as being on the 'beachfront'.

There is a 10% tax on all accommodation. In the cheaper places this is normally included in the price, or not payable at all, but check first. More expensive places add it on, along with an individual service charge of 5% to 15%, which can add substantially to your bill. If you are staying for a few days (or longer), you should always seek a discount. In the low season (November to April), discounts of 50% are not uncommon, so if you

normally stay in budget hotels, don't be afraid of checking out somewhere in the mid-range and asking for a discount.

In all categories in this section, the hotels are grouped by location, from Tuban to Seminyak, and then listed alphabetically. All prices were correct at the time of research (but are likely to increase in the future), and include all taxes and service charges.

PLACES TO STAY – BUDGET

The best type of losmen is a relaxed, family-run place built around an attractive garden. Look for a losmen which is far enough off the main roads to be quiet, but close enough so that getting to the beach, shops and restaurants is no problem. Many cheaper losmen still offer breakfast, even if it's only a couple of bananas and a cup of tea. Tea used to be included throughout the day on request, but this is becoming less common.

There will be many other places of similar standard and price in the same areas as the ones listed in this section, so if your first choice is full, check any others within walking distance.

For details about the Bali International Youth Hostel at Sidakarya, see the Around Denpasar section in the Denpasar chapter.

Tuban

South of Kuta, they're mostly mid-range and top-end places. The only budget place is *Mandara Cottages* (☎ 751775, fax 761770). It is within walking distance of the airport, the rooms are set back from the road, and there's a pool. The rooms have huge beds, hot water, and cost a very reasonable 45,000 rp.

Kuta

South Kuta There are a number of cheap places on, or just south of, Jl Pantai Kuta, although anywhere close to the road will be noisy.

Bamboo Inn (☎ 751935) A traditional little losmen, it's quiet and friendly but often full. Simple rooms cost 25,000 rp.

Budi Beach Inn (☎ 751610) This is an old-style losmen with a garden and large airy singles/doubles for a negotiable 39,000/44,000 rp to

77,000/88,000 rp, including air-con. It is central and nicer than it looks from the entrance.

Jensen's Inn II (☎/fax 752647) Quiet, friendly and central, this place is often full. Clean rooms cost US$12/15, but try to negotiate a more sensible price, and in rupiah.

Kuta Suci Bungalows (☎/fax 753761, email kutasuci@denpasar.wasantara.net.id) Well established, this place is a little noisy and the rooms could do with some renovations, but it is good value at 22,000/27,500/38,500 rp for singles/doubles/triples, or slightly more for a bungalow.

Zet Inn (☎ 753135) It lacks character, but is reasonable value with rooms for 25,000/35,000 rp, and up to 60,000/70,000 rp with air-con. It is popular with Indonesian visitors.

Central Kuta Many cheap places are along the tiny alleys and lanes between Jl Legian and the beach, but a few are also on the eastern side of Jl Legian. This is the best place to base yourself: it's quiet, only a short walk from the beach, and there are plenty of shops and restaurants nearby, so you rarely have to venture into the chaos along Jl Legian.

Adus Beach Inn (☎ 755326) This new, family-run place is quiet, spotlessly clean and excellent value, with singles/doubles for 25,000/30,000 rp.

Bali Duta Wisata (☎ 753534) It's certainly cheap, and popular, with rooms for 12,000/15,000 rp, but it's in a noisy area and is more of a hotel than a set of bungalows.

Bali Dwipa (☎ 751446) This place is often full, although it looks a bit run-down. The rooms have patios, and offer some privacy, and cost 15,000/20,000 rp.

Bali Sandy Cottages (☎ 753344) Secluded and close to the beach, the rooms here are pleasant and good value for 35,000/50,000 rp. It's in a large, quiet garden, where a pool ought to be, but isn't.

Jus Edith This no-frills place charges a no-frills 15,000/20,000 rp. Some rooms are better than others, and if you looked around elsewhere you could do better. It also produces custom-made didgeridoos!

Kempu Taman Ayu (☎ 751855) This is a long-running and friendly little place with rooms for 16,000/25,000 rp, although the rooms are not particularly private.

Komala Indah I (☎ 751422) Clean and great value considering the location, a room with a squat toilet and mandi costs 15,000 rp.

Komala Indah II (☎ 754258) This is a little gem, still set among the coconut palms that typified Kuta only 30 years ago. Some rooms are better than others, but priced at a bargain 15,000/20,000 rp. The attached restaurant is excellent. One female reader did complain, however, about unwarranted attention from staff.

Masa Inn (☎ 758507, fax 752606) This friendly and central place is very good value, so it's often full. The pool is an attraction, and rooms are cheap for 24,000/27,000 rp, or 35,000/45,000 rp with fan and hot water. Air-con family rooms are 45,500 rp.

Mimpi Bungalows (☎/fax 751848) This boasts plenty of foliage for shade and privacy, the rooms are nice, the staff are friendly and rooms are very reasonable for 40,000/60,000 rp.

Penginapan Maha Bharata (☎ 756754) This quiet place is recommended. Large, pleasant rooms cost 20,000/25,000 rp. Look for the sign from the main road.

Puri Ayodia Inn This small, standard losmen is in a quiet but convenient location and is good value, with rooms for 15,000/20,000 rp.

Rita's House (☎ 751760) This is not fancy, but good value, with rooms for 20,000/25,000 rp. It continues to get rave reviews from long-stay travellers. More rooms are being built, which will detract from the general cosiness.

Ronta Bungalows (☎ 754246) Clean, with a nice garden and central location, this place is often full. At 15,000/20,000 rp for rooms, it's not hard to understand why. The restaurant is also good, and popular.

Suka Beach Inn (☎ 752793) This is a popular place, and is better than others in the immediate area. Decent rooms go for only 15,000/20,000 rp.

Legian

A few places are crowded along the two busy main roads in Legian – Jl Padma and Jl Melasti, or in areas between. Jl Pura Bagus Taruna is a quieter stretch of road.

Legian Beach Bungalows (☎ 751087) Central, but noisy, it has a small pool. The rooms are also small and cost 35,000/45,000 rp for singles/doubles.

Losmen Made Beach Inn (☎ 752127) This unassuming place is excellent value in this neck of the woods. Rooms cost 35,000 rp.

Sinar Indah (☎ 755905) This standard losmen is handy to the beach, but try to negotiate as 55,000 rp per room, with fan and hot water, is a little high.

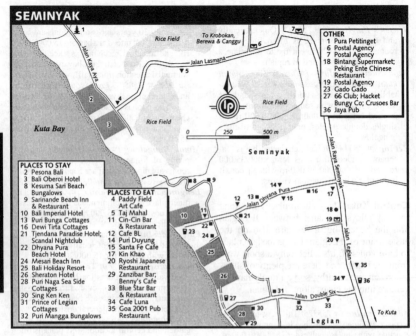

SEMINYAK

Rice Field

To Krobokan,
Berewa & Canggu

Jalan Lasmana

Kuta Bay

Rice Field

Rice Field

Seminyak

0   250   500 m

OTHER
1   Pura Petitinget
6   Postal Agency
7   Postal Agency
18 Bintang Supermarket;
    Peking Ente Chinese
    Restaurant
19 Postal Agency
23 Gado Gado
27 66 Club; Hacket
    Bungy Co; Crusoes Bar
36 Jaya Pub

PLACES TO STAY
2   Pesona Bali
3   Bali Oberoi Hotel
8   Kesuma Sari Beach
    Bungalows
9   Sarinande Beach Inn
    & Restaurant
10 Bali Imperial Hotel
13 Puri Bunga Cottages
16 Dewi Tirta Cottages
21 Tjendana Paradise Hotel;
    Scandal Nightclub
22 Dhyana Pura
    Beach Hotel
24 Mesari Beach Inn
25 Bali Holiday Resort
26 Sheraton Hotel
28 Puri Naga Sea Side
    Cottages
30 Sing Ken Ken
31 Prince of Legian
    Cottages
32 Puri Mangga Bungalows

PLACES TO EAT
4   Paddy Field
    Art Cafe
5   Taj Mahal
11 Cin-Cin Bar
    & Restaurant
12 Cafe BL
14 Puri Duyung
15 Santa Fe Cafe
17 Kin Khao
20 Ryoshi Japanese
    Restaurant
29 Zanzibar Bar;
    Benny's Cafe
33 Blue Star Bar
    & Restaurant
34 Cafe Luna
35 Goa 2001 Pub
    Restaurant

Jalan Dhyana Pura

Jalan Raya Seminyak

Jalan Legian

Jalan Double Six

Legian

To Kuta

Sorga Beach Inn (☎ 751609, fax 755328) Good
value at 15,000/20,000 rp for rooms, the
garden is shady, but the crickets will probably
keep you awake at night.

Surfers Paradise (☎ 751103) This quiet place is
good value, with rooms for 30,000/35,000 rp,
or 70,000 rp with air-con. The setting is pleasant, but the rooms could do with renovating.

Seminyak

There's very few budget places to be found
in Seminyak.

Kesuma Sari Beach Bungalows (☎ 730575) This
small, friendly place is tucked away. It has char-
acter-filled rooms, with enormous beds, hot
water and a sort of alfresco bathroom for 45,000
rp, which is excellent value for Seminyak.

Mesari Beach Inn (☎ 751401) Quiet and next to
some stables (where you can rent horses), it
has excellent value rooms for 20,000/25,000
rp, while charming bungalows cost 50,000 rp,
which is why it is often full.

Puri Mangga Bungalows (☎ 730447, fax 730307)
This pleasant, newish place has rooms with hot
water and fan, which the manager is willing to
negotiate down to a very reasonable 25,000 rp.

PLACES TO STAY – MID-RANGE

There are a great many mid-range hotels,
which in the Kuta region means US$15 to
US$50 for a double. The prices in US dollars
listed in this section are the 'published rates'
for the package-tour market. These rates are
normally negotiable to independent travellers
– often up to 50% off if business is quiet; new
hotels, especially, can have trouble filling
their rooms and give big discounts. Before
you agree on a price make sure you know
whether tax and service is included or extra,
and ask if breakfast is included.

The best of the mid-range hotels are
former budget places which have upgraded.
These places are normally family-owned and

have a vested interest in filling their hotel, so prices are more negotiable. Many of the new package-tour hotels are featureless and dull, with standard features like air-con and a swimming pool, but nothing in the way of Balinese style. All hotels listed in this section offer air-con rooms and hot water, and most places priced in US dollars have swimming pools.

Tuban

Adhi Jaya Cottages (☎/fax 753607) This place is nothing special. Fan-cooled singles/doubles/triples cost US$15/20/25, while the air-con cottages for US$30/35/42 are better value.

Cempaka Guest House (☎ 751621, fax 753529) This family-run place is close to the airport, but is noisy. Singles/doubles with air-con, TV and hot water can be easily negotiated down to 60,000/65,000 rp.

Dayu Beach Inn (☎ 752263) The rooms with fan and cold water for US$15/20 are too dear, but the best rooms for US$30/35/40 are good value.

Flamboyan Inn (☎/fax 752610) Rooms normally cost US$36/42/55 with air-con, but the manager is willing to negotiate. The place is quiet, and is recommended for families.

Pendawa Bungalows (☎ 752387, fax 757777) This is one of several decent places along a quiet laneway. It has a spacious garden, and six types of rooms priced from US$19/23/29 to US$48/58/79.

Sandi Phala Beach Resort (☎ 7537708, fax 754889) The rooms are in a two storey block facing onto the beach, and cost US$35/42.

Kuta

South Kuta The Kuta Square shopping development has revived this area; it's a good place to base yourself if you love shopping.

Asana Santhi Homestay (☎ 751281 at Willy I) This attractive, small hotel is surprisingly quiet and relaxed for its location. The well kept rooms have interesting furnishings, and the staff are very helpful. Rooms cost about US$30.

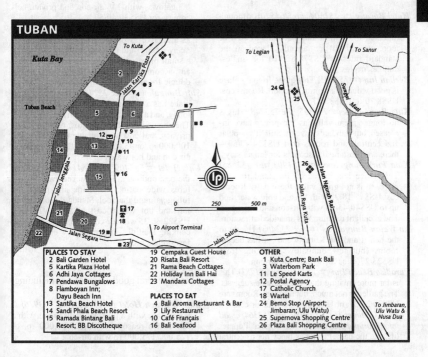

TUBAN

To Kuta / *To Legian* / *To Sanur*

Kuta Bay

Tuban Beach

Jalan Kartika Plaza
Jalan Jengala
Jalan Segara
To Airport Terminal
Jalan Satria
Sungai Mati
Jalan Ngurah Rai
Jalan Raya Kuta

0   250   500 m

To Jimbaran, Ulu Watu & Nusa Dua

PLACES TO STAY		OTHER
2 Bali Garden Hotel	19 Cempaka Guest House	1 Kuta Centre; Bank Bali
5 Kartika Plaza Hotel	20 Risata Bali Resort	3 Waterbom Park
6 Adhi Jaya Cottages	21 Rama Beach Cottages	11 Le Speed Karts
7 Pendawa Bungalows	22 Holiday Inn Bali Hai	12 Postal Agency
8 Flamboyan Inn;	23 Mandara Cottages	17 Catholic Church
Dayu Beach Inn		18 Wartel
13 Santika Beach Hotel	**PLACES TO EAT**	24 Bemo Stop (Airport;
14 Sandi Phala Beach Resort	4 Bali Aroma Restaurant & Bar	Jimbaran; Ulu Watu)
15 Ramada Bintang Bali	9 Lily Restaurant	25 Supernova Shopping Centre
Resort; BB Discotheque	10 Café Français	26 Plaza Bali Shopping Centre
	16 Bali Seafood	

Ida Beach Inn (☎ 751205, fax 751934) Its rooms are squashed together, but the place is quiet and has a nice garden. It's a little hard to find down a laneway. Singles/doubles/triples cost US$33/30/52.

Melasti Bungalows (☎ 751335, fax 751563, email melasti@denpasar.wasantara.net.id) This top-end hotel has a number of mid-range rooms for a reasonable US$30/36, with fan and hot water. Other rooms cost up to US$120/145.

Yulia Beach Inn (☎ 751893, fax 751055) This small hotel has been going for years, but is no longer the bargain it was. Nevertheless, it's friendly and quiet (except for the constant hum from the overworked air-con unit at the Matahari Department Store). Basic rooms start at US$7/10, but a bungalow with hot water costs US$20/25/29.

Central Kuta The back lanes between Jl Legian and the beachfront road have a number of mid-range places which are handy to the beach, shops and restaurants. They don't carry much traffic so it's a relatively quiet area.

Hotel Barong (☎ 751804, fax 761520) Although the rooms in this new place are too close together, it's central and discounts of 50% or more are almost permanently placed on the standard rates of US$78/85/110 for singles/doubles/triples.

Berlian Inn (☎ 751701) This quiet, friendly place is good value in a central location. Rooms cost US$8/10 to US$22/27.

Kuta Bungalows (☎ 754395, fax 753748) This is no longer great value as the prices have increased, but standards haven't. Still, it's popular and central, and rooms cost US$34/40/50 – there are substantial discounts for longer stays.

Kuta Puri Bungalows (☎ 751903, fax 752585) This place has increased its standards and price, so is not great value these days. Rooms cost US$15/18/22 with fan and cold water, and up to US$40/45/55 with air-con and hot water. The excellent restaurant is an added attraction.

La Walon Bungalows (☎/fax 752463) Handy to the beach and the Kuta 'scene', it has decent rooms (but few bungalows) ranging from US$23/27, plus 50% more for air-con.

Paradiso Beach Inn (☎ 752270, fax 751781) This is far more inviting than the entrance suggests. The garden is not much, but it's quiet. Rooms are US$20/25/37, or US$30/35/50 with air-con.

Poppies Cottages II (☎ 751059, fax 752364, email info@bali.poppies.net.id) The original Poppies (despite the name) is not as fancy nor as central

as Poppies I, and there are only a few cottages, but guests can use the pool at Poppies I. At US$30/36/51, Poppies II is no longer good value.

Hotel Puri Tanahlot (☎ 752281, fax 755626) These stylish bungalows are set around a pleasant garden and pool. It is quiet and rates are negotiable: standard rooms for US$8/10 are good value, while the most expensive bungalows cost only US$25/30.

Sari Bali Bungalows (☎ 753065) Nice bungalows and rooms in a spacious garden with a good pool range from 50,000/70,000 rp with fan and cold water to 100,000/120,000 rp with air-con.

Sari Yasa Samudra Bungalows (☎ 751562, fax 752948) It boasts an excellent location and a lovely pool. Rooms are US$24/27, and US$42/48 with air-con, fridge and private balcony.

Sayang Beach Lodging (☎/fax 751249) Although handy to the beach, it can be a little noisy. It has an excellent restaurant, and a range of rooms from US$10/12 up to US$47/59. One reader did complain about staff.

Sri Kusuma Hotel & Bungalows (☎ 751201, fax 756567) This pleasant, central and clean place has plenty of rooms for US$20/30/38, plus bungalows, with TV, air-con and private balconies, for US$30/40/50.

Sorga Cottages (☎ 751897, fax 752417) It's not as attractive as others, because there are too many rooms (and no cottages) squeezed on to a small piece of land, but the setting is pleasant. Rooms start from US$10/13.50; prices double for air-con, TV and hot water.

Suji Bungalow (☎/fax 752483) This family-run place has a pool table and satellite TV in the lobby, and a perfect little garden around a pool. The rooms have decent patios, offering some privacy, and cost a negotiable 60,000/80,000/100,000 rp, or 95,000/115,000/135,000 rp with air-con and hot water.

Un's Hotel (☎ 757409, fax 758414) This is one of the best options in Kuta. Tucked away, it features wide patios for shade and plenty of foliage around the pool. Standard rooms, with fan and hot water, cost US$17/20/24, and US$22/30/35 with air-con. A family room with cooking facilities, fridge and TV only costs a few dollars more.

Legian

There's several good options here, including:

Baleka Beach Hotel (☎ 751931, fax 753976) A good place with a pleasant pool, rooms with a fan cost a reasonable 75,000/90,000 rp, or 125,000/175,000 rp with air-con.

Bali Kelapa Hotel (☎ 754167, fax 754121) Also known as Bali Coconut Hotel, this is one of the best value places in the area. It is friendly, very close to the beach and rooms cost only 80,000 rp.

Garden View Cottages (☎ 751559, fax 753265) The rooms have hot water, telephone and fridge, but look a little like concrete boxes. The room rates of US$44/49/61 haven't changed for several years.

Puri Tantra Beach Bungalows (☎/fax 753195) These handful of charming traditional cottages are often full, because they're such good value at US$40/45.

Suri Wathi Beach House (☎ 753162, fax 758393) Off the main road, so it's very quiet, there are plenty of rooms and a swimming pool. It is friendly, and excellent value, with rooms for US$8/10, or US$12 for a bungalow.

Three Brothers Inn (☎ 751566, fax 756082) This long-standing and popular place has rooms scattered around a gorgeous garden, but the newer rooms have less character than the originals. Prices are US$22 with fan and hot water, and US$38 with air-con.

Seminyak

There are a few good mid-range options in this area. There are also houses and bungalows to rent by the week or month if you look around – ideal for families. If you pre-book a room by phone or fax, staff may pick you up from Kuta or the airport for no charge.

Dewi Tirta Cottages (☎ 730476) Decent rooms (not cottages) cost 65,000/75,000 rp with fan/air-con. It is quiet, and one of the few decent places willing to negotiate, but it lacks some character.

Prince of Legian Cottages (☎ 730733, fax 732144) These fully equipped bungalows sleep up to four people, and are popular with long-term visitors, especially families. The rates are US$40 per bungalow, but reductions of US$10 per night are possible for longer stays. Bookings are recommended.

Sarinande Beach Inn (☎/fax 730383) This delightful little hideaway is one of the best places in Seminyak. It is secluded, but offers free transfers to Kuta and the airport. Singles/doubles/triples, including TV, air-con and fridge, are excellent value for US$35/40/48.

Sing Ken Ken (☎ 752980, fax 730535) This is a slightly cramped, motel-style place which has comfortable rooms for US$36/42/51.

PLACES TO STAY – TOP END

Kuta, Legian, Tuban and Seminyak also have plenty of places in the top-end category, all with hot water, air-conditioning and a swimming pool (or two). As the price goes up, you'll get facilities like TV (with access to satellite stations and/or in-house video movies) and telephones (with International Direct Dialling to really augment your room bill). Other luxuries include room service, a hair dryer and a private safe for your valuables. Most top-end hotels in Tuban, Legian and Seminyak have a genuine beach frontage, but those in Kuta are separated by a busy main road.

Most visitors stay at top-end places as part of a package tour, getting special rates considerably lower than the prices listed in this section – these prices are rarely negotiable for independent travellers, however. Some hotels have the cheek to add variable high-season supplements in peak times.

Tuban

There are many top-end places along the main road through Tuban, but not all are on the beach.

Holiday Inn Bali Hai (☎ 753035, fax 754549, email holidayinn@denpasar.wasantara.net.id) Despite being part of an international chain, this hotel has excellent Balinese architecture, as well as a beautiful pool and gardens. Rooms cost from US$175, and bungalows from US$333.

Kartika Plaza Hotel (☎ 751067, fax 752475, email kartikaplz@denpasar.wasantara.net.id) This large hotel is right on the beach, has a gigantic pool and rooms cost from US$181.

Ramada Bintang Bali Resort (☎ 753292, fax 753288) Known for its nightly entertainment and sports facilities, there are about 400 rooms starting at US$176/187.

Risata Bali Resort (☎ 753340, fax 753354) The nice rooms are set around a pool in a lovely garden. It's only a short walk to the beach, but a fair way from most of Kuta's shops and nightlife. Room rates start at US$96/108.

Santika Beach Hotel (☎ 751267, fax 751260, email santika@denpasar.wasantara.net.id) This hotel has a beach frontage, swimming pools and tennis courts, and a variety of rooms from US$145.

Kuta

There's no shortage of top-end places in Kuta, and many of them are on or near the beach.

Hotel Aneka Kuta (☎ 752067, fax 752892, email anekuta@denpasar.wasantara.net.id) Boasting an excellent location, directly opposite the beach, the clean rooms have TV and cost US$66/72, or US$78/85 for some privacy in a villa. The 'full suite' costs US$303.

Bounty Hotel (☎/fax 753030) Centrally located, but a little way from the beach, the Bounty has a distinctive black-tiled pool, but it's not as luxurious as others in this range. Prices start at US$121 per room, but discounts of 50% are not uncommon for independent travellers.

Hotel Camplung Mas (☎ 751580, fax 751869) Marketed to young Aussie package tourists as part of the Ocean Blue Club, the nice, semi-detached cottages have high fences affording some privacy and cost US$59/61 for a twin/triple.

Hard Rock Beach Club (☎ 761869, fax 761868) An enormous new complex in a prime location, it's already very popular, not least for its gigantic pool, and rock art in the foyer. Rooms cost US$193, or US$205 if you want an ocean view.

Hotel Istana Rama (☎ 752208, fax 753078) This huge, impressive place is opposite the beach, and charges less than others for the same sort of luxuries: from US$102 a room.

Karthi Inn (☎ 754810, fax 751708) Close to south Kuta and the beach, it is also on the main road, and noisy. But it does offer all the mod cons packed around a pool for a reasonable US$55/72 for singles/doubles.

Hotel Kuta Jaya (☎ 752308, fax 752309) Another enormous place overlooking the beach, with prices starting at US$109/129.

Hotel Kuta Segara Ceria (☎ 751961, fax 751962, email kutasegara@denpasar.wasantara.net.id) Individual cottages set among some lovely gardens cost from US$91/110, and go much higher.

Natour Kuta Beach (☎ 751361, fax 753958) Although it's the successor to the original Kuta Beach Hotel, which was on this same site, the rebuilt version has no sense of history at all. There are nice views and the location is very central, however. Rooms cost US$108/121 to a massive US$363 for the 'executive'.

Poppies Cottages I (☎ 751059, fax 752364, email info@bali.poppies.net.id) Still setting the standard for what a good Bali hotel should be, Poppies I has an exotically lush garden with cleverly designed and beautifully built cottages,

with a sitting room, and quasi-alfresco bathroom. It's cheaper than most top-end places, and with a lot more character: US$93/99/114 for singles/doubles/triples. Make a reservation – it's very popular.

Hotel Ramayana (☎ 751864, fax 751866) A short walk to the beach, this is a well established place close to Kuta Square. Prices start from US$60/72, and are 20% more for a room closer to the pool.

Resor Kul Kul (☎ 752520, fax 752519, email kulkul@indosat.net.id) Separated from the beach by a busy road, this huge and popular hotel has two and three-storey blocks plus bungalows in relatively spacious grounds. Rooms start from US$114/127.

Hotel Sahid Bali (☎ 753855, fax 752019, email sahid-bl@dps.mega.net.id) Located along the beach road, this place is popular with packaged tours. It has all the mod cons, with rooms from US$108/121 – and prices go much, much higher.

Legian

Most of the top-end places in Legian are on the beach, but bring your wallet with you.

Bali Intan Legian (☎ 751770, fax 751891, email intan@denpasar.wasantara.net.id) Close to the beach, this is a standard package tour hotel with rooms in two storey blocks from US$96/108, and garden cottages for US$121/133.

Bali Mandira (☎ 751381, fax 752377, email balimandira@denpasar.wasantara.net.id) Yet another enormous complex with everything you want, with rooms starting at US$121/145.

Bali Padma Hotel (☎ 752111, fax 752149, email padma@denpasar.wasantara.net.id) A huge 400 room hotel by the beach, the Padma has lush gardens and lots of lotus ponds. Prices start at a whopping US$169/193.

Bali Sani Hotel (☎ 752314, fax 752313) This small hotel is a bit cramped, and it's a short walk to the beach. Rooms are small but attractively designed, some with a touch of eccentricity, and cost US$78, or US$96 for a cottage.

Hotel Jayakarta (☎ 751433, fax 752074, email jhrbali@indo.net.id) Formerly the Kuta Palace Hotel, this enormous place is right on the beach. It has pleasant swimming pools, but looks a little overdeveloped. Rooms cost from US$127/139.

Legian Beach Hotel (☎ 751711, fax 752651, email legiangroup@denpasar.wasantara.net.id) Right on the beach and in the heart of Legian, this large, popular hotel has a wide variety of rooms, some which would suit families. Prices start at US$108/121 and go higher and higher and ...

Seminyak

There are a few expensive hotels along the coast in Seminyak. All offer almost total seclusion, and a full range of services because there are very few shops and restaurants nearby. Most hotels provide a free shuttle bus service to Kuta and Legian.

Bali Holiday Resort (☎ 730847, fax 730848) In a beachfront location, and close to popular restaurants and nightclubs, this very nice resort is good value with singles/doubles from US$84/91.

Bali Imperial Hotel (☎ 730730, fax 730545) The Imperial is imposing, and the prices are substantial. Rooms cost from US$192; treble this if you want a private pool, jacuzzi etc.

Bali Oberoi Hotel (☎ 751061, fax 730791, email obrblres@indosat.net.id) Right on the beach, the Oberoi is isolated and unquestionably hedonistic. You'll need a map and compass to get from your room to the reception area. Prices range from a staggering US$393 to US$908.

Dhyana Pura Beach Hotel (☎ 730442, fax 730463, email dhyana-p@indosat.net.id) This standard, motel-style place has rooms from US$55/65, which is better value than most accommodation in this area. There is an interesting old Protestant Church in the grounds.

Pesona Bali (☎ 730814, fax 730815) An attractive beachfront hotel with friendly staff and all the usual luxury facilities, it's quite good value, with standard rooms for US$118.

Puri Bunga Cottages (☎ 730334) A newish place in the heart of Seminyak, it is well set up, if a little overdeveloped, and good value with rooms from US$66/72.

Puri Naga Sea Side Cottages (☎ 730761, fax 730524) This is a comfortable, well located hotel, with rooms from US$78/90 for a standard/deluxe, which is not that outrageous for this neck of the woods.

Tjendana Paradise Hotel (☎ 753573, fax 730518) Also known as Hotel Bali Saphir, the impressive Balinese foyer belies a standard layout of three storey motel-style rooms, which cost from US$96/109 and go higher still.

PLACES TO EAT

There are countless places to eat around the Kuta region, from tiny hawker's carts to gourmet hotel restaurants. The cuisine is international and multicultural – you could stay in the region for a month, eat in a different place for each meal and never have to face so much as a *nasi goreng*. The restaurant business is highly competitive, and is quick to pick up on new trends, whether it's sun-dried tomatoes, *pad thai* or *tapas*.

If you want to eat cheaply, try the places which cater to local workers. Every afternoon *food carts* appear at the end of the roads leading to Legian Beach; along the esplanade, opposite the Hard Rock Cafe in Kuta; and even along the chaotic Jl Legian. There are also cheap *warungs* in the back streets near the post office, and a few dotted around the alleys between Jl Legian and Kuta beach. You can also buy tinned and packaged food from *supermarkets* along the main roads (but you won't save much money doing this), and fruit and bread from the *public market*.

Most tourist restaurants offer standard Indonesian dishes (nasi goreng, *nasi campur* etc), as well as hamburgers, jaffles, spaghetti, salads etc from 3000 to 7000 rp. Most also have pizza, steak and seafood dishes from 9000 to 15,000 rp. The quality varies from indifferent to excellent, and seems to depend as much on when you go and what you order, as on the establishment and the price. Sometimes the menu is posted outside, but if not, you can always ask to see it. Always check the prices before you sit down, and look for the daily specials. As a rule, larger places on Jl Legian and those near upmarket hotels are more expensive than the outlets in the laneways of Kuta and Legian.

It makes sense to eat at a place which is reasonably busy – a high turnover means fresher ingredients and some of those other customers must know what they're doing. On the other hand, the very big, barn-like places can be inconsistent – an unexpectedly busy night can mean 100 extra meals, slow service and fish from the freezer instead of from the tanks out the front.

For fancier (and more expensive) cuisine, you'll find French, German, Italian, Japanese, Korean, Mexican, Swiss and Swedish restaurants. The more expensive places really specialise, but the cheaper ones have a variety of dishes regardless of the cuisine they claim to offer. Even if one place advertises that it's

SOUTH BALI

a 'Mexican' restaurant, the chances are that it will also serve good Indonesian, Italian, Chinese and Japanese food. Upmarket hotels will often feature traditional dancing (see the Entertainment entry later in this section), and buffets for guests and the public.

Tuban

Dotted along the main road through Tuban, there are a dozen or more huge seafood restaurants, where you can select your main course while it's still swimming. All of these places are expensive, and are about the same standard and price – count on about 35,000 rp per head for a fish meal, with bread, rice and soup, plus drinks. *Bali Seafood* is one of the best.

Cafe Français is a classy and popular patisserie for a croissant, coffee and fruit-juice breakfast. *Bali Aroma Restaurant & Bar* has very happy hours, and daily specials from 7000 to 8000 rp. *Lily Restaurant* has been recommended by a few readers for service and good value. At, or very near, the Kuta Centre shopping centre, fast-food junkies will be in heaven: there's *KFC*, *Dunkin' Donuts*, *Pizza Hut* and *McDonald's*.

All of the hotels in Tuban have one or more expensive restaurants inside the grounds, which are also open to the public.

Kuta

South Kuta One of the best seafood restaurants in this area is *Lenny's Seafood*. The service is good, and the seafood dishes from 9000 to 13,000 rp are not as expensive as you would imagine.

Bali Aget has a good range of cheap breakfasts, pizza specials at lunch and a long happy hour – so you could stay there the whole day!

East along Jl Bakung Sari are several good, inexpensive restaurants, including *Dayu I*. Above *Agung Supermarket*, which has a lot of western food items for sale, *Agung Cafe* serves Korean barbecue dishes and other Korean standards.

In Kuta Square shopping centre, there is a few fast-food joints, such as *McDonald's* and *KFC*.

Central Kuta Poppies Gang I is named for *Poppies Restaurant* (☎ 751059), one of the oldest and most popular restaurant in Kuta. The prices are quite high, around 15,000 rp for main courses, but the food is well prepared and presented. The garden setting and atmosphere are delightful – make a reservation. A few metres west, *TJ's* (☎ 751093) is a deservedly popular Mexican restaurant with a good ambience and main courses from 10,000 rp. Bookings may also be necessary.

Close by, *Bamboo Corner* is quaint, and a good place to try seafood specials (about 7000 rp), or something from the range of Chinese and Indonesian dishes for around 5000 rp. One of the best restaurants is the nearby *Bali Asi*. The service is friendly, and specials include lunchtime pizzas for about 5000 rp, and fish specials in the evening for about 7500 rp. It also boasts one of the cheapest and longest happy hours in Kuta.

Also nearby, *Nusa Indah Bar & Restaurant* is excellent for seafood specials (from a very reasonable 6000 rp), in a friendly atmosphere, and serves ice-cold Carlsberg and San Miguel beers for the same price as a Bintang. Other recommended places in the general area include: *Fat Yogi's*, which does tasty but pricey Italian meals for about 10,000 rp and decent pizzas for slightly more; and the popular *Made's Warung*, which offers delicious meals for 10,000 to 15,000 rp.

Poppies Gang II has dozens of cheap eateries. *Batu Bulong* is tasty and inexpensive, as is *Warung Nanas*, which is popular for its very happy hour and specials from 4500 to 9000 rp. Next door, the daily specials from 6000 to 7000 rp at *Warung Ziro* are excellent value, and it's not as crowded as others in the area. *Twice Pub* has been recommended by a few readers. These, and many others nearby, have laser disc video movies at night, which can detract from the ambience and service.

The lane heading north from Poppies Gang II has sprouted several good cheap eateries to cater to those staying in the nearby budget hotels. The service is friendly and the daily fish specials are excellent at *Warung 96*, while *Warung Dewi* and *The*

Corner Restaurant (or Bali Corner) are also deservedly popular. Further up, one of the best value places in Kuta has to be *Brasil Bali Restaurant*. It offers an amazing range of very cheap Brazilian, Indonesian and western-style dishes and breakfasts, and the drinks are always inexpensive. Many travellers end up eating there time and time again.

On the Beach There are kiosks spaced all along the beach serving drinks and snacks. Prices are predictably higher than you'd pay elsewhere, but it's worth it for some people-watching and sea breezes. The upmarket *Kuta Seaview Restaurant*, in the Hotel Kuta Segara Ceria, enjoys a great location. It features a Saturday night buffet and dance for 22,500 rp, but other prices are generally 'touristy'. One of the cheapest and nicest places is *Sari Yasa Coffee Shop*, in front of the Sari Yasa Samudra Bungalows. Pancakes cost 3000 to 4000 rp, and Chinese meals about 8000 rp, while the great views are free.

Along Jl Legian The possibilities along Jl Legian are endless. Most of the time the road is an almost continuous traffic jam, however, and a table near the road can mean you have to shout to be heard.

Just north of Bemo Corner, *Sushi Bar Kunti* offers set menus with delicious Japanese treats for 25,000 rp. *Mini Restaurant* is a huge place despite the name. It serves Chinese dishes for 10,000 to 12,000 rp, and also specialises in seafood. You can choose your intended meal from the tanks next to the street – prices will vary from day to day. Next door, *Expresso Bar & Pizzeria* has pizzas for 13,250 rp in a pleasant setting.

Several travellers have recommended *Aquarius Bar & Restaurant*, but servings can be a little small, and the chef hasn't quite worked out how to make the chips (French fries) crunchy. For something completely different, visit the incongruous *Bounty II*, a replica of the famous ship, standing at the back of a mall. On the 'deck', you can enjoy a good value buffet (30,000 rp).

Continuing northwards, *Mama's German Restaurant* has authentic German food, with sauerbraten, bratwurst, pork knuckles, and expensive draught beer. The Chinese *Gemini Restaurant* continues to get rave reviews from readers, in spite of its bare and basic appearance, but prices have risen and it is no longer the bargain it was. *Mama Luccia Italian Restaurant* is classy but expensive for about 15,000 to 22,000 rp a dish.

Aroma's Cafe was recently awarded Bali's Best Restaurant, and we continue to get lots of rave reviews from readers. It is a mid-priced vegetarian restaurant with good food and a delightful garden setting – the desserts and fruit drinks are particularly tasty.

A little further north and just east of Jl Legian is *Yanie's*, a popular place with good burgers, pizzas and steaks, as well as Indonesian standards. It's inexpensive, opens till late and has a good, fun atmosphere.

Also, you'll find *McDonald's* at the Matahari Department Store, and a few other well known and well signposted fast-food outlets, such as *Subway*, along this road.

Legian

Jl Padma and Jl Melasti, and the laneway between them (Jl Sahadewa), have numerous mid-range restaurants and bars; it is a great place to look around for buffet breakfasts (about 5000 rp), daily specials (from about 7500 rp) and hunt out cheap happy hours.

Some of the classier, but more expensive, places specialising in Chinese food and seafood are *Orchid Garden Restaurant*; *Legian Garden Restaurant*, which has an excellent happy hour and cheap breakfasts; and *Restaurant Puri Bali Indah*, with very tasty Chinese food. *Taman Garden* is very popular for its delicious food, happy hours and effusive staff; it attracts a lot of repeat customers. At *Joni Sunken Bar & Restaurant* you can eat and drink while semi-immersed in a swimming pool. It also offers live music, and good value buffet breakfasts for 8500 rp.

Further north, things get more expensive, but the standards are higher – this is the fashionable end of town. *Poco Loco* is a popular and upmarket Mexican restaurant and bar. *Warung Kopi* is well regarded for its varied

SOUTH BALI

menu of European, Asian and vegetarian dishes, plus good breakfasts and tempting desserts – prices start at around 9500 rp for a main dish. The long-standing *Glory Bar & Restaurant* does various buffets on various nights; its Balinese buffet (about 20,000 rp) is one of the few places in Kuta to try authentic local cuisine.

Right by the entrance to Jayakarta Hotel, *Topi Koki Restaurant* does a pretty good 'cuisine Français'. It is about the most expensive place around, with main courses from 15,000 rp, but it advertises daily specials from 8000 rp. A little further back from the beach, *Swiss Restaurant* is adjacent to the Swiss and Austrian consular agents so should have some credibility. Other classy, but pricey, restaurants along Jl Pura Bagus Taruna include: *Thai Restaurant, Bar & Bakery*; *Rum Jungle Road Bar & Restaurant*; and the distinctive *Bamboo Palace* (by the Losmen Made Beach Inn).

Other places which have been recommended by readers include *Surya Cafe & Beach Bar* and *Karang Mas Cafe*, which are both right on the beach, and *Rama Garden Restaurant*.

Seminyak

Seminyak has several good places to eat, but nothing is cheap. *Goa 2001 Pub Restaurant* is where trendy expats choose from a multicultural menu and a long list of fancy drinks – all at pretty fancy prices. Also recommended are *Ryoshi Japanese Restaurant* and *Cafe Luna* for a vast range of meals from about 10,000 rp. Further north, *Kin Khao* is the best in the area for Thai food. Nearby, a few *warungs* serve cheap and tasty Indonesian fare for local workers, but foreigners are always welcome.

Along Jl Dhyana Pura, *Santa Fe Cafe* is a pretty, and a pretty expensive, option for US south-western dishes; and *Puri Duyung* is also charming but not cheap – dishes start from about 11,000 rp. *Cin-Cin Bar & Restaurant* has sensible prices for this part of Seminyak (dishes start at about 8500 rp), and *Cafe BL* is also pretty good. It is a pleasant walk to the restaurant at *Sarinande Beach Inn*, where you can enjoy some cold drinks and snacks, by the hotel pool, for Kuta-style (as opposed to Seminyak-style) prices.

Along Jl Double Six, *Blue Star Bar & Restaurant* is one of the best value places, and offers tasty daily specials from 7000 rp.

On the beach front, it's hard to go past *Zanzibar Bar*, which also serves meals. Better still and worth a trip to Seminyak is *Benny's Cafe*, a great place for breakfast, or a beer and a meal while watching the sunset at the end of a 'hard day'. For something a little different, share a drink with some mock Easter Island statues at the slightly tacky *Crusoes Bar*.

If you are staying at Pesona Bali or Bali Oberoi hotels, or you have your own transport, visit the charming *Paddy Field Art Cafe* which, as the name suggests, has art for sale, and is set among glorious rice fields. Organised bus tours sometimes stop at the large *Taj Mahal* Indian restaurant on Jl Lasmana.

ENTERTAINMENT

Around 6 pm, the sunset at the beach is the big attraction, perhaps with a drink at one of the beach bars. After a good dinner, many visitors are happy with a video movie, another drink (or two) and a stroll in the cool evening air. But a lot of people are here to party, and around the Kuta region that means lots of drinking, loud music and late nights. There's also a selection of more sophisticated nightspots, mainly in Tuban and Seminyak, where the ambience is more relaxed and the music can be good – much of it from local bands. Check out the 'What's On in Bali' sections of the *Jakarta Post* and the *Observer* to find out what's happening, and what's cool.

Prostitutes are tolerated on the central part of Jl Legian after 11 pm, while 'Kuta cowboys' practise their pick ups in many of the busier tourist bars. There are also cruising transvestites *(orang bencong* or *waria)*, often on motorbikes, who can simultaneously perform oral sex and pick pockets, without even dismounting (from their motorbikes, that is). Seedy guys still offer grass and hash, but it's almost certainly a rip-off. Alcohol is the drug of choice.

It's generally safe to walk the main streets late at night, but avoid isolated parts of the beach and take care outside nightclubs. Foreigners, especially single women, should take a chartered bemo or, preferably, a metered taxi to and from more distant venues.

Bars, Clubs, Nightclubs & Discos

Bars are usually free to enter, and often have special drink promotions and 'happy hours' between about 6 and 9 pm – sometimes longer. For the serious drinker, the biggest concentration of bars is on Jl Legian, while Jl Melasti and Jl Padma have a lot of Aussie-style bars. Plenty of party animals go on the (in)famous Peanuts Pub Crawl (☎ 754226) on Tuesday and Saturday night. Special buses (5000 rp a ticket) go to a handful of local watering holes – you can also book at Peanuts or anywhere the Crawl is advertised.

Kuta, Legian & Tuban Some regular Kuta visitors would have been devastated to find out that *Peanuts* burned down in late 1997, but relieved to know that it's now up and running again. There's a big outer bar with pool tables and loud rock music, and a large dance floor inside with loud dance music. Some other places to check out along Jl Legian include *Lips*, a sleazy C&W bar; *001 Club*, a self-proclaimed 'rage spot' with an all-you-can-drink offer of 30,000 rp per night; and *Norm's Sports Bar*, a long-established Aussie favourite which is looking neglected and seedy these days.

One of the most popular places to party is *Sari Club* (or 'SC' for short), which features a giant video screen, dance music, a young crowd and lots of local guys – but drink prices are high. Around the corner, *Tubes Bar* is where surfers drink beer, play pool and watch surfing videos. Further up Jl Legian is *Bounty I*, built in the shape of a sailing ship and easy to spot. It gets people in early with happy hours, and packs them onto the dance floor till the wee hours.

For something a little different, have a drink (which includes a free swim at the pool)

at *Adrenalin Park*. You can watch a lunatic bungee jump off the tower, or find some Dutch courage yourself. (For the sake of other spectators, bungee jumping with a belly full of grog is not a good idea!)

Most upmarket hotels in Tuban have some sort of nightclub or karaoke bar. The most 'happening' place seems to be the *BB Discotheque* at Ramada Bintang Bali Resort.

Seminyak *Goa 2001 Pub Restaurant* is where a lot of people start the evening with a meal and a few drinks. Alternatively, *Jaya Pub* is a place for an older crowd to enjoy relaxed music and conversation, while *Cafe Luna* has street-side tables where you can see and be seen.

Later on, but *never* before 1 am, the action shifts to the beachside *66 Club* (pronounced 'double six'), particularly on Saturday night, or the chic *Gado Gado*. They both have a cover charge (about 10,000 rp) which should include one drink. When there aren't many people in town, these two seem to alternate, with only one open on a given night. Both places have sea breezes, good sounds and open-air dance floors, and attract a trendy, affluent crowd of tourists, expats and Indonesians, with quite a few gays and the occasional, expensive bar girl. For something a little more sophisticated, try *Scandal Nightclub* at Tjendana Paradise Hotel.

Live Music

Most patrons and bar owners seem satisfied with DJs playing taped music, so live music is not that popular. Jl Melasti has a few loud bars which feature some Indonesian bands singing decent reggae and top 40 hits in passable English. One of the newest and most extraordinary places is *The Macaroni Club* which features live jazz Monday to Saturday from 10.30 pm, and even invites guests to jam with the musos on Friday night. Entry is free, but prices for drinks and meals are not cheap.

Joni Sunken Bar & Restaurant is one place which consistently features decent acoustic guitar music. Some more upmarket venues, attracting older customers, include the glossy, new *Hard Rock Cafe*, with live music most nights and pricey drinks.

Several upmarket hotels have something a bit more sophisticated: in Tuban, *Santika Beach Hotel* has pianists and singers most nights, and *Ramada Bintang Bali Resort* regularly features top 40-type bands; and something is always happening at Legian's *Bali Padma Hotel*.

On the beach in Seminyak, *Crusoes Bar* usually has live music on Wednesday, Friday and Saturday, as well as happy hours every evening.

Video Movies & Sports Telecasts

Laser disc video movies are featured at an increasing number of restaurants and bars, particularly along or near Poppies Gang II. They are pretty loud and easy to find, and boards outside promote the shows. Many start from about 3 pm every day, and different movies run about every two hours. Only go if you want to see the movie – they are impossible to ignore and the service slows down as the staff get involved in the interesting bits. Some films are so recent they are probably still being shown at major cinemas in your home country.

For those who can't survive without seeing their favourite sport on TV, many bars and restaurants – especially around Poppies Gang II and along southern Jl Legian – show live telecasts of US basketball, football and baseball; Australian cricket, rugby league and Aussie Rules football; and European football (soccer). Two popular places are *The Pub* and *Casablanca Bar*.

Cinemas

There is a modern, three screen *cinema complex* on the 4th floor of the Matahari Department Store on Jl Legian. New release movies, mostly from the USA, are usually shown in the original language, with Indonesian subtitles. The cinemas are finding it hard to compete, however, because the same movies are often shown in a restaurant or bar for nothing, but you do get a large screen and no hawkers. Tickets cost 6500 rp, and shows start from 6 pm.

Balinese Dance

Large hotels and restaurants present tourist versions of the best known Balinese dances, and these are well publicised. They are usually included in a set menu, which can cost up to US$25 per head. Hotels which regularly hold dances include *Bali Padma*, Legian; *Ritz-Carlton*, Jimbaran (see the Bukit Peninsula section later in this chapter); and *Kartika Plaza*, Tuban.

Travel agents and hotels can also arrange evening trips to see traditional dances at Bona (near Gianyar in east Bali), Batubulan and Denpasar, usually charging from around 25,000 rp per head, including transport. A few dances are also held every evening at restaurants in nearby Sanur; and there's often a Ramayana ballet at the Taman Festival Bali park, near Sanur. The Kecak dances at the temple at Ulu Watu are enchanting and cheap. Refer to the relevant sections for details. Otherwise, if you are going to Ubud, see some dances there (for information, see the Ubud & Around chapter).

SHOPPING

Parts of the Kuta region are now almost door-to-door shops and over the years these have become steadily more sophisticated. There are still many simple stalls where T-shirts and beach wear are the main lines. Often these are crowded together in 'art markets' like the one at the beach end of Jl Bakung Sari and on Jl Melasti. Shops come and go, and the price you pay often depends on your ability to bargain, so recommending any particular shops is not worthwhile.

Don't be pressured into buying things during the first few days of your stay – shop around for quality and price first. Hawkers on the beach and the street ask astronomical prices at first, so you have to haggle like hell. You should also bargain at small stalls and shops. In bigger, more established shops, the 'first price' is more realistic and less negotiable. In shops with marked prices, that's it.

Shopping Centres

For everyday purchases, like food, toiletries and stationery, there are shops and mini-markets along the main streets. Galeal de Wata shopping centre on the road to Denpasar is a little inconvenient, so many people end up going to one or both of the two enormous Matahari department stores. Both have western fast-food outlets, Timezone video arcades, cheap eateries upstairs and plenty of other ways to spend your hard earned cash. The Kuta Square shopping centre is easily the largest and most sophisticated group of shops on Bali. In these shopping centres, and along the main streets in the Kuta region, you can also buy and develop slide and print film quickly at cheap prices.

Arts & Crafts

Kuta shops sell arts and crafts from almost every part of the island, from woodcarvings to paintings to textiles and just about everything else in between. There are also many interesting pieces from other parts of Indonesia, and it can be difficult to assess their authenticity and value – many of the 'Irian Jayan antiques' are made both locally and recently.

One of best areas to shop around is the public market and Kuta Art Market. There are also dozens of good shops along a stretch of Jl Legian, north of the intersection with Jl Melasti. In the Kuta Art Market, you may want to check out the Artists Cafe, a new place exhibiting the works of local artists. It ain't Ubud, but it *is* classy for Kuta.

Clothing

Plenty of places sell cool and practical surf gear and beach wear; there are also outlets for Australian brands like Hot Tuna and Billabong. The shop on the ground floor of the Hard Rock Cafe does a roaring trade in merchandise from T-shirts to jackets to baseball caps – none of which is cheap.

The local rag trade has now diversified into sports and casual wear, often with input from visiting European, Australian and US designers. Most of these shops are dotted along Jl Legian. Conventional clothing is sold in the Matahari department stores, and is not bad value. The Kuta Square shopping

centre has upmarket boutiques selling clothing by Nina Ricci, Fila and Benneton, among others.

Leather jackets and goods are a popular item, and currently good value – you will be approached by touts hoping you'll part with your money at their leather shop.

Silver Work & Jewellery

Many shops sell silver and jewellery, and some of it is beautifully made in stunning designs, but the quality can be suspect from street vendors and small stalls. If you have time, and your own transport, it is worth looking around at the plethora of shops lining the road between Denpasar and Ubud (see the Ubud & Around chapter for details).

Music

More and more music shops are springing up, offering an enormous range of cassette tapes and CDs of western, Indonesian and Balinese music – all at fixed prices. Imported tapes cost about 18,000 rp, and it's less for local music. With the current value of the rupiah, CDs are now good value. Most CDs cost 80,000 rp.

Watches

You'll be accosted repeatedly by guys selling fake fashion watches on the street. It's almost worth buying one so you have an excuse not to look at any others. The first price will be ridiculously high, but they will usually come down to around 30,000 rp, which is a lot cheaper than a real Rolex. Most of these 'copy watches' are pretty convincing, but some have token design deviations, like TG instead of TAG, on the watch face.

GETTING THERE & AWAY
Air

If you want to buy or change an airline ticket, you should visit the relevant airline office in Sanur, Denpasar or the airport (see the Bali Getting There & Away chapter for details). The myriad of travel agencies in the Kuta region will reconfirm your flight for a small fee, but any decent hotel should do this for its guests free of charge.

Bemo

Public bemos regularly travel between Kuta and the Tegal terminal in Denpasar from 450 to 500 rp (but tourists are generally charged slightly more). Most 'S' bemos go only to the terminal area in Kuta, just beyond Bemo Corner, but the S1 does a loop around Jl Pantai Kuta (see the Kuta Area Bemo Routes map for details).

If the public bemos will not stop for you in the tourist areas, you may have to go to Jl Pantai Kuta, east of Bemo Corner for a trip to Denpasar; or Jl Raya Kuta, outside the Supernova shopping centre, in Tuban, to anywhere south on Bukit Peninsula and the airport. For all other destinations you'll have to go to Tegal first, and then probably get a connection to another Denpasar terminal.

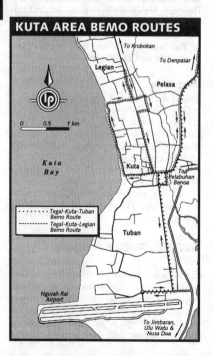

Public Bus

Lots of travel agents in the Kuta region sell bus tickets to Java and Lombok, but these are the same public buses that leave Ubung terminal in Denpasar, so you must still get to Ubung yourself anyway. Tickets will be slightly cheaper if you buy them at Ubung, but you won't save any money by going especially to Denpasar to buy the tickets. For public buses to anywhere else on Bali, you will have to go to Denpasar first, and buy a ticket at the relevant terminal.

The Bali Getting There & Away chapter has details about routes and fares between Denpasar and Java; and the Lombok Getting There & Away chapter has details of buses between Denpasar and Lombok.

Tourist Shuttle Bus

Several times a day, tourist shuttle buses travel between Kuta and Legian and almost every place you want to go on Bali. You can also get shuttle bus/boat connections to Lombok (including the Gili Islands) and Java directly from Kuta (see the Bali and Lombok Getting There & Away chapters for details).

Perama (☎ 751551, fax 751170) is the best known operator in Kuta, and around Bali. Other shuttle bus companies have similar fares and may offer more suitable times, but some, like Simpatik (☎ 755814), go only to Ubud, Sanur or Lovina. Some operators may pick you up from, and/or drop you at, your hotel (if the hotel is convenient). Usually, however, they pick up or drop off at a predetermined spot – often the place where you bought the ticket. Perama has a convenient office on Jl Legian, but you can also book tickets for Perama and other shuttle bus companies at any travel agent. The fares for services between Kuta and various destinations around Bali are listed in the relevant Getting There & Away sections throughout the book.

Car & Motorbike

There are many car and motorbike rental places around the Kuta region, so prices are the most competitive on Bali – as long as you look around. The Bali Getting Around chapter has details about the prices and standards you will get in the Kuta region.

One request: if you have rented a car, (or hired a taxi) *please* refrain from driving along the extremely narrow lanes in central Kuta – especially between Jl Legian and the beach – which are barely wide enough for two motorbikes. Either stay at a hotel along a main road, or park your vehicle (or get out of the taxi) on a main road and walk less than the 200m to your hotel.

GETTING AROUND
To/From the Airport
The Bali Getting There & Away chapter has details about catching taxis, shuttle buses and bemos, and walking, *from* the airport to the Kuta region.

From Kuta *to* the airport you should be able to charter a bemo for about 6000 rp (if you haggle hard), although even a metered taxi won't cost you much more. By public transport, you have to catch a bemo from the corner of Jl Raya Kuta and Jl Bakung Sari, or possibly even from outside the Supernova shopping centre in Tuban, and still walk for a few minutes to the airport terminal from the bemo stop. A taxi or tourist shuttle bus is more convenient.

Bemo
Dark blue bemos do a loop from Bemo Corner along and up Jl Pantai Kuta, along Jl Melasti, then up Jl Legian for a short while and then return down Jl Legian to Bemo Corner (about 500 rp for the loop). Another route goes from the airport to Denpasar via Kuta. Refer to the Kuta Area Bemo Routes map if you're confused.

In practice, bemo drivers can be reluctant to stop for tourists (the transport mafia influence), and bemos are less frequent and more expensive in the afternoon and evening. For many short trips, and certainly at night, you may have to charter a taxi or private car.

Chartered Bemo Bemos available for charter are easy to find – offers of 'transport' follow any tourist on foot. They don't have

meters so you'll have to negotiate the fare before you get on board. You should be able to get from the middle of Kuta to the middle of Legian for around 4000 rp, but bargain hard.

A full-day charter should run to about 90,000 rp, and you can estimate a price for shorter trips on a proportional basis, but you'll have to bargain hard. The 'first price' for transport can be truly outrageous. A chartered bemo will probably cost you about the same (or even more, if you don't haggle well) for an equivalent trip as a metered taxi, and taxis are a lot more comfortable. Vehicles which can legally be chartered have yellow licence plates – other vehicles offering rides may be a scam.

Taxi
There are plenty of taxis around the Kuta region, and they beep their horns at any tourist who is walking along the street. Most use their meters and are quite cheap – in fact, a metered taxi will often cost the same (or even less) than a chartered (unmetered) bemo or car, especially if you aren't good at haggling with bemo drivers. Taxis are very useful for trips around town at night, when they cost a little more, and they can be hired for trips to anywhere in south Bali, and even as far as Ubud.

Bicycle
Cycling is a good way to get around because the Kuta region is pretty flat – you can go up the narrowest gangs, park anywhere and even push your bike along the footpath, although the hawkers, window-shoppers, billboards and potholes make this easier said than done. The confusing one way streets and heavy traffic in Kuta also could also cause you some grief, but in Legian – and especially Seminyak – a bicycle is still the best way to get around.

These days there aren't many bikes for rent because many visitors prefer cars and motorbikes (which are still cheap). To find a bicycle, ask at your hotel and look around the streets – there are several rental agencies around Three Brothers Inn in Legian.

Bicycles only cost about 5000 rp per day, and for such a low price the agencies aren't interested in renting by the hour. The agency should provide a lock and key. Beware of thieves who might snatch things from the basket or luggage rack.

AROUND KUTA

Any place on Bukit Peninsula, and anywhere as far away as Bedugul, Padangbai, Ubud and Tanah Lot, can be easily visited on a day trip from Kuta by private transport, or even by public transport if you start early. There are also a couple of other beaches north of Kuta worth exploring.

Berewa

This greyish beach, secluded among stunning paddy fields, is a few kilometres up the coast from Kuta. There is no public transport in the area, but most of the hotels provide shuttle services to/from Kuta. The turn-off is along the road heading west from Krobokan.

There are three luxury resorts with pools, all next to each other along the beach. *Bolare Beach Hotel* (☎ 730258, fax 731663, email bolare@indosat.net.id) has a great beachfront location, and singles/doubles for US$72/85. *Legong Keraton Beach Cottages* (☎ 730280, fax 730285) has very nice individual cottages, set in a pretty garden right by the beach, for US$78/97. *Dewata Beach Hotel* (☎ 730263, fax 730290) has restaurants, tennis courts and a disco. The rooms are comfortable, but nothing special, and start from US$108/121.

You can eat in the *hotel restaurants*, or in one of the several decent *cafes* and *warungs* in the village, about 200m from the resorts.

Canggu

A popular surf spot with right and left-hand breaks, Canggu is surprisingly undeveloped. Surfers naturally congregate at the unnamed *warung* a few metres from the beach, but the only place to stay is the ultra-expensive *Hotel Tugu Bali* (☎ 731701, fax 731704, email bali@tuguhotels.com). It offers all the luxuries you would expect for US$302 to US$545.

To get to Canggu, go west at Krobokan and south at Kayutulang. Like Berewa, you will need your own transport.

Kites

Many Asian children do not enjoy the same variety and quantity of toys as children in the west, but they certainly do fly kites – almost anywhere in Asia the sky is likely to be full of kites of all sizes and types. Bali is no exception; you'll see children flying kites in towns and villages, and even in the middle of the rice paddies. At Sanur, however, kite flying is not just child's play – here the local *banjars* compete in kite-flying competitions, where size seems to be a major factor. July, August and September are the months for competitive kite flying.

The kites are enormous – traffic is halted when they're carried down the road and it takes half a dozen men to launch them, two men to carry the drum of heavy nylon cord, and a sturdy tree to tie the kite to once it's up and flying. Kites can be up to 10m long, and the cord tensioning the main cross-piece (itself a hefty length of bamboo) makes a low 'whoop-whoop-whoop' noise during flight. Not unexpectedly, such big kites are a danger to aircraft – one of these monsters could almost bring down a 747 – and kite flying has been restricted on the airport approaches, particularly across Pulau Serangan.

Many of the craft shops sell kites in the shape of birds, bats or butterflies. They come in a variety of sizes and fold up ingeniously so you can get them home. Look for ones with feathers and other details carefully painted – there's a lot of junk around.

Sanur

Sanur is an upmarket alternative to the Kuta region for those coming to Bali for sea, sand and sun, and a downmarket alternative to Nusa Dua for those who want a package-tour holiday in an air-conditioned hotel with a swimming pool. Good, inexpensive eateries abound, so you don't have to swallow the high prices at hotel restaurants. Other tourist services are here, with some charming craft, clothing, art and antique shops.

The beach is wide and white, and sheltered by a reef. At low tide it's very shallow, and you have to pick your way out over rocks and coral through knee-deep water. Many Indonesian families think it's ideal and you'll find many of them paddling here on Sunday and holidays, particularly at the northern end of the beach. At high tide the swimming is fine, and there's also a classic but fickle surf break.

A wide range of water sports is available, including windsurfing, water-skiing, snorkelling, parasailing and paddle boards – all for a price.

Sanur doesn't have the noise, confusion and traffic of the Kuta region, and you're not constantly badgered to buy things (badgered yes, but not constantly). The nightlife is sedate by comparison, but you can always go to the Kuta region for a wild night.

HISTORY

Inscriptions on a stone pillar found near modern Sanur tell of King Sri Kesari Varma, who came to Bali to teach Buddhism in 913 AD. The pillar, behind Pura Belangjong, is Bali's oldest dated artefact and also reveals ancient inscriptions recounting military victories of more than 1000 years ago. These inscriptions are in Sanskrit and are evidence of Hindu influence 300 years before the arrival of the Majapahit court.

The area was home to priests and scholars from the early days of Hinduism on Bali, and chronicles refer to Sanur priests from the 13th to the 16th century. Mads Lange, the Danish trader based in Kuta, document-ed close alliances between Sanur and the kings of Denpasar in the mid-19th century.

Sanur was one of the places favoured by westerners during their prewar discovery of Bali. Artists such as Miguel Covarrubias, Adrien Jean Le Mayeur and Walter Spies, and anthropologist Jane Belo and choreographer Katharane Mershon all spent time here. The first simple tourist bungalows appeared in Sanur in the 1940s and 50s, and more artists, including Donald Friend and Ian Fairweather, made their homes in Sanur. This early popularity made Sanur a likely locale for Bali's first big tourist hotel, the Bali Beach, built in the Soekarno era with war reparation funds from Japan.

Over this period, Sanur was fortunate to be ruled by insightful priests and scholars, who recognised both the opportunities and the threats presented by expanding tourism. Horrified at the high-rise Bali Beach Hotel, they imposed the famous rule that no building could be higher than a coconut palm. They also established village co-operatives that own land and run tourist businesses, ensuring that a good share of the economic benefits remains in the community.

The priestly influence remains strong, and Sanur is one of the few communities still ruled by members of the Brahman caste. It is known as a home of sorcerers and healers, and a centre for both black and white magic. The black-and-white chequered cloth known as *kain poleng*, which symbolises the balance of good and evil, is regarded as emblematic of Sanur.

ORIENTATION

Sanur stretches for about 5km along an eastern-facing coastline, with the landscaped grounds and restaurants of expensive hotels fronting right onto the beach. The conspicuous, 60s-style Hotel Bali Beach (now the Grand Bali Beach Hotel) is at the northern end of the strip. West of the beachfront hotels is the main drag, Jl Danau Tamblingan. It runs roughly parallel to the beach, with the hotel entrances on one side and wall-to-wall tourist shops and restaurants on the other side. For some reason, most of the streets are named after Indonesian lakes, such as Jl Danau Tamblingan and Jl Danau Buyan.

INFORMATION

Sanur is part of the Denpasar municipality, so you will have to go to the Denpasar Tourist Office for information, although your hotel may provide some local maps and information. Most international airlines offices, and some consular representatives, are sensibly based in Sanur rather than in Denpasar. See the Bali Getting There & Away chapter and the Bali Facts for the Visitor chapter, respectively, for details.

Money

The exchange rates offered by moneychangers in Sanur, especially in the big hotels, are poor – at least 10% lower than in Kuta. Even if you catch a return taxi to central Kuta to change your money, you will still be better off. The main American Express office on Bali is in the Grand Bali Beach Hotel. There are a couple of banks along the main road; Bank BCA, near Made's Kitchen restaurant, does cash advances on Visa.

Post & Communications

Sanur's post office is on the southern side of Jl Danau Buyan; more convenient postal agencies are listed on the Sanur map.

There's a Home Country Direct Dial telephone in the area where the airline offices are located at the Grand Bali Beach, and several wartels are dotted along the main road.

The Internet centre in the foyer of the Grand Bali Beach Hotel charges a ludicrous US$7.50 for the first 30 minutes, and US$1 for each subsequent five minutes. The Santai Hotel is far better value at 4000 rp for 15 minutes.

Emergency

The nearest hospital is in Denpasar, but there is a medical clinic (☎ 288271) in the Bali Hyatt hotel. The police station (☎ 288597) is on Jl Ngurah Rai.

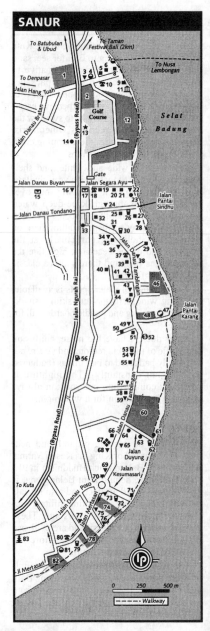

SANUR

PLACES TO STAY

1	Pura Dalem
2	Radisson Bali
5	Watering Hole Homestay
6	Alit's Beach Bungalows
8	Ananda Hotel
9	Diwangkara Beach Hotel
12	Grand Bali Beach Hotel; Airline Offices; Amex Office
19	Puri Kelapa Garden Cottages
20	Ratna Beach Hotel
21	Desa Segara
25	Queen Bali Hotel & Restaurant
27	Natour Sindhu Beach
29	La Taverna Bali Hotel
32	Puri Mango Guest House
35	Homestays Yulia, Luisa & Coca
39	Made's Homestay & Pub; Wartel
40	Bumi Ayu Bungalows
41	Bumas Hotel
44	Prima Cottages
45	Keke Homestay
46	Santrian Beach Resort
48	Laghawa Beach Inn
50	Hotel Bali Wirasana
51	Hotel Swastika; Hotel Ramayana
55	Santai Hotel; Kafe Jali Tawa; Internet Centre
58	Penginapan Jati; Warung Bali Sun

60	Bali Hyatt; Medical Clinic
66	Penginapan Lestari
71	Villa Kesumasari II
74	Sativa Sanur Cottages
78	Puri Santrian Hotel
82	Hotel Sanur Aerowisata

PLACES TO EAT

3	Si Pino Restaurant
16	Splash Bakery
22	Warungs
24	Kalimantan Bar & Restaurant
28	Mango Bar & Restaurant; Benno's Corner Cafe
31	Bali Hai Bar & Restaurant
34	Lotus Pond Restaurant
36	Warung Wina (Vienna Cafe)
38	Kuri Putih
42	Cumi Cumi
43	Taman Bayu
49	Swastika II Restaurant
54	Made's Kitchen; Bank BCA
57	Cafe Batu Kimbar; Postal Agency
59	Melanie's Restaurant; Wartel
65	Warung Agung
68	Legong Restaurant
69	Oka's
70	Kafe Jepun
73	Cafe Ketut
75	Tropika Kafe; Jaya Kesuma Art Market
76	Trattoria da Marco
77	Donald's Cafe & Bakery

OTHER

4	Bemo Stop; Perama Office
7	Boats to Nusa Lembongan
10	Wartel
11	Museum Le Mayeur; Water Sports Kiosk
13	Police Station
14	Supermarket
15	Main Post Office
17	Postal Agent
18	Telkom Wartel
23	Sanur Beach Market; Sanur Beach Market Bar & Restaurant; Water Sports Kiosk
26	Rumours Nightclub
30	Bali Janger
33	Pasar Sindhu Night Market & Art Market
37	Wartel
47	German Consulate
52	Bank Danamon
53	No 1 Club
56	Petrol Station
61	Surya Water Sports
62	Banjar Club
63	Duyung Art Market
64	Supermarket
67	Double U Shopping Centre
72	Bali International Sports Club
79	Trophy Pub; Postal Agency
80	Wartel
81	Bemo Stop; Warungs
83	Pura Belangjong

SOUTH BALI

MUSEUM LE MAYEUR

The Belgian artist Adrien Jean Le Mayeur de Merpes lived in this house from 1935 to 1958, when Sanur was still a quiet fishing village. The house must have been a delightful place then – a peaceful and elegant home right by the beach – but today it's squeezed between the Grand Bali Beach and Diwangkara Beach hotels. The museum is worth a quick look, but it's nothing special. It displays paintings and drawings by Le Mayeur; some are interesting, impressionist-style paintings from his travels in Africa, India, Italy, France and the South Pacific.

Paintings from his early period on Bali are romantic depictions of Balinese daily life and beautiful Balinese women but, unfortunately, many of them are yellowed, dirty and badly lit.

The paintings that look like they're done on hessian bags are actually on palm fibre, which Le Mayeur used during WWII when he couldn't obtain canvas. The more recent works, from the 1950s, are in much better condition, with the vibrant colours which later became popular with young Balinese artists.

All of the works have titles, descriptions and dates, in both Indonesian and English. The house itself is an interesting example of Bali-style architecture – notice the beautifully carved window shutters which recount the story of Rama and Sita from the *Ramayana*.

Entry costs 750/250 rp for adults/children.

The Artist from Belgium

Adrien Jean Le Mayeur de Merpes (1880-1958) arrived on Bali in 1932 and stayed at first near Denpasar, where he met Ni Polok, renowned as a beautiful Legong dancer, who began to model for him. He soon fell in love with the island, and with her, and they married – he was 55, she was 15. They rented land in Sanur and had a house built, which Le Mayeur decorated with antique stone and wood carvings collected from all over Bali. On his death, he willed the house to the Indonesian government to become a museum. His widow, Ni Polok, maintained the house until her death in 1985.

The museum (☎ 286201) is open from 8 am to 2 pm on Sunday, Tuesday and Wednesday; until 11 am on Friday; and until 12.30 pm on Saturday.

ACTIVITIES

There are numerous activities in Sanur, and all around south Bali. Also see the Activities entries in the Kuta and Tanjung Benoa sections in this chapter for more ideas of things to do if you are based in Sanur.

Diving

The diving off Sanur is not great, but there is a good variety of fish on the reef; at low tide they are in water shallow enough to be enjoyed by snorkellers. Sanur is not a bad place for divers to base themselves, and it's the best departure point for dive trips to Nusa Lembongan and other nearby islands. See the Diving section in the Bali Facts for the Visitor chapter for details about Sanur diving agencies.

Surfing

There are three good surf breaks on the reef, but mostly they need a big swell to work, and they are only good in the wet season (October to March) when winds are offshore. Better is Nusa Lembongan, which is easily accessible from Sanur (see the Nusa Penida chapter for details).

Water Sports

There are three kiosks where you can organise any number of water sports: near the Sanur Beach Market; close to the Museum Le Mayeur; and at Surya Water Sports. Prices at all three places are fairly similar, and are based on a minimum of two people. You can go parasailing (US$10 per go), jet-skiing (US$20, 15 minutes), water-skiing (US$20, 15 minutes), snorkelling by boat (US$15, one hour) and wind surfing (US$25, one hour). Alternatively, you can rent a banana boat (US$10, 15 minutes), hobie cat (US$25, one hour) or Balinese outrigger (US$15, one hour). Transport to and from your hotel is often included in the price.

For the Kids

A couple of kilometres north of Sanur, near the mouth of the Sungai Ayung, is **Taman Festival Bali** (☎ 289211). It's a nature reserve with some very lazy crocodiles (which do not reside in the public swimming pool), various rides for kids, and plenty of places to eat and drink. The official price (including all attractions) is US$15/7 for adults/children (aged two to 12). However, if you buy your ticket anywhere with a sign along the lines of 'buy your discount Taman Festival Bali tickets here', adults can get in for a more reasonable 35,000 rp, and about half that for children. It is worth asking a travel agent, or phoning the park, to find out the current deal.

Other Activities

If you want to ten pin bowl, the bowling centre in the Grand Bali Beach Hotel charges US$2.50 per person per game. For golfers, the Grand Bali Beach has a nine hole golf course, which costs US$50 per round, plus US$22 for a full-set of clubs, but only US$2.50 for the poor old caddie. If you're into war games, Bali Splat Mas (☎ 281693) offers 'jungle skirmishes' for US$49 a session.

COURSES

If you love Balinese food, you can register for the Lovina Cooking Course (☎ 287649), held in Sanur and identical to the popular course run in Lovina.

ORGANISED TOURS

Any of the hotels and travel agencies in Sanur can sell you tickets on the same tours that are also available from Kuta. See the Organised Tours section in the Bali Getting Around chapter for more details.

PLACES TO STAY

There are a few rock-bottom places in Sanur, and a handful of cheap mid-range hotels, but Sanur is primarily a medium to high-price resort, a place of 'international standard' hotels for package tours. Most places in the budget and mid-range include breakfast.

PLACES TO STAY – BUDGET

There is not much to choose from in the budget range. The three cheapest places are huddled together, and behind little art shops (which is where the staff will probably be). For these prices, in this part of Bali, don't expect much, but you may get a good deal on some batik or carvings. *Yulia Homestay* (☎ 288089) charges 30,000 rp per room, while *Luisa Homestay* (☎ 289673) and *Coca Homestay* (☎ 287391) charge 25,000 rp.

The best in this range is *Keke Homestay* (☎ 287282). Run by a friendly, English-speaking family, and set off the main road, the singles/doubles are quiet, clean and cost 30,000/40,000 rp.

PLACES TO STAY – MID-RANGE

All hotels listed in this entry offer hot water and air-con, and most also have cheaper rooms with fans and cold water. Most places charging US dollars have a swimming pool, but you will only be a few minutes walk from a glorious beach anyway.

In the northern part of Sanur, *Watering Hole Homestay* (☎/fax 288289), opposite the Grand Bali Beach Hotel entrance, has clean, pleasant rooms for 50,000/80,000 rp with

fan/air-con; and 100,000 r̶p̶ family-sized room with air-c̶o̶ ly, family-run place, with a good ̶r̶e̶ downstairs. Just down the road, *Ananda Hotel* (☎ 288327) is recommended: charming, clean and quiet singles/doubles are great value for 40,000/50,000 rp. It's the best place to base yourself before or after catching a boat to Nusa Lembongan.

Also good value is *Penginapan Lestari* (☎ 288867), further south, where rooms with fan/air-con cost 50,000/75,000 rp. None of the rooms have hot water, but it's quiet and friendly, and has some character.

One the best value places is *Penginapan Jati* (☎ 289157), although it doesn't have a pool. The outside decor is a bit ornate, but the staff are friendly and it's clean and quiet. Rooms costs US$15; the rooms for US$20 have a small kitchen.

Worth checking out is *Made's Homestay* (☎/fax 288152) at the back of the pub with the same name. It's a bit garish, but the staff are affable and there's a small pool. It is good value in this area: singles/doubles cost US$20/25 with a fan, or US$25 per room with air-con, bath and fridge.

Villa Kesumasari II (☎ 287824, fax 288876) is in a perfect, tranquil position, right on the beach, but is overpriced at 70,000/100,000 rp for fan/air-con rooms. Try to bargain with the manager if business is slow. *Prima Cottages* (☎ 286369, fax 289153) is in a scruffy area, but the cottages are good value for a negotiable US$20/30 with fan/air-con.

There are three central and good value places near where Jl Pantai Karang hits the main road. *Hotel Swastika* (☎ 288693, fax 287526) has pretty gardens, and comfortable singles/doubles for US$30/38 with a fan, and US$41/50 with air-con. *Hotel Ramayana* (☎ 288429) has air-con bungalows for US$30; it's slightly less for a room. *Hotel Bali Wirasana* (☎ 288632, fax 288561, email wirasana@indosat.net.id) is better value: from 36,000/48,000 rp for rooms with cold water and fan to 102,000/120,000 rp with all the mod-cons. It doesn't have a pool, but guests can use the one at Hotel Swastika.

Santai Hotel (π 287314) is a clean, comfortable two storey place with rooms facing a pool for US$30/37. It has been recommended by several readers for its 'environmental awareness', and decent library.

Other good hotels with air-con rooms for about US$35/45 include: **Laghawa Beach Inn** (π 288494, fax 289353); **Puri Mango Guest House** (π 288411, fax 288958), although it's on a noisy main road; and **Queen Bali Hotel** (π 288054), which also offers better bungalows for slightly more.

For a little more class at about US$60/72 (without breakfast) try: *Alit's Beach Bungalows* (π 288560, fax 288567); **Ratna Beach Hotel** (π 289109, fax 288418); **Diwangkara Beach Hotel** (π 288577, fax 288894); **Bumi Ayu Bungalows** (π 289101, fax 287517); **Bumas Hotel** (π 286306, fax 2883410); or **Puri Kelapa Garden Cottages** (π 286135, fax 287417).

PLACES TO STAY – TOP END

Most of the top-end hotels are on or near the beach. The prices given here are the low-season 'published rates' (including taxes and service charges), but prices will be considerably cheaper if you come on a package tour. Some places add a 'high supplement' in peak season (July to August and December to January).

Bali Hyatt (π 281234, fax 287693, email byhatt@dps.mega.net.id) This place blends in remarkably well. Singles/doubles start at around US$205/242, but you'll pay even more if you want a decent view.

Desa Segara (π 288407, fax 287242, email segara@denpasar.wasantara.net.id) The Segara has good facilities for kids. Rooms start from US$78/90, but the family bungalow for US$154 is steep.

Grand Bali Beach Hotel (π 288511, fax 287917, email gbb@indosat.net.id) Bali's first 'big' hotel is still one of the biggest on Bali. Dating from the mid-60s, it was built as a Miami Beach-style rectangular block facing the beach. Managed by the government Natour group, it has all the usual facilities from bars, restaurants and a nightclub to swimming pools and tennis courts, as well as a golf course and bowling

alley. Prices start at US$230, and the 'Presidential Suite' will set you back a mere US$4356.

La Taverna Bali Hotel (π 288497, fax 287126) Right on the beach, this attractive place has rooms from US$97 set in a beautifully landscaped garden.

Natour Sindhu Beach (π 288351, fax 289268, email nsindhu@denpasar.wasantara.net.id) Right on the beach and well set up, its rooms are reasonably priced at US$90/97, or US$115/121 for a bungalow.

Puri Santrian Hotel (π 288009, fax 287101, email santrian@denpasar.wasantara.net.id) This attractive and well located hotel has private cottages in a lush garden with two pools and beach frontage for a comparatively reasonable US$121/128.

Radisson Bali (π 281781, fax 281782) The four floors of rooms on either side of a long narrow pool are a bit cramped. It's not a good location, but compensates with an interesting programme of cultural demonstrations and activities, and a kid's club. Rooms start at US$170.

Santrian Beach Resort (π 288009, fax 288185) This features a great beach frontage, two swimming pools and tennis courts. Rooms start from US$80/85 and bungalows cost US$100/105.

Sativa Sanur Cottages (π/fax 287881) Right on the beach, its stylish rooms are attractively arranged around a swimming pool and gardens and cost US$82/95.

Hotel Sanur Aerowisata (π 288011, fax 287566, email sanurbch@dps.mega.net.id) This vast place has hundreds of rooms from US$170/182, as well as a full range of sporting facilities and entertainment options.

PLACES TO EAT

All the top-end hotels have their own restaurants, snack bars, coffee bars and cocktail bars – all at top-end prices, of course. Because Sanur is so spread out, most visitors end up choosing a restaurant close to their hotel.

A few restaurants along Jl Danau Tamblingan feature menus in German (probably because the German Consulate is nearby).

Northern Sanur

The best places to grab a cheap meal are the *food stalls* and *warungs* at the beach end of Jl Segara Ayu, and around the Pasar Sindhu Night Market.

On Jl Ngurah Rai, **Splash Bakery** has a

good selection of bread, cakes and pastries, as well as commendable local versions of the great Australian meat pie.

One of the best hotel restaurants is at **Queen Bali Hotel** – starters are about 4000 rp and western dishes 9500 to 12,000 rp, but Chinese and Indonesian meals are a lot cheaper. **Kalimantan Bar & Restaurant** (also called the Borneo) has main dishes for about 12,000 rp, in a tranquil, shady setting, and offers something called a 'Wyoming Cowboy breakfast'. The restaurant at the **Watering Hole Homestay** is popular for good meals at decent prices. It also features a delicious Indonesian buffet with Legong dancing on Thursday night for 20,000 rp per person. The nearby **Si Pino Restaurant** is also pretty good.

It is hard to go past **Bali Hai Bar & Restaurant**, especially during happy hours. Main meals range from 9000 to 11,000 rp, and the three course set menus for about 19,000 rp are very tempting. **Lotus Pond Restaurant** (☎ 289398) has an expensive a la carte menu, and features a 'grand *rijstaffel*' buffet every night for 50,000 rp, including free transport within Sanur if you ring in advance. Close by, **Warung Wina** (aka Vienna Cafe) has good prices, and will appeal to German-speakers because the menu is in German.

Along the noisy main road, **Puri Mango Guest House** has a restaurant which serves pizzas for 10,000 rp; and good value three course menus for about 19,000 rp.

Most of the walkway along central Sanur is cluttered with cafes and restaurants, where you can catch a sea breeze (some places don't have fans, anyway). The major disappointment is that you won't see the classic sunsets of Kuta, but the seafood in most places is very tasty. **Mango Bar & Restaurant** is friendly, although the servings can be small. **Benno's Corner Cafe**, next door, is excellent for snacks and drinks. **Sanur Beach Market Bar & Restaurant** is not bad value, and very popular; meals range from 9000 to 12,000 rp.

Dotted among these are some cheap **warungs** and **rumah makans**, mainly for local workers, but anyone can try a delicious nasi cap cai, for example, for about 3500 rp.

Southern Sanur

Heading south along Jl Dan there are dozens of great places to u, may want to just walk along and choose somewhere you fancy, or check out one of the following places. **Kuri Putih** has surprisingly reasonable prices for its 'mexi-bali' lunches (about 9000 rp), but prices are higher at night when it features Balinese dances. **Taman Bayu** (aka Bayu Garden) is classy, with main courses for about 15,000 rp, and has Balinese dancing most nights. **Cumi Cumi** has tasty seafood in pleasant surroundings.

Good budget places also along this street include: **Warung Bali Sun** (near Peningan Lestari), which is popular for sensible prices in a friendly atmosphere; **Warung Agung**; **Cafe Batu Kimbar**; and **Made's Kitchen**, a charming and cheap place for snacks and drinks.

The vegetarian restaurant, **Kafe Jali Tiwa**, in the Santai Hotel, has been recommended by a number of readers. **Melanie's Restaurant** has decent prices, such as pizzas for 10,000 rp and excellent Thai food for about 9500 rp, and a menu in English and German.

Near the roundabout where Jl Danau Poso starts, there are about a dozen cheap **rumah makans** where authentic Indonesian food is served for less than 5000 rp. In this area, **Tropika Kafe** has a menu in English and Swedish, and specialises in Balinese cuisine and seafood. The half-price drinks during happy hour is an added attraction.

Another place worth checking out is **Cafe Ketut**, which offers sensibly priced meals (8000 to 12,000 rp). **Kafe Jepun** doesn't specialise entirely in Japanese food these days, and the pasta for 12,000 rp and Indonesian food for 10,000 rp are both worth trying. **Oka's** has a pretty setting, but meals are pricey.

Other tempting places to try around town include: **Swastika II Restaurant**, **Legong Restaurant** and **Trattoria de Marco** for classy Italian cuisine.

For fresh baked goodies, head straight for **Donald's Cafe & Bakery**.

ENTERTAINMENT
Bars, Clubs, Nightclubs & Discos

Most of the big hotels have bars and sometimes discos, but there are not usually enough resident party animals to make them interesting; on week nights in the low season, venues can be depressingly empty.

Rumours Nightclub probably attracts the youngest crowd – mainly tourists plus some local beach boys. The slick *Bali Janger* disco is popular with Denpasar yuppies, but tourists also come along with bar girls and local boys. *No 1 Club* is one of Sanur's more popular nightspots, with flashy light shows and expensive drinks. These three places all have a cover charge of about 10,000 rp, and don't get going much before midnight.

Trophy Pub is a British-style pub, with a pool table, bar food and reasonably priced beer. Unashamedly catering to the Aussie sports fan, *Bali International Sports Club* promises 'ice cold beer from the esky' while you watch satellite sports telecasts from all over the world.

Live Music

For live reggae, try *Mango Bar & Restaurant* or *Banjar Club*. For something more sedate and expensive, dress up a little bit and enjoy the singers, pianists or classical ensembles at *Grand Bali Beach Hotel*, *Bali Hyatt* or *Hotel Sanur Aerowisata*.

Balinese Dance & Music

You can see tourist-oriented – but still charming and traditional – Balinese dances in tourist restaurants and hotels all over Sanur, or go on special tours to Denpasar, Batubulan or Bona. Taman Festival Bali (see the earlier Activities entry) also features regular performances of Ramayana ballet.

Restaurants which feature regular dances include: *Swastika II Restaurant*, *Kuri Putih*, *Watering Hole Homestay* and *Taman Bayu* (see the previous Places to Eat entry in this section). At the big hotels, a dinner-show will cost around US$25 per person, plus drinks. *Grand Bali Beach Hotel*, *Bali Hyatt* and *Hotel Sanur Aerowisata* have some of the most lavish productions.

SHOPPING
Markets

Shops on Jl Ngurah Rai are worth a browse, especially for antiques. For souvenirs and clothes, check out the following markets:

- Jaya Kesuma Art Market, near the Tropika Kafe.
- Double U shopping centre, a small place by the roundabout.
- Sanur Beach Market, off Jl Segara Ayu.
- Pasar Sindhu Art Market, off Jl Ngurah Rai.
- Duyung Art Market, near the Bali Hyatt.

Pasar Sindhu Night Market is open most of the day. It caters a bit to tourists, but mainly sells fresh vegetables, dried fish, pungent spices and other household goods.

For genuine art and carvings, visit three shops, which also double as homestays – Yulia, Luisa and Coco (see the earlier Places to Stay entry in this section).

For paintings, Ubud is a better choice and is not far away. Sanur is also close to many of the villages which produce stonecarving, woodcarving, jewellery, weavings and basketware (the Denpasar to Ubud section in the Ubud & Around chapter has details). Like in Kuta, sellers are not afraid to ask for an astronomical 'first price', so bargain hard.

Shopping Centres

For serious spending sprees, it's easy to commute to the modern shopping centres in Denpasar, Kuta and Nusa Dua. There is also a supermarket on Jl Ngurah Rai and another near the Bali Hyatt. A few other supermarkets were being built along Jl Danau Tamblingan at the time of research, and should be finished by the time you read this.

GETTING THERE & AWAY
Air

The Bali Getting There & Away chapter has information about flights to/from Bali, and contact details of international airline offices in Sanur.

Bemo

Public Bemo There is an official bemo stop at the southern end of Sanur on Jl Mertasari, and another directly outside the entrance to the Grand Bali Beach Hotel, but you can normally hail a bemo anywhere along Jl Danau Tamblingan and Jl Danau Poso.

Two different bemos operate between Sanur and Denpasar. From Sanur, blue bemos go through the Renon area and across town to Tegal terminal (where you change for a bemo to Kuta). Green bemos sometimes take a route through Denpasar, but usually go through the eastern outskirts straight to the Kereneng terminal. The fare is 500 rp, but don't be surprised if you are charged at least double that.

Chartered Bemo You can easily charter a bemo from the bemo stop outside the Grand Bali Beach Hotel to anywhere in southern Bali.

A chartered bemo is much faster and more convenient than a public bemo, and cheaper than a shuttle bus if you share with three or more people, but it might not be cheaper than a metered taxi if you don't bargain hard with the driver.

Tourist Shuttle Bus
Perama operates regular shuttle bus services to Kuta (5000 rp), and to Ubud (5000 rp) on the way to Lovina (12,500 rp), via Bedugul (7500 rp) or Kintamani (10,000 rp). A few other operators with slightly different prices, and departure times, also operate to/from Sanur.

You can book tickets for Perama buses at the Perama office, or book for Perama and other operators at any of the shops and travel agencies along the main road.

Boat
Public and shuttle boats to Nusa Lembongan leave from the Ananda Hotel. See the Nusa Penida chapter for details.

GETTING AROUND
One of Sanur's main attractions is the long, concrete walkway which stretches along most of the beach, past many upmarket hotels and seaside restaurants, and through the markets.

To/From the Airport
The Bali Getting There & Away chapter has information about how to get from the airport to Denpasar or Kuta, from where you'll have to get another bemo (or two) to Sanur. From the airport, pre-paid taxis to Sanur cost 17,500 rp, but to the airport from Sanur, a metered taxi will cost about half this price. There are also shuttle buses from Sanur to the airport (5000 rp), but these are hard to organise from the airport.

Public Bemo
Bemos go up and down Jl Danau Tamblingan and Jl Danau Poso for 500 rp. If the bemo is empty, make it clear that you want to take a public bemo, not charter it. Know where you want to go and accept that the driver may take a circuitous route to drop off or pick up other passengers.

Car, Motorbike & Bicycle
Numerous agencies along the main road in Sanur rent cars, motorbikes and bicycles. Vehicle rental is about 10% more expensive in Sanur than the Kuta region, and some heavy bargaining is often necessary, so it's probably worth going to the Kuta region and renting something there. Refer to the Bali Getting Around chapter for details about prices, standards and licences.

AROUND SANUR
Pulau Serangan
Very close to the shore, south of Sanur, is Pulau Serangan (Turtle Island). The beaches on Serangan's east coast were, for many years, turtle nesting sites and some of the islanders made a living catching turtles and collecting their eggs. Unfortunately, uncontrolled exploitation resulted in the complete elimination of the Serangan turtles over the last few decades, and none survive to lay eggs on the beach.

The island has two villages, Ponjok and Dukuh (see the South Bali map), and an important temple, **Pura Sakenan**, a 1km walk south from where the boats land. Architecturally, the temple is not much to see, but it's one of the holiest on Bali, and major festivals attract huge crowds of devotees, especially during the Kuningan and Galungan festivals.

Walking around Serangan is quite pleasant because there are no cars. The southern end of the island has nice beaches, and there's good snorkelling off the east coast. The problem is to negotiate a return trip which gives you enough time to walk the length of the island, enjoy the beach and then walk back. Boats can only go at high tide, so you need to plan for six hours on the island, which is more than a boat will normally wait.

Getting There & Away The easiest, but most expensive, way to the island is on an organised diving trip from one of the diving or water sports agencies in Sanur, Tanjung Benoa or Nusa Dua. A one hour trip costs about US$15 per person, but allows no time to really explore the island. During low tide, you may even be able to walk (albeit quickly) across to the island from Suwung.

The boat terminal for Serangan is at Suwung, a scruffy mangrove inlet south of Jl Ngurah Rai. (Bemos to Suwung leave from Sanglah terminal in Denpasar, but it's easier to take a taxi from Kuta or Sanur.) The starting price for chartering a boat (which holds up to ten people) is 25,000/50,000 rp one way/return.

There are occasional public boats (2000 rp per person), but they normally only run when there's an important festival on Serangan. Alternatively, you can charter a boat from Sanur (for about 50,000 rp return) or from Tanjung Benoa (for about 30,000 rp) – plus waiting time.

Pelabuhan Benoa

This wide but shallow bay is one of Bali's main ports. Benoa is actually in two parts – Pelabuhan Benoa, to the north, is connected by a 2km-long causeway to the main Kuta-Sanur road; and Benoa village is across the water to the south, on Tanjung Benoa (see the Tanjung Benoa section later in this chapter).

Benoa port consists of a wharf and a variety of offices. It is the port for ships run by Pelni (refer to the Bali Getting There & Away chapter for details); and for the fast *Mabua Express* boat to Lombok (refer to the Lombok Getting There & Away chapter for details). It is also the departure point for many luxury cruises, and fishing, diving and surfing trips (see the various Activities sections in the rest of this chapter for details).

Getting There & Away Visitors must pay a toll at a gate at the start of the causeway – 250 rp for pedestrians, and 600 rp per vehicle. Public bemos (1000 rp) leave from Sanglah terminal in Denpasar (the driver pays the toll). A chartered bemo or taxi from Kuta or Sanur should cost around 8000 rp one way, plus the toll.

Bukit Peninsula

The southern peninsula is known as Bukit (*bukit* means 'hill' in Indonesian), but was known to the Dutch as Tafelhoek (Table Point). Once a reserve for royal hunting parties, and a place of banishment for undesirables, Bukit was sparsely inhabited. Over the last few decades, luxury tourist hotels have been developed at Nusa Dua and along the south coast. A university campus and a cement industry have also been established. At the south-western tip of the peninsula is Ulu Watu, famous for its temple and surf.

SURFING

One of the most popular places for surfing on the peninsula is Pantai Suluban (see the South Bali map). Before the car park for the Ulu Watu temple, the road turns off to the Suluban Surf Beach, from where it's about 3km down a rocky road (passable for most vehicles). From the car park, continue on foot another 250m, down to the small gorge along a shaky and slippery path, to the beach. Half a dozen *warungs* give great views of the various surf breaks and the awesome sunsets, and serve simple meals and drinks, and allow you to doss down on the floor for about 5000 rp. You can also get ding repair stuff, and a massage, depending on what you need most.

There are other great surf breaks around the south-western tip of Bukit Peninsula, most notably **Padang Padang**, **Bingin** and **Balangan**. On the south coast are two more breaks, much more exposed and potentially dangerous. Both are accessible because they are next to fancy hotels. **Nyang Nyang** is reached by a track down the cliffs near Puri Bali Villas, and **Green Ball** is beside the Bali Cliffs Resort.

Most surfing spots are accessible by a passable (although occasionally rough) road, followed by a short walk from a car park. A few surf shops around Tubes Bar in Kuta offer shuttle bus services to surfing points around the peninsula for 25,000 rp return. For more details about surfing on Bukit, see the Surfing section in the Bali Facts for the Visitor chapter. These are some of the prettiest beaches on Bali, and are practically deserted when the surf isn't working. They are worth exploring even if you are not into surfing, but they are rarely suitable for swimming.

JIMBARAN

Just beyond the airport, south of Kuta, Teluk Jimbaran (Jimbaran Bay) is a superb crescent of white sand and blue sea. Jimbaran itself is a busy fishing village, somehow squeezed between the airport and a number of luxury hotels.

There's very little budget accommodation, but if you just want to see the beach or stay for a fresh seafood dinner it's very accessible from Kuta, Sanur or Nusa Dua.

The fishing fleet anchors at the northern end of the beach. Many of the boats (mostly traditional *prahus* and *jukungs*) are large, brightly coloured and elaborately decorated – and very photogenic. The main catch is large sardines, which are caught during the night and hauled up onto the shore early in the morning. There is also a daily fish market.

Enjoying the sunset and scenery, with a cool drink and a fresh fish on the fire, is a truly wonderful way to spend an evening.

Places to Stay
Places to Stay – Mid-Range There are only a couple of places resembling cheap accommodation, but more are likely to spring up in the near future. *Puri Indra Prasta* (☎ 701544) is uninspiring, noisy and over-priced, but there is a pool. Try to bargain prices down from 60,000/125,000 rp for a room, including breakfast, with fan/air-con.

Nelayan Jimbaran Cafe & Homestay (☎ 702253) is better value, with small clean singles/doubles for 75,000/90,000 rp, excluding breakfast.

Places to Stay – Top End *Puri Bambu Bungalows* (☎ 701377, fax 701440) has air-con rooms in three storey blocks around a pool, but it does have some character and the staff are friendly. Prices for singles/doubles start from US$66/78, which is cheap for Jimbaran, and 30% discounts are easy to obtain in quieter times.

Pansea Puri Bali (☎ 701605, fax 701320) has a full range of facilities and services,

SOUTH BALI

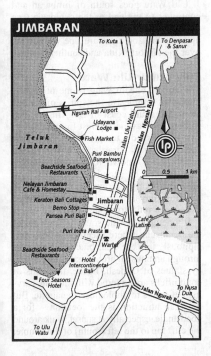

JIMBARAN

To Kuta
To Denpasar & Sanur

Ngurah Rai Airport

Udayana Lodge

Teluk Jimbaran

Fish Market

Jalan Ulu Watu

Jalan Ngurah Rai

Puri Bambu Bungalows

Beachside Seafood Restaurants

Nelayan Jimbaran Cafe & Homestay

Keraton Bali Cottages

Bemo Stop

Pansea Puri Bali

Jimbaran

Cafe Latino

Puri Indra Prasta

Wartel

Beachside Seafood Restaurants

Hotel Intercontinental Bali

Four Seasons Hotel

Jalan Ngurah Rai

To Nusa Dua

To Ulu Watu

0   0.5   1 km

including a huge swimming pool, two bars and two restaurants. Accommodation in air-con bungalows costs US$193/220 – but this does include breakfast, dinner and water sports facilities. *Keraton Bali Cottages* (☎ 701961, fax 701991) has spacious rooms from US$145/163 surrounded by tastefully landscaped gardens extending to the beach.

Further south, the massive *Hotel Intercontinental Bali* (☎ 701888, fax 701777) almost resembles a fortress. It's a very standard layout, but beautifully decorated with interesting Balinese arts and handcrafts. Room rates range from US$225 to US$400. *Four Seasons Hotel* (☎ 701010, fax 701020) has more than 100 individual villas spreading down a hillside on the southern edge of the bay. The accommodation is so spread out that little golf buggies are provided to transport guests between their villas and the reception area, restaurants, tennis courts and the beach. The villas are beautifully finished with great views and are yours from US$500 per night.

Between Jimbaran and the airport is the peaceful and eco-friendly *Udayana Lodge* (☎ 261204, fax 701098, email lodge@denpasar. wasantara.net.id), set in 70 hectares of bushland, with a swimming pool. Air-con rooms cost US$45, including breakfast.

Places to Eat

Many open-sided *shacks* along the beach serve delicious fresh seafood every evening; it's a perfect place for dining, sea breezes and sunset watching. The shacks are sited along the northern part of the beach, and along the quieter southern part, not far from the entrance to the Four Seasons. The standard deal is a whole fish, plus rice, bread, salad and maybe a dessert for 12,000 to 15,000 rp – the price depends on whether there are any seats (sitting on the sand is authentic and cheaper), and the cost of the day's catch. You pick your own fish from an ice box, and it's barbecued over coconut husks while you wait. As well as several types of fish, you can have lobster, crabs and prawns, but these are obviously more expensive.

The rooftop *cafe* at the Nelayan Jimbaran Homestay has spectacular views, but is more expensive than the beachside restaurants, and there are some unexciting *warungs* along Jl Ulu Watu. The big hotels all have their own *restaurants*, but expect to pay at least US$15 for lunch and US$20 for dinner, plus drinks.

On Jl Ngurah Rai, *Cafe Latino* is a popular Italian restaurant and nightspot, and features regular live entertainment.

Getting There & Away

Public bemos travel between Denpasar's Tegal terminal and Jimbaran (700 rp) on a southern loop from Kuta, but it's easier to catch any bemo heading towards Ulu Watu. Bemos don't run in the evening, however, so if you come for an evening meal you will need a taxi to get back. Taxis hang around the two beachside shack areas for this very reason.

ULU WATU

Jl Ulu Watu goes south of Jimbaran and continues to the end of the peninsula (see the South Bali map). On the way it climbs up to 200m, and there are fine views back over the airport, Kuta and southern Bali.

Pura Luhur Ulu Watu

The temple of Ulu Watu is one of several important temples to the spirits of the sea along the south coast of Bali. In the 11th century, the Javanese priest Empu Kuturan first established a temple here. The temple was added to by Nirartha, another Javanese priest who is known for seafront temples like Tanah Lot, Rambut Siwi and Pura Sakenan. Nirartha retreated to Ulu Watu for his final days, when he attained *moksa* (freedom from earthly desires).

It's perched on the south-western tip of the peninsula, where sheer cliffs drop precipitously into the clear blue sea. You enter through an unusual arched gateway flanked by statues of Ganesh. Inside, the walls of coral bricks are covered with intricate carvings of Bali's mythological menagerie. But the real attraction is the location – for a good angle, especially at sunset, walk around the cliff top to the left (south) of the temple.

Watch out for the local monkeys, which like to snatch spectacles and sunglasses, as well as handbags, hats and anything else they can get.

The temple complex is open daily, but the small temple itself is only open to Hindu worshippers. Tickets cost 1000 rp (which includes rental of a sarong and sash), and 300 rp to park a vehicle in the car park. Another attraction is that Ulu Watu is not nearly as touristy as Tanah Lot.

Balinese Dance On Wednesday and Saturday evening, an enchanting Kecak dance is held during sunset (from about 6 to 7 pm) in the temple grounds. Although obviously set up for tourists, it's the cheapest (7000 rp a ticket), and one of the best settings, of any Balinese dance on the island, and is worth the trip. A useful leaflet at the ticket office explains in English who are the baddies and goodies in this complex performance.

Places to Stay & Eat

On Jl Ulu Watu, a few kilometres south of Jimbaran, there are a couple places to stay which are convenient and have good views. *Hotel Villa Koyo* (☎ 702927) is a modern mid-range hotel which charges US$75 for a room, but may offer a 50% discount if business is slow (which is often). *Mr Ugly Cafe & Homestay* has small but comfortable rooms for about 35,000 rp; the cafe is a good stop for a drink or a snack.

There are other *restaurants* along Jl Ulu Watu, and plenty of *food stalls* in the incongruous shopping complex at the temple car park sell drinks and simple meals. It's nicer to stop for a meal or drink at Jimbaran.

Getting There & Away

Bemos travel between Tegal terminal in Denpasar and Ulu Watu village and temple (1100 rp), via Kuta (the stop is on Jl Raya Kuta, outside the Supernova shopping centre) and Jimbaran. However, public transport stops in the late afternoon, so to see the Kecak dance you'll have to go on an organised tour, or use private transport.

Many travel agencies in Kuta and Sanur arrange sunset trips to the temple, with a side trip to one or two nearby beaches, for about 20,000 rp per person – including an extra 10,000 rp for the waiting time while you watch the dance. If you are travelling in a group of two or more it's cheaper to charter a taxi or car.

SOUTH COAST

At the very southern end of Bukit Peninsula, perched on a cliff top, is a huge, luxury hotel, the *Bali Cliffs Resort* (☎ 771992, fax 771993, email bcr@indosat.net.id). Two transparent elevators go down the cliff to a restaurant, bar and beach. It's very expensive, of course: rooms range from US$235 to a whopping US$2662 for the presidential suite. If that's just a little out of your range, you can enjoy an expensive meal at the restaurant, which includes free use of the incredible elevator and the swimming pool.

A much smaller and more understated luxury option is *Puri Bali Villas* (☎ 701362, fax 701363), accessible by the road to the Nyang Nyang surf spot. It offers about half a dozen large private villas for US$250 per night, each with a magnificent view over a grassy field to the ocean.

NUSA DUA

Nusa Dua translates literally as 'two islands', which are actually two small raised headlands each with a little temple. But Nusa Dua is better known as Bali's top-end beach resort, a collection of suitably sumptuous five star hotels, successfully isolated from the realities of everyday life on Bali, with no schools, banjars or independent developments inside the enclave. This is where tourists pay almost exclusively in US dollars (and lots of them) to live where no hawkers are allowed, but the drawbacks are the lack of shops, other than the expensive shopping centre, and the general isolation.

As an alternative, less exclusive hotels are proliferating along the peninsula of Tanjung Benoa (see that section a little further on), while the village of Bualu, home to many hotel staff, is a burgeoning Indonesian town.

SOUTH BALI

Tourism – Nusa Dua Style

Nusa Dua is a luxury tourist enclave planned to ensure that the mistakes of Kuta would not be repeated, with advice from World Bank tourism experts. The site was chosen not just for its fine weather and white beaches, but also because the area was dry, relatively barren and sparsely populated. The objective was an isolated luxury resort, which would bring in the tourist dollars while having minimal impact on the rest of Bali.

The underlying philosophy reflected a change in tourism strategy. The idea of 'cultural tourism', which emerged in Ubud in response to the hedonism and 'cultural pollution' of Kuta, was to protect Bali's culture by selectively promoting and presenting aspects of it to tourists. There was an attempt to restrict tourism development to the Kuta-Sanur-Ubud area, but as mass tourism boomed, the sheer number of visitors was seen as a problem. The solution was a strategy of 'elite tourism', which would derive more revenue from fewer visitors. The authorities were probably not so naive as to think that rich tourists would be more culturally sensitive, but at least their impact could be largely confined to resort enclaves, where the cultural tourist attractions could be re-created with visiting dance troupes, gamelan muzak and Balinese decor.

Orientation & Information

As a planned resort, Nusa Dua is easy to make sense of when looking at a map, but it's very spread out. You enter the enclave through one of the big gateways, and inside there's expansive lawns, manicured gardens and sweeping driveways leading to the grand hotel entrances. In the middle of the resort is the enormous Galleria shopping centre, with everything you will probably need:

banks and moneychangers (offering lousy rates); ATMs which accept foreign credit cards; a postal agency; travel agencies; an American Express office (☎ 773334, fax 773306), which will collect mail for customers; plenty of restaurants; and Balinese dancing (see the Entertainment entry later in this section). There is also an Internet centre (sansan@indosat.net.id) in Bualu village, which costs 10,000 rp for the first 10 minutes, and 5000 rp for every subsequent five minutes.

The Klinik Gawat Darurat medical clinic (☎ 771118) is modern and well equipped, as you would expect, and should not be confused with the Nusa Dua Clinic in Tanjung Benoa.

Activities

Surfing The best surfing at Nusa Dua is on the reef to the north and south of the two 'islands'. Sri Lanka is a right hander in front of Club Med. The other breaks are reached by boat from the beach south of the Hilton. They work best with a big swell during the wet season. For more information, refer to the Surfing section in the Bali Facts for the Visitor chapter.

Diving & Water Sports Most diving and water sports are based in nearby Tanjung Benoa – refer to that section later in this chapter for details.

Golf In the middle of this luxury, there has to be a golf course, of course. The Bali Golf & Country Club (☎ 771791, fax 771797) has 18 holes, which will set you back US$135 per round, including buggy and caddie, or US$77 for just the front nine holes.

Camel Rides For something a little different, try a one hour Camel Safari (☎ 773377) for US$33/17 for adults/children.

Places to Stay

There is nothing even remotely cheap in Nusa Dua, but there are good budget and mid-range hotels in nearby Tanjung Benoa (see that section later on for details).

The Nusa Dua hotels all have swimming

Top: A losmen sign reflects the burgeoning surf travel market in south Bali.
Bottom left: Sunset on Kuta-Legian beach in south Bali.
Bottom right: Miniature boards for sale in a Kuta surf shop.

Top: Worshippers gather en masse at a temple festival in Ubud, Bali.
Bottom left: A woman performs her devotions at an Ubud temple festival.
Bottom right: Fruit, fruit and more fruit for sale at the frenetic Ubud produce market.

pools, a variety of restaurants, bars and all the other international hotel mod cons. They will charge the earth, and then an extra US$25 to US$50 for the 'high-season supplement', plus more for breakfast and other meals, and the use of sporting facilities.

We have not listed all the hotels in Nusa Dua. Some places are so exclusive that you may have to prove that you're a guest to get past the front gate, or that you can at least afford to pay for a meal or drink inside.

Bali Hilton International *(☎ 771102, fax 771199)* This is the most southerly hotel and it's massive. It has a full range of convention and leisure facilities, and rooms from US$175 to US$275, or heaps more for suites.

Hotel Bualu Village *(☎ 771310, fax 771313)* This was the first hotel at Nusa Dua. Away from the beach and not as elegant as its neighbours, it has a more friendly, informal atmosphere. Most sporting facilities are included in the price, which are comparatively modest at US$100/120 for singles/doubles.

Club Méditerranée Bali *(☎/fax 771521)* This package-tour operation includes all meals, activities and water sports facilities in its price, and the place is so self-contained that it's an enclave within an enclave. Rates start at around US$157 per person per night, and about half that for children.

Grand Hyatt Nusa Dua *(☎ 771234, fax 772038)* With extensive gardens and a river-like swimming pool, this is probably the best hotel in Nusa Dua, if not all of Bali. It charges US$193/220, and a lot more for villas.

Hotel Melia Bali Sol *(☎ 771510, fax 771360)* This hotel offers some Mediterranean touches with its food and entertainment. Rooms cost from US$212/240, and a lot more for suites.

Nusa Dua Beach Hotel *(☎ 771210, fax 771229)* It has all the luxuries you would expect for rooms costing from about US$200. It is attractively designed using Balinese architecture, and has good sporting facilities.

Sheraton Lagoon *(☎ 771327, fax 772326)* The Lagoon features all sorts of recreational facilities and a vast swimming pool with 'sandy beaches', landscaped 'islands' and cascading 'waterfalls'. Rooms start from US$280, plus more for ocean views.

Sheraton Nusa Indah Hotel *(☎ 771906, fax 771908)* With fewer Balinese decorative touches than others, it mainly pitches for the conference market, and has rooms from US$225.

Places to Eat

Each hotel has several restaurants. The public are welcome, but an evening meal will cost from US$25 per person, with drinks a very expensive extra. The various *restaurants* in the Galleria shopping centre are also expensive; do not go there if you baulk at spending 9500 rp for a hot dog or 13,000 rp for a large beer. Among many others at the Galleria, *Matsuri* is a 1st class Japanese restaurant, and the seafood at *Putri Duyung* is good, but courses start at 25,000 rp.

If you look around, and you're willing to walk or take a short taxi ride, you can find some value outside of the Nusa Dua complex. In Bualu, *Lotus Garden* is a classy place, with a tranquil setting more suited to Ubud than this busy main road.

Along Jl Pantai Peminge, there are several comparatively cheap eating places and watering holes, such as *Ulam*, which serves quality Balinese seafood, and *Poco Loco*, a Mexican restaurant and bar. The best value can be found at *Karmila Bar & Restaurant*, which has tasty food (for about 10,000 rp), a decent happy hour and friendly service. When business is slow, *Restorn Hann* advertises daily specials for about 10,000 rp.

Entertainment

If you're staying at Nusa Dua, you will return to the *Galleria* again and again. It offers Kecak and Legong dances, drum parades, live shows (including a Balinese Elvis impersonator!) – and it's all free, whether you're staying at Nusa Dua or not. Free Balinese dance classes are also held several times a week at the Galleria. Hotels in Nusa Dua will know the current schedule of attractions, or ask at the information booth (☎ 771662) at the shopping centre.

Major hotels like the *Grand Hyatt*, *Putri Bali* and *Hilton* feature Balinese dances in their restaurants during the evening, and always have western-style easy-listening singers and bands for guests and the public. Tanjung Benoa has other less formal possibilities. The 'What's On in Bali' section of the *Jakarta Post* and the *Observer* newspapers lists current and upcoming attractions.

SOUTH BALI

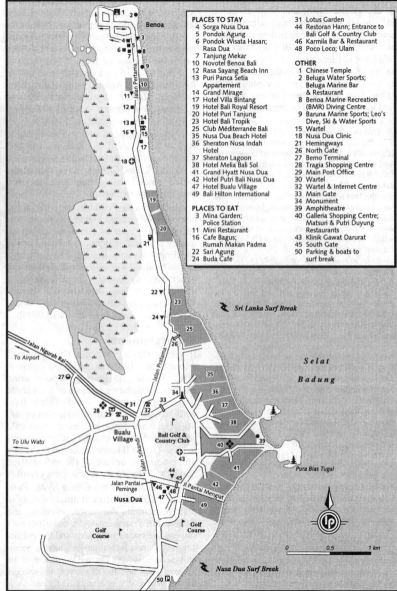

TANJUNG BENOA & NUSA DUA

PLACES TO STAY
4 Sorga Nusa Dua
5 Pondok Agung
6 Pondok Wisata Hasan;
  Rasa Dua
7 Tanjung Mekar
10 Novotel Benoa Bali
12 Rasa Sayang Beach Inn
13 Puri Panca Setia
  Appartement
14 Grand Mirage
17 Hotel Villa Bintang
19 Hotel Bali Royal Resort
20 Hotel Puri Tanjung
23 Hotel Bali Tropik
25 Club Méditerranée Bali
35 Nusa Dua Beach Hotel
36 Sheraton Nusa Indah
  Hotel
37 Sheraton Lagoon
38 Hotel Melia Bali Sol
41 Grand Hyatt Nusa Dua
42 Hotel Putri Bali Nusa Dua
47 Hotel Bualu Village
49 Bali Hilton International

PLACES TO EAT
3 Mina Garden;
  Police Station
11 Mini Restaurant
16 Cafe Bagus;
  Rumah Makan Padma
22 Sari Agung
24 Buda Cafe

31 Lotus Garden
44 Restoran Hann; Entrance to
  Bali Golf & Country Club
46 Karmila Bar & Restaurant
48 Poco Loco; Ulam

OTHER
1 Chinese Temple
2 Beluga Water Sports;
  Beluga Marine Bar
  & Restaurant
8 Benoa Marine Recreation
  (BMR) Diving Centre
9 Baruna Marine Sports; Leo's
  Dive, Ski & Water Sports
15 Wartel
18 Nusa Dua Clinic
21 Hemingways
26 North Gate
27 Bemo Terminal
28 Tragia Shopping Centre
29 Main Post Office
30 Wartel
32 Wartel & Internet Centre
33 Main Gate
34 Monument
39 Amphitheatre
40 Galleria Shopping Centre;
  Matsuri & Putri Duyung
  Restaurants
43 Klinik Gawat Darurat
45 South Gate
50 Parking & boats to
  surf break

Sri Lanka Surf Break

Selat Badung

Jalan Ngurah Rai
To Airport

To Ulu Watu

Bualu Village

Bali Golf & Country Club

Jalan Srikandi

Jalan Pratama

Jalan Pantai Peminge

Nusa Dua

Jl Pantai Mengiat

Golf Course

Golf Course

Pura Bias Tugal

Nusa Dua Surf Break

Benoa

Jalan Pertama

0   0.5   1 km

SOUTH BALI

Shopping

Markets Nusa Dua is a market-free and hawker-free zone, but bordering the edges of Nusa Dua, and especially along Jl Pantai Peminge, there are a few good souvenir shops with sensible prices.

Shopping Centres The Galleria shopping centre, with its 70 or more shops, is designed to ensure that visitors to Nusa Dua do not need to go anywhere else. It lacks the charm and bustle (and also the hawkers) of the Kuta region, and prices are higher.

A free shuttle bus (☎ 771662) connects all Nusa Dua hotels with the shopping centre about every hour. Pay a visit to the information booth for a map of the shopping complex (you'll need one), and for information about upcoming attractions and courses.

The Traiga shopping centre is the poor man's alternative to the Galleria, but it does boast ATMs which accept foreign credit cards, as well as a good book shop, a KFC, a decent supermarket and just heavenly air-conditioning.

Getting There & Away

The fixed taxi fare from the airport is 17,500 rp, but it will be cheaper in a metered taxi *to* the airport. Public bemos travel between Denpasar's Tegal terminal and the terminal at Bualu (the bemo also goes through Bualu village) for 500 rp. There's also a new bemo service between Batubulan terminal in Denpasar and Nusa Dua (2300 rp). From Bualu, it's about 1km to most hotels. Perama has tourist shuttle buses between Kuta and Nusa Dua several times a day for 5000 rp.

Getting Around

Firstly, find out what shuttle bus services your hotel provides. The Galleria provides a free shuttle bus to the shopping centre; otherwise you will have to order taxis, walk or rent a bicycle to get around.

The bigger hotels, and a few places in the Galleria, rent out bicycles for US$2/20 per hour/day (which is about 30 times the cost of rental in the Kuta region).

TANJUNG BENOA

The peninsula of Tanjung Benoa extends north from Nusa Dua, past Bualu village, and on to Benoa village. Benoa village is one of Bali's multi-denominational corners, with an interesting **Chinese temple**, as well as a mosque and Hindu temple nearby.

Orientation & Information

It is best to base yourself in the northern part of the peninsula; the area between the Villa Bintang and Club Med hotels is comparatively run down, and lacks shops and restaurants.

The wartels, police station, well equipped Nusa Dua Clinic (☎ 771324) and post office are all easy to find along the main road. Refer to the previous Nusa Dua section for information on services in Nusa Dua and Bualu village.

Activities

In the spaces along the coastal road between hotels there are many operators offering diving, cruises and water sports. Not all are experienced; nor do they always provide safe equipment, so check their gear and credentials before you go under water or parasail above it. Most operators provide free transport to/from anywhere in south Bali, and have a bar and restaurant attached to their premises. You can book directly or through any travel agency in south Bali.

Diving, Snorkelling & Water Sports

There are four reputable diving and water sports operators: Beluga Water Sports (☎/fax 771997), a long-established, upmarket outfit which also offers cruises; Benoa Marine Recreation (BMR, ☎/fax 771757), a reliable operator with a range of water sports, and diving and fishing trips; Leo's Dive, Ski & Water Sports (☎ 771592, fax 771989), which offers just about every possible water sport, and reasonably priced diving; and Baruna Marine Sports, which has offices all over Bali.

Prices for diving (a two person minimum is usually required) are about the same for each operator: it's US$40/60 for one/two dives around Tanjung Benoa; US$70 for two dives in eastern Bali; and US$95 for two dives at Nusa Penida. Certificate courses are also available for about US$350.

Snorkelling costs about US$10 per person per hour, including full gear and a boat ride to a nearby reef; or about US$15 if you want to go as far as Pulau Serangan (Turtle Island). You can rent full snorkelling gear at BMR (see the beginning of this entry) for US$5 per day.

Prices for water sports (which also normally require at least two people) are also similar among the operators: parasailing (US$10 per round); jet-skiing (US$20, 15 minutes); water-skiing (US$15, 10 minutes); banana boat ride (US$10, 15 minutes); and speedboat rental (US$125, one hour).

Cruises Several of the diving and water sports operators listed in the previous entry offer one hour cruises in a glass-bottom boat (US$15 per person); and three hour fishing trips for US$65 per person (with a minimum of three people). You might also want to try a Submarine Safari, run by Beluga Water Sports. It is an unusual sort of submarine in which you can admire marine life and coral for US$65 per person.

Places to Stay
Places to Stay – Budget & Mid-Range
Tanjung Benoa doesn't offer many budget or mid-range options. Although none of those listed in this entry are on the beach, they are only a short walk away.

There are four adjacent places near the top of Jl Pratama, so you can check them all out easily. All include breakfast. *Pondok Agung* (*☎/fax 771143*) is now more in the mid-range, but prices are negotiable. It charges US$20/25 for a fan-cooled/air-con room with hot water and TV, and there's a swimming pool. *Tanjung Mekar* (*☎ 772063*) is a small guesthouse, with nice rooms for 30,000 rp. *Rasa Dua* (*☎ 773515*) offers a few rooms in the home of one of the local boat operators for 35,000 rp. *Pondok Wisata Hasan* (*☎ 772456*) is another friendly, quiet option. Rooms with a fan cost 30,000 rp, or 60,000 rp with air-con and hot water.

Rasa Sayang Beach Inn (*☎ 771643*) is

friendly and clean, and great value at 30,000/37,500 rp for fan-cooled singles/doubles, and 48,000/60,000 rp with air-con. For a bit more comfort, try the quiet *Puri Pancia Setia Appartement* (*☎ 772243*), where the rooms (which aren't apartments) cost around 50,000 rp with air-con, but no hot water.

Places to Stay – Top End
In Benoa village, *Sorga Nusa Dua* (*☎ 771604, fax 771394*) is an attractive place, with a pool, gardens and tennis court. Singles/doubles cost US$96/103. *Novotel Benoa Bali* (*☎ 772239, fax 772237, email novobenoa @denpasar.wasantara.net.id*) straddles both sides of the road. (A guard with a 'stop' sign allows guests to cross the road unharmed.) Rooms cost US$157/181, or more for a *cabana* (bungalow).

Grand Mirage (*☎ 771888, fax 772148, email gmirage@denpasar.wasantara.net.id*) is another huge complex with all the trimmings for US$220/235. *Hotel Villa Bintang* (*☎ 772010, fax 772009, email vl_bintang@ denpasar.wasantara.net.id*) is another popular package tour place. Rooms cost US$102/115.

Heading further south, you reach *Hotel Bali Royal Resort* (*☎ 771039, fax 771885*), a small place with a pretty garden and just 14 air-con suites from US$170. *Hotel Puri Tanjung* (*☎ 772121*) is a little bigger, and a comparative bargain at US$73/110.

The last place before the northern gate to the Nusa Dua enclave is *Hotel Bali Tropik* (*☎ 772130, fax 772131, email btropik@ indosat.net.id*), a four star hotel with a pool, an eroded beach and rooms for US$122/190.

Places to Eat
There are several beachfront restaurants in or near Benoa village, such as *Mini Restaurant*, with a pleasant outdoor setting and meals for under 12,000 rp; and *Mina Garden*, a long-time favourite. For something really classy, *Beluga Marine Bar & Restaurant* (near the dive operation of the same name) has meals for about 15,000 rp, which is not outrageous considering the decor, location and service.

Cafe Bagus is away from the beach, but pretty cheap with some interesting items on the menu: the 6000 rp buffet breakfast is incredible value compared with the US$13 alternatives offered by most nearby hotels. *Rumah Makan Padma* has sensible prices (about 10,000 rp for seafood dishes), and a menu in German. *Sari Agung* is another standard tourist restaurant and bar.

Right on the 'border' with Nusa Dua, *Buda Cafe* often has daily specials, such as fish and chips and a small beer for 10,000 rp, but other prices are normally high. Nearby, cheap *warungs* cater to hotel staff and offer the best value for money.

Entertainment

Hemingways is a reasonably stylish piano bar, open from 8 pm until late, which features live music most evenings. *Beluga Marine Bar & Restaurant* has a classy bar and restaurant, and live jazz music every night. These are alternatives to the staid nightspots in the Nusa Dua hotels, but they are all pretty quiet outside the tourist seasons.

Getting There & Away

Refer to the previous Nusa Dua section for details on how to get to Bualu by public bemo and shuttle bus. From Bualu, green bemos hurtle along the Tanjung Benoa road, but not very often. It may be easier to take a taxi from Nusa Dua, Kuta or Sanur.

Getting Around

Travelling by taxi, or on foot, is the main way to get around because bemos are not frequent. A bicycle would be ideal along the flat, and relatively quiet, Tanjung Benoa road; however, no bikes are available for rent in Tanjung Benoa (budding local entrepreneurs, please take note of this deficiency), but there are some in Nusa Dua.

SOUTH BALI

Ubud & Around

Highlights

- Balinese dancing in Ubud is justly famous. The town has numerous accomplished dance troupes which perform regularly for both tourists and locals.

- Neka Museum boasts the finest collection of paintings on Bali – a veritable history of Balinese art.

- Arts, crafts and antiques are plentiful, with the galleries of Ubud – and the many workshops in the surrounding villages – offering an incredible assortment of things to buy.

- Ubud is Bali's culinary capital, with excellent restaurants serving superb Balinese, Asian and international cuisine at moderate prices.

- Gunung Kawi is the oldest monument on Bali, with imposing statues cut into the rock faces beside the picturesque Sungai Pakerisan.

Perched on the gentle slopes leading up towards the central mountains, Ubud is the centre of 'cultural tourism' on Bali, and a must-see destination for anyone interested in Bali's art, craft, music and dance. Apart from the many places of interest in Ubud itself, there are also numerous temples, ancient sites and craft centres in villages nearby. Although the growth of Ubud has engulfed several neighbouring villages, much of the surrounding countryside remains unspoilt, and offers gorgeous scenery and delightful possibilities for walking and cycling.

Denpasar to Ubud

The road between Denpasar and Ubud is lined with places making and selling hand-crafts. If it's your first trip to Ubud, try not to be put off by the rampant development and commercialisation – the craft villages are much more interesting when you stop and look. Many tourists shop along the route, sometimes by the bus load, but there are also some alternative, quieter routes and detours between the two towns, where much of the craftwork is done in small workshops and family compounds. You may enjoy these places more after visiting Ubud, where you'll see some of the best Balinese arts and develop your appreciation.

All bemos from the Batubulan terminal (see the Getting There & Away section in the Denpasar chapter) to Ubud stop at any of the craft villages along the main road. For serious shopping, it's worth renting or chartering your own transport from Ubud, so you can explore the back roads and carry your purchases. If you charter a vehicle, the driver may receive a commission – this can add 10% or more to the cost of purchases. Also, a driver is likely to steer you to somewhere which offers *him* a good commission, but does not offer *you* good value.

BATUBULAN

The start of the road from Denpasar is lined with outlets for stone sculptures – the main craft of Batubulan (which means 'moon stone'). Stone carvers are found all along the road to Tegaltamu, where the main road to Ubud does a sharp right turn. Batubulan is the source of the temple gate guardians seen all over Bali. The stone used is a porous grey volcanic rock called *paras*, which resembles pumice; it's surprisingly soft and light.

The temples around Batubulan are also noted for their fine stone sculptures. Just a couple of hundred metres to the east of the busy main road, **Pura Puseh** is worth a visit for its unusual decorations. The statues draw on ancient Hindu and Buddhist iconography and Balinese mythology, but they are not old – many are based on illustrations from books on Javanese archaeology.

Batubulan also has several venues offering regular performances of Barong & Rangda **traditional dances**. They are often held during the day, and are normally part of an organised tour from south Bali. Tickets cost about 10,000 rp. The dances held for tourists at Kuta, Sanur and Ubud are just as good, and more accessible for most visitors.

TAMAN BURUNG BALI BIRD PARK & RIMBA REPTIL PARK

This bird park (☎ 299352) boasts more than 1000 birds from over 250 species, including rare birds of paradise *(cendrawasih)* from Irian Jaya and highly endangered Bali starlings – many of which are housed in special walk-through aviaries. There are Komodo dragons, and a fine collection of tropical plants among two hectares of landscaped gardens. With some foreign assistance, the park is also actively involved in captive-breeding programmes.

Next door, Rimba Reptil reptile park (☎ 299344) has about 20 species of slithery creatures from Indonesia and Africa, as well as turtles, crocodiles, friendly Komodo dragons and a huge python called Gina – all set among more lush gardens.

Tickets are relatively expensive: 39,000/19,000 rp to either park for adults/children, or 70,000/35,000 rp for a ticket to both parks. Both places have pricey restaurants and gift shops, and are open daily from 9 am to 6 pm. Don't forget to bring your camera and plenty of film. Many organised tours stop at the parks, or you can take a Denpasar-Ubud bemo, get off at the junction at Tegaltamu, and follow the signs north for about 800m.

SINGAPADU

Singapadu is largely uncommercialised and preserves a traditional appearance, with walled family compounds and shady trees. The area has a strong history of music and dance, specifically the *gong gede* gamelan, and the older *gong saron*, and the Barong dance. Associated with this, local artisans

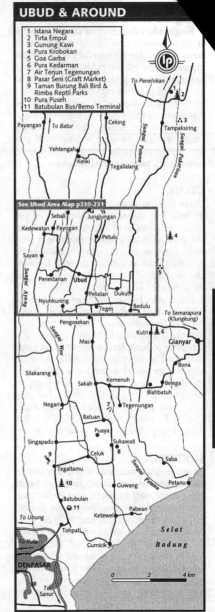

UBUD & AROUND

1	Istana Negara
2	Tirta Empul
3	Gunung Kawi
4	Pura Krobokan
5	Goa Garba
6	Pura Kedarman
7	Air Terjun Tegenungan
8	Pasar Seni (Craft Market)
9	Taman Burung Bali Bird & Rimba Reptil Parks
10	Pura Puseh
11	Batubulan Bus/Bemo Terminal

See Ubud Area Map p230-231

UBUD & AROUND

n producing masks for
dances.

rs now perform mostly
hotels in the tourist
are no regular public perfor-
...ces. There are not many obvious places
in the town to buy locally produced crafts,
as most of the better products are sold directly to dance troupes or quality art shops.
Ask around to find some of the workshops,
but even at the source, the best quality
masks will still be quite expensive. If you
are relying on public transport, wait for a
bemo at the junction at Tegaltamu.

CELUK

Celuk is the silver and goldsmithing centre
of Bali. The bigger showrooms are on the
main road, and have marked prices which
are quite high, although negotiation is possible. The variety and quality of the designs
is actually not as good as those in the well
known shops of Kuta, Sanur and Ubud, and
the prices are no cheaper.

Hundreds of silversmiths and goldsmiths
work in their homes on the back streets
north of the main road. Most of these artisans are from *pande* families, members of a
sub-caste of blacksmiths whose knowledge
of fire and metals has traditionally put them
outside the usual caste hierarchy. Their
small workshops are very interesting to
visit, and have the lowest prices, but they
don't keep a large stock of finished work.
They will usually make something to order
if you bring a sample or a good sketch.

SUKAWATI

Once a royal capital, Sukawati is now known
for a number of specialised crafts, and for its
huge, daily **craft market** called Pasar Seni.
One group of artisans, the *tukang prada*,
make temple umbrellas beautifully decorated with stencilled gold paint, which can be
seen at several roadside shops. The *tukang
wadah* make cremation towers, which you
are less likely to see. Other craft products
include *lontar* (palm) baskets, dyed with intricate patterns, and the wind chimes you
hear all over the island.

The craft market is an obvious, two
storey building on the east side of the main
road – public bemos stop right outside.
Every type of quality craftwork and touristy
trinket is on sale, at cheap prices for those
who bargain hard. Across the road is the
colourful morning **produce market**, with the
old **royal palace** behind.

Sukawati is also renowned for its **traditional dances** and *wayang kulit* (shadow
puppet) performances.

Puaya, about 1km north-west of Sukawati,
specialises in making high quality leather
shadow puppets and topeng masks.

BATUAN

Batuan's recorded history goes back 1000
years, and in the 17th century its royal family
controlled most of south Bali. The decline of
its power is attributed to a priest's curse,
which scattered the royal family to different
parts of the island.

In the 1930s, two local artists began experimenting with a new style of painting using
black ink on white paper. Their dynamic
drawings featured all sorts of scenes from
daily life – markets, rice fields, animals and
people crowded onto each painting – while
the black-and-white technique evoked the Balinese view of the supernatural.

Today, the distinct Batuan style of painting
is noted for its inclusion of some very modern
elements. Sea scenes often include a windsurfer, while tourists with video cameras or
riding motorbikes pop up in the otherwise
traditional Balinese scenery. There are good
examples in galleries along, or just off, the
main road in Batuan, and also in Ubud's
Museum Puri Lukisan.

Batuan is also noted for its traditional
dance, and is a centre for carved wooden
relief panels and screens. The ancient
gambuh dance is performed in Batuan's
Pura Puseh temple every full moon.

MAS

Although Mas is one way to spell 'gold' in
Indonesian, woodcarving is the principal
craft in this village. The great Majapahit
priest Nirartha once lived here, and the **Pura**

Taman Pule temple is said to be built on the site of his home. During the three day Kuningan festival, a performance of Wayang Wong (an older version of the Ramayana ballet) is held in the temple's courtyard.

Carving was a traditional art of the priestly Brahman caste, and the skills are said to have been a gift of the gods. Carving was limited to temple decorations, dance masks and musical instruments, but in the 1930s carvers began to depict people and animals in a naturalistic way, and the growth of tourism provided a market for woodcarving, which has become a major cottage industry. More abstract styles appeared in the 60s and 70s, with elongated figures and demonic forms emerging from the natural shapes of tree branches and roots.

North of Mas, woodcarving shops make way for art galleries, cafes and hotels, and you soon know that you're approaching Ubud. You can also use the back roads to the west of Mas and reach Ubud through Pengosekan or Padangtegal, or even the Monkey Forest Sanctuary if you are walking or cycling.

Places to Stay
Along the main road in Mas, **Taman Harum Cottages** (☎ 975567, fax 975149) has elegant individual bungalows, including some with balconies overlooking the rice paddies, plus a swimming pool. Prices range from US$79 for a standard room to US$145 for a family room. It can be found at the back of a gallery where you can enrol for art lessons (see the Courses entry in the Ubud section later in this chapter).

On the opposite side of the road, **Bima Cottages** (☎ 974538) charges US$25/35 for quiet single/double bungalows, with air-con and hot water, and the management is very willing to negotiate.

ALTERNATIVE ROUTES
Via the Coast
One alternative route between Denpasar and Ubud, bypassing Batubulan and Celuk, is little used. The road passes through the coastal village of **Gumicik** (which has a good beach) and, just back from the coast, Ketewel. The coast near Ketewel is good for **surfing** – the right-hand break is best in the wet season.

A road branches off from Ketewel to the beach at **Pabean**, the site for irregular religious purification ceremonies. Just north of Ketewel, before you rejoin the main road, is **Guwang**, another small woodcarving centre.

Via Blahbatuh
From Sakah, along the road between Batuan and Ubud, you can continue east for a few kilometres to the turn-off to Blahbatuh and continue to Ubud via Kutri and Bedulu.

In Blahbatuh, **Pura Gaduh** has a 1m-high stone head said to be a portrait of Kebo Iwa, the legendary strongman and minister to the last king of the Bedulu kingdom (see the Around Ubud section later in this chapter).

Carved timber lion figures are produced in Mas' many workshops. Along with their mirror-image twin, they appear as decoration on a traditional doorway.

UBUD & AROUND

Gajah Mada – the Majapahit strongman – realised that he could not conquer Bedulu, Bali's strongest kingdom, while Kebo Iwa was there. So Gajah Mada lured him away to Java with promises of women and song and had him killed. The stone head is very old, possibly predating Javanese influence on Bali, but the temple is a reconstruction of an earlier one destroyed in the great earthquake of 1917.

About 2km south-west of Blahbatuh, along Sungai Petanu (Petanu River), is **Air Terjun Tegenungan** waterfall (also known as Srog Srogan) at Belang Singa village. There is a signpost from the village of Kemenuh on the main road.

KUTRI

North of Blahbatuh, Kutri has the interesting **Pura Kedarman** (also known as Pura Bukit Dharma). If you climb Bukit Dharma hill behind the temple, there's a panoramic **view** and a **hilltop shrine** with a stone statue of the eight armed goddess Durga killing a demon-possessed water buffalo.

The Statue of Kutri

This statue on the hilltop shrine at Kutri is thought to date from the 11th century and shows strong Indian influences, although it's hard to make out the details.

Another theory is that the image is of Airlangga's mother, Mahendradatta, who married King Udayana, Bali's 10th century ruler. When her son succeeded to the throne she hatched a bitter plot against him and unleashed *leyaks* (evil spirits) upon his kingdom. She was eventually defeated, but this incident led to the legend of the *rangda*, a widow-witch and ruler of evil spirits. The temple at the base of the hill has images of Durga, and the body of a *barong* (mythical lion-dog creature) can be seen in the *bale barong* (pavilion which houses the barong; the sacred head is kept elsewhere).

BONA

Bona, on the back road between Gianyar and Blahbatuh, is credited as the modern home of the Kecak dance. Kecak and other dances are held here several times a week. Most visitors come from Ubud on organised tours which cost about 15,000 rp, including transport. Bona is also a basket-weaving centre and many other articles are also made from lontar leaves.

Nearby, **Belega** is a centre for bamboo furniture – roadside workshops and showrooms are stacked with the bamboo chairs, tables, beds and wardrobes which are standard issue in many of Bali's hotels.

Ubud

Ubud has been attracting and cultivating artistic talent since it became the seat of an aristocratic family in the late 19th century. When western artists and intellectuals began to visit the area in the 1930s, they provided an enormous stimulus to local art, introduced new ideas and techniques, and began a process of displaying and promoting Balinese culture around the world. As tourists arrived on Bali, Ubud became an attraction not for beaches or bars, but for its art, music, architecture and dance. These attractions are as rewarding as ever, combined with charming accommodation, great food and rustic surroundings. Ubud is just high enough to be cooler than the coast, but it's also noticeably wetter.

A mythical place called 'the real Bali' is supposed to exist somewhere near Ubud, and many who scorn Kuta will pretend that Ubud is untainted by tourism. In fact, Ubud is not a traditional Balinese rural village, nor is it typical of modern Bali. It has undergone tremendous development in the past few years, and now has traffic congestion in its centre and urban sprawl on the edges. It's still a pretty and relaxed place, however, especially if you're staying in a secluded family compound or eating in one of the delightful open-air restaurants, where the fragrant evenings are still quiet enough to hear a frog in a rice field.

There's an amazing amount to see in and around Ubud. You need at least a few days to appreciate it properly, and Ubud is one of those places where people planning to stay for a few days end up here for several weeks.

ORIENTATION

The once small village of Ubud has expanded to encompass its neighbours – Campuan, Penestanan, Padangtegal, Peliatan and Pengosekan are all part of what we see as Ubud today. The centre of town is the junction where the market and bemo stops are found. The main thoroughfare, Monkey Forest Rd, runs south to, naturally, the Monkey Forest Sanctuary – the road is one way (for cars, but not motorbikes, of course) heading south until the junction with Jl Dewi Sita.

The main east-west road is Jl Raya. West of Ubud, the road drops steeply down to the ravine at Campuan, where an old suspension bridge, next to the new one, hangs over Sungai Wos. Nearby is the pretty village of Penestanan, famous for its painters. East and south of Ubud proper, the villages of Peliatan, Pengosekan and Nyuhkuning are known variously for painting, traditional dance and woodcarving. North of Ubud it is less densely settled, with picturesque rice fields interspersed with small villages, many of which specialise in a local craft.

Maps

The maps in this guidebook will be sufficient for most visitors, but if you want to explore the surrounding villages on foot, the best map to buy is the very detailed and colourful *Ubud Surroundings* (25,000 rp), published by Travel Treasure. The pocket-sized *Ubud* map (12,500 rp) published by Periplus Handimaps, with the red cover, and the *Bali Pathfinder* (12,500 rp) are also worth picking up. All are available at the main bookshops mentioned in the following Information section.

INFORMATION

Unless otherwise indicated, all the places mentioned in this section appear on the Central Ubud map.

Tourist Office

The tourist office, or Yaysan Bina Wisata (☎ 96285), is open daily from 8 am to 8 pm. It doesn't hand out any maps or many brochures, but the staff are friendly and can answer most questions. They can tell you about authentic traditional dances and ceremonies in the region, and sell tickets to tourist-oriented dance and music performances. The tourist office is a local venture, set up in an effort to protect the village from the tourist onslaught by providing a service to inform and generate respect among visitors for Balinese culture and customs.

Money

All the major banks are represented in central Ubud, and most will change cash and travellers cheques. Bank Bali is the best for cash advances, while Bank Bali and Bank BII (see the Ubud Area map) have ATMs for Visa and MasterCard. The dozens of moneychangers along the main roads offer better rates and better service than the banks, however. The exchange rates are comparable to Kuta, but they often vary considerably from one moneychanger to another, so look around for the best rate.

Post

The charming little post office (see the Ubud Area map) is open Monday to Thursday from 8 am to 2 pm, until 11 am on Friday, and until 12.30 pm on Saturday. It has a sort-it-out-yourself poste restante – address mail to Kantor Pos, Ubud, Bali, Indonesia. The post office is inconvenient for most visitors, but there are several other handy postal agencies along the main roads (and indicated on the maps).

Telephone

The few *wartels* (public telephone offices) around Ubud can be used for local and international telephone calls and faxes, and there's a Telkom office along the eastern end of Jl Raya (see the Ubud Area map).

Home Country Direct Dial phones can be found outside the main Telkom office, Ary's Warung and the main post office.

Email & Internet Access

A few Internet centres are starting to pop up, and the prices are some of the lowest on Bali. Three cheap and reliable centres are:

Balinet
(yakin@deps.mega.net.id)
Charges are 5000 rp per15 minutes.
Pondok Pekak Library & Resource Center
(pondok@denpasar.wasantara.net.id)
It has the cheapest rates on Bali: 3000 rp for the first 15 minutes, and 1000 rp for every subsequent five minutes.
Roda Tourist Service
(rodanet@denpasar.wasantara.net.id – see the Ubud Area map)
It costs 5000 rp per 15 minutes; it's also recommended by readers for tours and car rental.

Travel Agencies

Jl Raya and Monkey Forest Rd are dotted with travel agencies, but most do little more than change money and sell tickets for dances and tourist shuttle buses. A few will book airline tickets (but you are better off doing this yourself in Kuta, Denpasar or Sanur) and can reconfirm your international flights for a negotiable fee (5000 to 10,000 rp).

Bookshops

Ubud is the best place on Bali to buy new and second-hand novels, and new books about Bali. The Ubud and Pandawa bookshops each sell a few foreign newspapers and magazines. Ganesha Bookshop (see the Ubud Area map) has a good selection of titles on travel, women's issues, arts and music, including a few titles in French. Ary's Bookshop has a fair stock of books and maps on Bali and Indonesia. Some of the museums mentioned later in this section have decent bookshops.

For second-hand books, in most major European languages, try Cinta Bookshop, Igna Bookshop or the Pondok Pekak Library.

Libraries

If you plan to spend some time in Ubud, you should visit the Pondok Pekak Library & Resource Center (☎ 976194). It's a relaxed and friendly place with Internet facilities; a

service for cheaply refilling plastic bottles with mineral water; a library and second-hand bookshop; and a useful message board. It is open daily from 9 am to 9 pm, but closes at 3 pm on Sunday.

Emergency

The Ubud Clinic (☎ 974911, mobile 081-1396069) is the best and most equipped medical centre in the region – see the Ubud Area map. It is open all day, every day, and charges 75,000 rp for a consultation at the clinic, and more for a visit to your hotel.

The *puskesmas* (community health centre, ☎ 974415) is pretty basic. Alternatively, head for Kuta or Denpasar.

The police station (☎ 975316) is to the east of the town centre in Andong – see the Ubud Area map.

MUSEUMS

Ubud is home to several fine museums. To most visitors, there's little difference between the exhibits at an art museum and an art gallery, except that galleries usually have items for sale. With the exception of the Museum Puri Lukisan, all can be found on the Ubud Area map.

Museum Puri Lukisan

The Museum of Fine Arts (☎ 975136) was opened in 1956, and displays fine examples of all schools of Balinese art. It was in Ubud that the modern Balinese art movement started; where artists first began to abandon purely religious and court subjects for scenes of everyday life. Rudolf Bonnet was part of the Pita Maha artists' co-operative, and together with Cokorda Gede Agung Sukawati (a prince of Ubud's royal family) they helped establish a permanent collection.

It's a relatively small museum, reached by crossing a river gully north of the main road. There are three gallery pavilions, set among beautiful gardens with decorative pools and statues. The pavilion straight ahead as you enter has a collection of early works from Ubud and the surrounding villages. These include examples of classical Wayang-style paintings, fine ink drawings by I Gusti

Nyoman Lempad and paintings by Pita Maha artists. The pavilion on the left as you enter has some colourful examples of the 'Young Artist' style of painting and a good selection of 'modern traditional' works. The pavilion on the right as you enter the grounds is used for temporary exhibitions, which are changed every month or so.

The museum has been restored in the last few years, and the paintings are well preserved and labelled in English. It's open from 8 am to 4 pm daily, and admission is 5000 rp. There are exhibitions of art for sale in other buildings in the gardens and in a separate display just outside the main gate.

Neka Museum

The Neka Museum (☎ 975074) was opened in 1976, and is the creation of Suteja Neka, a private collector and dealer in Balinese art. It has an excellent and diverse collection which is well exhibited, and is the best place to learn about the development of painting on Bali. A helpful pamphlet outlining the inclusions and directions is provided on entry, and the pictures are all well labelled.

The **Balinese Painting Hall** provides an overview of local painting, many influenced by wayang kulit puppetry. The **Arie Smit Pavilion** features Smit's works on the upper level, and examples of the 'Young Artist' school (which he inspired) on the lower level. The **Lempad Pavilion** houses Bali's largest collection of works by I Gusti Nyoman Lempad.

The **Contemporary Indonesian Art Hall** has paintings by artists from other parts of Indonesia, many of whom have worked on Bali. Works by Abdul Aziz, Affandi, Dullah and Anton Kustia Wijaya are among the most appealing. The upper floor of the **East-West Art Annex** is devoted to the work of foreign artists, such as Louise Koke, Miguel Covarrubias, Rudolph Bonnet, Han Snel, Donald Friend and Antonio Blanco. Finally, the **temporary exhibition hall** has changing displays of mostly contemporary paintings, with some items available for sale.

The museum is open daily from 9 am to 5 pm. Admission is 5000 rp, and no flash photography is allowed. There is a good bookshop in the lobby. It is worth stopping for a drink at the attached cafe, which has views normally found with a US$100 a night bungalow. Any bemo travelling between Ubud and Kintamani stops outside the museum.

Museum Rudana

This large imposing museum (☎ 976479), to the south of Ubud in Teges, was opened in December 1995. The three floors contain interesting traditional paintings, including a calendar dated to the 1840s; some Lempad drawings; and many more modern pieces from Affandi, among others. The collection is worth seeing, although it's not nearly as good as the other museums.

Museum Rudana is open from 8 am to 5 pm daily, and tickets cost 2500 rp. It's beside the **Rudana Gallery**, which has a large selection of paintings for sale, and there's a small cafe in the museum grounds. The museum is along the road to Denpasar, and easy to reach by bemo, or as a side-trip to Bedulu by bicycle.

Agung Rai Museum of Art (ARMA)

This new museum (☎ 976659), to the southeast of Monkey Forest Sanctuary, has two vast buildings housing works lent by patron Agung Rai, including the only publicly accessible works of the redoubtable Walter Spies, and rooms dedicated to the art of Raden Saleh, Affandi and Sadali. The entire collection is well labelled in English and Japanese. ARMA is interesting, although some visitors may be more than satisfied with what's on offer at the Neka or Puri Lukisan museums.

It's a good idea to visit ARMA late in the afternoon, have dinner nearby, and then watch some **traditional dances** inside the ARMA grounds in the evening – enquire and book at ARMA. There are also two coffee shops in the grounds, and a good bookshop with surprisingly low prices.

ARMA is open daily from 9 am to 6 pm. Tickets cost 5000 rp. The main entrance is

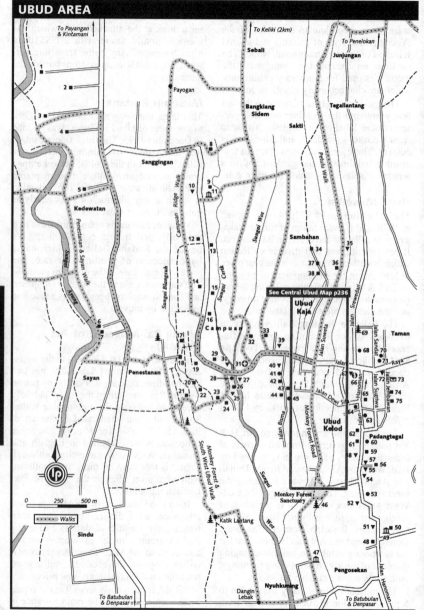

UBUD AREA

To Payangan & Kintamani

To Keliki (2km)

To Penelokan

Sebali

Junjungan

Payogan

Bangkiang Sidem

Tegallantang

Sakti

Petulu Walk

Sanggingan

Sambahan

Kedewatan

Penestanan & Sayan Walk

Campuan Ridge Walk

Sungai Blangsuh

Sungai Wos

Sungai Cerik

See Central Ubud Map p236

Ubud Kaja

Taman

Jalan Suweta

Jalan Sriwedari

Jalan Sandat

Campuan

Jalan Raya

Jalan Jembawan

Jalan Hanoman

Jalan Dewi Sita

Jalan Sugriwa

Ubud Kelod

Sayan

Penestanan

Padangtegal

Jalan Bisma

Monkey Forest Road

Monkey Forest & South West Ubud Walk

Sungai Wos

Sungai Ayung

Katik Lantang

Monkey Forest Sanctuary

Sindu

0   250   500 m

····· Walks

Dangin Lebak

Nyuhkuning

Pengosekan

Jalan Hanoman

To Batubulan & Denpasar

To Batubulan & Denpasar

UBUD AREA

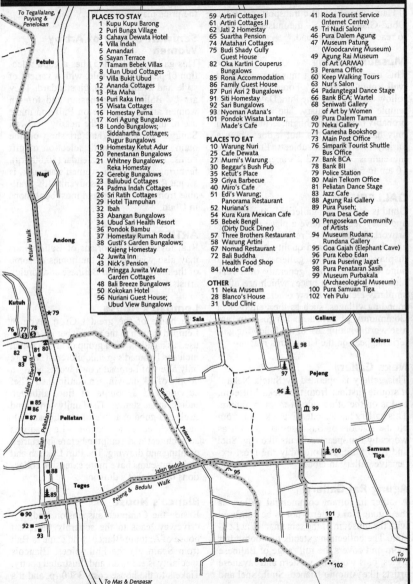

PLACES TO STAY
1 Kupu Kupu Barong
2 Puri Bunga Village
3 Cahaya Dewata Hotel
4 Villa Indah
5 Amandari
6 Sayan Terrace
7 Tamam Bebek Villas
8 Ulun Ubud Cottages
9 Villa Bukit Ubud
12 Ananda Cottages
13 Pita Maha
14 Puri Raka Inn
15 Wisata Cottages
16 Homestay Purna
17 Kori Agung Bungalows
18 Londo Bungalows;
    Siddhartha Cottages;
    Pugur Bungalows
19 Homestay Ketut Adur
20 Penestanan Bungalows
21 Whitney Bungalows;
    Reka Homestay
22 Gerebig Bungalows
23 Baliubud Cottages
24 Padma Indah Cottages
26 Sri Ratih Cottages
29 Hotel Tjampuhan
32 Ibah
33 Abangan Bungalows
34 Ubud Sari Health Resort
36 Pondok Bambu
37 Homestay Rumah Roda
38 Gusti's Garden Bungalows;
    Kajeng Homestay
42 Juwita Inn
43 Nick's Pension
44 Pringga Juwita Water
    Garden Cottages
48 Bali Breeze Bungalows
50 Kokokan Hotel
56 Nuriani Guest House;
    Ubud View Bungalows

59 Artini Cottages I
61 Artini Cottages II
62 Jati 2 Homestay
65 Suartha Pension
75 Budi Shady Gully
    Guest House
82 Oka Kartini Couperus
    Bungalows
85 Rona Accommodation
86 Family Guest House
87 Puri Asri 2 Bungalows
91 Siti Homestay
92 Sari Bungalows
93 Nyoman Astana's
101 Pondok Wisata Lantar;
    Made's Cafe

PLACES TO EAT
10 Warung Nuri
25 Cafe Dewata
27 Murni's Warung
30 Beggar's Bush Pub
35 Ketut's Place
39 Griya Barbecue
40 Miro's Cafe
51 Edi's Warung;
    Panorama Restaurant
52 Nuriana's
54 Kura Kura Mexican Cafe
55 Bebek Bengil
    (Dirty Duck Diner)
57 Three Brothers Restaurant
58 Warung Artini
67 Nomad Restaurant
72 Bali Buddha
    Health Food Shop
84 Made Cafe

OTHER
11 Neka Museum
28 Blanco's House
31 Ubud Clinic

41 Roda Tourist Service
    (Internet Centre)
45 Tri Nadi Salon
46 Pura Dalem Agung
47 Museum Patung
    (Woodcarving Museum)
49 Agung Rai Museum
    of Art (ARMA)
53 Perama Office
60 Keep Walking Tours
63 Nur's Salon
64 Padangtegal Dance Stage
66 Bank BCA; Wartel
68 Seniwati Gallery
    of Art by Women
69 Pura Dalem Taman
70 Neka Gallery
71 Ganesha Bookshop
73 Main Post Office
76 Simparik Tourist Shuttle
    Bus Office
77 Bank BCA
78 Bank BII
79 Police Station
80 Main Telkom Office
83 Jazz Cafe
88 Agung Rai Gallery
89 Pura Puseh;
    Pura Desa Gede
90 Pengosekan Community
    of Artists
94 Museum Rudana;
    Rundana Gallery
95 Goa Gajah (Elephant Cave)
96 Pura Kebo Edan
97 Pura Pusering Jagat
98 Pura Penataran Sasih
99 Museum Purbakala
    (Archaeological Museum)
100 Pura Samuan Tiga
102 Yeh Pulu

along the eastern road to Samuan Tiga, although you can also enter from a gate along Jl Hanoman. By public transport, catch the Ubud-Gianyar bemo – the museum is easy to reach from either road.

Museum Patung

This tiny woodcarving museum is a short walk south of Monkey Forest Sanctuary – follow the signs past the Pura Dalem Agung temple in the sanctuary. The walk there is probably more of a highlight, as the museum only has a few pieces, but it does show a variety of styles and subjects. Entry to the museum is 500 rp, and it's open daily from 10 am to 5 pm.

GALLERIES

Ubud is dotted with galleries – every street and alley seems to have a place exhibiting artwork for sale. They're enormously variable in the choice and quality of items on display. Three major galleries display a huge variety of work, generally of a very high quality, but at prices which are often similarly elevated. A few others in the surrounding villages, such as the Pengosekan Community of Artists in Pengosekan, are also worth visiting. All of the following galleries appear on the Ubud Area map.

Neka Gallery

This gallery is operated by Suteja Neka – it's quite distinct from the Neka Museum, and is on the other side of town in Taman. This gallery has an extensive selection from all the schools of Balinese art, as well as works by European residents like Han Snel and Arie Smit. It's probably the most expensive gallery in Ubud.

Agung Rai Gallery

Another important commercial gallery is the Agung Rai Gallery (not to be confused with the museum of the same name) at Peliatan. The collection extends for room after room and covers the full range of Balinese styles, plus works by western and Javanese artists like Antonio Blanco, Smit, Snel and Affandi. It works as a co-operative, with the work priced by the artist and the gallery adding a percentage. Some negotiation of the price may be possible.

Seniwati Gallery of Art by Women

This gallery (☎ 975485) has a good selection of paintings for sale, with a variety of style and a uniformly high standard. They are by Balinese, Indonesian and foreign women artists who live on Bali and make use of the facilities at the nearby Seniwati Sanggar workshop. The art shop on the main street has a small selection of gift items. Their colourful calendar (50,000 rp), featuring prints of the women's artwork, is a nice (but expensive) souvenir. It's available from the art shop and most bookshops in Ubud.

ARTISTS' HOMES

Real lovers and historians of Balinese art may also wish to visit the homes of some of the more renowned Balinese and foreign artists.

Lempad's House

The home of the great I Gusti Nyoman Lempad is open to the public, but it's mainly used as a gallery for a group of artists which includes Lempad's grandchildren. There are only a few of Lempad's own works here – a couple of ink drawings, an unfinished relief carving and a couple of fine, although fading, stone statues. The family compound itself is a good example of traditional Balinese architecture and layout – Lempad was an architect and sculptor before he started painting and drawing. The Puri Lukisan and Neka museums have more extensive collections of Lempad's drawings.

Blanco's House

Beside the Campuan suspension bridge, a driveway leads to the superbly theatrical house of Antonio Blanco, who came to Bali from Spain via the Philippines. Blanco's speciality is erotic art and illustrated poetry. Tickets to the house costs 3500 rp, and it's open daily from 8 am to 5 pm.

Other Artist's Homes

Arie Smit and Han Snel are other well known western artists currently residing in Ubud. In the 1960s, Smit sparked the 'Young Artists' school of painting in Penestanan. Han Snel's work is exhibited in a private collection at his restaurant and hotel in Ubud (see Places to Stay and Places to Eat later in this section), although his home is not open to the public.

The home of Walter Spies is now one of the rooms at the top-end Hotel Tjampuhan. Aficionados can stay in the room if they book well ahead. (See Places to Stay later in this section for details.)

MONKEY FOREST SANCTUARY

This charming, cool and dense piece of jungle at the end of, you guessed it, Monkey Forest Rd is inhabited by a band of avaricious monkeys, ever vigilant for passing tourists who just might have peanuts available for a handout. A sign says not to feed the monkeys, but they can put on ferocious displays of temperament if you don't come through with the goods – and quickly. The pamphlet you receive with your ticket provides an interesting summary of a 1991 study of the monkeys.

The interesting old **Pura Dalem Agung** (Temple of the Dead) is in the forest, for this is the inauspicious *kelod* side of town. Look for the rangda figures devouring children at the entrance to the inner temple.

Tickets to the sanctuary are 1100/600 rp for adults/children (still cameras are 500 rp, and video cameras 1000 rp). It is open daily during daylight hours. You can enter through one of the three gates: at the end of Monkey Forest Rd; another a few hundred metres east along the same road; or the third along a lane from Nyuhkuning to the south, via Museum Patung.

WALKS AROUND UBUD

The growth of Ubud has engulfed a number of nearby villages, although these have still managed to retain their distinct identities. There are lots of interesting walks in the area, to surrounding villages or through the rice paddies. You'll frequently see artists at work in open rooms and verandahs, and the timeless tasks of rice cultivation continue alongside luxury hotels. Refer to the earlier Maps entry for details about useful walking maps.

It's good to start walks very early in the day before it gets too hot. There are plenty of warungs around for a meal or drink, but bring your own water anyway. Also bring a good hat, decent shoes and wet weather gear for the afternoon showers; and long pants will make it easier to walk through thick vegetation. Don't leave your return too late if you're planning to get a bemo back to town, as they become infrequent after 5 pm, after which you may have to charter transport or walk back in the dark.

Monkey Forest & South-West Ubud

Monkey Forest Road is lined with hotels, restaurants and shops for its whole length, but at the far end, at the bottom of the hill, you'll arrive at a small but dense forest, inhabited by monkeys (see the earlier Monkey Forest Sanctuary entry). Continuing south along a path past a temple, you reach **Nyuhkuning**, noted for its woodcarving, and its small **woodcarving museum**. At the southern end of the village, turn right and cross Sungai Wos to Dangin Lebak. From there, follow paths north to **Katik Lantang** and Penestanan, both with substantial **temples**. **Penestanan** has numerous artists' homes, many with paintings for sale. Paved roads from there wind down across a stream and back to Campuan and Ubud.

This whole circuit is well under 10km, but could take a whole day, with lots of pleasant places to stop for eating, drinking and enjoying the sights.

Campuan Ridge

At the confluence of Sungai Wos and Sungai Cerik is **Campuan,** which means 'where two rivers meet'. An obvious path passes the marvellous Ibah hotel and leads north along the ridge between the rivers, with fields of elephant grass sloping away on either side. This grass *(aling aling)* is used for traditional thatched roofs, but demand from new construction work, especially big tourist facilities in Balinese style, has made it too expensive for many smaller users.

After about 2km, there are steep trails to the west which descend to Sungai Cerik, past areas where stone is cut from the slopes. Climbing the other side of the river will bring you near to the **Neka Museum**. Alternatively, you can go down across the eastern branch of Sungai Wos, then follow that ridge back to Ubud.

Continuing north along the main ridge, another trail to the west goes down to the river and comes up near Ulun Ubud Cottages. If you pass by this turn-off, the grassy fields give way to rice paddies, and you reach the small village of **Bangkiang Sidem**. From here you can continue walking north through **Sebali** for about 2km to **Keliki**, where you can stay at *Alam Sari*, with aircon, swimming pool and huge beds for about US$50 a double. It is another steep 20km or so all the way to Danau Batur on the edge of the great crater.

If you don't want to go that far, there are several options for looping back to Ubud. Just past the temples in Bangkiang Sidem, a trail goes west to reach **Payogan**, from where you can walk south to the main road. From the corner near the Ulun Ubud Cottages there is another trail south towards Penestanan, parallel to the main road back to Ubud.

Penestanan & Sayan

Just west of the Campuan bridge, a steep uphill road bends away to the left and winds across the forested gully of the Sungai Blangsuh to the 'Young Artists' village of Penestanan. West of Penestanan is **Sayan**, site of Colin McPhee's home in the 1930s, so amusingly described in his book, *A House in Bali*. The homes of a number of modern-day McPhees are perched overlooking the deep valley of the magnificent Sungai Ayung.

From Sayan, head north along the eastern side of the Ayung, where some of Bali's most expensive hotels offer magnificent

panoramas. You can cross a bridge to the western bank and head further north. If you have had enough, cross back to **Kedewatan**, and get back on to the main road through one of the public trails used by the upmarket hotels.

Petulu

In the late afternoon every day you can enjoy the spectacular sight of thousands of birds (including the Java pond heron and the plumed egret) arriving home in Petulu from all over Bali. They nest in the trees along the road through the village, and make a spectacular sight as they fly in and start squabbling over the prime perching places. Since the birds suddenly started to arrive in Petulu in 1965, villagers believe they bring good luck, although some locals do complain about the subsequent smell and mess.

You can wander around the village, or enjoy the spectacle while having a meal or drink in a local warung. Walk quickly under the trees if the herons are already roosting – the copious droppings on the road will indicate if it's wise not to hang around. Donations are requested.

There are two ways to Petulu – walk, or go by private vehicle or chartered bemo. (There are no direct bemos, but the bemo to Puyung will drop you off at the turn-off south of Petulu.) You can go to the eastern end of Jl Raya and head north through Andong, and look for the turn-off to Petulu. Alternatively, head north along Jl Suweta, continue through the village of **Junjungan**, which is heavily into the carving of garudas. Half a dozen shops by the roadside offer them in all sizes from a few centimetres high to giant 2m garudas which probably weigh a tonne. A little further up, on the right, a well marked turn-off leads to Petulu.

Pejeng & Bedulu

The temples of Pejeng and the archaeological sites of Bedulu (see the Around Ubud section later in this chapter) can be visited in a day's walk. As most of the attractions are on sealed roads, you can also go by bicycle. If you have the time and energy, do the entire loop by going to the far eastern end of Jl Raya, and find the small road which continues east from there. It passes the garbage dump and descends steeply to cross the Sungai Petanu, then climbs to the village of **Sala**. Some back roads will take you east to the main road. Going south along this road takes you past several important **temples**, and you can keep walking down to the carved cliffs of **Yeh Pulu** in Bedulu.

From there it's possible to follow Sungai Petanu upstream to **Goa Gajah** (Elephant Cave), but you may have trouble finding the right trail through the rice fields. If you've had enough, catch one of the many Ubud-Gianyar bemos which go past Goa Gajah. Alternatively, follow the trail by Sungai Petanu back to the small road by the garbage dump – most of it is pretty despite this landmark.

ACTIVITIES

Ubud is close enough to south Bali to enjoy some diving at Tanjung Benoa (or surfing at Kuta) for the day, but most visitors prefer more relaxed activities in the glorious countryside, or perhaps something soothing for the soul or body.

Cycling

Keep Walking Tours (☎/fax 96361, email balitrade@denpasar.wasantara.net.id) is based at Tegun Galeri shop on Jl Hanoman, and offers four or five hour cycling trips up and down the hills around Ubud. Prices start at 35,000 rp per person, including bike hire, but the cost is less per person in a large group.

Health & Beauty

Ubud has a few health and beauty salons where you can seriously pamper yourself. Milano Salon, Tri Nadi Salon and Nur's Salon have all been recommended by very satisfied customers. These salons provide manicures (17,500 rp, one hour), pedicures (15,000 rp, 45 minutes), Balinese massages (30,000 rp, one hour) and luxurious herbal baths (45,000 rp, one hour).

For the ultimate treatment, you can stay at Ubud Sari Health Resort (see Places to Stay later in this section). As well as tai chai and meditation classes for guests, the public can also enjoy massages from US$14 (one hour) and all sorts of herbal baths from US$15 to US$25.

Hiking

The legendary Victor Mason still runs the wonderful Bali Bird Walks (☎ 975009) from the Beggar's Bush Pub. The cost per person is US$33 for the day, including a guide book and lunch at the pub. The adventure agency, Sobek, offers the same walk for US$47, and can be booked at any local travel agency. Keep Walking Tours (see Cycling in this section) is more competitively priced. It offers three or four hour walks around the local area for about 18,000 rp per person, and longer hikes (six to seven hours) for about 25,000 rp. Ubud is also close enough to organise treks to places like Gunung Batur – see the Central Mountains chapter for details.

Rafting

Ubud is a great place to base yourself while you go rafting down the mighty Sungai Agung. The Rafting section in the Bali Facts for the Visitor chapter has more details.

COURSES

Ubud is just the sort of relaxed place to spend a few weeks and learn about Balinese and Indonesian culture, language music, dancing and cooking. To find out what courses are currently on offer, check out the noticeboards at the Pondok Pekak Library, Casa Luna restaurant, Bali Buddha Health Food Shop and tourist office. Some options include:

Art

Pondok Pekak Library, as well as a few art shops along Monkey Forest Rd, offer short courses in batik-making Classes in Balinese music, woodcarving and painting are often held at Studio B (☎ 975691) – 2½ hour elementary, medium or advanced courses cost 60,000 rp per person.

Taman Harum Cottages in nearby Mas (see the previous Denpasar to Ubud section) runs courses in woodcarving, batik painting, and Balinese dance and music from US$5 per person per hour.

Several places in Mas and Celuk also run classes in mask and metalwork. ARMA (see the earlier Museums section) offers courses in Balinese painting, music and dance, and children's programmes are offered.

Cooking

Noni Orti restaurant runs Balinese cooking courses three days a week for 40,000 rp per person. The popular Casa Luna restaurant (☎/fax 96282, email casaluna@denpasar. wasantara.net.id) also conducts classes three times a week for 80,000 rp. In both cases, book at the restaurants.

Language

The best place to ask about Bahasa Indonesia courses is the Pondok Pekak Library. A 20 hour course spread over one month costs 240,000 rp per person. Other courses are held on an ad hoc basis by local teachers; check out the noticeboards or ask around.

Music

Ganesha Bookshop (☎/fax 96359, email ganeshabks@denpasar.wasantara.net.id) conducts music workshops, where you can learn about and play Balinese instruments, every Tuesday night for 35,000 rp per person.

Spiritual

The Meditation Shop (☎ 976206) runs a number of free courses (in up to 10 different languages) between 6 and 7 pm every evening 'to direct your thoughts towards peaceful, positive experiences'. It also sells spiritual books and tapes. Pick up a pamphlet outside the centre. Ubud Sari Health Resort also runs courses – see the previous Activities entry.

ORGANISED TOURS

Taking an organised tour or two is a good idea as many of the attractions around Ubud are quite difficult to reach by public trans-

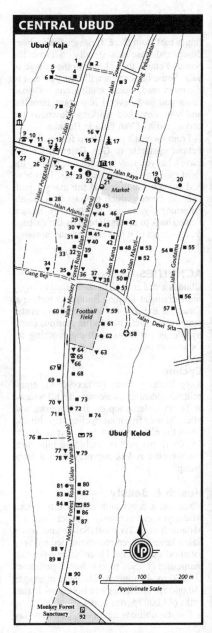

CENTRAL UBUD

PLACES TO STAY
1 Artja Inn
2 Arjana Accommodation
3 Suci Inn
4 Shanti Homestay
6 Siti Bungalows
7 Roja's Bungalows
11 Puri Saraswati Bungalows
28 Anom Bungalows; Jungut Inn
31 Alit's House
32 Puri Muwa Bungalows
33 Oka Wati Hotel
39 Gayatri Bungalows
41 Pandawa Homestay
& Bookshop
42 Gandra House
43 Hibiscus Bungalows
46 Yuni's House
47 Pondok Wisata Puri Widiana
48 Wija's House
49 Ning's House
50 Budi Bungalows
52 Dewi Putri Accommodation
53 Sayong House
54 Darta Homestay
55 Shana Homestay
56 Donald Homestay
57 Agung Cottages
60 Bendi's 2 Accommodation &
Bendi's Restaurant
61 Wahyu Bungalows
68 Frog Pond Inn; Postal
Agency; Wartel
69 Ubud Village Hotel
71 Pertiwi Bungalows
73 Puri Garden Bungalows
74 Rice Paddy Bungalows

76 Alamanda Accommodation
80 Ubud Bungalows
82 Saren Inn
83 Dewi Ayu Accommodation
84 Ubud Terrace Bungalows;
Hotel Argasoka
86 Fibra Inn
87 Ubud Inn
89 Pande Permai Bungalows
90 Monkey Forest Inn
91 Hotel Champlung Sari

PLACES TO EAT
5 Han Snel's Garden Restaurant
10 Mumbul's Cafe
12 Lotus Cafe
15 Bumbu Restaurant
16 Coconut Café; Cafe Angkasa
24 Ary's Warung
25 Ryoshi Japanese Restaurant
27 Casa Luna
29 Kul Kul Restaurant
30 Ayu's Kitchen
34 Lillies Garden Restaurant
36 Ibu Rai Bar & Restaurant;
Cafe Tirta
37 Bamboo Restaurant
38 Tutmak Cafe
40 Gayatri Cafe
44 Canderi's Warung
59 Aries Warung
63 Cafe Bali
64 Noni Orti; Milano Salon
66 Yogyakarta Cafe
70 Cafe Wayan
77 Lotus Lane Restaurant;
Dian Cafe; Mendra's Cafe

78 Jaya Cafe
79 Monkey Cafe
88 Warung Mama

OTHER
8 Museum Puri Lukisan
9 Wartel
13 Pura Taman Saraswati
14 Pura Desa Ubud
17 Pura Merajan Agung
18 Ubud Palace
19 Bank Danamon
20 Lempad's Home
21 Bemo Stops; Pasar Seni
(Art Market)
22 Yaysan Bina Wisata
(Tourist Office)
23 Ary's Bookshop
26 Bank Bali; Toko Tino
Supermarket; Ubud
Bookshop
35 Igna Bookshop
45 Bank BNI
51 Cinta Bookshop
58 Puskesmas (Community
Health Centre)
62 Pondok Pekak Library &
Resource Center (Internet
Centre)
65 Wartel
67 Putra Bar
72 Balinet Internet Center
75 Postal Agency
81 Meditation Shop
85 Postal Agency
92 Parking (for Monkey Forest
Sanctuary)

UBUD & AROUND

port, and finding your way around this part of Bali isn't easy, even with your own vehicle.

All travel agencies in Ubud can arrange organised tours, but it is worth shopping around as prices vary (for example, check if entrance fees are included in the price). The more interesting local half-day trips take in Mengwi, Alas Kedaton, Bedugul and Tanah Lot; or visit Goa Gajah, Pejeng, Gunung Kawi, Tampaksiring and Kintamani.

The Organised Tours section in the Bali Getting Around chapter has more information about tours which you can book from Ubud.

PLACES TO STAY

Ubud has hundreds of places to stay. We can't possibly mention them all, but we've tried to list a range of good value, charming and stylish places. A simple, clean room within a family home compound will cost from around 15,000/20,000 rp for single/ doubles, usually including a private bathroom and a light breakfast. In surrounding villages, there are also many cheap places, often in a much quieter, greener environment. It is often worth paying a little more, however – for about 25,000/40,000 rp, with breakfast, you can get a very nice room or bungalow, often well decorated with local arts and crafts, perhaps with a view of rice fields, jungle or garden.

Upper mid-range tourist hotels (ie those with swimming pools, hot water and US-dollar prices) are mostly on or near Monkey Forest Rd and Jl Raya. The really expensive hotels are perched on the edges of the deep river valleys, with super views and decorative art and craft works that rival many galleries.

A tax of 10% is added to the cost of a room, and fancier places add another 5% to 11% for service. Some accommodation is geared to long-stayers and offers cooking facilities, but no meals. In the low season, or if you are staying for a few days or longer (as many visitors do), it is certainly worth asking for a discount. While many streets are not named, large signs swinging in the breeze usually list the name of each hotel or losmen down that particular lane or road.

It is also worth noting that you should not try to find any hotel away from the main road in Penestanan or Campuan after dark, because there are no street lights.

PLACES TO STAY – BUDGET

Many cheap hotels are very small, often with just three or four rooms. What follows is a sample, as well as a guide to where to start looking; there are many other excellent places apart from those mentioned in this section.

Central Ubud

All of the following places appear on the Central Ubud map. The cheapest places are near the top of Monkey Forest Rd, but there are nicer places a few minutes walk away. Most are not very appealing, but they are central and only cost about 10,000/15,000 rp for singles/doubles. The best are *Pandawa Homestay* (☎ 975698), and *Anom Bungalows* and *Jungut Inn*, which are both along a quieter side street.

Off the main road, *Rice Paddy Bungalows* is one of three secluded, tranquil places with almost identical settings and prices: 30,000 rp, or 35,000 rp for upstairs rooms with the best views. Across from the foot-

ball field, *Wahyu Bungalows* (☎ 975055) is clean, shady and quiet. Rooms, with alfresco-style bathroom, start from 20,000 rp, and climb to 80,000 rp with hot water, balcony and views.

Bendi's 2 Accommodation (☎ 96410) has a quiet garden setting. Room prices are open to negotiation with the manager, and can be available for as little as 25,000 rp with hot water. *Saren Inn* (☎ 975704) is a mid-range place having trouble attracting guests, so the management is happily offering big discounts. Rooms for 30,000/40,000 rp with hot water and a fridge are excellent value.

Also recommended are *Gayatri Bungalows* (☎ 96391), with an immaculate garden and spacious rooms for 20,000/25,000 rp; and *Monkey Forest Inn*, which is friendly, and excellent value for 15,000/20,000 rp including hot water. Other clean places along, or near, Monkey Forest Rd, with rooms for about 15,000/20,000 rp, include: *Alit's House* (☎ 96284); *Puri Muwa Bungalows* (☎ 975441); *Dewi Ayu Accommodation* (☎ 976119); *Alamanda Accommodation*; and *Frog Pond Inn*.

Along Jl Maruti, *Dewi Putri Accommodation* (☎ 96304) is quiet, with a babbling brook at the back, and very good value for 10,000/15,000 rp. *Sayong House* (☎ 96305) is at the end of a quiet lane, with rooms for 20,000/30,000 rp, or 50,000 rp for a double with hot water. Also, *Budi Bungalows* is clean, quiet and comfortable, and has rooms for only 15,000/20,000 rp.

Jl Karna has several good places, although the noise from the motorbikes going to and from the market can be a little annoying at times. Places offering rooms for 15,000/20,000 rp include: *Gandra House* (☎ 976529); the charming *Ning's House* (☎ 973340); *Pondok Wisata Puri Widiana*, with a shady garden; and the friendly *Yuni's House* (☎ 975701).

Wija's House has rooms for 50,000 rp with hot water, but its prices will probably increase once the new swimming pool is completed. Nearby, along Gang Narada, *Hibiscus Bungalows* is pretty, but a little pricey for a negotiable 25,000/50,000 rp.

Jl Goutama is another cheap, quiet and central place to stay, where there are a dozen or more losmen. **Shana Homestay** is good value: large rooms, some with private patios, cost 15,000/20,000 rp. **Donald Homestay** (☎ 977156) is better than it looks from the outside. The setting is pretty, the staff are friendly and the rooms cost a negotiable 35,000/40,000 rp. **Darta Homestay** is good value, with a real farmyard atmosphere, with rooms for 10,000/15,000 rp.

East of Ubud

There's not that much on offer along Jl Hanoman (see the Ubud Area map), which is a shame given its central location and the number of cheap places to eat nearby.

Suartha Pension (☎ 974244) has a charming, traditional family setting, and rooms for 15,000/20,000 rp. A little off the main street, **Jati 2 Homestay** (☎ 975550) has a small number of delightful rooms for 20,000/25,000 rp, and views of rice fields that upmarket hotels charge the earth for. **Artini Cottages I** (☎ 975348) is a cheaper version of its more expensive partner across the road, and has rooms in an ornate setting from 25,000/40,000 rp.

A side road off Jl Hanoman leads to about six more peaceful places to stay. The wonderful views of the rice paddies from the more expensive room upstairs are worth a splurge. The recommended **Ubud View Bungalows** (☎ 974164) charges 40,000/ 50,000 rp per double for downstairs/upstairs rooms with hot water. Also worth trying is **Nuriani Guest House** (☎ 975346), where rooms in another lovely garden cost 20,000/ 35,000 rp for downstairs/upstairs; or 30,000/ 40,000 rp with hot water.

Jl Jembawan is yet another delightful street, with a number of good value places close to central Ubud. The new and spacious **Budi Shady Gully Guest House** (☎ 975033) charges 25,000/30,000 rp for singles/doubles with hot water, which is excellent value. Another good place is **Matahari Cottages** (☎ 975459), which has a charming setting. Bungalows are 30,000/35,000 rp, and larger rooms with three beds are 50,000 rp.

A little further east, Jl Tebesaya is reminiscent of a village street, and is still quite central; the places on the eastern side, overlooking the creek, are particularly attractive. **Puri Asri 2 Bungalows** (☎ 96210) has a lovely garden, and clean rooms for 20,000 rp with cold water; and a bargain 30,000 rp with hot water. **Rona Accommodation** (☎ 973229) is a well established favourite, not least for its bookshop and travel agency. Good rooms range from 20,000 to 40,000 rp with hot water. Another gem is the popular **Family Guest House** (☎ 974054). Set in a pleasant garden, it has friendly staff and rooms for 25,000/35,000 rp; 30,000/50,000 rp with hot water. There are another eight or so other good places to stay along the same street.

North of Ubud

Many visitors ignore anywhere north of Jl Raya, so this area is normally quiet and offers good value, but still close to central Ubud. All places in this section appear on the Central Ubud map, unless otherwise indicated.

Suci Inn (☎ 975304) is a long-established favourite. It's a friendly, relaxed place that's quiet, yet very close to the action. Clean singles/doubles cost 15,000/20,000 rp. Further up, **Pondok Bambu** (☎ 96421 – see the Ubud Area map) charges 40,000 rp for a large room with hot water, and is one of several friendly, cheap and family-run places up this street.

Jl Kajeng is another good place to base yourself, although it's barely wide enough for a vehicle. **Shanti Homestay** (☎ 975421) is a good option for 20,000/30,000 rp, or 40,000 rp for an upstairs room with hot water. **Roja's Bungalows** (☎ 975107) costs 25,000/30,000 rp in a friendly atmosphere, but try to negotiate as this price is a little high. **Arjana Accommodation** (☎ 975583) has nice rooms for 15,000/20,000 rp with an alfresco-style bathroom. **Artja Inn** is also friendly, and offers tasty breakfasts and endless tea. With negotiation, rooms for as little as 10,000 rp per person are possible.

There a few more places further up Jl Kajeng (see the Ubud Area map). **Homestay Rumah Roda** (☎ 975487) is a very

UBUD & AROUND

friendly, and understandably popular, place. Bungalows cost 25,000/30,000 rp, but it's on the wrong side of the road for the views. Opposite, *Kajeng Homestay* (☎ 975018) has a stunning setting – it's one of the nicest in the budget range in Ubud. Rooms with cold water cost 20,000/30,000 rp, but hot water costs only 5000 rp extra per person.

South of Ubud

More accommodation can be found closer to Pengosekan and Teges, but most of these hotels have little character, are inconvenient and located along a noisy main road (see the Ubud Area map).

Bali Breeze Bungalows (☎ 975410, fax 975546) has not raised its prices (nor maintained its garden, apparently) for years, and still charges 30,000/35,000 rp for ordinary rooms with cold water.

Going down Jl Peliatan, at the junction where the road bends sharply left to Denpasar, there is a cluster of decent places with rooms for about 12,000/15,000 rp. These include *Siti Homestay* (☎ 975599), *Sari Bungalows* (☎ 975541) and *Nyoman Astana's* (☎ 975661), which has the nicest garden and the possibility of hot water for 20,000/25,000 rp.

West of Ubud

For seclusion within walking distance of Ubud, many travellers find the places around Campuan and Penestanan very appealing, but most of the dozen or more places dotted around the rice fields are now priced in the mid-range market. They are accessible by very steep steps from the main road west of Ubud, or along a passable road from Penestanan. All appear on the Ubud Area map.

Among the better in the budget range are the popular *Londo Bungalows* (☎ 920361), with rooms for 40,000 rp, including hot water; the charmless *Siddahartha Cottages* (☎ 975748) for 50,000 rp, without hot water; and *Pugur Bungalows* (☎ 976672), which is overpriced, but often full, with rooms for 45,000/70,000 rp with hot water.

Along the road through Penestanan there are a few more options for about 15,000/

20,000 rp, such as *Whitney Bungalows* and *Reka Homestay*. Just up from the main road from Ubud (so it's a little noisy) is *Homestay Adur* (☎ 975072) for 25,000 rp a double.

About the only budget place in Campuan is *Homestay Purna* for 35,000 rp, which is overpriced for Ubud, but cheap in this area.

A little closer to town, Jl Bisma has a real countryside atmosphere. Of the handful of places stretching southwards, *Juwita Inn* (☎ 976056, fax 975162) is the closest and one of the best. It offers bungalows, with hot water, almost lost in a luscious garden, for a reasonable 35,000/55,000 rp.

PLACES TO STAY – MID-RANGE

There are dozens of decent mid-range places from 40,000/50,000 rp for singles/doubles, with hot water being the most touted feature (air-con is rarely offered in this range). There is also a growing number of new or renovated hotels for around US$40/50, which are almost always equipped with a swimming pool, hot water and air-con. These places are often never close to full, so prices are usually negotiable, especially if you're staying a few days.

Central Ubud

All of these places appear on the Central Ubud map. Straddling the budget and mid-range are two recommended places. *Hotel Argasoka* (☎ 976231) on Monkey Forest Rd has lovely gardens, spacious rooms and hot water, and is excellent value for 50,000/ 60,000 rp. Nearby, *Ubud Bungalows* (☎/fax 975537) also has spacious rooms starting at 50,000 rp, or 80,000 rp for a pleasant family room. Central, pleasant and well kept is *Puri Saraswati Bungalows* (☎/fax 975164). Singles/doubles/triples start at US$40/48/56. The quiet *Oka Wati Hotel* (☎ 96386, fax 975063, email okaati@mmm.net) still has a rice paddy in view, but is now a little overpriced with rooms from US$33 to US$55. One gem is *Agung Cottages* (☎ 975414), which is set in a lovely, quiet garden and has friendly staff. Huge, spotless rooms cost 75,000 rp with hot water.

Many of the places along the southern

part of Monkey Forest Rd are fairly dull and featureless. One place, with some imagination, taste and a pool, is *Ubud Village Hotel* (☎ 975701, fax 975069). The pleasant rooms, each with a separate garden entrance, cost US$40/45, or US$65/75 with air-con. *Puri Garden Bungalows* (☎ 975395), with its lush garden, is a nice place to stay for US$23/29. *Pertiwi Bungalows* (☎ 975236, fax 975559, email pertiwi@indosat.net.id) has comfortable rooms, plenty of outdoor space for kids and a swimming pool, but there's nothing that special about it. Rooms cost from US$42/48, and double that for the deluxe rooms.

The well established *Ubud Inn* (☎ 975071, fax 975188, email ubud-inn@indosat.net.id) has a variety of bungalows and rooms from US$30/40 to US$50/60, dotted around a spacious garden and swimming pool. Next door, *Fibra Inn* (☎/fax 975451) has a pool, and pleasant and comfortable bungalows from US$52/60. It has been recommended by several readers.

Two other good, central places to try in this range are *Pande Permai Bungalows* (☎ 975436), which is popular with tour groups, and charges US$28 per room, and *Ubud Terrace Bungalows* (☎ 975690), which is good value for a place with a pool – rooms cost 88,000/100,000 rp.

East of Ubud
Artini Cottages II (☎ 975689, fax 975348), on Jl Hanoman, has a stunning set-up with a pool, and is central to Ubud (see the Ubud Area map). For 100,000/150,000 rp for singles/doubles, this is excellent value. *Oka Kartini Couperus Bungalows* (☎ 975193, fax 975759) is central, with good value rooms for US$20/25 and it has a nice pool.

North of Ubud
To the north (see the Ubud Area map) there is nothing much in the mid-range, but one majestic place is worth booking ahead for – *Gusti's Garden Bungalows* (☎ 96311) may look unassuming from the street, but it opens on to a stunning garden, where large rooms, with hot water, are perched over-

looking a swimming pool. Normally you would expect to pay US$50 or more for this sort of place, but it only charges between 50,000 and 90,000 rp per double, depending on the view.

Another place where bookings are essential is *Ubud Sari Health Resort* (☎ 974393, fax 976305, email ubudsari@denpasar. wasantara.net.id). It offers a range of health treatments, massages and courses (see the earlier Activities and Courses sections), and the three charming bungalows are great value from 45,000/50,000 rp for singles/doubles to 100,000 rp for three people – including breakfast and hot water.

West of Ubud
All of the following places to stay appear on the Ubud Area map. Along or just off Jl Bisma, there are several stunning places. One of the best and most popular is *Nick's Pension* (☎ 975526), which has a pool and a tranquil setting, far from any main road, and offers rooms from US$20 to US$35 (with hot water). *Abangan Bungalows* (☎ 975977, fax 975082), up a steep driveway north of the main road, has a lovely setting with a pool, and is still close to Ubud. The small rooms cost US$20, and larger rooms in the rice-barn style are US$30 to US$35.

Further up the main road from Ubud, *Wisata Cottages* (☎/fax 975017) has a wonderful outlook over Sungai Cerik, although the rooms from US$27/44 are nothing special. A little further on, *Ananda Cottages* (☎ 975376, fax 975375) is popular, and has spacious gardens and a pool in a beautiful setting. Downstairs rooms cost US$42/48, and a two storey family unit is US$91.

In the rice fields around Penestanan, a few more mid-range places are being built. One of the better ones is *Baliubud Cottages* (☎ 975058, fax 974773), which has a pool, and rooms from US$35/46 to US$69/78 with air-con. Secluded and picturesque, is the impressive *Penestanan Bungalows* (☎ 975603, fax 288341).

Gerebig Bungalows (☎ 974582) has rooms with hot water for a negotiable 70,000 rp,

UBUD & AROUND

and wonderful views, but if you can manage without hot water there is better value to be found nearby.

Sri Ratih Cottages (☎ 975638, fax 976650) has a pool and is popular with tour groups. Rooms normally cost US$30/35, but are generally negotiable when business is quiet. Finally, *Kori Agung Bungalows (☎ 975166)* is not bad value, with rooms for US$15.

PLACES TO STAY – TOP END

Top-end hotels in Ubud feature some combination of artistic connections, traditional decor, lush landscaping, rice-field views and modern luxuries. They all charge up to 21% extra for tax and service – these taxes are included in the following prices.

Central Ubud

There are very few top-end places in central Ubud. *Hotel Champlung Sari (☎ 974686, fax 975473)* is convenient, and has nice views, but the singles/doubles are ordinary and cost US$95/106.

Close to central Ubud, *Pringga Juwita Water Garden Cottages (☎/fax 975734 –* see the Central Ubud map) has ponds and a swimming pool in one of the prettiest gardens in Ubud. Standard rooms cost from US$69/79; the luxurious deluxe rooms cost about US$15 more per person.

North & South of Ubud

Just off Jl Kajeng, one of the nicest places in Ubud is artist Han Snel's *Siti Bungalows (☎ 975699, fax 975643 –* see the Central Ubud map). The individual cottages are decorated with the artist's own work, and cost US$57 to US$115. Some are perched right on the edge of the river gorge – it's worth making a reservation for these.

The only convenient top-end place south of Ubud is *Kokokan Hotel (☎ 975742, fax 975332)*, owned by Agung Rai, patron of the ARMA museum nearby. It features nice views, fascinating architecture and fine decor. There is a range of singles/doubles/ triples from US$109/121/145, or US$302 for the complete 'Pondok Manis' house.

West of Ubud

Most of the upmarket places are located near, and overlooking, the superb Sungai Agung or Sungai Cerik (see the Ubud Area map).

Ibah (☎ 974466, fax 974467, email ibah @denpasar.wasantara.net.id) has a charming location overlooking a lush valley, and offers spacious and stylish individual suites from US$235, and US$423 for the 'Ibah Suite'. The delightful garden is decorated with stone carvings, handcrafted pots and antique doors, and the swimming pool is set into the hillside beneath an ancient looking stone wall.

Closer to Ubud, the long established *Hotel Tjampuhan (☎ 975368, fax 975137)* is beautifully sited above the confluence of Sungai Cerik and Sungai Wos. The hotel is built on the site of artist Walter Spies' 1930s home. Individual bungalows in a wonderful garden cost from US$63/73. The Spies' House (which fits four people) costs US$174, but you will have to make a reservation for this.

Padma Indah Cottages (☎/fax 975719) was established by a collector of Balinese art, whose collection is displayed in all of the cottages and in an on-site gallery. Rooms with a garden view cost US$105; it's a little more for a view of the rice fields.

In Sanggingan, the *Villa Bukit Ubud (☎ 975371, fax 975767)* is not bad value, with rooms for US$73/85. A little to the south, *Puri Raka Inn (☎/fax 975213)* has been recommended by readers, not least for its enormous bath and excellent swimming pool. It is struggling for business so it offers substantial discounts – standard rooms can cost only 100,000 rp, or 300,000 rp for the luxurious 'superior' room.

Pita Maha (☎ 974330, fax 974329, email pitamaha@dps.mega.net.id) is dramatically situated on the edge of Sungai Cerik. The individual villas, each in a small private compound, cost from US$302 to US$484 per night, but not all of them enjoy the best views.

Ulun Ubud Cottages (☎ 975024, fax 975524) has bungalows beautifully draped down the hillside overlooking the valley. The whole place is decorated with wonderful carvings and paintings. Standard rooms are good value for US$45/55, bungalows are US$50/65 and family rooms US$110/90.

In Kedewatan village, several places take advantage of the seclusion and magnificent views of Sungai Agung. *Amandari* (☎ 975333, fax 975335) has views over the rice paddies or down to the Ayung, and the main swimming pool seems to drop right over the edge. Rooms start at US$556, and go much higher.

Cahaya Dewata Hotel (☎ 975495, fax 974349) overlooks the same magnificent river gorge. The standard rooms are US$73/91, but if you want a view you'll have to pay from US$96/115. It features some fascinating artworks and decorations. Nearby, *Villa Indah* (☎/fax 95490) is pretty but nothing special, and costs US$120/145.

A little further to the north is *Kupu Kupu Barong* (☎ 975478, fax 975079). Clinging precariously to the steep sides of the Sungai Ayung gorge, each of the beautiful two storey bungalows costs US$405 to US$845. The views from the rooms, pool and restaurant are unbelievable, as you would hope for the price. *Puri Bunga Village* (☎ 975448, fax 975073) has a similarly dramatic location, but less spectacular prices: rooms start at US$139/195.

More affordable, and also overlooking Sungai Ayung, are two good places. *Sayan Terrace* (☎ 974384, fax 975384) has a brilliant view and attractive rooms for US $30/48, and family rooms for US$70. *Taman Bebek Villas* (☎ 975385, fax 976532, email tribwana@dps.mega.net.id) has a choice of elegant rooms, and villas with kitchenettes, starting from an affordable US$44; it's US$100 or more for a suite.

PLACES TO STAY – RENTALS

Anyone who wants to stay a while in Ubud can rent or share a house. Information can be obtained from the *Bali Advertiser* (see the Newspapers & Magazines section in the Bali Facts for the Visitor chapter); noticeboards mentioned in the Courses entry earlier in this section; or from Taking Care of Business estate agency (☎ 976410, fax 975052, email tcbnet@denpasar.wasantara. net.id) in Ubud.

PLACES TO EAT

Ubud's plethora of restaurants probably offers the tastiest and most diverse range of food on the island. You can get excellent western food, while authentic Indonesian and Balinese dishes will often be on the menu as well.

For the cheapest meals, the market has *food stalls*, but they often close early in the evening. The price of meals in restaurants and warungs is considerably cheaper in areas where budget travellers normally stay. In unassuming little places along the roads heading north of Jl Raya, and along Jl Sugiwa, Jl Hanoman and Jl Jembawan, you can pay as little as 2500 rp for a *nasi goreng*, 3500 rp for a passable spaghetti and 4500 rp for a fish meal with all the trimmings. You can easily pay three times this at many places along Jl Raya and Monkey Forest Rd – not including pricey drinks.

Central Ubud

Most places along Jl Raya and Monkey Forest Rd unashamedly cater to the tourist market, and blatantly charge tourist prices, but the service, setting and food in these places is usually very good. All of these places appear on the Central Ubud map, unless indicated otherwise.

Along Jalan Raya One place that has moved steadily upmarket, but remains incredibly popular is *Ary's Warung*. It serves a wide variety of excellent food, including dips, omelettes and wholemeal sandwiches for about 7500 rp, while main meals start from 15,000 rp. Nearby, *Ryoshi Japanese Restaurant* is one of a chain of upmarket Japanese eateries across Bali, and is always popular with Japanese visitors, which is a good sign.

Further along, *Casa Luna* has a superb international menu, and is so popular that you may have trouble getting a table in the evening. It also sells bread and pastry from its own bakery, great desserts (try the 'Death by Chocolate' cake) and half serves for kids. The service is efficient, and the atmosphere is pleasant and friendly.

Across the road, **Lotus Cafe** was for a long time *the* place to eat. A leisurely meal overlooking the lotus pond is still an Ubud institution, but the food is pricey – about 15,000 rp a main course. Close by, **Mumbul's Cafe** is the best place in Ubud for ice-cream, and scrumptious treats like sundaes and banana splits.

The best place along the eastern end is **Nomad Restaurant** (see the Ubud Area map). It offers standard Indonesian and Chinese dishes, but is mainly a spot for a sociable drink because it stays open later than many other places in Ubud.

North of Jalan Raya One of Ubud's real dining pleasures is **Han Snel's Garden Restaurant**. The setting is beautiful, with frogs croaking in the background. It's expensive (from 12,000 rp a dish), but the food is exquisite and the servings generous – it's the atmosphere and the hospitable owners which make this place attractive, however.

Ketut's Place (☎ 975304 – see the Ubud Area map) still runs the weekly Balinese Feast. For enquiries and bookings, contact Suci Inn closer to town (see the previous Places to Stay section). For 35,000 rp per person, you get a great meal of Balinese specialities, which is also an excellent introduction to Balinese life and customs. There's usually an interesting group, so it's very sociable.

Along Jl Suweta are **Coconut Cafe** and **Cafe Angkasa**, which rivals the Tutmak Cafe as Ubud's best coffee house. **Bumbu Restaurant** is popular with people staying in the area. The Indian and Indonesian food is cheap and tasty, and is served in a pleasant setting.

Along Monkey Forest Rd A lot of places are now overpriced, but a few good cheapies remain. **Canderi's Warung**, run by the irrepressible Ibu Canderi, is an Ubud institution. It offers large serves of Indonesian, western and vegetarian dishes at reasonable prices. **Kul Kul Restaurant** is also popular for its large serves at good prices. **Bendi's Restaurant**, in Bendi's 2 Accommodation,

features authentic Balinese food and is one of the few places which offers breakfast and an upstairs room. The *gado gado* (6500 rp) is particularly good. **Cafe Tirta** is also cheap and friendly, although the service is slow if it's busy. For something a bit nicer, without delving too deep into your pockets, **Gayatri Cafe** is excellent: seafood specials cost about 7500 rp, and it has a comfortable upstairs area.

For sheer elegance, in a wonderful setting, it's hard to go past **Ibu Rai Bar & Restaurant**. Prices are not as steep as you may imagine: pasta dishes are about 10,000 rp, and a large beer is 6500 rp. **Noni Orti** is about the same standard and price. For something a little more authentic, just as elegant but a little cheaper (9000 to 12,000 rp a dish), **Lillies Garden Restaurant** and **Cafe Bali** are romantically set among the rice fields.

Further south, **Cafe Wayan** is popular and relaxed, but pricey: meals start at 15,000 rp and go higher – the smoked duck is particularly good, but expensive. It offers regular Balinese feasts (60,000 rp), and some baked goodies to rival Casa Luna.

There are three good places virtually next to each other: **Mendra's Cafe** has cheap beer, but the serves are small; **Dian Cafe** has a good range and reasonable prices; and **Lotus Lane Restaurant** is one of the chain of classy places dotted around Bali. Also good is **Jaya Cafe**.

Yogyakarta Cafe looks unassuming from the outside, but it has a huge indoor and outdoor setting. It specialises in barbequed seafood from 8500 rp – you'll see the smoke, and smell the food, from the street. The new **Monkey Cafe** has a superb setting and is the best place for vegetarian food at reasonable prices (6000 to 9000 rp). **Ayu's Kitchen** also specialises in vegetarian dishes in the same price range. **Warung Mama** remains incredibly popular, more for the street-side table setting than anything else.

Across the football field, **Aries Warung** is cheap and cheerful (it should not be confused with the more popular and classy Ary's Warung). Along Jl Dewa Sita, **Bamboo Restaurant** has inexpensive Balinese dishes, pizzas (9500 rp), coconut pies (2500 rp) and a breezy upstairs setting. *Tutmak Cafe* is a stylish place which serves pasta, and about the best coffee in Ubud – use it to wash down its delicious chocolate cake.

East of Ubud

Along Jl Hanoman, especially further south of Jl Raya, many cheerful restaurants and warungs serve authentic and tasty Indonesian food for about 4000 rp, and western food, such as pasta and pizza, for about 6500 rp.

This is one of the best value areas in Ubud, and worth a short walk if you're not staying nearby. *Three Brothers Restaurant* is unpretentious, and offers simple food at honest prices in a very friendly atmosphere. *Warung Artini* has also been recommended by several readers.

Along Jl Tebesaya, there are also a few good and inexpensive places, including *Made Cafe*, where the Italian food will not disappoint you.

Just down Jl Jembawan, the new *Bali Buddha Health Food Shop* is a popular place to meet other travellers, and relax with something healthy to drink or eat. It also features a useful noticeboard with messages and ads about current and future courses and events.

South of Ubud

Padangtegal has some interesting options. *Bebek Bengil* (Dirty Duck Diner) does delectable deep-fried duck dishes in a delightful dining area. Going south, *Kura Kura Mexican Cafe* has substantial Mexican main courses from around 8000 rp – you can smell the chilli wafting across the main road.

Further south, there isn't a lot to get excited about; the busy main road destroys the atmosphere of most places. If you're staying in this part of Ubud, you may want to try *Edi's Warung*, which does seafood dishes for a reasonable 5000 rp; *Panorama Restaurant* which, as the name suggests, has great views, although meals start at 12,500 rp; and *Nuriani's*, also overlooking the rice fields.

West of Ubud

Up the slope south of Jl Raya, *Miro's Cafe* has a varied menu and a cool garden setting. Well prepared Indonesian dishes cost about 7500 rp and other main courses about 10,500 rp. It also has a good vegetarian selection. *Griya Barbecue* serves very good chicken, pork, steak and fish dishes for about 20,000 rp, but the pasta and Indonesian dishes are more reasonably priced at about 10,000 rp.

Continuing towards Campuan, *Murni's Warung* is an old Ubud favourite, with a four level dining room and bar. Prices are squarely set for the upmarket tourist. Opposite, *Beggar's Bush Pub* probably has the best views in Ubud and, while the meals are expensive (9000 rp for a snack; 12,000 rp for a main meal), the food is tasty and the serves are large.

Long-term stayers in Penestanan usually eat at their losmen, but the new *Cafe Dewata* is attracting plenty of customers for its good prices and breezy setting.

The public can eat in the *restaurants* of the upmarket hotels overlooking Sungai Ayung, but prices are usually in US dollars, and you'll need lots of them. *Amandari* has excellent food in a sophisticated atmosphere, and *Kupu Kupu Barong* has superb views – reservations for both are recommended, especially at lunch time. Further out, *Warung Nuri* is the place for drinks, meals and 'English breakfasts' before or after visiting the Neka Museum.

ENTERTAINMENT

Entertainment in Ubud is more cultural, and certainly more sedate, than you will find in Kuta, Lovina and Sanur.

Balinese Music & Dance

If you're in the right place at the right time you may witness an authentic dance during a temple ceremony – but these dances are often long and not as entertaining to the uninitiated. Dances performed for tourists are usually adapted and abbreviated to some extent to make them more enjoyable, but most are done with a high degree of skill and commitment, and usually have appreciative locals in the audience. It's also common to combine the features of more than one traditional dance in a single performance.

In a week in Ubud, you can see Kecak, Legong and Barong dances, Mahabharata and Ramayana ballets, wayang kulit puppets and gamelan orchestras in Ubud and at surrounding villages. The Agung Rai Museum of Art (see the earlier Museums section) also holds regular traditional dances – for these, book at ARMA. For details of these dances, ballets and puppet shows, see the Arts section in the Facts about Bali chapter and the Dance section on the facing page.

You can buy tickets (10,000 to 15,000 rp) from any of the travel agencies or hotels around Ubud, the tourist office, or the touts who hang around outside Ubud Palace. The most attractive and accessible setting is the central Ubud Palace, but for a seat in the front few rows get there at least 30 minutes early. If the dance is held in a local village, transport is usually included in the price.

Bars

There are very few bars in Ubud – mainly there's just restaurants which serve alcohol. Probably the closest thing to a bar is *Beggar's Bush Pub*. It's built on four levels – so take your pick of the best views. Glasses of draught beer cost 6000 rp. Opposite, *Murni's Warung* has an intimate lounge bar with high-priced drinks.

Closer to town, *Yogyakarta Cafe* also serves draught beer for 6500 rp in a classy setting, but the only views are of the TV and video screen. Happy hours are more of a 'Kuta thing', but *Jaya Cafe* and *Mendra's Cafe* offer discounted drinks in the evening.

Jazz fans will want to visit *Jazz Cafe* for its relaxed atmosphere, excellent food (about 12,000 rp for tasty pasta), live music on Tuesday, Thursday and Saturday evenings, and jam sessions on Saturday afternoon.

Videos & Sports Telecasts

Some of the central places which feature videos or laser discs every night are *Casa Luna* (which also shows children's movies in the afternoon); *Bamboo Restaurant*;

Coconut Cafe; and *Putra Bar*, which also boasts live international sports telecasts by satellite. The selling point at these places are the movies or TV telecasts, so the prices for drinks and meals are high, and servings of food can often be small.

SHOPPING

Ubud has such an incredibly vast array of shops that it seems unfair to highlight any particular places. The best advice is to visit a gallery or two and get an idea about the quality and price of the good stuff, and then shop around until you see something you really like at a price that suits – and don't forget to bargain hard.

Alternatively, you can use Ubud as a base to explore the amazing number of craft and antique shops all the way down to Batubulan. The craft market at Sukawati is a great place to look around, but you should get there early (see the Denpasar to Ubud section earlier in this chapter for details).

Paintings

You'll find paintings for sale everywhere. The main galleries have excellent selections, and they're very interesting to look through, but prices are typically well over the US$100 mark. You will get better prices directly from the artist or an artist's workshop. If your budget is limited, look for a smaller picture of high quality, rather than something that resembles wallpaper in size and originality. The common Balinese landscape paintings, with intricate wooden frames, make great souvenirs. Prices start from 50,000 rp depending on the quality – and they are only for sale in Ubud.

Woodcarvings

Small shops at the market and by Monkey Forest Rd often have good woodcarvings, particularly masks. There are other good woodcarving places along Jl Bedulu (between Pengosekan and Teges), and along the road between Nyuhkuning and the southern entrance to Monkey Forest Sanctuary.

continued on page 254

BALINESE DANCE

The most important thing about Balinese dances is that they're fun and accessible. Balinese dance is definitely not some sterile art form requiring an arts degree to appreciate – it can be exciting and enjoyable for almost anyone with just the slightest effort.

Balinese dances are not hard to find: there are dances virtually every night at all the tourist centres – admission is generally 10,000 to 15,000 rp for foreigners. Dances are put on regularly at the tourist centres to raise money, but are also a regular part of almost every temple festival and Bali has no shortage of these. Many of the dances put on for tourists offer a smorgasbord of Balinese dances – a little Topeng, a taste of Legong and some Baris to round it all off. A nice introduction perhaps, but some dances should be experienced in their entirety. It will be a shame if the 'instant Asia' mentality takes too strong a grip on Balinese dance.

Dances take various forms, but with a few notable exceptions (in particular, the Kecak and the Sanghyang trance dance), they are all accompanied by music from the gamelan orchestra. Some dances are almost purely for the sake of dancing – in this category you could include the technically precise Legong, its male equivalent (the Baris) or various solo dances like the Kebyar. Mask dances like the Topeng or the Jauk also place a high premium on dancing ability.

In the Barong & Rangda dance, powerful forces are at work and elaborate preparations must be made to ensure that the balance is maintained. All masked dances require great care as, in donning a mask, you take on another personality and it is wise to ensure that the mask's personality does not take over. Masks used in the Barong & Rangda dance are treated with particular caution. Only an expert can carve them and between performances the masks must be carefully put away. A *rangda* (bad) mask must even be kept covered until the instant before the performance starts (a rangda is a widow-witch and ruler of evil spirits). These masks can have powerful *sakti* (spirits) and the unwary must be careful of their magical, often dangerous, spiritual vibrations.

The Mexican artist Miguel Covarrubias pointed out that the Balinese like a blend of seriousness and slapstick, and this also shows in their dances. Some have a decidedly comic element, with clowns who serve both to counterpoint the staid, noble characters, and to convey the story. The noble characters may use the high Balinese language or classical Kawi, while the clowns, usually servants of the noble characters, converse in everyday Balinese. There are always two clowns – the leader, or *punta*, and his follower, the *kartala*, who never quite manages to carry off his mimicry.

Dancers on Bali are almost always ordinary people who dance in the evening or their spare time, just like painters or sculptors who indulge their artistry in their spare time. Dance is learned by performing, and long hours may be spent in practice, usually by carefully following the movements of an expert. There's little of the soaring leaps of western ballet or the smooth flowing movements often found in western dance. Balinese dance tends to be precise, jerky, shifting and jumpy, and is remarkably like Balinese music with its abrupt changes of tempo and dramatic contrasts between silence and crashing noise. There's also virtually no contact in Balinese dancing: each dancer moves completely independently.

To the expert, every movement of wrist, hand and fingers is important; even facial expressions are carefully choreographed to convey the character of the dance. Don't give the dancers your complete attention either – the audience can be just as interesting, especially the children. Even at the most tourist-oriented of dances there will be hordes of local children clustered around the stage. Watch how they cheer the good characters and cringe back from the stage when the demons appear.

Kecak

Probably the best known of the many Balinese dances, the Kecak is unusual in that it does not have a gamelan accompaniment. Instead the background is provided by a chanting 'choir' of men who provide the 'chak-a-chak-a-chak' noise. Originally this chanting group was known as the kecak and was part of a Sanghyang trance dance. Then, in the 1930s, the modern Kecak developed in Bona, near Gianyar in East Bali, where the dance is still held regularly.

The Kecak tells a tale from the *Ramayana*, one of the great Hindu holy books, about Prince Rama and his Princess Sita. With Rama's brother, Laksamana, they have been exiled from the kingdom of Ayodya and are wandering in the forest. The evil Rawana, King of Lanka, lures Rama

---

Where are the Dances?

Denpasar Kecak every evening at the Arts Centre (also see the Courses section in the Denpasar chapter).

South Bali Barong during festivals on Pulau Serangan; all sorts of dances at hotels and restaurants in Sanur, Nusa Dua, Jimbaran and the Kuta region; Ramayana ballet at Taman Festival Bali park, Sanur.

Ubud & Around All sorts of dances, Ramayana ballet and wayang kulit shadow puppets on dance stages in Ubud; Legong is famous in Peliatan, near Ubud; Barong & Rangda can be seen in Batubulan; wayang kulit can be seen at Sukawati; Kecak is very famous at Bona.

East Bali Barong, Topeng and Legong on a dance stage, and in restaurants, at Candidasa.

West Bali Legong at restaurants at Tanah Lot.

Top left: A young Oleg dancer in costume at Tirtagangga in east Bali.

Top right: A Puspanjali dancer during celebrations at a temple festival.

Bottom: A dancer performs the role of Sita from the *Ramayana* at a Blahbutah temple south of Ubud.

Left: The Sita character from the *Ramayana* performs at the entrance to a Blahbutah temple.

Bottom left: The Rejang, a traditional sacred dance from eastern Bali.

Bottom right: The most graceful and technically demanding of Balinese dances, the Legong, as performed at the Bali Arts Festival.

GREGORY ADAMS

RICHARD I'ANSON

RICHARD I'ANSON

Top left: A Rangda dancer (minus mask) rests up prior to a performance.

Top right: A group scene from a rendition of the Barong & Rangda dance at Batubulan in south Bali.

Bottom: The wicked widow-witch Rangda at her menacing worst during the Barong & Rangda dance.

Top left: A scene from the *Ramayana* ballet performed at Ubud.

Top right: Dolonan, a children's dance drama, performed with a women's gamelan orchestra at the Bali Arts Festival.

Middle: The masked Topeng dancer takes on the persona represented by the mask through stylised gestures and movement.

Bottom: The massed ranks of the monkey army, which help Prince Rama and Princess Sita in their fight against evil during the Kecak dance.

away with a golden deer (which is really Lanka's equally evil prime minister who has magically changed himself into a deer). When Rama fails to return, Sita persuades Laksamana to search for him. When the princess is alone, Rawana pounces and carries her off to his hideaway.

Hanuman, the white monkey god, appears before Sita and tells her that Rama is trying to rescue her. He brings her Rama's ring to show that he is indeed the prince's envoy and Sita gives him a hairpin to take back to Rama. When Rama finally arrives in Lanka he is met by the evil king's evil son Megananda, who shoots an arrow at him, but the arrow magically turns into a snake which ties Rama up. Fortunately, Rama is able to call upon a *garuda*, a mythical creature, part man and part bird, for assistance and thus escapes. Finally, Sugriwa, the king of the monkeys, comes to Rama's assistance with his monkey army and, after a great battle, good wins out over bad and Rama and Sita return home.

Throughout the dance the surrounding circle of men, all bare chested and wearing checked cloth around their waists, provide a nonstop accompaniment that rises to a crescendo as they play the monkey army and fight it out with Rawana and his cronies. The chanting is superbly synchronised; members of the 'monkey army' sway back and forth, raise their hands in unison, flutter their fingers and lean left and right, all with an eerily exciting coordination.

Barong & Rangda

The Barong & Rangda dance rivals the Kecak as Bali's most popular dance for tourists. Again it's a straightforward battle between good, the *barong*, and bad, the *rangda*. The barong is a strange creature, half shaggy dog, half lion, propelled by two men like a circus clown-horse. It's definitely on the side of good, but is a mischievous and fun-loving creature. By contrast, the widow-witch rangda is bad through and through, and certainly not someone you'd like to meet on a midnight stroll through the rice paddies.

Barongs can take various forms, but in the Barong & Rangda dance it will be as the *barong keket*, the most holy of the barongs. The barong flounces in, snaps its jaws at the gamelan, dances around a bit and enjoys the acclaim of its supporters – a group of men with krises. Then rangda makes her appearance, her long tongue lolling, human entrails draped around her neck and her terrible fangs protruding from her mouth.

The barong and rangda duel, using their magical powers, but when things look bad for the barong its supporters draw their krises and rush in to attack the rangda. Using her magical powers the rangda throws them into a trance and the men try to stab themselves with their krises. But the barong also has great magical powers and casts a spell which stops the krises from harming the men. This is the most dramatic part of the dance. As the gamelan rings crazily the men rush back and forth, waving their krises around, all but foaming at the mouth, sometimes even rolling on the ground in a desperate attempt to stab themselves.

There often seems to be a conspiracy to terrify tourists in the front row!

Finally, the rangda retires, defeated, and good has won again. This still leaves, however, a large group of entranced barong supporters to bring back to the real world. This is usually done by sprinkling them with holy water, sanctified by dipping the barong's beard in it. Performing the Barong & Rangda dance is a touchy operation – playing around with all that powerful magic, good and bad, is not to be taken lightly. Extensive ceremonies have to be performed, a *pemangku* (priest) must be on hand to end the dancers' trance and at the end a chicken must be sacrificed to propitiate the evil spirits.

Legong

The Legong is the most graceful of Balinese dances and, to sophisticated Balinese connoisseurs of dancing, the one arousing most interest and discussion. A *legong* (as a Legong dancer is known) is a girl – often as young as eight or nine years, and rarely older than her early teens. Such importance is attached to the dance that in old

The stuff of Balinese nightmares – Rangda the witch-widow.

age a classic dancer will be remembered as a 'great legong', even though her brief period of fame may have been 50 years ago.

There are various forms of this dance, but the Legong Keraton (Legong of the Palace) is the one most often performed. Peliatan's famous dance troupe, which visitors to Ubud often get a chance to see, is particularly noted for its Legong. The story behind the Legong is very stylised and symbolic – if you didn't know the story it would be impossible to tell what was going on.

The Legong involves just three dancers – the two legongs and their 'attendant', the *condong*. The legongs are identically dressed in gold brocade, so tightly bound that it is something of a mystery how they manage to move so rapidly and agitatedly. Their faces are elaborately made up, their eyebrows plucked and repainted, and their hair decorated with frangipanis. The dance relates how a king takes a maiden, Rangkesari, captive. When Rangkesari's brother comes to release her, Rangkesari begs the king to free her rather than go to war. The king refuses and on his way to the battle meets a bird bringing ill omens. He ignores the bird and continues on to meet Rangkesari's brother and gets killed.

That's the whole story, but the dance only tells of the king's preparations for battle and ends with the bird's appearance – when the king leaves the stage it is to join the battle where he will meet his death. The dance starts with the condong dancing an introduction and then departing as the legongs come on. The two legongs dance solo, in close identical formation and in mirror image, as when they dance a nose-to-nose 'love scene'. The dance tells of the king's sad departure from his queen, Rangkesari's bitter request that he release her and then the king's departure for the battle. The condong reappears with tiny golden wings as the bird of ill fortune and the dance ends.

Baris

The warrior dance, known as the Baris, is traditionally a male equivalent of the Legong – femininity and grace give way to energetic and warlike martial spirit. The Baris dancer has to convey the thoughts and emotions of a warrior preparing for action, and then meeting an enemy in battle. It's a solo dance requiring great energy and skill. The dancer has to show his changing moods through facial expression as well as movement – chivalry, pride, anger, prowess and finally a little regret all have to be there. It's said that the Baris is one of the most complex of the Balinese dances.

Kebyar

The Kebyar is a male solo dance like the Baris, but with greater emphasis on the performer's individual abilities. Development of the modern Kebyar is credited in large part to the famous prewar dancer Mario. There are various forms of Kebyar, including the Kebyar Duduk, where the 'dance' is done from the seated position and facial expressions, as well as movements of the hands, arms and torso, are all important. In the Kebyar Trompong, the dancer joins the gamelan and plays the trompong drum while dancing.

Ramayana Ballet

The *Ramayana* is a familiar tale on Bali, but the dance is a relatively recent addition to the Balinese repertoire. Basically, it tells the same story of Rama and Sita as told in the Kecak, but without the monkey ensemble and with a usual gamelan gong accompaniment. Furthermore, the *Ramayana* provides plenty of opportunity for improvisation and comic additions. Rawana may be played as a classic bad guy, Hanuman can be a comic clown and camera-clicking tourists among the spectators may come in for a little imitative ribbing.

Barong Landung

The giant puppet dances known as Barong Landung are not an everyday occurrence – they take place annually on the island of Pulau Serangan and a few other places in southern Bali. The legend of their creation relates how a demon Jero Gede Macaling popped over from Nusa Penida (see that chapter for details) disguised as a standing barong to cause havoc on Bali. To scare him away, the people had to make a big barong just like him.

The Barong Landung dances, a reminder of that ancient legend, feature two gigantic puppet figures – a horrific male image of black Jero Gede and his female sidekick, white Jero Luh. Barong Landung performances are often highly comic.

Janger

The Janger is a relatively new dance which suddenly popped up in the 1920s and 30s. Both Miguel Covarrubias and Hickman Powell commented on this strange, almost un-Balinese, courtship dance. Today, it has become part of the standard repertoire and no longer looks so unusual. It has similarities to several other dances, including the Sanghyang, where the relaxed chanting of the women is contrasted with the violent 'chak-a-chak-a-chak' of the men. In the Janger, formations of 12 young women and 12 young men do a sitting dance, and the gentle swaying and chanting of the women contrasts with the violently choreographed movements and loud shouts of the men.

Topeng

This is a mask dance where the dancers have to imitate the character represented by the mask. (*Topeng* means 'pressed against the face', as with a mask.) The Topeng Tua is a classic solo dance where the mask is that of an old man and the dancer has to dance like a creaky old gentleman. In other dances there may be a small troupe who dance various characters and types. A full collection of Topeng masks may number 30 or 40.

Jauk

The Jauk is also a mask dance, but strictly a solo performance – the dancer plays an evil demon, his mask an eerie face with bulging eyes and fixed smile, while long wavering fingernails complete the demonic look. Mask dances are considered to require great expertise because the dancer is not able to convey the character's thoughts and meanings through his facial expressions – the dance has to tell all. Demons are very unpleasant, frenetic and fast-moving creatures, so a Jauk dancer has to imitate all these things.

Sanghyang

The Sanghyang trance dances originally developed to drive out evil spirits from a village. The Sanghyang is a divine spirit which temporarily inhabits an entranced dancer. The Sanghyang Dedari dance is performed by two young girls who dance a dream-like version of the

Kepada Yang Terhormat :

Tuan ....

Toko ....

....

NOTA NO._____ ....

Banyaknya	NAMA BARANG	Harga	JUMLAH
10 rt	Internet		10.000
			10.000

PERHATIAN
Barang-barang yang sudah dibeli
tidak dapat dikembalikan/ditukar.

Jumlah Rp.

Tanda Terima

Hormat kami,

tidak dapat dikembalikan/ditukar

Legong, but with their eyes closed. The dancers are said to be untrained in the intricate pattern of the Legong, but dance in perfect harmony, with their eyes firmly shut. Male and female choirs, the male choir being a Kecak, provide a background chant, but when the chant stops the dancers slump to the ground in a faint. Two women bring them around, and at the finish a *pemangku* (temple guardian and priest for temple rituals) blesses them with holy water and brings them out of the trance. The modern Kecak dance developed from the Sanghyang.

In the Sanghyang Jaran, a boy in a trance dances around and through a fire of coconut husks, riding a coconut palm 'hobby horse'. It's labelled the 'fire dance' for the benefit of tourists. Like other trance dances (such as the Barong & Rangda dance) great care must be taken to control the magical forces at play. Experts must always be on hand to take care of the entranced dancers and to bring them out of the trance at the close, but in tourist centres the 'trance' is often staged.

Other Dances

Old dances fade out and new dances or new developments of old dances still appear: dance on Bali is not a static activity. The Oleg Tambulilingan was developed in the 1950s, originally as a solo female dance. Later, a male part was added and the dance now mimics the flirtations of two *tambulilingan* (bumblebees).

Pendet, an everyday dance of the temples, is a small procedure to go through before making temple offerings. You may often see the Pendet being danced by women bringing offerings to a temple for a festival, but it is also sometimes danced as an introduction and a closing for other dance performances.

One of the most popular comic dances is the Cupak, which tells a tale of a greedy coward (Cupak) and his brave but hard-done-by younger brother Grantang, and their adventures while rescuing a beautiful princess.

The Arja is a sort of Balinese soap opera, long and full of high drama. Since it requires much translation of the noble's actions by the clowns, it's hard for westerners to understand and appreciate. Drama Gong is in some ways a more modern version of the same romantic themes.

continued from page 246

Surrounding villages also specialise in different styles or subjects. Along the road from Teges to Mas, look for masks and some of the most original carved pieces with natural wood finishes. North of Ubud, look for carved garuda birds in Junjungan, and painted flowers and fruit in Tegallalang, about 1km east of Petulu. Near the ARMA Museum, wood chimes are a common item for sale.

Other Items

The two storey art market (Pasar Seni, near the bemo stops) sells a wide range of clothing, sarongs, footwear and souvenirs of variable quality at negotiable prices. Some other souvenirs include leather goods, batik, baskets and silverware (but the range is far better at Celuk). If you are after antiques, remember that in Ubud they tend to be overpriced – bargain hard or go back to Batubulan, Denpasar or even Kuta.

Toko Tino Supermarket is quite large, and sells most things, including current editions of *Indonesian Observer* and *Jakarta Post*. A few shops along Monkey Forest Rd offer a small range of CDs for about 5000 rp more than you'd pay in Kuta. In central Ubud, several photography shops sell slide and print film, and develop your snaps quickly. Ubud's colourful produce market, adjacent to the art market, operates every third day. It starts early in the morning, but pretty much winds up by lunch time.

GETTING THERE & AWAY
Bemo

You can reach Ubud on two bemo routes. Small orange bemos travel from Gianyar to Ubud, and on to Pujung, and larger brown bemos travel from Batubulan terminal in Denpasar to Ubud, and then head to Kintamani via Payangan. Official fares are 700 rp to Gianyar, 1500 rp to Denpasar and 2000 rp to Kintamani, but don't be surprised if you're overcharged a little. To Bedugul, go back to Denpasar; to Lovina, get a connection in Kintamani. Surprisingly, Ubud does

not have a bemo terminal; bemos stop at one of two convenient points, north and west of the market in the centre of town. Alternatively, you can charter a bemo. See the Chartering a Bemo entry in the earlier Bali Getting Around chapter for information.

Tourist Shuttle Bus

Shuttle buses are very useful for places which are not particularly easy to reach by public transport, such as Sanur, Lovina, Kuta and Bedugul. Plenty of companies offer shuttle buses at regular times; just check out the billboards outside shops and travel agencies advertising current prices and times. Perama (☎ 96316) is the major operator, while Simpatik (☎ 977364) only has services to Kuta, Sanur and Lovina.

Prices (and departure times) do vary among operators, so you may want to shop around. Perama, for example, charges 5000 rp to Sanur; 7500 rp to Kuta, the airport, Bedugul, Kintamani, Padangbai and Candidasa; and 12,500 rp to Singaraja and Lovina. Perama, and a few other companies, also have shuttle bus/boat services as far as Senggigi (17,500 rp), on Lombok, and the Gili Islands (22,500 rp), off the coast of Lombok. You can buy tickets at one of the dozens of shops, travel agencies and hotels along the main roads in Ubud, particularly Monkey Forest Rd – don't bother booking directly with the shuttle bus company.

Car & Motorbike

Rental prices for cars and motorbikes are quite competitive, and with several nearby attractions which are often difficult to reach by bemo, renting a vehicle is an attractive idea. The ubiquitous Suzuki *jimny* jeep costs about 50,000/60,000 rp per day without/with insurance; and the bigger Toyota Kijang costs from 70,000/80,000 rp. A motorbike costs from 15,000/20,000 rp, plus about 5000 rp more per day for something newer.

Cars and motorbikes can be easily rented from one of the numerous agencies, mostly found along Monkey Forest Rd, Jl Hanoman and Jl Raya, or from your hotel. If an agency asks for large sums of US dollars, or substantial deposits, try somewhere else.

Taxi

There are very few taxis in Ubud – the few which will honk their horns at you have normally dropped off passengers in Ubud from south Bali, and are hoping for a fare back. They should use their meters, but check first.

GETTING AROUND
To/From the Airport

Regular tourist shuttle buses go to the airport from Ubud – but they are hard to organise *from* the airport to Ubud. Pre-paid taxis from the airport cost 47,000 rp, but taxis are not always available in Ubud. If your plane leaves at an unreasonable hour, you will have to pre-book a taxi at your hotel or at a travel agency in Ubud for about 40,000 rp. By bemo, go to Batubulan terminal in Denpasar, catch another bemo to Tegal, and then another to the airport. Or you can charter a bemo yourself. It's best to arrange this the previous day, and be sure to confirm a price and time of departure with the driver.

Bemo

Bemos don't directly link Ubud with nearby villages; you'll have to catch a bemo going to Denpasar, Gianyar, Pujung or Kintamani and get off where you need to. Small orange bemos to Gianyar travel along eastern Jl Raya, down Jl Peliatan and east to Bedulu. To Pujung, bemos head east along Jl Raya and then north through Andong and past the turn-off to Petulu. Larger brown bemos to Denpasar go east along Jl Dewi Sita and down Jl Hanoman.

To Kintamani, they travel along western Jl Raya, past Campuan and turn north at the junction after Sanggingan.

Ojek

If you are staying in the 'suburbs' of Ubud and want to get into town (or vice versa), ask around for an *ojek* (paying pillion passenger on a motorbike). Prices are negotiable, of course, but the young Balinese drivers seem more interested in taking pretty, single, female passengers.

Bicycle

Many shops, agencies and hotels in central Ubud rent out mountain bikes. The standard charge is 5000 rp per day, or 4000 rp per day for a longer rental. Make sure the bike works properly because some of the roads are not conducive to long bike rides. A general guide to the lay of the land is:

East along Jl Bedulu, the road is reasonably flat and quiet, although the other eastern road towards Sala is steep and windy.
South towards Denpasar, the roads via Teges and Pengosekan are flat but very, very busy, so you'll spend more time trying to stay on your bike than enjoying the scenery.
North towards Penelokan the roads are fairly uninteresting and steadily slope upwards. The road though Junjungan is quietest; it's very busy via Andong.
West towards Campuan and Sanggingan, the road is steep in both directions – mainly for those with strong leg muscles and good bikes.

Around Ubud

The region east and north of Ubud has many of the most ancient monuments and relics on Bali. Many of them predate the Majapahit era and raise as yet unanswered questions about Bali's history. Some sites are more recent, and in other instances newer structures have been built on and around the ancient remains. They're interesting to history and archaeology buffs, but not that spectacular to look at – with the exception of Gunung Kawi which is very impressive. Perhaps the best approach is to plan a whole day walking or cycling around the area, stopping at the places which interest you, but not treating any one as a destination in itself. Refer to the Ubud & Around map in this chapter.

If you're travelling by public transport, start early and take a bemo to the Bedulu intersection south-east of Ubud, and another due north to Tirta Empul (about 15km from Ubud). See the temple of Tirta Empul, then

The Legend of Bedulu

A legend relates how Bedulu possessed magical powers which allowed him to have his head chopped off and then replaced. Performing this unique party trick one day, the servant entrusted with lopping off his head and then replacing it unfortunately dropped it in a river and, to his horror, watched it float away. Looking around in panic for a replacement he grabbed a pig, cut off its head and popped it upon the king's shoulders. Thereafter the king was forced to sit on a high throne and forbade his subjects to look up at him; Bedulu means 'he who changed heads'.

follow the path beside the river down to Gunung Kawi. From there you can return to the main road and walk due south about 8km to Pejeng (see the Ubud Area map), or flag down a bemo going towards Gianyar.

The temples and museum at Pejeng and the archaeological sites at Bedulu are all within about 8km of each other. For ideas about walking and cycling to some of these places, refer to the Walks Around Ubud section and the Bicycles entry in the Getting Around section earlier in this chapter.

BEDULU

Bedulu was once the capital of a great kingdom. The legendary Dalem Bedaulu ruled the Pejeng dynasty from here, and was the last Balinese king to withstand the onslaught of the powerful Majapahits from Java. He was eventually defeated by Gajah Mada in 1343. The capital shifted several times after this, to Gelgel and then later to Semarapura (Klungkung).

Goa Gajah

Only a short distance east of Teges is Goa Gajah (Elephant Cave – see the Ubud Area map). There were never any elephants on Bali; the cave probably takes its name from the nearby Sungai Petanu which at one time was known as Elephant River, or perhaps because the face over the cave entrance might resemble an elephant.

The origins of the cave are uncertain – one tale relates that it was created by the fingernail of the legendary giant Kebo Iwa. It probably dates at least to the 11th century, and it was certainly in existence at the time of the Majapahit takeover of Bali. In modern times, the cave was rediscovered by Dutch archaeologists in 1923; the fountains and bathing pool were not unearthed until 1954.

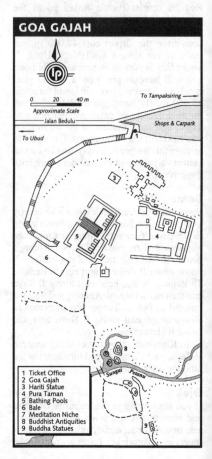

GOA GAJAH

0   20   40 m
Approximate Scale

Jalan Bedulu

To Ubud

To Tampaksiring

Shops & Carpark

Sungai Petanu

1 Ticket Office
2 Goa Gajah
3 Hariti Statue
4 Pura Taman
5 Bathing Pools
6 Bale
7 Meditation Niche
8 Buddhist Antiquities
9 Buddha Statues

The cave is carved into a rock face and you enter through the cavernous mouth of a demon. The gigantic fingertips pressed beside the face of the demon push back a riotous jungle of surrounding stone carvings.

Inside the T-shaped cave you can see fragmentary remains of *lingam*, the phallic symbol of the Hindu god Shiva, and its female counterpart the *yoni*, plus a statue of Shiva's son, the elephant-headed god Ganesh. In the courtyard in front of the cave are two square bathing pools with water gushing into them from waterspouts held by six female figures. To the left of the cave entrance, in a small pavilion, is a statue of Hariti, surrounded by children. In Buddhist lore, Hariti was an evil woman who devoured children, but under the influence of Buddhism she reformed completely to become a protector of children and a symbol of fertility.

From Goa Gajah you can clamber down through the rice paddies to Sungai Petanu, where there are crumbling **rock carvings** of *stupas* (domes for housing Buddhist relics) on a cliff face, and a small **cave**.

Goa Gajah is open daily from 8 am to 6 pm. If you're travelling independently, arrive before 10 am, when a number of large tourist buses start to arrive. Admission costs 1100/600 rp for adults/children – plus 500 rp for your camera, 1000 rp for a video, 400 rp to park your car and 500 rp or more to rent a sarong. There are some *eateries* in the carpark, amid the slew of souvenir shops and stalls.

Yeh Pulu

This 25m-high carved cliff face is believed to be a hermitage dating from the late 14th century. Apart from the figure of elephant-headed Ganesh, the son of Shiva, there are no obviously religious scenes here. The energetic frieze includes various scenes of everyday life, although the position and movement of the figures suggests that it could be read from left to right as a story. One theory is that they are events from the life of Krishna, the Hindu god.

One of the first recognisable images is of

The ornately carved entrance to Goa Gajah – the Elephant Cave.

a man carrying a shoulder pole with two jugs, possibly full of *tuak* (palm wine). He is following a woman whose jewellery suggests wealth and power. There's a whimsical figure peering round a doorway, who seems to have armour on his front and a weapon on his back. The thoughtful seated figure wears a turban which suggests he is a priest.

The hunting scene starts with a horseman and a man throwing a spear. Another man seems to be thrusting a weapon into the mouth of a large beast, while a frog imitates him by disposing of a snake in like manner. Above the frog, two figures kneel over a smoking pot, while to the right two men carry off a slain animal on a pole. Then there's the controversial depiction of the woman holding the horse's tail – is she begging the rider to stay or being dragged off as his captive?

The Ganesh figures of Yeh Pulu and Goa Gajah are quite similar, indicating a close relationship between the two sites. You can walk between the sites, following small paths through the rice fields, but you might need to pay a local kid to guide you. By car or bicycle, look for the signs to 'Relief Yeh Pulu' or 'Villa Yeh Pulu' east of Goa Gajah.

Admission is 1100/600 rp for adults/children; cameras are 500 rp; videos 1000 rp; and sarong rental is negotiable. The ticket includes a small brochure with an explanation in English, but if you want more information about Yeh Pulu buy Madi Kertonegoro's book *The Talking Stones*, available from bookshops in Ubud.

Next to the entrance, *Made's Cafe* offers cold drinks and snacks, and you can stay at *Pondok Wisata Lantar* (☎ 942399), which has small, clean rooms for 15,000 rp, including breakfast.

From the entrance, it's a pleasant 300m walk to Yeh Pulu. There's a sacred fountain opposite the mural, and an old woman anoints you with holy water, and expects a small donation in return.

Pura Samuan Tiga

The majestic Pura Samuan Tiga (Temple of the Meeting of the Three) is about 200m east of the Bedulu junction. The name is possibly a reference to the Hindu trinity, or it may refer to meetings held here in the early 11th century. Despite these early associations, all the temple buildings have been rebuilt since the 1917 earthquake. The imposing main gate was designed and built by I Gusti Nyoman Lempad, one of Bali's renowned artists and a native of Bedulu.

Museum Purbakala

This archaeological museum (☎ 942447) has an ill-assorted collection of artefacts from all over Bali. The exhibits include some of Bali's first pottery from near Gilimanuk, and sarcophagi dating from as early as 300 BC – some originating from Bangli were carved in the shape of a turtle, which has important cosmic associations in Balinese mythology. Next to the pond inside the complex, a noticeboard offers a reasonable explanation of the exhibits in English.

The museum is open Monday to Thursday from 8 am to 2 pm, and until noon on Friday and Saturday. It is about 500m north of the Bedulu junction, and easy to reach by bemo or bicycle.

Getting There & Away

About 3km east of Teges, the road from Ubud reaches a junction where you can turn south to Gianyar or north to Pejeng, Tampaksiring and Penelokan. Ubud-Gianyar bemos will drop you off at this junction, from where you can walk to the attractions. The road from Ubud is reasonably flat, so coming by bicycle is a good option.

PEJENG

Continuing up the road towards Tampaksiring you soon come to Pejeng and its famous temples. Like Bedulu, this was once an important seat of power, the capital of the Pejeng kingdom which fell to the Majapahit invaders in 1343.

Pura Kebo Edan

Also called the Crazy Buffalo Temple, this is not an imposing structure, but it is famous for its 3m-high statue, known as the Giant of Pejeng, thought to be about 700 years old. The temple is on the western side of the road. You might have to pay 1000 rp to enter.

The Legend of the Drum

A Balinese legend relates how the drum known as Moon of Pejeng came to earth as a fallen moon, landing in a tree and shining so brightly that it prevented a band of thieves from going about their unlawful purpose. One of the thieves decided to put the light out by urinating on it, but the moon exploded, killed the foolhardy thief and fell to earth as a drum – with a crack across its base as a result of the fall. Variations on the story say it was the wheel of a chariot which carried the moon goddess.

Pura Pusering Jagat

The large Pura Pusering Jagat (Navel of the World Temple) is said to be the centre of the old Pejeng kingdom. Dating from 1329, this temple is visited by young couples who pray at the stone lingam and yoni. Further back is a large stone urn, with elaborate but worn carvings of gods and demons searching for the elixir of life in a depiction of the *Mahabharata* tale 'Churning the Sea of Milk'. The temple is on a small track running west of the main road.

Pura Penataran Sasih

This was once the state temple of the Pejeng kingdom. In the inner courtyard, high up in a pavilion and difficult to see, is the huge bronze drum known as the **Moon of Pejeng**. The hourglass-shaped drum is more than 2m long, the largest single-piece cast drum in the world. Estimates of its age vary from 1000 to 2000 years, and it is not certain whether it was made locally or imported. Even in its inaccessible position, you can make out these patterns and the distinctive heart-shaped face designs.

TAMPAKSIRING

Tampaksiring is a small town (see the Ubud & Around map) with probably the most impressive ancient monument on Bali, and a large and important temple, with public baths.

Gunung Kawi

On the southern outskirts of town a sign points east off the main road to the wondrous Gunung Kawi. From the end of the access road, a steep stone stairway leads down to the river, at one point making a cutting through an embankment of solid rock. There, in the bottom of this lush green valley, is one of Bali's oldest, most charming and certainly largest, ancient monuments.

Gunung Kawi consists of 10 rock-cut *candi* (shrines), memorials cut out of the rock face in imitation of actual statues. They stand in 7m-high sheltered niches cut into the sheer cliff face. A solitary candi stands about 1km further down the valley to

the south; this is reached by a trek through the rice paddies on the west side of the river.

Each candi is believed to be a memorial to a member of the 11th century Balinese royalty, but little is known for certain. Legends relate that the whole group of memorials was carved out of the rock face in one hard working night by the mighty fingernails of Kebo Iwa.

The five monuments on the eastern bank are probably dedicated to King Udayana, Queen Mahendradatta, their son Airlangga and his brothers Anak Wungsu and Marakata. While Airlangga ruled eastern Java, Anak Wungsu ruled Bali. The four monuments on the western side are, by this theory, to Anak Wungsu's chief concubines. Another theory is that the whole complex is dedicated to Anak Wungsu, his wives, concubines and, in the case of the remote 10th candi, to a royal minister.

Entry to Gunung Kawi costs 1100/600 rp for adults/children. It's 1000 rp for a video and 500 rp for a still camera. It is open daily from 7 am to 5 pm.

Tirta Empul

A well signed-posted fork in the road north of Tampaksiring leads to the holy springs at Tirta Empul. Founded in 962 AD, the springs are believed to have magical powers, so the temple is important. The springs are a source of Sungai Pakerisan, which rushes by Gunung Kawi only 1km or so away. The actual springs bubble up into a large, crystal-clear tank within the temple and gush out through waterspouts into a bathing pool. Despite its antiquity, the temple is glossy and new – it was totally restored in the late 1960s.

There is an admission charge (1100/600 rp for adults/children), plus more for a video or camera. You must have a sarong or long pants, and you may also need to rent a scarf. The complex is open from 8 am to 6 pm; come in the early morning or late afternoon to avoid the tourist buses. You can also use the clean, segregated and free **public baths** in the grounds.

Overlooking Tirta Empul is Soekarno's palace, **Istana Negara**. It is an unspectacular, single storey structure, designed by Soekarno himself and built in 1954 on the site of a Dutch rest house.

Soekarno, whose mother was Balinese, was a frequent visitor to the island. It's said that he had a telescope here to spy on girls bathing in the pools below.

Other Sites

There are other groups of candi and monks' cells in the area of Bali encompassed by the ancient Pejeng kingdom, notably **Pura Krobokan** and **Goa Garba**, but none so grand as Gunung Kawi. Between Tirta Empul and Gunung Kawi, **Pura Mengening** temple has a freestanding candi similar in design to those at Gunung Kawi. There's another spring at this temple which also feeds into Sungai Pakerisan.

Getting There & Away

Tampaksiring is an easy day trip from Ubud, or a stopover between Ubud and Danau Batur. By bemo, get a connection in Bedulu. Tirta Empul and Gunung Kawi are easy to find along the Penelokan-Ubud road, and are only about 1.5km apart. There is nowhere to stay in Tampaksiring.

East Bali

Highlights

- The scenery of East Bali is spectacular, with superbly sculpted rice terraces, spectacular volcanoes, rugged seascapes and beautiful bays.

- At Semarapura (Klungkung), pavilion ceilings at the palace are covered with paintings depicting Bali's most lurid legends.

- Pura Besakih is Bali's 'mother temple'; an extensive complex with many temple structures. It's at its most spectacular during one of the frequent festivals.

- Padangbai is a small bustling port, with a pretty beach and an attractive coastline nearby.

- Diving and snorkelling on the famous wreck of the *Liberty* at Tulamben attracts many visitors, but there are superb sites all along the north-eastern coast.

- There's plenty of good hiking, including treks up Gunung Agung, Gunung Lempuyang and Gunung Seraya, and walks near Tirta Gangga and Putung.

The eastern end of Bali is dominated by the mighty Gunung Agung, known as the 'navel of the world' and Bali's 'mother mountain'. Towering at 3142m, Agung has not always been a kind 'mother' – as the disastrous 1963 eruption attests (see the boxed text 'The 1963 Eruption' later in this chapter).

Today Agung is quiet, but the 'mother temple' of Pura Besakih, perched high on the slopes of the volcano, attracts a steady stream of devotees and tourists.

The main route east from Denpasar and Ubud goes through Gianyar and Semarapura (also known as Klungkung), and then close to the coast past Kusamba, the bat-infested temple of Goa Lawah and the turn-off to the pretty beach and port of Padangbai. There are plenty of wonderful places to stay – and great diving opportunities – between Padangbai and Candidasa. The road finally reaches Amlapura, another former capital. From there you can continue north past Tirta Gangga until you hit the coast, or travel along the coast itself, which is a developing area of diving opportunities and new bungalows.

GIANYAR

Gianyar is the administrative centre, and main market town, of the Gianyar district, which also includes Ubud. On the main road from Denpasar, and still in the heavy traffic region of south Bali, the town has a number of small textile factories and the palace of the surviving royal family, but Gianyar is of minimal interest.

Information

The tourist office is not very helpful, and is often closed through lack of interest from staff and travellers. There's a handy *wartel* (public telephone office) and a police station (☎ 93110), while and the Bank BRI and Bank Danamon will change cash. A huge, white statue of Arjuna in his chariot is the main feature at the west end of Jl Ngurah Rai, the main street.

Textile Factories

The textile factories at the western end of town have showrooms where you can buy material by the metre, or have it made into shirts, skirts, robes and so on. You can go out the back to the workshops and see the thread-dyeing technique before it is woven into the cloth called *endek*. Prices range from 15,000 to 20,000 rp per metre, depending on how fine the weaving is – or much more if it has silk in it.

EAST BALI

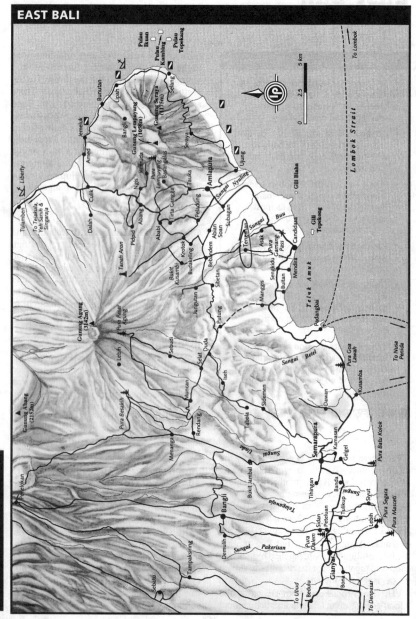

EAST BALI

GIANYAR

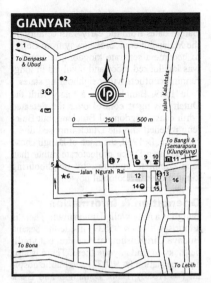

GIANYAR

1 Cap Togog Textile Factory
2 Cap Cili Textile Factory
3 Hospital
4 Post Office
5 Statue
6 Police Station
7 Tourist Office
8 Bemo Terminal (for Ubud & Tampaksiring)
9 Dunkin' Donuts; Bank Danamon
10 Wartel
11 Puri Gianyar
12 Market; Bemo Terminal (for Bangli);
   Rumah Makaus
13 Bank BRI
14 Main Bemo Terminal (for Denpasar)
15 Pondok Wisata Gianyar I
16 Alun-alun (Sports Ground)

Puri Gianyar

This old palace is little changed from the time the Dutch arrived in the south and the old kingdoms lost their power. The palace dates from 1771, but was destroyed in a conflict with the neighbouring kingdom of Klungkung in the mid-1880s and rebuilt, only to be severely damaged in the 1917 earthquake. It's still a fine example of traditional palace architecture. Tourists are not normally allowed inside, but if you report to the guard inside the complex, you may be allowed a quick look around. Otherwise, you can see some of it through the gates.

Places to Stay & Eat

The best and most central place to stay is **Pondok Wisata Gianyar 1** (☎ 942165) which costs 22,000 rp for small, clean double rooms. Gianyar's **warungs** along the main street are noted for their fine roast piglet *(babi guling)*, and excellent traditional food is available at the **rumah makans** around the market. The incongruous **Dunkin' Donuts** stand is presumably more for passing traffic than the local populace.

Getting There & Away

Regular bemos (1000 rp) travel between the main terminal in Gianyar and Batubulan terminal in Denpasar. Bemos from Gianyar to Ubud and Tampaksiring leave from another stop over the road from the market; and to Bangli, they leave from inside the market area.

LEBIH & THE COAST

South of Gianyar the coast is fringed by black sand beaches and small coastal villages like Lebih, but you will need you own transport to get around. Sungai Pakerisan (Pakerisan River), which starts near Tampaksiring, reaches the sea near Lebih. Here, and at other coastal villages south of Gianyar, funeral ceremonies reach their conclusion when the ashes are consigned to the sea. Ritual purification ceremonies for temple artefacts are also held on these beaches. The impressive **Pura Segara** temple looks across the strait to Nusa Penida, home of Jero Gede Macaling – the temple helps protect Bali from his evil influences (for details see the Nusa Penida chapter).

Further west is **Pura Masceti**, one of Bali's nine directional temples. On the beach, the local villagers have erected a huge and somewhat horrific 'swan' in an attempt to create a tourist attraction. One of the best **beaches** along this stretch of coast is just south of Siyut.

EAST BALI

SIDAN

Continuing east from Gianyar you come to the turn-off to Bangli at Peteluan, about 2km out of town. Follow this road for about 1km until you reach a sharp bend. Here you'll find Sidan's **Pura Dalem**, a good example of a temple of the dead, with very fine carvings. Note the sculptures of Durga with children by the gate and the separate enclosure in one corner of the temple – this is dedicated to Merajapati, the guardian spirit of the dead.

BANGLI

Halfway up the slope to Penelokan, Bangli, once the capital of a kingdom, is said to have the best climate on Bali. Bangli has an interesting temple, and the town makes a pleasant base for exploring the area, but the range of accommodation is poor.

BANGLI

1 Ticket Office (Pura Kehen)
2 Pura Kehen
3 Pondok Wisata Jaya Giri
4 Tourist Office; Sasana Budaya Giri Kusuma
5 Penginapan Pada Liang
6 Police Station
7 Tirta Buana Swimming Pool
8 Hospital
9 Telkom Wartel

To Penelokan
To Rendang
To Bukit Demulih & Tampaksiring
Sungai Sangsang
Park

10 Post Office
11 Losmen Dharmaputra
12 Bank BNI
13 Bemo Terminal
14 Artha Sastra Inn
15 Bangli Inn
16 Market; Warungs
17 Bank Danamon
18 Petrol Station
19 Pura Dalem Penunggekan

Jalan Ngurah Road
Jalan Merdeka

0   250   500 m

To Sidan & Gianyar

History

Bangli dates from the early 13th century. In the Majapahit era it broke away from Gelgel to become a separate kingdom, although it was landlocked, poor and involved in long-running conflicts with neighbouring states.

In 1849, Bangli made a treaty with the Dutch, giving it control over the defeated north coast kingdom of Buleleng, but Buleleng rebelled and the Dutch imposed direct rule there. In 1909, the rajah of Bangli chose to become a Dutch protectorate rather than face complete conquest by neighbouring kingdoms or the colonial power.

Orientation & Information

Bangli is a neat, well planned town. There is a tourist office (☎ 91537) inside the Sasana Budaya Giri Kusuma arts centre, but you'll be lucky to find anyone there. There is also a police station (☎ 91072) and public hospital (☎ 91020). Bank Danamon and Bank BNI will change cash, and the former will provide cash advances on Visa cards.

Pura Kehen

Pura Kehen, the state temple of the Bangli kingdom, is one of the finest temples in east Bali; a little like a miniature version of Pura Besakih.

It is terraced up the hillside, with a great flight of steps leading to the beautifully decorated entrance. The first courtyard has a huge banyan tree with a *kulkul* (warning drum) entwined in its branches. Chinese porcelain plates were set into the walls as decoration, but most of the originals have been damaged or lost. The inner courtyard has an 11 roofed *meru* (multi-roofed shrine), and a shrine with thrones for the Hindu trinity – Brahma, Shiva and Vishnu. The carvings are particularly intricate.

Tickets at a gate about 100m to the west cost 1100 rp. Otherwise, walk via the road past the arts centre and make a donation at the counter opposite the temple, where you can rent a sarong (1000 rp). The temple is open daily from 8 am to 5 pm. The requisite souvenir stalls are at the car park, a few metres to the east of the temple gate.

Sasana Budaya Giri Kusuma

Supposedly a showplace for Balinese dance, drama, gamelan and visual arts, this arts centre rarely seems to have anything on. A regular schedule isn't available, but you may be lucky enough to stumble across something, or ask around the center or tourist office inside. In any case, it's worth a quick wander around on your way to or from the temple.

Bukit Demulih

Three kilometres west of Bangli is the village of Demulih, and a hill called Bukit Demulih. If you can't find the sign pointing to it, ask local children to direct you. After a short climb to the top, you'll see a small **temple** and good **views** back over Bangli and south Bali.

On the way, a steep side road leads down to Tirta Buana, a **public swimming pool** in a lovely location deep in the valley.

Pura Dalem Penunggekan

Just south of Bangli, this fascinating temple of the dead features reliefs of particularly vivid scenes of wrong-doers getting their just desserts in the afterlife. They're not really inspiring, and definitely adults-only viewing.

Places to Stay & Eat

There's a poor choice of accommodation and restaurants in Bangli, probably because most people speed through here on day trips. *Artha Sastra Inn (☎ 91179)* is a former palace residence. It is pleasant, friendly and popular, and singles/doubles cost from 15,000/ 20,000 rp. *Bangli Inn (☎ 91419)* is the most comfortable place in town, and quite good value for a negotiable 25,000 rp per room.

The other cheapies are grim: *Losmen Dharmaputra* has unappealing rooms with a shared bathroom for 10,000 rp; *Penginapan Pada Liang (☎ 91639)* is overpriced at 15,000 rp; and *Pondok Wisata Jaya Giri (☎ 92255)* is close to the temple, but rarely open. Bangli has very few restaurants, but it does boast good *food stalls* and *warungs* in the market area.

Getting There & Away

Bangli is easy to reach: it's on the main road between Denpasar's Batubulan terminal (1100 rp) and Gunung Batur, via Penelokan. Bemos also regularly leave Gianyar and go up the pretty, shaded road to Bangli, although it's often quicker to get a connection at the junction near Peteluan.

Tourist shuttle buses travelling between Ubud and Gunung Batur usually go via Tampaksiring, and bypass Bangli.

SEMARAPURA (KLUNGKUNG)

Semarapura was once the centre of Bali's most important kingdom, and a great artistic and cultural focal point. Today it's a major public transport junction, with an interesting palace and a busy market. It's a reasonable place to base yourself while you explore the surrounding area, although the range of accommodation is not good. The town is still commonly called Klungkung, but has been officially renamed Semarapura, and this new name appears on most signs and maps these days.

History

Successors to the Majapahit conquerors of Bali established themselves at Gelgel (just south of modern Semarapura) in around 1400, and the Gelgel dynasty strengthened with the growing Majapahit presence on Bali. During the 17th century the successors of the Gelgel line established separate kingdoms and the dominance of the Gelgel court was lost. The court moved to Klungkung (as it was called then) in 1710, but never regained a pre-eminent position.

In 1849, the rulers of Klungkung and Gianyar defeated a Dutch invasion force at Kusamba. Before the Dutch could launch a counter attack, a force from Tabanan arrived and the trader Mads Lange was able to broker a peace settlement.

For the next 50 years, the south Bali kingdoms squabbled, until the Rajah of Gianyar persuaded the Dutch to support him. When the Dutch finally invaded the south, the king of Klungkung had a choice between a suicidal *puputan* (fight to the death) like the

EAST BALI

SEMARAPURA (KLUNGKUNG)

PLACES TO STAY
17 Losmen Cahay Pusaha
18 Loji Ramayana Hotel

PLACES TO EAT
13 Bali Indah
14 Sumber Rasa

To Besakih

To Kusamba,
Candidasa &
Amlapura

Jalan Gajah Mada

Jalan Gunung Batukaru

Jalan Gunung Rinjani

Jalan Besakih

Jalan Surapati

Jalan Diponegoro

Jalan Nakula

Jalan Sahadewa

Jalan Puputan

To Terminal Klod (2km),
Tihingan, Gianyar & Denpasar

To Gelgel &
Kamasan

0   125   250 m

OTHER
1   Police Station
2   Post Office
3   Puputan Monument
4   Museum Semarajaya
5   Bale Kambang
6   Kertha Gosa;
    Wartel
7   Parking
8   Bemo Terminal
    (for Besakih & Rendang)
9   Pura Taman Sari
10 Bank Pembangunan;
    Bank Danamon
11 Bank BCA
12 Market
15 Temple
16 Mosque

rajah of Denpasar, or an ignominious surrender as Tabanan's rajah had done. He chose the former. In April 1908, as the Dutch surrounded his palace, the Dewa Agung and hundreds of his relatives and followers marched out to certain death from Dutch gunfire, or the blades of their own kris. It was the last Balinese kingdom to succumb.

Information

Bank Danamon, Bank BCA and Bank Pembangunan will change cash. There is a post office, wartel and police station (☎ 21115).

Semara Pura

When the Dewa Agung dynasty moved here in 1710, a new palace – the Semara Pura (sometimes referred to as Taman Gili, the 'Island Garden') – was established. It was laid out as a large square, believed to be in the form of a mandala, with courtyards, gardens, pavilions and moats, and was built by the best artisans available. Most of the original palace and grounds were destroyed by Dutch attacks in 1908, and the **Pemedal Agung**, the gateway on the south side of the

square, is all that remains of the palace itself – it's worth a close look to see the carvings. The complex is open daily from 7 am to 6 pm, and tickets are 2000/1000 rp for adults/children.

Kertha Gosa In the north-eastern corner of the complex, the 'Hall of Justice' was effectively the supreme court of the Klungkung kingdom, where disputes and cases which could not be settled at the village level were eventually brought. This open-sided pavilion is a superb example of Klungkung architecture, and its ceiling is completely covered inside with fine paintings in the Klungkung style. The paintings, done on asbestos sheeting, were installed in the 1940s, replacing the cloth paintings which had deteriorated.

The rows of ceiling panels actually depict several different themes. The lowest level illustrates five tales from Bali's answer to the *Arabian Nights*, where a girl called Tantri spins a different yarn every night. The next two rows are scenes from Bima's travels in the afterlife, where he witnesses the torment of evildoers. The gruesome tortures are shown clearly, but there are different interpretations of what punishment goes with what crime. (There's a pretty authoritative explanation in *The Epic of Life – A Balinese Journey of the Soul*, available for reference in the pavilion.) The fourth row of panels depicts the story of Garuda's search for the elixir of life, while the fifth row shows events on the Balinese astrological calendar. The next three rows return to the story of Bima, this time travelling in heaven, with doves and a lotus flower at the apex of the ceiling.

Bale Kambang The ceiling of the beautiful 'Floating Pavilion' is painted in Klungkung style. Again, the different rows of paintings deal with different subjects. The first row is based on the astrological calendar; the second on the folk tale of Pan and Men Brayut and their 18 children; and the upper rows on the adventures of the hero Sutasona.

Museum Semarajaya This museum has some archaeological pieces, and some quite interesting contemporary accounts of the 1908 puputan. It's nothing special, but entry is included in the ticket to the complex, so you might as well have a quick look.

Pura Taman Sari

The quiet lawns and ponds around this temple make it a relaxing stop. The towering 11 roofed meru indicates that this is a temple built for royalty.

Places to Stay & Eat

If you want to stay, the best place is *Loji Ramayana Hotel* (☎ 21044). It's pleasant, with a restaurant in a pavilion out the back, and far enough from the main road to be reasonably quiet. The better rooms are quite big, and cost a negotiable 30,000 rp. Directly opposite, the only other option is *Losmen Cahay Pusaha* (☎ 22118), with noisy rooms from 15,000 rp.

Apart from the charming restaurant in the *Loji Ramayana*, the Chinese *Bali Indah* and *Sumber Rasa* restaurants are both neat, clean and cheap.

Shopping

Several shops along Jl Diponegoro sell Klungkung-style paintings, temple umbrellas and some good textiles from nearby villages. There may be some interesting antiques if you look hard. The chaotic market is definitely worth a look around.

Getting There & Away

Very frequent bemos and minibuses from Denpasar (Batubulan terminal) pass through Semarapura (1100 rp) on the way to Padangbai and Amlapura. They can be hailed from the main road in Semarapura.

Bemos heading north to Rendang and Besakih leave from the centre of Semarapura. Most other bemos leave from the inconvenient terminal Klod, about 2km south of the city centre.

Perama shuttle buses travelling between south Bali or Ubud and Padangbai or Candidasa will stop in Semarapura on request. The town is also a regular stop-off on organised bus tours around east Bali.

AROUND SEMARAPURA

There are a number of interesting things to see within a few kilometres of Semarapura, and several roads north and east lead to Pura Besakih, Gunung Agung and some of Bali's most attractive coast and countryside. Public transport around these parts is not frequent, so it's best to rent or charter your own vehicle. Organised tours of east Bali usually stop at a few of these places.

Gelgel

Once the seat of Bali's most powerful dynasty, Gelgel's decline started in 1710 when the court moved to Klungkung (now called Semarapura), and finished when the Dutch bombarded the place in 1908.

Today the wide streets and the surviving temples are only faintly evocative of past grandeur. The **Pura Dasar** is not particularly attractive, but its vast courtyards are a clue to its former importance, and festivals here attract large numbers from all over Bali.

A little to the east, the **Masjid Gelgel** is Bali's oldest mosque. It was established in

EAST BALI

century for the benefit of
sionaries from Java, who were
to return home after failing to
make any converts.

Gelgel is about 3km south of Semarapura, past the intersection by the Semara Pura complex.

Kamasan

Another quiet, traditional village, Kamasan is the origin of the Kamasan style of classical painting (see the Balinese Arts & Crafts colour section earlier in the book). Several artists have workshops and small showrooms along the main streets. The work is often a family affair, with one person doing the outlines, while another mixes the paints and another applies the colours. The paintings depict traditional stories or Balinese calendars, and although they are sold in souvenir shops all over Bali, the quality is better here. Look for smooth and distinct linework, evenly applied colours and balance in the overall composition.

From Semarapura, head south towards Gelgel, and look for the turn-off to Kamasan.

Tihingan

Tihingan has several workshops producing *gamelan* instruments. Small foundries make the resonating bronze bars and bowl shaped gongs, which are then carefully filed and polished until they produce the correct tone. Some pieces are on sale, but most of the instruments are produced for musical groups all over Bali. It's not really set up for visitors, but the workshops with signs out the front will receive visitors. From Semarapura, head west along Jl Diponegoro, and look for the signs.

Museum Seni Lukis Klasik

Nyoman Gunarsa, one of the most respected and successful modern artists in Indonesia, established this museum and arts centre near his home town of Banda. The three storey building houses a wide variety of older pieces, including stone and wood carvings, architectural antiques, masks, ceramics and textiles. Many of the classical paintings are on bark paper, and are some of the oldest surviving examples of this style. The top floor is devoted to Gunarsa's own work, with many vibrant, colourful, semi-abstract depictions of traditional dances and musicians.

There's a large performance space downstairs, and some fine examples of traditional architecture just outside. The museum opens Tuesday to Sunday from 9 am to 5 pm, and admission is 5000 rp. It is about 6km from Semarapura, near a bend on the road to Denpasar – look for the mannequin policemen at the base of a large statue nearby.

Goa Jepang

About 1km further west of the museum, these mildly interesting Japanese caves are probably of more interest to WWII historians, and children who will enjoy scurrying through the caves. It is well signposted, near a bridge, and there is the requisite *restaurant* at the entrance.

Bukit Jambal

The road north of Semarapura climbs steeply into the hills, via Bukit Jambal, which is understandably popular for its magnificent views. Inevitably, several *restaurants* have appeared (two are unimaginatively named Restaurant Bukit Jambal I and II) to provide buffet lunches for tour groups. This road continues to Rendang and Pura Besakih.

Sidemen Road

A less travelled route goes north-east from Semarapura, via Sidemen and Iseh, to the Rendang-Amlapura road. The area boasts marvellous scenery and a delightful rural character, and is easily accessible by bemo from Semarapura, although most of the road is fairly rough.

Sidemen was a base for Swiss ethnologist Urs Ramseyer, and is also a centre for culture and arts, particularly *songket*, a cloth woven with threads of silver and gold. German artist Walter Spies lived in Iseh for some time from 1932. Later, the Swiss painter Theo Meier, nearly as famous as Spies for his influence on Balinese art, lived in the same house.

Places to Stay & Eat In Sideman, *Sidemen Pondok Wisata (☎ 23009)* is pleasantly old-fashioned, with four-poster beds and great views. It costs 50,000 rp per person with breakfast, or 70,000 rp per person with full board (three meals). *Subak Tabola Inn (☎ 23015)*, along a small track, 1.5km on your right as you head south from Sidemen, is set among rice fields and has a lovely outlook. It has a small pool and comfortable rooms from US$35, or more with full board.

Another wonderful place in Sidemen is *Sacred Mountain Sanctuary (☎/fax 23456, email sacredmt@dps.mega.net.id)*. It has two storey bamboo huts, with what one reader described as a 'delightful courtyard bathroom that has to be seen to be believed', and a small pool. Rooms cost about 150,000 rp, including breakfast.

Pondok Wisata Patal Kikian (☎ 23001) is delightful, and offers almost total seclusion and tranquillity, as well as awesome views of Gunung Agung. Stylish singles/doubles cost US$25/50, but you should book first to ensure they have adequate staff and food. Look for the poorly signposted turn-off on the left, not far south of Iseh.

The Coast

The coast south of Semarapura is striking, with seaside temples, black sand beaches and pounding waves, but the sea is not suitable for swimming. Roads don't run along the coast; you need to take side tracks to the sea at places like **Siyut** and **Pura Batu Kolok**. It's difficult without your own transport.

East of Semarapura, the main road crosses Sungai Unda (Unda River), location of occasional rafting trips (see the Rafting section in the Bali Facts for the Visitor chapter). The road then swings south towards the sea. Lava from the 1963 eruption of Agung destroyed villages and cut the road, but lava flows are now overgrown.

Kusamba A side road goes south to this fishing and salt-making village, where you'll

A Short History of Kusamba

In 1849, Kusamba was the site of a key battle which delayed Dutch control of south Bali for more than 50 years. The Dutch had landed an invasion force here, which outraged the Balinese by desecrating a temple. While the Dutch were weakened by an outbreak of dysentery, Dewa Agung Isteri, known as the 'virgin queen' of Klungkung, led an attack in which the Dutch suffered numerous casualties and their leader was fatally wounded.

Historically, Kusamba was also one of the original Muslim settlements on Bali, and a centre for metal workers who produced weapons, including the sacred kris. Kusamba still has mosques and kris-makers, although neither wants to attract visitors.

see lines of colourful fishing *prahus* (outriggers) lined up on the beach. Fishing is usually done at night and the 'eyes' on the front of the boats help navigation through the darkness. Regular boats travel to the islands of Nusa Penida and Nusa Lembongan, which are clearly visible from Kusamba. East and west of Kusamba, there are thatched roofs of salt making huts along the beach – see the boxed text 'Saltmakers of the East Coast' later in this chapter.

Pura Goa Lawah Three kilometres east of Kusamba is the Bat Cave Temple. The cave in the cliff face is packed, crammed, jammed full of bats – the complex is equally overcrowded with tour groups later in the day. A distinctly batty stench exudes from the cave, and the roofs of the temple shrines in front of the cave are liberally coated with bat droppings. Superficially, the temple is small and unimpressive, but it is very old and of great significance to the Balinese.

The cave is said to lead all the way to Besakih, but it nobody has yet volunteered to confirm this: the bats provide sustenance for

Pura Goa Lawah (Bat Cave Temple) is one of nine directional temples on Bali and is devoted to the diety Naga Basuki.

ly dressed devotees turn up with beautifully arranged offerings. The panoramic view and moutain backdrop are impressive too, but try to arrive early, before the mist rolls in, along with the tour buses.

Despite its importance to the Balinese, Pura Besakih can be a disappointment. The architecture is not particularly impressive, tourists are not allowed inside any of the temples, the views are usually obscured by mist, and the number of entry charges, hustlers and souvenir sellers can be infuriating. The tourist information office can answer basic questions, but has no printed information and does nothing to make the site more comprehensible.

Warning Many unofficial and unscrupulous guides hang around the temple. If someone latches on to you, let them know quickly whether you want their services and for how much. There are a few minor scams. Some 'guides' claim that you need to pay a 5000 rp 'fee' for going further into the temple complex during a festival, although this is not true.

History

The precise origins of the Pura Besakih complex are not clear, but it almost certainly dates from prehistoric times. The stone bases of Pura Penataran Agung and several other temples resemble megalithic stepped pyramids, which date back at least 2000 years. There are legendary accounts of Sri Dangkyang Markendaya conducting meditation and ceremonies here in the 8th century, while stone inscriptions record a Hindu ritual on the site in 1007 AD. There are some indications of Buddhist activity here, but it was certainly used as a Hindu place of worship from 1284 when the first Javanese conquerors settled on Bali, and this is confirmed by accounts from the time of the Majapahit conquest in 1343. By the 15th century, Besakih had become a state temple of the Gelgel dynasty.

The central temple was added to over the years, and additional temples were built for specific family, occupational and regional

the legendary giant snake, Naga Basuki, which is also believed to live in the cave. The cave and temple are open every day (tickets are 500 rp), plus rental of a sash. There's also a car park (200 rp), souvenir shops and extremely pushy souvenir sellers.

PURA BESAKIH

Perched nearly 1000m up the side of Gunung Agung is Bali's most important temple, Pura Besakih. In fact, it is an extensive complex of 23 separate but related temples, with the largest and most important being Pura Penataran Agung. It's most enjoyable during one of the frequent festivals, when hundreds, perhaps thousands, of gorgeous-

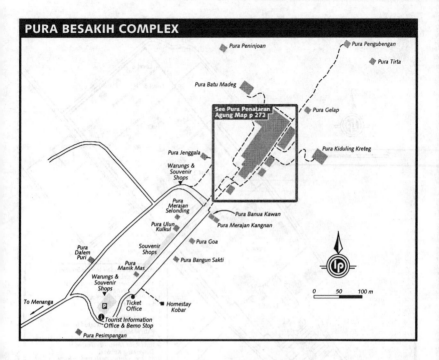

PURA BESAKIH COMPLEX

Pura Peninjoan
Pura Pengubengan
Pura Tirta
Pura Batu Madeg
See Pura Penataran Agung Map p 272
Pura Gelap
Pura Kiduling Kreteg
Pura Jenggala
Warungs & Souvenir Shops
Pura Merajan Selonding
Pura Banua Kawan
Pura Ulun Kulkul
Pura Merajan Kangnan
Pura Dalem Puri
Pura Goa
Souvenir Shops
Pura Manik Mas
Pura Bangun Sakti
Warungs & Souvenir Shops
To Menanga
Ticket Office
Homestay Kobar
Tourist Information Office & Bemo Stop
Pura Pesimpangan

0   50   100 m

groups. The complex was neglected during the colonial period, perhaps because of the lack of royal patronage, and was virtually destroyed in the 1917 earthquake. The Dutch assisted with its reconstruction, and the dependent rajahs were encouraged to support the maintenance of the temples.

Entrance

As well as being Bali's Mother Temple, Besakih is also the Mother of Balinese Money-Making. You pay to park (600 rp per car and 200 rp for a motorbike) and to enter (1100 rp per person). Buy your tickets at the entrance of the complex, or at a bus lay-off about 1km before the complex. If you don't have a sarong, you have to rent one for 2000 to 3000 rp – although 5000 rp may be the first price asked. You have to brave a swarm of souvenir sellers, and then pay more entry fees for other temples.

The best time to come is at about 8 am, before the souvenir stalls open and the tourist buses start to unload their passengers. The complex is open every day during daylight hours.

Pura Penataran Agung

This is the central temple of the complex – in significance, if not in exact position. It is built on six levels, terraced up the slope, with the entrance being approached from below, up a flight of steps. This entrance is an imposing split gateway *(candi bentar)*, and beyond it, the even more impressive *kori agung* is the gateway to the second courtyard.

Tourists are not permitted inside, so for the best view climb the steps to the left of the main entrance and follow the path around the western side. From here you can just see over the wall into the second courtyard

EAST BALI

PURA PENATARAN AGUNG

1 Pura Ratu Pande - temple for metal workers guild
2 11 Roof Meru - dedicated to Ida Ratu Sunarang Jagat
3 11 Roof Meru - dedicated to Sanghyang Widhi
4 Pura Ratu Penyarikan
5 Pura Pedharman
6 11 Roof Meru - dedicated to Ida Ratu Maspahit
7 Seven Roof Meru - dedicated to Saraswati
8 Nine Roof Meru - dedicated to Sanghyang Kubakal
9 11 Roof Meru - dedicated to Ratu Manik Makatel
10 Padmasana Tiga - triple throne for Brahma, Wisnu and Shiva
11 Pura Ratu Pasek
12 Kori Agung - gateway to the inner courtyard
13 Kulkul Tower
14 Candi Bentar - split gate
15 Kulkul Tower
16 Pura Dukuh Segening
17 Seven Roof meru
18 Pura Basukian

(don't climb up on the wall), where the *padmasana* is. In most modern temples this is a single throne for the supreme god, but Besakih stresses the Hindu trinity, and it has a triple throne called *padmasana tiga*, or *padmasana trisakti*, with separate seats for Brahma, Wisnu and Shiva. This point is the spiritual centre of the temple, and indeed of the whole Besakih complex.

Continuing on the footpath around the temple, you can see quite a few imposing meru, the multi-roofed towers through which gods can descend to earth, but otherwise the temple is unspectacular. The upper courtyards are usually empty, even during festivals. One of the best views is from the path at the north-eastern end, where you can look down past the many meru and over the temple to the sea.

Other Temples

None of the other temples is striking, except when decorated for festivals, but each one has a particular significance, sometimes in conjunction with other temples. The Hindu trinity, *trimurti*, is represented by the combination of Pura Penataran Agung as Shiva, Pura Kiduling Kreteg as Brahma and Pura Batu Madeg as Vishnu. Just as each village on Bali has a *pura puseh* (temple of origin), *pura desa* (village temple) and *pura dalem* (temple of the dead), Pura Besakih has three temples which fulfil these roles for Bali as a whole – Pura Basukian, Pura Penataran Agung and Pura Dalem Puri respectively.

The Balinese concept of *panca dewata*, which embodies a centre and four cardinal points, is represented by Pura Penataran Agung (the centre), Pura Kiduling Kreteg (south), Pura Batu Madeg (north), Pura Gelap (east) and Pura Ulun Kulkul (west). Each district of Bali is associated with a specific temple at Besakih, and the main temples of Bali are also represented by shrines here. Some temples are associated with families descended from the original Gelgel dynasty, and there are shrines and memorials going back many generations. Various craft guilds also have their own temples, notably the metalworkers, whose Pura Ratu Pande is built onto the side of the main temple.

Special Events

With so many temples and gods represented at Besakih, there seems to be at least one festival or ceremony every week – the booklet *Calendar of Events*, available from the main tourist offices in south Bali, lists the important ones.

The founding of Besakih itself is celebrated at Bhatara Turun Kabeh, around the full moon of the 10th month (usually in March and April), when all the gods descend at once. The annual rites at Pura Dalem Puri, usually in January, attract thousands who make offerings for the dead. In addition, each individual temple has its own *odolan* (temple birthday), held annually according to the 210 day *wuku* calendar.

Even more important are the great purification ceremonies of Panca Wali Krama, theoretically held every 10 years, and the Eka Dasa Rudra, every 100 years. The exact dates of these festivals are determined after long consideration by priests and have never been exactly regular. An Eka Dasa Rudra was held in 1963, but was disrupted by the disastrous eruption of Gunung Agung, and restaged successfully in 1979. The last Panca Wali Krama was in 1989.

Places to Stay & Eat

Staying at Besakih is useful if you want an early start to climb Gunung Agung, but surprisingly there is nowhere decent or central to stay. There are some unsigned *losmen* within the complex, but you'll have to ask at the tourist office or the gate for directions. One place, *Homestay Kobar*, offers basic doubles for 15,000 rp.

There are many cheap *warungs* around the car park, and plenty of shops selling food along the road inside the complex. Naturally, there are several pricey *restaurants* along the main roads to the temple complex.

Seven kilometres below Besakih, *Lembah Arca Restaurant & Accommodation* (☎ 23076) is a reasonable place to stay and eat, and only a short bemo ride from Besakih. It's prettily situated in a valley by a bend in the road, although the singles/doubles are overpriced for 25,000/40,000 rp.

Getting There & Away

The usual route to Besakih is by minibus or bemo from Semarapura (1500 rp). Ask the driver to take you to the temple entrance, not to the village of Besakih about 1km south of the temple complex. It may be quicker to get a connection in Rendang or Menanga. You may want to charter a vehicle because public transport is not frequent; make sure you leave the temple by 3 pm if you want to return by bemo.

If you have your own transport, you can reach Besakih along a turn-off from the road between Menanga and Penelokan, or from near Rendang. Besakih is a *major* feature on any organised tour of east and north Bali. Visiting on a tour will save you the hassle of getting to the complex, and allow you to see other places nearby.

EAST BALI

GUNUNG AGUNG

Bali's highest and most revered mountain, Gunung Agung is an imposing peak from most of south and east Bali, although it's often obscured by cloud and mist. Most books and maps give its height as 3142m, but some say it lost its top in the 1963 eruption and is now only 3014m. The summit is an oval crater, about 500m across, with its highest point on the western edge above Besakih.

The 1963 Eruption

The most disastrous volcanic eruption on Bali this century took place in 1963, when Gunung Agung blew its top in no uncertain manner at a time of considerable prophetic and political importance.

The culmination of Eka Desa Rudra, the greatest of all Balinese sacrifices and an event which only takes place every 100 years on the Balinese calendar, was to be on 8 March 1963. At the time of the eruption, it had been more than 100 Balinese years (115 years on the lunar calendar) since the last Eka Desa Rudra, but there was dispute among the priests as to the correct and most propitious date.

Naturally the temple at Besakih was a focal point for the festival, but Agung was already acting strangely as preparations were made in late February. The date of the ceremony was looking decidedly unpropitious, but Soekarno, then the president of Indonesia, had already scheduled an international conference of travel agents to witness the great occasion as a high-light of their visit to the country, and he would not allow it to be postponed. By the time the sacrifices began, the mountain was glowing, belching smoke and ash, and rumbling omi-nously, but Gunung Agung contained itself until the travel agents had flown home.

On 17 March Agung exploded. The catastrophic eruption killed more than 1000 people (some estimate 2000) and destroyed entire villages – 100,000 people lost their homes. Streams of lava and hot volcanic mud poured right down to the sea at several places, com-pletely covering roads and isolating the eastern end of Bali for some time. The entire island was covered in ash and crops were wiped out everywhere.

Torrential rainfall followed the eruptions, and compounded the damage as boiling hot ash and boulders were swept down the mountain side, wreaking havoc on many villages, in-cluding Subagan, just outside Amlapura, and Selat, further along the road towards Rendang. The whole of Bali suffered a drastic food shortage, and many Balinese were resettled in western Bali and Sulawesi.

Although Besakih is high on the slopes of Agung, only about 6km from the crater, the temple suffered little damage from the eruption. Volcanic dust and gravel flattened timber and bamboo buildings around the temple complex, but the stone structures came through un-scathed. The inhabitants of the village of Lebih, also high up on Agung's slopes, were all but wiped out. Most of the people killed at the time of the eruption were burnt and suffocated by searing clouds of hot gas that rushed down the volcano's slopes. Agung erupted again on 16 May, with serious loss of life, although not on the same scale as the March eruption.

The Balinese take signs and portents seriously – that such a terrible event should happen as they were making a most important sacrifice to the gods was not taken lightly. Soekarno's political demise two years later, following the failed Communist coup, could be seen as a con-sequence of his defiance of the volcanic deity's power. The interrupted series of sacrifices finally recommenced 16 years later in 1979.

Climbing

It's possible to climb Agung from various directions, but the two shortest and most popular routes are from the temple at Besakih, and up the southern flank from Selat or Muncan. The latter route goes to the lower edge of the crater rim, but you can't make your way from there around to the very highest point. You'll have great views south and east, but you won't be able to see central Bali. If you want to say you've been to the very top, or if you want the 360° view, climb from Besakih.

To have the best chance of seeing the view before the clouds form, get to the top before 8 am, and get there by 6 am to see the sunrise. You'll have to start well before dawn, so plan your climb when there will be some moonlight, and take a strong torch (flashlight). Also take plenty of water and food, waterproof clothing, a warm jumper and extra batteries – just in case.

You should take a guide for either route, although it's not strictly necessary. Before you start, or early in the climb, the guide will stop at a shrine and make an offering and some prayers. This is a holy mountain and you should show respect. Besides, you will want to have everything going for you.

It's best to climb during the dry season (April to September); July to September are the most reliable months. At other times, the paths can be slippery and dangerous, and you probably won't see anything of the view. Climbing Agung is not allowed when major religious events are being held at Besakih, which generally includes most of April. No guide will take you up at these times, from either Besakih, Selat or Muncan, and there are horror stories about those who defied the ban and came to a sticky end on Agung.

From Selat or Muncan This route involves the least walking because there is a serviceable road from Selat or Muncan to the Pura Pasar Agung (Agung Market Temple), high on the southern slopes of the mountain. From the temple you can climb to the top in as little as two hours, but allow at least three or four – it's a pretty demanding trek. You must report to the police station at Selat before you start from either town, and again when you

return. You should pre-arrange a guide in Muncan or Selat – ask around the markets in either town, or contact the helpful guys at the police station in Selat. A guide will charge about 35,000 rp per person, including food – transport will cost extra.

You can stay the night near Muncan or Selat (see the following Rendang to Amlapura section), and drive up early in the morning, or drive up the day before and stay overnight at the temple. If so, a donation and some devotions are appropriate. Pura Pasar Agung has been greatly enlarged and improved, in part as a monument to the 1963 eruption which devastated this area.

Start climbing from the temple at around 3 or 4 am. There are numerous trails through the pine forest – this is where you'll need your guide – but after an hour or so you'll climb above the tree line. The ground is stony and can be loose and broken towards the summit. Allow plenty of time to get down again. From the temple you can walk down to Sebudi, from where there are bemos, or arrange for a chartered bemo to pick you up at the temple.

From Besakih This climb is tougher than from the south. You must leave no later than 6.30 am if you want to get down before nightfall; it's best to leave at midnight if you want a clear view before the clouds close in. Allow five to six hours for the climb, and four to five for the descent. The starting point is Pura Pengubengan, north-east of the main temple complex, but it's easy to get lost on the lower trails, so hire a guide. The tourist information office near the car park at Besakih can arrange a guide, but they'll charge around US$25 per person, which is way too much, so try to negotiate. Arrange the guide the day before, and stay in a losmen at or near Besakih so you can start early.

From Tirta Gangga The trekking agency in Tirta Gangga (☎ 22436 – see that section later in this chapter) can arrange trips via Pura Pasar Agung temple. It is better to stay overnight in the Pasar Agung Temple, otherwise you have to leave Tirta Gangga at about 2 am. It's more expensive from Tirta Gangga, because you must charter a vehicle (90 minutes) to the start of the trek. It will cost about US$20 per person, including transport, for a group of four – the rate per person is higher for a smaller group.

From Dalah The most daunting way, although it's less congested in peak season, is from Dalah on the mountain's eastern flank. Because there is no recognised trail, you will certainly need a knowledgeable guide. You can drive as far as Dalah, and as you climb the eastern side of Agung, you'll appreciate the sea breezes and earlier sunrise. You will have to start very early; the return trip will take about eight hours. The best place to arrange this trek is one of the hotels along the coast between Amed and Lipah (see the North-East Coast section later in this chapter). Eco-dive is a good place to start organising a guide, and haggling about his fee.

RENDANG TO AMLAPURA

A scenic road goes around the southern slopes of Gunung Agung from Rendang to near Amlapura. It runs through some superb countryside, descending more or less gradually as it goes further east. If you have your own wheels, you'll find it very scenic, with some interesting places to stop, but it can take some time by public bemo. You can do it in either direction, but by bicycle it is better going eastward.

Starting from the west, **Rendang** is an attractive town, easily reached by bemo from Semarapura or via the very pretty, minor road from Bangli. About 4km along a winding road, the old-fashioned village of **Muncan** has quaint shingle roofs. The road then passes through some of the prettiest rice country on Bali before reaching **Selat**, where you turn north for Pura Pasar Agung, a starting point for climbing Gunung Agung. You can stay at *Pondok Wisata Puri Agung*, on the road between Selat and Duda. It has clean and comfortable rooms for 40,000 rp, although the service can be erratic and staff may even be absent when you arrive.

Further on is **Duda**, where another scenic route branches south-west via Sidemen to Semarapura (see the previous Around Semarapura section). Further east, a side-road (about 800m) leads to **Putung**, which has a car park, some souvenir stalls and *Pondok Hilltop Resort* (☎ 23039), where you can enjoy wonderful views down the southern slopes to the coast. The resort charges US$20/25 for very ordinary singles/doubles, which are all in drastic need of renovation. It is, however, still worth coming for the views, a meal (about 9000 to 15,000 rp) or an expensive drink. This area is superb for **hiking**: there's an easy-to-follow track from Putung to **Manggis**, about 8km down the hill.

Continuing east, **Sibetan** is famous for growing *salaks*, the delicious fruit with a curious 'snakeskin' covering – you can buy them between December and April from stalls along the road. Nearby, a poorly signposted road leads north to Jungutan with its **Tirta Telaga Tista** – a pleasant pool and garden complex built for the water-loving old Rajah of Karangasem.

The scenic road finishes at Bebandem, where there's a **cattle market** every three days, and plenty of other stuff for sale as well. Bebandem and several nearby villages are home to members of the traditional metalworkers caste, which includes silversmiths as well as blacksmiths.

Further east in **Abian Soan**, the delightful *Homestay Lila* is a good place to base yourself while you hike around the area; you can arrange a guide at the homestay. Very basic singles/doubles, in a friendly atmosphere, cost 10,000/15,000 rp. For more information about hiking in this area, see the Hiking Around Tirta Gangga section later in this chapter.

PADANGBAI

Located on a perfect little bay, Padangbai is the port for Bali-Lombok ferries, and passenger boats to Nusa Penida. It is also a popular place to break up a journey and relax while you plan your assault on Bali or Lombok (depending on which way you're heading) – and it's a better alternative than Candidasa.

Cruise ships visiting Bali use Padangbai, but have to anchor offshore because only small ships and ferries can actually enter the bay. When the ships are in, Padangbai is temporarily transformed into a cacophonous souvenir market with sellers flocking in from all over the island, but otherwise there is a gloriously relaxed atmosphere. The most lasting memory for most visitors is the constant sound of blaring horns from incoming ferries.

Information

The tourist information booth is rarely open or staffed, but still check it out if you need some information.

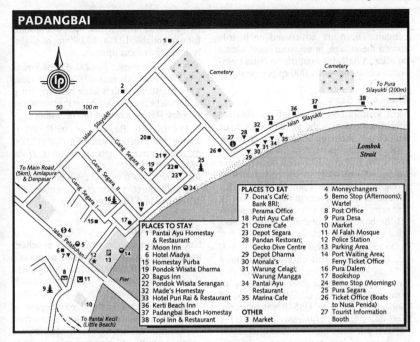

PADANGBAI

To Pura Silayukti (200m)

Lombok Strait

To Main Road, (5km), Amlapura & Denpasar

To Pantai Kecil (Little Beach)

PLACES TO STAY
1 Pantai Ayu Homestay & Restaurant
2 Moon Inn
6 Hotel Madya
15 Homestay Purba
19 Pondok Wisata Dharma
20 Bagus Inn
22 Pondok Wisata Serangan
32 Made's Homestay
33 Hotel Puri Rai & Restaurant
36 Kerti Beach Inn
37 Padangbai Beach Homestay
38 Topi Inn & Restaurant

PLACES TO EAT
7 Dona's Café; Bank BRI; Perama Office
18 Putri Ayu Cafe
21 Ozone Cafe
23 Depot Segara
28 Pandan Restoran; Gecko Dive Centre
29 Depot Dharma
30 Monala's
31 Warung Celagi; Warung Mangga
34 Pantai Ayu Restaurant
35 Marina Cafe

OTHER
3 Market
4 Moneychangers
5 Bemo Stop (Afternoons); Wartel
8 Post Office
9 Pura Desa
10 Market
11 Al Falah Mosque
12 Police Station
13 Parking Area
14 Port Waiting Area; Ferry Ticket Office
16 Pura Dalem
17 Bookshop
24 Bemo Stop (Mornings)
25 Pura Segara
26 Ticket Office (Boats to Nusa Penida)
27 Tourist Information Booth

Moneychangers at the hotels and along the main streets offer very poor rates (about 15% lower than the Kuta region) – check the rates at Bank BRI first. The bookshop along the esplanade has a small selection of second-hand novels in major European languages, and some useful maps of Bali and Lombok. Some travellers have complained about being overcharged at the wartel – always ask to see the print out before paying.

Things to See & Do

If you walk south-west from the ferry terminal and follow the trail up the hill, you'll eventually come to the idyllic **Pantai Kecil** (Little Beach) on the exposed coast outside the bay. Be very careful in the water, because there's a couple of *warungs*, and the occasional night-time beach party. A few other pretty and secluded beaches can be found around Padangbai – it's a great area for **walks**.

On a headland at the north-eastern corner of the bay, a path uphill leads to three **temples**, including Pura Silayukti where Empu Kuturan – who introduced the caste system to Bali in the 11th century – is said to have lived.

Diving There's some pretty good diving on the coral reefs around Padangbai, but the water can be a little cold, and visibility is not always ideal. Many of the operators based in Sanur, Kuta, Tulamben and along the north-east coast organise dives around Padangbai, but one local agency has started: Gecko Dive Centre on Jl Silayukti. It will take you to the main sites, including Pura Jepun and the Blue Lagoon, both to the east. The coral isn't spectacular, but there's a good variety of fish, and a 40m wall at the Blue Lagoon.

Boating & Fishing Locals are starting to offer snorkelling, diving and fishing trips around Padangbai, and as far as Nusa Lembongan. These are advertised on boards around the village, or ask your hotel what's on offer. A half-day boat trip to Nusa Lembongan costs about 20,000 rp per person.

Places to Stay

Most visitors stay at one of the pleasant beachfront places – the gentle arc of coast with colourful fishing boats drawn up on the sand is postcard perfect. In the high season, hotels can fill up quickly and become more expensive, especially when a ferry-load of foreigners arrive from Lombok late in the afternoon. Don't just accept the first room or first price – it may be a 'here's-a-sucker-just-off-the-boat-from-Lombok' price. Almost none of the hotels include breakfast.

On the beach, *Hotel Puri Rai* (☎ *41385, fax 41386)* has a collection of two storey cottages looking rather like traditional rice barns. Considering the other choices it is not great value: US$20 to US$30 for fan-cooled rooms, or US$30 to US$40 with air-con. Next door, *Made's Homestay* (☎ *41441)* is popular, and the English-speaking manager is a mine of information, but at 30,000/50,000 rp for singles/doubles, you can do better.

Kerti Beach Inn (☎ *41391)* offers basic rooms at the front for a bargain 10,000 rp, and double storey thatched cottages for 20,000 rp. *Padangbai Beach Homestay* (☎ *41517)* is the only place with genuine, individual bungalows, even if they could do with some renovation. The price is good – 25,000 rp – and it is popular. At the end of the bay, *Topi Inn* (☎ *41424)* is in a serene location. The bamboo building has small doubles upstairs for 15,000 rp, and some dorm beds for a very reasonable 3000 rp per person.

Away from the beach there are several good alternatives. *Pantai Ayu Homestay* (☎ *41396)* is very friendly, and offers great views (although the cemetery does spoil them somewhat). Singles cost 15,000 rp, and doubles range from 20,000 to 25,000 rp. In the village, there's three tiny places down an alley. *Pondok Wisata Dharma* (☎ *41394)* is probably the best, with rooms for a negotiable 12,000/17,000 rp, or slightly more for rooms upstairs.

Around the corner, *Pondok Wisata Serangan* (☎ *41425)* charges 40,000 rp for clean rooms upstairs, with a large balcony, but it will soon be overshadowed by the two storey *Pondok Wisata Kembar Inn* next door.

The friendly *Bagus Inn* (☎ *41398)* is simple, but excellent value for 8000/12,000 rp, and the mossie nets are a bonus. *Hotel Madya* (☎ *41393)* is clean and good value for 15,000/20,000 rp, and the rooms are surprisingly quiet. Other cheap options are *Moon Inn* and *Homestay Purba*.

Places to Eat

Not surprisingly, the seafood is excellent and cheap: a tuna steak or plate of prawns costs from 4000 to 6000 rp, including chips (French fries) and salad. Each has a restaurant, and a few have some entertainment.

Along the esplanade, *Depot Segara* is about the best place for breakfast – the fruit juices (1500 rp) are excellent, and the pancakes are tasty and prepared in an unusual way. *Putri Ayu Cafe* has seafood specials, and the related *Pantai Ayu Restaurant* is very popular for its wide range and reasonable prices. *Warung Celagi* and *Warung Mangga* offer tempting seafood specials and pizzas, while *Marina Cafe* is cheap, but ask if you want your beer cold. Other reasonable cheapies are *Monala's*, *Dona's Cafe* and *Depot Dharma*.

Ozone Cafe is an evening gathering place, and *Pandan Restoran* is also relaxed, but a little more expensive than others. The restaurant at *Topi Inn* is the fanciest place in Padangbai. It features a colourful menu of fish dishes, health foods and Indonesian regulars, as well as live guitar music and occasional Balinese dancing. It is the perfect place for a late night dessert and coffee.

The quaint restaurant on top of *Pantai Ayu Homestay* offers great food and views (you can't see the cemetery at night). *Hotel Puri Rai* has the town's one and only (so far) video show.

EAST BALI

Getting There & Away

Bemo Padangbai is a couple of kilometres south of the main Semarapura to Amlapura road. For no particularly obvious reason, there are two bemo stops. The one used before midday is along the esplanade, while in the afternoon they congregate along the road out of town. Regular bemos go to Amlapura (1500 rp) via Candidasa (1000 rp), Semarapura (1500 rp) and occasionally on to Denpasar (1700 rp). Alternatively, walk along the shady 2km road to the main road and hail down a passing bemo.

Sadly, there is some form of transport Mafia in Padangbai, so it's almost impossible for tourists to pay the *harga biasa* (normal price) for public transport, but the extra few hundred rupiah is probably not worth quibbling about.

Public Bus Several buses travel between Denpasar (Batubulan terminal) and Padangbai (2200 rp) every day. These theoretically are timed to connect with ferries to Lombok, but do not depend on it. Buses also pass through Padangbai on the way to Surabaya and Yogyakarta on Java – you can purchase tickets at the travel agencies along the esplanade in Padangbai.

Tourist Shuttle Bus Perama shuttle buses stop here on trips around the eastern coast from Kuta (10,000 rp) to Lovina (15,000 rp), stopping at Candidasa (2500 rp), Tirta Gangga (5000 rp) and Tulamben (7500 rp). Its office (☎ 41419) is at Dona's Cafe.

Perama, and a few other agencies along the esplanade, can also organise services to Senggigi and the Gili Islands (using the public ferry), but if you haven't organised connections by the time you get to Padangbai, it's easy enough to organise everything when you arrive on Lombok.

Ferry Ferries travel between Padangbai and Lembar on Lombok every 60 to 90 minutes, all day and night. (The Lombok Getting There & Away chapter has full details.) The ticket office for private vehicles is well signposted in the northern part of the car park;

other passengers pay at another office in the waiting area.

Refer to the Nusa Penida chapter later in the book for information about boats to these islands from Padangbai.

PADANGBAI TO CANDIDASA

It's 11km along the main road from the Padangbai turn-off to the beach resort of Candidasa, and there are bemos or buses every few minutes. Between the two is an attractive stretch of coast which has some tourist development and a large, new oil storage depot, which explains the oil tankers you'll see in Teluk Amuk (Amuk Bay).

After about 4km, there is a turn-off to the pretty village of **Manggis**, along a road with views of rice paddies.

Back on the main road, a badly marked turn-off leads to the *very* exclusive **Amankila** hotel (☎ *41333, fax 41555*). It features an isolated seaside location and understated architecture which complements the environment quite well (except for the hideous walkways). Almost absolute luxury will cost you a mere US$555 to $1573 per double. It costs nothing to walk up the road to the hotel and admire the marvellous views of the coastline.

Buitan (Balina Beach)

The pretty and quiet Balina Beach is the name bestowed on the tourist development in the village of Buitan. It is losing its beach to erosion, and beach lovers may be disappointed with the black sand and rocks. To find the turn-off, look for the small yellow sign 'Balina' from the main road.

Diving The beach is an increasingly popular departure point for diving trips around the east Bali coast. The Spicedive and Baruna diving centres are easy to find on the main street. They offer the same sort of packages and prices for dives around east Bali as the agencies listed in the North-East Coast and Tulamben sections later in this chapter.

Places to Stay & Eat From the street to Buitan, it's easy to follow the signs to the

EAST BALI

various accommodation options. **Balina Beach Resort** (☎ 41002, fax 41001) has a variety of rooms, including some very attractive cottages. The pretty gardens and pool face a reasonably good bit of beach, but it's no longer good value: doubles range from US$66 to US$85.

Opposite, **Puri Buitan** (☎ 41021) offers modern, motel-style singles/doubles from US$30/35 to US$65/75, but it often offers large discounts.

Further east, with its own entrance from the main Padangbai-Candidasa road, is **The Serai** (☎ 41011, email serai@ghmhotels.com) with elegant, white thatched-roof buildings in a spacious garden facing the beach. Very comfortable, although not really outstanding, rooms cost from US$151 to US$264.

If you walk east along the beach (access is not so easy from the main road), you'll find two pleasant, budget places. **Matahari Beach Bungalows** (☎ 41008) is also called Sunrise Bungalows (and the new owner threatens to change the name again soon). It offers pleasant, secluded bungalows for 35,000 rp, or 75,000 rp with air-con and hot water. **Pondok Purina** (☎ 41029) is a very pleasant collection of bungalows costing US$7/10/15 for singles/doubles/triples.

You will probably end eating at your hotel, or another hotel, but the main street through Buitan does have a couple of decent, tourist-oriented **warungs**.

Mendira & Sengkidu

Mendira also has a few hotels and losmen. Even this far out, the beach is still eroded, however, and sea walls have been constructed. Purists may be disappointed with the black sand which all but disappears at high tide, but it's a pretty area and a quieter alternative to Padangbai or Candidasa. From Sengkidu village, look for, and follow, the turn-off with signs to the hotels.

The friendly little **Homestay Dewi Utama** (☎ 41053) offers basic accommodation, but the price can't be beaten in this area: 12,000 rp per room, including bathroom and breakfast. Just a little further up the road, **Pondok Wisata Pisang** (☎ 41065) has simple bungalows which cost 15,000/25,000 rp for singles/doubles.

Candi Beach Cottages (☎ Kuta 0361-751711, fax 752651) has all the mod cons and rooms from US$109/121, which is not great value. Nearby, **Amarta Beach Inn Bungalows** (☎ 41230) has a gorgeous location and friendly atmosphere, and is great value for 25,000/30,000 rp, including breakfast. Opposite, **Anom Beach Inn Bungalows** (☎ 41902, fax 41998) is a bit fancier, and has a pool. It offers a huge range of rooms and bungalows from US$25/31 to US$49/61 for the 'superior bungalow'.

There are a couple of cheap **warungs** in the main street, such as the one belonging to Homestay Dewi Utama, but you will probably end up eating at your hotel, or another one nearby. Exquisite seafood awaits.

About 1km west of the start of Candidasa, **Nirwana Cottages** (☎ 41136) has only 12 rooms in a quiet location, with rates from US$43 to US$61. Another mid-range place nearby is **Hotel Rama Candidasa** (☎ 41974), with pool, tennis court, satellite TV etc, for US$43 to US$82.

TENGANAN

Tenganan is occupied by Bali Aga people, the descendants of the original Balinese who inhabited Bali prior to the Majapahit arrival. The village is surrounded by a wall, and consists basically of two rows of identical houses stretching up the gentle slope of the hill. The Bali Aga are reputed to be exceptionally conservative and resistant to change, but even here the modern age has not been totally held at bay – a small forest of TV aerials sprouts from those oh-so-traditional houses. The most striking feature of Tenganan, however, is its exceptional neatness, with the hills providing a beautiful backdrop.

A peculiar, old-fashioned version of the gamelan known as the *gamelan selunding* is still played here, and girls dance an equally ancient dance known as the Rejang. There are other Bali Aga villages nearby, including **Asak**, where another ancient instrument, the *gamelan gambang*, is still played.

Scenes from the annual Usaba Sambah festival at the Bali Aga village of Tenganan in East Bali: Girls costumed festival finery (top); the bright and vibrant festival procession (bottom left); and *pandanus* fighters at close quarters attempt to draw blood with the spiky leaves (bottom right).

RICHARD I'ANSON

Top: The mighty volcano Gunung Agung looms over the coastal village of Tulamben in east Bali.
Middle: Dozens of fishing boats crowd the port at Padangbai on Bali's south-eastern coast.
Bottom: Despite a disappearing beach, due to the destruction of the sheltering reef, Candidasa in east Bali remains a popular destination for visitors interested in diving, temples and dance.

Special Events

Tenganan is full of strange customs, festivals and practices. The *Calendar of Events* booklet has a whole section devoted to Tenganan's festivals. At the month-long Usaba Sambah Festival, which usually starts in May or June, men fight with sticks wrapped in thorny pandanus leaves – similar events occur on the island of Sumba, far to the east in Nusa Tenggara. At this same festival, small, hand-powered Ferris wheels are brought out and the village girls are ceremonially twirled around.

Handcrafts

A magical cloth known as *kamben gringsing* is woven here – a person wearing it is said to be protected against black magic. Traditionally this is made using 'double ikat' technique, in which both the warp and weft threads are resist dyed before being woven.

The Legend of Tenganan

There's a delightful legend about how the villagers of Tenganan came to acquire their land. The story pops up in various places in Indonesia, but in slightly different forms.

The Tenganan version relates how Dalem Bedaulu (the king with a pig's head described in the Bedulu section of the Ubud & Around chapter) lost a valuable horse. When its carcass was found by the villagers of Tenganan, the king offered them a reward. They asked that they be given the land where the horse was found – that is, all the area where the dead horse could be smelled.

The king sent a man with a keen nose who set off with the village chief and walked an enormous distance without ever managing to get away from the foul odour. Eventually accepting that enough was enough the official headed back to Bedaulu, scratching his head. Once out of sight the village chief pulled a large hunk of dead horse out from under his clothes.

It's very time consuming, and the few pieces of double ikat available for sale are expensive. Other interesting textiles are sold here – some are handmade by local craftswomen, but much is from other parts of Bali and Indonesia. Many locally made baskets are on sale, made from *ata* palm. Another local craft is traditional Balinese calligraphy, with the script inscribed onto *lontar* palm strips, in the same way that ancient lontar books were created.

Getting There & Away

Tenganan is at the end of a road 4km uphill from a turn-off just west of Candidasa. At the turn-off, a posse of motorbike riders can offer an *ojek* (paying pillion passenger) to the village for about 1500 rp; otherwise you can wait for an infrequent bemo (500 rp) at the turn-off. The best idea is to take an ojek or bemo up there, and enjoy the gentle walk back downhill to the main road.

CANDIDASA

Until the 1970s, Candidasa was a just a quiet little fishing village, then beachside losmen and restaurants sprung up and suddenly it was *the* new beach place on Bali. Now it's shoulder-to-shoulder tourist development, and many find it overbuilt and unattractive. The main drawback is the lack of a beach; except for the far eastern stretch, it has eroded away as fast as the new hotels have been erected. Most of the coastline has breakwaters, so you can't even walk along any of the coastline.

Despite this, some visitors enjoy Candidasa, especially the eastern part – it's less hectic than the Kuta region and is a good base from which to explore east Bali. The budget and mid-range accommodation is surprisingly good value, and is also popular with divers (scuba and snorkelling), although beach-lovers will prefer Padangbai, Mendira or Buitan.

Information

Candidasa boasts a tourist office which was open, but never staffed, each time we visited – you may have better luck. Easily found along the main street are bookshops, postal agencies and wartels. The rates offered by the many moneychangers along the main road are not that attractive; Bank Danamon usually has a better rate.

Things to See & Do

Candidasa's temple, **Pura Candidasa**, is on the hillside across from the lagoon at the eastern end of the village strip. The fishing village, just beyond the lagoon, has colourful **prahus** drawn up on what's left of the beach. In the early morning you can watch them coasting in after a night's fishing. The owners canvas visitors for snorkelling trips to the reef and the nearby islets.

The main road east of Candidasa spirals up to **Pura Gamang Pass** (*gamang* means 'to get dizzy') from where there are fine **views** down to the coast. If you follow the coastline from Candidasa towards Amlapura, a trail climbs up over the headland with fine views over the rocky islets off the coast. The diving around these islands is good. Beyond this headland there's a long sweep of wide, exposed, black sand **beach**.

Diving & Snorkelling

Gili Tepekong, which has a series of coral heads at the top of a sheer drop-off, is perhaps the best diving site. Other features include an underwater canyon which can be dived in good conditions. It offers the chance to see lots of fish, including some larger marine life. The currents here are strong and unpredictable, the water is cold and visibility is variable – it's recommended for experienced divers only. The Diving section in the Bali Facts for the Visitor chapter has a list of dive sites in the region.

Three reputable agencies arrange dives all over east Bali. Costs are fairly high – about US$65 for one dive at Tepelong, US$55 at Amed and Padangbai, and about US$300 for an open-water PADI course – but discounts are certainly possible. Baruna has a kiosk (☎ 41185), and an office (☎ 41217) in the Puri Bagus Candidasa Hotel. One reader did complain about faulty equipment and bad information, however – but this may have been a one-off problem. Calypso Bali Dive (☎ 41126, fax 41537) is based inside the Candidasa Beach Bungalows II; and

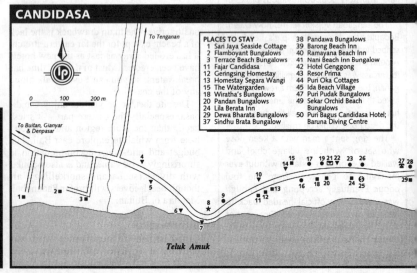

CANDIDASA

To Tenggana

0   100   200 m

To Buitan, Gianyar & Denpasar

EAST BALI

Teluk Amuk

PLACES TO STAY
1 Sari Jaya Seaside Cottage
2 Flamboyant Bungalows
3 Terrace Beach Bungalows
11 Fajar Candidasa
12 Geringsing Homestay
13 Homestay Segara Wangi
15 The Watergarden
18 Wiratha's Bungalows
20 Pandan Bungalows
24 Lila Berata Inn
29 Dewa Bharata Bungalows
37 Sindhu Brata Bungalow

38 Pandawa Bungalows
39 Barong Beach Inn
40 Ramayana Beach Inn
41 Nani Beach Inn Bungalow
42 Hotel Genggong
43 Resor Prima
44 Puri Oka Cottages
45 Ida Beach Village
47 Puri Pudak Bungalows
49 Sekar Orchid Beach Bungalows
50 Puri Bagus Candidasa Hotel; Baruna Diving Centre

Stingray Diver Services (☎ 41063) is located in the Puri Bali Bungalows.

A few hotels and shops along the main road rent snorkelling gear. With the sheltered breakwaters, it is a safe area to snorkel, even for children, although tragically there is not much coral near the shore to admire.

Places to Stay

Candidasa has a number of large and luxurious places with air-con and swimming pools – most of them are on the beach side of the main road, but very few actually have, or are even close to, a beach. These places also often add a high-season supplement.

Some of the mid-range places are very ordinary, but there is plenty of good-value budget accommodation to choose from. Easily the best place to base yourself is the original fishing village hidden in the palm trees east of the lagoon: it is far quieter than the rest of Candidasa and there is a beach, but the lack of transport in the area means a short walk to most restaurants and public transport. Most places in the budget range include breakfast.

Places to Stay – Budget

There are three reasonable places to check out on the western side of town, but this is far from the centre of Candidasa and the beach. *Sari Jaya Seaside Cottage* (☎ 41212) charges 20,000 rp for decent individual bungalows; *Flamboyant Bungalows* (☎ 4127) is reasonable for 12,500/15,000 rp for singles/doubles; and *Terrace Beach Bungalows* (☎ 41232) is the nicest of the bunch and charges 15,000/20,000 rp.

Geringsing Homestay (☎ 41084) has attractive cottages in a quiet garden from 10,000/12,000 rp – they are excellent value. Next door, the *Homestay Segara Wangi* (☎ 41159) has rooms for 15,000 rp; the ones closer to the shore are better. Continuing east, the inexpensive rooms at *Wiratha's Bungalows* (☎ 41973) are also good value at 15,000/30,000 rp.

In the centre of town, the popular *Lila Berata Inn* (☎ 41081) is no-frills for 8000/10,000 rp: as long as you don't mind traffic noise, squat toilets and chickens in the garden.

Immediately east of the lagoon is a good place to check out a few alternatives: *Sindhu*

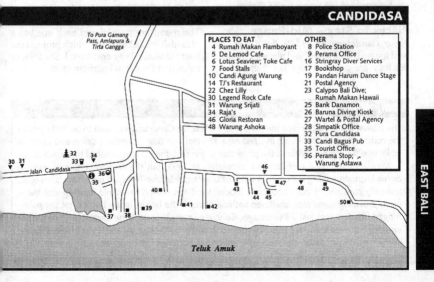

CANDIDASA

PLACES TO EAT	OTHER
4 Rumah Makan Flamboyant	8 Police Station
5 De Lemod Cafe	9 Perama Office
6 Lotus Seaview; Toke Cafe	16 Stringray Diver Services
7 Food Stalls	17 Bookshop
10 Candi Agung Warung	19 Pandan Harum Dance Stage
14 TJ's Restaurant	21 Postal Agency
22 Chez Lilly	23 Calypso Bali Dive;
30 Legend Rock Cafe	Rumah Makan Hawaii
31 Warung Srijati	25 Bank Danamon
34 Raja's	26 Baruna Diving Kiosk
46 Gloria Restoran	27 Wartel & Postal Agency
48 Warung Ashoka	28 Simpatik Office
	32 Pura Candidasa
	33 Candi Bagus Pub
	35 Tourist Office
	36 Perama Stop;
	Warung Astawa

To Pura Gamang Pass, Amlapura & Tirta Gangga

Jalan Candidasa

Teluk Amuk

EAST BALI

Brata Bungalow (☎ *41825*) has rooms and bungalows for 36,000/45,000 rp; and *Pandawa Bungalows* (☎ *41925*) has a quaint corridor of rooms for 20,000/25,000 rp.

The eastern part of Candidasa is the best place to base yourself, and there are several good options. *Barong Beach Inn* (☎ *41137*) is quiet, laid-back and has rooms for 20,000/30,000 rp, depending on the views. *Ramayana Beach Inn* (no telephone) for a negotiable 15,000/25,000 is very quiet, with great views from the tiny garden. *Nani Beach Inn Bungalow* (☎ *41829*) has quaint, spotless rooms with something that could be described as a 'beach' in front for 40,000/50,000 rp. *Hotel Genggong* (☎ *41105*) actually has a tiny beach (full of traditional *prahu* boats, however) and a very pretty garden. Rooms and cottages are great value for 30,000 to 40,000 rp.

Puri Pudak Bungalows (☎ *41978*) is open to negotiation and excellent value if you can get a bungalow for only 20,000 rp. Another great option is *Sekar Orchid Beach Bungalows* (☎ *41977*). Standard bungalows around a pleasant garden cost 35,000 rp, but it is worth splurging on the one and only upstairs room, which offers gorgeous views, sea breezes and hot water for 65,000 rp.

Places to Stay – Mid-Range

Fajar Candidasa (☎ *41539, fax 41538*) is well located, with a pool and pleasant rooms, but they are crowded together. Fan-cooled rooms cost US$30/36, and with air-con they're US$48/60. The more pleasant eastern end of Candidasa has *Puri Oka Cottages* (☎ *41092, fax 41093*), with nice rooms and a small beach and pool. Prices are normally US$36/40, but can be negotiated down to as little as 40,000/75,000 rp. *Dewa Bharata Bungalows* (☎ *41090, fax 41091*) has a pool, bar and restaurant, and is good value for US$23/28, including breakfast.

The nicest place in Candidasa is *Ida Beach Village* (☎/fax *41096*). There are only six tastefully decorated bungalows in a huge garden, with scattered palm trees. At only 35,000 to 45,000 rp per room, including breakfast, this place is very popular, so bookings are essential.

Other options include: *Pandan Bungalows* (☎/fax *41541*) for 69,000/80,000 rp, and the uninspiring *Resor Prima* (☎ *41373, fax 41971*), which is overbuilt and overpriced at US$40 a double, but the rooms have satellite TV and a fridge.

Places to Stay – Top End

The Watergarden (☎ *41540,* email *water garden@denpasar.wasantara.net.id*) is a delightfully different place, with a swimming pool and fish-filled ponds that wind around the buildings and through the lovely garden. The rooms are tasteful and each one has a verandah area like a jetty, which projects out over the water. They cost from US$85/96, or twice that for a two bedroom suite.

Um, What Happened to the Beach?

The answer lies a few hundred metres offshore where the Candidasa reef used to be. To help with the construction of new hotels in Candidasa, the reef was dug up, ground down and burnt to make lime for cement. Without the protection of the reef, the sea soon washed the beach away.

Mining of the coral reef stopped completely in 1991, but the erosion continues, even a dozen kilometres along the coast. A series of large and intrusive T-shaped piers have been built, ironically constructed out of concrete blocks. Sand has started to rebuild itself against these piers, providing some nice, sheltered bathing places if the tide is right – but it's not the palm-fringed beach it was just 25 years ago. Concrete seawalls protect the foreshore from further erosion, but even these are being destroyed in places by the sea. At least it has been a lesson in the fragility of coastal environments, which has not been lost on other beach resorts.

Puri Bagus Candidasa Hotel (☎ *41131, email pbcandi@denpasar.wasantara.net.id)* is right at the end of the beach, hidden away in the palm trees that surround the original fishing village. It's a handsome beachfront place, with nicely designed rooms which cost from US$102/115, or twice that for the villas.

Places to Eat

The food in Candidasa is pretty good – particularly the fresh seafood. Restaurants are dotted along the main road (mostly between the police station and where the road veers north to Amlapura), but the traffic noise will shatter any thoughts of a peaceful meal. The cheapest places to eat are the *food stalls* which spring up every evening – normally about where the main road almost crashes into the sea.

Standard tourist-oriented dishes at decent prices (4000 rp for Indonesian food and 6000 rp for seafood) can be found at *Rumah Makan Hawaii*, *Rumah Makan Flamboyant* and *De Lemod Cafe*.

Worth trying is *Toke Cafe* which offers a good range of meals with sensible prices, and an idyllic setting (except for the traffic noise). *Warung Astawa* offers seafood specials for 6500 rp, and continues to receive rave reviews from readers who appreciate the music, service and food.

Warung Srijati promises 'the best Balinese food in town'. For only about 4000 rp a dish, it's probably worth a visit to find out if you agree.

Further up the price range, *Lotus Seaview*, part of the Bali-wide chain of upmarket tourist restaurants, has a wonderful outlook. *TJ's Restaurant* is related to the popular TJ's in Kuta, but the food is not as Mexican and not as good.

At *Raja's*, the seafood is average, so it's best to stick with what it knows best: pizzas for about 12,500 rp.

If you're based in eastern Candidasa, you will have to walk to the main road for meals, eat at a nearby hotel or try one of two decent places: the classy *Warung Ashoka* or *Gloria Restoran*.

Entertainment

Barong, Topeng and Legong dance performances take place at 9 pm on Tuesday and Friday at the Pandan Harum dance stage in the centre of Candidasa. Tickets costs 6000 rp. Some restaurants, such as *Candi Agung Warung*, and a number of places where the main road turns north, offer free Legong dances most nights. Billboards around town advertise current performances.

Some restaurants, like *Raja's* and *Chez Lilly*, show video movies most evenings; these are advertised outside, or on noticeboards along the main road. *Legend Rock Cafe* has live music and dancing some nights, but less often in the low season when Candidasa is very quiet. Sports fans will want to visit *Candi Bagus Pub* for live satellite telecasts of their favourite sports, or to play pool.

Shopping

Sarongs, silver, souvenirs and beachwear are available in the many shops along the main road. Hand woven textiles are produced locally, as are fine baskets, but the nearby village of Tenganan (see that section earlier in this chapter) has a better range. Some interesting ceramics are also produced locally. Prices are naturally set for tourists, but there is enough competition along the main road for prices to be kept down and negotiable.

Getting There & Away

Candidasa is on the main road between Amlapura and Denpasar, so plenty of bemos and buses hurtle along the main road, and stop anywhere in Candidasa. There is no bus or bemo terminal, so hail down public transport anywhere along the main road.

Most visitors prefer the more comfortable and direct tourist shuttle buses which travel between Kuta (about 10,000 rp) and Lovina (about 15,000 rp) and stop anywhere in between. Check around because prices do vary considerably. Perama has an office (☎ 41114) at the western end of the strip, plus a pick-up and drop-off point near the lagoon; and Simpatik (☎ 41262) is near the

Legend Rock Cafe. It is easier to book a ticket at just about any hotel, restaurant or shop.

Getting Around

Suzuki jeeps (about 55,000 rp per day, including insurance and petrol), motorbikes (about 17,000 rp per day) and bicycles (4000 rp per day) can be rented from a few agencies along the main road.

AMLAPURA

Amlapura is the main town and transport junction in east Bali, and the capital of the Karangasem district.

It is not worth staying here overnight, especially considering the lack of accommodation, but it is still worth a detour from nearby Tirta Gangga or a stop off while skirting along the main road around east Bali.

Information

Amlapura is the smallest of Bali's district capitals; a sleepy, sprawling place with a confusing array of one way streets. The friendly staff at the tourist office (☎ 21196) will be spellbound if any traveller goes in and asks for information. There is a police station, and Bank BRI and Bank Danamon will change money, but it may be easier in Candidasa or Padangbai.

Puri Agung Karangasem

Amlapura's three palaces along Jl Teuku Umar are decaying reminders of Karangasem's period as a kingdom in the late 19th and early 20th centuries. Only Puri Agung Karangasem has been restored and is open to visitors, but you can wander around the other two.

Outside Puri Agung Karangasem, there is an impressive three tiered entry gate and

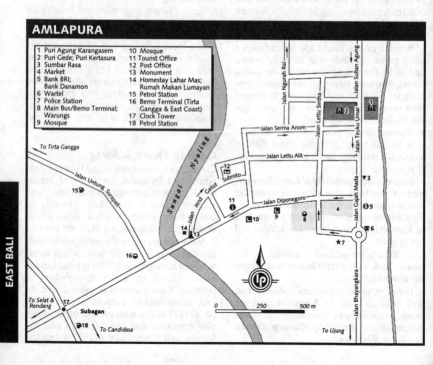

AMLAPURA

1 Puri Agung Karangasem
2 Puri Gede; Puri Kertasura
3 Sumbar Rasa
4 Market
5 Bank BRI; Bank Danamon
6 Wartel
7 Police Station
8 Main Bus/Bemo Terminal; Warungs
9 Mosque
10 Mosque
11 Tourist Office
12 Post Office
13 Monument
14 Homestay Lahar Mas; Rumah Makan Lumayan
15 Petrol Station
16 Bemo Terminal (Tirta Gangga & East Coast)
17 Clock Tower
18 Petrol Station

To Tirta Gangga

Jalan Ngurah Rai
Jalan Lettu Sintha
Jalan Sultan Agung
Jalan Teuku Umar
Jalan Serma Anom
Jalan Lettu Alit
Jalan Untung Surapati
Jalan Jend Gatot Subroto
Jalan Diponegoro
Jalan Gajah Mada
Sungai Nyuling
Jalan Bhayangkara

To Selat & Rendang
Subagan
To Candidasa
To Ujung

0   250   500 m

beautiful sculptured panels. After you pass through the entry courtyard, a left turn takes you to the Bale London, so called because of the British royal crest on the furniture. The main building is known as Maskerdam, after Amsterdam in the Netherlands, because it was the Karangasem kingdom's acquiescence to Dutch rule which allowed it to hang on long after the demise of the other Balinese kingdoms. Inside you can see several rooms, including the royal bedroom and a living room with furniture which was a gift from the Dutch royal family. On the other side is the Bale Kambang, surrounded by a pond. The ornately decorated Bale Pemandesan, in between Maskerdam and the pond, was used for royal tooth-filing and cremation ceremonies.

Puri Agung Karangasem is open every day from 8 am to 6 pm, and admission costs 2000 rp. Ask for an explanation sheet at the entrance, which tells you all you need to know (in English). You don't need a sarong, because it's more a museum than a place of worship.

Places to Stay & Eat

There is very little reason to stay here, especially considering the far better options in Tirta Gangga only 6km away. *Homestay Lahar Mas* (☎ 21345) is very basic and noisy, but clean enough, with singles/doubles for 13,500/15,000 rp.

There's the usual collection of *warungs* around the main bus/bemo terminal, plus the *Sumbar Rasa* restaurant in town, and *Rumah Makan Lumayan* next to the Lahar Mas. Amlapura tends to shut down early so don't leave your evening meal until too late.

Getting There & Away

Amlapura is the major transport hub in east Bali. Buses and bemos regularly ply the main road to Batubulan terminal (2500 rp) in Denpasar, via Candidasa, Padangbai and Semarapura. Bemos also climb the road around the southern slopes of Gunung Agung to Rendang and Besakih, but it is much better to do this with your own transport (see the earlier Rendang to Amlapura

section). Plenty of buses also go around the north coast to Singaraja (about 2500 rp), via Tirta Gangga, Amed and Tulamben, but these leave from the special terminal in the south-west of town.

TAMAN UJUNG

Five kilometres south of Amlapura, Taman Ujung is an extensive, picturesque and crumbling ruin of a once-grand water palace complex. The last king of Karangasem completed this grand palace in 1921, but it has been deteriorating for some time and was extensively damaged by an earthquake in 1979. You can wander around the remnants of the main pool, admire the **views** from the pavilion higher up the hill above the rice paddies, or continue a little further down the road to Ujung, a **fishing village** on the coast. Regular bemos leave from the main terminal in Amlapura.

TIRTA GANGGA

The tiny village of Tirta Gangga (Water of the Ganges) is an increasingly popular place to stop off and relax for a day (or more) while touring around east Bali. It is quiet (if you stay away from the main road), there's a good selection of cheap restaurants and hotels, excellent trekking in the region and a pretty palace to admire. Almost everything is within a few hundred metres along the main road from the palace.

Taman Tirta Gangga

Amlapura's water-loving rajah, after completing his masterpiece at Ujung, had another go at Tirta Gangga. This water palace, originally built in 1948, was damaged in the 1963 eruption of Agung and again during the political events that wracked Indonesia two years later. It isn't grand, but it's still a place of beauty and a reminder of the former power of the Balinese rajahs. The palace has a **swimming pool**, as well as ornamental ponds.

The palace never closes, but the ticket office is only open between 7 am and 6 pm daily. Tickets cost 1100/600 rp for adults/children; cameras and video cameras cost

2500 p. It costs 4000/2000 rp to swim in the nicer, cleaner 'pool A' in the top part of the complex; or 2000/1000 rp in 'pool B'.

Places to Stay

All places include breakfast. Opposite the water palace, *Hotel Rijasa* (☎ 21873) is a small and simple place where extremely neat and clean bungalows cost 15,000/20,000 rp for singles/doubles, and a little more for hot water. The manager is a good source of local information. Actually within the palace compound, *Tirta Ayu Homestay* (☎ 22697) has bungalows for 30,000/40,000 rp or more spacious ones for 60,000/70,000 rp. This is worth a splurge for the superb setting, and the free use of the swimming pools.

Right by the palace, the peaceful *Dhangin Taman Inn* (☎ 22059) is a relaxed place, and the owner is a bit of a character. The cheaper rooms are fairly ordinary and a bit claustrophobic, but cheap at 10,000/15,000 rp; the larger rooms have some charm for 25,000/30,000 rp. Every room is different, so look around. Just up the road from the palace, on the left, a driveway leads to *Puri Sawah Bungalows* (☎ 21847, fax 21939), which has a handful of comfortable and spacious rooms with great views. The standard rooms cost 65,000 rp, which seems a lot compared with the other places nearby, but the larger, two bedroom bungalows (with hot water) are ideal for families at 120,000 rp.

About 200m further up the hill, some very steep steps on the left lead to *Kusuma Jaya Inn* (☎ 21250). It boasts wonderful views, and rooms for a negotiable 15,000 rp for singles, and 20,000 to 30,000 rp for doubles. The staff are friendly, and some readers have raved about the food. Finally, another 600m further up, *Prima Bamboo* (☎ 21316) also offers outstanding views (and easier steps), but it is close to the main road and noisy. The rooms are reasonably pleasant, however, for 20,000/25,000 rp.

Places to Eat

All hotels have *restaurants*, but the ones up the hill are a fair hike if you aren't staying there.

About a dozen *warungs* cluster around the entrance to the water palace, and serve the usual fare at cheap prices. The best of the bunch are the unassuming *Warung Rawa* on the main road; and *Tirtagangga Cafe*, near the entrance to the palace, which serves good pizzas (about 12,000 rp) and ice-cold beer.

The restaurants in the *Pura Sawah* and *Tirta Ayu* hotels are worth a splurge for their great views and ambience. One reader claimed that *Good Karma* served 'the best food in Indonesia'. This place and *Genta Bali* are the hippest places to hear western music and meet other travellers. Hotel Rijasa often holds traditional Balinese dances on Sunday night for 5000 rp.

Getting There & Away

Regular bemos and minibuses travelling between Amlapura and Singaraja stop at Tirta Gangga, right outside the water palace, or any hotel further north. The fare to Amlapura should be 500 rp, but beware of blatant overcharging.

Perama tourist shuttle buses pass through once or twice a day in either direction to Lovina (12,500 rp) and Kuta (12,500 rp). Several shops in Tirta Gangga sell tickets – look for the noticeboards.

HIKING AROUND TIRTA GANGGA

The rice terraces around Tirta Gangga are some of the most beautiful on Bali. They sweep out from Tirta Gangga, almost like a sea surrounding an island. A few kilometres beyond, on the road to the east coast, there are more dramatically beautiful terraces, often seen in photographs of Bali. From Tirta Gangga, or Abian Soan (see the earlier Rendang to Amlapura section), tiny paths take you to many picturesque traditional villages.

Most villages are connected by obvious roads or paths, but to ensure a warm welcome in the smaller villages, and to find your way there from Tirta Gangga, it would be sensible to engage a guide. You could arrange this from your hotel at Tirta Gangga, or contact

Nyoman Budiasa who runs the only trekking agency (☎ 22436) in Tirta Gangga, based at the Genta Bali warung. Another good place to arrange hikes is Homestay Lila in Abian Soan.

Prices for guides are, of course, negotiable, but expect to pay about 6000 rp per person per hour, plus transport and food; considerably more if trekking up the mighty Agung mountain. Here are a few ideas of where to head:

Pura Lempuyang This is one of Bali's nine directional temples, perched on a hilltop at 768m. Regular bemos go to Ngis from Amlapura, via Tirta Gangga. From Ngis, follow the signs for 2km to Kemuda (ask directions if the signs confuse you). From Kemuda, a daunting 1700 steps (allow at least two hours, one way) takes you to the Lempuyang temple.

You can climb between Kemuda and the temple without a guide, but you'll need one if you: (a) want to use the more interesting route through Basangalas (four hours, one way); (b) continue to the peaks of Lempuyang (1058m) or Seraya (1175m); or (c) climb from Bunutan or Jemeluk on the east coast. Start any climb at about 7 am to allow plenty of time to get up and down before it gets too hot.

Bukit Kusambi This small hill has a big view – at sunrise, Lombok's Gunung Rinjani throws a shadow on Gunung Agung. It is easy to reach from Abian Soan – look for the obvious large hill to the north-west, and follow the tiny canals through the rice fields. On the western side of the hill, a set of steps leads to the top.

Budakeling This village, home to several Buddhist communities, is about six hours return from Tirta Gangga – the path goes through rice fields, via Krotok, home of traditional blacksmiths and silversmiths. It takes about two hours less (return) if you start at Abian Soan.

Tauka A pretty trail takes about five hours return to Tauka, via Peladung, from Tirta Gangga.

Tanah Aron Tanah Aron is home to a famous monument, and is gloriously situated on the slope of Gunung Agung. It is about six hours return from Tirta Gangga.

Gunung Agung Refer to the previous Gunung Agung section for details.

THE NORTH-EAST COAST

The north-east coast from Amed to Selang is starting to attract a number of visitors, who come for the secluded seaside accommodation and excellent, accessible diving and snorkelling. There is a downside though – public transport services are infrequent, facilities are limited, the beach is often black and rocky, and there are no telephones to directly pre-book your dive trips or accommodation.

The coastline is superb and unspoilt, however, with views across to Lombok and back to Gunung Agung. Colourful *jukung* boats are lined up on every available piece of beach, and you'll see rows of troughs used to extract salt.

Diving & Snorkelling

Snorkelling is excellent at several places along the coast; no better than Jemeluk where you can admire stunning coral only 10m from the beach. Almost every hotel rents snorkelling equipment for about 10,000 rp per day.

Only a few hotels seriously cater for divers, however. The best diving spots are Jemeluk, with coral reefs only minutes away by boat; Tulamben (see that section later in the chapter); a shipwreck near Lipah; and coral gardens and fish at Selang.

Also a few kilometres north of Ujung, you can explore some great coral reefs, but there is no decent accommodation nearby and it's difficult to reach, even by private transport. By chartering a local boat, you can also dive around the three tiny islands east of Selang. The Diving section in the Bali Facts for the Visitor chapter has more details about diving in other parts of eastern Bali.

The main operators along the coast are: Mega Dive (email megadive@dps.mega.net.id), based at Amed Beach Cottage; Arni Dive Centre, at Hotel Indra Udhyana; and Eco-dive, at Jemeluk, which is cheaper than most operators in east Bali. The diving centres charge about US$30/45 for one/two dives in Amed or Tulamben, and also offer PADI courses.

Saltmakers of the East Coast

In the volcanic areas near Kusamba, and around the north-east coast between Amed and Selang, you can see the thatched roofs of salt-making huts along the beach.

The process of collecting the salt is complicated. Sand which has been saturated with sea-water is collected from the beach, dried out and then taken inside in the hut where more sea water is strained through a basket called a *tinjung* to wash out the salt. This very salty water is then poured into a shallow trough, or *palungan*, made of palm tree trunks split in half. Hundreds of these troughs are lined up in rows along the beaches during the salt-making season, and as the hot sun evaporates the water, the almost dry salt is scraped out and put in baskets. It's a laborious process, yielding a meagre income in the dry season and none at all in the wet season when rain stops production. The salt is used mainly for processing dried fish, not as table salt.

Trekking

An increasingly popular diversion from the glorious diving and snorkelling is a trek up Gunung Seraya (1175m), or Gunung Agung from Dalah (see the previous Gunung Agung section for details).

Seraya is best attempted from the trails starting at Jemeluk or Bunutan. Allow the best part of a day to get to the top of Seraya, see the sulphur springs at Bangli, and visit a remote village or two.

To find these trails, you will need a guide, which can be arranged at most hotels along this part of the coast. Eco-dive at Jemeluk is a good place to start organising something.

Places to Stay & Eat

More and more hotels and bungalows are being built along the coast between Amed and Selang, and once the road improves and the telephone cables are laid, it will lose its tranquillity and isolation. All places include breakfast.

About 1km east of Amed is the *Pondok Kebun Wayan* (aka Amed Cafe). It offers small but charming rooms for 15,000 rp, with outside toilet, or 30,000 rp if you want a bathroom, mossie net and fan. About 500m further on, *Divers Cafe* has a delightful restaurant on the beach, and two bungalows for 30,000 rp. The village of Jemeluk is another 500m. Here, *Eco-dive* has some simple bungalows. They are overpriced at 28,000 rp, but this is a wonderful area for snorkelling, and the best place to arrange trekking.

Less than 1km to the east is Amed Beach Cottage, on a small, rocky beach. This tranquil place charges a reasonable 20,000/ 30,000 rp for spacious, if a little airless, singles/doubles. Another 100m further along, Kusumajaya Indah Bungalows has more character and a prettier garden than others in this range. It charges 35,000/45,000 rp. From there it's another 1.5km to Bunutan, from where public transport to the south-east is hard to find.

About 800m past Bunutan, the very classy

and very expensive *Hotel Indra Udhyana* (bookings ☎ 0370-26336, fax 36797) has grabbed the best location along the coast. The 33 luxurious cottages, with all the mod cons, range from US$120 to about US$350.

In Lipah, which has some white sand (but not much), there are several *warungs* and more hotels: *Wawa-Wewe Bar, Restaurant & Bungalows* and *Tiyung Petung Cafe Homestay* both charge 30,000 rp per room. The latter has a lovely cafe area, and often features live music.

Nearby, the *Hidden Paradise Cottages* (bookings: ☎ 0361-431273, fax 423820) has cottages around a picturesque pool, but they don't compete with other places for value: US$35/46 for rooms with fan/air-con. Also in Lipah, the popular *Pondok Vienna Beach* is probably the best in the mid-range. It is located right on the beach and has charming rooms for 60,000 rp.

Finally, close to Selang, the most popular place along this coast is *Good Karma Bungalows*. Overlooking a black beach, these Sulawesi-style bungalows are sprawled all over the place. They range from 30,000 to 60,000 rp for singles, 40,000 to 75,000 for doubles, and 'homes' sleeping up to six people are 115,000 rp.

Getting There & Away

It's easy to find these places if you have your own transport, but not if you're relying on public transport. Plenty of minibuses and bemos run to Culik from Singaraja and Amlapura, and some detour to Amed. Tourist shuttle buses will also drop you off at Culik. About every hour in the morning a bemo goes from Culik to the T-junction in the middle of Bunutan. Further south-east, you can continue on an ojek, or take an ojek all the way from Culik – they congregate at the turn-off to Amed. From Selang to Ujung, via Seraya village, public transport is very limited, so allow plenty of time to get around – it may even be quicker to walk.

The road from Amed to Selang is narrow, winding and potholed, and it gets steadily worse as it heads south and then back to Amlapura. Although the road can be nego-tiated with a Suzuki *jimny* jeep, take your time and look out for oncoming traffic. The road mostly follows the slopes of Gunung Seraya way above the sea, and there's spectacular coastal scenery. From Amed to Ujung is only 25km, but allow at least two hours to enjoy the trip, and stop off at the market town of Seraya.

TULAMBEN

Most travellers seem to ignore this part of the island, and prefer the short cut between Padangbai or Candidasa and Lovina, via Gunung Batur, but the village of Tulamben is becoming a popular stopover. The major attraction is the submerged wreck of the US cargo ship *Liberty* – probably the most popular dive site on Bali. Tulamben also offers clear water for swimming and snorkelling, and a few restaurants and places to stay, but the grey rocky beach is disappointing. There are no telephones in this area, so no hotel or diving agency can be contacted directly.

Diving & Snorkelling

The wreck of the *Liberty* is a few metres out from a parking area, with a change room, shop and Puri Madhya Bungalows. You can swim straight out from here and you'll see the stern rearing up from the depths. It's heavily encrusted with coral, and is swarming with 400 or so species of colourful fish – and with scuba divers most of the day. The ship is more than 100m long, but the hull is broken into sections and it's easy to get inside. The bow is in quite good shape, the midships region is badly mangled and the stern is almost intact – the best parts are between 15 and 30m deep.

Many divers commute to Tulamben from Candidasa or Lovina, and it can get quite crowded between 11 am and 4 pm, with up to 50 divers around the wreck at a time. It's better to stay the night in or near Tulamben, and get an early start. You will want at least two dives to really explore the site.

Every hotel has a diving centre attached, but not all of them are particularly reliable or cheap. Prices do vary from one operator

EAST BALI

Wreck of the *Liberty*

On 11 January 1942, the armed US cargo ship USAT *Liberty* was torpedoed by a Japanese submarine off the south-western coast of Lombok. It was then towed by the destroyers HMNS *Van Ghent* and USS *Paul Jones* with the intention of beaching it on the coast of Bali and retrieving its cargo of raw rubber and railway parts. When its condition looked perilous the crew were evacuated and the ship was successfully beached. The rapid spread of the war through Indonesia prevented the cargo from being salvaged, but everything which could be taken was stripped in the ensuing years.

The *Liberty* sat on the beach at Tulamben until 1963 when the violent eruption of Gunung Agung toppled it beneath the surface of the water. Or at least that's one version of the story. Another relates that it sank some distance offshore and the lava flow from the eruption extended the shoreline almost out to the sunken vessel. Much of the ship remains intact, and is now a haven for a quantity and variety of marine life that astounds biologists and divers alike.

to another, so check around. Expect to pay about US$35/55 for one/two dives at Tulamben; or a little more from Jemeluk or Amed (see the previous North-East Coast section); and about US$35 for a night dive at Tulamben.

Mimpi Tulamben Dive Centre (bookings: ☎ 0361-701070, fax 701074), at the Mimpi Resort, also offers four-day PADI courses in major European languages for US$320 to US$370, and can arrange expensive cruises. PT Tulamben Segara Wisata, based at Puri Madhya Bungalows, is right at the jump off point to the wreck. PT Wisnu Dewa Segara, based at the new Bali Coral Bungalows, is probably the best value because it normally negotiates.

Most hotels and diving centres rent out snorkelling gear for anything from 15,000 rp to US$5 per day. Shop around if you can, and ask for a cheaper rate if you don't want to snorkel for the whole day.

Places to Stay & Eat

The hotels (all of which have *restaurants*) and occasional *warungs* are spread along a 3km stretch of the main road. All hotels, except the Mimpi Resort, include breakfast; and each hotel has different room rates depending on the proximity to the beach.

The first as you approach from Lovina, and the only one right by the wreck, is *Puri Madhya Bungalows*. It has a few small, clean rooms with sea views for 30,000 rp. If you're using their dive centre for two or more dives, they will often provide free accommodation.

About 400m further south-east, *Bali Coral Bungalows* has a cluster of new and clean bungalows for 40,000 rp, with a fan and mossie net; or US$15 if you want views and hot water. It is worth negotiating because right next door is *Gandu Mayu Bungalows*. The rooms here are also clean and comfortable, but more spread out and cheaper: 15,000 to 25,000 rp per room. Both have excellent *restaurants*, which are worth visiting if you're only coming for the day.

Another 500m east, there are three places in a row. *Paradise Palm Beach Bungalows (bookings: ☎ 0363-41052)*, also known as Bali Sorga Cottages, has a large number of neat and clean bungalows, with verandahs overlooking a pretty garden. They are 30,000 to 35,000 rp, or US$35 if you want hot water, air-con and the best views. *Matahari Bungalows*, also known as Puri Tulamben Bungalows, is the least appealing option, but cheap at 20,000 to 25,000 rp. The luxurious and very comfortable *Mimpi Resort (bookings: ☎ 0361-701070, fax 701074)* offers a wide range of upmarket singles/doubles for US$66/90; and up to US$180 for a seaside cottage.

A few kilometres south of Tulamben, there are a few more places like the top-end *Emerald Tulamben Hotel (bookings: ☎ 0361-22490)* from US$130; and the budget *Penginapan Agung Cottages* from 25,000 rp.

Getting There & Away

Plenty of minibuses, buses and bemos travel between Amlapura and Singaraja and stop anywhere in Tulamben – but they tend to be less frequent after 2 pm. Perama tourist shuttle buses, based at the Gandu Mayu Bungalows, will drop you off anywhere along the main road on its daily trip in either direction between Kuta (15,000 rp) and Lovina (10,000 rp).

TULAMBEN TO YEH SANIH

Beyond Tulamben the road continues to skirt the slopes of Agung, with frequent evidence of lava flows from the 1963 eruption. Beyond Agung, Gunung Abang and the outer crater of Gunung Batur also slope down to the sea. The scenery is stark, but provides an interesting contrast to the rest of Bali – there are frequent vistas of the sea, and the rainfall is so low you can generally count on sunny weather.

The only place to stay is *Alamanda* (no telephone) in **Sambirenteng**. It is a tasteful place on the beach with a fine coral reef just

offshore. It boasts its own diving centre, a pretty pool and very attractive bungalows in a garden setting for US$45/50 for singles/doubles, and cheaper rooms for US$30/36. The beachfront *restaurant* is an excellent place to stop for lunch.

Les is home to a lovely **waterfall**, reputedly one of Bali's highest. Bemos or minibuses may make the 1.5km detour south of the main road to Les; if not, walk or look for an ojek at the turn-off. To the waterfalls, follow the main road for 500m from the right of the market place, temple and public baths in Les, and then continue along the obvious path which virtually hugs the stream for another 2.5km. This is a pleasant stop if you have your own vehicle, or a side trip from Tulamben by public transport.

The next main town is **Tejakula** famous for its **horse bath**. Although it was actually built as a place to wash horses, it's now the town's public bathing place, and has quite graceful, but somewhat run-down rows of white arches. Apart from this, it's a quaint village, with some finely carved kulkul towers.

At Pacung, about 10km before Yeh Sanih you can turn inland to **Sembiran**, which is believed to be a Bali Aga village, although it doesn't promote itself as such. The most striking thing about the place is its hillside location and the brilliant coastal **views** it offers.

Nusa Penida

Highlights

- For expert surfers, there's some classy right-hand reef breaks off Nusa Lembongan.

- Coral walls, caves and big pelagic formations are there for experienced divers to explore in the waters around Nusa Penida. Bring your gear with you, as there are no dive centres on the islands.

- For adventurous travellers with plenty of time, Nusa Penida has rugged coastal scenery and remote villages to explore. Nusa Lembongan is better set up for the short-stay visitor.

Nusa Penida, an administrative region within the Klungkung district, comprises three islands – Nusa Penida itself, the smaller Nusa Lembongan to the north-west and tiny Nusa Ceningan in between. Nusa Lembongan attracts most visitors for its surf, seclusion and quiet beaches. The island of Nusa Penida has several villages, but is right off the tourist track and has few facilities for visitors. Nusa Ceningan is very sparsely populated.

Lembongan is a wonderful place, where surfers and nonsurfers alike can get away from the relative chaos of mainland Bali. There's been talk of luxury resorts on Nusa Penida, and even a golf course, but currently most upmarket tourists visit only Nusa Lembongan on expensive day cruises from the mainland (diving, snorkelling or surfing from a boat, or making brief forays ashore), while the rest stay on Lembongan for a few days or longer.

Economic resources are limited on the islands. It has been a poor region for many years and there has been some transmigration from here to other parts of Indonesia.

Thin soils and a lack of fresh water do not permit the cultivation of rice, but other crops are grown – maize, cassava and beans are staples here. Seaweed is the main crop on Lembongan.

Diving

There are great diving possibilities around the islands, but no dive operators. You will have to arrange a trip with a diving centre in Sanur, Candidasa or the Kuta region. Stick with the most reputable operators, as diving here is demanding with cold water and difficult currents – local knowledge is essential.

A particular attraction is the large marine animals, including turtles, (harmless) sharks and rays. The most bizarre is the *mola mola* (sunfish) which can be seen around the islands between July and September. They can be over 3m long, and look odd, and even a little scary, but they are harmless.

NUSA PENIDA

Clearly visible from anywhere along Bali's south-eastern coast, the island of Nusa Penida is a limestone plateau with a population of around 45,000. It was once used as a place of banishment for criminals and other undesirables from the kingdom of Klungkung.

The northern coast has white sand beaches and views over the water to the volcanoes on Bali, but they're not good for swimming as most of the shallows are filled with the bamboo frames used for seaweed farming. The south coast has limestone cliffs dropping straight down to the sea and a row of offshore islets – it's rugged and spectacular scenery.

The interior is hilly, with sparse-looking crops, and poor, old-fashioned villages. The rainfall is low, and there are large tanks called *cabangs* in which water is stored for the dry season.

The population is predominantly Hindu,

although there are some Muslims (and a mosque) in Toyapakeh. The culture is distinct from that of Bali: the language is an old form of Balinese no longer heard on the mainland, and there is also local dance, architecture and craft, including a unique type of red *ikat* weaving.

Cruises

As an alternative to the busy little island of Nusa Lembongan, at least one company organises day cruises to Penida from Bali. Beluga (see the Tanjung Benoa section in the South Bali chapter for details) sails to a pontoon and beach area, with all the luxuries, at Bodong. The trip costs US$95 per person, including a buffet lunch.

Sampalan

There's nothing inspiring about Sampalan, the main town on Penida, but it's quiet and pleasant, with a market, schools and shops strung out along the curving coast road. The market area, where the bemos congregate, is in the middle of town. Pelabuhan Buyuk, where the boats leave for Padangbai, is a few hundred metres west of the market.

Between the market and the harbour is a small side road, with the friendly *Losmen Made*, which charges around 15,000 rp for a small, clean room with breakfast. The government rest house, *Bungalow Pemda*, opposite the police station a few hundred metres east of the market, also has rooms for 15,000 rp.

There are a few simple *warungs* along the main road and around the market. *Kios Dewi*, east of the market, serves Padang-style food.

Toyapakeh

If you come by boat from Lembongan, you'll probably be dropped at (or just off) the beach at Toyapakeh, a pretty town with lots of trees. The beach has clean white sand, clear blue water and Gunung Agung as a backdrop. Step up from the beach and you're at the roadhead, where bemos can take you to Sampalan (500 rp).

Few travellers stay here, but *Losmen*

Terang, near the waterfront, has singles/doubles for 7500/10,000 rp.

Around the Island

A trip around the island, following the north and east coasts, and crossing the hilly interior, can be completed in a few hours by motorbike. You could spend much longer, lingering at the temples and the small villages, and walking to less accessible areas, but there's no accommodation outside the two main towns. The following description goes clockwise from Sampalan.

The coastal road from Sampalan curves and dips past bays with rows of fishing boats and offshore seaweed gardens. After about 6km, just before the village of Karangsari, steps go up on the right side of the road to the narrow entrance of **Goa Karangsari** caves. There are usually people who can provide a pressure lantern and guide you through the cave for about 5000 rp. The limestone cave extends more than 200m through the hill and emerges on the other side to overlook a verdant valley.

Continue south past a naval station and

Jero Gede Macaling – Demon

Nusa Penida is the legendary home of Jero Gede Macaling, the demon who inspired the Barong Landung dance (see the Dance section in the Ubud & Around chapter). Many Balinese believe the island is a place of enchantment and evil power *(angker)* – paradoxically, this makes it an attraction. Although few foreigners visit, thousands of Balinese come every year for religious observances aimed at placating the evil spirits.

The island has a number of interesting temples dedicated to Jero Gede Macaling, including Pura Dalem Penetaran Ped, near Toyapakeh. It houses a shrine, which is a source of power for practitioners of black magic, and a place of pilgrimage for those seeking protection from sickness and evil.

NUSA PENIDA

To Sanur • Nusa Lembongan • Jungutbatu • Lembongan • Nusa Ceningan • Sakti • Sebunibus • ▲(139m) • Toyapakeh • Prapat • Bodong • Ped • Pura Dalem Penetaran Ped • Biyaung • Sentalkawan • Sentalkangin • To Kusamba • Mentigi • Kutampi • Telga • To Padangbai • Pelabuhan Buyuk • Sampalan • Batumalapan • Lombok Strait • (289m)▲ • Jurangpait • Glagan • Goa Karangsari • Karangsari • Klumpu • Pulagan • Celagilandan • Suana • Pura Batukuning • Semaya • Selat Badung • Pundukakaja • Bukit Mundi (529m) • Nusa Penida • Penangkidan • Karangjawa • Batumadeg • Pejukutan • Karang • Tanjung Sari • Batukandik • Air Terjun • (439m)▲ • Dungkap • Tanglad • Tanjung Abah • Debuluh • (422m)▲ • Ramuban • Sekartaji • Tanjung Moling • Tanjung Bakung

0 2 4 km

several charming **temples** to Suana. Here the main road swings inland and climbs up into the hills, while a very rough side track goes south-east, past more interesting temples to **Semaya**, a fishing village with a sheltered **beach** and one of Bali's best **dive sites** off-shore.

About 9km south-west of Suana, **Tanglad** is a very old fashioned village and a centre for **traditional weaving**. Rough roads south and east lead to isolated parts of the coast.

A scenic ridge-top road goes north-west from Tanglad. At Batukandik, a rough road leads to a spectacular **air terjun** (waterfall). Sheer limestone cliffs drop hundreds of feet into the sea, with offshore rock pinnacles surrounded by crashing surf. At the base of these cliffs, underground streams discharge fresh water into the sea. You can descend the cliff face on an exposed metal stairway (which is not as scary as the rickety wooden

scaffolding nearby which local women used to clamber down every day with large pots on their heads for collecting water).

Back on the main road, continue to Batumadeg, past **Bukit Mundi** (the highest point on the island at 529m), through **Klumpu** and **Sakti**, which has traditional stone buildings. Return to the north coast at Toyapakeh.

The important temple of **Pura Dalem Penetaran Ped** is near the beach at Ped, a few kilometres east of Toyapakeh. It houses a shrine for the demon Jero Gede Macaling. The temple structure is crude, even ugly, which gives it an appropriately sinister ambience. From there, the road is straight and flat back to Sampalan.

Getting There & Away

The strait between Nusa Penida and southern Bali is very deep and subject to heavy swells – if there is a strong tide, boats often have to wait. You may also have to wait a while for the public boat to fill up with passengers. The shuttle boat between Sanur and Nusa Lembongan (see the Sanur entry in the Nusa Lembongan section of this chapter) is the best way to get to the islands.

Padangbai Fast public boats operate daily between Padangbai and Nusa Penida. The trip takes less than one hour and costs 4000 rp. It's an exciting ride as the boat bounces across the water beneath the looming Gunung Agung volcano.

At Padangbai, the boats leave at about 8 am from the beach just north-east of the car park for the Bali-Lombok ferry. The ticket office is unsigned, but indicated on the Padangbai map in the East Bali chapter. On Penida, the boats land at Pelabuhan Buyuk, just west of Sampalan.

Kusamba Slower *prahus* (traditional boats) carry goods, and the occasional passenger, between Sampalan and Kusamba, the port closest to Semarapura, the district capital. The boats leave when they're full, weather and waves permitting, and cost about 3000 rp one way. This is definitely only for the adventurous.

Nusa Lembongan Some public boats travel between Sampalan or Toyapakeh and Jungutbatu or Toyapakeh on Nusa Lembongan. You will have to ask your hotel or someone along the beaches or terminals about departure times, but they tend to travel in both directions between 5 and 6 am. You can charter a whole boat between the two islands for around 25,000/50,000 rp one way/return, but bargain hard.

Getting Around
Bemos regularly travel along the sealed road between Toyapakeh and Sampalan, and sometimes on to Suana and up to Klumpu, but beyond these areas the roads are rough or nonexistent and transport is very limited. You may be able to negotiate an *ojek* (paying pillion passenger on a motorbike) for about 15,000 rp per hour, but this is very

expensive. If you really want to explore, bring a mountain bike and camping equipment from the mainland (but remember Penida is hilly). Alternatively, plan to do some serious hiking, but come well prepared.

NUSA LEMBONGAN
The most developed island for tourism is Nusa Lembongan, with about 7000 people, mainly based in two small villages, Jungutbatu and Lembongan. Most visitors come for the surf that breaks on the reefs, or the quiet beach, but it's still a great place to relax, even if you're not into swimming, surfing or diving. Reefs protect the lovely arcs of white sand with clear blue water, and from the north there are superb views across the water to Gunung Agung on mainland Bali. Lembongan has a range of good budget accommodation, most with their own patch of glorious beach.

Information
Other than a few hotels and restaurants, facilities are very limited on the island. For

---

Sea Grass of Lembongan

The cultivation of sea grass, or *rumput laut*, is a recent, but well established, industry on Nusa Lembongan. The island has very little rainfall, so the seawater maintains a high level of salinity, which is ideal for seaweed. At low tide traditional fishing boats head out to collect mature seaweed, while the immature stuff is left to grow. The seaweed is laid on the beach for a few days, and then stored in special sheds. It is shipped to Padangbai, and then exported to Hong Kong, Japan and Europe where it is used as a thickening agent in processed foods and cosmetics.

If you walk up the north-west coast of Nusa Lembongan, past the hotels, you can watch the men and women at work – just follow your nose.

NUSA LEMBONGAN

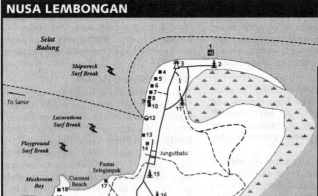

Selat Badung

To Toyapakeh

Shipwreck Surf Break

To Sanur

Lacerations Surf Break

Playground Surf Break

Pantai Selegimpak

Jungutbatu

Mushroom Bay

Coconut Beach

Nusa Lembongan

Lembongan

Ceningan Reef Surf Break

Nusa Ceningan

Nusa Penida

0   0.5   1 km

PLACES TO STAY
4 Puri Nusa Bungalows
5 Bungalo Tarci
   & Restaurant
6 Nusa Lembongan
   Bungalows
7 Agung's Lembongan
   Lodge
8 Main Ski Inn
   & Restaurant
9 Ketut Bungalows
10 Nusa Indah
13 Pondok Baruna
14 Johnny's Losmen
17 Villa Wayan Lodge
18 Mushroom Beach
   Bungalows
20 Waka Nusa Resort

OTHER
1 Snorkelling Area
2 Pura Sakenan
3 Lighthouse
11 Pura Empuaji
12 Perama Office
15 Pura Segara
16 Pura Dalem
19 Bali Hai
21 Adi Warung
22 Underground House

diving trips, and other happenings, check out the noticeboard at the Main Ski Inn, or ask around your hotel. Main Ski also has a book exchange. Don't expect to change any money on the island.

Electricity operates from 5 pm to 7 am (from 12 pm on Sunday), and only the up-market places will have generators. There's a doctor on the island who specialises in coral cuts and surfing injuries – he can be contacted through your hotel.

Surfing

Surfing here is best in the dry season (April to September), when the winds come from the south-east. It's definitely not for beginners, and can be dangerous even for experts. There are three main breaks on the reef, all aptly named. You can paddle out to **Shipwreck**, but for **Lacerations** and **Playground** it's better to hire a boat. Prices are very negotiable, and

depend on demand and your negotiation skills; about 8000 rp for a return trip, plus waiting time, if necessary, is reasonable.

Strangely, the surf can be crowded even when the island isn't. Charter boats from Bali sometimes bring groups of surfers for day trips from the mainland, or as part of a longer surfing trip between Bali and Sumbawa. Most surfers and snorkellers stay at (or hang around) the Main Ski Inn, Agung's Lembongan Lodge and Puri Nusa Bungalows – all are well set up and offer information, trips, equipment rental and repairs.

See the Surfing section in the Bali Facts for the Visitor chapter for detailed information on each break.

Snorkelling

There's good snorkelling on the reef, especially off the north of the island, and some spots are accessible from the beach. To get to other snorkelling spots, you'll need to charter a boat, which costs a standard 15,000 rp per hour per boat, depending on demand, distance and number of passengers.

Also ask around the hotels – particularly Puri Nusa Bungalows and Main Ski Inn – about organised trips. A half day/one day trip will cost about 20,000/30,000 rp per person, with up to ten other passengers. Snorkelling gear can be rented at (or from locals who hang around) Puri Nusa and Main Ski for about 8000 rp per day.

Cruises

Some visitors come for the day, seeking sun, surf and diving, and then return to Sanur, Nusa Dua or the Kuta region in the evening. There are a number of cruise operators. Most leave from Pelabuhan Benoa on Bali, and sail to a beach on, or a large pontoon just off, Nusa Lembongan, where you can enjoy a substantial buffet lunch and water activities. Cruises can be booked through any travel agency in south Bali.

Bali Hai (☎ 0361-720331) has been doing day cruises around Lembongan for years. Prices are normally US$85 per person, but are sometimes reduced to US$68. A similar day trip is offered on Waka Louka (☎ 0361-723629) for US$86, based at the Waka Nusa Resort (see Places to Stay later in this chapter).

Less luxurious, but less expensive, options for day trips can be arranged with the 'superfast' Quick Cat (☎ 0361-240032), from US$69; Island Explorer Cruises (☎ 0361-289856) from US$59; or Nusa Lembongan Express Service (☎ 724545) from US$35; the latter are run in connection with Villa Wayan Lodge (see Places to Stay in this section).

Lembongan Village

About 4km south-west along the sealed road from Jungutbatu is Lembongan village. Leaving Jungutbatu you pass the Balinese-style **Pura Segara** temple with an enormous banyan tree; a steep climb up a knoll offers a wonderful view back over the beach. It's possible to continue right around the island,

following the rough track which eventually comes back to Jungutbatu, but the roads are steep for cyclists and walkers. As you enter Lembongan, you may want to ask directions to the **Underground House**.

Mushroom Bay

This perfect little bay, unofficially named for the mushroom corals offshore, is home to several gorgeous beaches. Predictably, it's also the focus of Lembongan's upmarket tourist developments (see the following Places to Stay entry). To get there from Jungutbatu, you'll need to walk or cycle, and turn right as you enter Lembongan village. If you can arrange it with the boatman (or there are other passengers who want to get off there), public boats from Kusamba, Sanur and Padangbai may stop here, as well as Jungutbatu.

Places to Stay

Most of the accommodation is along a beach on the north-western coast, so that's where

The Underground House

For a few thousand rupiah, some kids will take you through the labyrinthine underground 'house', 100m off the road. They will provide a candle, but it would be a good idea to bring your own torch (flashlight). Be very careful, there are big holes in unexpected places. It's not very exciting, however – just a crawl and scramble through many small passages, rooms and chambers, supposedly dug by one man.

The story goes that the man lost a dispute with an evil spirit and was condemned to death, but begged to be allowed to first finish his house. The spirit relented, and the man started excavating his cave with a small spoon. He always started a new room before he finished the last one, so of course the house was never completed, and thus his death sentence was postponed indefinitely.

many visitors go. A few places are just flimsy, bamboo bungalows, sometimes with a shared bathroom, but these days most are solid, brick structures. Prices are negotiable and do vary, depending on the season and how long you want to stay. Surfers often get a good rate if the owner thinks they will spend plenty on food and drink. Peak season is around Christmas and July-August.

Don't deal with any touts – go to the desk or the manager of the hotel yourself, and don't give any money to anyone else. There are no telephones on the island, but some places have offices on Bali, which can be contacted by radio from the island, so you can book ahead. Most places don't include breakfast. Only a few are signposted from along the main road; it is best to walk along the beach to find any hotel on the north-western coast.

Jungutbatu In the village, about 30m up a laneway, is *Johnny's Losmen*, a classic Indonesian losmen which opened 17 years ago. It's basic, but quite OK and very good value at 3000/6000 rp for singles/doubles. It is mostly empty, because most visitors prefer to stay somewhere on the beach. The obvious, light-green *Pondok Baruna* has a few spotless rooms, and friendly staff, for 20,000/25,000 rp. It doesn't have a lot of character, but it's quieter than the party-oriented places to the north, and is on the beach.

North-West Coast *Nusa Indah* is nothing special and doesn't overlook the beach, but it has adequate rooms for 20,000/30,000 rp downstairs/upstairs. The *Main Ski Inn & Restaurant* (☎ 0361-289213) is very popular with long-stay surfers, and all budget travellers. Bungalows are priced from 20,000 to 50,000 rp, depending on the season and whether you want an upstairs room with views and breezes.

Bungalo Tarci (also known as Ocean View Bungalows) has rooms for 25,000 rp, and two storey bungalows for 40,000 rp – but prices will be higher in peak season. *Nusa Lembongan Bungalows* is a hotch-potch of unexciting bungalows for about 30,000 rp, but some readers have commented favourably about very friendly staff. One place not overrun with surfers and divers is the friendly, family-run *Ketut Bungalows*, with clean and quiet rooms from 25,000 to 40,000 rp. *Agung's Lembongan Lodge* (☎ 0361-422266) has cheap double rooms from 20,000 rp, and bungalows for 40,000 rp. The bungalows are a little close together, denying much privacy, but it's a friendly and popular place.

At the far northern end of the beach, *Puri Nusa Bungalows* (☎/fax 0361-298613) is more upmarket, but is very popular with surfers and divers, especially from Japan. Smart rooms in a solid, two storey block range from 25,000 rp at the back to 50,000 rp at the front.

Mushroom Bay The only cheap place is *Mushroom Beach Bungalows*, a collection of charming Balinese-style bungalows with a five star setting, overlooking a gorgeous beach. Prices range from a very reasonable US$10 to US$15, including breakfast. There is no telephone, but you should be able to get a room if you just turn up. The classy thatched bungalows at *Waka Nusa Resort* (☎/fax 0361-261130) cost about US$157 a night, plus meals.

Pantai Selegimpak A little more realistic in price is *Villa Wayan Lodge* (☎ 0361-724545), on Selegimpak beach. Rooms cost from US$21 to US$28 a night. The food is excellent and the management can arrange snorkelling trips, and transport to/from Bali. It is recommended for families, but is quite remote.

Places to Eat

Every hotel, except Johnny's Losmen, has a *restaurant*. The two storey restaurant at *Main Ski Inn*, right on the beach, serves tasty, reasonably priced western and Indonesian food. It has stupendous views and often features movies on the island's only video machine. The restaurant at *Bungalo*

Tarci has a great cook, but watch out for the occasional bit of furtive overcharging.

At Mushroom Bay, you can eat at your hotel, or there are a couple of warungs along the main street, such as *Adi Warung*.

Getting There & Away

There is no jetty on Nusa Lembongan – boats land at Jungutbatu (and sometimes Mushroom Bay) and you have to jump off into the shallow water. The strait between Bali and Nusa Lembongan is very deep and huge swells can develop during the day. You may get wet with spray, so be prepared.

Nusa Penida Refer to the previous Nusa Penida section for details on getting to/from the main island.

Kusamba & Padangbai Most boats from Kusamba or Padangbai go to Toyapakeh on Nusa Penida, but sometimes they also go to Jungutbatu. Ask the boatmen around the beach near Johnny's Losmen and Pondok Baruna on Nusa Lembongan for details. Shuttle boats and public boats from Sanur are far safer and quicker.

Sanur A public boat leaves at about 8 am every day from the northern end of Sanur Beach, in front of the Ananda Hotel. There is a ticket office, so don't buy from a tout – if in doubt, ask someone at the Ananda. The fixed 'tourist price' to Jungutbatu is 15,000 rp. The trip takes about 90 minutes, or more if conditions are unfavourable.

Tourist Shuttle Boat Perama has at least one shuttle bus/boat trip every day, with good connections to all tourist centres on Bali. The company normally uses its own boat rather than the public one (but double-check this with Perama). The Perama boat also leaves from in front of the Ananda Hotel in Sanur, and lands in front of the Perama office (well, hut) at Jungutbatu.

Current one way fares to Lembongan are: 20,000 rp from Sanur; 25,000 rp from the Kuta region and Ubud; 30,500 rp from Candidasa and Padangbai; and 40,000 rp from Mataram or Senggigi on Lombok (using the public Lembar-Padangbai ferry). Book at any Perama office, or travel agent, on Bali or Lombok, or the Perama hut on Nusa Lembongan.

Getting Around

There is a main road as far as the hills and mangroves will allow, stretching from Pura Sakenan in the north to the bridge to Nusa Ceningan. You can walk around the island in about three hours, which is just as well because finding a motorbike to rent is not easy. If you do find one, it will probably be in bad condition and expensive: around 15,000 rp per hour. A bicycle is a better option, although still not cheap: 5000 rp per hour from Ketut Bungalows; or about 15,000 rp per day from one of the villagers who may approach you. And be prepared: the hills can be steep.

NUSA CENINGAN

A narrow suspension bridge crosses the lagoon between Nusa Lembongan and Nusa Ceningan, so it's quite easy to explore its network of tracks on foot or a rented motorbike or bicycle – not that there's much to see. The lagoon is filled with frames for seaweed farming, which is the main money-spinner. There's also a fishing village and several small agricultural plots. The island is quite hilly and you'll get glimpses of great scenery as you go around the rough tracks.

West Bali

Highlights

- Although heavily hyped, the superbly situated temple of Tanah Lot is still a great sight at sunset, and one of Bali's most photogenic attractions.

- Margarana is a moving memorial in Marga to those who died on Bali during the struggle for Indonesian independence from the Dutch.

- The charming 'sea temple' of Pura Rambut Siwi has a magnificent location on the remote and rugged Jembrana coast.

- Short, guided treks are possible in the huge national park of Taman Nasional Bali Barat, where you might just see the rare and endangered Bali starling.

- Pulau Menjangan is within the national park area, and the reefs around this island offer excellent scuba diving and snorkelling.

Most of the places regularly visited in west Bali, like Sangeh or Tanah Lot, are easy day trips from Denpasar, Ubud or the Kuta region. The rest of the west tends to be a region travellers zip through on their way to or from Java, but it does offer a few secluded places to stay, the Taman Nasional Bali Barat national park, and long stretches of wide black sand beach and rolling surf. Countless tracks run south of the main road, usually to fishing villages which rarely see a tourist despite being so close to a main transport route.

In the latter half of the 19th century this was an area of warring kingdoms. With the Dutch takeover in the early 20th century, however, the princes' lands were redistributed among the general population. With this bounty of rich agricultural land, the region around Tabanan was cultivated with beautiful rice fields and became one of the wealthiest parts of Bali.

KAPAL

About 10km north of Denpasar, Kapal is the garden gnome and temple curlicue centre of Bali. If you're building a new temple and need a balustrade for a stairway – or any of the other countless standard architectural motifs – the numerous shops which line the road through Kapal will have what you need. Alternatively, if you want some garden ornamentation, from a comic-book deer to a brightly painted Buddha, you've also come to the right place.

Kapal's **Pura Sadat** is the most important temple in the area. It was possibly built in the 12th century, then damaged in an earthquake earlier this century, and subsequently restored after WWII.

TANAH LOT

The spectacularly located Tanah Lot is possibly the best known, and most photographed, temple on Bali. The tourist crowds here are phenomenal, especially at sunset, and the commercial hype is appalling, but the temple, perched on a little rocky islet, looks superb – whether delicately lit by the dawn light, or starkly outlined at sunset.

For the Balinese, Tanah Lot is one of the important and venerated sea temples. Like Pura Luhur Ulu Watu, at the southern end of the island, Tanah Lot is closely associated with the Majapahit priest Nirartha. It's said that Nirartha passed by here and, impressed with the tiny island's superb setting, suggested to local villagers that this would be a good place to construct a temple.

Tanah Lot is a well organised tourist trap. Around the car park (parking costs 350 rp), dozens of souvenir shops are on a sort of sideshow alley, which you can easily bypass. Follow the crowds, past the entrance (tickets cost 1100/600 rp for adults/children), and down to the sea. You can walk over to the temple itself at low tide, or climb up to the left and sit at one of the many tables along the cliff top. Order an expensive drink, or a more expensive dinner, get your camera ready – and wait for 'The Sunset'.

Places to Stay & Eat

To really appreciate the area, you can stay nearby. *Losmen Puri Lukisan*, directly opposite the entrance to the car park, charges 20,000/25,000 rp for simple singles/doubles. A better option is *Pondok Wisata Astiti Graha* (☎ 812955), about 800m before the car park. Decent rooms away from the main road cost 45,000 rp, including breakfast. *Dewi Sinta Restaurant & Villa* (☎ 812933, fax 813956) is on souvenir shop alley, not far from the ticket office. The rooms are clean, but unexciting, and cost US$14/19, or US$28/36 with air-con. Just inside the entrance, the slightly better *Mutiara Tanah Lot* (☎ 812939) charges 175,000 rp per double, including breakfast.

One of the most controversial hotels on Bali is *Le Meridien Nirwana Golf Spa & Resort* (☎ 815900, fax 815901). It offers an 18 hole golf course, three swimming pools and everything else imaginable. Rooms cost from US$250 to US$1080. (The Ecology & Environment section in the Facts about Bali chapter has more information about the impact of this hotel on the local people.)

There are oodles of *warungs* around the car park, and expensive *restaurants* inside the grounds. *Dewi Sinta* has an elegant restaurant, with set menus from 16,000 to 20,000 rp, and Legong dances on Saturday and Thursday nights.

Getting There & Away

If you have your own transport, turn off the Denpasar to Gilimanuk road near Kediri and follow the signs – or follow the traffic late in the afternoon. You may want to avoid the traffic jams on the way home and leave before the sun completely sets, or leave later, after enjoying a leisurely dinner.

To Tanah Lot, regular bemos leave Kediri (600 rp), which is well connected to Denpasar's Ubung terminal (850 rp). Bemos usually stop running by nightfall, so if you stay for the sunset, you may need to stay nearby, charter a vehicle or walk back to Kediri. Tanah Lot is the main attraction of many, *very* popular organised tours, which often include other sites such Bedugul, Mengwi and Sangeh. The Organised Tours section of the Bali Getting There & Around chapter has more details.

MENGWI

The huge state temple of **Pura Taman Ayun**, surrounded by a wide, elegant moat, was the main temple of the Mengwi kingdom, which survived until 1891 when it was conquered by the neighbouring kingdoms of Tabanan and Badung. The large, spacious temple was built in 1634, and extensively renovated in 1937. It's a lovely place to wander around, especially before the tour buses arrive.

The first courtyard is a large, open grassy expanse and the inner courtyard has a multitude of *merus* (multi-tiered shrines). In a beautiful setting across the moat from the temple is a rather lost-looking **Mandala Wisata Arts Centre** (☎ 811910). There is also a small **museum**, featuring unspectacular and uninformative dioramas of Balinese festivals.

Sari Royal Garden Restaurant, overlooking the moat, is not too expensive considering the charming view. The complex is open from 8 am to 6 pm, every day, and costs 1000/500 rp for adults/children.

Any bemo running between Denpasar (Ubung terminal) and Bedugul or Singaraja can drop you off at the roundabout in Mengwi, where signs indicate the road (250m) to the temple. Pura Taman Ayun is a stopoff on many organised tours from Ubud and towns in south Bali.

TAMAN BUAYA & REPTIL

About 4km north of Mengwi, the Reptile and Crocodile Park (☎ 243686) displays a number of slithery creatures languishing in many depressing cages and pools, with nothing labelled in any language. Entrance costs 40,000 rp, which normally includes a

...ue wrestling show'. You'd be better off visiting the reptile park next to the Taman Burung Bali Bird park (for information see the Denpasar to Ubud section of the Ubud & Around chapter).

The park is open from 9 am to 6 pm daily, and is a few kilometres north of Mengwi, along the Denpasar-Bedugul road.

BELAYU

In the small village of Belayu, 3km north of Mengwi, traditional *songket* sarongs are woven with intricate gold threads. These are for ceremonial use only, not for everyday wear. Take any bemo or bus between Denpasar and Bedugul or Singaraja, get off at the turn-off to Belayu, and walk about 1km west.

MARGA

Between the walls of traditional family compounds, there are some beautifully shaded roads in Marga, but this town wasn't always so peaceful. On 20 November 1946, a force of 96 independence fighters was surrounded by a much larger and better-armed Dutch force fighting to regain Bali as a colony after the departure of the Japanese. The outcome was similar to the *puputan* of 40 years before – Ngurah Rai and every one of his 95 men was killed. There was, however, one important difference – this time the Dutch suffered heavy casualties too, and this may have helped weaken their resolve to hang onto the rebellious colony.

The independence struggle is commemorated at the **Margarana**, north-west of Marga village. It's seldom visited by tourists, but every Balinese school child comes here at least once, and there's a ceremony on 20 November every year. In a large compound stands a 17m-high pillar with the text of Ngurah Rai's letter engraved in stone panels on the sides; the final words are 'Merdeka atau mati!' (Freedom or death!). Behind the Margarana is a compound with 1372 small stone memorials to those who gave their lives for the cause of independence. There's also a **museum**, with a few photos, homemade weapons and other artefacts from the conflict. The complex is open daily from 9 am to 5 pm, and tickets cost 1000 rp.

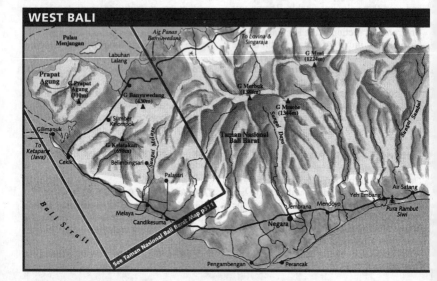

Take any bemo from Denpasar heading for Bedugul or Singaraja, and get off at Marga, about 6km north of Mengwi. Walk westward about 2km through Marga. Even with your own transport it's easy to get lost, so ask directions.

SANGEH

About 20km north of Denpasar, near the village of Sangeh, stands the **monkey forest** of Bukit Sari. There's a rare grove of nutmeg trees in the monkey forest and a temple, **Pura Bukit Sari**, with an interesting old Garuda statue. Take care: the monkeys will jump all over you if you have a pocketful of peanuts and don't dispense them quickly enough. The Sangeh monkeys have also been known to steal hats, sunglasses and even thongs (flip-flops) from fleeing tourists.

This place is touristy, but the forest is cool, green and shady, and the monkeys are cute as well as cheeky. The souvenir sellers are restricted to certain areas and are easy to avoid. You can reach Sangeh on any bemo from Denpasar (Wangaya terminal).

There is also road access from Mengwi

The Legend of Sangeh

The monkey forest at Sangeh is featured, so the Balinese say, in the *Ramayana*. To kill the evil Rawana, king of Lanka, Hanuman had to crush him between two halves of Mahmeru, the holy mountain. Rawana, who could not be destroyed on the earth or in the air, would thus be trapped between the two elements. On his way to perform this task, Hanuman dropped a piece of the mountain near Sangeh, complete with a band of monkeys.

and Ubud, but no public transport. Most people visit on an organised tour.

TABANAN

Tabanan is the capital of the district of the same name. It's a large, well organised place, with shops, hospital, police station (☎ 91210) and a market, but little specifically for tourists, such as decent accommodation.

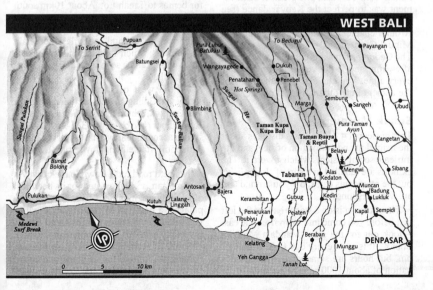

WEST BALI

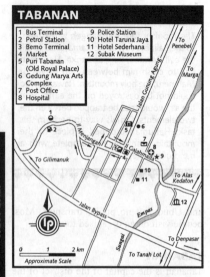

TABANAN

1 Bus Terminal
2 Petrol Station
3 Bemo Terminal
4 Market
5 Puri Tabanan
   (Old Royal Palace)
6 Gedung Marya Arts
   Complex
7 Post Office
8 Hospital
9 Police Station
10 Hotel Taruna Jaya
11 Hotel Sederhana
12 Subak Museum

To Penebel
To Marga
To Gilimanuk
To Alas Kedaton
To Denpasar
To Tanah Lot

Jalan Gunung Agung
Jl Menjangan
Jl Galahnada
Jalan Bypass
Empas
Sungai

0   1   2 km
Approximate Scale

Tabanan is also a renowned centre for dancing and *gamelan* playing. Mario, the renowned dancer of the prewar period, hailed from Tabanan. His greatest achievement was to perfect the Kebyar dance (see the Balinese Dance section in the Ubud & Around chapter) and he is also featured in Miguel Covarrubias' classic *Island of Bali*. The **Gedung Marya** arts complex was named after him, and is the venue for an arts fair every June. You can also visit the ruins of the ancient **Puri Tabanan** royal palace.

Subak Museum

This museum (☎ 810318) has displays about the irrigation and cultivation of rice, and the intricate social systems which govern it. The exhibits are labelled in a sort of 'Indoglish', but the attendants can show you around and answer questions.

The museum is up a steep road on the left just before you come into town from the east – look out for the sign 'Mandala Mathika Subak'. It is open every day from 8 am to 7 pm, but hours are somewhat erratic. A donation of about 1000 rp is requested.

Places to Stay & Eat

Hotel Taruna Jaya (☎ *812478)* was closed at the time of research. The only alternative, the very dreary *Hotel Sederhana*, 50m to the south, has a virtual monopoly. It charges 30,000 rp for an airless cubicle. There are plenty of *warungs* along the main road through town.

Getting There & Away

All bemos and buses between Denpasar and Gilimanuk stop at the Ubung terminal in the western end of Tabanan. The bemo terminal in the town centre only has transport to nearby villages. If you're driving, note that most main streets are one way, with traffic moving in a clockwise direction around the central blocks.

SOUTH OF TABANAN

There's not a lot of tourist attractions in the southern part of Tabanan district, but it's easy to access with your own transport. You can reach the main villages by local bemo from Tabanan, especially in the mornings.

Kediri has Pasar Hewan, one of Bali's busiest **cattle markets**, and is the terminal for bemos to Tanah Lot. About 10km south of Tabanan is **Pejaten**, a centre for the production of traditional pottery, including elaborate, ornamental roof tiles. Porcelain clay objects, which are made purely for decorative use, can be seen in a few workshops in the village.

A little west of Tabanan, a road goes south via Gubug to the secluded coast at **Yeh Gangga**, where the *Yeh Gangga Beach Bungalows (bookings:* ☎ *0361-261354)* has stylish accommodation. It's a well run place, with comfortable bungalows from US$40 a double.

The next road turns down to the coast via **Kerambitan**, a village noted for its beautiful old buildings, including two 17th century **palaces**; a tradition of *wayang*-style painting; and its own styles of music and dance, especially *tektekan*, a ceremonial procession.

South of Kerambitan, you pass through **Penarukan**, known for its stone and wood carvers, and also its dancers. Continue down to the coast, where the beach at **Kelating** is wide, black and usually deserted.

A small road leads about 4km from southern Kerambitan to **Tibubiyu**, where you'll find *Bee Bees Bungalows & Restaurant*. It's wonderfully isolated, perfectly tranquil, and has tasteful, two storey thatched bungalows for about 40,000/50,000 rp for singles/doubles, including breakfast. It's surrounded by rice fields, the beach is close and it serves good meals.

NORTH OF TABANAN

The area north of Tabanan is good to travel around with your own transport, as the only bemo route is along the road to Penebel.

Another monkey forest, **Alas Kedaton**, is a stopoff on many organised tours from Ubud and south Bali. It is open daily from 7.30 am to 6.30 pm, and costs 1100/600 rp for adults/children. Your ticket includes a guide, who may do little more than fend off avaricious monkeys and lead you to a cousin's sarong shop nearby. Near the entrance, a small shop puts on a 'Bat Show'. For a donation, you can be photographed with one of the hideous creatures draped around your body – if you dare.

In the village of Wanasari, **Taman Kupu Kupu Bali** (☎ 814282) features thousands of pretty, indigenous butterflies in a huge, enclosed area. Admission is around US$4/2 for adults/children and it's worth a visit if you're in the area. The northern road then reaches a fork: take a left to **Pura Luhur Batukau** (see the Central Mountains chapter), via the **hot springs** at Penatahan. There are several pools where you can soak, as well as *Yeh Panes* (☎ 262356), where well finished singles/doubles cost from US$144/178. The road to the right continues to Penebel, and then to Dukuh, where *Taman Sari Bungalow & Coffee House* (☎ 812898) has rooms for US$10. It's a friendly and secluded place, and an ideal base for exploring the area if you have your own vehicle.

LALANG-LINGGAH

On the road from Tabanan to Gilimanuk, near the village of Lalang-Linggah, *Balian Beach*

Pejaten village is noted for its traditional pottery. The terracotta tiles above feature typical astrological and Hindu motifs.

Bungalows overlooks Sungai Balian river, and is close to the sea. Most of the accommodation is in pavilions sleeping from three to six, and costs from 45,000 rp to 72,000 rp per room. There are more basic singles/doubles for 22,500/32,5000 rp. It's a peaceful, relaxed place, and the management is friendly. Across the river, *Sacred River Retreat* (☎ 730904) offers 'transformational seminars' and 'inspirational holidays', with yoga, meditation and massage for around US$250 per night, all inclusive.

A little further to the west, the new **Taman Rekreasi Indah Soka** is a group of *warungs*

WEST BALI

and a huge car park, with a road leading to the surf breaks near the mouth of the river. The break is sometimes called Soka.

JEMBRANA COAST

About 34km west of Tabanan you cross into Bali's most sparsely populated district, Jembrana. There are some interesting back roads to the north coast, but the main road follows the south coast most of the way to Negara, the district capital. There's some beautiful scenery, but little tourist development along the way.

Medewi

Along the main road, a large sign points down the paved road (200m) to Pantai Medewi. The beach is black and rocky, but Medewi is noted for its *long* left-hand wave. It works best at mid to high tide on a 2m swell – get there early before the wind picks up.

Medewi Beach Cottages (☎ 40029, fax 41555) dominates the beach. It is a pleasant place to relax for a while, and the pool is an added attraction. Standard singles/doubles for US$17/23, and a cheap *restaurant*, are on one side of the road; the more expensive rooms, from US$46/52, and a classier *restaurant*, are on the other. Traditional dancing is held during evening meals on Sunday.

The unsignposted *Homestay Gede*, about 50m west of the Cottages, has a few, very basic rooms for 10,000 rp, with a shared bathroom, but they are almost permanently full of surfers.

A few hundred metres west of the Medewi turn-off, *Tinjaya Bungalows* has pleasant rooms in two storey cottages (25,000/30,000 rp downstairs/upstairs), plus some smaller rooms inside for 20,000 rp. The *restaurant* is particularly good, as is the breezy *Pondok Wisata & Rumah Makan Pulukan*, which, despite its name, is not a hotel. It is about 200m east of the turn-off.

Pura Rambut Siwi

Picturesquely situated on a cliff top overlooking a long, wide stretch of beach, this superb temple is one of the important coastal temples in south Bali. It is another of the temples established in the 16th century by the priest Nirartha who had such a good eye for ocean scenery (see also Tanah Lot and Ulu Watu). Legend has it that when Nirartha first came here, he donated some of his hair to the local villagers. The hair is now kept in a box buried in this temple, the name of which means 'worship of the hair'.

The effusive caretaker rents sarongs and provides a rapid-fire commentary about the temple in passable English. He then opens the guest book, indicating that previous visitors have apparently 'donated' an exorbitant 40,000 rp – 5000 rp is more than enough.

The temple is at the end of a 300m paved road, between Air Satang and Yeh Embang. It is not particularly well signposted – look for the turn-off at the predictable cluster of *warungs* along the main road. Any of the regular bemos and buses between Denpasar and Gilimanuk will stop at the turn-off.

NEGARA

Negara is a friendly, prosperous little town, and not a bad place to break up a journey. Most banks change money, but you are more likely to be successful at the Bank BNI. The town is most famous for the bull races nearby.

Places to Stay & Eat

Hotel Ana (☎ 41063) is the cheapest place in town: singles/doubles without a bathroom cost 7000/9000 rp; with a bathroom they're 9000/11,000 rp. *Hotel Tis* (☎ 41634) has more character than most others, and costs 10,000/12,500 rp. The Denpasar to Gilimanuk road (Jl Sudirman), which bypasses the town centre, has several cheap options, but the road is very noisy. The quietest and friendliest is *Hotel Ijogading* for 10,000/15,000 rp.

The best place in town is *Hotel Wira Pada* (☎ 41161). The grounds are spacious and it has off-street parking. Pleasant, quiet rooms cost 20,000/25,000 rp with a fan, or 35,000/40,000 rp with air-con. It's the only hotel where the price includes breakfast.

The *restaurant* at the Wira Pada serves

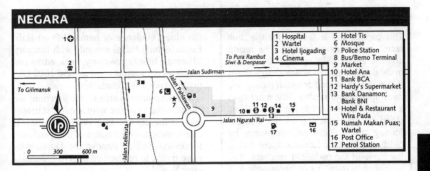

NEGARA

1	Hospital	5	Hotel Tis
2	Wartel	6	Mosque
3	Hotel Ijogading	7	Police Station
4	Cinema	8	Bus/Bemo Terminal
		9	Market
		10	Hotel Ana
		11	Bank BCA
		12	Hardy's Supermarket
		13	Bank Danamon; Bank BNI
		14	Hotel & Restaurant Wira Pada
		15	Rumah Makan Puas; Wartel
		16	Post Office
		17	Petrol Station

good food, although it's a little pricey. *Rumah Makan Puas* offers decent Padang-style food, and there are many *warungs* in the market area. Hardy's Supermarket is home to a small *eatery*, a *CFC* fried chicken stall and a cheap roof-top *bar*.

Getting There & Away
Negara is a stopoff for every type of bemo, bus and minibus travelling between Gilimanuk and the Ubung terminal (2500 rp) in Denpasar.

AROUND NEGARA
At the southern fringe of Negara is **Loloan Timur**, a largely Bugis community (originally from Sulawesi), which retains 300-year-old traditions. Look for their distinctive houses on stilts, some decorated with wooden fretwork.

The southern coast has a few beaches, but none are particularly attractive, and some are downright dangerous. One of the best, **Candikesuma**, just off the road to Gilimanuk, is only accessible with your own vehicle.

Perancak
This is the site of Nirartha's arrival on Bali in 1546, commemorated by a small temple, **Pura Gede Perancak. Taman Wisata Peran-cak** (☎ 42173) is a tourist spot where **bull races** (see the boxed text of the same name later in this chapter) and Balinese buffets are sometimes staged for organised tours from south Bali. If you're travelling independently, give the park a ring before you

go out there. In Perancak, ignore the depressing little zoo, and go for a **walk** along the picturesque fishing harbour.

Jembrana
Once capital of the region, Jembrana is the centre of the *gamelan jegog*, a gamelan using huge bamboo instruments that produce a very low-pitched, resonant sound. Performances often feature a number of gamelan groups engaging in musical contest. To see and hear them in action, time your arrival with a local festival, or ask in Negara where you might find a group practising.

BELIMBINGSARI & PALASARI
Christian evangelism on Bali was discouraged by the Dutch, but sporadic missionary activity resulted in a number of converts, many of whom were rejected by their own communities. There was little room for them in Denpasar, so in 1939 they were encouraged to resettle in Christian communities in the wilds of west Bali.

Belimbingsari was established as a Protestant community, and now has the largest **Protestant church** on Bali. It's an amazing structure with features of church architecture rendered in a distinctly Balinese style – there is a *kulkul* (warning drum) in place of a church bell, an *aling-aling*-style entrance gate and some very attractive Balinese angels. Come on Sunday to see inside.

Palasari is home to a Catholic community, and their new **cathedral** is also large and

WEST BALI

Bull Races

This part of Bali is famous for the 'bull races' known as *mekepung*. The racing animals are actually water buffalo, normally docile creatures which charge down a 2km stretch of road or beach pulling tiny decorative chariots, often little more than a sort of plough used in the fields. Riders stand or kneel on top of the chariots forcing the bullocks on, sometimes by twisting their tails to make them follow the curve of the makeshift racetrack. The winner, however, is not necessarily first past the post. Style also plays a part and points are awarded for the most elegant runner. Gambling is not legal on Bali but …

Important races are held throughout this part of west Bali in August, September and October; occasional races are set up for tourist groups at a park in Perancak on the coast; and minor races are held in the general area (best in Perancak) from daybreak every Sunday, often finishing by noon.

impressive (there could be a little competition here). It also shows Balinese touches in the spires which resemble the multi-roofed meru in a Balinese temple and a facade with the same shape as a temple gate. A few kilometres north of Palasari, a **dam** has created a fine looking lake among the hills, but it hasn't been developed for tourists.

These villages are north of the main road, and the best way to see them is with your own transport by doing a loop starting from Melaya. The network of back roads and tracks is very confusing and poorly mapped and signposted, so be prepared to get lost and ask for directions. Otherwise, get a bemo or bus to drop you near one of the turn-offs, where you can arrange an *ojek*.

CEKIK

Cekik is the junction where the road either continues to Gilimanuk or heads east towards Lovina. All buses and bemos to/from Gili-manuk pass through Cekik. Archaeological excavations here during the 1960s yielded the oldest evidence of human life on Bali. Finds include burial mounds with funerary offerings, bronze jewellery, axes, adzes and earthenware vessels from around 1000 BC, give or take a few centuries.

On the southern side of the junction, the pagoda-like structure with a spiral stairway around the outside is a **War Memorial**. It commemorates the landing of independence forces on Bali to oppose the Dutch who were trying to reassert control of Indonesia after WWII.

TAMAN NASIONAL BALI BARAT

The West Bali National Park covers 19,003 hectares of the western tip of Bali. An additional 50,000 hectares are protected in the national park extension, as well as almost 7000 hectares of coral reef and coastal waters. On an island as small and densely populated as Bali, this represents a major commitment to nature conservation.

The **park headquarters** (☎ 40060), right at the junction in Cekik, was being renovated at the time of research. Here you can organise guides for local trekking and check out the relief map of the park. The headquarters is open daily from 7 am to 4 pm. There is also a small **visitors' centre** (no telephone) at Labuhan Lalang on the northern coast, which is the starting point for trips to Pulau Menjangan (see the Trekking entry later in this section).

The main roads to and from Gilimanuk go through the national park, but you don't have to pay an entrance fee just to drive through. If you want to visit Pulau Menjangan or trek in the park, however, you must buy a ticket at Labuhan Lalang. Tickets, valid for one day, cost 2000 rp per person (plus 2000 rp to park a car, or 1000 rp for a motorbike, at Lalang).

Flora & Fauna

Most of the natural vegetation in the park is not tropical rainforest, which requires rain all year, but coastal savanna, with deciduous trees which become bare in the dry season. The southern slopes receive more regular rainfall, and hence more tropical vegetation, while the coastal lowlands have extensive mangroves.

More than 200 species of plants inhabit the park. Local fauna includes black monkeys, leaf monkeys and macaques (seen in the afternoon along the main road near Sumber Kelompok); and barking, sambar, Java and mouse deer *(muncak)*. You may also see squirrels, wild pigs, buffalo, iguanas, pythons and green snakes. There were once tigers, but the last confirmed sighting was in 1937 – and that one was shot. The bird life is prolific, with many of Bali's 300 species found, including the very rare Bali starling.

Trekking

All trekkers must be accompanied by an authorised guide. It is best to arrive the day before you want to trek, and make inquiries at the park headquarters at Cekik, the visitors' centre at Labuhan Lalang or any hotel in Gilimanuk or along the coast east of Gilimanuk. A guide may miraculously appear at your hotel within minutes of your arrival, anyway – but make sure he is authorised.

The cost of hiring a guide is negotiable, but expect to pay about 10,000 rp per hour per group (of up to four people), plus return transport and food. Early morning is the best time to start – it's cooler and you're more likely to see some wildlife.

These are some of the more popular treks:

From a trail west of Labuhan Lalang, hike around the mangroves in Teluk Terima bay. Then partially follow the Sungai Terima river into the hills and walk back down to the road along the steps at Makam Jayaprana. You may see grey macaques, deer, and black monkeys. Allow two to three hours.

A longer trek (four hours) starts at Kelatakan village, passes the microwave tower on Gunung Kelatakan and returns down to Ambyasari.

From Sumber Kelompok, go up Gunung Kelatakan (698m), and hike back to the main road near Kelatakan village. This hike takes six to seven hours, but with some preparation, and permission from the park headquarters, you can extend this to a two day hike. Bring a tent, or your guide can make a makeshift shelter.

The best way to explore the mangroves of Teluk Gilimanuk is by chartering a boat (maximum of three people) for about 15,000 rp per boat per hour from the makeshift port in front of Penginapan Nusantara II in Gilimanuk (see the Gilimanuk map). This is the ideal way to see bird life, including the kingfisher, and, very rarely, the Bali starling.

From about June to September (when the sensitive Bali starlings move further inland) you can trek around some of Prapat Agung. Allow at least five hours (one way) from Sumber Kelompok to a point near Lampu Merah (Red Light), via the Bali Starling Pre-Release Centre. Save some time and energy and charter a boat.

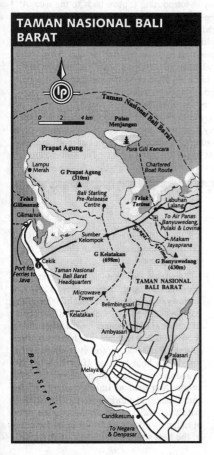

TAMAN NASIONAL BALI BARAT

WEST BALI

The Bali Starling

Also known as the Bali myna, Rothschild's mynah, or locally as *jalak putih*, the Bali starling *(Leucopsar rothschildi)* is Bali's only endemic bird. It is striking white in colour, with black tips to the wings and tail, and a distinctive bright blue mask. It breeds readily in captivity, and is greatly valued as a caged bird, but in its natural environment it is bordering on extinction. The wild population has been estimated to be as low as 25, well below the number needed for sustainable reproduction, although experts believe that perhaps several hundred are successfully breeding in captivity around the world.

The internationally supported Bali Starling Project is attempting to rebuild the population by re-introducing captive birds to the wild. At the Bali Starling Pre-Release Centre, formerly caged birds are introduced to the food sources of the natural environment and encouraged to nest in native trees before being released around Taman Nasional Bali Barat national park. It's a difficult process, and many attempts have been sadly unsuccessful: birds are often killed by predatory falcons and poachers. The starlings are also constantly disadvantaged by a reduced habitat caused by development, and there are precious few resources to protect the birds.

While it is possible to visit the Pre-Release Centre for much of the year, the areas where the birds are most likely to be seen are not normally open to visitors, especially during the breeding season when they congregate on Prapat Agung peninsula. Your chances of spotting a Bali starling in the wild are extremely low; it is best to see them in captivity. The Taman Burung Bali Bird Park (see the Ubud & Around chapter) also has a captive-breeding programme.

Pulau Menjangan

This uninhabited island boasts what is believed to be Bali's oldest temple, **Pura Gili Kencana**, which dates from the Mahajapit period in Java. You can walk around the island in any hour or so, but the attractions are mainly underwater. The scuba diving is excellent: there is great visibility; superb unspoiled coral; caves; lots of tropical fish, such as clown fish and parrot fish, as well as (harmless) sharks and barracuda; a spectacular drop-off; and a small shipwreck 600m out. Snorkellers can find some decent spots not far from the jetty on the island – ask the boatman where to go. Diving trips to the island can be arranged with most dive operators throughout Bali, but it's easier at the diving centres at Pemuteran, Pulaki or

Lovina. Mimpi Dive Centres (Jimbaran – ☎ 0361-701070) are planning a diving centre on the island, which should be completed by the time you get there.

The jetty for boats to Menjangan is at Labuhan Lalang, where there's several *warungs* and a pleasant beach 200m to the east (which you may be charged 3500 rp to use). Local boat owners have a strict cartel: it costs 60,000 rp for a four hour trip to the island (and 5000 rp for every subsequent hour) in a boat holding 10 people, or five scuba divers with equipment.You can rent snorkelling gear at Lalang (10,000 rp per four hours), so snorkellers may be satisfied with the coral formations close to the shore at Lalang – ask locals for the exact locations of the best sites.

Top: Temple offerings and crowds during a festival at Pura Besakih in east Bali.
Bottom: Festival procession at Candikuning's Pura Ulun Danu Bratan in central Bali.

SARA-JANE CLELAND

ADAM McCROW

Balinese workers during the rice harvest in central Bali. The island's production techniques are among the best in the world, with most regions producing two crops a year.

Makam Jayaprana

A 20 minute walk up some stone stairs from the southern side of the road, a little west of Labuhan Lalang, will bring you to Jayaprana's grave. There are fine views to the north at the top. Jayaprana, the foster son of a 17th century king, planned to marry Leyonsari, a beautiful girl of humble origins. The king, however, also fell in love with Leyonsari and had Jayaprana killed. Leyonsari learned the truth of Jayaprana's death in a dream, and killed herself rather than marry the king. This Romeo and Juliet story is a common theme in Balinese folklore, and the grave is regarded as sacred, even though the ill-fated couple were not deities.

Air Panas Banyuwedang

According to a local brochure, water from these hot water springs will 'strengthen the endurance of your body against the attack of skin disease'. It's an unappealing place – the springs at Banjar, near Lovina, are far, far better. It costs 1100/600 rp (for adults/children) to soak in the little bath house. The owners of the *Mimpi Menjangan Resort* believe the place is worthwhile, so they're hurriedly building bungalows nearby.

Places to Stay

There is nowhere to stay within the national park, but there is a *campground* at the park headquarters at Cekik. The closest hotels are in Gilimanuk and along the northwestern coast.

Getting There & Away

Refer to the following Gilimanuk section for details about public transport. The national park is far from Ubud and south Bali, so day trips are either impractical or expensive. Most day trips (12 hours), come via Lovina and Pupuan, or Tanah Lot, and cost from US$60 per person. Hiring or chartering your own vehicle will cost far less.

GILIMANUK

Gilimanuk is the terminus for ferries which shuttle back and forth across the narrow strait to Java. There is a bank, which offers horrendously low rates; post office; wartels; and an uninformative tourist office underneath the unmistakably hideous stone *thing* stretching across the road. There are also masses of voracious mosquitoes, so take precautions.

Most travellers to/from Java don't need to stop in Gilimanuk. There's little of interest, but it is the closest accommodation to the national park if you want to start a trek early. The most striking feature is the profiles of Gunung Merapi and Gunung Raung, which loom over Gilimanuk from the other side of the Bali Strait when the weather is clear. They make a detour to East Java very tempting.

Places to Stay & Eat

Most places are along Jl Raya, the busy main road between Cekik and the terminal/port. If you have a tent, you can camp at

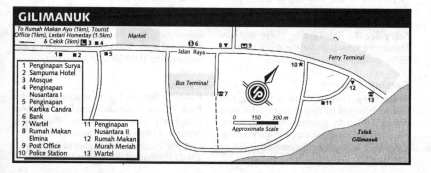

GILIMANUK

To Rumah Makan Ayu (1km), Tourist Office (1km), Lestari Homestay (1.5km) & Cekik (3km)

Market

Jalan Raya

Ferry Terminal

Bus Terminal

0   150   300 m
Approximate Scale

Teluk Gilimanuk

1 Penginapan Surya
2 Sampurna Hotel
3 Mosque
4 Penginapan Nusantara I
5 Penginapan Kartika Candra
6 Bank
7 Wartel
8 Rumah Makan Elmina
9 Post Office
10 Police Station
11 Penginapan Nusantara II
12 Rumah Makan Murah Meriah
13 Wartel

WEST BALI

the grounds of the park headquarters at Cekik free of charge. The grounds are not pristine, but the bathroom is clean enough.

Penginapan Nusantara II is closest to the ferry terminal, and has a view over the bay which is magic at sunrise. However, the rooms are dingy, airless and overpriced for 25,000 rp.

In the centre of Gilimanuk, *Penginapan Kartika Candra*, *Penginapan Nusantara I* and *Penginapan Surya* are also airless and cheerless, and charge about 12,500/17,500 rp for singles/doubles.

Much better is the new *Sampurna Hotel* (☎ 61250) which costs 15,000 to 25,000 rp for a room with a fan, or 55,000 rp with air-con. Breakfast is included. If you have your own transport, *Lestari Homestay* is a good option. It has a range of rooms, from 12,000 rp for grotty doubles to 50,000 rp for plush, new bungalows.

There are *warungs* and *rumah makans* around the market and ferry terminal, such as *Rumah Makan Murah Meriah*, but the best and most central is *Rumah Makan Elmina*. If you have your own transport, try a few other places along the road to Cekik, such as *Rumah Makan Ayu*.

Getting There & Away

Bus & Bemo Buses frequently hurtle along the main road between Gilimanuk and the Ubung terminal (3900 rp) in Denpasar, or along the north coast to Singaraja (2700 rp). Cheaper minibuses and bemos leave from outside the market in Gilimanuk, but they are very crowded and will stop at every place along the way.

Ferry See the Bali Getting There & Away chapter for details about the ferry between Gilimanuk and Ketapang in Java.

Getting Around

At the ferry, bemo and bus terminals, you will be thronged by ojek drivers, who want 500 to 1000 rp for a short ride across town. More leisurely and comfortable, particularly if you have luggage, are the numerous *dokars* (pony carts).

NORTH-WEST COAST

The road between Gilimanuk and Lovina is sparsely populated, but a few resorts and diving centres take advantage of the secluded beaches and coral reefs. These places are listed on the map at the start of the North Bali chapter.

Sumberkerta

Along the main road in this sleepy village, *Penginapan & Restaurant Nikmat* charges 30,000 to 40,000 rp for a simple room. This is too much, but it's the cheapest place to stay and eat along this part of the coast.

Pemuteran

The spacious *Taman Sari Hotel* (bookings: ☎ 0361-288096, fax 286297) faces its own pretty beach. Gorgeous bungalows in the dramatic foothills start from US$40, but 20% off-season discounts are possible. Next door, *Pondok Sari* (☎ 92337) also attractively faces the same beach and has a similar set-up for a very similar price. Not far away, *Taman Selini Beach Bungalows* (☎/fax 93449) costs US$57, including breakfast, but is not as nice as the other two.

There are three local dive operators: Yos Diving Centre at Pondok Sari; Arkipelago at Taman Sari; and the independent Reef Seen Aquatics (☎/fax 92339, email reefseen @denpasar.wasantara.net.id). Prices for each operator are very similar: US$30/55 for one/two local dives; US$35 for a night dive; and US$70 for two dives at Pulau Menjangan. They also rent snorkelling gear for about US$3 per day.

Reef Seen, which is well regarded for its local marine conservation programmes and community projects, also offers sunset and sunrise cruises, glass-bottom boat trips and horse riding (US$30 for two hours).

Pulaki

Pulaki is famous for its vineyards and for **Pura Pulaki**, a coastal temple which was completely rebuilt in the early 1980s, and is home to a large troop of monkeys.

A few hundred metres east of the temple, a well signposted, 3km paved road leads to

Turtle Project at Pemuteran

One pleasing example of how tourism has benefited the local community and marine life is the Turtle Project at Pemuteran, a village on the far north-west coast.

The project started in 1994 at a local diving centre. Local fisherfolk are encouraged to rescue turtles which are entangled in their fishing nets, and 'sell' them to the project managers. The turtles are well fed and kept in tanks until they are ready to be released into the sea.

In four years, more than 800 turtles have been born in captivity, or rescued and then later released into the sea. It is hard to determine just how successful the project is because released turtles are hard to keep track of, but just as important to the project coordinators is the education of the local community about their environment.

Foreigners can make donations, or fund the release of a turtle into the sea for 25,000 to 50,000 rp. Contact the Reef Seen Aquatics Dive Centre (☎/fax 0362-92339, email reefseen @denpasar.wasantara.net.id), or visit the hatchery at the dive centre in the village of Pemuteran. But please remember: this is a community project, and not a tourist attraction.

Pura Melanting. This temple is set dramatically in the foothills, and gloriously devoid of tourists and hawkers. A 1000 rp donation is expected to enter the complex, although you're not permitted in the main worship area. The elegant *Matahari Beach Resort* (☎ 92312, fax 92313) has beautifully finished bungalows in attractive gardens, with a big pool and direct beach frontage. It is the base for David's Dive Sport, and offers tennis, windsurfing and mountainbiking.

Singles/doubles start at US$165/192 and go much higher.

Banyupoh

From Pulaki, the road continues east to *Segara Bukit Seaside Cottages*, a secluded place on a small black beach. It charges 55,000 to 66,000 rp for a double with fan, and 132,000 rp with hot water and air-con (all with breakfast), which is not particularly good value.

Central Mountains

Highlights

- Gunung Batur offers awe-inspiring landscapes with its vast crater, lake, volcanic cones, solidified lava flows and smoking volcanoes.

- Trekking to the peak of Batur to watch the sunrise is very popular, but there are many other possibilities around the central mountains and lakes.

- The cool, green Botanical Gardens in Candikuning have magnificent trees, extensive lawns and more than 500 species of orchid.

- Rent a canoe or speedboat to explore the delightful mountain lake of Danau Bratan.

- Scenic roads lead to the village of Munduk, with fields of blue hydrangeas, Dutch villas to stay in and some curious art installations nearby.

Most of Bali's mountains are volcanoes – some are dormant, some are definitely active. The mountains divide the gentle sweep of fertile rice land to the south from the narrower strip to the north. In east Bali there is a small clump of mountains right at the end of the island, beyond Amlapura. Then there's the mighty volcano Gunung Agung (3142m), the island's 'mother mountain'. North-west of Agung is the stark and spectacular caldera which contains the volcanic cone of Gunung Batur (1717m), the lake of Danau Batur and numerous smaller craters.

In central Bali, around Bedugul, there's another complex of volcanic craters and lakes, with much more lush vegetation. A string of smaller mountains stretches off to the sparsely inhabited western region.

The popular round trip to the north coast crosses the mountains on one route (eg via Gunung Batur) and returns on another (from Singaraja, via Bedugul), thus covering the most interesting parts of the central mountain region. You can do the circuit easily in either direction, and while getting to more remote areas by public transport is a little tricky, it's not impossible.

The mountain areas can be considerably more cool and damp than Lovina, Ubud or the Kuta region, so come prepared. Fans are not normally provided in hotel rooms, but hot water is more readily available, and welcome.

Gunung Batur

Most day-trippers come on organised tours and stop on the crater rim at Penelokan for views and lunch; most overnight visitors stay in the villages around the lake.

ORIENTATION

The area is like a giant dish, with the bottom half covered with water and a set of volcanic cones growing in the middle. The road around the southern and western rim is part of the main road between Gianyar and Singaraja, and has a series of villages which have grown together in a continuous, untidy strip. The smaller, nicer villages are at the bottom of the crater, mostly around the edges of Danau Batur.

INFORMATION
Tourist Office

The tourist information office, or Yayasa Bintang Danu (☎ 23370), at Penelokan has some limited information about local transport fares and trekking routes. It's a good idea to check with them before you're taken in by one of the local hustlers. It is open daily from 9 am to 3 pm. The ticket offices at Kubupenelokan, Toya Bungkah and Penelokan also act as quasi-tourist offices.

Entry Tickets

If you arrive by private vehicle from the south (but not from Singaraja), you will be stopped at ticket offices at Penelokan or Kubupenelokan. Tickets, valid for one visit to anywhere along the road between Penelokan and Penulisan, cost 1100/550 rp for adults/children, plus more for a car (1000 rp), motorbike (200 rp), camera (1000 rp) or video (2500 rp). If you arrive from anywhere by public bemo, you normally don't have to pay anything; and the toll should be included in any organised tours.

If you then travel to Toya Bungkah, you have to pay the same amount *again* – valid for one visit to the village. Keep the tickets if you drive back and forth around the crater rim, or you may have to pay again and again.

Money

You can change money at Bank BRI in Kintamani; at Hotel Segara, in Kedisan; at Lakeview Hotel and a number of nearby stalls in Penelokan; and at Jero Wijaya travel agency and another moneychanger in Toya Bungkah.

Dangers & Annoyances

Everybody seems to try to get as much money out of every tourist as possible. This makes us want to get out of the area quickly after climbing Gunung Batur.

Dr Christoph Eingartner, Germany

Gunung Batur has a well deserved reputation as a money-grubbing place where visitors (mainly around Penelokan) are hassled by hawkers as persistent as they are in the Kuta region, and by plenty of wannabe guides (mainly around the lake area). It is not uncommon for tourists to pay US$60 *each* for a four hour trip up the mountain. This is more than a school teacher makes in a month, so it's hardly ssurprising that people are prepared to spend days or weeks trying to catch just one group of gullible trekkers.

Guides will usually provide breakfast on the summit, and this often includes the novelty of cooking eggs or bananas in the steaming holes at the top of the volcano.

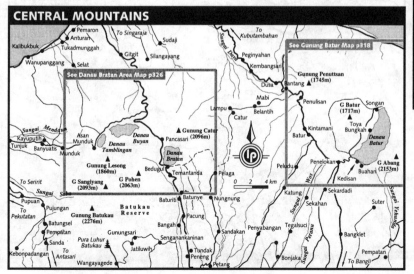

Unfortunately, the practice has resulted in an accumulation of litter – egg shells, banana peels, plastic bags etc – around the summit. Please take your rubbish with you.

In addition, keep an eye on your gear, and don't leave any valuables in your car, especially at any car park at the start of any trail up the volcano.

THE CLIMB

Soaring up in the centre of the huge outer crater is the cone of Gunung Batur (1717m)

and a cluster of smaller cones. You can take one route up and another one down, then get a bemo back to your starting point. Start early in the morning (depending which route you take), before mist and cloud obscure the view. Ideally, you should get to the top for sunrise (about 6 am) – it's a magnificent sight, although it can get crowded; throngs of about 100 on top are not uncommon in peak season.

You should think twice before taking a longer route in the wet season (October to March), because the trails can be muddy and

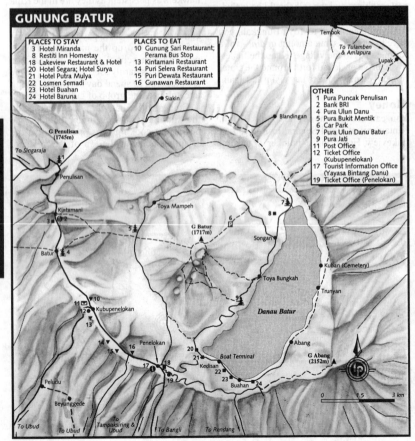

GUNUNG BATUR

PLACES TO STAY
3 Hotel Miranda
8 Restiti Inn Homestay
18 Lakeview Restaurant & Hotel
20 Hotel Segara; Hotel Surya
21 Hotel Putra Mulya
22 Losmen Semadi
23 Hotel Buahan
24 Hotel Baruna

PLACES TO EAT
10 Gunung Sari Restaurant;
   Perama Bus Stop
13 Kintamani Restaurant
14 Puri Selera Restaurant
15 Puri Dewata Restaurant
16 Gunawan Restaurant

OTHER
1 Pura Puncak Penulisan
2 Bank BRI
4 Pura Ulun Danu
5 Pura Bukit Mentik
6 Car Park
7 Pura Ulun Danu Batur
9 Pura Jati
11 Post Office
12 Ticket Office
   (Kubupenelokan)
17 Tourist Information Office
   (Yayasa Bintang Danu)
19 Ticket Office (Penelokan)

slippery, and the views will almost always be blocked by clouds anyway. Always take a torch (flashlight), unless your guide provides one; a hat; proper walking shoes; trousers and jumper (sweater); water; and plenty of film. You will need to charter or rent a vehicle to the starting point if you climb very early in the morning, unless you start directly from Toya Bungkah. Your guide will arrange transport for an extra charge.

Guides

If you have a strong torch, reasonable sense of direction, your own transport to the starting point and it's not completely dark when you start climbing, you won't need a guide for the usual routes. But a guide is still useful if you can hire one for a decent price – not easy. Before you commit yourself to anyone on the street, talk to other travellers and visit one of the tourist or ticket offices for some independent advice.

Gunung Batur – The Stats

Gunung Batur has been volatile for hundreds of thousands of years: there were more than 20 minor eruptions between 1824 and 1994, and major eruptions in 1917, 1926 and 1963. As recently as November 1997, about 3000 minor tremors were recorded.

Vulcanologists describe Gunung Batur as a 'double caldera' – ie one crater inside another. The outer crater is about 14km by 10km, and the road along the western rim is about 1500m above sea level. The smaller, inner and more recent crater is about 8km in diameter. The central cone is 1717m above sea level, and comprises three smaller cones, called Batur I, II and III.

Although Gunung Batur is not recognised as 'dangerous', the Vulcanology Survey of Indonesia does issue occasional warnings about steam explosions, which are particularly hazardous if visibility is poor. If a local guide says that Batur is too dangerous to climb, believe him.

In and around Toya Bungkah and Kedisan (and sometimes several kilometres before you get there), you'll be hassled by people offering to guide you up the mountain – sometimes for outrageous amounts in US dollars. If you do want a guide, 15,000 to 20,000 rp per group (of up to four people), plus transport, is reasonable – but haggle long and hard. Some trips include breakfast at the top and take longer, more interesting routes on the way down, and they cost more. Guides who speak good English will also charge more. Many of the guides have photocopied brochures with glowing testimonials from previous 'satisfied customers', – take all this with a (very) large grain of salt.

Trekking Agencies

The easiest – but certainly the most expensive – option is to organise a trip through a trekking agency. All hotels around the lake have trekking agencies, but many are little more than a guide with a telephone. The following agencies offer treks up Gunung Batur, as well as other places, eg Gunung Abang and Gunung Agung. Prices include transport to and from the starting point, and breakfast at the top, or after the climb.

Arlina's Bungalows
  (☎ 51165)
  This hotel in Toya Bungkah charges US$10/15/25 per person for the short/medium/long trip via Pura Jati.
Jero Wijaya
  (☎ 51249, fax 51250)
  This agency in Toya Bungkah charges from US$10 per person for the short trip with a 'trainee guide' to US$25 for the longer trip with an 'informative' English-speaking guide.
Mutiara Tourist Service
  (☎ 0361-975145)
  This agency in Ubud works through Jero Wijaya, but charges more because of extra transport, and hotel accommodation in Toya Bungkah.
Pineh Trekking Agent
  (☎ 51378)
  Based at the Hotel Surya, it charges a reasonable 20,000/25,000/30,000 rp per person. This also includes free pick-up in Ubud, Gianyar or Bangli, but you'll have to stay at the Surya.

Routes

For an interesting round trip, you can climb Gunung Batur from Toya Bungkah, follow the rim around to the western side, then go south through the area of the most recent volcanic activity, descend to the east and traverse through the lava field to Pura Jati. The area south-west of the summit has the most interesting volcanic features, with smoking craters, bright yellow sulphur deposits and steep slopes of fine black sand.

At the summit it's possible to walk right around the rim of the cone, or descend into the cone from the southern edge. Climbing up, spending a reasonable time on the top and then strolling back down takes four or five hours, but allow a little more for a really good look around.

There are several refreshment stops along the way, and people with ice buckets full of cold drinks. The drinks are expensive, but very welcome. The *warungs* at the top have tea and coffee, jaffles and, of course, brilliant views.

You can reach the summit from Batur village or Kintamani, but most travellers use one of three routes.

From the North-East The easiest route is from the north-east, where a track enables you use private transport within about 45 minutes walk from the top. From Toya Bungkah take the road north-east towards Songan and take the left fork after about 3.5km. Follow this small road for another 1.7km to a well signposted track on the left, which climbs another kilometre or so to a parking area. From here the walking track is easy to follow to the top.

The parking area is not secure, however, so don't leave anything of value in your car, or even a helmet with your motorbike. You cannot rely on public transport after you finish the climb, but you could probably ask for a lift from other climbers with rented vehicles.

From Toya Bungkah The route from Toya Bungkah is also pretty straightforward, and ideal for those without private transport.

Walk out of the village towards Kedisan and turn right just after the ticket office. There are a few separate paths at first but they all rejoin sooner or later – just keep going uphill, tending south-west and then west. After about 30 minutes you'll be on a ridge with quite a well defined track; keep going up. It gets pretty steep towards the top and it can be hard walking over the loose volcanic sand – climbing up three steps and sliding back two. Allow about two hours to the top.

From Kedisan If you stay at Kedisan, you might want to start at Pura Jati. There are three options: the shortest trek is straight up (about three hours return); a slightly longer detour (about four hours return) goes via crater number two or three; and a longer trek (five or six hours return) goes directly to crater number four, and to the summit via the other two.

PENELOKAN

Penelokan, which appropriately means 'place to look', has superb views across to Gunung Batur and down to the lake at the bottom of the crater. It is basically a junction, with a large hotel, several restaurants and numerous pushy souvenir sellers. Don't be put off by the touts, hawkers and tourist buses if you plan to stay in a village around the lake.

Places to Stay & Eat

There's only one place to stay, right on the edge of the crater. *Lakeview Restaurant & Hotel* (☎/fax 51464) has firmly gone upmarket and charges US$36 for a superior room, and US$48 for deluxe with the best views. Prices include breakfast.

The road around the rim has a crowd of restaurants geared to bus-loads of tour groups, such as *Gunawan Restaurant*, *Puri Selera Restaurant*, *Puri Dewata Restaurant* and *Kintamani Restaurant*. They all have fine views, and provide buffet-style lunches for 20,000 to 25,000 rp, plus 21% tax. The a la carte alternatives are still very expensive. Dotted among these are decent *warungs* with similar views, and meals for about 5000 rp.

BATUR & KINTAMANI

The village of Batur used to be down in the crater. A violent eruption in 1917 killed thousands of people and destroyed more than 60,000 homes and 2000 temples. Although the village was wiped out, the lava flow stopped at the entrance to the village temple.

Taking this as a good omen, the village was rebuilt, but Gunung Batur erupted again in 1926. This time the lava flow covered all but the loftiest temple shrine. Fortunately, the Dutch administration anticipated the eruption and evacuated the village. It was relocated up on the crater rim, and the surviving shrine was also moved up and placed in the new temple, **Pura Ulun Danu** (not to be confused with Pura Ulun Danu Batur, north of Songan by the lake). Spiritually, Gunung Batur is the second most important mountain on Bali (only Agung outranks it) so this temple is of considerable importance.

The villages of Batur and Kintamani now virtually run together. Kintamani is famed for its large and colourful **market** held every three days. It starts and ends early – by 11 am it's all over. High rainfall, cool climate and reliable water supplies from the lake make this a very productive fruit and vegetable growing area.

Places to Stay & Eat

Kintamani is not a good base. The only hotel, *Hotel Miranda*, is very basic but cheap at 10,000/20,000 rp for singles/doubles, without breakfast. It does provide good food, an open fire at night and the friendly, informative owner also acts as a guide.

PENULISAN

The road gradually climbs along the crater rim beyond Kintamani. If you come up from the south, you may find yourself ascending through the clouds around Penelokan and Kintamani, then coming out above them as you approach Penulisan.

At a bend in the road, several steep flights of steps lead to Bali's highest temple, **Pura Puncak Penulisan**, at 1745m. Inside, the highest courtyard are rows of old statues and fragments of sculptures in the open *bale* (pavilions). Some of the sculptures date back as far as the 11th century. The views from the temple are superb: facing north you can see over the rice terraces clear to the Singaraja coast – clouds and mist permitting. It costs 1000 rp to enter, and you can rent a sash and/or sarong from someone outside the entrance.

With your own transport you can continue further around the crater rim, with a great view of the northern side of Gunung Batur. After a while, the road leaves the ridge top and descends towards the north coast – you'll get glimpses of brilliant coastal scenery through the tall trees, but the road doesn't yet go all the way down.

KEDISAN

A hairpin-bend road winds its way down from Penelokan to Kedisan on the shore of the lake. The road is longer (about 4km) than it looks on the map, and very steep. There are a few places to stay in the immediate area, and it's a more pleasant alternative to Toya Bungkah.

Places to Stay & Eat

Not actually in the village, but around the corner towards Toya Bungkah, are two good places. *Hotel Surya* (☎ 51378) has a number of clean, comfortable rooms for 20,000 rp, or 30,000 rp with hot water. The staff are friendly, and the views from the *restaurant* are superb. The 'economy rooms' at *Hotel Segara* (☎ 51136) next door are the same price and standard, but the better rooms for 50,000 to 80,000 rp have extra attractions like TV and hot water.

Closer to the village, *Hotel Putra Mulya* has slightly nicer 'economy' rooms than the Surya or Segara – they go for 20,000 rp. *Losmen Semadi* is the same price as Putra Mulya, but not as clean.

All the hotels operate their own *restaurants*, and include breakfast in their rates. Opposite the boat terminal in Kedisan, *Cafe*

Segara is good for breakfast and lunch, but it closes at 7 pm. Fish is obviously a speciality, and costs about 6500 rp.

BUAHAN

A little further around the lake (a pleasant 15 minute stroll from Kedisan) is Buahan, a friendly village with market gardens going right down to the lakeshore.

Hotel Baruna (☎ 51221) is your best option – it is friendly and almost guaranteed 'guide-free'. Simple, clean singles/doubles cost 20,000/25,000 rp, with cold water and breakfast. Alternatively, the *Hotel Buahan (☎ 51217)* is good value for 30,000 rp with hot water, and the rooms are new and clean, but unfortunately, the views are obstructed by a brick wall.

TRUNYAN & KUBAN

The village of Trunyan is squeezed tightly between the lake and the outer crater rim. This is a Bali Aga village, inhabited by descendants of the original Balinese, the people who predated the Majapahit arrival. Unlike the other well known Bali Aga village, Tenganan (in east Bali), this is not an interesting or friendly place. It's famous for the **Pura Pancering Jagat** temple, but you're not allowed to go inside. There are also a couple of traditional Bali Aga-style dwellings, and a large banyan tree, said to be over 1100 years old.

A little beyond Trunyan, and accessible only by boat (there's no path) is the **village cemetery** at Kuban. The people of Trunyan do not cremate or bury their dead – they lie them out in bamboo cages to decompose, although strangely there is no stench. A macabre collection of skulls and bones lies on a stone platform.

The only way to get to Kuban, and the main way to Trunyan, is by chartered boat from Kedisan (see the Getting Around entry later in this section). Sadly, both places (and the boat trip) are now blatant tourist traps: touts and guides want very large tips for a three minute, barely comprehensible explanation, and then firmly urge you to 'donate' the 'same offerings' (10,000 to 20,000 rp) to

the temple or the graves that already lay in the bowl – 1000 rp is enough.

TOYA BUNGKAH

The major village on the lake is Toya Bungkah, also known as Tirta, with its hot springs – *tirta* and *toya* both mean 'water'. Toya Bungkah is a scruffy little village, but despite this, many travellers stay here so they can climb Gunung Batur early in the morning – then most get out as quickly as possible afterwards.

Hot Springs

The hot springs *(air panas)* bubble out in a couple of spots, and feed an unattractive **public bathing pool** before flowing out into the lake. The water is soothingly hot, and ideal for aching muscles after a climb up the volcano, but if you use the *very* public baths, you may be stared at by locals and hassled by hawkers.

Alternatively, you have to pay through the nose at the new Tirta Sanjiwani Hot Springs Complex (☎ 51204). Although it mainly caters to packaged tours, anyone can use the spa (US$20) or swimming pool (US$5).

Places to Stay

There are quite a few places to stay; most are basic and cheap, while some are now a little overpriced. The main road to Penelokan is used by large trucks all day and night, so try to get a room at the back of the hotel.

Many places offer similar prices and standards, and include breakfast. For around 15,000/20,000 rp for singles/doubles, the following places are reasonably good value: *Hotel Dharma Putra (☎ 51197)* has a mandi (ie no shower) and squat toilet; *Under the Volcano I (☎ 51666)* offers large, clean rooms around a small garden; and *Nyoman Pangus Bungalows (☎ 51667)* has signposts claiming that it's 'recommended by Lonely Planet' – and it is (at least this time around anyway).

Arlina's Bungalows (☎ 51165) is clean, comfortable and friendly, but is now firmly overpriced. Standard rooms are 45,000 rp, or 60,000 rp with hot water.

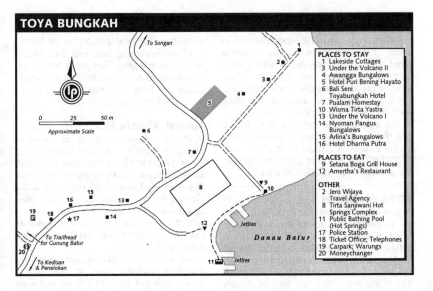

TOYA BUNGKAH

To Songan

0   25   50 m
Approximate Scale

Jetties

Danau Batur

Jetties

To Trailhead
for Gunung Batur

To Kedisan
& Penelokan

PLACES TO STAY
1 Lakeside Cottages
3 Under the Volcano II
4 Awangga Bungalows
5 Hotel Puri Bening Hayato
6 Bali Seni
   Toyabungkah Hotel
7 Pualam Homestay
10 Wisma Tirta Yastra
13 Under the Volcano I
14 Nyoman Pangus
   Bungalows
15 Arlina's Bungalows
16 Hotel Dharma Putra

PLACES TO EAT
9 Setana Boga Grill House
12 Amertha's Restaurant

OTHER
2 Jero Wijaya
   Travel Agency
8 Tirta Sanjiwani Hot
   Springs Complex
11 Public Bathing Pool
   (Hot Springs)
17 Police Station
18 Ticket Office; Telephones
19 Carpark; Warungs
20 Moneychanger

The principal attraction of *Bali Seni Toya-bungkah Hotel* (☎ 51173) is a quiet location off the main road, and the fact that you may be the only guest. The rooms could do with some renovation, and cost 20,000/30,000 rp. *Pualam Homestay* is cheap, clean and costs a negotiable 10,000/15,000 rp. The cheapest place, *Wisma Tirta Yastra*, also has the best location, but the rooms are very basic for 12,000 rp.

The path leading to the Lakeside Cottages is quiet, but most budget places here are not good value. Charging about 25,000 rp with cold water, or 30,000 rp with hot water, are *Under the Volcano II* (☎ 51666) and the motley bunch of poorly maintained rooms at *Awangga Bungalows*.

Lakeside Cottages (☎ 51249, fax 51250) is popular with packaged tours. Standard rooms cost US$8/10, and 'superior' rooms with hot water and TV are US$20/25.

Dominating the village, the incongruous *Hotel Puri Bening Hayato* (☎ 51234, fax 51248) has modern, comfortable rooms for US$54/66, or US$84/96 with everything, including the best views.

Places to Eat

Small fish known as *mujair* are the local speciality, and are usually barbecued with onion and garlic – but be warned, these little critters have heaps of bones. A few *warungs* huddle around the car park, and all the hotels have *restaurants*, mostly with similar menus and prices.

Amertha's Restaurant has the best views, especially of the chaos at the public bathing pool in the late afternoon, but prices are a little high. *Arlina's Bungalows* has a popular restaurant, which offers large serves at fair prices. The only independent restaurant is the *Setana Boga Grill House* which has fish dishes for about 6000 rp.

SONGAN

The road continues around the lake from Toya Bungkah to Songan, which is a large and interesting village with some old buildings and market gardens which extend to the edge of the lake. At the end of the road is **Pura Ulun Danu Batur**. Along a 150m path towards the lake, another part of the same temple sits majestically at the northern tip of the lake. From the temples, you can climb to the top of the outer crater rim in about 20 minutes and see the north-eastern coast. It's an easy downhill **walk** (about 6km) to the coastal road at Lupak, where you can get public transport back to the lake, via Singaraja and Penelokan (although these are both a long way around).

The only place to stay, the small *Restiti Inn Homestay*, is on the left, past the centre of the village. A clean simple room costs 15,000 rp, and it's as far away from pestering guides as you can be in the area.

TOYA MAMPEH

A turn-off in Songan takes you on a rough but passable road around the crater floor. Much of the area is very fertile, with bright patches of market garden and quite strange landforms. On the north-western side of the volcano is Toya Mampeh village (also called Yeh Mampeh), with a vast field of chunky black lava – a legacy of the 1974 eruption.

Further on, **Pura Bukit Mentik** was completely surrounded by molten lava from this eruption, but the temple itself, and its impressive banyan tree, were quite untouched – it's now called the 'Lucky Temple' in the local language. The serenity is constantly shattered, however, by trucks hauling out volcanic stone for more hotel construction.

GETTING THERE & AWAY

This section deals with how to get to and from the whole Gunung Batur area. The two main routes to Penelokan, via Bangli and Tampaksiring, meet just before Penelokan, and are both good roads. The other roads are OK, but have very little public transport.

You can also take the rougher road to Rendang, which turns off a couple of kilometres east of Penelokan, and goes on to Semarapura (Klungkung) via Menanga. If the weather is clear, you'll have fine views of Gunung Agung along this route.

Public Bus & Bemo

From the Batubulan terminal in Denpasar bemos regularly go to Kintamani, via Ubud

and Payangan for 2500 rp. These bemos do not come through Penelokan, but it is easy enough to find local transport to the lake.

If you're coming from east Bali, bemos leave regularly from Gianyar or Bangli, via Penelokan. Buses and minibuses also travel frequently from Singaraja, through Kintamani and Penelokan (2000 rp).

Tourist Shuttle Bus

A shuttle bus will minimise the hassle of changing bemos and carrying luggage. Perama has a service at least once a day from Kuta and Sanur (10,000 rp from both places). It travels via Ubud (7500 rp), stops at the Gunung Sari Restaurant and then continues to Lovina (7500 rp). If you pre-arrange it with the driver, he will drop you anywhere between Kubupenelokan and Penulisan, but not to anywhere else.

Some hotels and trekking agencies in Toya Bungkah advertise buses to other tourist areas, such as Ubud (10,000 rp) and Kuta (12,000 rp), but they are often just charter services. Prices are based on a minimum of six people, which may be difficult to muster ae many visitors have their own transport.

Organised Tours

This area is a main attraction for many organised tours, which is why Penelokan is chock-a-block with expensive restaurants and hawkers. The Organised Tours section in the Bali Getting Around chapter has more details.

Two trekking agencies, Sobek (☎ 287059, fax 289448) and Nature Treks (☎ 0361-285354; email nature@denpasar.wasantara. net.id), organise descents of the volcano by mountain bike through luscious scenery to Ubud. Costs are about US$55 per person, including bike hire, transport from south Bali and lunch, and the tours take about two to three hours.

GETTING AROUND

Travelling between Penulisan and Penelokan by public transport is very easy. From Penelokan to Toya Bungkah, it is less frequent. Along the sparsely inhabited, western side of the inner rim, public transport is virtually nonexistent. There is a passable road around the volcano, via Toya Mampeh, but only as far as Abang on the eastern side of the lake.

Bemo
From Kintamani, via Penelokan, there are public bemos to Kedisan (500 rp), Toya Bungkah (1000 rp) and Songan (1500 rp). They are supposed to run about every half hour in the morning, and hourly in the afternoon, but they only depart when full – which is not often. Orange bemos regularly shuttle back and forth around the crater rim, between Penelokan and Kintamani (200 rp). To Penulisan, catch a bus or minibus going to Singaraja.

Ojek
One quick and easy way to get around is by *ojek* (paying pillion passenger on a motorbike). Although it's not necessary between Penulisan and Penelokan, ojeks can be very handy for the roads around the lake and volcano. Fares are very negotiable, but from Penelokan try not to pay more than 2000 rp to Kedisan, 3000 rp to Buahan or 5000 rp to Toya Bungkah.

Boat
A chartered trip around the lake on a motorised wooden boat is very enjoyable – but certainly overpriced. Boats leave from a large terminal in Kedisan, where there is a ticket office, car park and very persistent hawkers. The fare allows you to visit the tourist traps of Trunyan and Kuban, but if you also want to go to Toya Bungkah, you'll have to negotiate an extra payment.

The trip takes less than two hours, and costs a minimum of 40,000 rp per boat, plus about 2000 rp in fees and insurance per person. A maximum of seven people can share one boat, but you may find it hard to find others to share the cost. The terminal opens at 8 am, and the last boat leaves at about 4 pm. Try to go before 10 am, when the waves are less choppy and the mighty Gunung Batur is most photogenic.

If you want to do it on the cheap, don't consider the alternative of hiring a dugout canoe and paddling yourself – the lake is *far* bigger than it looks from the shore and it can get very choppy. One alternative is to follow the footpath around the lake to Trunyan, an easy two hour walk from Kedisan. From Trunyan, you can negotiate a boat back to Kedisan or Toya Bungkah, but it won't be cheap.

Danau Bratan

Approaching from the south, you gradually leave the rice terraces behind and ascend into the cool, damp mountain country around Danau Bratan. This lovely area is an excellent place to relax, and use as a base while hiking around the other lakes and surrounding hills. There is also a picturesque temple, botanical gardens, a colourful market, a golf course and a variety of water sports on the lake. Thankfully, the area lacks the tourists and touts found around Gunung Batur.

While the choice of accommodation is not great, prices for most things are geared towards Balinese, not foreign, tourists. Try not come on Sunday or a public holiday, as the lake area will be teeming with courting couples on motorbikes, and families from south Bali squeezed into Kijangs.

ORIENTATION & INFORMATION
Although Bedugul is often used to describe the general area around the lake, there are three main villages. Bedugul is little more than a hotel, restaurant and water sports centre at the southern end of the lake; Candikuning is the main village, and home to a colourful market, bemo stop and several hotels; and Pancasari has more hotels and the main bemo terminal. The market in Candikuning has a *wartel* (public telephone office) and several moneychangers.

ACTIVITIES
Water Sports
Where there's a lake on Bali, a variety of water sports is normally available, but at Danau Bratan prices are geared towards

DANAU BRATAN AREA

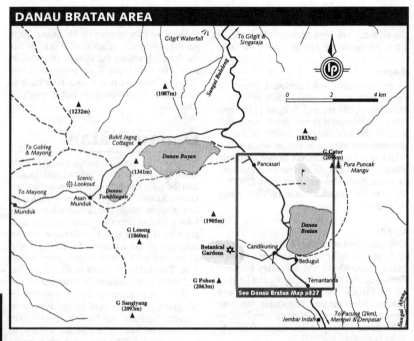

Gitgit Waterfall
To Gitgit &
Singaraja

(1087m)

(1232m)

(1833m)

Bukit Jegeg
Cottages

G Catur
(2096m)

Pura Puncak
Mangu

To Gobleg
& Mayong

Danau Buyan

Pancasari

Scenic
Lookout

(1341m)

To Mayong

Danau
Tamblingan

Asan
Munduk

Munduk

(1905m)

Danau
Bratan

G Lesong
(1860m)

Botanical
Gardens

Candikuning

Bedugul

G Pohon
(2063m)

Temantanda

See Danau Bratan Map p327

G Sangiyang
(2093m)

To Pacung (2km),
Mengwi & Denpasar

Jembar Indah

0   2   4 km

Balinese and Indonesian visitors. Paddling a rowboat across part of the lake is a wonderful experience, especially at sunrise (about 6 am). It is wise to tee this up with a boatman the day before for an 'extra fee', although you may find a boat and boatman at the gardens of the Pura Ulun Danu Bratan temple at sunrise. At the temple gardens, it costs 20,000 rp for a four person speedboat (15 minutes). A two person *sepeda air* (water bicycle) costs 7500 rp (30 minutes), and a five person rowboat with a boatman is 10,000 rp (30 minutes). The cost of a rowboat from the lane leading to the Ashram Guest House is 15,000/25,000 rp (30 minutes) without/with a boatman. The price is about the same at Bedugul.

Bedugul is the place to go for something more sophisticated, and noisy. Ignore the list of prices in US dollars on the window of the ticket office. Foreigners *can* pay local prices, which are cheap compared with Kuta and Sanur: para-sailing (22,000 rp per go); speed-boats (US$15, 30 minutes); jet-skiing (33,000 rp, 15 minutes); and water-skiing (US$10, 15 minutes).

Hiking

From the **Goa Jepang** (Japanese Cave), a well marked path ascends to the top of **Gunung Catur** (2096m). It takes about two hours from the caves (another 30 minutes if you start at Bedugul) and about one hour back down. The final bit is steep and you should take some water. At the summit, the old **Pura Puncak Mangu** temple is popular with monkeys. The Around Danau Bratan section later in this chapter has more information about local hikes. The guys at the Lila Graha Bungalows can arrange guided treks throughout the area for negotiable fees.

Golf

One of the most spectacular courses in the world must be the Bali Handara Kosaido Country Club (☎ 22646, fax 23048) near Pancasari. Green fees during the week are US$80 for 18 holes (US$95 on the weekend). To that, add club hire (US$25), caddy fees (US$9) and a golf buggy (US$25). It also offers upmarket accommodation (see Places to Stay later in this section).

BEDUGUL

Bedugul is the name of the area at the southern end of the lake, sometimes known as the Taman Rekreasi Bedugul (☎ 21197), or Bedugul Recreation Park. There's a hotel and restaurant (see Places to Stay and Places to Eat later in this section), souvenir shops and facilities for various water sports. Bedugul costs 1000 rp to enter, and 500 rp to park a car. It is open 24 hours a day.

KEBUN RAYA EYA KARYA BALI

At the intersection in Candikuning, identifiable by the enormous sculpture of a corn cob, a road (1km) leads to these botanical gardens. Established in 1959 as a branch of the national botanical gardens at Bogor, near Jakarta, they cover more than 120 hectares on the lower slopes of Gunung Pohon, and boast an extensive collection of trees and some 500 species of orchid. Some plants are labelled with their botanical names, but apart from that there is little information for visitors. But it's a lovely place – cool, shady and scenic. Usually there are very few visitors, but groups of Balinese like to come for picnics, especially on Sunday and public holidays, when the traffic can be horrendous. Tickets costs 1000 rp, and it is open from 7 am to 6 pm every day. Parking costs 200 rp for a motorbike, which for some reason cannot be taken into the park, and 500 rp for a car which can (for 3000 rp). It's best to take a long, leisurely walk around.

PURA ULUN DANU BRATAN

This Hindu/Buddhist temple was founded in the 17th century, and is dedicated to Dewi Danu – the goddess of the waters. It is the focus of ceremonies and pilgrimages to ensure the supply of water. It has classical

CENTRAL MOUNTAINS

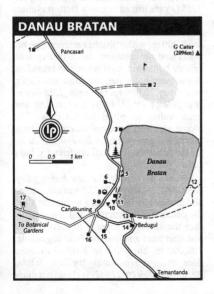

DANAU BRATAN

PLACES TO STAY
1 Pancasari Inn
2 Bali Handara Kosaido Country Club
3 Enjung Beji Resort; Wisma Beratan Indah
6 Lila Graha Bungalows
7 Ashram Guest House
13 Bedugul Hotel & Restaurant; Boat Hire
14 Bukit Strobeli (Strawberry Hill)
15 Hotel Bukit Permai
16 Pondok Wisata Dahlia Indah
17 Penginapan Cempaka; Pondok Permata Firdous

PLACES TO EAT
10 Rumah Makan Ananda
11 Bedugul Cafe

OTHER
4 Pura Ulun Danu Bratan; Boat Hire; Restoran Ulun Danu
5 Car Park; Boat Hire; Food Stalls
8 Perama Bus Stop; Sari Artha Inn
9 Candikuning Market; Wartel; Bemo Stop
12 Goa Jepang (Japanese Cave)

Hindu thatched-roof *merus* (multi-roofed shrines) and an adjoining Buddhist stupa. While you cannot enter the temple itself, it is definitely worth visiting for the surrounding, immaculate gardens, and views of the majestic, and often permanently clouded, Gunung Catur. The area is very picturesque, especially at sunrise. In the gardens, there is a restaurant (see Places to Eat later in this section) and water sports (see the Activities entry earlier in this section).

The gardens are open every day from 8.30 am to 6 pm, but if you come any time after 6 am (for the sunrise), someone will still want the entrance fee of 1000/500 for adults/children. Parking costs another 500 rp.

PLACES TO STAY

The area is a weekend getaway for wealthy Balinese, so accommodation is of indifferent quality and generally overpriced. In this cooler part of Bali, a fan is not normally provided (or needed), while hot water is often included (and welcome). Unless otherwise stated, all places include breakfast.

Pacung

There are a few places in Pacung, about 3km south along the main road towards Denpasar. The upmarket *Pacung Mountain Resort (☎ 21038)* is expensive, and the budget-priced *Jembar Indah* is noisy – you are far better off finding somewhere quiet and close to the beautiful lake.

Bedugul

Opposite the turn-off to Bedugul is *Bukit Strobeli (☎ 21265)* – also known as Strawberry Hill. It has a huddle of uninspiring, but cheap, rooms for 22,000 rp, although the noise from the main road is deafening. A little closer to the lake, *Hotel Bukit Permai (☎/fax 21445)* is away from the road and has excellent views, but it lacks some character and charm. Rooms range from 50,000 rp to 100,000 rp with the best views and TV.

In the recreation park, *Bedugul Hotel (☎ 21197, fax 21198)* has motel-style rooms and bungalows, in a good location, but without much charm, for 84,000/108,000 rp

for singles/doubles. However, regular discounts of up to 50% make this an attractive option.

Candikuning

Along the road to the botanical gardens, signs point to several cheap hotels, mostly about 100m or so off the road. *Penginapan Cempaka (☎ 21042)*, near the entrance to the gardens, has clean, quiet rooms for 25,000 to 40,000 rp. Next door, the simple *Pondok Permata Firdous (☎ 21531)* is reasonable value for 20,000 rp a double, but at that price don't expect hot water.

In the village, *Pondok Wisata Dahlia Indah (☎ 21233)*, along a lane near the road to the gardens, is a decent mid-range option, with comfortable rooms, for a negotiable 40,000 rp without breakfast. *Sari Artha Inn (☎ 21022)* costs from 15,000 to 20,000 rp for simple, and very noisy, rooms. Better bungalows, with hot water, cost 35,000 rp, but while it is further from the main road, the walls are paper thin. The Perama tourist shuttle bus stops here, so it is convenient.

The best two places are closest to the lake. *Ashram Guest House (☎ 21450, fax 21101)* gets mixed reviews from travellers and is often busy in the peak season, so book ahead. It has a range of rooms starting at 15,000 rp, with a shared bathroom, no hot water and no breakfast, to 30,000 rp with private bathroom, cold water and breakfast. If you want hot water, breakfast and views, you'll pay 70,000 rp. Opposite, *Lila Graha Bungalows (☎ 21446)* is charming and better value, but offers limited views. The rooms are clean, have real sheets and a huge bathroom, and go for 35,000/40,000 rp for singles/doubles. The staff are friendly, but a little work-shy.

Next to the temple, the new *Enjung Beji Resort (☎ 21490, fax 21022)* has many clean and pleasant cottages, and a tennis court, but the cottages lack character and few actually face the lake. All come with a colour TV, and start from a reasonable (and negotiable) 100,000 rp, but climb to 300,000 rp. Next door, and not even facing the lake, *Wisma Beratan Indah (☎ 21342)* is cheap but fairly cheerless. Rooms range from 30,000 to 60,000 rp for a family room with a TV and garage, but no views.

Pancasari

Further up north, and further up the price range, there are a few places in Pancasari, such as *Pancasari Inn* (*☎/fax 21148*), with rooms for US$42. If you are really flush with funds, you can stay at *Bali Handara Kosaido Country Club* (*☎ 22646, fax 23048*) where 'standard bungalows' start at US$91; rooms are US$121 and go as high as US$423. The attraction is obviously the golf course (see the earlier Activities section), but it also boasts a sauna, tennis court, fitness centre and traditional Japanese bath.

PLACES TO EAT

The cheapest places are the *food stalls* at the Candikuning market, and at the car park overlooking the lake, but they tend to close by about 7 pm. Naturally, there are plenty of *warungs* along the road to the botanical gardens, and outside the entrance to the gardens at Pura Ulun Danu Bratan. In Candikuning, *Rumah Makan Ananda* has the best range and prices for Indonesian food, while closer to the lake *Bedugul Cafe* has cheap snacks, cold beer and fish meals (6500 rp).

All hotels have *restaurants*, which are also open to the public. The restaurant at *Ashram Guest House* is overpriced and has a limited menu, while the restaurant at *Lili Graha Bungalows* has better prices, range and service. *Bukit Strobeli* has an excellent restaurant, and is worth the walk if you are not staying there.

Inside the temple gardens, *Restoran Ulun Danu* offers a large a la carte menu or a buffet lunch for 20,000 rp. It is a perfect place for a relaxing drink, but is not open for dinner.

Bedugul Restaurant (at the hotel of the same name) overlooks the lake and has superb views. However, the a la carte menu is deliberately limited and overpriced, so you are almost forced to take the buffet for 24,000 rp.

GETTING THERE & AWAY

The lake is on a main north-south road, so it's easy to reach from Denpasar or Singaraja, but not from anywhere else.

Bemo, Minibus & Bus

Regular bemos, minibuses and buses travel between Denpasar's Ubung terminal and the Sukasada terminal in Singaraja. They stop anywhere along the main road between Bedugul and Pancasari. To get to Ubud, you will have to change bemos in Denpasar. For Gunung Batur, get a connection in Singaraja – or walk.

Tourist Shuttle Bus

Shuttle buses, run by Perama and a few other operators, are the easiest way to the region, especially from Ubud. They start in Kuta and Sanur (7500 rp from both places), stop at Ubud (7500 rp) and continue on to Lovina (7500 rp). The Perama stop is at Sari Artha Inn in Candikuning, but the driver may drop you off anywhere between Bedugul and Pancasari if you ask nicely.

GETTING AROUND

If you're staying in Candikuning, it's walking distance to Bedugul and the temple. To anywhere else, jump on one of the frequent blue Denpasar-Singaraja bemos for about 500 rp. There isn't a recognised walking trail between the Ashram Guest House and Bedugul, but locals somehow make their way through the forest.

Around Danau Bratan

DANAU BUYAN & DANAU TAMBLINGAN

North-west of Danau Bratan are two more lakes, Buyan and Tamblingan, connected by a thin canal called Telaga Aye. Neither lake is developed like Danua Bratan. There are several tiny villages and abandoned **temples** along the shores of both lakes, but the frequently swampy ground makes it unpleasant in parts to explore.

Activities

Hiking There's a hiking trail around the southern side of Danau Buyan, then over the saddle to Tamblingan, and on to Asan Munduk, but you spend too much time in the forest and not enough admiring the lakes. The paved road, along the northern edge of the lakes towards Munduk, is better for hiking – it is flat and elevated, and parallels the lakes for about 7km, offering stunning views. Take a Denpasar-Singaraja bemo to the turn-off, wait for irregular transport to about Asan Munduk, and then walk back down to the Denpasar-Singaraja road.

The rafting outfit, Sobek (π 287059, fax 289448), organises treks through this region for US$49 per person, including transport from south Bali, and lunch.

Kayaking Sobek also organises kayaking trips across Danau Tamblingan for US$68, including transport from south Bali and a 'champagne lunch'. Either lake would be superb for kayaking or canoeing if you can hire some equipment, and have your own transport.

NORTH TO SINGARAJA

Heading north from Pancasari, the main road climbs steeply up the rim of an old volcanic crater. It's worth stopping along the way to look back at the **views** of the lakes, but beware of the monkeys which scuttle across the road. Turning right at the top will take you on a scenic descent to the coastal town of Singaraja, via Gitgit waterfalls (see the North Bali chapter).

ASAN MUNDUK & MUNDUK

To the west of the lake at Asan Munduk, you'll see a strange, stepped pyramid about 4m high. This is the **Pyramid Plastic**, one of several art installations in the area. It is in fact made of melted down plastic waste, partly as a statement about the environmental problems plastic has caused on Bali.

If you turn left at this junction, a trail leads to near Danau Tamblingan, among forest and market gardens. Turning right takes you along beautiful winding roads to Munduk

(see the Central Mountains map). Two kilometres before Munduk, a sign points to a 500m path leading to a pretty **waterfall**, one of many in the area.

There's archaeological evidence of a developed community in the Munduk region between the 10th and 14th centuries, and accounts of the first Majapahit emissaries to visit the area. When the Dutch took control of north Bali in the 1890s, they experimented with commercial crops, establishing plantations for coffee, vanilla, cloves and cocoa. Quite a few old Dutch buildings are still intact along the road in Munduk and further west, and there are some **Bali Aga villages** in the region.

Hiking

The 'environmental trekking centre' at Puri Lumbung Cottages offers a series of two to three hour hikes to nearby coffee plantations, waterfalls and villages, as well as around Tamblingan and Buyan lakes. Fees for the guides seem to be fairly relaxed, and often up to the hiker, but about 15,000 rp per hour seems to be the standard fee for a local guide who speaks good English, plus transport costs.

Places to Stay & Eat

On the road to Munduk, the new *Bukit Jegeg Cottages* (π/fax 0361-239895 in Denpasar) is luxurious and spacious, although the cottages amazingly don't face the lakes at all. Standard rooms cost US$58, and family suites US$109; the cottages are new, so discounts are definitely possible.

Puri Lumbung Cottages (π/fax 92810), on the right side of the road as you enter Munduk from Bedugul, is co-run by the local community. It can provide hiking information and guides, a yoga teacher, a meditation centre and traditional healer. It's a delightful place to stay, and has well finished, thatched bungalows for US$60/66/97 for singles/doubles/family rooms, including breakfast. *Warung Kopi Bali* restaurant in the hotel has a wonderful outlook and serves an excellent lunch or dinner, with main courses starting from around 8000 rp.

The other charming option is one of the seven spotless, renovated Dutch villas run by *Penginapan Guru Ratna (☎ 92812, fax 92810)* and Puri Lumbung Cottages. Prices (including breakfast) range from 40,000 rp per double, with a shared bathroom, to US $24 for a mini-home, with a kitchen large enough for a family. The prices are high, but this is a lovely village, and the managers are helpful and friendly. The meals (about 10,000 rp) have been described by readers as a real 'Balinese feast'. If this is too dear, ask around the village for a room in other former *Dutch villas* for 20,000 rp per person.

Getting There & Away

There is no public transport to Munduk, but if you take the Denpasar-Singaraja bemo to the turn-off and wait, something will come along. From Seririt (see the North Lombok chapter), transport is even more scarce. You may have to charter a bemo from Candikuning for about 15,000/25,000 one way/return. If you're driving to or from the north coast, a pretty good road west of Munduk goes through a number of picturesque villages to Mayong, then down to the sea at Seririt.

PELAGA & PETANG

A scenic road heads north from Ubud, via Sangeh and Petang, and finishes at the pretty village of Pelaga. Pelaga holds infrequent bull races, and is a wonderful place for **hiking** to Danau Bratan and Gunung Catur. The **views** from Petang of Gunung Agung are glorious, and there is **swimming** in nearby rivers, plus hiking.

In Pelaga village, *Pondok Wana Plaga (☎ 702218)* is a delightful place – prices were not available at the time of research, but it should cost about US$10 per person. In Petang, you can stay at an unnamed *losmen (☎ 232550)*, just outside the village, for US$20 per person, including three delicious meals. There are occasional bemos up this road all the way from Wangaya terminal in Denpasar (1300 rp), but it's best with your own transport. With some directions, you could walk (about 8km) from Bedugul to Pelaga.

GUNUNG BATUKAU

West of the Mengwi-Bedugul-Singaraja road rises Gunung Batukau (2276m), the 'coconut-shell mountain'. This is the third of Bali's three major mountains and the holy peak of the western end of the island.

If you want to climb it, you'll need a guide because there are many false trails and it's easy to get lost. From the temple, a guide will cost from 70,000 to 100,000 rp. It takes about five or six hours to the top, and four hours to get down, through quite thick forest. If you want to get to the top before the mist rolls in, you'll need a tent and spend a night near the summit. Alternatively, arrange a guide at Candikuning or Munduk, and leave at about 2 or 3 am.

Pura Luhur Batukau

On the slopes of Batukau, this was the state temple when Tabanan was an independent kingdom. It has a seven roofed meru to Maha Dewa, the mountain's guardian spirit, as well as shrines for the three mountain lakes: Bratan, Buyan and Tamblingan. It's surrounded by forest, and often damp and misty.

There are several routes to the temple, but none of the roads is particularly high class – it's a remote place. The most straightforward way is to follow the road north from Tabanan to Wangayagede, the last village before the temple.

Jatuluih

For an alternative route to Pura Luhur Batukau, turn off the Mengwi-Singaraja road, south of Pacung, and follow the rough road to Senganankaninan. From there, an even rougher road goes in a westerly direction to Wangayagede, via Jatuluih. The name Jatuluih means 'truly marvellous', and the view truly is – it takes in a huge chunk of south Bali.

ROUTES VIA PUPUAN

The two most popular routes between the south and north coast are the roads via Kintamani and Bedugul, but there are two other routes to cross the mountains. Both branch north from the Denpasar to Gilimanuk road, one from Pulukan and the other from Antasari, and meet at Pupuan before dropping down to Seririt, west of Lovina. Both are accessible by bemo, but there is nowhere to stay along the way.

The Pulukan-Pupuan road climbs steeply up from the coast providing fine views back down to the sea. The route runs through spice-growing country. At one point, the narrow and winding road actually runs right through an enormous *bunut* tree, a type of ficus, which bridges the road. Further on,

the road spirals down to Pupuan through some of Bali's most beautiful rice terraces. It is worth stopping off at the magnificent **waterfall** at Pujungan, which is a few kilometres south of Pupuan.

The road from Antasari starts through rice paddies, climbs into the spice-growing country, and then descends through the coffee plantations to Pupuan. If you continue 12km or so towards the north coast you reach Mayong, where you can turn east to Munduk and on to Tamblingan and Buyan lakes.

North Bali

North Bali, the district of Buleleng, makes an interesting contrast with the south of the island. The Lovina beaches are popular with budget travellers, and boast a large variety of places to stay and eat, but nothing like the chaos of the Kuta region. Many travellers coming from Java go straight from Gilimanuk to the north coast, rather than taking the south-coast road which would leave them in Denpasar or, horror of horrors, Kuta.

Buleleng has a strong artistic and cultural tradition. Its dance troupes are highly regarded and a number of dance styles have originated here, including Janger. Gold and silver work, weaving, pottery, instrument making and temple design all show distinctive local styles. The Sapi Gerumbungan is a bull race in which style is as important as speed. This is a Buleleng tradition, and quite different from the races of Negara in south-west Bali.

Events are held at villages near Lovina, on Independence Day (August 17), Singaraja Day (March 31) and other occasions.

HISTORY

The north coast has been subject to European influence for a long time. Having first encountered Balinese troops on Java in the 18th century, the Dutch became the main purchasers of Balinese slaves. Many slaves served in the Dutch East India Company armies.

Various Balinese kings provided the Dutch with soldiers, but in the 1840s, disputes over shipwreck salvage, together with fears that other European powers might establish themselves on Bali, prompted the Dutch to make treaties with a number of the Balinese rajahs. However, the treaties proved ineffective, the plundering continued apace and disputes arose with Buleleng's rajah.

During 1845, the rajahs of Buleleng and Karangasem formed an alliance, possibly to conquer other Balinese states or, equally possibly, to resist the Dutch. In any case, the Dutch became worried and attacked Buleleng and Karangasem in 1846, 1848 and 1849, seizing control of north Bali on the third attempt.

SINGARAJA

With a population of around 100,000, Singaraja (which means Lion King) is Bali's second-largest city, but it's orderly – even quiet – compared with Denpasar. With its pleasant tree lined streets and some interesting Dutch colonial houses, it is not unlike Ambon, the capital of the Maluku Province. You can stay in Singaraja, but most people come on a day trip from Lovina.

Singaraja was the centre of Dutch power on Bali and remained as the administrative centre for the Lesser Sunda Islands (Bali through to Timor) until 1953. It is one of the few places on Bali where there are visible reminders of the Dutch period, but there are also Chinese and Muslim influences. The port of Singaraja was for years the usual arrival point for visitors to Bali – it's where all the prewar travel books started. Ironically, some early travel writers complained it was too commercial and found south Bali much less developed.

Singaraja today is a major educational and cultural centre, and its two university campuses provide the city with a substantial student population. The 'suburb' of Beratan, south of Singaraja, is the silver-work centre of north Bali, and a few workshops in and around Singaraja also produce hand-woven sarongs – especially *songket*, woven with silver or gold threads.

Orientation & Information

The main commercial areas are in the northeast part of town (immediately south of Buleleng harbour) and along Jl Pramuka and Jl Ngurah Rai. Most hotels, restaurants and offices of bus companies are along Jl Jen Achmed Yani. Traffic does a few complicated one way loops around town, but it's easy enough to get around on foot or by bemo.

The main banks will change money, as will the moneychanger on Jl Pramuka.

The tourist office (☎ 25141), on the corner of Jl Veteran and Jl Gajah Mada, is reasonably helpful. If you are exploring the north coast in depth, it's certainly worth picking up their excellent, free booklet *Discover the Sights & Sounds of Buleleng*.

The largest hospital in north Bali is the RSUP Umum (☎ 22046), and there is a major police station (☎ 41510). There are several *wartels* (public telephone offices) along the main streets, and an inconvenient Telkom office on Jl Udayana.

Pelabuhan Buleleng

Buleleng port, just north of Jl Erlangga, is an interesting area to walk around. Singaraja is rarely used as a harbour these days, because it has little protection from bad weather, and the provincial capital (that is, Denpasar) was transferred to the south of the island. Shipping for the north coast now uses the port at Celukanbawang, and visiting cruise ships anchor at Padangbai.

The conspicuous **Yudha Mandala Tama**

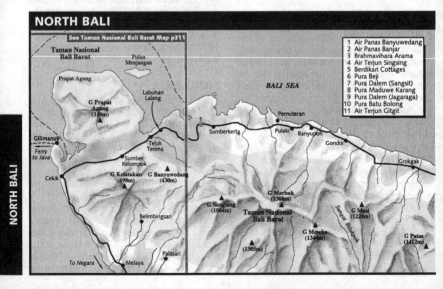

NORTH BALI

See Taman Nasional Bali Barat Map p311

1 Air Panas Banyuwedang
2 Air Panas Banjar
3 Brahmavihara Arama
4 Air Terjun Singsing
5 Berdikari Cottages
6 Pura Beji
7 Pura Dalem (Sangsit)
8 Pura Maduwe Karang
9 Pura Dalem (Jagaraga)
10 Pura Batu Bolong
11 Air Terjun Gitgit

Taman Nasional Bali Barat
Pulau Menjangan
Prapat Agung
G Prapat Agung (310m)
Labuhan Lalang
Gilimanuk
Ferry to Java
Teluk Terima
Sumber Kelompok
Cekik
G Kelatakan (698m)
G Banyuwedang (430m)
Belimbingsari
Palasari
To Negara
Melaya

BALI SEA
Pemuteran
Sumberkerta
Pulaki
Banyupoh
Gondoi
Grokgak
G Merbuk (1388m)
G Sangiang (1004m)
Taman Nasional Bali Barat
G Musi (1224m)
Sungai Blukbuk
G Mesehe (1344m)
G Patas (1412m)
(1305m)

monument commemorates a freedom fighter who was killed by gunfire from a Dutch warship early in the struggle for independence. Close by, there's a colourful **Chinese temple**.

Gedong Kirtya Library

Tourists are welcome to visit this small historical library (☎ 22645), next to the tourist office, but it's of more interest to scholars. It opens from 7 am to 2 pm, Monday to Thursday, and closes a little earlier on Friday and Saturday. A donation is requested.

Pura Jagat Natha

Singaraja's main temple, and the largest in north Bali, this is impressively large. It is not usually open to foreigners, but you can appreciate its majesty – and admire the elaborate carved stone decorations – from the outside.

Places to Stay

There are a number of places to stay, but many tourists go straight to the beaches at Lovina, only a few kilometres away. Most hotels cater for Indonesian business people,

so they are located along noisy main roads and have squat-style toilets and a *mandi*. All places include breakfast.

Along Jl Jen Achmed Yani, *Hotel Sentral* (*☎ 21896)* is OK for 15,000 rp a room; *Hotel Duta Karya (☎ 21467)* is slightly better for

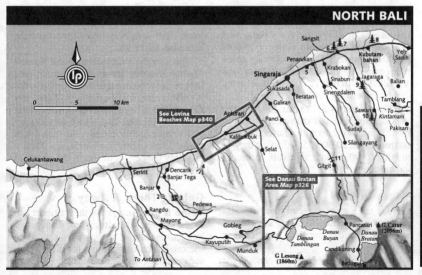

NORTH BALI

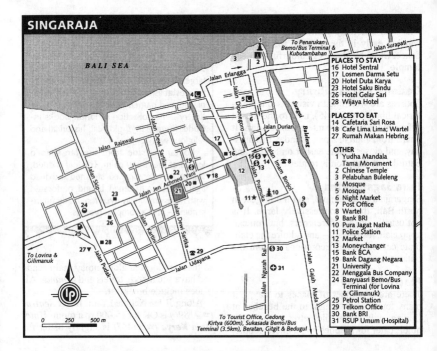

SINGARAJA

BALI SEA

To Penarukan
Bemo/Bus Terminal &
Kubutambahan

PLACES TO STAY
16 Hotel Sentral
17 Losmen Darma Setu
20 Hotel Duta Karya
23 Hotel Saku Bindu
26 Hotel Gelar Sari
28 Wijaya Hotel

PLACES TO EAT
14 Cafetaria Sari Rosa
18 Cafe Lima Lima; Wartel
27 Rumah Makan Hebring

OTHER
1 Yudha Mandala
  Tama Monument
2 Chinese Temple
3 Pelabuhan Buleleng
4 Mosque
5 Mosque
6 Night Market
7 Post Office
8 Wartel
9 Bank BRI
10 Pura Jagat Natha
11 Police Station
12 Market
13 Moneychanger
15 Bank BCA
19 Bank Dagang Negara
21 University
22 Menggala Bus Company
24 Banyuasri Bemo/Bus
  Terminal (for Lovina
  & Gilimanuk)
25 Petrol Station
29 Telkom Office
30 Bank BRI
31 RSUP Umum (Hospital)

To Lovina &
Gilimanuk

0   250   500 m

To Tourist Office, Gedong
Kirtya (600m), Sukasada Bemo/Bus
Terminal (3.5km), Beratan, Gitgit & Bedugul

17,500/20,000 rp for singles/doubles, or 35,000/40,000 rp with air-con; and *Hotel Saku Bindu* (☎ *21791*) and *Hotel Gelar Sari* (☎ *21495*) are reasonable value for 15,000/20,000 rp. The only place to offer any peace in this area is the basic *Losmen Darma Setu* (☎ *23200*) for 10,000/12,000 rp. Look for the sign from the main road.

Wijaya Hotel (☎ *21915, fax 25817*) is the most comfortable and convenient place in town. Standard rooms with a fan and outside bathroom cost 20,000/25,000 rp, or they're 60,000/65,000 rp with a private bathroom and air-con.

Places to Eat
There is not a great range of places in Singaraja; you are better off taking a 10 minute bemo ride to one of the many restaurants in Lovina.

In the evening, there are *food stalls* in the night market on Jl Durian, and during the day at the main market on Jl Jen Achmed Yani. There are always *warungs* around the bemo/bus terminals.

Opposite the Wijaya Hotel, the *Rumah Makan Hebring* serves cheap, traditional Indonesian food in a family atmosphere, but it's often not open in the evenings. *Cafe Lima Lima* is one of three places in a huddle along Jalan Jen Achmed Yani which serve cheap and unmemorable Indonesian meals and seafood, but no beer. *Cafetaria Sari Rosa* is probably the best of the lot in the centre of town.

Getting There & Away
Bemo & Bus Singaraja is the transport hub for the northern coast. It has three main bemo/bus terminals, and knowing which one to use can be confusing. From the main Sukasada terminal, on the southern side of town,

minibuses go to Denpasar (Ubung terminal) via Bedugul about every 30 minutes from 6 am to 4 pm (3400 rp); and to Semarapura (Klungkung) (3000 rp) via Kintamani. There is also a tiny bemo stop, next to the *puskesmas* (community health centre) in Sukasada, with services to Gitgit.

Closer in from the Banyuasri terminal, buses and minibuses leave for Gilimanuk (2700 rp) and Seririt, and buses go to Denpasar (Ubung terminal) about every 20 minutes. From this terminal, plenty of blue bemos also go to Lovina.

Finally, from the Penarukan terminal, a couple of kilometres east of town, bemos go to Yeh Sanih (800 rp) and Amlapura (2500 rp) via the coastal road; and buses go to Denpasar (Batubulan terminal), via Amlapura or Kintamani, for 3500 rp.

Java From Singaraja, several bus companies have overnight services to Surabaya on Java, so you can bypass Denpasar and the rest of south Bali if you want. Many travel agencies along the western end of Jl Jen Achmed Yani sell bus tickets. One of the more reliable bus companies is Menggala (☎ 24374), which charges 28,500 rp to Surabaya.

Tourist Shuttle Bus All of the shuttle buses going to Lovina from south Bali, whether via the east coast, Bedugul or Kintamani, can drop you off in Singaraja – refer to Getting There & Away in the Lovina section later in this chapter for more details.

Getting Around
Plenty of bemos link the three main bemo/bus terminals, and hurtle along all main roads in between. The bemos are all well signed and colour-coded, and cost about 500 rp for a ride anywhere around town. The green Banyuasri-Sukasada bemo goes along Jl Gajah Mada to the tourist office; and this bemo, as well as the brown one between Penarukan and Banyuasri terminals, also goes along Jl Jen Achmed Yani. For shorter trips, take a *dokar* (pony cart). There are also plenty of *ojeks* (paying pillion passenger on a motorbike) around the place.

AROUND SINGARAJA
Interesting sites around Singaraja include some of Bali's best known temples. The north-coast sandstone is very soft and easily carved, allowing local sculptors to give free rein to their imaginations. You'll find some delightfully whimsical scenes carved into a number of the temples here.

Although the basic architecture of the temples is similar in both north and south Bali, there are some important differences. The inner courtyards of southern temples usually house a number of multi-roofed shrines *(merus)* together with other structures, whereas in the north, everything is grouped on a single pedestal. On the pedestal you'll usually find 'houses' for the deities to use on their earthly visits; they're also used to store important religious relics.

Sangsit
A few kilometres east of Singaraja (see the North Bali map), you can see an excellent example of the colourful architectural style of north Bali. Sangsit's **Pura Beji** is a *subak* temple, dedicated to the goddess Dewi Sri who looks after irrigated rice fields. The sculptured panels along the front wall set the tone with their Disneyland-like demons and amazing *nagas* (mythological serpents). The inside also has a variety of sculptures covering every available space, and the courtyard is shaded by a frangipani tree. It's about 500m off the main road towards the coast.

Pura Dalem shows scenes of punishment in the afterlife, and other pictures which are humorous and sometimes erotic. It's in the rice fields, about 500m north-east of Pura Beji.

The best accommodation option is the nearby **Berdikari Cottages** (☎ 25195), where a huge range of decent rooms range from 25,000 to 125,000 rp.

All forms of public transport between Singaraja's Penarukan terminal and Amlapura stop at Sangsit, and at the hotel.

Jagaraga

It was the capture of the local rajah's stronghold at Jagaraga that marked the arrival of Dutch power on Bali in 1849. The village, which is a few kilometres south of the main road, has an interesting **Pura Dalem** (see the North Bali map). The small temple has delightful sculptured panels along its front wall, both inside and out. On the outer wall look for a vintage car driving sedately past, a steamer at sea and even an aerial dogfight between early aircraft. Jagaraga is also famous for its Legong troupe, said to be the best in north Bali, but performances are irregular. Regular bemos from the Penarukan terminal in Singaraja stop at Jagaraga on the way to Sawan.

Sawan

Several kilometres inland from Jagaraga, Sawan is a centre for the manufacture of gamelan gongs and gamelan instruments. You can see the gongs being cast and the intricately carved gamelan frames being made. The strange looking **Pura Batu Bolong** is also worth a look (see the North Bali map). Around Sawan, there's **cold water springs** that are believed to cure all sorts of illnesses. Regular bemos travel from Penarukan terminal in Singaraja to Sawan.

Kubutambahan

About 1km east of the turn-off to Kintamani is **Pura Maduwe Karang** (Temple of the Land Owner – see the North Bali map). Like Pura Beji at Sangsit, the temple is dedicated to agricultural spirits, but this one looks after unirrigated land.

This is one of the best temples in north Bali and is particularly noted for its sculptured panels, including the famous bicycle panel depicting a gentleman riding a bicycle with flower petals for wheels. The cyclist may be WOJ Nieuwenkamp, a Dutch artist who, in 1904, probably brought the first bicycle to Bali. It's on the base of the main plinth in the inner enclosure, and there are other panels worth inspecting.

The temple is easy to find in the village. Kubutambahan is on the road between Singaraja and Amlapura, and there are regular bemos and buses.

Yeh Sanih

About 15km east of Singaraja, Yeh Sanih (also called Air Sanih) is a popular spot where freshwater springs are channelled into some pleasant swimming pools before flowing into the sea. The area is attractively laid out with pleasant gardens and a restaurant. Admission to the springs and pool is 450/250 rp for adults/children, and it is open from 8 am to 6 pm every day. The inevitable hotels, restaurants and warungs stretch along the main road for about 2km east of the springs.

Places to Stay & Eat Some visitors may want to stay here if Lovina appears too crowded. In any case, Yeh Sanih is a great place for a meal, especially after a swim.

The first place on your right, as you come from Singaraja, is *Puri Rena Restaurant & Bungalows* (☎ 26589). It has quiet singles/doubles in a lovely garden on a hill for 15,000/25,000 rp, including breakfast. The *restaurant* is secluded and has great views.

Across the road, the *Puri Sanih Bungalows* (☎ 23508) has a picturesque *restaurant* in the gardens, overlooking the pools, and two sets of bungalows nearby. The cheaper ones are closer to the pools, and the main road, and cost 20,000 rp, while the better ones have views, huge beds and tranquillity for 55,000 rp.

About 300m further to the east, the two charming and luxurious bungalows at *Cilik's Beach Garden* (☎/fax 26567) are attractively laid out in a lovely, quiet garden. They cost US$55/70, including breakfast. Just over the road, *Puri Rahayu Bungalows & Restaurant* (☎ 26565) is noisy, but pleasant and friendly. Bungalows with a fan cost 25,000 rp, or it's 50,000 rp with air-con.

More hotels are springing up further east, but they're too far from the springs.

Getting There & Away Yeh Sanih is on the main road along the north coast. It's an easy trip with your own vehicle; and frequent public transport from Singaraja (800 rp) to Amlapura stops outside the gardens.

Gitgit

About 11km south of Singaraja, is the pretty, and pretty touristy, **Air Terjun Gitgit** waterfalls. The well signposted path (800m) from the main road in the village is predictably lined with souvenir stalls, but the workers are quite friendly. The 40m waterfalls are quite pretty, and a great place for a picnic, but they are not pristine. You buy a ticket (1100/600 rp for adults/children) about half way down the path.

There is another small waterfall, sometimes called **Gitgit Multi-Tier Waterfall**, about 2km further up the hill from the main falls, and about 600m off the main road. It is not as impressive, but is wonderfully devoid of hawkers and touts, and you can swim here. There is no entrance fee, but a donation is expected. This area is being developed, so it may become more touristy.

Places to Stay & Eat Opposite the path to Air Terjun Gitgit falls, *Gitgit Hotel & Restaurant* (☎ 26212, fax 41840) has clean, uninteresting and overpriced rooms from 50,000 rp. The *restaurant* is also way overpriced. It's cheaper, and more atmospheric, to eat at one of the *warungs* along the path to the main falls.

Getting There & Away Regular buses and minibuses travel between the main Sukasada terminal in Singaraja and Denpasar (Ubung terminal), via Bedugul, and stop at Gitgit. More regular, and direct, bemos to Gitgit (700 rp) also leave from outside the puskesmas in Sukasada (see the previous Singaraja section for details). Let the driver know where you want to get off, because he may speed through the village and miss the paths. Gitgit is also a major stopoff on tours of north and central Bali.

LOVINA

West of Singaraja is a string of coastal villages – Pantai Happy (Tukad Mungga), Anturan, Kalibukbuk and Temukus – which have become a popular beach resort collectively known as Lovina. There are plenty of shops, bars, hotels and other tourist facilities, but the place isn't totally overrun (yet?) by tourist developments and, surprisingly, rice paddies still dominate the area. Visitors may be hassled by people wanting to sell dolphin and snorkelling trips and sarongs, but they don't sell as hard as they do in the Kuta region. Lovina is a convenient base for trips around the north coast, a good place to meet other travellers, and there's a bit of nightlife if you look hard.

The sand is black and volcanic, not like the white stuff found in the south. The beaches are also thin and don't offer much privacy, but it's mostly clean and fine to walk along (but where there are no hotels, the beaches are quite scruffy). There is no surf – a reef keeps it calm most of the time. The sunsets are as spectacular as those in the Kuta region, and as the sky reddens, the lights of the fishing boats appear as bright dots across the horizon. Earlier in the afternoon, at fishing villages like Anturan, you can see *prahus* (outriggers) being prepared for the night's fishing.

Orientation

It's hard to know where one village ends and the next one begins, but the signposts along the main road indicating the location of the various hotels and restaurants are good landmarks. The tourist area stretches out over about 8km, but the main focus of Lovina is Kalibukbuk, 10.5km west of Singaraja.

Information

The tourist office, which shares the same premises as the police station, is not worth visiting: it has a poor map of Lovina on the wall, and staff offer limited information. There are plenty of moneychangers around Lovina; their rates are better than the solitary bank.

The main post office is inconvenient for most visitors, but postal agencies and wartels are dotted along the main road.

Spice Dive Centre (spicedive@singaraja. wasantara.net.id) runs an Internet service for a reasonable 500 rp per minute. The friendly people at the nearby Warung Karma (karma@singaraja.wasantara.net.id) also have an Internet service.

Cruises

Dolphin trips are Lovina's special tourist attraction – so much so that a large concrete statue has been erected in honour of the overtouted cetaceans. There is no evidence that the dolphins are harmed by the attention, but there is some suggestion that boats have to go further and further to see fewer dolphins. Some days, no dolphins are sighted, but about 80% of the time you'll see at least a few.

At times, tourists are hassled by touts selling dolphin trips, but the problem seems to vary depending on the season. It is best to buy a ticket the day before; your hotel is as good a place as any. The price of a trip is supposedly fixed at 15,000 rp per person by a boat-owners' cartel, but competition is often so intense that discounts are possible. Some operators will give a refund of 50% if you don't see dolphins; others offer break-fast and/or tea or coffee on the boat – but some readers have reported being ripped off with these 'offers'.

One local outfit offers glass-bottom boat trips (90 minutes), so you can see some fine coral without getting wet. They cost about 18,000 rp per person, and leave from Kalibukbuk. During the peak season, there's also an expensive dinner cruise. Get your tickets from your hotel or any of the shops-cum-travel agencies around Lovina.

Snorkelling

Generally, the water is clear and the reef is good for snorkelling. It's not the best coral you'll find, but it's not bad and reaching it is very easy. In many places you can simply swim out from the beach, or get a boat to take you out; the boatman should know where the best coral is. Various organised snorkelling tours are available from your hotel or the travel agencies. They cost about 25,000 rp per person (minimum of two) for a half-day trip, including transport. The best time to go snorkelling from the beach is before 11 am.

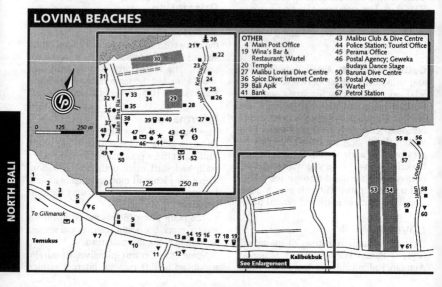

LOVINA BEACHES

OTHER
4 Main Post Office
19 Wina's Bar & Restaurant; Wartel
20 Temple
27 Malibu Lovina Dive Centre
36 Spice Dive; Internet Centre
39 Bali Apik
41 Bank
43 Malibu Club & Dive Centre
44 Police Station; Tourist Office
45 Perama Office
46 Postal Agency; Geweka Budaya Dance Stage
50 Baruna Dive Centre
51 Postal Agency
64 Wartel
67 Petrol Station

To Gilimanuk

Temukus

Kalibukbuk

See Enlargement

Full snorkelling gear can be rented from numerous shops along the main streets of Kalibukbuk, and possibly from your hotel, for about 10,000 rp per day. Scuba diving agencies may charge as much as US$3 for two hours.

Diving

Scuba diving on the local reef is nothing special, but it's a good area for beginners. Local diving operators do trips to other sites in the area, particularly Pulau Menjangan island, off the north-west coast, and Tulamben or Amed to the east. As always, it's wise to check the qualifications of the instructor or dive master, as well the equipment, before you sign up.

Costs don't vary much between the reliable operators, but in the off season prices are more negotiable. For two dives, including transport, expect to pay about US$45 around Lovina (US$30 for one local night dive); US$60 around Amed or Tulamben; and at least US$60 as far as Pulau Menjangan. The three most reputable and long-running operators in Lovina also run introduction and

PADI certificate courses. They are: Baruna Dive Centre (☎ 41084), one of the branches of a well regarded Bali-wide company; Malibu Lovina Dive Centre (☎/fax 41225) and the associated Malibu Dive Centre (☎ 41310); and Spice Dive Centre (☎ 41305, email spicedive@singaraja.wasantara.net.id), which has a very good reputation.

Water Sports

Baruna Dive Centre can also organise all sorts of expensive water sports, including parasailing (US$10 per go), windsurfing (US$10, one hour), water-skiing (US$20, 15 minutes) and jet-skiing (US$20, 15 minutes).

Courses

An interesting diversion is the Lovina cooking course held at the popular Adjani's Restaurant (see the Places to Eat entry later in this section). It offers private, two hour classes (in English), including shopping at the morning market, for 40,000 to 80,000 rp, depending on the meals. You can then sample the results with friends at the restaurant afterwards.

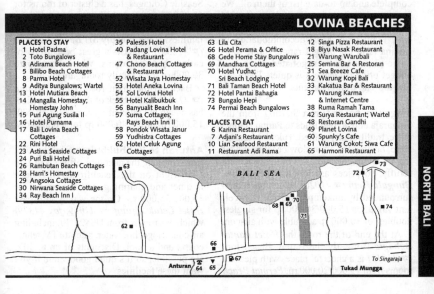

LOVINA BEACHES

PLACES TO STAY
1 Hotel Padma
2 Toto Bungalows
3 Adirama Beach Hotel
5 Billibo Beach Cottages
8 Parma Hotel
9 Aditya Bungalows; Wartel
13 Hotel Mutiara Beach
14 Mangalla Homestay; Homestay John
15 Puri Agung Susila II
16 Hotel Purnama
17 Bali Lovina Beach Cottages
22 Rini Hotel
23 Astina Seaside Cottages
24 Puri Bali Hotel
26 Rambutan Beach Cottages
28 Harri's Homestay
29 Angsoka Cottages
30 Nirwana Seaside Cottages
34 Ray Beach Inn I

35 Palestis Hotel
40 Padang Lovina Hotel & Restaurant
47 Chono Beach Cottages & Restaurant
52 Wisata Jaya Homestay
53 Hotel Aneka Lovina
54 Sol Lovina Hotel
55 Hotel Kalibukbuk
56 Banyualit Beach Inn
57 Suma Cottages; Rays Beach Inn II
58 Pondok Wisata Janur
59 Yudhistra Cottages
62 Hotel Celuk Agung Cottages

63 Lila Cita
66 Hotel Perama & Office
68 Gede Home Stay Bungalows
69 Mandhara Cottages
70 Hotel Yudha; Sri Beach Lodging
71 Bali Taman Beach Hotel
72 Hotel Pantai Bahagia
73 Bungalo Hepi
74 Permai Beach Bungalows

PLACES TO EAT
6 Karina Restaurant
7 Adjani's Restaurant
10 Lian Seafood Restaurant
11 Restaurant Adi Rama

12 Singa Pizza Restaurant
18 Biyu Nasak Restaurant
21 Warung Warubali
25 Semina Bar & Restoran
31 Sea Breeze Cafe
32 Warung Kopi Bali
33 Kakatua Bar & Restaurant
37 Warung Karma & Internet Centre
42 Surya Restaurant; Wartel
48 Restoran Gandhi
49 Planet Lovina
60 Spunky's Cafe
61 Warung Cokot; Siwa Cafe
65 Harmoni Restaurant

■ 63

■ 73

72 ■

BALI SEA

68 ■ 70
69 ■
71

■ 74

62 ■

66
■

■ 67

Anturan ☎ ▼
64 65

To Singaraja

Tukad Mungga

NORTH BALI

Organised Tours

While it may seems touristy and a bit rushed, the most effective way of maximising your time is to take one of the many organised tours around north and central Bali. Prices range from 20,000 to 35,000 rp per person (minimum of two) and can take in such attractions as Gitgit, Bedugul, the hot water springs and Buddhist temple at Banjar, Yeh Sanih and, possibly, Kintamani. You can buy tickets at any of the shops-cum-travel agencies around the streets.

Lovina and Singaraja are also stopoffs on organised day tours from south Bali – refer to the Organised Tours section in the Bali Getting Around chapter.

Places to Stay

The first hotel is only about 6km from Singaraja; the last is about 8km further west. During peak times (July to August and December to January) accommodation may be tight and prices higher – sometimes even double the prices listed here. Generally, the cheapest places are away from the beach.

There's so many places along the Lovina Beach strip that it's impossible to give a complete and up-to-date list of them all. We have tried to include places that are good value, close to the beach and away from the busy main road. Most accommodation in Lovina is in the budget range. Some mid-range places can be negotiated down to a budget price if business is quiet. There are few top-end establishments.

Singaraja to Anturan Starting from the Singaraja end, a road leads to Pantai Happy, more traditionally called Tukad Mungga. Here, business is often slow because it's far from Kalibukbuk and parts of the beach are scruffy, so prices are low and negotiable. *Bungalo Hepi* (☎ 41020), which has a pool surrounded by unkempt gardens, is excellent value for 15,000/30,000 rp for singles/doubles, or 30,000 rp a double with air-con.

At the end of the road, the *Hotel Pantai Bahagia* (formerly the Happy Beach Inn) (☎ 41017) is a cheerful place, with pleasant rooms from 15,000/20,000 rp. *Permai Beach Bungalows* (☎ 41471, fax 41224) has a nice setting and a pool. The rooms are normally expensive – 50,000/70,000 rp with fan/air-con – but these prices are often negotiable, especially if you use their diving centre.

Facing the main road, but extending out to the beach, is the upmarket *Bali Taman Beach Hotel* (☎ 41126, fax 41840). It's small but attractive, and has a pool and nice gardens. Prices range from US$13/17 for a room with a fan to US$125 for a luxurious family suite – good value in this range.

Anturan Continuing west, a turn-off leads to this scruffy little fishing village, which now has an excess of places to stay. Most of the rooms and bungalows are crowded together, but it is a popular spot (probably because there's a Perama tourist shuttle bus office just up the road).

Gede Home Stay Bungalows (☎ 41526) is friendly and popular, and has small rooms from 15,000 rp, plus some better ones with hot water for 30,000 rp. *Mandhara Cottages* (☎ 41476) has a good location and decent rooms for 50,000 rp. *Hotel Yudha* (☎ 41183, fax 41160), formerly known as Simon's Seaside Cottages, has a cluster of rooms for 50,000/55,000 rp, which seems a lot as there is no pool. Recommended, especially for families, is the friendly *Sri Beach Lodging* (☎ 42235). It boasts a great beachfront location, but the rooms, which cost up to 30,000 rp for a family room, are small.

Back on the main road, *Hotel Perama* (☎ 41161), at the back of the Perama office, has cheap but unexciting rooms for 10,000/15,000 rp, or it's 40,000 rp for a bungalow.

Anturan to Kalibukbuk Continuing west from Anturan, the next turn-off leads to *Lila Cita*, right on the beachfront. This place is quiet and charming, and has rooms for 15,000/25,000 rp. On the way, you'll pass *Hotel Celuk Agung* (☎ 41039, fax 41379) which has rooms from US$25/30, including air-con, fridge, hot water, satellite TV, tennis courts and a pool. Discounts of up to 30% are possible, so it's quite good value if you want these facilities.

Jl Loviana has about a dozen hotels, and is a good place to look around for something suitable. The pleasant *Hotel Kalibukbuk* (☎ 41701) has rooms from 35,000 rp with fan, and 50,000 rp with air-con. One reader was mugged in the hotel, but hopefully this was a one-off occurrence. Back from the beach, the *Banyualit Beach Inn* (☎ 417889, fax 41563) has a pool, plus fan-cooled doubles for 30,000 rp, cottages with air-con for 65,000 rp, and a range of options in between.

Other budget places along this road include: *Yudhistra Cottages* (☎ 41552), with rooms set around a pleasant garden, for 15,000 rp with a fan and 35,000 rp with air-con and hot water; the friendly and quiet *Suma Cottages* for a negotiable 25,000/30,000 rp; *Rays Beach Inn II* (☎ 41088), with a bit more space than Suma's, for 25,000 rp; and the *Pondok Wisata Janur* (☎ 41056), with a small cluster of rooms for 15,000/20,000 rp.

The only two upmarket places in Lovina are along this part of the main road, but extend back to the beach. *Sol Lovina Hotel* (☎ 41775, fax 41659) has all the luxuries, and a huge swimming pool. Standard rooms cost from US$100/110, and go much, much higher for the presidential suite. Next door, the *Hotel Aneka Lovina* (☎/fax 23827) has similar facilities, a huge pool in a lovely garden, and rooms from US$85/95.

Kalibukbuk A little over 10km from Singaraja, the 'centre' of Lovina is the village of Kalibukbuk. Many visitors choose to stay here because it is convenient and central.

Down Jl Ketepang, *Rambutan Beach Cottages* (☎ 41388, fax 41057) has a swimming pool set in charming gardens, but there is little that is authentically 'Balinese' about the place. It offers 'budget' singles/doubles/triples for US$10/12/17, or US$20/20/25 with hot water. It is recommended for families. At *Puri Bali Hotel* (☎ 41485), all the rooms have hot water and cost a negotiable 40,000 rp with fan, or 100,000 rp with air-con.

Close to the beach is the super clean and well run *Rini Hotel* (☎ 41386). Normally a popular, budget priced option, it recently underwent renovation and now features a saltwater pool, so check the latest prices. The long-standing *Astina Seaside Cottages* (☎ 41187) has some character, and a garden setting, and is still good value. Rooms range from 17,000/20,000 rp with a shared bathroom to 35,000/40,000 rp for a cottage.

Along the busy main road, the homely *Wisata Jaya Homestay* offers reasonable rooms for 11,000/12,000 rp. Further west, *Chono Beach Cottages* is central, but noisy, yet the price of 15,000/20,000 rp is good value if you negotiate a little. The next turn-off, Jl Bina Ria, has a handful of bars and restaurants before it ends at the beach. A driveway leads to the rambling *Nirwana Seaside Cottages* (☎ 41288, fax 41090), on a large slab of privileged beachfront property. Rooms start at 45,000/75,000 rp with fan and hot water, or it's 85,000/100,000 rp for an air-con bungalow. The bungalows and rooms are pleasant, but the service could be improved.

A side track also goes to *Angsoka Cottages* (☎ 41841, fax 41023), which has a pool and a range of rooms from 20,000/40,000 rp with fan, or 105,000 rp with air-con and hot water. *Ray Beach Inn I* (☎ 41087) has rooms in a cell-block style for 15,000 rp, and is a last resort. *Palestis Hotel* (☎ 41035) has the most ornate decorations, a welcome pool inside and promises 'a good sleep'. Rooms are good value, and start from 40,000 rp with a fan.

Another small track, next to the Palestis, leads to several other cheap, but pleasant, places, such as the family-run *Harri's Homestay* (☎ 41152) for 15,000/25,000 rp; and *Padang Lovina Hotel* for 30,000 rp a double.

West of Kalibukbuk Back on the main road, there's a string of other cheapies, including: *Hotel Purnama* (☎ 41043) for 15,000 rp a room; *Mangalla Homestay* for the same price; the popular but small *Homestay John* (☎ 41260), north of the Mangalla and actually on the beach, for 25,000 rp;

Puri Agung Susila II (☎ *41080*), about the cheapest around for 10,000 rp a room; and *Hotel Mutiara Beach* (☎ *41132*) for a reasonable 20,000 rp for a room upstairs.

Mid-range places nearby include: *Bali Lovina Beach Cottages* (☎/fax *41285*) from US$35/42 to US$55/68; and *Aditya Bungalows* (☎ *41059, fax 41342*), a big place with a beach frontage, pool, shops and a variety of rooms from US$24 with TV, phone, fridge etc. *Parma Hotel* (☎ *41555*) has cottages from 20,000/25,000 rp, and cheaper rooms (15,000 rp) by the road – all set in a garden extending down to the beach. Further along, *Billibo Beach Cottages* (☎ *41358*) charges 45,000/80,000 rp with TV, air-con and hot water; and the nearby *Adirama Beach Hotel* (☎/fax *41759*) costs from US$15 to US$30 with air-con and TV. Near the bend in the road, *Toto Bungalows* (☎ *41107*) has very basic rooms for 10,000/15,000 rp.

Further west there are even more places – these are either secluded or isolated, depending on your point of view. One of the best is the new *Hotel Padma* (☎ *41140*). It is noisy, but until it's better known the rooms are good value for a mid-range place. Prices range from 20,000 to 60,000 rp. The pool is a real attraction.

Places to Eat

Just about every hotel has a restaurant and bar, and guests, as well as the public, are always welcome. Some of the dozens and dozens of places to eat are listed here, but you'll do well to just look around and eat somewhere that takes your fancy. Even the nicest looking restaurants will have main courses for under 8000 rp. Always keep an eye out for daily specials.

A few shops in Kalibukbuk offer a cheap, and environmentally friendly, Aqua mineral water refill service; it costs 1000 rp to refill a 2L bottle.

Anturan Starting from the Singaraja end, the *Harmoni Restaurant* has delicious fresh fish and other seafood dishes, but the service is often slow, so be prepared for a leisurely meal. Further west, *Warung Cokot* serves good, cheap Balinese food, such as *babi guling* (pork in lemongrass sauce), while the swish *Siwa Cafe* caters more for the passing bus tour crowd, and charges accordingly. *Spunky's Cafe* may have a corny name, but it's a bright, friendly place, with good food for about 6000 rp. It is one of several newer places along Jl Loviana.

Kalibukbuk Along the main road, *Surya Restaurant* is very popular, and offers reasonable pizzas (5000 rp) for lunch and tasty seafood specials (about 7500 rp) all day long. Next door, *Malibu Club* has a bakery and serves pizzas, but it's overpriced, and more interested in catering for the evening crowd. *Chono Beach Restaurant* is also popular, perhaps because of the happy hour as much as the food.

On Jl Ketepang, *Semina Bar & Restoran* has buffets, Balinese dancing and a reasonably priced a la carte menu in a nice setting. The road finishes at the wonderful *Warung Warubali*, one the best places to watch the sunset during happy hour. It is open 24 hours, and meals cost from 10,000 to 13,000 rp.

The popular *Ruma Ramah Tama,* on Jl Bina Ria, features a more imaginative menu than many other places, including a wide range of vegetarian dishes and children's serves.

Further down, *Kakatua Bar & Restaurant* offers Mexican, Thai and Indian cuisine, as well as pizzas, so most people should be catered for. Opposite, *Warung Kopi Bali* is deservedly popular and gets a lot of repeat business. The servings are large, the food is tasty and prices are reasonable (8000 to 12,500 rp). Left at the end of the road, *Sea Breeze Cafe*, on the beach, has tasty food and a wonderful outlook.

West of Kalibukbuk Heading west on the main road, the once popular Arya's Cafe has become *Planet Lovina*, but it doesn't quite capture the atmosphere of the similarly named American chain. *Restoran Gandhi* and *Biyu Nasak Restaurant* both specialise in vegetarian food, as well as seafood, with most dishes about 7500 rp.

Top left: Gamelan musicians at Candikuning's Pura Ulun Danu Bratan in central Bali.
Top right: A Muslim tourist from Jakarta at a temple festival in Candikuning in central Bali.
Bottom: Boats for hire on the shores of Danau Batur in Kedisan, against a backdrop of the active volcano of Gunung Batur, central Bali.

Top: Fishing boat at sunset off Legian beach in south Bali.
Bottom left: A statue at Brahmavihara Arama, Bali's only Buddhist monastery at Banjar in north Bali.
Bottom right: A boy relaxes at Air Panas Banjar, the hot springs at Banjar, which feature carved stone *nagas* that spew the hot water into the baths.

Further along, *Singa Pizza Restaurant* is one of the best places for pizzas (about 9500 rp). *Adjani's Restaurant* is a popular place for genuine Indonesian and Balinese food (for about 6500 rp) in a friendly atmos-phere, and the owners run cooking classes (see the earlier Courses entry in this section). If you are staying in this part of Lovina, *Restaurant Adi Rama* and *Karina Restaurant* are OK, while the seafood dishes (about 11,500 rp) at *Lian Seafood Restaurant* are worth a short bemo ride.

Entertainment

Balinese Dancing A number of the hotel restaurants offer Balinese dancing with a Balinese buffet meal, or Dutch-style *rijstaffel* (banquet). At about 15,000 rp for entertainment and unlimited food, this is good value and worth a splurge at least once. These are held at the restaurant at *Rambutan Beach Cottages* on Wednesday and Sunday; and at least weekly at *Chono Beach Restaurant* and *Semina Bar & Restoran*. Otherwise, try to find out what is happening at *Geweka Budaya Dance Stage* along the main road in Kalibukbuk. A huge billboard normally advertises Legong and other Balinese dances several times a week for about 7500 rp per person.

Bars & Nightclubs Lovina's social scene seems to centre on the *Malibu Club*, which has pulsating discos on Wednesday and Saturday nights, and live music on other nights. The local equivalent of the Kuta cowboys comes here, and sometimes a contingent of students from Singaraja. Another bar, which only seems busy during the tourist season, is *Wina's Bar & Restaurant*.

Bali Apik, and several places nearby such as *Surya Restaurant*, have started a happy-hour war, much to the delight of thirsty patrons. From about 6 to 9 pm, large Bali Hai beers cost from 4500 rp.

Videos Particularly popular with families are video nights. Admission is free, but drinks and food are more expensive than elsewhere. *Warung Karma*, the restaurant

at Padang Lovina Hotel, *Malibu Club* and *Bali Apik* advertise current and future attractions on noticeboards along the main road, and on notices nailed to the trees around Lovina.

Shopping

Lovina isn't nearly as well set up for shopping as Sanur, Candidasa and the Kuta region. There are a few shops, but little in the way of souvenirs, art markets or sarong shops. So, you'll find shopping in Lovina a pleasure, rather than a chore, but prices are not as competitive as other tourist centres on Bali.

Getting There & Away

Public Bus & Bemo To Lovina from south Bali by public transport, you will probably need to change in Singaraja (see the earlier Singaraja section for details). The normal fare on the regular blue bemos from the Banyuasri terminal in Singaraja to Kalibukbuk is 800 rp, but don't expect any change from 1000 rp.

Java There are direct public buses between Surabaya (on Java) and Singaraja (see the earlier Singaraja section), so if you're coming from the west you can get off anywhere along Lovina rather than backtrack from Singaraja. Alternatively, catch a regular public bus from Singaraja to Gilimanuk (or hail it down along the main road in Lovina), and take the ferry to Java.

Many Lovina travel agencies sell 'tourist bus' trips to major Javanese cities, but beware: these are often just tourist shuttle buses from Singaraja all the way to Ubung terminal in Denpasar, and then a deluxe public bus (which is still reasonably comfortable) to Java.

Tourist Shuttle Bus Lovina is the most northern and western point for all shuttle bus services on Bali – they do not continue to Gilimanuk. At least once a day, Perama links Lovina with Kuta, Sanur and Ubud (all for 12,500 rp) via Bedugul (7500 rp) or Kintamani (7500 rp).

The main Perama office (☎ 41104) is

next to the tourist office, and there's another office in Anturan. Simpatik (☎ 21234) and Marga Sakti Transport (no telephone) have identical shuttle bus runs for about the same price as Perama. These buses can be booked at your hotel or at the numerous shops-cum-travel agencies along the streets. And remember: these buses don't go any further west than Kalibukbuk (Lovina).

There are also shuttle bus services from Lovina to Java – the Bali Getting There & Away chapter has details.

Getting Around
The Lovina strip is *very* spread out, but you can easily travel back and forth on bemos. The standard fare is 500 rp, but foreigners are regularly overcharged by a few hundred rupiah. If you are staying in the outer 'suburbs' of Lovina, or want to explore some coastal areas, several shops in Kalibukbuk rent bicycles for about 6000 rp per day. The main road is nice and flat, but busy; the side roads are often sandy.

Car & Motorbike Lovina is an excellent base from which to explore north and central Bali, and rental prices are quite reasonable. Approximate rates per day are: 17,500 rp for a motorbike; and 60,000 rp for a Suzuki *jimny* jeep, plus about 20,000 rp per day for insurance. A chartered jimny or bemo with a driver will cost about 75,000 rp per day.

Rentals and charters can be organised through your hotel, or at a shop-cum-travel agency, but look around because prices do vary between operators.

AROUND LOVINA
The area immediately west of Lovina has several worthwhile attractions. The North-West Coast section in the West Bali chapter has information about places further west (ie between Celukanbawang and Gilimanuk).

Air Terjun Singsing
About 5km west of the middle of the Lovina beach strip, a sign leads to Air Terjun Singsing (Daybreak Waterfall – see the North Bali map). About 1km from the main road, there

is a *warung* on the left and a car park on the right. Walk past the warung and along the path for about 200m to the lower falls. The waterfall is not huge, but the pool underneath is good for a swim. The water isn't crystal clear, but it's cooler than the sea and very refreshing.

You can clamber further up the hill to another **waterfall** (Singsing Dua), which is slightly bigger and has a mud bath which is supposedly good for the skin. This one also cascades into a deep pool in which you can swim.

The area is pretty and makes a nice day trip from Lovina. The falls are more spectacular in the wet season, of course, but may turn into a trickle in the dry season.

Banjar
Brahmavihara Arama Bali's single Buddhist monastery is only vaguely Buddhist-looking, with colourful decorations, a bright orange roof and statues of Buddha, but it has very Balinese decorative carvings and door guardians. It's quite a handsome structure in a commanding location, with **views** down the valley and across the paddy fields to the sea. You'll need a sarong, but this can be hired for a small donation. The monastery doesn't advertise any regular courses or programmes, but visitors are welcome to meditate in special rooms.

The temple is about 4km up an obvious turn-off from the main road. If you don't have your own transport, arrange an ojek at the turn-off. The road continues past the monastery, winding further up into the hills to Pedewa, a **Bali Aga village**.

Air Panas Banjar Not far from Brahmavihara Arama temple, these hot springs are beautifully landscaped with lush tropical plants. You can relax here for a few hours and have lunch at the restaurant, or even stay the night and really indulge yourself.

Eight carved stone nagas spew water from a natural hot spring into the first bath, which then overflows (via the mouths of five more nagas), into a second, larger pool. In a third pool, water pours from 3m-high spouts to give you a pummelling massage. The water is slightly sulphurous and pleasantly hot, so you might enjoy it more in the morning or the evening than in the heat of the day. You must wear a swimsuit and you shouldn't use soap in the pools, but you can do so under an adjacent outdoor shower.

Buy your ticket (1000/500 rp for adults/children) from the little office at the end of the road, and cross the bridge to the baths. There are changing rooms under the restaurant, on the right-hand side. It is open every day from 8 am to 6 pm.

Places to Stay & Eat The wonderful *Pondok Wisata Grya Sari (☎ 92903, fax 92966)* is set in the hills, very close to the baths – this is one place you may wish to splurge on a night's accommodation. Very nice singles/doubles start at US$36/41; the suites are twice as expensive, but only slightly better quality. The Grya Sari also has an expensive *restaurant* in a lovely setting. The Indonesian food at *Restoran Komala Tirta*, which overlooks the baths, is also pretty good and inexpensive.

Getting There & Away The monastery and hot springs are both well signposted along separate roads south of the main road. If you don't have your own transport, it's easy to catch a bemo to the turn-off to Banjar Tega village, then get an ojek up to the monastery. From there you can walk to the hot springs – it's about 3km and mostly downhill. Look for signs or ask for directions.

Alternatively, go back down to Banjar Tega, and turn left along Jl Sekar in the centre of the village. The small road runs

west and then north for about 2km to Banjar village. From there it's only a short distance uphill before you see the 'air panas 1km' sign on the left. Follow the road to the car park where you'll be shown a place to park (200 rp). From the springs you should be able to get an ojek back to the main road (2.4 km), or it is a pleasant walk.

Seririt
Seririt is a junction for roads that run south over the mountains to Pulukan or Antasari, on the way to Denpasar. The road running west along the coast towards Gilimanuk is quite good, with pretty coastal scenery and few tourists.

Seririt has a petrol station and a reasonable selection of shops. If you need to stay, *Hotel Singarasari (☎ 92435)*, near the bus/bemo stop, has rooms from 12,000 rp to 30,000 rp with air-con and TV. There are many *warungs* and *rumah makans* in the market area, just north of the bemo stop.

Celukanbawang
Celukanbawang, is the main cargo port for north Bali, and has a large wharf. Bugis schooners – those magnificent sailing ships which take their name from the seafaring Bugis people of Sulawesi – can sometimes be seen anchoring here.

There isn't a lot of reason to come here or stay, but if you need accommodation there are two places along the road towards the port: the brand-spanking new *Hotel Puri Mustika Permai (☎ 93444)* has rooms from 50,000 to 100,000 rp, including breakfast; and the dreary *Hotel Drupa Indah (☎ 93242)* has double rooms for 25,000 rp.

LOMBOK

LOMBOK

Facts about Lombok

HISTORY

The earliest recorded society on Lombok was the relatively small kingdom of the Sasaks. The Sasak people were agriculturalists and animists who practised ancestor and spirit worship. The original Sasaks are believed to have come overland from north-west India or Myanmar (Burma) in waves of migration that predated most Indonesian ethnic groups. Few relics remain from the old animist kingdoms, and the majority of Sasaks today are Muslim, although animism has left its mark on the culture. Not much is known about Lombok before the 17th century, at which time it was split into numerous, frequently squabbling states each presided over by a Sasak 'prince' – a disunity exploited by the neighbouring Balinese.

Balinese Rule

In the early 17th century, the Balinese from the eastern state of Karangasem established colonies and took control of west Lombok. At the same time, the roving Makassarese crossed the strait from their colonies in west Sumbawa and established settlements in east Lombok. This conflict of interests ended with the war of 1677-8, in which the Makassarese were booted off the island and east Lombok temporarily reverted to the rule of the Sasak princes. Balinese control was soon reasserted and by 1740 or 1750 the whole island was in their hands.

While the Balinese were now the masters of Lombok, the basis of their control in west and east Lombok was quite different. In west Lombok, relations between the Balinese and the Sasaks were relatively harmonious. The Sasak peasants, who adhered to the mystical Wektu Telu interpretation of Islam, easily assimilated Balinese Hinduism, participated in Balinese religious festivities and worshipped at the same shrines. Intermarriage between Balinese and Sasaks was common.

The western Sasaks were organised into similar irrigation associations *(subak)* that the Balinese used for wet-rice agriculture. The traditional Sasak village government, presided over by a chief, who was a member of the Sasak aristocracy, was done away with and the peasants were ruled directly by the rajah or a land-owning Balinese aristocrat.

Things were very different in the east, where the recently defeated Sasak aristocracy hung in limbo. Here the Balinese had to maintain control from garrisoned forts and, although the traditional village government remained intact, the village chief was reduced to little more than a tax collector for the local Balinese district head *(punggawa)*.

The Balinese ruled like feudal kings, assuming control of the land from the Sasak peasants and reducing them to the level of serfs. With their power and land-holdings slashed, the Sasak aristocracy of eastern Lombok was hostile to the Balinese. The peasants remained loyal to their former Sasak rulers, and supported rebellions in 1855, 1871 and 1891.

Dutch Involvement

The Balinese succeeded in suppressing the first two revolts, but the third uprising, in 1891, was a different story. Towards the end of 1892 it too had almost been defeated, but the Sasak chiefs sent envoys to the Dutch resident in Buleleng (Singaraja) asking for help, and inviting the Dutch to rule Lombok. Although the Dutch planned to take advantage of the turmoil on Lombok, they backed off from military action – partly because they were still fighting a war in Aceh (Sumatra) and partly because of the apparent military strength of the Balinese on Lombok.

Dutch reluctance to use force began to dissipate when the ruthless Van der Wijck succeeded to the post of Governor General of the Dutch East Indies in 1892. He made a treaty with the rebels in east Lombok in 1894 and then, with the excuse that he was setting out to free the Sasaks from tyrannical Balinese rule, sent a fleet carrying a large army to Lombok. Although the Balinese rajah quickly capitulated to Dutch demands, the younger Balinese princes of Lombok overruled him and attacked and routed the Dutch. It was a short-lived victory – the Dutch army dug its heels in at Ampenan and was reinforced from Java. The Dutch counterattack began, Mataram was overrun and the Balinese stronghold of Cakranegara was bombarded with artillery.

The rajah eventually surrendered to the Dutch and the last resistance collapsed when a large group of Balinese, including members of the aristocracy and royal family, were slain in a traditional, suicidal *puputan*, deliberately marching into the fire from Dutch guns.

Dutch Rule

Dutch rule of Lombok is a case study in callous colonial rule. New taxes resulted in the impoverishment of the majority of peasants and the creation of a new stratum of Chinese middlemen. Peasants were forced to sell more of their rice crop in order to pay the taxes; the amount of rice available for consumption declined by about a quarter between 1900 and the 1930s. Famines took place from 1938 to 1940 and in 1949.

For nearly half a century, by maintaining the goodwill of the Balinese and Sasak aristocracy and using a police force that never numbered more than 250, the Dutch were able to maintain their hold on more than 500,000 people. The peasants wouldn't act against them for fear of being evicted from their land and losing what little security they had. There were several failed peasant uprisings, but they were never more than localised rebellions; the aristocracy never supported them and the peasants themselves were ill-equipped to lead a widespread revolt. Even after Indonesia won independence, Lombok continued to be dominated by its Balinese and Sasak aristocracies.

Post-Colonial Lombok

Under Dutch rule the eastern islands of Indonesia were grouped together as the Lesser Sunda Islands. When Soekarno proclaimed Indonesian independence on 17 August 1945,

the Lesser Sunda Islands were formed into the single province of Nusa Tenggara, which means 'islands of the south-east'. This proved far too unwieldy to govern and the province was subsequently divided into three separate regions – Bali, Barat (West) Nusa Tenggara and Timur (East) Nusa Tenggara. Lombok became part of West Nusa Tenggara in 1958, and Mataram was named the administrative capital of the region.

Lombok & the New Order

Immediately after the attempted coup in 1965, Lombok experienced mass killings of communists, sympathisers and ethnic Chinese, as did Bali and other parts of Indonesia. Under President Soeharto's 'New Order', Lombok enjoyed stability and some growth, but nothing like the booming wealth of Java and Bali, and it remained a poor island with uneven development. Crop failures led to famine in 1966 and to severe food shortages in 1973.

Lombok Today

Lombok is a small and remote island in a large country which has a very centralised power structure. The people are among the poorest in Indonesia, and suffer one of the highest rates of infant mortality and illiteracy in the country. People have moved away from Lombok under the *transmigrasi* programme, and several foreign aid projects have attempted to improve water supply, agricultural output and health. Small scale agriculture is still the main activity, but many locals rely heavily on a tourist industry which attracts a lot of development and speculation – but not enough tourists.

In late 1997, well before the Jakarta riots, there were other publicised riots in Praya and Mataram, led by students dissatisfied with the current economic situation. These riots, together with the fires in Kalimantan and Irian Jaya and the riots in Java and Sulawesi in early 1998, led many foreigners cancelled their planned holidays in Indonesia. Lombok was particularly hard hit, and it may be several years before the tourist industry on the island recovers.

GEOGRAPHY

Lombok lies eight degrees south of the equator and stretches some 80km east to west and about the same distance north to south. It is dominated by the second-highest mountain in Indonesia, Gunung Rinjani, which soars to 3726m. It has a large caldera with a crater lake, Segara Anak, 600m below the rim, and a new volcanic cone which has formed in the centre. Rinjani last erupted in 1994, and evidence of this can be seen in the fresh lava and yellow sulphur around the inner cone.

Central Lombok, to the south of Rinjani, is similar to Bali, with rich alluvial plains and fields irrigated by water flowing from the mountains. In the far south and east it is drier, with scrubby, barren hills. This area gets little rain and often has droughts which can last for months. In recent years, several dams have been built, so the abundant rainfall of the wet season can be retained for irrigation throughout the year.

Most of the population is concentrated in the fertile but narrow east-west corridor sandwiched between the dry southern region and the slopes of Rinjani to the north.

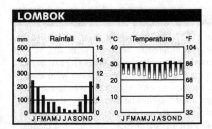

CLIMATE

In Lombok's dry season – from June to September – the heat can be scorching. At night, particularly at higher elevations, the temperature can drop so much that a sweater and light jacket are necessary. The wet season extends from October to May, with December and January the wettest months.

ECOLOGY & ENVIRONMENT

Lombok is often described as 'Indonesia's best kept secret' or 'an undeveloped, un-ruined alternative to Bali'. A few lessons about the effects of unrestrained development in the tourist centres of Bali have been learnt and put into practice on Lombok, but tourism still has a dramatic effect on the local environment and community:

- In Senggigi, Kuta and the Gili Islands large stretches of coastline have been commandeered for luxury resorts, but often for speculative purposes, so hotels are rarely built.
- Resort areas that used to be owned by locals are now owned mostly by Javanese and foreign companies.
- Sewage and rubbish is often not disposed of properly.
- New roads to Kuta have destroyed natural landscapes.
- Boats and scuba divers around the Gilis often damage fragile coral reefs.
- Top-end hotels create chronic water shortages, especially in the dry area around Kuta.
- Development in Kuta has destroyed the local fishing and seaweed industries, and the fisher-man have lost access to beaches and ocean in Senggigi.
- There is often conflict when conservative Islamic people are offended by foreigners who drink alcohol and dress inappropriately.

There is some encouraging news, however: some tourist ventures, including a dive centre on the Gilis and a hotel in Senggigi al-locate profits to the local community, and are involved in conservation projects, such as saving endangered turtles. Every visitor to Lombok can also do their bit: for example, you can support businesses run by local people, take heed of the advice in the boxed texts in the Bali Facts for the Visitor chapter about responsible diving and trekking, and consider issues raised in the Avoiding Offence section later in this chapter.

FLORA & FAUNA

Apart from banana and coconut palms, which grow in profusion over most of Lombok, the forests are confined largely to the mountain regions where they are extensive and dense, although logging is taking its toll. Teak and mahogany are among the forest timbers. Other native trees are bintangur, kesambi, bungur and fig, which is used widely for building houses and furniture. Much of the rest of the island is devoted to rice cultivation and the rice fields are every bit as picturesque as Bali's – including the ducks. There's several species of deer in the forests, as well as wild pigs, porcupines, snakes, lizards, frogs, turtles, long-tailed monkeys, civets and feral cattle. Lombok is the furthest point to the west of Australia where the sulphur-crested cockatoo can be found.

GOVERNMENT & POLITICS

Lombok and Sumbawa are the two main islands of the province of Nusa Tenggara Barat (NTB). Its capital is Mataram, complete with a civilian governor and a military commander. Lombok itself is divided into three *kabupaten* (districts): Lombok Barat (capital Mataram); Lombok Tengah (Praya); and Lombok Timur (Selong).

See the Government & Politics entry in the Facts about Bali chapter for detailed information about the Indonesian system of government.

ECONOMY
Agriculture & Fishing

Lombok's economy is based on agriculture and the rice grown here is noted for its excellent quality. However, the climate on Lombok is drier than Bali's and, in many areas, only one crop can be produced each year. In some years, water shortages caused by poor rains can limit rice production, or even cause a complete crop failure, leading to rising prices and unstable markets. The last major crop failure was caused by a drought in 1966, and many people perished. In 1973, there was another bad crop, and although the outcome was not as disastrous, rice on Lombok rose to double the price it was on Bali.

There are plantations of coconut palms, coffee and cotton. Tobacco is a common cash crop, and the square brick drying towers are often seen. In the fertile areas the land is intensively cultivated, often with a variety of crops planted together. Look for the vegetables and fodder trees planted on the levees between the paddy fields. Crops such as cloves, vanilla, pepper and pineapples are being introduced. Where possible, two rice

The Wallace Line

The 19th century naturalist Sir Alfred Wallace (1822-1913) observed great differences in fauna between Bali and Lombok – as great as the differences between Africa and South America. In particular, there were no large mammals (elephants, rhinos, tigers etc) east of Bali and very few carnivores. He postulated that during the ice ages when sea levels were lower, animals could have moved by land from what is now mainland Asia all the way to Bali, but the deep Lombok Strait would always have been a barrier. Thus he drew a line between Bali and Lombok, which he believed marked the biological division between Asia and Australia.

Plant life, on the other hand, does not display such a sharp division, but there is a gradual transition from predominantly Asian rainforest species to mostly Australian plants like eucalypts and acacias, which are better suited to long dry periods. This is associated with the lower rainfall as one moves east of Java. Environmental differences, including those in the natural vegetation, are now thought to provide a better explanation of the distribution of animal species than Wallace's theory about limits to their original migrations.

Modern biogeographers do recognise a distinction between Asian and Australian fauna, but the boundary between the regions is regarded as much fuzzier than Wallace's line. This transitional zone between Asia and Australia is nevertheless referred to as 'Walacea'.

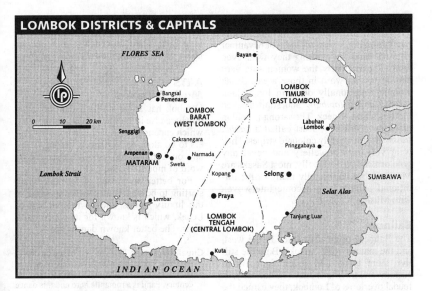

LOMBOK DISTRICTS & CAPITALS

FLORES SEA

Bayan

Bangsal
Pemenang

LOMBOK
TIMUR
(EAST LOMBOK)

Labuhan
Lombok

LOMBOK
BARAT
(WEST LOMBOK)

Senggigi

Cakranegara

Pringgabaya

0   10   20 km

Ampenan
MATARAM   Narmada
Sweta

Kopang

Selong

SUMBAWA

Lombok Strait

Selat Alas

Lembar

Praya

Tanjung Luar

LOMBOK
TENGAH
(CENTRAL LOMBOK)

Kuta

INDIAN OCEAN

crops are grown each year, with a third crop, perhaps of pineapples, grown for cash.

Fishing is widespread along the coastline which, edged by coral reefs, has many good spawning areas. Stock-breeding on Lombok is done only on a small scale. Pumice stone is a profitable export, especially when stone-washed denim is in fashion.

Tourism

Inspired by Bali's obvious success, Lombok is keen to develop its tourist industry. The number of tourists increased seven-fold between 1983 and 1993, but the Indonesian and regional governments want to attract 'quality tourists' (which is a euphemism for big-spending tourists), and are promoting the construction of expensive resort hotels.

Most of the initial development is at Senggigi, but large tracts of beachfront land all around the island, particularly at Kuta and the Gili Islands, have been acquired for 'co-developments' with Javanese and foreign interests. Some local people who sold their land used the money for a pilgrimage to Mecca and now live in poverty.

At the time of research, the majority of hotels, restaurants and shops were suffering badly from the lack of tourism. Upmarket places were offering substantial discounts, mid-range hotels were often virtually empty and owners of budget places in more remote areas, such as Lendang Nangka and Senaru, complained that they have had no guests for weeks; some *losmen* (family-run hotels) have overcapitalised and have no other form of income. There is also a growing disquiet among owners of budget hotels and restaurants around Lombok who may be driven from their properties to make way for upmarket tourist developments; and unease among investors about the current dire state of the tourist industry.

POPULATION & PEOPLE

Lombok has a population of 2.4 million (1990 census), with the majority living in and around the principal centres of Mataram, Praya and Selong. Almost 90% of the people are Sasak, about 10% are Balinese, and there are minority populations of Chinese, Javanese and Arabs.

Sasaks

The Sasaks are assumed to have originally come from north-western India or Myanmar (Burma), and the clothing they wear even today – particularly the women – is very similar to that worn in those areas. Sasak women traditionally dress in long black sarongs called *lambung* and short-sleeved blouses with a V-neck. The sarong is held in place by a 4m-long scarf called a *sabuk*, trimmed with brightly coloured stripes. They wear very little jewellery and never any gold ornaments. Officially, most Sasaks are Muslims, but unofficially many of the traditional beliefs have become interwoven with Muslim ideology.

Balinese

The Balinese originally settled in the west, and the majority of Lombok's Balinese still live there today and retain their Hindu customs and traditions intact. Historically, as feudal overlords of Lombok, they earned the ill will of the Sasaks. Even today, the Sasaks regard the Dutch as liberating them from an oppressive power, but by and large the Balinese and Sasaks coexist amicably. The Balinese contributed to the emergence of Lombok's Wektu Telu religion, and Balinese temples, ceremonies and processions are a colourful part of west Lombok's cultural life.

Other Groups

The Chinese first came to Lombok with the Dutch as cheap labour and worked as coolies in the rice paddies. Later they were given some privileges and allowed to set up and develop their own businesses – primarily restaurants and shops. Many shops and restaurants in Mataram are run or owned by Chinese, which has resulted in resentment and occasional anti-Chinese riots.

Ampenan (in Mataram) has a small Arab quarter known as Kampung Arab. The Arabs living here are devout Muslims who follow the Koran to the letter, and marry among themselves. They are well educated and relatively affluent.

In the late 19th century, seafaring Buginese from south Sulawesi started to settle on the coastal areas of Lombok, such as Labuhan Lombok, Labuhan Haji and Tanjung Luar. Their descendants still operate much of the fishing industry.

ARTS
Music & Dance

Lombok has some brilliant dances found nowhere else in Indonesia. But unlike Bali, which encourages (in fact hustles) westerners to go along to its dances, getting to see any on Lombok has usually depended on word of mouth or pure luck.

For better or worse, performances are starting to be staged for tourists in some of the luxury hotels and in the village of Lenek, which is known for its dance traditions. The better known dances are:

Cupak Gerantang This dance is based on one of the Panji stories, an extensive cycle of written and oral stories originating on Java in the 15th century. Panji is a romantic hero and this dance is popular across Lombok. It's often performed at traditional celebrations, such as birth and marriage ceremonies, and at other festivities.

Kayak Sando This is another version of a Panji story, but here the dancers wear masks. It is only found in central and east Lombok.

Gandrung This one is about love and courtship – *gandrung* means being in love or longing. It is a social dance, usually performed outdoors by the young men and women of the village. Everyone stands around in a circle and then, accompanied by a full *gamelan* orchestra, a young girl dances dreamily by herself for a time, before choosing a male partner from the audience to join her. The Gandrung is common to Narmada, Lenek and Praya.

Oncer This war dance is performed by men and young boys. It is a highly skilled and dramatic performance which involves the participants playing a variety of unusual musical instruments in time to their movements. The severe black of the costumes is slashed with crimson and gold waist bands, shoulder sashes, socks and caps. The dance is performed with great vigour at traditional *adat* festivals, both in central and eastern Lombok.

Rudat The Rudat is performed by pairs of men dressed in black caps and jackets and black-and-white check sarongs. The dancers are backed by singers, tambourines and cylindrical drums called *jidur*. The music, lyrics and costume used in this dance show a mixture of Islamic and Sasak cultures.

Tandak Gerok This combines dance, theatre and singing to music played on bamboo flutes and the bowed lute called a *rebab*. Its unique and most attractive feature is that the vocalists imitate the sound of the gamelan instruments. It is usually performed after harvesting or other hard physical labour, but is also put on at adat ceremonies.

Genggong Using a simple set of instruments which includes a bamboo flute, a rebab and knockers, seven musicians accompany their music with dance movements and stylised hand gestures.

Architecture

Lombok's architecture is governed by traditional laws and practices, as are most aspects of daily life. Construction must begin on a propitious day, always with an odd-numbered date, and the building's frame must be completed on that day. It would be bad luck to leave any of the important structural work to the following day.

In a traditional Sasak village there are three types of buildings – the communal meeting hall *(beruga)*, family houses *(bale tani)* and rice barns *(lumbung)*. The beruga

---

The Lumbung

The *lumbung* (rice barn), with its characteristic horseshoe shape, has become something of an architectural symbol on Lombok. You'll see lumbung shapes in the design of hotel foyers, entrances, gateways and even phone booths.

The lumbung design is often also used for tourist bungalows. On an island that has been regularly afflicted with famine, a rice barn must be a powerful image of prosperity. Ironically, the new strains of high-yield rice, which have done so much to increase the food supply in Indonesia, cannot be stored in a traditional rice barn. It is said that the only lumbung built these days are for storing tourists.

---

and the bale tani are both rectangular, with low walls and a steeply pitched thatched roof, although, of course, the beruga is much larger. The arrangement of rooms in a bale tani is also very standardised. There is an open verandah *(serambi)* at the front and two rooms on two different levels inside – one for cooking and entertaining guests, the other for sleeping and storage.

Weaving

Lombok is renowned for its traditional weaving, the techniques being handed down from mother to daughter. Each piece of cloth is woven on a hand loom in established patterns and colours. Some fabrics are woven in as many as four directions and interwoven with gold thread, and many take at least a month to complete. Flower and animal motifs of buffalos, dragons, lizards, crocodiles and snakes are sometimes used to decorate this exquisite cloth. Several villages specialise in weaving, basketware, bags and mats. The Lombok Arts & Crafts colour section in this chapter has more information.

SOCIETY & CONDUCT
Traditional Culture

Traditional law is still fundamental to the way of life on Lombok today, particularly customs relating to courting and marriage rituals, and circumcision ceremonies. In west Lombok you can witness Balinese dances, temple ceremonies, and colourful processions with decorative offerings of flowers, fruit and food. Sasak ceremonies are often less visible, but you may see some colourful processions. Ask around and you can probably find when and where festivals and celebrations are being held.

Birth One of the Balinese rituals adopted by the Wektu Telu religion is a ceremony which takes place soon after birth involving offerings to, and the burial of, the placenta. This ceremony, called *adi kaka*, is based on the belief that during the process of each birth, four siblings escape from the womb, symbolised by the blood, the fertilised egg, the placenta and amniotic fluid that protects the foetus during pregnancy. If the after-birth is treated with deference and respect, these four siblings will not cause harm to the newborn child or its mother. The priest then names the newborn child with a ritual-istic scattering of ashes known as *buang au*. When the child is 105 days old (ie half a year according to the Balinese *wuku* calen-dar) it receives its first haircut in another ceremony called the *ngurisang*.

Circumcision The laws of Islam require that all boys be circumcised *(nyunatang)*, and in Indonesia this is usually done some-where between the ages of six and 11. Much pomp and circumstance mark this occasion on Lombok. The boys are carried through the village streets on painted wooden horses and lions with tails of palm fronds. The cir-cumcision is performed without anaesthetic as each boy must be prepared to suffer pain for Allah. As soon as it is over, they must enact a ritual known as the *makka* – a kind of obeisance involving a drawn kris dagger which is held unsheathed.

Courting Traditionally, teenage girls and boys are kept strictly apart, except on certain festival occasions such as weddings, cir-cumcision feasts and the annual celebration of the first catch of the strange *nyale* fish at Kuta (explained in the 'Nyale Fishing Festi-val' boxed text in the Lombok Facts for the Visitor chapter). On these occasions they are allowed to mingle freely. However, if at one of these occasions a girl publicly accepts a gift from a boy – food for example – she is committed to marrying him.

Harvest time is another opportunity for courting. Traditionally, the harvesting of rice was women's work and the men carried the sheaves away on shoulder-poles. Under the watchful eyes of the older men and women, a group of girls approaches the rice paddy from one side, and a group of boys from the other. Each group sings a song, ap-plauds the other and engages in some circumspect flirting. This courtship ritual is still carried on in the more isolated, tradi-tional villages.

Marriage Rituals Young couples have the choice of three rituals. The first is a formal arranged marriage, the second is a union between cousins, and the third is elopement. The first two are uncomplicated; the parents of the prospective bridal couple meet to discuss the bride's dowry and sort out any religious differences. After concluding the business arrangements, the ceremony *(sorong serah)* is performed.

The third method is far more complicat-ed and dramatic. Theoretically a young girl is forbidden to marry a man of lower caste, but this rule can be broken through kidnap-ping and eloping. As a result, eloping is still a widespread practice on Lombok, despite the fact that in most instances the parents of the couple know what's afoot. Originally it was used as a means of eluding competitors for the girl's hand, or in order to avoid family friction, but it also minimised the heavy expenses of a wedding ceremony.

The rules of this ritual are laid down and must be followed step by step. After the girl is spirited away by the boy, he is required to report to the *kepala desa* (village headman) where he has taken refuge. He receives 44 lashes for such a 'disrespectful' action and has a piece of black cotton string wound around his right wrist to indicate to all that he has kidnapped his future bride. The kepala desa then notifies the girl's family through the head of their village. A delega-tion from the boy's family visits the girl's parents, and between them they settle on a price for the bride, which is distributed among members of the bride's family in recompense for losing her.

Traditional dowries are worked out ac-cording to caste differences; the lower his caste and the higher hers, the more he has to pay. Payment is in old Chinese coins *(bolong)* and other ceremonial items, rather than in cash. Once this has been settled the wedding begins.

Generally the bride and groom, dressed in ceremonial clothes, are carried through the streets on a sedan chair on long bamboo poles. The sounds of the gamelan (known as the *barong tengkok*) mingle with the shouts and laughter of the guests, as the couple are swooped up and down and around on their way to the wedding place. Throughout the whole ceremony the bride must look downcast and unhappy at the prospect of leaving her family.

Death The Balinese inhabitants of Lombok conduct cremation ceremonies identical to those on Bali (for information see the Facts About Bali chapter).

Followers of the Wektu Telu religion, however, have their own rituals. The body is washed and prepared for burial by relations in the presence of a holy man, and then wrapped in white sheets and sackcloth. The corpse is placed on a raised bamboo platform, while certain sections of the Koran are read out and relations pray to Allah and call upon the spirits of their ancestors. The body is then taken to the cemetery and interred with the head facing towards Mecca. During the burial, passages of the Koran are read aloud in Sanskrit and afterwards more quotations from the Koran are recited in Arabic.

Relatives and friends of the deceased put offerings on the grave – pieces of hand-carved wood if it's a man, and decorative combs if it's a woman. Several ceremonies, involving readings from the Koran, are performed on the third, seventh, 40th and 100th days after the death. A special ceremony, known as *nyiu*, is carried out after 1000 days have elapsed – the grave is sprinkled with holy water and the woodcarvings or combs removed and stones put in their place.

Contests Sasaks are fascinated by physical prowess and heroic trials of strength, fought on a one-to-one level. As a result they have developed a unique contest of their own and adapted others from nearby Sumbawa. Contests are most frequently seen in July, August and September – August is the best month to see them.

Peresehan This peculiar type of man-to-man combat is a great favourite all over Lombok. Usually held in the late afternoon in the open air, a huge crowd of men gather together to watch two men battle it out with long rattan staves, protected only by small rectangular shields made from cow or buffalo hide. The staves are ceremoniously handed around the crowd. With great drama the gamelan starts and two men, dressed in exquisite finery featuring turbans or headscarves and wide waist sashes, feign the movements of the contest about to be fought.

Having shown everyone how it is supposed to be done, the two men look around the crowd for contestants, who are carefully chosen to match each other as closely as possible in height and strength. Anyone can be chosen; some perform several times during the afternoon, others refuse to take part at all. While it is quite permissible to refuse, it is clearly of great status to win. Those who agree to participate must quickly find scarves to wrap around their heads and waists if they aren't already wearing them (the head gear and waist sash are supposed to have magical protective powers). They next take off their shirts and shoes, roll up their trousers, pick up their staves and shields, and begin laying into each other.

It goes for three rounds (five with more experienced fighters) or until one of the two is bleeding or surrenders. The referee *(pekembar)* can also declare the contest over if he thinks things are getting too rough. This often happens; although the movements are very stylised, there is nothing choreographed or rigged about the peresehan.

Lanca This particular trial of strength originated in Sumbawa, but the Sasaks have also adopted the lanca and perform it on numerous occasions, particularly when the first rice seedlings are planted. Like the peresehan, it is a contest between two well matched men who use their knees to strike each other. It involves a lot of skill and strength.

Avoiding Offence

Most of Lombok is conservative, and very different in this respect from Bali. Immodest dress and public displays of affection between couples can cause offence. Brief shorts, tank tops (singlets) and swimwear are acceptable around the beaches and streets of Senggigi and the Gili Islands (although Kuta is quite conservative). Elsewhere, long pants or skirts, and T-shirts or shirts are the norm. Nude or topless bathing (by women) is also *very* offensive anywhere on Lombok.

Many people on Lombok fast during the month of Ramadan. At this time it is insensitive and offensive for foreign visitors to eat, drink or smoke in public during the day.

Islamic law forbids Muslims from drinking alcohol and, although booze is widely available on Lombok, public drunkenness is frowned upon and is particularly offensive near a mosque.

The corresponding section in the Facts about Bali chapter has more information about how to avoid offence on Lombok.

RELIGION
Islam

The great majority of Lombok's population are Muslims. Islam reached Indonesia in the 13th century with peaceful Gujarati merchants arriving on the eastern coast of Lombok via the Celebes (now Sulawesi), and on the western coast via Java.

Today Islam is the professed religion of 90% of the Indonesian people, and its traditions and rituals affect all aspects of their daily life. Friday afternoon is the officially decreed time for believers to worship, and all government offices and most businesses are closed. Arabic is taught in all Indonesian schools, so the Koran can continue to be read and studied by successive generations. Scrupulous attention is given to cleanliness, including ritualistic washing of hands and face. The pig is considered to be unclean and is not kept or eaten in strict Muslim regions. Indonesian Muslims may have more than one wife, but this is not common on Lombok, partly because few men can afford to keep a second wife. Those who make the pilgrimage to Mecca are known as *haji* if they are men, *haja* if they are women, and are highly respected.

The founder of Islam, Mohammed, was born in 571 AD and began his teachings in 612. He combined an early Hebraic kind of monotheism and a latent Arab nationalism, and by 622 was beginning to gain adherents. Mohammed did not demonstrate supernatural powers, but did claim he was God's only teacher and prophet, charged with the divine mission of interpreting the word of God. Mohammed's teachings are collated and collected in the scripture of Islam, the Koran, which was compiled from his oral and written records shortly after his death. It is divided into 14 chapters, and every word in it is said to have emanated from Mohammed and been inspired by God himself, in the will of Allah.

The fundamental tenet of Islam is 'there is no god but Allah and Mohammed is his prophet'. The word *islam* means submission, and the faith demands unconditional surrender to the wisdom of Allah, not just adherence to a set of beliefs and rules. It involves total commitment to a way of life, philosophy and law. Aspects of Islam have been touched by animist, Hindu and Buddhist precepts, influencing both peripheral details like mosque architecture and fundamental beliefs like the attitudes to women.

Muslim women on Lombok, and the rest of Indonesia, are allowed more freedom and shown more respect than women in some other Islamic countries. They do not have to wear veils, nor are they segregated or considered to be 2nd class citizens. There are a number of matrilineal and matriarchal societies and sometimes special mosques are built for women.

Wektu Telu

This unique religion originated in the village of Bayan, in north Lombok. Officially only a very small proportion of the population belongs to this faith, which is not one of Indonesia's 'official' religions. More and more young people are turning to Islam.

The word *wektu* means 'result' in the Sasak language, while *telu* means 'three' and signifies the complex mixture of the three religions which comprise Wektu Telu: Balinese Hinduism, Islam and animism.

LOMBOK ARTS & CRAFTS

SARA-JANE CLELAND

On Lombok, where periodic droughts and famine beset the countryside, there are relatively few objects made for purely decorative purposes – in other words, there's more craft than art. However, these functional objects show a high degree of skill and artisanship. The finer examples of Lombok's weaving, basketware and pottery are highly valued by collectors.

Perhaps the best place to get an idea of Lombok's arts and crafts is the vast, covered market in Sweta. This is the largest market on Lombok, and you'll find a number of stalls specialising in local crafts like woodcarving, weaving and pottery.

Villages specialise in certain crafts, and it's interesting to travel to a number of them, seeing handweaving in one village, basketware in another and pottery in a third.

Carving

Most carving on Lombok is to decorate functional items; typical applications are containers for tobacco and spices, and the handles of betel-nut crushers and knives. Materials include wood, horn and bone. Sindu and Senanti are centres for carving.

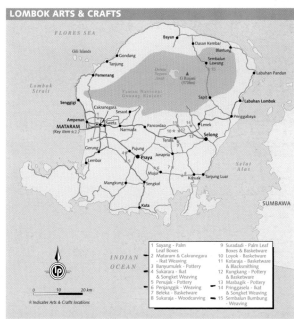

Box: Detail from a traditional Sumbanese ikat weaving pattern. Sumbanese ikat is widely available on Lombok.

LOMBOK ARTS & CRAFTS

1 Sayang - Palm Leaf Boxes
2 Mataram & Cakranegara - Ikat Weaving
3 Banyumulek - Pottery
4 Sukarara - Ikat & Songket Weaving
5 Penujak - Pottery
6 Penjanggik - Weaving
7 Beleka - Basketware
8 Sukaraja - Woodcarving
9 Suradadi - Palm Leaf Boxes & Basketware
10 Loyok - Basketware
11 Kotaraja - Basketware & Blacksmithing
12 Rungkang - Pottery & Basketware
13 Masbagik - Pottery
14 Pringgasela - Ikat & Songket Weaving
15 Sembalun Bumbung - Weaving

★ Indicates Arts & Crafts locations

0   10   20 km

INDIAN OCEAN

Weaving

A number of classic Indonesian weaving techniques are used. Weaving factories around Cakranegara and Mataram produce ikat on old hand-and-foot-operated looms. You can visit them, see the dyeing and weaving processes, and buy fabrics by the metre or made up as shirts, blouses etc.

Sukarara and Pringgasela are villages which specialise in traditional ikat and *songket* weaving. Sarongs, Sasak belts and clothing edged with brightly coloured embroidery are sold.

RICHARD I'ANSON

SARA-JANE CLELAND

Top & bottom: Plying the loom in central Lombok – an industry that supports many villagers throughout the region.

Basketware

Lombok is noted for its spiral woven rattan basketware, bags made of lontar or split bamboo, small boxes made of woven grass and plaited rattan mats. Decorative boxes of palm leaves made in the shape of rice barns and decorated with small shells are another Lombok exclusive. Much of the work is sold directly for export, and may be easier to find on Bali than Lombok.

Beleka, Suradadi, Kotaraja and Loyok are noted for fine basketware, while Rungkang, about 1km east of Loyok, combines pottery and basketware, as pots are often finished with a covering of woven cane for decoration and extra strength. Sayang is known for palm-leaf boxes.

Bottom left & right:
Women at work weaving baskets in the village of Loyok in central Lombok.

RICHARD I'ANSON

RICHARD I'ANSON

Ceramics

Lombok pots have become widely known. The small village of Penujak, 6km south of Praya, is well known for its *gerabah* pottery, made from a local red clay. You can watch the pots being handmade and fired in traditional kilns in the roadside workshops along the main street. Some of the larger pots would be difficult to carry, but there are also small animal-shaped figurines. Banyumulek and Masbagik are also centres for the production of traditional pottery.

SARA-JANE CLELAND

RICHARD I'ANSON

Top left, top right & bottom: While they can be a little difficult to transport, the distinctive ceramic pots of Lombok are keenly sought by collectors across the world.

RICHARD I'ANSON

Members of the Wektu Telu religion regard themselves as Muslims, although they are not officially accepted as such by mainstream Muslims.

The fundamental tenet of Wektu Telu is that all important aspects of life are underpinned by a trinity. One example of this principle is the trinity of Allah, Mohammed and Adam. Allah symbolises the one true God, Mohammed is the link between God and human beings, and Adam represents a being in search of a soul. The sun, the moon and stars are believed to represent heaven, earth and water. The head, body and limbs represent creativity, sensitivity and control.

On a communal basis, the Wektu Telu believe they have three main duties – to believe in Allah; avoid the temptations of the devil; and co-operate with, help and love other people. The faithful must also pray to Allah every Friday, meditate and undertake to carry out good deeds.

The Wektu Telu do not observe Ramadan, the month-long period of abstinence so important in the Islamic faith. Their concession to it is a mere three days of fasting and prayer. They also do not follow the pattern of praying five times a day in a holy place – one of the basic laws of Islam. While prayer and meditation are of supreme importance in their daily rituals, the Wektu Telu believe in praying from the heart when and where they feel the need, not at appointed times in places specifically built for worship. According to them, all public buildings serve this purpose and all are designed with a prayer corner or a small room which faces Mecca. Wektu Telu do not make a pilgrimage to Mecca, but their dead are buried with their heads facing in that direction.

As for not eating pork, the Wektu Telu believe that everything which comes from Allah is good.

Castes Unlike the Muslims, the Wektu Telu have a caste system. There are four castes, the highest being Datoe, then (in order) Raden, Buling and Jajar Karang.

LANGUAGE

Most people on Lombok are bilingual, and speak their own ethnic language (Sasak), as well as the national language, Bahasa Indonesia, which they are taught at school and use as their formal and official mode of communication.

Apart from those working in the tourist industry, few people on Lombok speak English, and this includes police and other officials. Nevertheless, English is becoming more widely spoken on Lombok. Travellers without a grasp of Bahasa Indonesia can get by in the tourist centres, but some knowledge of the local tongue will enhance your visit to the island and endear you to its people – it could also be invaluable in an emergency!

Outside the main centres, finding anyone who can say more than a few phrases of English is extremely rare. If you can't speak Indonesian, arm yourself with a phrasebook and dictionary.

The Language chapter at the end of this book has some useful words and phrases in Bahasa Indonesia and Sasak.

Facts for the Visitor

Most of the information covered in the Bali Facts for the Visitor chapter is also relevant to Lombok. This chapter has information specific to Lombok.

SUGGESTED ITINERARIES
You'll need at least one week to fully appreciate Lombok, plus another few days if you plan to climb Gunung Rinjani. Two weeks is about all you need, unless you plan to do a lot of trekking, sunbaking and exploring of traditional villages. Whether you begin in Labuhan Lombok (by ferry from Sumbawa), Lembar (by ferry from Bali) or Mataram (by air), you can easily follow each of these suggested itineraries.

One Week
West & North Lombok Wander around Ampenan and Mataram (one day; or a day trip from Senggigi), laze around Senggigi (one/two days), visit the glorious Gili Islands (maybe one day on each island) and relax in Senaru (one/two days).

The Lombok Circle If you're pressed for time, try this: Mataram (one day), Senggigi (one day), the Gilis (two days), Senaru (one day), Tetebatu (one day) and Kuta (one day).

Sun, Surf & Sand Some people spend their whole time on the Gilis, but you can also enjoy Senggigi and Kuta, and explore the remote coastlines east and west of Kuta and along the remote south-west peninsula.

Two Weeks
West & North Lombok This allows you to really explore the places previously mentioned, with more time to snorkel, dive, hike and visit pretty villages around Mataram.

The Lombok Circle Two weeks is idea for this loopl: Mataram & around (two days), Senggigi (one/two days), the Gilis (three/four days), Senaru (two days, or longer if you want to climb Rinjani), Selong or Labuhan Haji to explore the east coast (one day), Tetebatu and visits to traditional villages (two days), and Kuta and around (two days).

Beaches & Trekking Some people come for the fresh air and landscapes, or diving and surfing. Try: the Gilis (three days), a trek up Rinjani

from Senaru (four days), Selong or Labuhan Haji (one day), Tetebatu (two days), Kuta and around (three days), and the south-west peninsula (one day).

PLANNING
When to Go
The dry season (June to September) is hotter than Bali, but is better for trekking and travel to remote areas. The wet season is a little hotter and considerably more humid, but quite OK; in some ways it's more pleasant than dry, dusty conditions, and the landscape is greener and more attractive.

The Muslim fast of Ramadan is not the best time to visit Lombok, especially the traditional rural areas (see the Public Holidays & Special Events section later in this chapter).

Maps
The maps in this guidebook will be sufficient for most visitors, except perhaps the serious trekkers, cyclists, divers and surfers. Periplus' *Lombok & Sumbawa* is the best map around; you can buy it in most foreign countries and on Bali, but not on Lombok.

Two good maps are available on Lombok and Bali: the colourful *Lombok* map, published by Travel Treasure Maps, has useful maps of the main tourist areas on the back; and the *P. Lombok* map, published by PT Karya Pembina Swajaya, is large and detailed. The free maps provided by both tourist offices in Mataram are useful; tourist maps of Bali rarely include anything useful about Lombok.

TOURIST OFFICES
There are two regional tourist offices in Mataram, and a tiny one at the ferry terminal at Lembar. Staff are friendly and helpful.

VISAS & DOCUMENTS
Visa requirements are the same as for Bali (see the Bali Facts for the Visitor chapter).

There is an immigration office *(kantor imigrasi)* in Mataram. If you want to hire a car or motorbike on Lombok, you'll need an International Driving Permit.

MONEY
Exchanging Money
You can change cash and travellers cheques in major currencies at banks and money-changers in Mataram and the tourist centres (Senggigi, the Gilis and Kuta). Money-changers normally offer more attractive exchange rates than banks, but their rates are 10% to 15% lower than at tourist centres on Bali, so it's worth stocking up on rupiah if you are arriving from Bali. You can have money transferred to Bank Exim in Mataram. In remote areas of Lombok it's often difficult to get change for large notes, so always carry a lot of small notes and loose change.

Costs
Costs are similar to those on Bali for an equivalent standard of food and accommodation, but there are not as many mid-range places to stay or eat, and generally not as many temptations, so you'll probably spend less money on Lombok. Entry charges are not so common, but you will often be asked for a donation on some pretext and it's good manners to make one. If you share a double room in the budget range, eat in simple restaurants and travel by public transport, about 40,000 rp per person per day will be enough.

POST & COMMUNICATIONS
The main post office in Mataram is the only one with a poste restante service; other post offices will accept poste restante mail, but then redirect it to Mataram. You can have mail sent to your hotel, but it may take time.

You can send and receive international calls and faxes from private and Telkom *wartels* (public telephone offices) in most larger towns, for about the same cost as in Bali. There is a Home Country Direct Dial telephone inside the waiting room at the Mataram airport. The emergency telephone numbers for Lombok are the same as on Bali. All of Lombok is in the ☎ 0370 telephone area code.

There are Internet centres in Senggigi, and on Gili Air. Like on Bali, access is slow, but the costs are reasonable.

BOOKS
Western publications about Lombok are a rarity compared with the many works available about Bali. Most of the information about Lombok can be found in more general works about Nusa Tenggara and Indonesia. Alfons van der Kraan's book, *Lombok: Conquest, Colonisation & Underdevelopment, 1870-1940*, is a history of the colonial period.

Very few bookshops on Lombok sell books in English. There is a small selection at the supermarket in Senggigi, and second-hand bookshops in Kuta and Tetebatu. Some of the popular *losmen* (family-run hotels) around the island may have a few second-hand paperbacks for sale. You should stock up on reading material (and maps) on Bali.

PHOTOGRAPHY & VIDEO
Colour print film is easy to buy and develop in Senggigi and Mataram; the price is similar to Bali. You should buy and develop slide film at home or on Bali. Bring your own video tapes.

Most people on Lombok are happy to have their photo taken, but ask anyway. If they're reluctant, it may be because they don't think they look their best. However, if someone's dressed up for a ceremony, they may be disappointed if you *don't* photograph them.

ELECTRICITY
In most towns the electricity supply is 220V, but some smaller places still have 110V. In less developed parts of Lombok, including Gili Air, Gili Meno and Kuta, electricity supply is limited, erratic or nonexistent. In these three tourist areas, mid-range and upmarket hotels normally have small generators, but the cheaper places may have no

electricity at all, so bring candles and a torch (flashlight).

TOILETS

Lombok is relatively poor and undeveloped, so toilets in most restaurants and budget hotels are more likely to be the squat-style variety, and they won't provide toilet paper. Toilet paper is available at general stores throughout Lombok, but if there's a bin next to the toilet, use it to dispose of the paper so you don't clog up their systems.

HEALTH

Most of the health considerations are the same as for Bali, except that malaria is a real risk on Lombok. See the Health section in the Bali Facts for the Visitor Chapter for details.

Malaria

The risk is greatest in the wet months and in remote areas. The very serious *P. falciparum* strain causes cerebral malaria and may be resistant to many drugs. For a full discussion, see the Health section in the Bali Facts for the Visitor chapter.

Medical Services

There are a few decent hospitals in Mataram, as well as less salubrious public hospitals in Praya (Central Lombok) and Selong (East Lombok). There is also a medical clinic for tourists in Senggigi. For anything serious, go to Denpasar or even Singapore or Darwin. There are pharmacies in the main towns and tourist centres, but the choice of medicines is limited.

WOMEN TRAVELLERS

People are pretty reserved on Lombok, and women are generally treated with respect. The sort of harassment that western women sometimes experience in some other Muslim countries is very unusual, although not unheard of in tourist centres such as Senggigi, where there a growing number of beach boys/guides/gigolos. One female reader wrote complaining of 'Indonesian men running around at midnight grabbing my crotch area' on Gili Trawangan.

Please dress with more respect than you may on Bali: beachwear is OK around Senggigi and the Gilis (but less so at Kuta); elsewhere on Lombok, shorts and loose tops are definitely frowned upon by locals. And attitude is often as important as what you wear.

TRAVEL WITH CHILDREN

Lombok is generally quieter than Bali and the traffic is much less dangerous. People are fond of kids, but a little more reserved about it than the Balinese. The main reservation about bringing kids to Lombok is the risk of malaria. Discuss malaria prevention with your doctor. Weekly tablets are probably easier for kids than daily ones. You can also get antimalarials for children in syrup form. For a full discussion of malaria and its prevention, see the Health section in the Bali Facts for the Visitor chapter.

DANGERS & ANNOYANCES

The traffic is much lighter here than on Bali, but there is still a danger of traffic accidents. Trekkers sometimes hurt themselves, and there have been some deaths from falls on Gunung Rinjani or drowning in the crater lake. Most beaches are protected by coral reefs, and are quite safe, but there are strong currents at places around the Gili Islands and Kuta, and no lifeguards anywhere.

There is a growing problem of theft on Lombok, most commonly from hotel and losmen rooms in tourist centres. Generally, you are less likely to be hassled by hawkers than on Bali, but it's becoming more of a problem, especially at Senggigi and Kuta. In less touristy areas, the main annoyance may just be the curiosity of locals, especially youngsters.

PUBLIC HOLIDAYS & SPECIAL EVENTS

The Bali Facts for the Visitor chapter has a list of public holidays in Indonesia.

Lombok has many of its own festivals and holidays. Most festivals take place at the beginning of the rainy season (around October to December) or at harvest time (around April to May). During these periods there are celebrations in villages all over the island, and people dress in their most resplendent clothes. Wooden effigies of horses and lions are carried in processions through the streets, and the sound of the gamelan reaches fever pitch. While most of these ceremonies and rituals are annual events, most of them do not fall on specific days in the western calendar.

Ramadan

Ramadan, the month of fasting *(puasa)*, is the ninth month of the Muslim calendar. During Ramadan people rise early for a big breakfast, then abstain from eating, drinking and smoking until sunset. Many visit family graves and royal cemeteries, recite extracts from the Koran, sprinkle the graves with holy water and strew them with flowers. Special prayers are said at mosques and at home.

During this period, many restaurants are closed, and foreigners eating, drinking (especially alcohol) and smoking in public are regarded with a contempt which can border on aggression. During Ramadan, Muslims may be preoccupied with fasting and other religious obligations, and have little or no time for business or socialising.

The end of Ramadan, Idul Fitri (also called Hari Raya), is a major celebration and holiday, so transport and accommodation is crowded, but it's an interesting time to be on Lombok. Don't plan on travelling anywhere. Stay put, ideally in a Balinese-run hotel, but don't miss the celebrations on the streets.

The Muslim year is shorter than the western one so their festivals and events fall at a different time each year.

Ramadan will occur between the following dates for the next few years:

9 December 1999	to	8 January 2000
27 November 2000	to	27 December 2000
17 November 2001	to	16 December 2001
6 November 2002	to	6 December 2002
27 October 2003	to	25 November 2003

You should remember though that these dates are approximate and that, depending on the cycles and more importantly actual sightings of the moon, Ramadan could actually fall a few days either side of these dates. You would be advised to seek more current information if you are considering travelling around any of these times.

Other Religious Festivals

Other occasions observed on Lombok include:

Bersih Desa – a festival occurring at harvest time, when houses and gardens are cleaned, fences whitewashed, and roads and paths repaired. Once part of a ritual to rid villages of evil spirits, it is now held in honour of Dewi Sri, the rice goddess.

Hari Raya Ketupat – a Wektu Telu celebration held at Batulayar, near Senggigi, seven days after the end of Ramadan.

Harvest Ceremony – held at Gunung Pengsong, near Mataram, some time around March or April as a thanksgiving for a good harvest. This Bali Hindu ceremony involves a buffalo being dragged up a steep hill and then sacrificed.

Idul Adha – a day of sacrifice held on the 10th day of the 11th month of the Muslim calendar. People visit the mosque and recite passages from the Koran.

Idul Fitri – also called Hari Raya, this is the first day of the 10th month of the Muslim calendar and the end of Ramadan. This climax to a month of austerity and tension is characterised by wild beating of drums all night, fireworks and no sleep. At 7 am everyone turns out for an open-air service. Women dress in white and mass prayers are held followed by two days of feasting. Extracts from the Koran are read and religious processions take place. Gifts are exchanged and pardon is asked for past wrongdoings. Everyone dresses in their finest and newest clothes, and neighbours and relatives are visited with gifts of specially prepared food. It is traditional to return to one's home village, so many Indonesians travel at this time. At each house visited, tea and sweet cakes are served, and visiting continues until all the relatives have been seen.

Maulid Nabi Mohammed – also called Hari Natal, Mohammed's birthday is held on the 12th day of the 12th month of the Arabic calendar.

Mi'raj Nabi Mohammed – a festival celebrating the ascension of Mohammed.

Puasa – a Wektu Telu festival held in deference to the Muslim period of abstinence. The three days of fasting and prayer begin at the same time as Ramadan.

Perang Ketupat – an annual rain festival held at Lingsar, near Mataram, between October and December. Adherents of the Wektu Telu religion and Balinese Hindus give offerings and pray at the temple complex, then come out and pelt each other with *ketupat*, sticky rice wrapped in banana leaves. (The Lingsar section in the West Lombok chapter has more information.)

Pujawali – a Bali Hindu celebration held every year at Pura Kalasa temple at Narmada, near Mataram, in honour of the god Batara, who dwells on Lombok's most sacred mountain, Gunung Rinjani. At the same time, the faithful who have made the trek up the mountain and down to Danau Segara Anak hold a ceremony called *pekelan*, where they throw gold trinkets and objects into the lake.

Pura Meru – a special Bali Hindu ceremony held every June at full moon in the Balinese Pura Meru temple at Cakranegara (in Mataram).

ACTIVITIES

Lombok doesn't quite offer the same range of activities as Bali, but you can enjoy a round of golf at Golong (near Mataram), boat trips around the Gili Islands and horse riding at Sembalun Lawang in the north, as well as trekking, diving, snorkelling and surfing elsewhere on the island.

Trekking

Gunung Rinjani (3726m) and its surroundings is a superb area for trekking. It's possible to get up to the crater rim and back in a single day, but it's much more rewarding to do a longer trip, which will involve about three nights' camping. Equipment, guides and porters can be hired in Sapit, Sembulan Lawang and Senaru, but most people start from Senaru.

If you just want to explore the countryside on foot and visit a number of villages, the area of central Lombok, between the main east-west road and the southern slopes of Rinjani, is highly recommended. Other shorter hikes include the waterfalls around Tetebatu, also on the southern slopes; villages around Mataram, especially Air Nyet and in Hutan Wisata Suranadi; Loang Gali; Sapit; the remote coastline east and west of Kuta; and Gili Trawangan.

Surfing

The south and east coasts of Lombok get the same swells that generate the big breaks on Bali's Bukit Peninsula. The most accessible surfing beach is Kuta, where there are hotels, restaurants and a surf shop. Other south-coast places which you can get to by land, with a little difficulty, include Selong Blanak, Mawun and Ekas – lots of breaks are accessible by boat from these areas. Desert Point on the south-west peninsula is Lombok's best known break (a classic, fast, tubular left), but it doesn't work regularly as it needs a good size swell. You can reach it by land, but there's no regular public transport, nor is there any visitor facilities.

The easiest way to get around is on a surf tour on a chartered yacht, usually from Bali. These cost about US$200 per person (depending on demand and the number of passengers) for a seven day, all-inclusive trip around Nusa Lembongan, Lombok and Sumbawa. Enquiries and bookings can be made at surf shops in the Kuta region on Bali.

Nyale Fishing Festival

On the 19th day of the 10th month in the Sasak calendar – generally February or March – hundreds of Sasaks gather on the beach at Kuta, Lombok. When night falls, fires are built and young people sit around competing with each other in rhyming couplets called *pantun*. At dawn the next day, the first *nyale* (a worm-like fish), are caught, after which it's time for teenagers to have fun. In a colourful procession boys and girls sail out to sea – in different boats – and chase one another with lots of noise and laughter. The nyale are eaten raw or grilled, and are believed to have aphrodisiac properties. A good catch is a sign that the rice harvest will also be good.

Diving & Snorkelling

There is great scuba diving and snorkelling off the Gili Islands, and some less exciting options near Senggigi. A few dive operators are located on the Gilis and in Senggigi, but some are better than others, so stick with a reputable operator. (More details can be found in the West Lombok and Gili Islands chapters.) New diving areas are still being explored on Lombok, such as Gili Petangan off the east coast, but you'll need the help of a good operator and guide to reach remote areas. In the current economic climate, and with the dearth of tourists on Lombok, large discounts at diving centres are often possible, so diving is often considerably cheaper than on Bali.

The Diving section in the Bali Facts for the Visitor chapter has more detailed information about accredited courses, prices, dive sites and equipment.

ACCOMMODATION

Accommodation is not widely available throughout the island. Senggigi has the only 'international' hotels; Mataram has a good range of budget and mid-range hotels, mainly catering to businessmen; Senggigi, the Gili Islands, Senaru, Tetebatu and Kuta have many losmen, and a few mid-range places; more remote stretches of the coastline have a few tourist hotels; and the main regional towns have a few basic options. If you are stuck in a remote area, ask to stay with the *kepala desa* (village head).

On the Gilis, a typical Lombok beach bungalow is a hut on stilts with a small verandah out the front and a concrete bathroom out the back. Almost all of them are at the bottom of the price range, usually starting from 12,500/15,000 rp for singles/doubles, including a light breakfast. Some of these places are depressing and dirty, but others are an absolute delight.

FOOD

There are tourist-oriented restaurants in the tourist centres, but elsewhere you'll mainly eat Indonesian or Chinese food, but ensure you also try some delicious Sasak food. In Bahasa Indonesia, the word *lombok* means 'chilli pepper' and it's used liberally in the local cooking.

Sasak food uses white rice as a staple, served with vegetables and hot chilli. A little chicken is used, some fish, very little red meat and no pork. The meat component is frequently offal, such as liver, brains or intestine. For some regional specialities, see the glossary at the rear of this book.

Sweets

Sweet sticky things are popular in Sasak cooking. They are typically combinations of sticky rice or rice flour, with palm sugar, coconut and coconut milk, wrapped in a banana leaf or pressed into a small cake. They are commonly offered to visitors with coffee or tea.

DRINKS

Although the water on Lombok is generally OK to drink, you may want to pop in a purifying tablet to be on the safe side. Bottles of mineral water, however, are widely available, and there is a refill service on the Gilis and at Senggigi. Tea *(teh)* is commonly served with meals.

Alcohol is not common on Lombok, because the population is predominantly Muslim, but beer and spirits are available at bars and restaurants in tourist centres. *Brem* (rice wine) and *tuak* (palm beer) are made locally, but are not conspicuous.

For a mild intoxicant, some people chew betel nut. It's mainly used by older men and women in the more isolated villages, but is becoming less common. It helps to relieve the pain of toothache and gum disease, and improved dental health is one reason for declining use.

ENTERTAINMENT

The local population is not big on nightlife – the cinema or *bioskop* (if it's still functioning) in larger towns is about as exciting as it gets. Traditional dances for tourists can be seen in Senggigi. Ask around, or enquire at the tourist offices in Mataram, about genuine traditional dances and ceremonies in the villages.

There are some bands, singers and acoustic guitarists playing in Senggigi, but little elsewhere on the island. On the Gilis – particularly Gili Trawangan – there is lots of western-style dancing, drinking and late-night loitering in the beachside bars and restaurants. Video nights at restaurants are common in tourist centres, but not as much as on Bali.

SPECTATOR SPORTS

Sasaks (males anyway) are keen on competitive sports. There's quite a large football (soccer) stadium near Mataram, and every town has a makeshift football field. Volleyball, badminton and table tennis are also popular. Late in the afternoon in almost any village you will find young men enjoying an enthusiastic game of volleyball or soccer, often with an enthusiastic audience as well.

SHOPPING

Handcrafts on Lombok are traditional, practical articles like boxes, basketware and pottery, handmade from natural materials such as palm leaf, bamboo, grass fibres and rattan. Handwoven sarongs and fabrics are especially interesting and attractive. For more details, see the Lombok Arts & Crafts colour section in the Facts About Lombok chapter, and study the Lombok Arts & Crafts map which highlights villages that specialise in certain crafts. Shops in Mataram and the tourist centres also stock items from all over Lombok, as well as other parts of Indonesia.

Nearly every village on Lombok has basic shops, and a market at least once a week, with numerous stalls selling food, clothes, handcrafts and many other items. The largest daily market with the broadest variety is at Sweta (in Mataram). Supermarkets in Mataram and Senggigi have the best range of western-style goods.

Getting There & Away

Lombok is easy to reach by air and sea from neighbouring islands, but is not as accessible from other parts of Indonesia or nearby countries. The vast majority of visitors come from Bali, less than 100km away, while those island-hopping from the east will normally come from Sumbawa.

AIR

The economic problems at the time of research has resulted in significant changes in the schedules of all airlines which used to fly to Lombok. Just prior to publication of this book, the Indonesian government increased the prices for internal flights by 40%; further increases are not out of the question either. Be sure to check the latest schedules with individual airlines.

Airline Offices

The offices for the airlines currently represented on Lombok are:

Bouraq
   (☎ 27333) Hotel Selaparang, Mataram. This office will remain open for bookings on flights elsewhere in Indonesia, but Bouraq flights to/from Lombok have been cancelled.
Garuda Indonesia
   (☎ 32305) Hotel Lombok Raya, Mataram
Merpati Airlines
   (☎ 36745) Main office: Jl Selaparang, Mataram
   (☎ 33844) Agency: Jl Selaparang (opposite Perama office), Mataram
Sempati
   (☎ 21612, fax 25037) Cilinaya shopping centre, Mataram. This office is currently closed, and Sempati flights to/from Lombok have been temporarily cancelled.
Silk Air
   (☎ 36924) Jl Raya Senggigi, Senggigi
   (☎ 93877, fax 93822) Airport Office

A number of travel agents in Mataram and Senggigi sell tickets and reconfirm flights, and you can also buy tickets at the airport. It's important to reconfirm because all flights are on small planes and it's very easy to get bumped. Flights are often cancelled at short notice. If you buy return or onward tickets on Bali for flights leaving Lombok make sure the domestic tax is included; it should be, but isn't always.

Departure Tax

The departure tax for domestic flights is 8000 rp. The tax for international flights is the same as on Bali (ie 30,000 rp).

Singapore

The Singapore Airlines subsidiary, Silk Air, has direct flights from Singapore five times a week for US$220/321 (one way/return), but given the current economic circumstances, this flight may be cancelled in the future. You will have to go to Denpasar or Jakarta for other international flights.

Bali

Merpati Airlines is now the only domestic airline flying to and from Lombok. At the time of research, there are 10 flights a day from Denpasar to Mataram and back for 119,000 rp. While the ferry is much cheaper, the flight only takes about 25 minutes, so you can probably get from your hotel in Kuta Beach, Bali, to another hotel in Senggigi in less than two hours if you travel by air. Because foreigners can pay for the flight in rupiah, and the exchange rate is very favourable, this flight is an attractive alternative to taking a ferries between the ports of Padangbai (Bali) and Lembar (Lombok).

Other Indonesian Islands

From Mataram, Merpati also has direct flights every day to Sumbawa Besar (149,800 rp) and Bima (284,100 rp) in Nusa Tenggara, and Surabaya (266,600 rp) on Java. To other places – such as Yogyakarta, Jakarta and Ujung Pandang – you will have to change planes in Denpasar or Surabaya.

LAND
Public Bus
Many public buses travel every day between the Mandalika terminal at Sweta (in Mataram) and the major cities on Sumbawa, Java and Bali. For long-distances, book your ticket a day or two ahead at the terminal, or from a travel agency along Jl Pejanggik/ Selaparang in Mataram. If you get to the terminal before 8 am, there may be a spare seat on a bus going in your direction, but this is especially risky during any major public holiday. You may also get a spare seat on a bus at the ports of Labuhan Lombok and Lembar, but don't count on it.

Sometimes you have the choice between a cheaper (economy) bus and a more expensive (luxury) one with air-con and reclining seats, but often there is no option. The official fares are displayed on a green board outside the Mandalika terminal, but prices do vary from one company to another. All fares include ferry charges. The fares listed here were current at the time of writing, but are prone to change. Where there's two prices, they denote economy/luxury.

Destination	Time	Cost (rp)
Bima	12 hours	16,100/27,500
Denpasar	6 hours	20,000
Dompu	10 hours	14,400/22,500
Jakarta	two nights	90,000
Ruteng	20 hours	60,000
Sape	14 hours	17,400
Semarang	28 hours	60,000
Sumbawa Besar	5 hours	8950/15,000
Surabaya	20 hours	40,000
Yogyakarta	30 hours	70,000

Tourist Shuttle Bus
The Bali-based company, Perama, has tourist shuttle bus/boat services between the main tourist centres on Lombok, including Senggigi, the Gili Islands and Kuta, and most tourist centres on Bali, such as Ubud, Sanur and the Kuta region. A few other companies offer similar services at similar prices. Tickets can be booked directly or at any travel agency on Lombok or Bali, and prices include boat or ferry charges. Most companies use the public Padangbai-Lembar ferry, but it's worth checking to see if Perama uses its quicker shuttle boat.

Shuttle buses are more expensive than public transport, but they save you considerable hassle changing bemos and waiting for ferries. For example, a ticket on a shuttle bus/boat between Ubud (Bali) and Kuta (Lombok) costs about 25,000 rp. By public transport, the trip would only cost about 10,000 rp (if you weren't overcharged), but involves about five bemo connections.

SEA
Bali
Ferry Ferries travel from Padangbai (Bali) to Lembar (Lombok) every 60 to 90 minutes, 24 hours a day, every day. The cost for VIP (1st) class is 9000/5000 rp for adults/children; for *economi* (2nd) class, it's 5500/2900 rp. VIP class has an air-con area with a snack bar and video entertainment. Economy passengers sit on bench seats or wherever they can find a spot.

Bicycles cost an extra 700 rp, motorbikes 6200 rp, and cars and jeeps 35,700 rp. Food and drinks are available on board or from the numerous hawkers who hang around the wharves until the ferry leaves. The trip takes at least four hours, and sometimes up to seven.

Mabua Express The luxury jet-powered *Mabua Express* (☎ 0361-721212 on Bali or ☎ 0370-81225 on Lombok) travels once or twice a day in both directions between the Pelni port at Lembar (Lombok) and Pelabuhan Benoa (Bali). The official fare is US$25/ 17.50 for 'diamond/emerald' (1st/2nd) class, but at the time of research this was dearer than the flight, so prices were slashed to 80,000 rp for one class only. This should include transfer from any hotel in south Bali and west Lombok, but double-check this. You can book directly or at just about any travel agency on Lombok or Bali.

Pelni Boat They're neither frequent nor reliable, but two boats from the national shipping line, Pelni, travel from Lembar (Lombok) to Pelabuhan Benoa (Bali) about every week. Tickets on *Awu* and *Tilongkabila* cost 33,000/25,500/13,000 rp for 1st/2nd/economy class and can be booked at the Pelni office in Mataram – see the Other Islands entry later in this section for details.

Sumbawa

Ferries travel between Labuhan Lombok (Lombok) and Poto Tano (Sumbawa) every 45 to 60 minutes, 24 hours a day, every day. *Ekonomi B* (2nd) class fares are 2350/1550 rp for adults/children, and *ekonomi A* (1st) class is 3650/2000 rp. Motorbikes cost 6050 rp, and cars 36,900 rp. If you are coming from Sumbawa, start early so you can reach Labuhan Lombok by 4 pm, because public transport is limited after this time.

Other Indonesian Islands

Currently three Pelni boats, *Kelimutu*, *Awu* and *Tilongkabila*, do regular loops through the islands of Indonesia, stopping at Lembar about once a fortnight. You can book tickets at the Pelni office (☎ 37212) in Mataram Monday to Saturday from 8.30 am to 12 pm, and 1 to 3 pm, except Friday when it closes at 11 am.

ORGANISED TOURS

Many companies organise tours around Lombok from Bali. They normally use the rapid *Mabua Express*, before tearing through Senggigi, Kuta and several handcraft villages in central Lombok by bus. From Bali, day trips cost about US$75 per person and can be booked at any travel agent on Bali. Longer (and more expensive) tours are also available.

Boat Trips to Komodo

Boat trips from Lombok to islands further east are widely promoted. The main destination is Pulau Komodo island, near Flores, to see the giant monitor lizards called Komodo dragons, but the boats also make stops at other islands for snorkelling, trekking and beach parties.

Some of these trips are pretty rough, with minimal safety provisions. Try to get a recent personal endorsement and find out *exactly* what the cost includes. One reader savagely complained about one company which does not apparently have the appropriate licence (nor the expertise and equipment) to take tours to Komodo and beyond.

The tourist shuttle bus/boat company, Perama, is usually pretty reliable, although the trip gets mixed reviews from readers – some say its a waste of time and money; others had great fun. Costs are approximately 450,000/775,000 rp for four/seven days.

One of the several upmarket options is offered by Spice Island Cruises (☎ 0361-286283 on Bali, email cruzresv@denpasar.wasantara.net.id).

Getting Around

Lombok has an extensive network of roads, although there are many outlying villages that are difficult to get to by public transport. There is a good road across the middle of the island between Mataram and Labuhan Lombok, and quite good roads to the south of this route. The road around the north coast is rough but passable, while the roads to the extreme south-west and south-east are very rough or nonexistent.

Public buses and bemos are generally restricted to the main roads. Away from these, you will have to hire a pony cart *(cimodo)*, get a lift on a motorbike, or walk. In the north-east and south there is usually some public transport between the bigger towns, but it might mean waiting a long time and riding in the back of a truck. Most public transport becomes scarce in the afternoon and ceases after dark (or earlier in more remote areas). If you find yourself in the sticks without your own wheels, you could try to charter a bemo or just make yourself comfortable as you can until sunrise.

During the wet season many unsealed roads are flooded or washed away, while others are impassable because of fallen rocks and rubble, making it impossible to reach out-of-the-way places. The damage may not be repaired until the dry season.

As methods of transport around Lombok are very similar to those on Bali, you may also wish to refer to the Bali Getting Around chapter for more information.

BUS
Public Bus, Minibus & Bemo

Buses are the cheapest and most common way of getting around – public bemo for shorter distances, and bus or minibus for longer stretches. On rough roads in remote areas, trucks may be used as public transport. The main terminal for all of Lombok is at Sweta (part of the capital city, Mataram). There's other regional terminals are at Praya, Kopang, Anyar, and Pancor, near Selong.

You may have to go via one or more of these transport hubs to get from one part of Lombok to another.

Public transport fares are fixed by the provincial government, and displayed on a noticeboard outside the terminal in Sweta. This does not stop the bus and bemo drivers from trying to overcharge you, however, so check what the locals are paying. Children on a parent's knee are free, and kids up to the age of 11 cost around half price. You may have to pay more if you have a large bag or surfboard.

As with all public transport in Indonesia, drivers wait until their vehicles are filled to capacity before they leave. If you offer to pay extra for the one or two fares the driver is *still* waiting for, you will depart sooner, and become instant friends with other passengers. The maximum permitted number of passengers is usually written somewhere in or on the vehicle – but an extra one or two are usually somehow squeezed in.

Bemos can be an uncomfortable way to get around, and you often won't see much of the scenery. On the other hand, people are very friendly, the fares are very cheap and transport is fairly frequent around most of the island.

Chartering a Bemo If you're pressed for time or flush with cash, chartering a bemo (or private car) from one place to another, or even for one or more days, is convenient and affordable, especially if you can share costs. Drivers may be reluctant to venture off sealed roads, however, because they don't want to damage their precious vehicles.

Some bemos are restricted to a certain route or area (for example, the yellow bemos that shuttle around Mataram cannot be chartered for a trip to Lembar), but most bemos and minibuses can be chartered anywhere around Lombok. Prices are strictly negotiable, and depend on your bargaining skills. About 80,000 rp per day (from 8 am to 5 pm) plus petrol, is not unreasonable. The driver will want more for long waits, rough roads and any other reason he can come up with. You can often arrange this through your *losmen* (family-run hotel), or simply go to a bemo terminal and negotiate with a driver.

Check that the vehicle is roadworthy. A straightforward trip can quickly turn into a nightmare if you find yourself out after dark, in the rain, with a wiperless and unlit bemo.

Tourist Shuttle Bus As on Bali, shuttle buses link the main tourist centres on Lombok. Currently this service links Mataram with Kuta, Senggigi, Bangsal and Tetebatu – so you cannot travel from, say, Kuta to Bangsal without changing shuttle buses first in Mataram, but you can normally connect on the same day. From Senggigi, there are also shuttle boats to the Gili Islands (see the Boat section later in this chapter).

Shuttle buses are certainly more comfortable, reliable and expensive than public transport, but not as frequent. They are also cheaper than renting or chartering a vehicle, but if you're travelling in a group of three to five, it's cheaper to charter a bemo for the trip, and the departure times and itineraries on a chartered bemo will be more flexible.

You should try to book a seat on a shuttle bus the day before you want to travel; you can buy tickets at the shuttle bus offices or from most travel agencies and shops in the tourist centres. Perama is the most established operator and has the widest network, but some smaller outfits, notably Lombok Mandiri (☎ 36796) in Senggigi are a little cheaper.

CAR & MOTORBIKE
Renting and driving a car or motorbike is much the same as on Bali, so please refer to the Bali Getting Around chapter for details. One main advantage is that Lombok traffic is more bearable, but this is offset by the bad roads in some parts.

Petrol is available at stations in and around the larger towns; out in the villages, petrol is sold from plastic containers at small wayside shops, and costs about 50 rp more.

Rental
There are several car and motorbike rental companies in Mataram and Senggigi. It may be more convenient and less expensive to arrange something through your hotel (if you are staying somewhere cheap), so ask them first. Senggigi has the best choice of vehicles and most competitive prices for rentals on Lombok.

Car Car rental is becoming more organised on Lombok, although in some cases you are still just borrowing a car from a private owner. The ubiquitous Suzuki *jimny* jeep will cost about 60,000 rp per day, plus petrol and insurance. Larger Toyota Kijang jeeps are not common, but if you can find one they cost about 90,000 rp per day, plus insurance (which is dearer than on Bali). Prices will be less per day for longer rentals. The requirements regarding insurance and deposits are the same as on Bali, and you must have an International Driving Permit.

Motorbike A motorbike is ideal for the tiny, rough roads which are difficult or impassable by car. Once you get out of the main centres there's not much traffic, apart from people, dogs and water buffalos – and watch out for the numerous potholes.

Expect to pay about 17,500 rp per day, including insurance, for a normal scooter, and more for a Yamaha trail bike (110cc). The police on Lombok don't seem to mind if your International Driving Permit is not endorsed for motorbikes, but no-one (especially the police) has a definite policy about the matter. It is best to ask the rental agency/owner about the current requirements.

If you get a motorbike licence on Bali, it is valid for Lombok. Always check the condition of the motorbike, as some are not well maintained and you can quickly get into areas where there's no spare parts or mechanical help.

Bringing a Car or Motorbike from Bali
If you deal with a reputable rental agency on Bali, they should allow you to take a car or motorbike to Lombok for up to one week,

on the condition you return it to Bali. For anything longer, they may be more anxious and require a substantial deposit. As cars on Bali are only registered for driving on that island, you'll need a special permit (25,000 rp) from the police in Denpasar. The rental agency can arrange this quickly and easily.

Taking a rented motorbike from Bali to Lombok is no problem: for some reason, no special permit is needed.

Generally, it's less hassle and possibly cheaper (if you factor in the ferry charges), to make your own way across to Lombok, and rent a car or motorbike over there. If your rental car from Bali breaks down, for example, contacting the agency on Bali and arranging repairs can be problematic.

OJEK

An ojek is a motorbike on which you ride as a paying pillion passenger. The cost is highly negotiable, but about 1000 rp per 5km is not unreasonable. They are very convenient where bemos are infrequent (such as between Pomotong and Tetebatu), and they are not nearly as frightening as ojeks on Bali.

BICYCLE

Travelling around on a bicycle – especially a mountain bike – is ideal on Lombok; the roads are reasonably flat (although they get steepish anywhere around Gunung Rinjani) and the traffic is far less dangerous than on Bali. If you plan to explore remote regions, remember that food and water are often scarce so carry your own, and take a good hat. Bicycles are available for rent in and around the main tourist centres of Lom-bok, including the Gili Islands, but you normally can't take them very far. If you are keen, bring a bike from home or Bali.

The best area for cycling is just east of Mataram (see the Around Mataram section in the West Lombok chapter). Other routes you could try are: Mataram to Banyumulek, via Gunung Pengsong, and return; or the coastal road from Mataram to Pemenang, via Senggigi and (if you feel energetic),

return via the steep road through the Pusuk Pass.

Alternatively, there's two agencies that arrange bicycle tours around Lombok: Mega Handika Tour (☎ 33321, fax 35049, email megatourim@mataram.wasantara.net.id), at Jl Panca Usaha 3, Mataram; and PT Lombok Independent (☎ 32497; fax 36796), at Jl Gunung Kerinci 4, Mataram. Trips cost from US$35 to US$45 per day, including gear and food, and can be booked directly, or at the West Lombok tourist office in Mataram.

CIDOMO

The pony cart used on Lombok is known as a cidomo, a typically complex contraction of cika (traditional handcart), dokar (the usual Indonesian word for a pony cart) and mobil (because car wheels and tyres are used). They are normally brightly coloured with decorative motifs, and are fitted out with bells that chime when in motion. A typical cidomo has bench seating on either side which can comfortably fit three people, or four if they're all slim. It's not unusual, however, to see half a dozen or more passengers, plus several bags of rice and other paraphernalia piled up in a cart.

The ponies appear to some visitors to be heavily laden and harshly treated, but they are usually looked after reasonably well, if only because the owners depend on them for their livelihood. Cidomos are a very popular form of transport in many parts of Lombok, and often go to places that bemos don't, won't or can't.

Fares are not set by the government. For foreigners, the price will always depend on demand, the number of passengers, the destination and your negotiation skills, so there's little point in listing prices. The best idea is to ask other passengers what they are paying.

BOAT

The only regular public boat is between Bangsal and the Gili Islands, but the tourist shuttle bus operator, Perama, and a few other companies, offer shuttle boat services to the Gilis, mainly from Senggigi.

Chartered Boat

You can also charter a boat to the Gilis from Senggigi or Bangsal if the public or shuttle boats have left. To reach the more remote islands, snorkelling spots and surf breaks, you'll have to rent a *prahu* (outrigger boat). They often use a small outboard motor, but sail-powered ones are still common. Rental prices are negotiable, but as a rule of thumb about 10,000 rp per hour, or 60,000 to 80,000 rp per day (including petrol and labour) is reasonable.

LOCAL TRANSPORT

Only Mataram and Senggigi are large enough to warrant any intra-city public transport. There are plenty of bemos and taxis around Mataram, and a few in Senggigi. Taxis can be chartered with or without the meter to anywhere within the immediate area. The taxis at the airport have fixed prices (see the Mataram section in the West Lombok chapter).

To get around town, most locals walk, take a cidomo or hire an ojek.

ORGANISED TOURS

Organised tours provide a quick introduction to the highlights of the island, and you can always re-visit your favourite places later. Most tours are half-day trips around Mataram; or full-day trips to Kuta and the south coast, to the central craft villages, or to the Gili Islands and north coast. Prices start at about 25,000/40,000 rp per person for a half-day/full-day tour.

You can arrange a tour with any travel agency in Senggigi or Mataram, or ask the West Lombok tourist office in Mataram for some suggestions. Don't forget: you can always rent or charter a vehicle and create your own itinerary.

Bali-based Perama shuttle bus company, which has main offices in Mataram and Senggigi, is a budget-minded outfit with a range of interesting tours. One fascinating option is a tour run by Alternative Lombok (☎/fax 25508), which gives visitors a chance to stay in a traditional home and learn about the Sasak way of life. The profits are used to fund community projects.

Alternatively, you can tour by bicycle or on horseback; for the latter try Lotus Asia Tours (☎ 36781, fax 35753, email lombok @mataram.wasantara.net.id), Jl Raya Senggigi, Senggigi.

The Bali Getting There & Away chapter has more information about organised tours to Java, Sumbawa and the rest of Nusa Tenggara from Lombok.

West Lombok

- Ampenan, Lombok's port in colonial times, retains a quaint down-at-heel charm, with picturesque streets and interesting antique shops.

- The villages and scenery east of Mataram are very similar to Bali, and perfect for picnics, hikes and bicycle riding.

- Senggigi, the main resort area, has a good range of accommodation, and the beachfront restaurants are delightful.

- The huge, covered market at Sweta sells a vast array of food, spices, baskets, sarongs and hand-made utensils.

Most travellers end up spending some time in West Lombok, which has the bustling capital of Mataram, the resort town of Senggigi and the ferry service to/from Bali. There are also several beautiful villages just to the east of Mataram which you should try to explore any way you can.

MATARAM

The capital and Lombok's main city, Mataram is actually a conglomeration of four towns – Ampenan, Mataram, Cakranegara and Sweta. Some travellers use Mataram as a base, but most head straight to Senggigi or the Gili Islands, and don't stay here at all. There are banks, travel agencies, airline offices, some interesting shops and markets, and a few other things to see, but the city is not a major attraction, and it can be visited easily on a day trip from Senggigi.

Orientation

The four towns are spread along one main road which starts as Jl Pabean in Ampenan,

quickly becomes Jl Yos Sudarso, changes to Jl Langko then Jl Pejanggik, and finishes up in Sweta as Jl Selaparang. It runs from west to east and is one way for it's entire length. A parallel one way road, Jl Tumpang Sari/Panca Usaha/Pancawarga/Pendidikan, takes traffic back towards the coast.

Ampenan Once the main port of Lombok, Ampenan is now little more than a small fishing harbour. While it's a bit run-down and dirty, it still has some character. The main road does not quite reach the coast at Ampenan; it simply fades out just before it gets to the port's grubby beach. Ampenan has a curious mixture of people. Apart from the Sasaks and Balinese, there are also some Chinese, plus a small Arab quarter known as Kampung Arab. The Arabs living here are devout Muslims and usually well educated.

Mataram Mataram is the administrative capital of the province of Nusa Tenggara Barat (West Nusa Tenggara). Some of the public buildings, such as the banks, post office and governor's office and residence, are substantial.

Cakranegara Now the main commercial centre of Lombok, bustling Cakranegara is usually referred to as Cakra. Formerly the capital of Lombok under the Balinese rajahs, Cakra today has a thriving Chinese community, as well as many Balinese residents.

Sweta Sweta has the central transport terminal of Lombok – Mandalika terminal. This is where you catch bemos and buses to other parts of the island and to Bali and Sumbawa. Stretching along the eastern side of the terminal is a vast, covered market, the largest on Lombok. If you wander through its dim alleys you'll see stalls spilling over with coffee beans, fruit, eggs, fabrics, rice, fish, crafts and hardware.

Top: A diver examines acropora coral near the Gili Isands off Lombok's north-western coast.
Middle left: The long nosed hawkfish *(Oxycirrhites typus)*.
Middle right: Feather duster worms *(Protula magnifica)*.
Bottom left & right: Schooling jacks from the diver's perspective and close up.

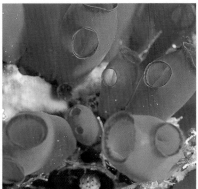

Top left: Thorny oyster *(Spondylus varians)*.
Top right: The Royal Blue Tunicate *(Rhopalaea sp)*.
Middle: A group of scalefin anthias *(Pseudanthias squamipinnis)*.
Bottom left & right: A diver swims among seafans, and a seascape with soft coral and sea whips.

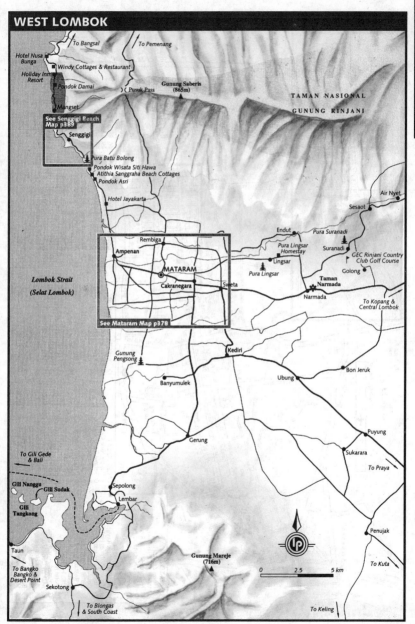

WEST LOMBOK

To Bangsal
To Pemenang

Hotel Nusa Bunga
Windy Cottages & Restaurant
Holiday Inn Resort
Pondok Damai

Mangset

See Senggigi Beach Map p388

Senggigi

Pura Batu Bolong
Pondok Wisata Siti Hawa
Atithia Sanggraha Beach Cottages
Pondok Asri

Hotel Jayakarta

Pusuk Pass

Gunung Saberis (865m)

TAMAN NASIONAL
GUNUNG RINJANI

Air Nyet

Sesaot

Endut
Pura Suranadi

Pura Lingsar Homestay
Suranadi
GEC Rinjani Country Club Golf Course

Rembiga

Ampenan

MATARAM

Cakranegara
Sweta

Lingsar
Pura Lingsar
Golong

Taman Narmada

Narmada

To Kopang & Central Lombok

See Mataram Map p378

Lombok Strait
(Selat Lombok)

Gunung Pengsong

Kediri

Banyumulek

Ubung

Bon Jeruk

Puyung

To Gili Gede & Bali

Gerung

Sukarara

To Praya

Gili Nanggu
Gili Sudak

Gili Tangkong

Sepolong

Lembar

Taun

To Bangko Bangko & Desert Point

Sekotong

To Blongas & South Coast

Gunung Mareje (716m)

Penujak

To Kuta

To Keling

0   2.5   5 km

WEST LOMBOK

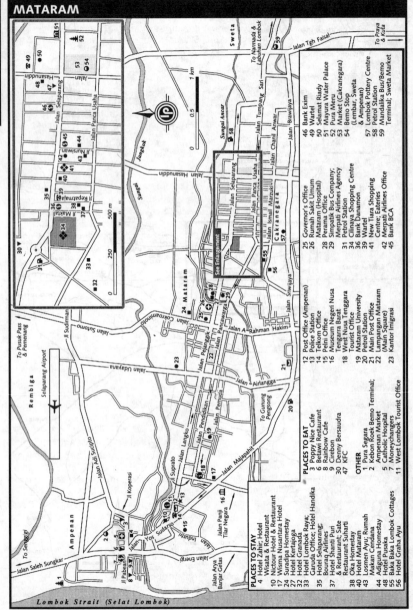

MATARAM

1 km

0.5

0

500 m

250

0

Lombok Strait (Selat Lombok)

PLACES TO STAY
4   Hotel Zahir; Hotel
    Wisata & Restaurant
10 Nictour Hotel & Restaurant
17 Wisma Nusantara Hotel
24 Suradipa Homestay
27 Hotel Kertajoga
32 Hotel Granada
33 Hotel Lombok Raya;
    Garuda Office; Hotel Handika
35 Hotel Selaparang;
    Bouraq Airlines
37 Hotel Shanti Puri
    Restaurant Sate
    Restaurant Suharti
38 Oka Homestay
40 Hotel Mataram
43 Losmen Ayu; Rumah
    Makan Cendana
44 Adiguna Homestay
48 Hotel Pusaka
55 Baka Baka Lombok Cottages
56 Hotel Graha Ayu

PLACES TO EAT
3   Poppy Nice Cafe
6   Betawi Restaurant
8   Rainbow Cafe
9   Grebon
30 Denny Bersaudra
47 KFC

OTHER
1   Pura Segara
2   Kebon Roek Bemo Terminal;
    Ampenan Market
5   Catholic Hospital
7   Moneychangers
11 West Lombok Tourist Office
12 Post Office (Ampenan)
13 Police Station
14 Telkom Office
15 Pelni Office
16 Museum Negeri Nusa
    Tenggara Barat
18 West Nusa Tenggara
    Tourist Office
19 Mataram University
20 Petrol Station
21 Main Post Office
22 Lampangan Mataram
    (Main Square)
23 Kantor Imigrasi
25 Governor's Office
26 Rumah Sakit Umum
    Mataram (Hospital)
28 Telkom Office
29 Perama Bus Company;
    Sinjara Bus Company;
    Merpati Airlines Agency
31 Petrol Station
34 Cilinaya Shopping Centre
36 Bank Danamon
39 Wartel
41 New Tiara Shopping
    Centre; Eateries
42 Merpati Airlines Office
45 Bank BCA
46 Bank Exim
49 Wartel
50 Selamat Riady
51 Mayura Water Palace
52 Pura Meru
53 Market (Cakranegara)
54 Bemo Stop
    (Lembar, Sweta
    & Ampenan)
57 Lombok Pottery Centre
58 Petrol Station
59 Mandalika Bus/Bemo
    Terminal; Sweta Market

Information

Tourist Offices Mataram has two tourist offices. The office responsible for the province of West Nusa Tenggara (☎ 21658), which includes Lombok, is on Jl Suprato, just north of the museum in Ampenan. It is overflowing with helpful staff, but is only worth visiting if you need information or maps for Sumbawa. It also has brochures about other provinces in Indonesia, but little about Lombok.

The office for West Lombok (☎ 31730), which includes Mataram and Senggigi, is on Jl Langko near the Ampenan post office. It actually serves as an unofficial tourist office for all of Lombok. The staff are friendly and well informed, and it's worth visiting to check the latest airline and Pelni schedules, and to book organised tours. It's open Monday to Thursday from 7 am to 2 pm, closing at 11 am on Friday, and 1 pm on Saturday.

Lombok's *kantor imigrasi* (immigration office, ☎ 22520) is on Jl Udayana, the road out to the airport.

Money There are a number of banks along the main road in Cakra. Most will change money and travellers cheques, although it may take some time. There are also money-changers in Ampenan and in the Cilinaya shopping centre which are efficient, open for longer hours and have slightly better rates than the banks – but the rates in Senggigi will generally be better. You can also change money at the airport.

Post The main post office is inconvenient, in the south of Mataram, but it does have the only poste restante service on Lombok. It is open Monday to Saturday from 8 am to 2 pm, except Friday when it closes at 11 am.

A more convenient post office is located opposite the West Lombok tourist office in Ampenan.

Telephone The Telkom office in Ampenan provides telegram and fax services, and is open 24 hours a day. The international telephone service from this office is efficient, and you can usually get an overseas call connected within a minute or so. There's also a few *wartels* (public telephone offices) around town, and a Home Country Direct Dial telephone in the waiting room of the airport.

Emergency The two best hospitals on Lombok are in the city: Rumah Sakit Umum Mataram (☎ 21345) has English-speaking doctors; and the Catholic Hospital (☎ 21397) in Ampenan is also good. The main police station (☎ 110), where you may have to go for a local motorbike licence (if you haven't obtained one from Bali), is on Jl Langko.

Pura Segara

This Balinese sea temple is on the beach about 1km north of Ampenan. Nearby are the remnants of a **Muslim cemetery** and an old **Chinese cemetery** – both are worth a wander through if you're visiting the temple.

Museum Negeri Nusa Tenggara Barat

This modern museum has exhibits on the geology, history and culture of Lombok and Sumbawa, and is worth a look around if you have a free hour or so. If you intend buying any antiques or handcrafts, have a look at the *krises*, *songket* (silver or gold-threaded cloth), basketware and masks to give you a starting point for comparison. It's open Tuesday to Sunday from 8 am to 2 pm, but closes at 11 am on Friday. The admission price for tourists is 2500 rp.

Mayura Water Palace

On the main road through Cakra, this palace was built in 1744, and once part of the Balinese kingdom's royal court on Lombok. The main feature is a large artificial lake with an open-sided pavilion in the centre, connected to the shoreline by a raised footpath. This *bale kambang* (floating pavilion) was used as both a court of justice and a meeting place for the Hindu lords. There are other shrines and fountains dotted around the surrounding park.

The entrance to the walled enclosure of the palace is on the western side (tickets

WEST LOMBOK

cost 500 rp). Although not a patch on Tirta Gangga on Bali, it's a pleasant retreat. Less than a century ago it was the site of bloody battles with the Dutch.

Pura Meru

Directly opposite the water palace is Pura Meru, the largest temple on Lombok. It was built in 1720 under the patronage of the Balinese prince, Anak Agung Made Karang of the Singosari kingdom, as an attempt to unite all the small kingdoms on Lombok, and as a symbol of the universe, dedicated to the Hindu trinity of Brahma, Vishnu and Shiva.

The outer courtyard has a hall housing the wooden drums that are beaten to call believers to festivals and special ceremonies. In the middle courtyard are two buildings with large raised platforms for offerings.

The inner court has one large and 33 small shrines, as well as three *meru* (multi-roofed shrines) which are in a line: the central one, with 11 tiers, is Shiva's house; the one to the north, with nine tiers, is Vishnu's; and the seven tiered one to the south is Brahma's.

Battleground of Yesteryear

The grounds of the Mayura Water Palace today are used as a place to unleash fighting cocks and make offerings to the gods. However, less than a century ago it was the site of bloody battles with the Dutch.

In early 1894 the Dutch sent an army to back the Sasaks in a rebellion against their Balinese rajah. The rajah quickly capitulated, but the crown prince decided to fight on while the Dutch-backed forces were split between various camps.

The Dutch camp at the Mayura Water Palace was attacked late at night by a combined force of Balinese and western Sasaks. The camp was surrounded by high walls, and the Balinese and Sasaks took cover behind them as they fired on the exposed army, forcing the Dutch to take shelter in a nearby temple compound. The Balinese also attacked the Dutch camp at Mataram, and soon after the entire Dutch army on Lombok was routed and withdrew to Ampenan where, according to one eyewitness, the soldiers 'were so nervous that they fired madly if so much as a leaf fell off a tree'. The first battles resulted in enormous losses of men and arms for the Dutch.

Although the Balinese had won the battle, they had just begun to lose the war. Now they would not only have to continue to fight the eastern Sasaks, but also the Dutch, who were quickly supplied with reinforcements from Java.

The Dutch attacked Mataram a month after their initial defeat, fighting street to street against Balinese and west Sasak soldiers, and also the local population. The Balinese crown prince was killed in the battle for the palace and the Balinese retreated to Cakranegara, where they were well armed and the complex of walls provided good defence against infantry. Cakra was attacked by a combined force of Dutch and eastern Sasaks. As occurred in Mataram, the Balinese men, women and children opted for the suicidal *puputan* (fight to the death) rather than surrender, and were cut down by rifle and artillery fire. The rajah and a small group of *punggawas* (commanders) fled to the village of Sasari near the pleasure gardens at Lingsar. A day or two later the rajah surrendered to the Dutch, but even his capture did not lead the Balinese to surrender. In late November the Dutch attacked Sasari and, again, a large number of Balinese chose the puputan. With the downfall of the dynasty, the local population abandoned its struggle against the Dutch. The conquest of Lombok, considered for decades, had taken the Dutch barely three months. The old rajah died in exile in Batavia (now Jakarta) in 1895.

The meru are also said to represent the three great mountains, Rinjani, Agung and Bromo.

The temple is open every day, and a donation is expected (about 500 rp) for the caretaker who will lend you a sash, and a sarong if you need one. A major festival is held here every June – ask either tourist office in Mataram for details.

Places to Stay – Budget

Although some budget places in Ampenan and Mataram are cheap and popular, Cakra is the most central, convenient and pleasant place to base yourself. Most budget and mid-range hotels include breakfast.

Ampenan A short stroll from the centre is the unassuming *Hotel Zahir* (☎ 34248). The rooms at this Balinese-style losmen each have a small verandah facing a central courtyard, and go for 8000/10,000/15,000 rp for singles/doubles/triples. The staff are friendly and helpful, and can arrange cheap motorbike rental.

On the same street, the *Hotel Wisata* (☎ 26971) has a good choice of clean and comfortable rooms ranging from 12,500/ 15,000 rp for singles/doubles to 35,000/ 40,000 rp with air-con. It's the best option in Ampenan, even if it lacks character.

Mataram The cheapest place in the whole city is *Suradipa Homestay* (☎ 24576), on the tiny Gang Macan VII alley – look for the sign off Jl Cockroaminoto. Don't expect too much luxury, but it is very good value at 7500/10,000 rp for singles/doubles with a fan and private bathroom. Close to the Perama office, on Jl Perjanggik, *Hotel Kertajoga* (☎ 21775) is noisy but good value, with fan-cooled rooms for 19,500/23,000 rp and air-con rooms for 27,500/ 33,000 rp. *Wisma Nusantara Hotel* (☎ 23492) is central and has a large number of clean (but noisy) rooms, so you will always be guaranteed a bed. The rooms are US$11, but the manager is certainly willing to negotiate.

Cakranegara Along the side streets south of Jl Selaparang there are a number of good,

cheap Balinese-style losmen, although there seems to be an inordinate number of mosques within earshot. Look for the signs to the losmen along Jl Selaparang.

On Jl Repatmaja, the quaint *Oka Homestay* (☎ 22406) is family-run, has a quiet garden and is often full. Singles/doubles cost 12,500/15,000 rp. On Jl Nursiwan, *Adiguna Homestay* (☎ 25946) is another good budget place with rooms from 12,500/ 15,000 rp. The popular and friendly *Losmen Ayu* (☎ 21761), on the same street, is well set up for budget travellers. It offers comfortable rooms for 12,500/15,000 rp, and a range of better, cleaner and newer rooms over the road for 20,000/25,000 rp. Rooms with air-con cost considerably more, and it has a kitchen which guests can use.

On Jl Maktal, the *Hotel Shanti Puri* (☎ 32649), is almost of mid-range quality, with rooms for 20,000/25,000 rp. More expensive rooms are available with air-con and hot water for 45,000/50,000 rp. It is on a quiet street, and is a good place to get travel information.

Places to Stay – Mid-Range

Ampenan The *Nictour Hotel* (☎ 23780, fax 36579) is quiet and comfortable, with carpets, air-con and telephone. 'Superior' rooms cost 90,000/110,000/130,000 rp for singles/doubles/triples, and another 30,000 rp per person for the 'deluxe' rooms. It is often quiet, and at such times discounts of up to 40% are possible.

Mataram The location of *Hotel Granada* (☎ 36015) is a little inconvenient, but pleasant enough. All rooms have air-con, hot water and TV, and there's a swimming pool. Singles/doubles start at 70,950/76,450 rp; ask for a low-season discount regardless of the time of year. Nearby, the new *Baka Baka Lombok Cottages* (☎ 25378) has a range of quaint, clean and large cottages for 57,500 rp, with hot water. This is currently excellent value – no doubt an introductory offer to entice guests.

Hotel Handika (☎ 33321) is in a noisy part of town on Jl Pancawarga. Fan-cooled rooms cost from US$8/10 to US$28/30, but the management is happy to offer discounts of 50%.

The central *Hotel Pusaka (☎/fax 33119)* has rooms with air-con and TV from 47,500/55,000 rp to 100,000/125,000 rp. The *Hotel Graha Ayu (☎ 35697)* offers rooms from 55,000/66,500 rp with all the mod cons, but it's unappealing.

Cakranegara There are quite a few good-value, mid-range places in Cakra, although anywhere along the main road will be noisy. *Hotel Selaparang (☎ 32670)* has a good range of rooms from 25,410/30,250 rp with a fan, to 51,425/57,475 rp with air-con, hot water and TV. The management will happily offer discounts of about 20%. Across the road, *Hotel Mataram (☎/fax 34966)* has a small pool and cluster of standard rooms for 30,000/37,500 rp; air-con rooms with TV and hot water cost 40,000/45,000 rp.

Places to Stay – Top End

Hotel Lombok Raya (☎ 32305, fax 36478) in Mataram is the only top-end place in the city. It offers attractively furnished, fully equipped US$55/60 singles/doubles, and a big swimming pool. It's pretty good value compared with equivalent places on Bali.

Places to Eat

Ampenan There are several decent Indonesian and Chinese restaurants, including the popular *Cirebon*, with a standard menu, and dishes from around 5000 rp. A little further west, the *Rainbow Cafe* is a cheap, friendly little place with reggae-inspired decor, a few books, cold beer and reasonable food. *Poppy Nice Cafe* is as appealing as its name, with a good range of well prepared dishes and very hospitable management. *Hotel Wisata* and *Nictour Hotel* also have decent restaurants.

The best place in Ampenan is *Betawi Restaurant*, right on the corner of Jl Sungkar and Jl Yos Sudarso. From the upstairs area you can look down and watch Ampenan go about its business. There is a good range of

Indonesian, Chinese and western dishes (for about 7500 rp), and the beer is cold.

Mataram *Denny Bersaudra* is a good place to try some authentic Sasak-style food from about 6000 rp a dish. Look for the sign at the roundabout along western Jl Selaparang.

Cakranegara The *Hotel Shanti Puri* is a friendly place with a wide range of tasty food. The nearby *Sate Restaurant Suharti* is worth visiting for its selection of delicious sates from 3500 to 5000 rp. Near the junction of Jl Selaparang and Jl Hasanuddin, and around the nearby market, there are many unexciting Javanese-style *rumah makans*, but none is particuialrly memorable nor worth recommending.

Rumah Makan Cendana is handy to the Losmen Ayu and Adiguna Homestay, and offers a good range of meals from 3500 rp. There are also decent *restaurants* in most of the hotels along Jl Selaparang, and some cheap *eateries* in the New Tiara shopping centre. Most visitors, and affluent locals, end up at the conspicuous *KFC* – the only fast food outlet on the island.

Shopping

If you don't have time to visit the villages where traditional handicrafts are made (see the Lombok Arts & Crafts colour section in the Facts about Lombok chapter), you'll find a good selection at shops and markets in town. Shops also sell 'primitive' objects like masks and carvings, imported from other parts of Indonesia – although some are locally made imitations. Items that are used or dirty are often described as antiques, but very few pieces are more than a few years old. Objects like wooden cowbells show some patina if they are genuinely old, but the best advice is to buy things for what they are, and not because they purport to be from a certain period or a certain place.

Handcrafts & Antiques There's two areas in Ampenan which have a good selection of handcraft shops and are interesting to browse around. Look on and around the western side of Jl Saleh Sungkar (the road north to Seng-gigi), and around the shops close to Hotel Zahir. An excellent place to look for local products is the Sweta market.

Pottery The Lombok Pottery Centre, on the southern edge of Cakra, displays and sells some of the best products available. While it's more interesting to go to the villages and see the pots being made, this centre has an excellent selection from all of the main pottery places. Their prices are reasonably competitive; it's cheaper than in Senggigi, but more expensive than buying directly from the villagers.

Textiles There's a couple of weaving factories in Cakra, where you can see dyeing and weaving, and buy *ikat* or handwoven *songket* sarongs. Selamat Riady, on Jl Tanun, just east of Jl Hasanuddin, is open on most mornings, and has a shop with textiles and a few other crafts.

Getting There & Away
Air Refer to the Lombok Getting There & Away chapter for details of flights to/from Lombok, and for contact details of airline offices in Mataram.

Bus & Bemo The Mandalika terminal in Sweta is the main bus and bemo terminal for the entire island. It is also the terminal for long-distance buses to Sumbawa, Bali and Java (see the Lombok Getting There & Away chapter for details), and is the eastern terminus for local bemos which shuttle back and forth to Ampenan.

The terminal is fairly chaotic, so you may have to rely on the touts to show you which bus or bemo to catch. Long-distances buses leave from behind the main terminal building; bemos and smaller buses for Lombok leave from one of two car parks either side. Any vehicle without a destination sign on top can usually be chartered for very negotiable prices.

The distances and current fares for buses and bemos from Sweta to major towns and terminal junctions on Lombok are:

Destination	Distance	Price (rp)
Bayan	79km	2100
Kopang	25km	600
Kuta	54km	1250
Labuhan Lombok	69km	2050
Lembar	22km	700
Pancor	47km	1400
Pemenang	31km	700
Pomotong	34km	800
Praya	27km	700
Tanjung	45km	1150

The Kebon Roek terminal at Ampenan is for bemos to Sweta and Senggigi. A trip up the coast to Senggigi costs 500 rp from Ampenan, but you'll probably end up paying a little more for the 'tourist price'. Some bemos also travel between Sweta and Senggigi, although you often have to change in Ampenan.

Ojek You can always arrange a trip around Mataram, or anywhere else on Lombok, on the back of a motorbike. Ask around the hotels in Ampenan, or look for any motorcyclist hanging around the markets in Cakra, Ampenan and Sweta. Hotel Zahir can arrange day trips by *ojek* to anywhere you want from 35,000 rp per day.

Getting Around
To/From the Airport Selaparang airport to the north is nice and convenient. Pre-paid taxis to anywhere in Mataram cost 7500 rp; it's 12,000 rp to Senggigi; 26,000 rp to Bangsal and Lembar; and 41,000 rp all the way to Tetebatu. Alternatively, you can walk out of the airport carpark to the main road and take one of the frequent No 7 bemos which run to the Ampenan terminal, or look for a *cidomo* (pony cart) to Mataram from the corner of Jl Sutomo and Jl Sudirman.

Bemo Ampenan-Mataram-Cakra-Sweta is very spread out, so don't plan to walk from place to place. Impressive new yellow bemos shuttle back and forth every half-second between the Kebon Roek terminal in Ampenan and the Mandalika terminal in Sweta. Some make slight detours, but they generally travel along the two main thoroughfares. The fare is a standard 400 rp regardless of the distance. Outside the market in Cakra there is a handy bemo stop for services to Ampenan, Sweta and Lembar. The terminals at Sweta and Ampenan are good places for chartering bemos.

Car & Motorbike Most hotels in the city can arrange the rental of cars and motorbikes. Several rental agencies are based along Jl Pendidikan and Jl Pancawarga, and near Hotel Zahir in Ampenan. The West Lombok tourist office in Ampenan can also help. However, you are better off renting in Senggigi where prices are more competitive, and the range of vehicles is larger.

AROUND MATARAM

Not far east of Sweta, there are some gorgeous areas of villages, rice fields and temples; reminiscent of some of the best landscapes and scenery that Bali has to offer. You can easily visit all the following places in half a day if you have your own transport; if you don't, it's worth chartering a bemo or taxi. Riding a bicycle would be an excellent alternative (see the Bicycle section in the Lombok Getting Around chapter for other ideas).

Taman Narmada

Laid out as a miniature replica of the summit of Gunung Rinjani and its crater lake, Taman Narmada (Narmada Park) takes its name from an Indian sacred river. Its temple, **Pura Kalasa**, is still used and the Balinese Pujawali celebration is held here every year in honour of the god Batara, who dwells on Gunung Rinjani.

Taman Narmada was constructed by the king of Mataram in 1805, when he was no longer able to climb Rinjani to make offerings to the gods. Having set his conscience at rest by placing offerings in the temple, he spent at least some of his time in his pavilion on the hill, lusting after the young girls bathing in the artificial lake.

Along one side of the pool is the remains of an aqueduct built by the Dutch and still in use. Land tax was tied to the productivity of the land, so the Dutch administration was keen to maximise the agricultural output. They achieved this by extending the irrigation systems to increase the area under cultivation. The Balinese had already built extensive irrigation networks, particularly in the west of Lombok.

This is a beautiful place to spend a few hours, but don't go there on weekends when it tends to become very crowded. Apart from the lake there are two **swimming pools** in the grounds. It is open daily from 7 am to 6 pm. Tickets cost 500/250 rp for adults/children, plus another 500/250 rp to swim in the pools.

Places to Eat Right at the Narmada bemo stop is the local **market**, which sells mainly food and clothing, but is well worth a look. A number of *warungs* scattered around sell *soto ayam* (chicken soup) and other dishes. Otherwise, take some food and drink and enjoy a picnic on the grounds.

Getting There & Away Narmada is on a hill about 6km east of Sweta, on the main east-west road crossing Lombok. Frequent bemos from Sweta take you to the Narmada market (400 rp), directly opposite the entrance to the gardens.

Pura Lingsar

This large temple complex, built in 1714, is the holiest place on Lombok. The temple combines the Bali Hindu and Wektu Telu religions in one complex. Designed in two separate sections and on different levels, the Hindu temple in the northern section is higher than the Wektu Telu temple in the southern section.

The Hindu temple has four shrines. On one side is Hyang Tunggal, which looks towards Gunung Agung, the seat of the gods on Bali. The shrine faces north-west rather than north-east as it would on Bali. On the other side is a shrine devoted to Gunung Rinjani, the seat of the gods on Lombok. Between these two shrines is a double shrine symbolising the union between the two islands. One side of this double shrine is named in honour of the might of Lombok, and the other side is dedicated to a king's daughter, Ayu Nyoman Winton; according to legend, she gave birth to a god.

The Wektu Telu temple is noted for its small enclosed pond devoted to Lord Vishnu. It has a number of holy eels that look like huge swimming slugs – they can be enticed from their hiding places with hard-boiled eggs which can be bought from stalls outside and inside the temple complex. You will be expected to rent a sash and/or sarong (or bring your own) to enter the temple, but this is not necessary just to enter the outside buildings.

During the annual rain festival at the start of the wet season – somewhere between October and December – the Hindus and Wektu Telu make offerings and pray in their own temples, then come out into the communal compound and pelt each other with *ketupat* – rice wrapped in banana leaves. The ceremony is to bring the rain, or to give thanks for the rain.

Places to Stay & Eat There are a few basic *food stalls* and shops in the parking area. The only place to stay is *Pura Lingsar Homestay*, about 500m from the temple, on the road towards Suranadi. Pleasant singles/doubles cost 15,000/20,000 rp.

Getting There & Away Lingsar is not on the main east-west road from Sweta. First take a bemo from Sweta to Narmada (400 rp), and catch another to Lingsar (400 rp). Ask to be dropped off near the entrance to the temple complex, which is 300m down a well marked path off the main road.

Suranadi

Suranadi is a pleasant little village in the sort of gorgeous countryside that is becoming difficult to find on Bali. There is a temple, a small pocket of forest, a hotel and several good restaurants all in the middle of the village.

Pura Suranadi This is one of the holiest Hindu temples on Lombok. Set in pleasant gardens, it is noted for its bubbling, icy cold spring water and restored baths with ornate Balinese carvings. The eels (and even tuna) are also sacred and seldom underfed. Like the temples on Bali, you will be asked for a 'donation' for the rental of a sash and/or sarong.

Hutan Wisata Suranadi Just opposite the village market, an entrance leads to a small forest sanctuary. It is a bit neglected, but it's a shady and quiet area for some short **hikes** and is good for **birdwatching**. It now also proudly boasts what is probably Lombok's only elephant. Tickets cost 1000 rp, and it is open daily during daylight hours.

Places to Stay & Eat *Suranadi Hotel* (☎ 33686, fax 35630) has decent rooms for US$30, and cottages which are overpriced at US$60 – breakfast is not included. It is an old Dutch building, which was originally an administrative centre, but it's no great example of colonial architecture. There are two swimming pools, tennis courts, a restaurant and a bar. It's a lovely place to stay for a while, particularly if you can negotiate a better price. The public can stop for a swim in the refreshingly cool pool at the hotel for 2000/1000 rp for adults/children.

Pondok Surya has basic rooms, a nice outlook and an excellent *restaurant*, which is mainly for guests. It's casual and friendly, and the rooms, which are a bit dark, cost 15,000 rp per person. Look for the sign at the market.

A little further away (charter a bemo), *Teratai Cottages* is better. Bungalows cost from 30,000 to 60,000 rp, and there's a swimming pool and tennis court.

Several upmarket *restaurants* are dotted along the main road, opposite the entrances to the temple and forest, hoping to catch the occasional tour groups. You can also eat in cheap *warungs* at the market.

Getting There & Away You will have to wait for a public bemo from Narmada; if that fails, charter one for a negotiable 10,000 rp one way.

Golong

About half way between Suranadi and the main road, on a quiet back road, Golong is the site of Lombok's only golf course, **GEC Rinjani Country Club** (☎ 33488, fax 33839). A round of golf will cost US$46 on weekdays and US$69 on weekends, plus caddie fees (US$12) – which is far cheaper than anywhere on Bali. Accommodation is US$81 in a comfortable motel-style room, or US$69 for a villa. There's a great swimming pool, which the public can enjoy for 10,000/5000 rp for adults/children. You will have to charter a vehicle to get there.

Sesaot

About 5km north-east from Suranadi is Sesaot, a charming, quiet market town on the edge of a forest where wood-felling is the main industry. There are some gorgeous spots for a **picnic**, and you can **swim** in the river. The water is very cool and is considered holy as it comes straight from Gunung Rinjani. There is regular transport from Narmada, and you can eat at the **warungs** along the main street.

Air Nyet

Further east, Air Nyet is another pretty village with more places for **swimming** and **picnics**. Ask directions for the unsigned turn-off in the middle of Sesaot. The bridge and road to Air Nyet are rough, but it's lovely **walk** (about 3km) along the forest path. You have to buy tickets (500 rp) on Sunday and holidays, when the place is very busy, but otherwise the forest is gloriously empty and serene. You may have to charter a vehicle from Sesaot or Narmada.

GUNUNG PENGSONG

This Balinese temple is built – as the name suggests – on top of a hill. It's 9km south of Mataram and has great views of rice fields, volcanoes and the sea. The whole area was used by retreating Japanese soldiers to hide during WWII, and remnants of **cannons** can be found, as well as lots of pesky monkeys.

Try to get there early in the morning before the clouds envelop Gunung Rinjani.

Beautifully handcarved ornaments were once regular temple offerings, particularly to Dewi Sri, the rice goddess. Today, rice cakes, fruit and paste ornaments are more commonly seen.

Once a year, generally in March or April, a buffalo is taken up the steep 100m slope and sacrificed to give thanks for a good harvest. The Bersih Desa festival also occurs here at harvest time – houses and gardens are cleaned, fences whitewashed, and roads and paths repaired. Once part of a ritual to rid the village of evil spirits, it is now held in honour of the rice goddess Dewi Sri.

There's no set admission charge, but you will have to tip the caretaker about 500 rp. There is very little direct public transport from Sweta, so you might have to charter or rent a vehicle.

BANYUMULEK

This is one of the main pottery centres of Lombok, specialising in decorated pots and pots with a woven fibre covering, as well as more traditional urns and water flasks. It is close to the city, a couple of kilometres west of the Sweta-Lembar road, which carries frequent bemos. It's easy to combine Banyu-mulek with a visit to Gunung Pensong if you have your own transport, if you want to walk, or (better still), use a bike. For details, refer to the Bicycle section in the Lombok Getting Around chapter.

LEMBAR
Lembar is the main port on Lombok. The ferries to and from Bali dock here, as do the *Mabua Express* and Pelni boats. The ferry terminal is small, and manageable, with a small tourist office, some telephones and a few *warungs* and *food stalls*. The terminal for Pelni and the *Mabua Express* has a separate entrance, but is only a few hundred metres away.

Places to Stay & Eat
There are two budget hotels nearby, although it is easy enough to carry on to Mataram, Senggigi or the Gili Islands on the same day. *Sri Wahyu* (☎ 81048) is just off the main road, about 1km north of the terminals – look for the sign on the main road. Reasonable singles/doubles cost 8800/9900 rp, and better ones are 13,200/14,800 rp. Around 200m further north, opposite the obvious weighbridge, *Serumbung Indah* (☎ 81153) is a better option, and has good rooms for 20,000 rp.

Getting There & Away
Bemo Plenty of bemos go to Lembar from the terminal in Sweta, or you can catch one at the stop next to the market in Cakra. In Lembar, walk out of the ferry or Pelni terminal and simply catch anything heading to Sweta from the main road. The official fare to Sweta is 700 rp, but tourists are usually charged a 'special fare' of 2000 rp – staff at the ferry terminal tourist office will tell you the current fare.

Boat Refer to the Lombok Getting There & Away chapter for details about all types of ferries and boats between Bali and Lembar.

SOUTH-WESTERN PENINSULA
If you approach Lembar by ferry you'll see a hilly and little-developed peninsula on your right. A road from Lembar goes round the eastern side of the harbour, some distance inland and after almost 20km reaches a T-junction at Sekotong. From there the road left goes to the south coast, while the other road follows the coast, more or less, around Lombok's south-west peninsula. The further you go on this road, the rougher it gets and it may become impassable for ordinary cars past Labuhan Poh.

Taun
The road goes past Taun, which has a stunning, empty, white sandy beach. Nearby, *Sekotong Indah Beach Cottages* provides comfortable accommodation near a beach. Basic singles/doubles with shared bathroom cost 15,000/20,000 rp; better rooms go for 20,000/25,000 rp; and individual cottages are about 30,000 rp. It also has a *restaurant*. Other *bungalows* were being built along this coastal road at the time of research, and will offer alternative accommodation at similar prices.

Bangko Bangko
If you keep following this track, you'll eventually reach **Bangko Bangko**, and from there it's about 2km to **Desert Point**, the famous surf break. There is nowhere to stay or eat, but if you have time to explore the tip of the peninsula, you will probably come across a few **Japanese cannons** left over from WWII.

Islands
There are two groups of picturesque islands off the northern coast of this peninsula, which are all visible from the boats going to Lembar. You can reach them by chartered *prahu* outrigger from Lembar (for around 40,000 rp), Tuan (for a little less) or Labuhan Poh, but it's hard to get there, and the chances of chartering a decent boat at a reasonable price are not good.

Only a few of these islands are inhabited with truly traditional Sasak villages, but most have unspoilt white **beaches** with lots of palm trees, and wonderful **snorkelling** and **diving** opportunities (bring your own gear).

The only tourist accommodation is on **Gili Nanggu**, where the ***Cempaka Cottages*** *(☎ Mataram 22898)* charge about 45,000 rp per person, including all meals.

Further west, **Gili Gede** is in the second group of islands and is the largest of all of them. It has a number of traditional villages (where some Bugis settlers make a living from boat building), more glorious beaches and clear water for snorkelling.

SENGGIGI

On a series of sweeping bays, north of Mataram, Senggigi is the most developed tourist area on Lombok, with a range of tourist facilities and budget, mid-range and top-end accommodation. Senggigi has experienced a lot of development in the last few years, and much of it is still pretty raw, and not yet softened by landscaping. The current economic climate, along with the dearth of tourists, means that Senggigi is also looking quite forlorn these days, with empty shops, hotels and restaurants – but this means potential discounts for visitors.

Senggigi has fine beaches, although they slope very steeply into the water, and there are signs that erosion is starting to eat away the sand and foreshore. There are beautiful sunsets over the Lombok Strait which you can enjoy from the beach, a nearby temple or one of the beachfront restaurants. As it gets dark the fishing fleet lines up offshore, each boat with its bright lanterns.

Orientation

The Senggigi area is spread out along almost 10km of coastal road. Most of the shops and other facilities, and a fair concentration of hotels, are on the main road, Jl Raya Senggigi, about 6km north of Ampenan. This road continues north to Bangsal (the port for the Gili Islands) and follows the coast with lots of turns, hills and fantastic scenery.

Information

Money You can exchange money and travellers cheques at most of the big hotels (if they have the cash), but you are far better off using one of the moneychangers along the main road – but their rates are about 10% lower than in tourist centres on Bali.

Post & Communication The post office is on the main street, near the shopping centres. The Telkom office is a little inconveniently located, but there are other wartels along the main road. There are two Internet centres. Bulan Cybercafe (bulan @mataram.wasantara.net.id) charges 4000 rp per 15 minutes. It also has a message board and a fax machine. Planet Internet (planet@mataram.wasantara.net.id) charges 5000 rp per 15 minutes.

Other Services Senggigi has some photo processing places and a well stocked supermarket.

Emergency The nearest hospitals are in Mataram, but there is a medical clinic in Hotel Senggigi Aerowisata.

The police station (☎ 110) is along the northern stretch of central Senggigi.

Pura Batu Bolong

This temple sits on a rocky point which juts into the sea around 1km south of Senggigi, and about 5km north of Ampenan. The rock underneath the temple has a natural hole which gives the temple its name – *batu bolong* ('rock with hole'). A Balinese temple, it's oriented towards Gunung Agung, Bali's holiest mountain, across the Lombok Strait. Legend has it that beautiful virgins were once thrown into the sea from the top of the rock. Locals like to claim that this is why there are so many sharks in the water here.

There's a fantastic view of Senggigi from the point, and it is a wonderful place to watch a sunset. During the day, you'll probably be urged to 'donate' 5000 rp in return for renting a sash before you enter, but 1000 rp is generally enough. At other times, you can wander in and out like the locals do.

Activities

Senggigi is not another Kuta Beach, Bali – there's no go-karts or bungee jumping here.

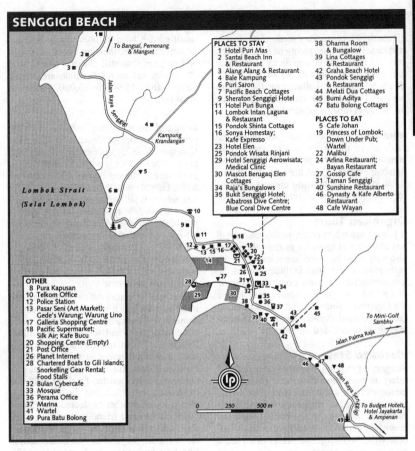

SENGGIGI BEACH

To Bangsal, Pemenang & Mangset

Jalan Raya Senggigi

Kampung Krandangan

Lombok Strait (Selat Lombok)

PLACES TO STAY
1 Hotel Puri Mas
2 Santai Beach Inn & Restaurant
3 Alang Alang & Restaurant
4 Bale Kampung
6 Puri Saron
7 Pacific Beach Cottages
9 Sheraton Senggigi Hotel
11 Hotel Puri Bunga
14 Lombok Intan Laguna & Restaurant
15 Pondok Shinta Cottages
16 Sonya Homestay; Kafe Expresso
23 Hotel Elen
25 Pondok Wisata Rinjani
29 Hotel Senggigi Aerowisata; Medical Clinic
30 Mascot Berugaq Elen Cottages
34 Raja's Bungalows
35 Bukit Senggigi Hotel; Albatross Dive Centre; Blue Coral Dive Centre
38 Dharma Room & Bungalow
39 Lina Cottages & Restaurant
42 Graha Beach Hotel
43 Pondok Senggigi & Restaurant
44 Melati Dua Cottages
45 Bumi Aditya
47 Batu Bolong Cottages

PLACES TO EAT
5 Cafe Johan
19 Princess of Lombok; Down Under Pub; Wartel
22 Malibu
24 Arlina Restaurant; Bayan Restaurant
27 Gossip Cafe
31 Taman Senggigi
40 Sunshine Restaurant
46 Dynasty & Kafe Alberto Restaurant
48 Cafe Wayan

OTHER
8 Pura Kapusan
10 Telkom Office
12 Police Station
13 Pasar Seni (Art Market); Gede's Warung; Warung Lino
17 Galleria Shopping Centre
18 Pacific Supermarket; Silk Air; Kafe Bucu
20 Shopping Centre (Empty)
21 Post Office
26 Planet Internet
28 Chartered Boats to Gili Islands; Snorkelling Gear Rental; Food Stalls
32 Bulan Cybercafe
33 Mosque
36 Perama Office
37 Marina
41 Wartel
49 Pura Batu Bolong

To Mini-Golf Sambhu

Jalan Palma Raja

Jalan Raya Batu Bolong

To Budget Hotels; Hotel Jayakarta & Ampenan

0   250   500 m

Diving Dive trips from Senggigi normally only go to sites around the Gili Islands, so it is better and cheaper to base yourself there, unless, of course, you prefer the swankier hotels in Senggigi.

There are several diving centres along the main road in Senggigi, but it's best to stick with the two reliable dive operators: Blue Coral (☎ 93441, fax 93251, email blue_coral @mataram.wasantara.net.id) and Albatross (☎ 93399, fax 93388). They both offer PADI open-water courses (for about US$300) and trips to the Gilis for US$50/65 for one/two

dives. See the Gili Islands chapter for more details on what is on offer there.

Snorkelling For some local snorkelling, or if you're going to the Gilis for the day, you can rent snorkelling gear (7500 rp per day) from several spots along the beach near the Hotel Senggigi Aerowisata. Both the local diving agencies offer snorkelling trips and rent more expensive snorkelling equipment.

There's some reasonable snorkelling off the point and in the sheltered bay around the headland. One excellent spot is the reef about

WEST LOMBOK

50 to 70m out from the front of the Windy Cottages, a few kilometres north of Senggigi (see the Places to Stay section later in this chapter). The reef has plenty of fish, lobsters, eels and turtles (if you're lucky), and there are other good spots closer to the beach. The hotel rents snorkelling gear for 5000 rp per day. The best time for snorkelling is the dry season (June to September).

Mini Golf Golf enthusiasts (and those who can't afford the green fees at normal golf courses) may want to head out to Mini-Golf Sambhu (☎ 93138), at the end of Jl Palma Raya in the new housing complex. Phone for free pick-up and current prices.

Organised Tours

It is easy enough to organise day tours from any of the travel agencies, or from shops that also purport to be travel agencies, along the main road. These tours include most of the usual attractions in west Lombok and some of the craft villages in central Lombok. See the Organised Tours section in the Lombok Getting Around chapter for more information about prices, and other tours.

Places to Stay

Senggigi is moving steadily upmarket, and many of the former shoestring places have increased their standards and prices. Make sure you get a fan: the heat and mosquitoes can be a nuisance. All the budget and mid-range places include breakfast, unless stated otherwise. Some top-end places often add a high season supplement.

Places to Stay – Budget

South of Senggigi The following places appear on the West Lombok map. *Pondok Wisata Siti Hawa (☎ 93414, fax 23912)* is a funky little homestay fronting a fantastic beach and run by a local community group. The bamboo cottages cost 10,000/13,000 rp for singles/doubles. It caters well for budget travellers – there are cheap home-cooked meals, and you can rent motorbikes, bicycles and boats. *Atithi Sanggraha Beach Cottages (☎ 93070)* is also worth checking

out. It may lack some character, but the cottages are clean, quiet and dotted around a small garden with its own beach. And for 20,000/25,000 rp, they are excellent value. Not as good, but still cheap, *Pondok Asri (☎ 93075)* has rooms – which are a little noisy – from 15,000 to 25,000 rp without breakfast.

Senggigi The remaining budget options appear on the Senggigi Beach map. The *Lina Cottages (☎ 93237)* is central, friendly and good value – which is why it is often full (so book ahead). Rooms cost 40,000/50,000 rp, and a bungalow with sea views, hot water and air-con is still reasonable value for Senggigi at 100,000 rp. Prices do not include breakfast, however. Also worth trying is the oft-ignored *Melati Dua Cottages (☎ 93288, fax 93028)*. The quaint individual cottages are good value from 30,000 to 60,000 rp with air-con (but no hot water), but they are close to the main road.

The smaller places off the main road and away from the beach are quiet and less costly. *Bumi Aditya* has bamboo bungalows (which are small, clean, and somehow appealing) for 5,000 to 25,000 rp. You may have to look hard to find a member of staff sometimes. *Pondok Wisata Rinjani (☎ 93274)* has cottages in a pretty garden for 15,000/20,000 rp, without breakfast, but the whole complex is looking rather neglected these days. For seclusion and friendly atmosphere, try *Raja's Bungalows (☎ 93569)*. The modern clean rooms, with what one reader called 'the best bathrooms on Lombok', go for 30,000 rp. It is about 200m up a path past the mosque – look for the hotel sign from the main road.

Sonya Homestay (☎ 63447) is a basic, family-run losmen that has been recommended by several readers. The atmosphere is friendly, and the small rooms (which are clustered together) are only 15,000 rp. Not far away, *Pondok Shinta Cottages* is a last resort: very ordinary rooms, with no fan and next to the main road, cost 8000/10,000 rp.

One of the best places is the new *Hotel Elen (☎ 93014)*, which is very easy to miss behind the Hero Photo shop. Clean, modern rooms with a ceiling fan, and some style, cost 17,500/25,000 rp.

North of Senggigi The *Bale Kampung*, in Kampung Krandangan, is billed as a backpackers' place. It provides cheap food and good information about local attractions – it's not too far away from the sea, but seems like light years from the Senggigi scene. Rooms cost 16,500/21,000 rp, and quaint but tiny bungalows are 14,300/17,600 rp. The bathrooms are a bit rustic, however, and have squat-style toilets.

Pondok Damai (☎ *93019*), in Mangset village, is a quiet, seaside retreat. It's a comfortable, charming collection of cottages for 40,000/55,000 rp, but there's no hot water. It is not great value, but it's cheap for this part of the beach.

Places to Stay – Mid-Range

Unless otherwise indicated, the following places appear on the Senggigi Beach map.

South of Senggigi *Batu Bolong Cottages* (☎ *93065, fax 93198*) has spacious and well finished bungalows on both sides of the road from 35,000 rp to 86,000 rp (with hot water and air-con). This is very good value compared with some of the soulless midrange concrete places nearby.

Senggigi Once the main budget hotel in town, *Pondok Senggigi* (☎ *93273*) has gone steadily upmarket. The rooms run off a long verandah and face a pleasant garden; there's also a nice swimming pool. Singles/doubles start from US$9/12, but most rooms cost at least twice this – with air-con and hot water, rooms cost US$39/45. In the centre of town, *Dharma Room & Bungalow* (☎ *93050*) has a lovely garden down to the beach. The rooms with a fan for 45,000 rp are often full; bungalows with air-con and hot water cost 130,000 rp.

Graha Beach Hotel (☎ *93101, fax 93400*) has a good, central beachside location, but the rooms are small and lack character. They start at US$45 (or US$50 for an ocean view).

Mascot Berugaq Elen Cottages (☎ *93365, fax 93236*) has almost top-end facilities and location for mid-range prices. It offers pleasant 'Seaview' or 'Sasak-style' bungalows for US$49 and US$42. It provides air-con, hot water and phone, but the best feature is the quiet garden setting which extends to the beach.

North of Senggigi The *Santai Beach Inn* (☎ *93038*) has a homey atmosphere and a lush garden. There's a good library and book exchange, and it offers traditional meals in a pleasant pavilion. Economy bungalows, without a fan, cost 26,000/33,000 rp; standard ones with a fan are 40,000/52,000 rp; and the one family room has hot water and costs 80,000 rp. Advanced bookings are recommended.

Next door, the small but classy *Hotel Puri Mas* (☎/fax *93023*) has attractively decorated bungalows and villas surrounded by trees and shrubs, a pretty pool and a wide range of prices – from US$23 for the 'standard bungalow' to US$143 for the 'villa'.

Another perfect place to get away from it all is the spacious and charming *Windy Cottages* (☎ *93191, fax 93193* – see the West Lombok map). It charges 60,000 rp for standard rooms; 75,000 rp to 90,000 rp for bigger bungalows with hot water. These prices are very reasonable, and it is a great spot for snorkelling (see the Activities entry earlier in this section).

Places to Stay – Top End

In line with Lombok's tourist development strategy, Senggigi has acquired a few luxury hotels. None of them is well patronised, even in the high season, so discounts on the prices listed here are quite possible. The following places appear on the Senggigi Beach map, unless otherwise indicated.

South of Senggigi Huge and impossible to miss (the central building is quite massive) is the *Hotel Jayakarta* (☎ *93045, fax 93043 email jayakarta@mataram.wasantara.net.id)*. The rooms are plain and clean, with fridge, phone and TV, and cost from US$85/97 for singles/doubles, plus an extra USS$20 per person for ocean views. It has a vast garden and a huge swimming pool, and is popular with tour groups.

Senggigi The first big 'international standard' hotel built at Senggigi is right on the headland. Operated by Garuda, *Hotel Senggigi Aerowisata (☎ 93210, fax 93200, email senggigi@lombokisland.com)* has a beautiful setting, lovely garden, swimming pool, tennis courts and other mod cons. Rooms cost from US$157, but discounts of 30% are regularly advertised.

At least as classy is the *Lombok Intan Laguna (☎ 93090, fax 93185, email intan@mataram.wasantara.net.id).* It's a large, central and handsome hotel, with a big pool. Rooms start from U$121, and are about double that for suites.

Bukit Senggigi Hotel (☎ 93173, fax 93226, email bukit@mataram.wasantara.net.id) has motel-like rooms staggering up the side of a small hill – some of them have views over the sea. Prices start from US$90/97, but 40% discounts are often available. There's also a swimming pool, a disco and karaoke lounge.

A similar but older place is *Hotel Puri Bunga (☎ 93013, fax 93286),* also built up the hillside on the inland side of the road, with even better views. It's a bit of a trek to the higher rooms and to the beach, but the rooms have air-con, telephone, TV and hot water, and the pool is good. The published rate is US$72/78, but they are only good value if you can get a 50% discount, although this is not too hard. Further north, *Sheraton Senggigi Hotel (☎ 93333, fax 93140, email ssbr_sgg@mataram.wasantra.net.id)* is the best hotel in Senggigi and also the most expensive, with rooms starting from US$181. It's all very tasteful, the pool and gardens are lovely, and the staff are friendly and efficient. There's also a children's playground and pool.

North of Senggigi The *Pacific Beach Cottages (☎ 93006, fax 93027)* have all the standard luxuries – air-con, TV, hot water,

swimming pool – but the rooms are ordinary and the whole place has limited character. Standard rooms cost US$55, and bungalows are US$67. Nearby, *Puri Saron (☎ 93424, fax 93266)* has the same sort of facilities and the same lack of character. It asks US$67/73 for ordinary rooms, but will discount.

Holiday Inn Resort (☎ 93444, fax 93092 – see the West Lombok map) offers all the comforts you would expect from US$170, but gives 50% discounts in the low season. The small number of luxury bungalows at *Alang Alang* is gradually increasing, and although they overlook the ocean, they're close to the main road. Rooms cost US$70, including breakfast.

Continuing north along the coast, a few upmarket options offer some character and style. One of the better ones is the well run *Hotel Nusa Bunga (☎ 93035* – see the West Lombok map). It has a splendid beachfront position, a pool, and air-con bungalows in a pretty garden from US$55/65.

Places to Eat

You can eat pretty well in Senggigi for a reasonable price, but there isn't the range or quality you'd find in Bali's tourist areas. Beachside dining is a Senggigi speciality; it's especially delightful in the evening, with cool sea breezes, blazing sunsets and great views, but the hawkers on the beach can be annoying.

Most of the hotels have their own restaurants, and some of those north and south of Senggigi have minibuses that cruise along the main road in the evening hoping to pick up (and later drop off) some customers – it's a free service and worth considering. There is not much at the bottom end of the scale, except a couple of *warungs* along the main road near the mosque, and a few *food stalls* along the beach, especially at the end of the road past the Hotel Senggigi Aerowisata.

South of Senggigi The upmarket *Cafe Wayan (☎ 93098)* is related to the excellent Cafe Wayan in Ubud (this is recommendation enough for some visitors). Pizzas go for 10,000 rp, but other meals cost considerably more. The freshly baked pastries and cakes are a delight. Two long-term favourites, the Dynasty Restaurant and Kafe Alberto, have joined forces to form the *Dynasty & Kafe Alberto Restaurant (☎ 93313)*. It provides Chinese and Italian food with great views for reasonable prices – 9000 to 13,000 rp for seafood and other dishes. Both places provide a free transport service to and from Senggigi.

Senggigi The restaurant at *Pondok Senggigi* is an old favourite Senggigi standby. It's not the cheapest, but is still popular from breakfast until late at night. The large open dining area is comfortable and convivial, and there's a wide selection of well prepared western and Indonesian food, with some interesting Sasak specialities as well.

The beachfront restaurant at *Lina Cottages* is also very good. Although meals are pricey at about 10,000 rp, the setting is superb and the happy hours are competitive. Next door, *Sunshine Restaurant* has cheap drinks during the magnificent sunsets, and meals are also priced from about 10,000 rp. For seaviews and seabreezes – again, at high prices – try *Gede's Warung* and *Warung Lino*. Both are lost at the back of the Art Market.

Princess of Lombok has a bar downstairs, and a pleasant open dining area upstairs. It offers a good line in Mexican food, which makes a change, but it is quite expensive – most dishes are 17,500 rp, while steaks cost 20,000 rp. *Arlina Restaurant* is central and more reasonably priced, with meals from 6000 to 10,000 rp. For decent coffee, pasta and Indonesian food, try *Kafe Expresso* near Sonya Homestay. *Malibu* has decent happy hours, but otherwise meals cost 9,000 to 14,000 rp. It remains popular because of friendly staff, and the fresh seafood which you can select from the table along the road.

It is worth checking out what specials the restaurant at *Lombok Intan Laguna* is advertising. Most days there are buffets of seafood or sates, or a *rijsttafel* (banquet) for about 30,000 rp per person. The other upmarket place in town is the popular and stylish *Taman Senggigi*. The setting is quite charming, but most meals cost around the 20,000 rp mark.

North of Senggigi *Alang Alang* and the new *Cafe Johan* offer superb views, and the prices aren't too bad – both provide a free transport service to/from Senggigi. The restaurant at *Windy Cottages*, even further up the coast, is in an open-sided pavilion facing the sea. It's a scenic area and the beach is nice; a trip up here for lunch makes a lovely outing. The vegetarian restaurant at *Santai Beach Inn (☎ 93038)* is worth a trip north. Bookings are advisable during the evening in peak season.

Entertainment

Senggigi has about the only nightlife on Lombok – it's mostly pretty low key, but it can be good fun. *Pondok Senggigi, Kafe Bucu, Bayan Restaurant* and *Marina* often have live music, either acoustic guitarists or local bands doing passable rock and reggae music with an Indonesian flavour. The late afternoon happy hour at the *Lombok Intan Laguna* often coincides with live traditional music; more upbeat dance bands usually feature later in the evening.

Contact the *Dynasty & Kafe Alberto Restaurant (☎ 93313)* to find out what night it features traditional dancing (at the time of research, it was Thursday). There may also be traditional dancing at the Art Market in the peak season. A couple of the pubs can be quite sociable – *Down Under Pub* at the Princess of Lombok has good music plus pool tables. *Gossip Cafe* often has a disco.

Shopping

The Pacific Supermarket has most of the basics you'll need, and a small selection of books in English and maps of Lombok and Bali. The Pasar Seni art market has a variety of craft stalls and shops, including a pottery outlet and an antique shop – but many shops are empty. The new Galleria shopping centre, and another multi-coloured one near the Pacific Supermarket, are completed but empty – a sad sign of the times.

If you have the time and interest, it's worth making a day trip to the craft and antique shops in Ampenan, the huge market at Sweta or the small villages in central Lombok which specialise in various handcrafts.

Getting There & Away

Bemo Regular bemos travel between Senggigi and the terminal at Ampenan (500 rp), and usually continue north as far as Pemenang or Bayan. There are also sometimes bemos from Sweta for 600 rp. Don't be surprised if you are overcharged a little on any bemo going to or from Senggigi.

Tourist Shuttle Bus/Boat The Perama company has several daily bus/boat connections between Senggigi and the main tourist centres on Bali, eg to Kuta (20,000 rp) and Ubud (17,500 rp); and to the main tourist centres on Lombok, eg Bangsal (5000 rp), Tetebatu (7500 rp) and Kuta (on Lombok; 10,000 rp). Another local company, Lombok Mandiri offers very similar fares and connections. You can buy tickets for either company at travel agencies along the main road in Senggigi; tickets for Perama can also be bought at the Perama office (☎ 93007).

Boat Refer to the Gili Islands chapter later in this book for information about boats trips between Senggigi and these delightful islands.

Getting Around

A pre-paid taxi from the airport to Senggigi costs about 12,000 rp; *from* Senggigi to the airport, a metered taxi will cost less. Taxis regularly ply the main road looking for customers. To get to or from the airport by public transport, get a connection at the terminal in Ampenan – see the Getting Around entry in the Mataram section earlier in this chapter. for more information.

The roads just south and north of Senggigi are perfect for cycling, but unfortunately only one place bothers to rent bicycles – Pondok Wisata Siti Hawa (see Places to Stay earlier in this section).

A dearth of travellers has translated into genuine discounts on the rental of cars and motorbikes, so Senggigi is the best place to rent a vehicle on Lombok. There are several operators along the main road in Senggigi – look for an advertising sign, negotiate with the rental guys, check the fine print and off you go.

Central, South & East Lombok

Highlights

- Many villages specialise in particular crafts. You can watch the craftspeople working, and buy some beautiful pieces.

- Small, friendly rural villages such as Tetebatu and Lendang Nangka offer simple accommodation and some great hiking opportunities.

- Lombok's Kuta Beach has a limited range of accommodation in a lovely, isolated location.

- The undeveloped south coast has perfect bays and beaches, 'secret' surf spots and few facilities – so far.

The opening section in this chapter, Central Lombok, covers the inland towns and villages in the rich agricultural area south of Gunung Rinjani. The second section, South Lombok, covers the towns further south and the beautiful south coast, which is targeted for massive tourist development, but at the moment has little infrastructure. The third section, East Lombok, covers the east coast, which is rarely visited by foreigners except for those using the ferry port at Labuhan Lombok.

Central Lombok

The southern slopes of Gunung Rinjani are well watered and lush, offering opportunities for scenic walks through the rice fields and jungle. Further to the south, the country is drier, and dams have been built to provide irrigation during the dry season. Most of the places in central Lombok are more or less traditional Sasak settlements, and several of them are known for particular types of local handcrafts.

It is best to base yourself in Tetebatu, and rent or charter private transport from there to visit nearby villages, or hike to picturesque waterfalls. The usual method of public transport to most villages in this region is the very slow *cidomo* (pony cart).

KOTARAJA

Kotaraja means 'city of kings', although no kings ruled from here and it's hardly a city. Apparently, when the Sasak kingdom of Langko (at Kopang) fell to the Balinese invaders, the rulers of Langko fled to Loyok, the village south of Kotaraja. After the royal compound in that village was also destroyed, two of the ruler's sons went to live in Kotaraja. The aristocracy of Kotaraja can trace their ancestry back to these brothers, but the highest caste title of *raden* has now petered out through intermarriage.

Kotaraja is a road junction. Take any bus or bus travelling between Sweta and Labuhan Lombok, get off at Pomotong, and take a bemo, ojek or cidomo up the hill.

Various villages nearby (see the Lendang Nangka and Loyok & Rungkang entries later in this chapter) are noted for blacksmithing and basketware products. Traditional blacksmiths still use human-powered bellows and an open hearth, but old car springs are now the favoured 'raw material' for knives, farm implements and other tools.

TETEBATU

Wonderfully located at the foot of Gunung Rinjani, Tetebatu is a lovely, cool mountain retreat, similar to Senaru, on the other side of Gunung Rinjani. Although treks up to the volcano's rim can be arranged from Tetebatu, it's often misty and rainy here, particularly between November and April (for full details of the Gunung Rinjani trek, see the North Lombok chapter).

There are magnificent views over southern Lombok, east to the sea and north to Gunung

Rinjani, and its a perfect place to relax for a few days, and go hiking to nearby waterfalls.

Information

Tetebatu is not set up for mass tourism (yet). The only facilities here are a moneychanger at the bottom of the village and a book exchange at Warung Harmony. Otherwise, friendly advice and a photocopy of a local map (1000 rp) are available from the shop marked 'Coffee Shop Tourist Information', just up from the junction at Pomotong on the main road. The closest post office and *wartel* (public telephone office) are in Kotaraja.

Taman Wisata Tetebatu (Monkey Forest)

A shady, 4km walk off the main road leads to this little pocket of forest, or you could take an ojek from the turn-off. It is inhabited by little black monkeys, which you are more likely to hear than see. From the end of the rough track, which is no good for cars, you will need a guide (ask at your losmen) to find the several tiny **waterfalls** in the area. A tiny, unmarked path at the end of the track leads to *Kios Monkey Forest*, a compound with a few huts where a handful of visitors can stay and eat (for a donation). Please note that this place is run by a Sasak community which is not interested in mass tourism.

Waterfalls

On the southern slopes of the Taman Nasional Gunung Rinjani national park, there are two more waterfalls. Both are accessible only by private transportation, or a lovely 90 minute walk (one way) through the rice fields from Tetebatu. You will need a guide, so ask at your losmen. Locals believe that the water from **Air Terjun Jukut** (also known as Jeruk Manis and Air Temer) will increase

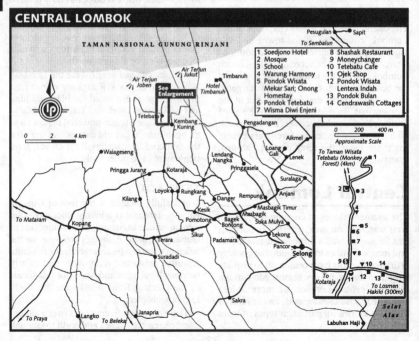

hair growth, so the follicularly challenged may want to try this. Tickets costs 1500 rp. The falls are a steepish 2km walk from the car park at the end of the road.

To the north-west, **Air Terjun Joben** (also known as Otak Kokok Gading) is more of a public swimming pool; locals also believe the water here can cure all sorts of ailments. The place is swamped by locals on Sunday, but it is virtually empty during the rest of the week. Tickets cost 500/250 rp for adults/children; there's some *food stalls* nearby.

Places to Stay

There is a string of small, friendly losmen along the two main roads. Almost identical in price (about 15,000/20,000 rp for singles/doubles) and standard are four places, next to each other. *Pondok Tetebatu* has a large number of rooms, but few can be classed as 'bungalows'. *Pondok Wisata Mekar Sari* only has a few rooms, but they have some character. *Wisma Diwi Enjeni* boasts the best views and setting. *Onong Homestay*, just beyond Pondok Wisata Mekar Sari, has been recommended by readers, with rooms a little cheaper than the others, friendly staff and an English-speaking manager.

The northern road ends at the charming, colonial *Soedjono Hotel*. It has great views, a large swimming pool (empty during our visit) and a range of rooms: bungalows cost from 16,500/22,000 rp and 'superior' rooms are 55,000/66,000 rp. One reader did, however, complain about being hassled by guides at the hotel.

Along the road heading east there are several slightly nicer and more expensive places. *Cendrawasih Cottages* is newer and cleaner than most, and good value for 15,000/20,000 rp. *Pondok Wisata Lentera Indah* (also known as Green Orry) has a range of comfortable bungalows from 20,000/25,000 rp, while the quaint bungalows at *Pondok Bulan* are similar in standard and price. The last is probably the best: *Losmen Hakiki* has charming bungalows for 15,000/25,000 rp, and larger ones for 30,000 rp. They all surround a tiny rice field. One weary traveller described it as 'heaven on earth'.

Places to Eat

Every hotel has a *restaurant* serving the usual tourist-oriented and Indonesian dishes. For some Sasak food for 3000 to 6000 rp, try *Shashak Restaurant* where the service is slow but the food is excellent. They also run classes in Sasak cuisine. A little trendier is *Tetebatu Cafe*, but the best place is probably *Warung Harmony*, where western, Indonesian and Sasak meals are cheap, the setting is pleasant and the owners are very friendly.

Getting There & Away

From Kotaraja, and from Pomotong (on the main east-west road), bemos to Tetebatu are infrequent – and they may only drop you off at the bottom of the village. The cidomos are painfully slow, so it's best to take a quick and direct ojek from the junction at Pomotong. In Tetebatu, ojek drivers hang around the crossroads near the Shashak Restaurant. Perama runs one tourist shuttle bus per day between Tetebatu and Mataram (7500 rp) – book at Pondok Wisata Lentera Indah.

Getting Around

Pondok Wisata Lentera Indah rents out mountain bikes (8000 rp per day), but the roads are too steep for most cyclists. A motorbike (for about 17,000 rp per day) is an ideal way to visit nearby attractions. These are available at the Shashak Restaurant, Warung Harmony, Pondok Wisata Lentera Indah and Pondok Tetebatu.

LOYOK & RUNGKANG

Loyok is noted for its fine **handcrafts**, particularly basketware and weaving using natural fibres, especially bamboo. Most of the craftspeople work from their homes, or you can buy from shops on the main street. Rungkang is known for its **pottery**, which is made from a local black clay. The pots are often finished with attractive canework for decoration and increased strength. Similar pottery is made in a number of other villages in the area south of the main road.

From Pomotong, catch a bemo or ojek to Rungkang. You can walk about 1km or get a cidomo to Loyok.

MASBAGIK

Quite a large town on the main road at the turn-off to Selong, Masbagik has a colourful morning **market** every day, and a huge **cattle market** on Monday afternoon. There's also a post office and wartel. Masbagik Timur, 1km east, is one of the centres for clay **pottery** and ceramic production. Both places are easily accessible by any bemo heading along the main road that runs east from Mataram.

LENDANG NANGKA

This Sasak village is surrounded by picturesque countryside, with small roads and friendly people. In and around the village you can see blacksmiths who still make knives, hoes and other tools using traditional techniques. Silversmiths are also starting to work here.

During August, you should be able to see traditional Sasak stick fighting at Lendang Nangka. It's quite a violent affair with leather-covered shields and bamboo poles.

Traditional dances are sometimes performed in the area, but they're not scheduled events – ask at your losmen, and you might be lucky.

Places to Stay & Eat

All these places have communal bathrooms, with a *mandi* (cold water 'bath') and squat toilet; and prices include three Sasak meals. *Radiah's Homestay* offers simple hospitality, and the scruffy rooms cost 17,500 rp for a single room, and 25,000 to 30,000 rp for a double. Around 200m west of Radiah's, *Pondok Wira* is a little better. It's a decent place with rice barn-style singles/doubles, including some with views, for 20,000/25,000 rp. Better bungalows are 25,000/30,000 rp. About 2km further towards Kotaraja, *Pondok Sasak* has more character, but the staff can be surly. Simple rooms cost about 15,000 rp per person.

Getting There & Away

First catch a bus or bemo to Masbagik, on the main east-west road, then hop on a cidomo to Lendang Nangka. Otherwise, look for an ojek from Pomotong or Tetebatu.

PRINGGASELA

This village is a centre for traditional weaving done on simple backstrap looms. The materials made here feature beautifully coloured stripes which run the length of the cloth, with decorative details woven into the weft. You can see the weavers in action and buy some of their beautiful work, such as sarongs, blankets etc. Most of the work here is superb quality and takes the women a long time to make. There are a dozen or so **art shops** at the crossroads.

Two losmen offer simple, family-style accommodation with communal (and fairly basic) bathroom facilities; and prices include three Sasak meals. Both are on the road that heads north to Timbanuh. *Akmal Homestay* is run by a friendly family and charges 15,000/20,000 rp for singles/doubles. *Rainbow Cottages*, next door, is not as welcoming and charges 15,000 rp per person.

If you don't have your own transport, take a bemo to Masbagik or Rempung, and then a cidomo or ojek to Pringgasela.

TIMBANUH

At the end of another road, up the southern slope of Rinjani, stands the Dutch colonial *Hotel Timbanuh*, a cool respite with simply glorious views. The place (and the staff, it appears) has seen better days. The rooms are uninspiring and cost about 15,000/25,000 rp for singles/doubles, and you will have to pre-arrange any meals with the staff. To reach Timbanuh, you'll need to charter or rent your own transport.

LOANG GALI

At Loang Gali, there's a public **swimming pool** in the forest, fed by springs, and plenty of **hiking trails**, begging to be explored.

Overlooking the pools, *Loang Gali Cottages* charges 15,000 rp per person. The rooms are nothing special, and you will have to pre-arrange meals with them, but it is a serene place.

Loang Gali is at the end of an unsigned dirt road, off the main road north of Lenek. You will need your own transport, and probably have to ask directions.

South Lombok

South Lombok is appreciably drier than the rest of the island; it is also sparsely populated, and has few roads and limited public transport. Most visitors head for Lombok's more serene version of Kuta, but if you have your own transport – and especially if you're into surfing – you can visit several excellent surfing spots and take in some stunning coastal scenery.

PRAYA

This is the main town in the south-west. It's quite attractive, with spacious gardens, tree-lined streets, a few old Dutch buildings and no tourists. The bemo terminal, on the north-western side of town, is the transport hub for the area, and the town is well connected to Mataram and Kuta.

Dienda Hayu Hotel (☎ *54319*), at Jl Untung Surapati 28 just up from the market, is clean and comfortable. Economy rooms cost 27,500 rp, and VIP rooms with air-con are 38,500 rp – these prices include breakfast. There aren't a lot of reasons to stay in Praya, unless you use it as a base to explore local craft villages.

AROUND PRAYA

Several of the villages around Praya are noted for different handcrafts. Most of the villages are close to main roads from Praya so you can reach them by public transport (mainly by cidomo), but if you want to explore several of them, and buy lots of things, it's useful to have your own transport. Several small back roads wind through the hills to join the main east-west road, enabling a very pretty tour through central Lombok. A lot of these places are included in organised tours of the region.

Sukarara

According to the brochures, Sukarara, to the west of Praya, is a 'traditional weaving centre', although it doesn't look very traditional. Much of the main street is given over to commercial **craft shops**, so it is pretty touristy, but it's still worth a visit to see the various styles of weaving. There are looms set up outside workshops along the main street and displays of sarongs hanging in bright bands. Typically they have attractive young women working out the front, in traditional black costumes featuring brightly coloured edging. More women work inside, often wearing jeans and watching TV as they work, but most of the material is actually made in homes in surrounding villages. There's also bigger showrooms, with professional salespeople who can be informative but very persuasive. These places are geared to tour groups and have a good range, but higher prices.

Get a bemo along the main road to Puyung (where a huge **market** is held every Sunday). From there, hire a cidomo or walk the 2km to Sukarara.

Penujak

Penujak is noted for its traditional *gerabah* pottery, which is made from local clay using the simplest of techniques. The elegant pots range in size up to a metre high. There are also various kitchen vessels and decorative figurines, usually in the shape of animals. This traditional pottery has a rich terracotta colour, and is unglazed, but hand burnished to a lovely soft sheen. Some new designs are brightly coloured. Penujak is on the main road from Praya to the south coast; any bemo to Sengkol or Kuta will drop you off.

Pejanggik

This village is also known for traditional weaving, but it's much more low key than Sukarara. There are a few workshops near the main road and just off to the south, but to find them you'll have to stop and look, and listen for the clack-clack of the looms.

Beleka

The main products of this village, to the north of the main road at Ganti, are baskets, mats and boxes made from natural fibres, such as rattan, grass, palm leaf and bamboo. Showrooms along the main road display and sell some fine examples of this quality work – it's strong, simple and beautifully made.

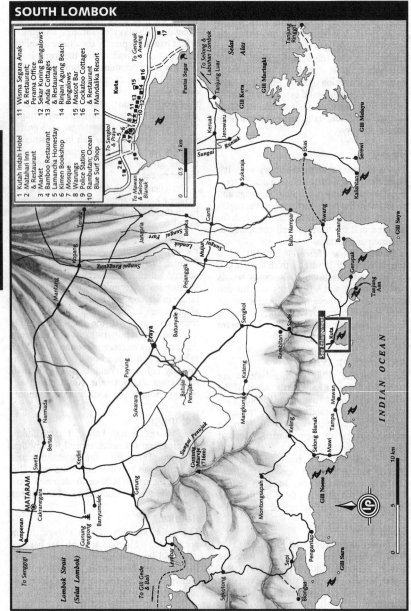

SOUTH LOMBOK

1 Kutah Indah Hotel
2 Matahari Inn & Restaurant
3 Market
4 Bamboo Restaurant
5 Lamancha Homestay
6 Kimen Bookshop
7 Mosque
8 Warungs
9 Police Station
10 Rambutan; Ocean Blue Surf Shop
11 Wisma Segara Anak & Restaurant; Perama Office
12 Sekar Kuning Bungalows
13 Anda Cottages & Restaurant
14 Rinjani Agung Beach Bungalows
15 Mascot Bar
16 Cockatoo Cottages & Restaurant
17 Mandalika Resort

The Sasak village of Sade – traditional architecture or a purpose-built tourist trap?

Rembitan & Sade

The area from Sengkol down to Kuta Beach is a centre of traditional Sasak culture. There are regular bemos on this route, particularly in the morning, so you can get off at the villages and flag down another when you are ready to move on. Donations are requested at both villages.

Rembitan is on a hill just west of the main road. It's a slightly sanitised Sasak village, but is nevertheless an authentic cluster of thatched houses and lumbung, surrounded by a wooden fence. On top of the hill is **Masjid Kuno**, an old thatched-roof mosque.

A little further south is Sade. It's another 'traditional' village which some say was constructed purely for tourists, but it may have been merely an extensive renovation. It has concrete footpaths, plenty of houses displaying goods for sale, and hawkers giving the hard sell.

KUTA

The best known place on the south coast is Lombok's Kuta (often spelt Kute), a magnificent stretch of white sand and turquoise sea with rugged hills rising around it. It has far, *far* fewer tourists and tourist facilities than the (in)famous Kuta Beach on Bali, but there have always been big plans to develop a whole stretch of the superb southern coast with luxury hotels.

After many years of speculation, there are signs that something may happen; the road from Praya has been completely remade and there's roads running to as-yet-undeveloped beaches. Meanwhile, losmen at Kuta are all on limited leases. The lack of tourists means that the hawkers (often kids selling blankets and coconuts) are annoying, and often quite aggressive.

Every year, people, celebrities and TV crews flock to Kuta for the *nyale* fishing celebration, in February or March (see the boxed text 'Nyale Fishing Festival' in the Lombok Facts for the Visitor chapter). Thousands sleep on the beach. The main tourist season is August; for the rest of the year, Kuta is very quiet and very laid-back.

Information

Guests can change money at Matahari Inn, Mandalika Resort and Kuta Indah Hotel, while anyone can change at Anda Cottages and Wisma Segara Anak (which is also a postal agency).

There are telephones in the hotels, but no wartel. You can buy new books at Wisma Segara Anak, and old paperbacks at Kimen Bookshop. The mossies can be bad at times, so come prepared.

Surfing

Plenty of good waves break on the reefs around here. Many are supposedly 'secret'. There are lefts and rights in the bay in front of Kuta, and some more on reefs east of Tanjung Aan. Local boatmen will take you out for a negotiable fee. Go about 7km east of Kuta to the fishing village of Gerupak, where there are several potential breaks on the reefs at the entrance of Teluk Gerupak. Again, access is by local fishing boat. There are more breaks further east and west, but nearly all require a boat. The current charter rate is about 80,000 rp per day.

For surfing tips and repairs, and rental of surfboards (15,000 rp per day; or less for longer rentals) and boogie boards (10,000 rp), visit the office (well, shack) belonging to Ocean Blue surf shop.

Places to Stay

Places to Stay – Budget Most places will include breakfast, and should also provide a fan and mosquito net. Along the esplanade, the cheaper places are pretty much alike – mostly bamboo cottages (often semi-detached) on stilts in a scruffy garden, with an attached concrete bathroom and a small balcony.

Anda Cottages (☎ 54836) was the first in Kuta and is still good value at 12,500/15,000 rp for singles/doubles around a spacious garden. The modern rooms for 25,000/35,000 rp are large and clean. *Sekar Kuning Bungalows* (☎ 54856) is very similar.

Wisma Segara Anak (☎ 54834) is well set up, although possibly getting a little complacent because it is popular and convenient. Bungalows go for 10,000/15,000 rp. *Rinjani Agung Beach Bungalows* (☎ 54849) asks 15,000 rp for rooms and 20,000 rp for bungalows. The bungalows with air-con are good value for 30,000 rp.

Cockatoo Cottages (☎ 54830) is a little more secluded, and also good value. Simple bungalows cost 7000/10,000 rp; and the one modern bungalow for 20,000 rp is worth asking for. The quiet and homely *Lamancha Homestay* is not on the beach, but it has one lovely bungalow for 20,000 rp, and a few smaller rooms for 15,000 rp. *Rambutan* is scruffy, and definitely a last resort.

Places to Stay – Mid-Range & Top End

The two mid-range places are a short walk from the beach. *Kuta Indah Hotel* (☎ 53781, fax 54628) charges US$21/26 to US$42/49 for decent singles/doubles around a grassy area; breakfast is extra. The pool is probably its main attraction, although the sea is certainly swimmable. There's also free transport to local beaches and surfing spots.

The popular *Matahari Inn* (☎ 54832, fax 54909, email matahari@mataram.wasantara.net.id) is jointly managed by Swiss expats. The economy rooms for 25,000/30,000 rp are decent, and often full; the range of rooms with air-con and hot water is excellent value for 60,000 to 110,000 rp.

The top-notch place is the brand-spanking new *Mandalika Resort* (☎ 53333, fax 53555, email novotel@lombokonline.com), run by Novotel. It looks a bit like a Sasak village from the stone age, but it is very luxurious and modern, and boasts a superb beach. It provides a range of rooms starting from US$156. Children are welcome and well catered for.

Places to Eat

There are several cheap *warungs* along the esplanade, plus each hotel has a *restaurant*.

Cockatoo Cottages probably offers the best value, with western meals for 8000 rp, and tasty Indonesian dishes for about 6000 rp. *Wisma Segara Anak* is large, breezy and has the only happy hour in town (large beers are 7000 rp), but the meals are a little overpriced.

Matahari Inn has pretty reasonable pizza from 10,000 rp, while *Anda Cottages* is popular with tour groups because of its airy setting, and reasonable prices. *Bamboo Restaurant* is also good value, but some items may be *habis* (unavailable). *Mascot Bar* is the only pub in town; and *Rinjani Agung Beach Bungalows* boasts the only video nights in Kuta (this is a far cry from its cousin on Bali).

Getting There & Away

Public transport directly to Kuta from Mandalika terminal in Sweta (1250 rp) is not frequent; you may have to catch a bemo to Praya, and then another to Kuta. Travel early or you may get stuck and have to charter a vehicle some of the way.

Bemos also hurtle through Kuta going east to Awang, west and north to Keling or north along another road to Sengkol (and sometimes they continue to Praya and Mataram). Perama (☎ 54846), based at Wisma Segara Anak, has one tourist shuttle bus per day to Mataram (10,000 rp).

Getting Around

Surprisingly, the only place that rents out motorbikes is Matahari Inn (17,000 rp per day), but this may change in the future. Occasional cidomos plod along the main road; otherwise, you'll have saunter around like everyone else.

EAST OF KUTA

Quite good roads go around the coast to the east, passing a series of beautiful bays punctuated by headlands. There's some public transport, but you will see more with your own transport – a mountain bike would be good (bring your own). All the beachfront land has been bought by speculators for planned tourist resorts.

Pantai Segar is about 2km east around

the first headland and you can easily walk there. An enormous rock 2km to the east offers superb views across the countryside if you climb up it early in the morning.

The road goes 5km east to Tanjung Aan, where there are two classic beaches with very fine, powdery white sand. It comes as no surprise to discover that this is another area slated for upmarket resort hotels.

The road continues another 3km to the fishing village of Gerupak, where there's a market on Tuesday. From there you can get a boat across the bay to Bumbang.

Alternatively, you can turn to the north just before Tanjung Aan and go to Awang, a fishing village with a sideline in seaweed harvesting. You could get a boat from here across to Ekas and some of the other not-so-secret surf spots in this bay (see the East Lombok section later in this chapter for more information).

WEST OF KUTA

The road west of Kuta has been sealed as far as Selong Blanak, a lovely sandy bay – although some readers have complained about unsavoury characters hanging around the beach. The road doesn't follow the coast closely, but there are regular and spectacular ocean vistas. In between are more fine beaches like Mawan, Tampa and Mawi, but you have to detour to find them. They are all known to have surfing possibilities in the right conditions.

For accommodation, the isolated *Selong Blanak Cottages*, roughly 1.5km north of Selong Blanak, has a variety of rooms from 35,000 rp, and a decent *restaurant*, but the place is looking rather neglected these days.

To go further west, turn off this road at Keling. The road goes through pleasantly forested hills to Montongsapah, where it swings back to the coast, with a brilliant ocean view as you descend to Pengantap.

From Pengantap, you can climb across a headland to descend to another superb bay, which you follow around for about 1km. Keep your eyes peeled for the turn-off west to Blongas, which is a very steep, rough and winding road with breathtaking scenery.

There are some good places for **surfing** and **diving**, but you'll need to charter a boat to find them.

This is as far west as you can go on this road – return to the junction and turn north to Sekotong, by another scenic road, and on to Lembar. For information on the towns west of Sekotong, see the West Lombok chapter.

The trip from Kuta around to Lembar is excellent, but it's pretty rugged, especially the detour to Blongas. The best option is to go by motorbike, but only of you're a competent rider – in places it may be too steep, narrow and rutted even for a little *jimny* jeep. The distance is not great (less than 100km), but allow plenty of time and don't try it in the wet season.

East Lombok

All that most travellers see of the east coast is Labuhan Lombok – the port for ferries to Sumbawa – but improvements to the road around the eastern and north-eastern coasts make a round-the-island trip quite feasible and enjoyable. Similarly, the once-remote south-eastern peninsula is becoming more accessible, particularly to those with their own transport.

ANYAR TO LABUHAN LOMBOK

This road is sparsely populated, so public transport is limited. The road east from the main northern junction at Anyar (mentioned in the North Lombok chapter) is very steep and windy. There are isolated black-sand **beaches** along the way, particularly at Obel Obel.

Further south, the pleasant and secluded *Siola Cottages*, just before the village of **Labuhan Pandan**, is set in a coconut grove on the seashore. Bungalows cost around 20,000 rp, or more for a rate that includes three meals. You can also just stop there for a meal or a snack at the *restaurant*.

Two kilometres to the south, *Gili Lampu Cottages* offers simple bamboo bungalows a little way back from the beach for around 15,000 rp.

From Labuhan Pandan, or further north at Sugian, you can charter a boat to the uninhabited islands of Gili Sulat and Gili Pentangan. Both islands have lovely **white beaches** and good coral for **snorkelling**, but no facilities. A boat costs about 40,000 rp for up to five passengers for a day trip there and back, with a few hours on an island.

The Perama tourist shuttle bus company has a camp on Gili Pentangan. As you approach Labuhan Lombok, look for the **giant trees** about 5km north of the harbour.

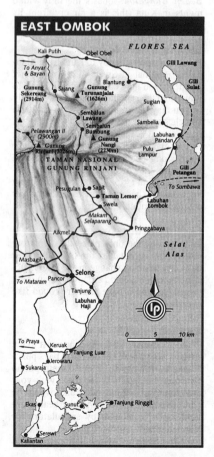

EAST LOMBOK

LABUHAN LOMBOK

Labuhan Lombok, also known as Labuhan Kayangan, is the main port for ferries and boats to Sumbawa. There's fantastic views of mighty Gunung Rinjani from the port, and from the hill on the southern side of the harbour you can gaze across the Selat Alas strait to Sumbawa.

The town of Labuhan Lombok, about 3km from the ferry terminal, is a scruffy place. If you are on your way to or from Sumbawa there's no need to stay overnight, and the choice of hotels is very poor.

Places to Stay & Eat

In the village, *Losmen Dian Dutaku* has very depressing singles/doubles for 5000/10,000 rp – it's a last resort only. On the road to the port, *Losmen Munawar* is also noisy and uninspiring, but a little better for the same price.

The best option, *Hotel Melati Lima Tiga*, costs 12,500/18,000 rp, but is still noisy. There is food available at some *warungs* in the town, and around the ferry terminal.

Getting There & Away

Bus & Bemo Frequent buses and bemos travel between Labuhan Lombok and Mandalika terminal in Sweta (Mataram) for 2050 rp, and head north to Bayan and Anyar. If you're zipping straight across Lombok and bound for Bali, you can easily get a connection in Sweta to Lembar. Note that public transport to/from Labuhan Lombok is often marked Labuhan Kayangan or Tanjung Kayangan, which are common names for the port and peninsula, respectively.

Buses and bemos that do not go *directly* to Labuhan Lombok, but just travel the main road along the east coast, will only drop you off at the port entrance, from where you'll have to catch another bemo to the ferry terminal. Don't walk; it is too far.

Boat Regular passenger ferries leave Labuhan Lombok for Poto Tano in Sumbawa (see the Lombok Getting There & Away chapter for details). Ferries depart from the terminal, roughly 3km from the village of Labuhan

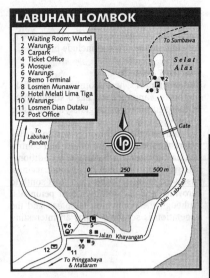

LABUHAN LOMBOK

1 Waiting Room; Wartel
2 Warungs
3 Carpark
4 Ticket Office
5 Mosque
6 Warungs
7 Bemo Terminal
8 Losmen Munawar
9 Hotel Melati Lima Tiga
10 Warungs
11 Losmen Dian Dutaku
12 Post Office

Lombok. The port is easy enough to work out. There are a few *food stalls*, and vendors also board the boat.

SOUTH OF LABUHAN LOMBOK
Selong & Pancor

Selong, the capital of the East Lombok administrative district, has some old buildings dating from the Dutch period. *Hotel Erina* (☎ 21297), at Jl Pahlawan 164 (the road towards the sea), is not a bad place to stay. Decent rooms cost 15,000 to 20,000 rp. There is a dearth of *restaurants* in Selong.

The transport junction for the region is **Pancor**, where you can stay at *Hotel Melati*, about 2km north of the bemo terminal.

Labuhan Haji

On the coast is Labuhan Haji, which is accessible from Selong and Tanjung Luar by bemo. Formerly a port for those departing on a *hajj* (pilgrimage to Mecca), the port buildings are abandoned and in ruins. The black sand beach here is a bit grubby, but the water is OK for swimming.

Melewi's Beach Hotel (☎ 21241), almost

on the beach about 300m from the bemo stop, is isolated and has great views across to Sumbawa. Bungalows cost 20,000/25,000 rp for singles/doubles, and include breakfast.

Further South

Tanjung Luar One of Lombok's main fishing ports, Tanjung Luar has a strong smell of fish and plenty of Bugis-style houses on stilts.

From here the road swings west to **Keruak** where wooden boats are made, and continues past the turn to **Sukaraja**, a traditional village where you can buy woodcarvings. Just west of Keruak there's a road south to **Jerowaru** and the south-eastern peninsula. Although the population is sparse and the vegetation is scrubby, it has an interesting

coastline. If you want to explore, you'll need your own transport, but it's easy to get lost and the roads go from bad to worse.

A sealed road branches west past Jerowaru – it gets pretty rough but eventually reaches **Ekas** from where you can charter a boat to Awang across the bay (see the South Lombok section earlier in this chapter). It is a popular region for **surfing** and it has a lovely little **beach**, but it's a long way to come.

On the eastern coast of the peninsula, Tanjung Ringgit has some large **caves** which, according to a local legend, are home to a demonic giant. The road there is rough, and may be impassable after heavy rains. It might be easier to charter a boat from Tanjung Luar.

North Lombok

Highlights

- Gunung Rinjani, a spectacular active volcano of great spiritual significance, offers superb trekking and stunning scenery.

- Danau Segara Anak is a brilliant blue-green lake in Rinjani's volcanic crater; the milk-white water from the nearby hot springs is believed to have curative powers.

- Traditional villages such as Segenter have rectangular bamboo and thatch houses, laid out in traditional Sasak style.

- Senaru, a pretty village on the northern flank of Gunung Rinjani is a relaxing place to stay, even if you aren't going to climb the mountain.

The sparsely populated northern region of Lombok is very picturesque, with a variety of landscapes and seascapes, few tourists and even fewer facilities. Public transport is not frequent, nor does it detour from the main road. With your own transport, however, you can stop along the way to admire the views, and make side trips to the coast, waterfalls and inland villages. The major attraction unquestionably is the mighty Gunung Rinjani mountain.

BANGSAL TO BAYAN

The road between Senggigi and Bangsal is scenic, especially the inland route through Pusuk Pass. However, the road north of Bangsal is windy and often steep, and public transport is less frequent.

Several minibuses a day go from Mandalika terminal in Sweta (Mataram) to Bayan (2100 rp), and stop off at any place along the way, but you may have to get connections in Pemenang and Anyar.

Bangsal

The junction for boats to the Gili Islands is not an unpleasant place to hang out at for a while. Travel agents, moneychangers, shaded *warungs* and shops have cropped up to take advantage of the fact that travellers using public transport to the Gilis often have to wait here. If you get stuck, *Taman Sari Guesthouse*, at the entrance to the port, has neat, clean singles/doubles for 20,000/5,000 rp.

Getting There & Away From the boat terminal, walk about 800m straight up the road for a bemo along Jl Raya Tanjung to Bayan (for connections to Senaru) or back down to Mataram, via Senggigi. You can avoid the hassles of public transport – and enjoy the scenery – by chartering a bemo or jeep at Bangsal; as an example, a vehicle to Senaru costs about 35,000 rp.

Refer to the Gili Islands chapter for information about passing through Bangsal on the way to or from the Gilis.

Sira

On the coast facing Gili Air, Sira has a white-sand beach and good snorkelling on the nearby coral reef. The whole area has been acquired for luxury tourism developments, but so far only the stunning *Oberoi Lombok* (☎ 38444, fax 32496) has been built. It is an extraordinarily opulent, isolated and luxurious place with a private swimming pool and rooms from US$221 – and more for ocean views. It is not signposted from the main road, but your driver will know where it is.

Tanjung

This village and transport terminal is quite large and attractive, and hosts a big cattle market every Sunday.

Just before Tanjung, *Manopo Homestay* (fax 32688), which is also known as Le Club des Explorateurs, has eccentric management, a lovely seaside location and several basic rooms from 15,000 to 25,000 rp. This is definitely not your average Indonesian *losmen*, and is easy to miss from the main road.

Karang Kates

A little further on is Karang Kates (Krakas for short), where five springs spurt out freshwater from the sea bed 400m offshore – the people here collect their drinking water from the sea. The sign announcing 'Water in the Sea' is not quite as daft as it may appear. It is a great area for **snorkelling**, but bring your own gear or hire it at Senggigi.

Gondang

In the village of Gondang, *Suhardi Home Stay* has simple but pleasant singles/doubles for about 15,000/25,000 rp. It's the best place to base yourself while exploring the nearby beaches and waterfalls.

Air Terjun Tiu Pupas

The 30m Tiu Pupas waterfall is about 4km inland along a rough track from Gondang – the track is passable by motorbike, but ask around before driving a car. There are other nearby **waterfalls** on the northern slopes of Rinjani, but they're only worth seeing up until the beginning of the dry season, and most are very difficult to reach. The falls on the southern slopes are more accessible (see the Tetebatu section in the Central, South & East Lombok chapter).

Segenter

Further up the coast, this traditional Sasak village is a bit hard to find, but it's worth the effort. A track (usually not accessible by car) heads south off the main road, about 1km west of Sukadana. Follow it for about 2km until you see the thatched roofs and woven wooden fence of the village compound. It's

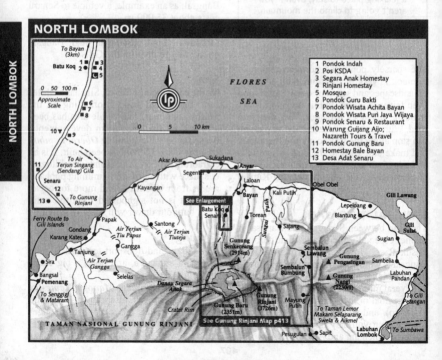

NORTH LOMBOK

To Bayan (3km)
Batu Koq

0   50 100 m
Approximate Scale

To Air Terjun Singang (Sendang) Gila
Senaru
To Gunung Rinjani

1 Pondok Indah
2 Pos KSDA
3 Segara Anak Homestay
4 Rinjani Homestay
5 Mosque
6 Pondok Guru Bakti
7 Pondok Wisata Achita Bayan
8 Pondok Wisata Puri Jaya Wijaya
9 Pondok Senaru & Restaurant
10 Warung Guijang Aijo; Nazareth Tours & Travel
11 Pondok Gunung Baru
12 Homestay Bale Bayan
13 Desa Adat Senaru

FLORES

SEA

0   5   10 km

Akar Akar   Sukadana
Segenter   Anyar
Kayangan   Laloan
See Enlargement   Bayan   Kali Putih   Obel Obel
Batu Koq   Senaru   Toreah   Gili Lawang
Ferry Route to Gili Islands   Papak   Santong   Lepeloang
Gondang   Air Terjun   Air Terjun   Sajang   Blantung
Karang Kates   Tiu Pupas   Tiuteja   Gili
Tanjung   Gangga   Gunung   Sugian   Sulat
Sira   Air Terjun   Senkereang   Sembalun
Bangsal   Gangga   Selelas   (2914m)   Lawang   Gunung   Sambelia
Pemenang   Sembalun   Pengasingan
To Senggigi   Danau Segara Bumbung   Labuhan
& Mataram   Anak   Gunung   Pandan
                                                          Nangi
                           Gunung   Gunung   Mayung   (2330m)
                    Crater Rim Baru   Rinjani Putih   To Gili
                            (2351m) (3726m)   To Taman Lemor   Petangan
TAMAN NASIONAL GUNUNG RINJANI See Gunung Rinjani Map p413 Makam Selaparang, Labuhan
                                              Swela & Aikmel Lombok
                              Pesugulan Sapit   To Sumbawa

Top: Workers in the fields at Tetebatu in central Lombok.
Middle Left: Lombok's Kuta beach – a far cry from its Bali namesake.
Bottom left: Scene from a circumcision ritual in west Lombok.
Right: Patchwork fields in central Lombok.

Top: Danau Sengara Anak (Child of the Sea), the stunning, crescent-shaped crater lake of Gunung Rinjani in north Lombok.
Bottom left: Clothing and fabric sellers on Kuta beach in south Lombok.
Bottom right: Doing business in a west Lombok market.

very neatly laid out, with rows of identical rectangular houses facing each other, and communal pavilions in between. The homes are bamboo, with a stone hearth, cane baskets and wooden implements, but everything is perfectly made, precisely arranged, and interesting to see. Afterwards, make a donation (2000 rp is sufficient) and sign the visitors' book.

Bayan

This northernmost part of Lombok's coast is the birthplace of the Wektu Telu religion, as well as a home for traditional Muslims. The mosque at Bayan, on the road east of the junction, is said to be the oldest on Lombok – perhaps over 300 years old.

SENARU

This quiet, picturesque village is the usual starting point for a climb up Gunung Rinjani, but even if you're not interested in climbing, or it's the wrong season, Senaru is still worth a visit. It has a good range of budget accommodation – some places have superb views over the valley to the east and up to the rim of Rinjani.

Trekking

Most losmen can provide information and guides for Rinjani, so Senaru is the best place to base yourself for the climb (see the Gunung Rinjani section later in this chapter). Ignore the notice at the Pos KSDA (park ranger's office) as you enter the village – you only have to report at Pos I, past Senaru, if trekking up Rinjani.

Air Terjun Singang (Sendang) Gila

Make sure you visit these magnificent waterfalls, which you can also admire from the car park next to Pondok Senaru. From the entrance to the falls (where you pay 250 rp), it's a pleasant 30 minute walk – partly through forest and partly alongside an irrigation canal – which follows the contour of the hill, occasionally disappearing into tunnels where the cliffs are too steep. Watch for the sleek black monkeys swinging through the trees.

Another 30 minutes or so further up the hill are some more **waterfalls**, where you can swim. The track is steep and tough at times, so it's a good idea to take a guide. Some boys will probably approach you and offer their services (for a negotiable fee).

Desa Adat Senaru

The traditional village compound of Senaru has an air of untainted antiquity, but it has become a bit of a tourist trap lately. As recently as the 1960s, Senaru was completely isolated from the rest of the world, and it still seems remote, although trekkers pass through all the time. You must report to the village head, sign a visitors' book and make a donation – at least 5000 rp is urged, but 1000 rp is enough.

Places to Stay & Eat

Most of the losmen are similar in standards and almost identical in price, and they all include breakfast. *Segara Anak Homestay* has good views from some rooms and a helpful manager who charges 15,000 rp a room. *Pondok Guru Bakti* (Guru Bakti is the school teacher who first helped visitors to 'discover' this area) and *Pondok Indah* also cost about 15,000 rp, and are good places to organise treks.

Other good options are: *Rinjani Homestay*, which is basic but one of the cheapest (10,000 rp a room); *Pondok Wisata Achita Bayan*, which charges 10,000/12,000 rp for singles/doubles; and *Pondok Wisata Puri Jaya Wijaya*, the cheapest for 7500/10,000 rp. *Homestay Bale Bayan*, opposite the traditional village, is quite atmospheric and the closest to the trailhead. Decent rooms cost 15,000 rp. *Pondok Gunung Baru* is identical in standard and price.

The rooms at *Pondok Senaru (Mataram ☎ 22868)* are large, quaint and offer views from the small patios, but they now cater to tour groups, and charge 50,000 rp to the independent traveller.

Every losmen has a *restaurant* or 'coffee shop' (a common term in the village for some reason). The best spot for views is the restaurant at *Pondok Senaru*, which also has good food at surprisingly reasonable prices. The only independent restaurant is the basic *Warung Guijang Aijo*.

Getting There & Away

From the west, catch a bemo to Anyar, from where bemos travel to Senaru for about 700 rp about every 20 minutes until 4 pm. If you are coming from, or going to, east Lombok, get off at the junction near Bayan (your driver will know it), where bemos regularly connect with Senaru.

SEMBALUN LAWANG & SEMBALUN BUMBUNG

On the eastern side of Gunung Rinjani is the beautiful Sembalun valley. The inhabitants of the valley claim descent from the Hindu Javanese, and a relative of one of the Majapahit rulers is said to be buried here. The valley is also home to mystic cow callers, who attract wild cattle on the mountain by whirling a bamboo tube filled with salt and water to produce a low humming sound.

The main Sasak village of Sembalun Bumbung is a sprawling and relatively wealthy village lying just off the main road. It is often referred to simply as Sembalun; 'Bumbung' is used to differentiate it from Sembalun Lawang, 2.5km north along the main road. Sembalun Lawang is a satellite village, with a 'big onion' monument and not a lot else, but it's at the start of a trek to Rinjani and therefore the better place to stay.

Places to Stay & Eat

Along the main road to the start of the trail in Sembalun Lawang are two places to stay, which also serve meals and arrange guides, porters and hiking gear. *Pondok Sembalun* is an attractive place where small single/ double bungalows go for 10,000/12,500 rp. *Wisma Cemara Siu* (☎ 21213) offers good rooms in a spacious, spotless house with views of the mountain for 10,000/15,000 rp. The management is switched on and helpful with arranging treks.

In Sembalun Bumbung, *Puri Rinjani* has basic rooms in the house for 10,000 rp or new bungalows out the back for 15,000 rp.

It can arrange horse rides for around 15,000 rp, and there are plans to provide mountain bikes for guests.

Getting There & Away

From Kali Putih (on the main road to the north), a few bemos rattle along the rough road to both villages, usually only in the morning. From the south, a scenic, sealed road twists over the mountains, normally only as far as Bumbung. Bemos run about every hour from 9 am and 4 pm between Bumbung and Aikmel, on the Mataram to Priggabaya road, (2500 rp). From Aikmel, regular bemos and buses run to Mataram and Labuhan Lombok.

SAPIT

To the south-east of Gunung Rinjani, Sapit has stunning views across to Sumbawa, with Rinjani forming a spectacular backdrop. It is another place to organise a climb up Rinjani, but the trek involves more effort and time. Even if you are not climbing Rinjani, Sapit is still worth visiting if you want somewhere cool and relaxing.

Things to See & Do

Between the towns of Swela and Sapit (see the East Lombok map in the Central, South & East Lombok chapter), a side road goes down into **Taman Lemor**, where there's a refreshing spring-fed pool and a few pesky monkeys. Tickets are 400/250 rp for adults/ children, and it's open from 8 am to 4 pm daily. Down the road towards Pringgabaya, a side road goes to **Makam Selaparang**, the burial place of ancient Selaparang kings. Neither is particularly exciting, but both provide a good excuse for some **hiking**.

You could also visit a few **hot springs** and small **waterfalls** near Sapit. Ask either homestay for directions.

Places to Stay & Eat

Hati Suci Homestay (☎ 36545, fax 35753, email hatisuci@mataram.net.id) has several pleasant bungalows in a splendid location. They cost from 20,000/35,000 rp to 30,000/ 50,000 rp for singles/doubles, and breakfast is included. The *restaurant* is worth a visit, if only for the breeze and views. The associated *Balelangga Bed & Breakfast* (same contact details as the Hati Suci) is not as good, but cheaper. Simple bungalows, with outside bathroom facilities, cost 15,000/25,000 rp, including breakfast. It is around 700m past the Hati Suci.

Getting There & Away
First get a bus to Pringgabaya on the main road between Labuhan Lombok and Mataram, then catch a bemo to Sapit (1000 rp). Ask the driver to take you the extra few hundred metres to the hotel you want.

There is no public transport between Sembalun Bumbung and Sapit, so if you don't have your own transport, you must come from the south.

GUNUNG RINJANI

The trek was demanding, but well worth the effort – definitely the best sunset ever; watching the sun sink below the horizon of the fluffy clouds, and the colours, were amazing. It was like something out of a fairy story.

Eriko Taninoto & Jason Creek, Britain

Rinjani is the highest mountain on Lombok and the second highest in Indonesia (after Puncak Jaya in Irian Jaya). At 3726m, it soars above the island and dominates the landscape, but by mid-morning on most days the summit is shrouded in cloud. There is a huge crater containing a large, green, crescent-shaped lake called Segara Anak (Child of the Sea), which is about 6km across at its widest point.

It has a series of natural hot springs known as Kokok Putih, on the north-eastern side of this crater, said to have remarkable healing powers, particularly for diseases of the skin. The lake is 600m below the crater rim, and in the centre of its curve there is a new cone, Gunung Baru (also known as Gunung Barujari), which is only a couple of hundred years old. Rinjani is an active volcano and last erupted in 1994, changing the shape of this inner cone and sprinkling ash over much of Lombok.

Both the Balinese and Sasaks revere the volcano. To the Balinese it is equal in stature to Gunung Agung, a seat of the gods, and many Balinese make a pilgrimage here each year. In a ceremony called *pekelan,* the people throw jewellery into the lake and make offerings to the spirit of the mountain. Some Sasaks make several pilgrimages a year – full moon is their favourite time for paying respects to the mountain and curing ailments by bathing in its hot springs.

Many foreign visitors make the climb too, although very few people go the extra 1700m or so to the very summit of Rinjani. Even the climb to the crater lake is not to be taken lightly. Do not try it in the wet season (November to April) because the tracks will be slippery and very dangerous; in any case you would be lucky to see any more than mist and cloud. June to August is the only time you are guaranteed (well, almost) no rain or cloud.

There are a few options for the climb, from a strenuous dash to the rim and back, to a four or five day trek around the summit. Most visitors stay in Senaru, climb from there to the crater lake and return the same way; this northern route is more easily accessible and has better services for trekkers.

Alternatively, you could trek between Senaru and Sembalun Lawang on the eastern side of Rinjani, or start from Sapit to the south-east.

Organised Tours
A number of agencies in Mataram and Senggigi can arrange guided, all-inclusive treks. They are very expensive, but they save time and hassle. Prices include transport to the mountain (even from Mataram or Senggigi), equipment, an English-speaking guide, porters, and food and water for a two night/three day trek. They will need at least two people to make it worthwhile, and it will be up to you to find other travellers to cut the costs. Remember there's fewer tourists on Lombok these days.

Discover Lombok
   (☎ 36781) It has an office in the Pasar Seni art market, Senggigi; and charges US$150 per person.

Nazareth Tours & Travel
(☎ 31705) This agency has offices in Senggigi, Ampenan and Senaru, and offers a variety of treks from US$150 to US$220.

Perama
(☎ 35928) Treks can be arranged at its offices in Mataram and Senggigi; they cost around US$120 from Senaru and US$150 from Sembalun Lawang.

Sahir Generations
(☎ 21688) Based in Masbagik, central Lombok, it offers a variety of treks from US$150 in a group of four.

Segara Anak Trekking Club
Based at the Segara Anak Homestay, Senaru, it charges about US$85/120 for one/three night trips.

Do-It-Yourself

If you have time, there is no reason why you cannot organise a trek yourself in Sapit, Senaru or Sembulan Lawang for about 20% of the cost charged by trekking agencies. In Sapit, contact the Hati Suci Homestay; in Senaru, contact any of the losmen, particularly Pondok Indah, Pondok Guru Bakti and Homestay Bale Bayan which are helpful and have equipment to rent; or the two losmen in Sembulan Lawang. If they start talking in American dollars (and lots of them), try somewhere else.

Guides & Porters You can trek from Senaru to the hot springs and back without a guide – the trail is pretty well defined. From Sembulan Lawang, however, the starting point is clear, but after that there's a number of trails branching off and you could get lost. When scaling the summit of Rinjani, you have to start in the dark, so it's good to have someone who knows the way.

The cost for guides and porters is fairly standard at each of the three villages that you can set out from – Sapit, Senaru and Sembulan Lawang. You must provide food, water and transport for each guide and porter, and probably cigarettes as well. A good guide will be informative, manage all the arrangements and add greatly to the enjoyment of the trek, but won't carry anything, so you might have to get at least one porter as well. In Senaru, the charges are

30,000 rp per day for a guide and 20,000 rp for a porter; in Sembulan Lawang and Sapit, the standard fees are 40,000 rp per day for a guide, and 25,000 rp for a porter.

Equipment There are some crude shelters on the way, but don't rely on them – a sleeping bag and tent are essential. In Senaru, rent of a two/four person tent will cost about 15,000/30,000 rp, a sleeping bag 6000 rp, and sleeping mattress 3000 rp (prices are for a two night/three day trek). Take a stove so you don't need to deplete the limited supply of firewood – this will cost 10,000 to 15,000 rp in Senaru, plus fuel, for the three days.

Prices in Sapit and Sembulan Lawang are slightly higher, because there is little or no competition. You'll also need to bring solid footwear, layers of warm clothing and wet weather gear (these items can't be rented).

Supplies Bring rice, instant noodles, sugar, coffee, eggs, tea, biscuits or bread, some tins of fish or meat (and a can opener), onions, fruit and anything else that keeps your engine running. It's better to buy most of these supplies in Mataram or Senggigi, where it is cheaper and there's more choice, but you can find a fair range in Senaru. Also bring plenty of water, matches and a torch (flashlight). Don't forget to carry all your rubbish out with you.

The Climb

The walk is usually begun from Senaru in the north, from where independent trekkers usually go halfway and back to Senaru. You can, however, go all the way from Senaru to Sembalun Lawang, and then take public transport or charter a bemo back to Senaru, but the trail from Pelawangan II down to Sembalun Lawang is lightly travelled and indistinct. A guide is strongly recommended for this section – and essential if you start in Sembalun Lawang.

Masochists in a hurry could walk from Senaru to Sembalun Lawang (or vice versa) in two full days with one night at the hot springs, but the first day would be very difficult and it doesn't include the climb to most reliable source on the ascent. Water should be treated or boiled.

Another 1½ hours steady walk uphill brings you to Pos III (2300m), where there is another two shelters in disrepair. Water is 100m off the trail to the right, but sometimes dries up in the height of the dry season. Pos III is the usual place to camp at the end of the first day.

Pos III to Pelawangan I (1½-2 hours)
From Pos III it takes about 1½ hours to reach the rim, Pelawangan I, at an altitude of 2634m. Set off very early to arrive at the crater rim for the stunning sunrise. It's possible to camp at Pelawangan I. If you extend yourself to walk here at the end of the first day, you'll be treated with a spectacular sunset and an equally spectacular sunrise the next morning. The drawbacks are that level camp sites are limited, there is no water and it can be very blustery.

Pelawangan I to Lake & Hot Springs (2-3 hours)
It takes about two hours to descend to Segara Anak and around to the hot springs. The first hour is a very steep descent and involves low-grade rock climbing in parts. Watch out for rubble – in certain spots it's very hard to keep your footing, especially with a heavy pack. At the bottom of the crater wall, it is then an easy one hour walk across undulating terrain around the lake edge.

There are several places to camp, but most prefer to be near the hot springs, where you can soak your weary body and recuperate. If you find the water too hot near the lake, follow the river further downstream to any pool where the water is slightly cooler. Although the sulphur scum may look off-putting, this is a natural occurrence, and the water is superb to soak in.

There are two dilapidated shelters beside the lake, but the nicest camp sites are at the lake's edge. Fresh water can be taken from a spring near the hot springs. You can boil the lake water, but no amount of boiling will take away the acrid taste.

Gunung Baru (2351m), the 'new' cone in

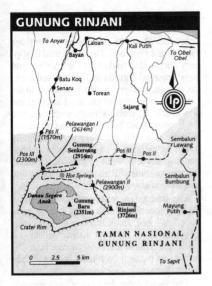

GUNUNG RINJANI

the top. More customary is either a walk to the hot springs and return from Senaru in three days, or a four or five day full circuit including the ascent of Gunung Rinjani. The minimum time for the full circuit is three days/two nights.

The last day of the full circuit is a long slog, but it's downhill all the way after the hard climb to Rinjani. Many walkers return to Senaru after climbing the summit, as part of a five day trip that includes another night at the hot springs.

Senaru to the Pos III (5-6 hours) At the end of the village is Pos I (the PHPA post on some maps; 860m). Sign in here and pay the entrance fee (2000 rp). Just beyond the post is a small *warung* and then the trail forks – continue straight ahead on the right fork. The trail steadily ascends through scrubby farmland for about half an hour to the sign at the entrance to Taman Nasional Gunung Rinjani. The wide trail climbs for another 2½ hours until you reach Pos II (1570m), where there are two shelters. Water can be found 100m down the slopes from the trail and this is the

the middle of Segara Anak, may look tempting but it's a very dangerous climb. The track around the lake to the base of Baru is narrow and people have drowned after slipping off it. The climb itself takes you over a very loose surface, and if you start sliding or falling, there is nothing to stop you and nothing to hang on to. Also, many of the tracks around here were wiped out in the 1994 eruption.

Some hikers spend two nights – or even more – at the lake, but most head back to Senaru the next day. The climb back up the rim is certainly taxing – allow at least three hours and start early to ensure you make it back to Senaru in one day. Allow five hours from the rim down to Senaru. The last bemo down the mountain from Senaru leaves at round 4 pm.

Rather than retrace your steps, the better option is to press on to Sembulan Lawang if you can work out what to do with your gear.

Hot Springs to Pelawangan II (3-4 hours) The trail starts beside the last shelter at the hot springs and heads away from the lake for 100m or so before veering right. The trail traverses the northern slope of the crater, away from the lake, and it is an easy walk for one hour along the grassy slopes. Then it's a steep and constant climb; from the lake it takes about three hours until you finally reach the crater rim.

At the rim a sign points the way back to Segara Anak. Water can be found down the slope near the sign. The trail forks here – go straight on to Sembulan Lawang, or continue along the rim to the campsite of Pelawangan II (2900m). It is only about 10 minutes more to the campsite on a bare ridge. When clear, you can watch the sun set behind the rim on the other side. Bali's Gunung Batur as well as Gunung Agung are visible. Try to find a sheltered spot to camp in case the wind springs up.

Pelawangan II to Rinjani Summit (5-6 hours return) Gunung Rinjani stretches in an arc above the campsite at Pelawangan II and looks deceptively close. The usual time to start the climb is at 3 am, in order to reach

the summit in time for the sunrise before the clouds roll in.

It takes about 45 minutes up to the ridge that leads to Rinjani. The steep trail is slippery and hard to find in the dark, unless you have engaged a guide or have sussed it out the evening before. Don't try to climb to the peak when strong winds are blowing; the winds are icy, dust swirls in your eyes and it can upset your balance. Once you hit the ridge, it is a relatively easy walk gradually uphill for an hour or so. After about an hour heading towards what looks like the peak, the real summit of Rinjani looms up behind and towers above you.

The trail gets steeper and steeper. About 500m before the summit, there is scree composed of loose, fist-sized rocks – it's easier to scramble on all fours than try to stay on your feet. This section can take an hour. Finally, you make it onto solid rock and then the summit.

The views from the top are truly magnificent on a clear day, but even on a clear day don't expect to be able to see forever. Low level cloud can obscure the land mass and it is often hazy. But even if the views are not clear, it is certainly an achievement to have climbed the second highest peak in Indonesia. The descent is much easier, but take care on the scree. All up it takes three hours or more to reach the summit, and two more to get back down.

Pelawangan II to Sembalun Lawang (5 to 6 hours) After having negotiated the peak it is possible to reach Sembalun Lawang the same day. After a two hour descent, it is a long and hot, but easy, three hour walk. Head off early to avoid as much of the heat of the day as possible and make sure you have plenty of water to reach Sembalun Lawang.

From the camp site head back to the main trail and follow it for only a couple of hundred metres. The trail almost becomes a road but don't keep following it – the trail to Sembalun Lawang is a small side trail branching off. It's not signposted. Keep looking over the edge until you find it – it follows the next ridge along from Rinjani, not the valley. Once on the trail, it is easy to follow and takes around two hours to the bottom.

At the bottom of the ridge the trail levels out and crosses undulating to flat grassland all the way to Sembalun Lawang. An hour's walk will bring you to Pos III, a relatively new shelter, and then it is another half hour to Pos II. Long grass obscures the trail, once a road, and in places you cannot see it more than a couple of metres ahead. A half hour beyond Pos II the trail crosses a bridge and then crests a small rise to a lone shade tree. The trail seems to fork here; take the right fork.

Having orientated Sembalun Lawang firmly in your mind, experienced hikers with plenty of water should be able to reach it without too much difficulty – as a general rule the trail follows the flank of Rinjani before swinging around to Sembalun Lawang at the end. However, the area is not populated and, unless you meet other hikers, there is no one to ask directions. A guide is strongly recommended for this part of the trip.

Starting from Sembalun Lawang It is six or seven hours to Pelawangan II and a guide is essential. It is much harder to get your bearings walking up the mountain and the trail is all but impossible to find on your own. This is an easier walk to the rim than from the Senaru side, with only a three hour walk up the ridge to tax you.

Before you head off, sign in at the Departemen Kehutanan (Forest Department) office in Sembalun Lawang (where the road to Rinjani starts) and hand over the 2000 rp fee. Horses can be hired to take you to Pos III for 30,000 rp.

A Night Climb From Senaru If you travel light and climb fast, you can reach the crater rim from Senaru in about six hours – it's approximately a 1770m altitude gain in 10km. Armed with a torch and some moonlight (and/or a guide), set off at midnight and you will be there for sunrise. The trip back takes about five hours, so you can be down in time for lunch. Take lots of snack food and at least 1L of water.

Around the Rim If you reach Pelawangan I early in the day, you can follow the crater rim around to the east for about 3km to Gunung Senkereang (2914m). This point overlooks the break in the rim where the stream from the hot springs flows out of the crater and north-east towards the sea. It's not an easy walk however, and the track is narrow and very exposed in places.

Other Routes on Rinjani You can climb up to the crater from Torean, a small village south-east of Bayan. The trail follows Sungai Putih, the stream that flows from Segara Anak and the hot springs, but it is hard to find; you'll need a guide.

You can also climb the southern side of Rinjani from either Sesaot (see the West Lombok chapter) or Tetebatu (see the Central, South & East Lombok chapter). Both routes involve at least one night camping in the jungle, and you may not see any views at all until you get above the tree line. Again, a guide is essential.

A better option from the south is from Sapit or Pesugulan, towards Sembalun Bumbung, then to Pelawangan II.

Gili Islands

Highlights

- The scenery is beautiful, with white-sand beaches, blue sea, great views, and spectacular sunrises and sunsets.
- Gili Air has peaceful cottages under coconut palms.
- Gili Meno is a great place to play Robinson Crusoe.
- Gili Trawangan, the 'party island', has the best diving and snorkelling on Lombok.
- The absence of cars, motorbikes or hawkers!

Off the north-western coast of Lombok are three small, coral-fringed islands – Gili Air, Gili Meno and Gili Trawangan – each with superb, white sandy beaches, clear water, coral reefs, brilliantly coloured fish and the best snorkelling on Lombok. Although they are known to travellers as the 'Gili Islands', *gili* actually means 'island', so this is not a local name. There's lots of other gilis around the coast of Lombok.

Many years ago, descendants of Bugis immigrants were granted leases to establish coconut plantations on the islands. The economic activities expanded to include fishing, raising livestock, and growing corn, tapioca and peanuts. As tourists started to visit Lombok, some came to the Gilis on day trips and then began to stay for longer periods in local homes. Many of the people on the islands soon fund that the most profitable activity was 'picking white coconuts' – providing services to tourists.

The islands have become enormously popular with visitors, who come for the very simple pleasures of sun, snorkelling and socialising. They are cheap, and the absence of cars, motorbikes and (especially) hawkers

adds greatly to the pleasure of staying on the Gilis.

Dangers & Annoyances

Security There are occasional thefts on the islands, and they are not always dealt with effectively – there are no police on any of the Gilis. Make sure your room, including the bathroom, is well secured. Keep your things locked in a bag and well away from windows, doors or other openings. Report any theft to the island *kepala* (head), and if there is no response, go to the police station in Tanjung (on the mainland) or, better, Ampenan (Mataram).

Gili Trawangan has a reputation as the 'party island'. With poorly lit beach parties, lots of alcohol and no police, it is perhaps unsurprising that a few foreign women have complained of (so far) minor cases of sexual harassment and assault from Indonesian and foreign men. Please be careful.

Stonefish & Jellyfish Although not common, stonefish are found on coral reefs where they are camouflaged and almost invisible. If you stand on one, the venomous spines can cause excruciating pain and sometimes death. Do not walk on the coral reefs. If you need more encouragement to not walk on reefs, see the boxed text 'Coral Conservation' in this chapter.

Jellyfish are also common when strong winds blow from the mainland, and they can leave a painful rash.

Snorkelling & Diving

The coral around the islands is good for snorkelling; probably the best area is off the north-west coast of Gili Trawangan. Many snorkelling areas can be reached from the shore, or you can rent a boat – the boatman will know the best spots. Equipment can be rented on the islands.

For scuba divers, the visibility is fair to good (best in the dry season), and there are some very good coral reefs accessible by boat. Marine life includes (harmless) sharks, turtles, giant clams and rays. A particularly interesting attraction is the blue coral, with an almost luminous colouring.

There are reputable scuba diving operations on each island. At the time of research, a dearth of tourists meant that discounts of up to 50% off the prices listed in this chapter were possible.

Accommodation

The Gilis standard is a plain little bamboo bungalow on stilts, with a thatched roof, a small verandah out the front and a concrete bathroom block at the back. Inside, there will be one or two beds with mosquito nets. Prices start from about 12,500/15,000 rp for singles/doubles in the low season. When the islands are usually busy (in July and August and around Christmas), owners ask more – possibly double the prices listed. Upmarket places may add a 'high season supplement'.

Most places include a light breakfast. Like everywhere in north Lombok, a 10% local government tax is added to your restaurant

---

Coral Conservation

In the past, much damage was done to coral reefs by fish bombing and careless use of anchors. There is a much greater awareness of this now and rehabilitation of damaged reefs is possible. Unfortunately, many visitors are unwittingly causing more damage by standing and walking on the reefs, often while snorkelling, boating or windsurfing. Perfectly formed corals are easily broken and take years to recover; the reef ecology is very sensitive.

If you're not into conservation, then think about the stonefish. These fish – with their venomous spines – are well camouflaged on the coral reefs of the Gilis, and at times they are virtually invisible. Standing on a stonefish can cause excruciating pain and sometimes death. So keep off the reefs!

---

bill, although it is often already included in your hotel bill. Make sure you have lots of small notes because even getting 2000 rp change from a 5000 rp note can be a hassle – although this is sometimes a subtle way to encourage travellers to offer the change as a 'tip'.

Touts often meet boats as they land. Once they take your luggage, you are normally committed to wherever they take you. If you want to stay in a particular place, don't let a tout convince you that it's full, expensive, closed or doesn't exist.

Getting There & Away

All boats pull up on the beaches, so you will have to wade ashore with your luggage. And sometimes the weather can be rough:

The sea was so rough that the boat couldn't reach the beach, so luggage and passengers went from the beach one by one in a small canoe. The captain and the two boatmen got more and more serious, non-smiling and stressed. After one hour, the rudder broke off. We took four hours to reach Gili Trawangan from Bangsal.

Moura Modiman, the Netherlands

Public Bemo & Boat Firstly, catch a bus or bemo to Pemenang, from where it's about 1km by *cidomo* (pony cart) to the harbour at Bangsal. The fare should be about 500 rp, but tourists are charged three or four times more. The North Lombok chapter has more information about Bangsal.

The Koperasi Angkutan Laut (Sea Transport Co-operative) is the boat owners' cartel which monopolises public transport between Bangsal and the islands. It's a matter of sitting and waiting until there is a full boat load – about 15 people. Public boats normally start departing Bangsal – and each of the three islands – at about 8 am, but check the departure times at the Koperasi's offices the day before. Boats normally stop running by 4 pm. From Bangsal, the fare is 1200 rp to Gili Air, 1500 rp to Gili Meno and 1600 rp to Gili Trawangan.

Tourist Shuttle Bus & Boat The main shuttle service operator, Perama (Senggigi

GILI ISLANDS

☎ 93007), is reliable and well established. It has a service to the Gilis which leaves Senggigi at 9 am and returns at 3 pm, you can take a day trip from Senggigi. This boat normally connects with tourist shuttle bus services to tourist centres on Lombok (ie Kuta, Mataram and Tetebatu) and Bali (see further in this entry).

From Senggigi, the fare per person to Gili Trawangan is 10,000/20,000 rp (one way/return). This service will also go to Gili Meno (12,500/25,000 rp) and Gili Air (15,000/30,000 rp) if passengers ask. Sunshine (based at the restaurant of the same name in Senggigi) also has a daily boat service to the Gilis from Senggigi at the same time and for the same price.

Perama, and a few other operators, also offer direct shuttle bus/boat services to the Gilis from Kuta (in Bali), Ubud and most tourist centres in south Bali. However, this service often involves a shuttle bus to Padangbai, the *public* ferry to Lembar, a shuttle bus to Mataram or Senggigi (where you may have to stay the night at your own expense), and a shuttle boat to the Gilis the next morning. Check the precise details before you book. It may be just as easy (and cheaper too) to travel between Bali and the Gilis under your own steam using public transport.

Chartering a Boat If you are too late for the public or shuttle boat you can always charter a boat. From Bangsal, the Koperasi charges 15,000/25,000 rp (one way/return) to Gili Air; 18,000/35,000 rp to Gili Meno; and 21,000/40,000 rp to Gili Trawangan. To visit all three islands from Bangsal will cost about 60,000 rp return, plus waiting time. The Perama offices on the three islands can arrange chartered boats, but costs are higher.

From in front of the Hotel Senggigi Aerowisata in Senggigi you can also charter a boat to the Gilis for the day. The set cost is 100,000 rp for a four person boat; or 200,000 rp for a boat holding up to ten.

Island Hopping Perama runs a convenient shuttle boat service between the islands, so you can stay on one island and look around another one – but the schedules don't allow you to visit two other islands and return to your original island on the same day. The one way fares are 4000 rp between Gili Air and Gili Trawangan, and 3000 rp between Gili Meno and the other two islands. The boats do two runs a day at about 9 am and 3 pm – check the times, and book with the individual Perama offices, or at any of the shops-cum-travel agencies on the islands.

GILI AIR

Gili Air is the closest island to the mainland and has the largest population. There are beaches around most of the island, but some are not suitable for swimming because they are quite shallow with a sharp coral bottom. Because the hotels and restaurants are so scattered, the island has a pleasant, rural character; it is more secluded and a delight to wander around. There are plenty of other people to meet, but if you stay in one of the more isolated places, socialising is optional.

Orientation & Information

It is surprisingly easy to become disoriented on the network of tiny tracks across the island. The simplest option is to follow the coast. Boats stop at the southern end of the island, near (but not at) the jetty.

The Perama office (☎ 36341) and *wartel* (public telephone office) are next to the Gili Indah Hotel, and the Koperasi boat operators have an office next to the jetty.

You can exchange money at the better hotels, but the rates are lousy. Hotel Gili Air offers a fax and 'e-mile' service (giliair @mataram.wasantara.net.id); while Pondok Cafe provides an Aqua mineral water refill service, and runs a small book exchange. At budget-range hotels, and restaurants without generators, electricity comes on at about 6 pm.

Activities

Boat Trips One local company (☎ 64018) operates glass bottom boat tours to the other two islands between 5.30 pm and midnight, including snorkelling (gear is provided) and

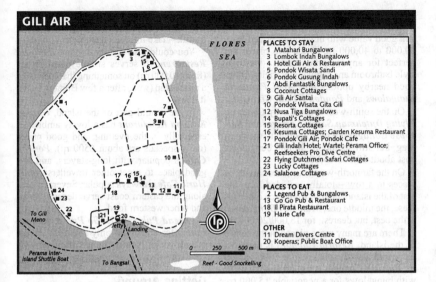

GILI AIR

FLORES
SEA

PLACES TO STAY
1 Matahari Bungalows
3 Lombok Indah Bungalows
4 Hotel Gili Air & Restaurant
5 Pondok Wisata Sandi
6 Pondok Gusung Indah
7 Abdi Fantastik Bungalows
8 Coconut Cottages
9 Gili Air Santai
10 Pondok Wisata Gita Gili
12 Nusa Tiga Bungalows
14 Bupati's Cottages
15 Resorta Cottages
16 Kesuma Cottages; Garden Kesuma Restaurant
17 Pondok Gili Air; Pondok Cafe
21 Gili Indah Hotel; Wartel; Perama Office;
   Reefseekers Pro Dive Centre
22 Flying Dutchmen Safari Cottages
23 Lucky Cottages
24 Salabose Cottages

PLACES TO EAT
2 Legend Pub & Bungalows
13 Go Go Pub & Restaurant
18 Il Pirata Restaurant
19 Harie Cafe

OTHER
11 Dream Divers Centre
20 Koperas; Public Boat Office

To Gili
Meno

Jetty
Boat
Landing

Perama Inter-
island Shuttle Boat

To Bangsal

0   250   500 m

Reef - Good Snorkelling

a BBQ fish dinner. A minimum of five people is required and it costs 70,000 rp per head. You can enquire at your hotel or one of the makeshift travel agencies around the island.

Snorkelling & Diving There's quite good snorkelling off the eastern and northern sides of the island. There is also excellent scuba diving within a short boat ride, with lots of whitetip sharks and underwater canyons.

It is best to deal with the two main diving centres:

Dream Divers Centre
(☎ 93738) This German-run outfit charges US$45 for two dives; US$40 for subsequent dives; and US$275 for open water courses.
Reefseekers Pro Dive
(☎/fax 34387) This very professional company charges US$25/45/80 for one/two/four dives; and offers a number of courses. It has a strong commitment to conserving the marine environment, and promoting local community projects.

Places to Stay
The best beach is on the northern part of the island, but surprisingly few losmen are set

up there. Along the western coast there are several places, but the beach is virtually nonexistent. The eastern coast is slightly more developed, with more places to eat nearby, and you can probably admire the sunrise from your room. Many travellers stay somewhere in between. There are many other good places to stay, apart from those listed in this section.

Places to Stay – Budget
Although the staff at *Lombok Indah Bungalows* are fairly lackadaisical, the setting overlooking the beach is superb. The bungalows are fairly standard and cost 15,000 rp. Another good option is the bungalows at the back of *Legend Pub*, which cost 12,000/15,000 rp for singles/doubles – but they can be noisy if the pub gets rowdy (which is rare). If these are full, try *Pondok Wisata Sandi* or *Pondok Gusung Indah* which are about the same price and standard as the Lombok Indah.

On the eastern coast, *Coconut Cottages* (☎ 35365) offers a set of clean, charming cottages in a pretty garden from 25,000 to

50,000 rp. Not far away, *Gili Air Santai* (☎ 641022) is a little classier than most, and still good value with bungalows priced from 20,000 to 40,000 rp. These two places are perfect for anyone who wants a western-style bathroom and regular electricity. Other good nearby options are: *Abdi Fantastik Bungalows* and *Pondok Wisata Gita Gili*.

On the south-west coast, *Lucky Cottages*, *Flying Dutchman Safari Cottages* and *Salabose Cottages* are near enough to the main drag, but still secluded. Simple bungalows cost about 12,500/15,000 rp.

On the far north-west coast, there are three places in a row – totally secluded from the rest of the island, but not from each other. Of these, the middle one, *Matahari Bungalows*, is the best, but dearest, for 18,000/20,000 rp.

There are many more places in the centre of the island. *Resorta Cottages* is the most basic and also the cheapest at 7000/10,000 rp. *Bupati's Cottages* is a good, quiet option, with bungalows for a negotiable 15,000 rp. *Nusa Tiga Bungalows* is also quiet, spacious and very good value, with bungalows for 12,000/15,000 rp.

Also in this price range, the *Kesuma Cottages* and *Pondok Gili Air* are friendly and convenient.

Places to Stay – Mid-Range

Gili Indah Hotel (☎ 36341) is the biggest place on Gili Air. It features a variety of bungalows in a wonderful garden, virtually on the beach. The 'standard' bungalows are not particularly great value at 20,000/25,000 rp, but it is worth splurging on the 'superior' bungalows for 50,000/60,000 rp; you will need to book ahead, though.

On the nicer, northern end of the island, *Hotel Gili Air* (☎/fax 34435, email giliair@ mataram.wasantara.net.id) is another up-market option. The beautiful bungalows in a large garden, facing a superb beach, cost from US$23/28 to US$28/34, with hot water and air-con – all prices include breakfast.

Places to Eat

Most hotels and losmen have decent *restaurants* serving cheap western, Chinese and Indonesian food. The restaurant at *Hotel Gili Air* has a delightful setting and is worth a walk – take a torch (flashlight) at night.

You could also try the unique *Il Pirata Restaurant*. It serves simple pasta dishes (from 10,000 rp) on something that looks like a pirate ship (well, after a few Bintang beers, it does).

In the central part of the island, *Garden Kesuma Restaurant* has a lovely ambience, especially in the evening, and good prices (daily specials are about 6500 rp). *Pondok Cafe* is popular with long-stayers, and is a good place to meet other travellers; while *Harie Cafe* is always popular. Several places along the eastern coast serve decent pizzas, and other western food.

Legend Pub and *Go Go Pub & Restaurant* offer about the only nightlife on the island, which is fairly tame compared with Gili Trawangan and Senggigi.

Getting Around

Walking is the usual form of transport, but there are a few cidomos. If you hire one outside the Hotel Gili Air you will be charged an extortionate (by Indonesian standards) 5000 rp to the jetty area.

GILI MENO

Gili Meno, the middle island, has the smallest population – only about 60 families, plus ancillary hotel staff. It is also the quietest island, and one which many visitors strangely ignore.

It is perfect for anyone who wants almost total seclusion, and a chance to wallow on a private beach. The salt lake produces salt in the dry season, and mosquitoes in the wet season.

Information

The Perama office is next to Taro Warung. You can change money at the Gazebo and Kontiki Meno Bungalows, and make telephone calls at the wartel by Gazebo Hotel. While normal food and drink supplies are adequate, there are no real shops on the island, so stock up on anything else you may need.

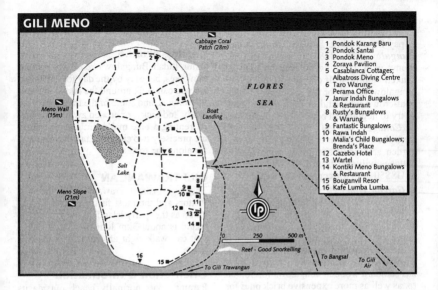

GILI MENO

Cabbage Coral Patch (28m)

FLORES SEA

Meno Wall (15m)

Boat Landing

Meno Slope (21m)

Salt Lake

Reef - Good Snorkelling

To Bangsal
To Gili Air

To Gili Trawangan

1 Pondok Karang Baru
2 Pondok Santai
3 Pondok Meno
4 Zoraya Pavilion
5 Casablanca Cottages;
   Albatross Diving Centre
6 Taro Warung;
   Perama Office
7 Janur Indah Bungalows
   & Restaurant
8 Rusty's Bungalows
   & Warung
9 Fantastic Bungalows
10 Rawa Indah
11 Malia's Child Bungalows;
   Brenda's Place
12 Gazebo Hotel
13 Wartel
14 Kontiki Meno Bungalows
   & Restaurant
15 Bouganvil Resor
16 Kafe Lumba Lumba

Activities

Local people can organise fishing, dolphin and boating trips if you can gather enough passengers to share the costs. Look around for notices posted on the trees near the losmen, or ask at Janur Indah Bungalows. The beach on the eastern side of the island is very nice, and there's good snorkelling just offshore and further north – you can rent gear from most losmen for about 7500 rp per day. The blue coral around Meno is particularly beautiful.

Zoraya Pavilion losmen, and a couple of other places, claim to have 'dive centres', but you should stick with the reputable Albatross Diving Centre, based at Casablanca Cottages.

Places to Stay

The accommodation is mostly on the eastern coast, and there are several places that are pretty upmarket by Gili standards. All of the places on the north coast, and many cheapies all over the island, have no electricity or generators, which means no fans for the heat or mosquitoes (although most places provide

a mosquito net anyway). For some reason, most places do not include breakfast. If you are after seclusion and private beaches, head for the northern coast.

Places to Stay – Budget

Pondok Meno is quiet and relaxed, although the garden is a bit scruffy. Simple bungalows go for 15,000 rp. **Pondok Santai** is very similar in standard and price, while **Pondok Karang Baru** looks newer and sturdier, and worth paying a little more – 20,000/25,000 rp for singles/doubles. **Zoraya Pavilion** (☎ 27213) has a variety of interesting rooms in a large shady area. Prices are negotiable, and cost 25,000 to 70,000 rp.

Unfortunately, the most central and convenient places are the most uninspiring, and many are badly signed, or not all. **Fantastic Bungalows** is certainly a misnomer; **Rawa Indah** is slightly better for 12,000 rp. **Malia's Child Bungalows** cost 16,500/20,000 rp, but, unusually, the bathroom and toilet are outside the bungalows. **Rusty's Bungalows** is probably the best of the lot, with bungalows for 15,000/20,000 rp.

GILI ISLANDS

Places to Stay – Mid-Range

If you want reliable electricity, you'll have to pay for a mid-range place. *Janur Indah Bungalows (☎ 33284)* is clean, and has rooms with a ceiling fan and an unusual sunken bathroom. It charges 50,000 rp per bungalow, priced for the just-come-off-the-boat-crowd who land in front of the hotel, so try to negotiate a better price. *Casablanca Cottages (☎ 33847, fax 93482)* is back from the beach, but is nicely set up with a garden and small swimming pool. Quaint cottages will cost from US$11/14 with fan to US$50 with air-con and hot water.

Gazebo Hotel (☎/fax 35795) has tastefully decorated Bali-style bungalows with private bathrooms and air-con, comfortably spaced among shady coconut trees. Cottages cost US$45/55; more for full-board. It is closed from mid-January to mid-March. *Kontiki Meno Bungalows (☎/fax 32824)* has standard wooden bungalows for 30,000 rp, as well as more expensive brick ones for 50,000 rp – all with fans.

The upmarket *Bouganvil Resor (☎/fax 35295)* has a swimming pool and large comfortable rooms with air-con and hot water from US$30 to US$72 – considerably more in the high season.

Places to Eat

The best place to eat is at one of the beachfront *restaurants* – but don't expect any snappy service on this laidback island. *Janur Indah Bungalows* has reasonable prices: 4000 to 7000 rp for most dishes. *Brenda's Place*, the beachfront restaurant at Malia's Child Bungalows, is one of the best places: it has a wide range of cheap western and Indonesian food, and a breezy upstairs area.

Rusty's Warung is deservedly popular for its good value western and Indonesian meals from 3000 to 7000 rp. *Kontiki Meno Bungalows* has good food in a big pavilion, but it's more expensive than others.

Although it is a fair walk, *Kafe Lumba Lumba* has decent Padang-style food, and promises outstanding sunsets, as well as live music most nights and a 'party night' every Wednesday – it's still tame compared with Gili Trawangan, however.

Getting Around

Janur Indah Bungalows rents new mountain bikes, but only by the day for 15,000 rp. As you can walk around the island in about 90 minutes, and some of the tracks are very sandy and rocky, or eroded away completely, renting a bike makes little sense. There are precisely two cidomos, but they can't go far along the tracks.

GILI TRAWANGAN

The largest island, Trawangan, has the most visitors and the most facilities, and a reputation as the 'party island' of the group. The island is about 3km long and 2km wide – you can walk right around it in about two hours.

Orientation & Information

Perama boats normally beach outside its office; other boats anchor near (but not at) the jetty. Most of the cheap hotels, restaurants and tourist facilities are on the eastern side of the island. Several places will change money or travellers cheques, but you'll get a far better rate at Senggigi on the mainland. The Blue Marlin Dive Centre may give cash advances on Visa or MasterCard, for a 3% commission (but don't count on it); and it has an expensive fax service.

The wartel sells stamps (there is no post office), and there are a few bookshops in the Pasar Seni (Art Market).

Activities

Boat Trips One or two local outfits run four hour trips on glass bottom boats to the other two islands for 15,000 rp per person – enquire and book at any shop-cum-travel agency. If you ask around, you can rent a boat holding up to ten people for 80,000 to 100,000 per day, but you will have to find other passengers yourself.

Diving Some excellent scuba diving sites are within a short boat ride, especially off Trawangan's west coast. Several dive oper-

ators are based in the main tourist area, but
you should select from one of the three
long-established centres. Blue Marlin Dive
Centre (☎ 32424, fax 93043, email bmdc@
mataram.wasantara.net.id) is an impressive
outfit; Albatross (☎ 38134) was the first operator on Gili Trawangan; and Blue Coral
(☎ 34497) has fairly comprehensive facilities. Beware of a bogus operation calling
themselves Reefseekers, the same name as
the reputable company on Gili Air.

Official prices are very similar among all
three operators, but check for discounts of
up to 50% if business is quiet – an open-
water PADI course costs about US$320; a
two day advanced diving course, US$220;
one two local dives, US$30/45; and a night
dive is US$35.

Snorkelling The best area for snorkelling
is off the north-eastern coast. There is coral

around most of the island, but much of the
reef on the eastern side has been damaged.
Beware of strong currents on the eastern
side, between Trawangan and Meno. Snorkelling gear can be hired for around 5000 rp
per day from shacks near the boat landing.

Walking Trawangan is great for wandering
around (and, often, getting a little lost).
There are some remains of an old **Japanese
cannon** behind the Dewi Sri Bungalows,
and the hill in the south-western corner is a
good place to take in the view across the
straits to Bali's Gunung Agung, especially
at sunset. The sunrise over Lombok's Gunung Rinjani is also impressive.

Places to Stay

Some places want you to check out before
10 am. Note that anywhere close to Rudy's
Pub is bound to be loud at night, especially

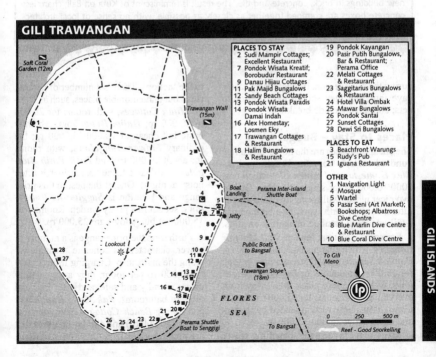

The Wisdom of Government

In recent years, Gili Trawangan has attracted an incredible number of visitors, and consequently the attention of the Lombok government and outside business interests.

The islanders only lease the land on which they developed their plantations, and later their tourist businesses. In the early 1990s, the government decided that all the small bungalows should be located away from the north-east part of the island, and rumours began to circulate about a proposed luxury hotel and golf course on the island. There was some negotiation and compensation, and alternative leases were offered further south. But some of the people refused to move, and in 1992, after repeated requests, the authorities ordered in the army, and closed down the bungalows by the simple but effective means of cutting the posts off with chainsaws.

It's not clear whether this was to make way for a grandiose development project, or because the bungalows contravened the lease conditions, or because they did not meet environmental and health standards. A new power station has been established at the northern end of the island, but four years after relocating the bungalows there were still no signs of a big new hotel, and this whole area, which fronts the best beach on the island, is looking very desolate indeed.

Meanwhile, the southern end of Gili Trawangan has been neatly subdivided into narrow allotments, where most of the accommodation and facilities for low-budget travellers are now concentrated. In 1993, a fire destroyed 15 or 20 bungalows, and the authorities encouraged new buildings in brick, concrete and tile. The result is reminiscent of Kuta on Bali; charmless concrete boxes are cramped together as closely as possible, with no sense of local architectural style, and no sensitivity at all to the natural environment.

during the busy season. Budget places rarely have fans, but they should have mosquito nets; and most include breakfast.

Places to Stay – Budget

The cheapest places are the homestays a few hundred metres from the beach, such as *Alex Homestay* or *Losmen Eky* which cost 8000/10,000 rp for singles/doubles. One or two nicer places will spring up nearby in the future, but it's worth spending a bit more for a Gili-standard bamboo bungalow on stilts.

For some isolation, look at *Sudi Mampir Cottages*, which charges 10,000/15,0000 rp; *Pondok Santai*, spread out in a nice garden for 15,000 rp a double; or *Dewi Sri Bungalows*, which is a tidy place, well away from everything, with rooms for 15,000 rp. *Sunset Cottages* has been recommended by readers and costs about 25,000/35,000 rp.

Many visitors look for something closer

to the 'action'. There's a number of central, clean but unmemorable places, such as *Danau Hijau Cottages*, with rooms for 20,000 to 30,000 rp; *Halim Bungalows*, which is basic but cheap at 10,000/15,0000 rp; the ordinary *Mawar Bungalows*, with rooms for about 20,000 rp; and *Pasir Putih Bungalows*, with an attached bar (which is often noisy at night). One of the best in this price range and location is *Saggitarius Bungalows*, set out in a pretty garden. Rooms cost 15,000 rp; bungalows are 25,000 rp.

Further up the price range is a number of newer, characterless concrete 'bungalows' along the main strip. Charging from 25,000 to 40,000 rp per room, they are generally clean, friendly and safe, and offer fans and modern bathrooms. *Pak Majid Bungalows* and *Sandy Beach Cottages* have identical prices (30,000 rp) and similar facilities, but are nothing special.

Both *Pondok Wisata Kreatif (☎ 34893)* and *Trawangan Cottages (☎ 23582)* are overpriced, with singles/doubles at 35,000/40,000 rp, but are still popular and friendly. Similar in price and standard, but quieter and friendlier, is *Pondok Kayangan (☎ 37932)*. Also worth trying are *Melati Cottages*, with rooms for 25,000 to 30,000 rp; and *Pondok Wisata Paradis* and *Pondok Wisata Damai Indah*, which both offer rooms for 20,000/30,000 rp.

Places to Stay – Mid-Range

The upmarket option is *Hotel Villa Ombak (☎ 22093)*. It offers some stylish lumbung-style rooms with a fan for US$35, and better bungalows for US$50 – including breakfast. It has a nice garden, but no swimming pool Prices are negotiable.

Places to Eat

Most of the hotels have *restaurants*, but none of them stands out as a gourmet treat. They generally offer a decent selection of inexpensive western and Asian dishes, and fresh seafood. The cheapest places for meal and drink during the day (but not during the evening, because there's no electricity) are any of the makeshift *warungs* strung along the beach, north of the boat landing.

Some of the hotels with better restaurants include *Trawangan Bungalows*, which does passable pizzas for 10,000 rp; *Melati Cottages*; and *Saggitarius Bungalows*. The best is arguably *Borobodur Restaurant*, where an excellent tuna steak costs 7500 rp, and a cold beer is 8000 rp.

A couple of places, such as *Halim Bungalows*, offer fresh fish on a table along the path – just choose something, agree on a price and enjoy. Most divers swap stories at the restaurant at *Blue Marlin Dive Centre*. It is worth a short walk up to the modestly named *Excellent Restaurant*, and *Iguana Restaurant* is one of the better independent restaurants.

Entertainment

A few places show videos most nights, such as the restaurants at *Halim*, *Melati* and *Pasir Putih* hotels. Each screening starts at 7 pm.

The major party spot is at *Rudy's Pub*, which advertises upcoming attractions on trees along the path.

Getting Around

The best way to get around is on foot. Otherwise, you can rent a cidomo for a short trip or all around the island for a *very* negotiable price.

A cartel of bicycle renters at the beachfront warungs have set rental prices at a ludicrous 5000 rp per hour or 20,000 rp per day. It only takes about one hour to cycle around the island – if the bike works, and the tracks aren't too sandy.

Language

BAHASA BALI

The national language of Indonesia, Bahasa Indonesia, is widely used on Bali, but is not Balinese.

Balinese, or Bahasa Bali, is another language entirely, with a completely different vocabulary and grammar, and much more complex rules of use. It's a difficult language for a foreigner to come to grips with; it isn't a written language, so there's no definitive guide to its grammar or vocabulary, and there is considerable variation in usage from one part of the island to another. Bahasa Bali isn't taught in schools either, and those dictionaries and grammars that do exist are attempts to document current or historical usage, rather than set down rules for correct syntax or pronunciation.

Balinese is greatly complicated by its caste influences. In effect, different vocabularies and grammatical structures are used, depending on the relative social position of the speaker, the person being spoken to and the person being spoken about. Even traditional usage has always been somewhat arbitrary because of the intricacies of the caste system.

The forms of the language (or languages) have been categorised as follows:

Basa Lumrah, also called *Biasa* or *Ketah*, is used when talking to people of the same caste or level, and between friends and family. It is an old language of mixed origin, with words drawn from Malayan, Polynesian and Australasian sources.

Basa Sor, or *Rendah*, is used when talking with people of a lower caste, or to people who are non-caste.

Basa Alus is used among educated people, and is derived from the Hindu-Javanese court languages of the 10th century.

Basa Madia, or *Midah*, a mixture of Basa Lumrah and Basa Alus, is used as a polite language for speaking to or about strangers, or people to whom one wishes to show respect.

Basa Singgih, virtually a separate language, is used to address persons of high caste, particularly in formal and religious contexts. Even the Balinese are not always fluent in this language. It is based on the ancient Hindu Kawi language, and can be written using a script that resembles Sanskrit, as seen in the *lontar* (palm) books where it's inscribed on strips of leaf (see the boxed text 'Gedong Kirtya Library' in the North Bali chapter). Written Basa Singgih is also seen on the signs that welcome you to, and farewell you from, most villages on Bali.

The different vocabularies only exist for about 1000 basic words, mostly words concerned with people and their actions. Other words (in fact, an increasing proportion of the modern vocabulary), are the same regardless of relative caste levels.

Usage is also changing with the decline of the traditional caste system and modern tendencies towards democratisation and social equality. It is now common practice to describe the language in terms of only three forms:

Low Balinese, or *Ia*, equivalent to Basa Lumrah, is used between friends and family, and also when speaking with persons of equal or lower caste, or about oneself.

Polite Balinese, or *Ipun*, the equivalent of Basa Madia, is used for speaking to superiors or strangers, and is becoming more widespread as a sort of common language not so related to caste.

High Balinese, or *Ida*, a mixture of Basa Alus and Basa Singgih, is used to indicate respect for the person being addressed or the person being spoken about.

The polite and high forms of the language frequently use the same word, while the low form often uses the same word as Bahasa Indonesia. The polite form, Basa Madia or Midah, is being used as a more egalitarian language, often combined with Bahasa Indonesia to avoid the risk of embarrassment in case one does not make the correct caste distinctions.

So how does one Balinese know at which level to address another? Well, initially, a conversation between two strangers would commence in the high language. At some point the question of caste would be asked and then the level adjusted accordingly. However, among friends a conversation is likely to be carried on in low Balinese no matter what the caste of the conversationalists may be.

Bahasa Bali uses very few greetings and civilities on an everyday basis. There are no equivalents for 'please' and 'thank you'. Nor is there a usage that translates as 'Good morning' or 'Good evening', although the low Balinese *kenken kebara?* ('How are you?' or 'How's it going?') is sometimes used. More common is *lunga kija?*, which literally means 'where are you going?' (in low, polite and high Balinese).

Some other Balinese expressions that a visitor might encounter are listed below in Low, Polite and High forms. Some of them may also occur in place names.

Try to pronounce them as you would a Bahasa Indonesia word of the same spelling; they are Romanised here on the same basis. The Indonesian equivalents are are also provided for comparison.

BAHASA INDONESIA

Like any language, Indonesian has a simplified colloquial form and a more developed literary form. It is among the easiest of all languages to learn – there are no tenses, plurals or genders and, even better, it's easy to pronounce.

Apart from the ease of learning a little Indonesian, there's another very good reason for trying to pick up at least a handful of words and phrases – few people are as delighted with visitors learning their language as Indonesians. They will not criticise you if you mangle your pronunciation or tangle your grammar. They make you feel like you're an expert if you know only a dozen or so words. And bargaining seems to be a whole lot easier and more natural when you do it in their language.

Pronunciation

Most letters have a pronunciation more or less the same as their English counterparts. Nearly all the syllables carry equal emphasis, but a good approximation is to stress the second to last syllable.

The main exception to the rule is the un-

Choose Your Words Carefully!

English	Indonesian	Low Balinese	Polite Balinese	High Balinese
yes	ya	nggih, saja	inggih, patut	patut
no	tidak	sing, tuara	tan	nenten, tan wenten
good, well	bagus, baik	melah	becik	becik
bad	jelek	jele, corah	corah	kaon, durmaga
sleep	tidur	pules	sirep sare	makolem
eat	makan	madaar, neda	ngajeng, nunas	ngrayunang
this/these	ini	ne	niki, puniki	puniki
that/those	itu	ento	punika	punika
big	besar	gede	ageng	agung
small	kecil	cenik, cerik	alit	alit
water	air	yeh	toya	tirta
stone	batu	watu	watu	batu
north	utara	kaja	kaler	lor
south	selatan	kelod	kelod	kidul
east	timur	kangin	kangin	wetan
west	barat	kauh	kulon	kulon

stressed **e** in words such as *besar* (big), pronounced 'be-SARR'.

a	as in 'father'
e	as in 'bet' when unstressed, although sometimes hardly pronounced at all, as in the greeting *Selamat*, which sounds like 'slamat' if said quickly. When stressed it's like the 'a' in 'may', as in *becak* (rickshaw), pronounced 'baycha'. There's no general rule as to when the 'e' is stressed or unstressed.
i	as in 'unique'
o	as in 'hot'
u	as in 'put'
ai	as in 'Thai'
au	as the 'ow' in 'cow'
ua	as a 'w' when at the start of a word, eg *uang* (money), pronounced 'wong'

Most consonants mirror their English counterparts with the following exceptions:

c	as the 'ch' in 'chair'
g	as in 'get'
ng	as the 'ng' in 'sing'
ngg	as the 'ng' in 'anger'
j	as in 'John'
r	slightly trilled, as in Spanish 'r'
h	a little stronger than the 'h' in 'her'; almost silent at the end of a word
k	like English 'k', except at the end of a word when it's more like a closing of the throat with no sound released, eg *tidak* (No/not), pronounced 'tee-da'
ny	as the 'ny' in canyon

Addressing People

Pronouns, particularly 'you', are rarely used in Indonesian. When speaking to an older man (or anyone old enough to be a father), it's common to call them *bapak* (father) or simply *pak*. Similarly, an older woman is *ibu* (mother) or simply *bu*. *Tuan* is a respectful term, like 'sir'. *Nyonya* is the equivalent for a married woman, and *nona* for an unmarried woman. *Anda* is the egalitarian form designed to overcome the plethora of words for the second person.

Basics

Please. (asking for help)	*Tolong.*
Please. (giving permission)	*Silahkan.*
Thank you. (very much)	*Terima kasih. (banyak)*
You're welcome.	*Kembali.*
Sorry.	*Ma'af.*
Maybe.	*Mungkin.*
Excuse me.	*Permisi.*
Another/One more.	*Satu lagi.*
Good.	*Bagus.*
Good, fine, OK.	*Baik.*
Yes	*Ya.*
No. (not)	*Tidak.*
No. (negative)	*Bukan.*

To indicate negation, *tidak* is used with verbs, adjectives and adverbs; *bukan* with nouns and pronouns.

Greetings & Civilities

Welcome.	*Selamat datang.*
Good morning. (before 11 am)	*Selamat pagi.*
Good day. (11 am to 3 pm)	*Selamat siang.*
Good day. (3 to 7 pm)	*Selamat sore.*
Good evening. (after dark)	*Selamat malam.*
Good night. (to someone going to bed)	*Selamat tidur.*
Goodbye. (to person staying)	*Selamat tinggal.*
Goodbye. (to person going)	*Selamat jalan.*

Useful Phrases

How are you?	*Apa kabar?*
I'm fine.	*Kabar baik.*
What's your name?	*Siapa nama anda?*
My name is ...	*Nama saya ...*
Are you married?	*Sudah kawin?*
Not yet.	*Belum.*
How old are you?	*Berapa umur anda?*
I'm ... years old.	*Umur saya ... tahun.*

Language Difficulties

I (don't) understand.	Saya (tidak) mengerti.
Do you speak English?	Bisa berbicara bahasa Inggris?
I can only speak a little (Indonesian).	Saya hanya bisa berbicara (bahasa Indonesia) sedikit.
Please write that word down.	Tolong tuliskan kata itu untuk saya.

Getting Around

I want to go to ...	Saya mau ke ...
Where is ...?	Di mana ...?
How many kilometres?	Berapa kilometre?

What time does the ... leave?	Jam berapa ... berangkat?
boat/ship	kapal
bus	bis
plane	kapal terbang
train	kereta api

Where can I hire a ...?	Dimana saya bisa sewa ...?
bicycle	sepeda
motorbike	sepeda motor

station	stasiun or terminal
ticket	karcis

Directions

Which way?	Ke mana?
Go straight ahead.	Jalan terus.
Turn left/right.	Belok kiri/kanan.
Stop!	Berhenti!

here/there/ over there	di sini/situ/sana
north	utara
south	selatan
east	timur
west	barat

Accommodation

Is there a room available?	Ada kamar kosong?
How much is it per day?	Berapa harganya sehari?

Is breakfast included?	Apa harganya termasuk makan pagi/sarapan?

one night	satu malam
one person	satu orang
bed	tempat tidur
room	kamar
bathroom	kamar mandi
soap	sabun

Around Town

bank	bank
immigration	imigrasi
market	pasar
police station	kantor polisi
post office	kantor pos
public telephone	telepon umum
public toilet	WC ('way say')

What ... is this?	Ini ... apa?
street	jalan
town	kota
village	desa

What time does it open/close?	Jam berapa buka/tutup?
May I take photos?	Boleh saya ambil foto?

Food & Shopping

What is this?	Apa ini?
How much is it?	Berapa (harga)?
expensive	mahal
this/that	ini/itu
big	besar
small	kecil

food stall	warung
restaurant	rumah makan
I can't eat meat.	Saya tidak boleh makan daging.
without meat	tanpa daging

Time

When?	Kapan?
What time?	Jam berapa?
How many hours?	Berapa jam?
7 o'clock	jam/pukul tujuh
five hours	lima jam
yesterday	kemarin

tomorrow	*besok*
hour	*jam*
day	*hari*
week	*minggu*
month	*bulan*
year	*tahun*

Monday	*hari Senen*
Tuesday	*hari Selasa*
Wednesday	*hari Rabu*
Thursday	*hari Kamis*
Friday	*hari Jum'at*
Saturday	*hari Sabtu*
Sunday	*hari Minggu*

Numbers

1	*satu*
2	*dua*
3	*tiga*
4	*empat*
5	*lima*
6	*enam*
7	*tujuh*
8	*delapan*
9	*sembilan*
10	*sepuluh*

A half is *setengah*, which is pronounced 'stenger', eg *stenger kilo* (half a kilo). 'Approximately' is *kira-kira*. After the numbers one to 10, the 'teens' are *belas*, the 'tens' are *puluh*, the 'hundreds' are *ratus*, the 'thousands' are *ribu* and 'millions' are *juta* – but as a prefix *satu* (one) becomes 'se', eg *se-ratus* (one hundred). Thus:

11	*sebelas*
12	*duabelas*
13	*tigabelas*
20	*dua puluh*
21	*dua puluh satu*
25	*dua puluh lima*
30	*tiga puluh*
99	*sembilan puluh sembilan*
100	*seratus*
150	*seratus limapuluh*
200	*dua ratus*
888	*delapan ratus delapan puluh delapan*
1000	*seribu*
one million	*sejuta*

Emergencies

Help!	*Tolong!*
Fire!	*Kebakaran!*
Call a doctor!	*Panggillah dokter!*
Call an ambulance!	*Panggillah ambulin!*
I'm ill.	*Saya sakit.*
I'm allergic to ...	*Saya alergi ...*
Where are the toilets?	*Dimana ada WC?*
I'm lost.	*Saya kesasar.*
doctor	*dokter*
hospital	*rumah sakit*
chemist/pharmacy	*apotik*

SASAK

Sasak is not derived from Malay, so don't expect to be able to understand Sasak if you can speak Bahasa Indonesia. Nevertheless, some words are similar, and Sasak speakers use an Indonesian words when there is no Sasak equivalent.

Sasak mostly expresses the concepts that are important in traditional contexts, but in these it can be both precise and subtle. For example, where the English langauge has one word for rice, Indonesian has three – *padi* for the growing rice plant, *beras* for uncooked grain, and *nasi* for cooked rice. Sasak has equivalents for those (*pare*, *menik* and *me*), and it also has *gabah*, for grains with their husks ready for planting; *binek* for a seedling up to three days old; *ampar* for plants up to 20 days old; and *lowong* for plants which are ready to be transplanted from the seed beds into the paddy field.

Sasak is a difficult language to learn – it does not have a written component, so its usages are not well documented, and there are substantial variations between one part of Lombok and another. Nor is there an English-Sasak dictionary.

Learning Bahasa Indonesia is a much more practical option for a visitor to Lombok, but the following expressions may prove useful. Pronounce them as if they were written in Bahasa Indonesia.

Many thanks to Haji Radiah of Lendang Nangka for help in preparing this language section.

Greetings & Civilities

Sasak does not have greetings such as 'Good morning'. A Sasak nearing a friend might ask, in the local language, 'What are you doing?' or 'Where are you going?' simply as a form of greeting.

Local people will frequently ask foreigners questions such as these in English as a greeting (and it may be their only English!). Don't get annoyed – they are just trying to be polite. A smile and a 'hello', or a greeting in Indonesian, is a polite and adequate response.

Useful Phrases

How are you?	*Berem be khabar?*
Where are you going?	*Wah me aning be?*
I'm going to Sweta.	*Sweta wah mo ojak ombe.*
Which way is Sweta?	*Embe langan te ojok Sweta?*
How far is Sweta?	*Berembe kejab ne olek te ojok Sweta?*
Where is Radiah's place?	*Embe tao' balem Radiah?*
I want to go to the toilet.	*Tiang melet ojok aik.*
Leave me alone!	*Endotang aku mesak.*
	Endotang aku mesak mesak! (stronger)
Go away!	*Nyeri to!*
	(said forcefully, emphasising the 'to')

Useful Words

day	*jelo*
good	*solah*
big	*belek*
small	*kodek*
hot	*beneng*
cold	*enyet*
north	*daya*
south	*lauk*
east	*timuk*
west	*bat*

Monday	*senin*
Tuesday	*selasa*
Wednesday	*rebo*
Thursday	*kamis*
Friday	*jumat*
Saturday	*saptu*
Sunday	*ahat*

People & Families

person	*dengan*
woman	*dengan mine*
man	*dengan mama*
baby	*bebeak*
child	*kanak*
girl	*kanak mine*
boy	*kanak mama*
young unmarried woman	*dedera*
widow	*bebalu mine*
widower	*bebalu mama*
mother	*inak*
father	*amak*
wife	*senine*
husband	*semama*

Numbers

1	*skek*	11	*solas*
2	*dua*	12	*dua olas*
3	*telu*	13	*telu olas*
4	*empat*	14	*empat olas*
5	*lima*	20	*dua pulu*
6	*enam*	30	*telung dasa*
7	*pituk*	40	*petang dasa*
8	*baluk*	50	*seket*
9	*siwak*	60	*enam pulu*
10	*sepuluh*	70	*pituk pulu*

100	*satus*
200	*satak*
300	*telungatus*
400	*samas*
500	*limangatus*
700	*pitungatus*
800	*bali ratus*
900	*siwak ratus*
1000	*sia*

Glossary

ABRI – Angkatan Bersenjata Republik Indonesia; Indonesia's Armed Forces

adat – tradition, customs and manners

adi kaka – birth ritual

angklung – portable form of the *gamelan* used in processions as well as in other festivals and celebrations

angkutan kota – literally, city transport, and is the official name for the ubiquitous bemo

arak – colourless, distilled palm wine; the local firewater

arja – refined operatic form of Balinese theatre

Arjuna – a hero of the *Mahabharata* epic and a popular temple gate guardian image

badawang – the mythological 'world turtle'

bahasa – language; Bahasa Indonesia is the national language of Indonesia

bale – an open-sided pavilion with a steeply pitched thatched roof; the basic structure used in Balinese architecture

bale banjar – communal meeting place of a *banjar* (a sort of community club); a house for meetings and gamelan practice

bale gede – reception room or guesthouse in the home of a wealthy Balinese

bale kambang – floating pavilion; a building surrounded by a moat

bale tani – family house; see also *serambi*

Bali Aga – the 'original' Balinese; these people managed to resist the new ways brought in with the Majapahit migration

balian – see *dukun*

banci – a less polite term for *waria*, a female impersonator

banjar – local division of a village consisting of all the married adult males

banyan – a type of ficus tree, often considered holy; see *waringin*

bapak – father; also a polite form of address to any older man; see also *pak*

Baris – warrior dance

Barong – mythical lion-dog creature, star of the Barong & Rangda dance and champion of the good

Barong Landung – literally, tall *Barong*; these enormous puppet figures are seen at the annual festival on Pulau Serangan

Barong Tengkok – name for the portable *gamelan* used for wedding processions and circumcision ceremonies on Lombok

Batara – title used to address a deceased spirit, particularly that of an important person

batik – process of colouring fabric by coating part of the cloth with wax, then dyeing it and melting the wax out; the waxed part is not coloured, and repeated waxing and dyeing builds up a pattern. Although a Javanese craft, the Balinese also produce batik.

Bedaulu, Dalem – legendary last ruler of the Pejeng dynasty

bejak – bicycle rickshaw, no longer used on Bali or Lombok

bemo – popular local transport on Bali and Lombok, traditionally a small pick-up truck with a bench seat down each side in the back; small minibuses are now commonly used as bemos; contraction of *becak mobil*

bensin – petrol (gasoline)

beruga – communal meeting hall

bhoma – fierce looking guardian spirit represented in many temples

Bima – another hero of the *Mahabharata*, the biggest and strongest of the Pandava brothers

bioskop – cinema

Boma – son of the earth, a temple guardian figure

Brahma – the creator, one of the trinity of Hindu gods

Brahmana – the caste of priests and highest of the Balinese castes; although all priests are Brahmanas, not all Brahmanas are priests

brem – rice wine

bu – shortened form of *ibu* (mother)

buang au – naming ritual

bukit – hill; also the name of the southern peninsula of Bali

bumbu – a hot spice

bupati – government official in charge of a *kabupaten* (district)

camat – government official in charge of a *kecamatan* (subdistrict)

candi – shrine, originally of Javanese design; also known as *prasada*

candi bentar – gateway entrance to a temple

caste – the Balinese caste system is nowhere near as important or firmly entrenched as India's caste system. There are four castes: three branches of the 'nobility' *(Brahmana, Ksatriyasa* and *Wesia)*, and the common people *(Sudra)*.

catur yoga – ancient manuscript on religion and cosmology

cidomo – on Lombok, pony cart with car wheels

dalang – puppet master and storyteller in a *wayang kulit* performance; a man of varied skills and considerable endurance

danau – lake

desa – village

dewa – deity or supernatural spirit

dewi – goddess

Dewi Danau – goddess of the lakes

Dewi Sri – goddess of rice

dokar – pony cart; still a popular form of local transport in many towns and larger villages throughout Bali; known as a *cidomo* on Lombok

dukun – 'witch doctor', actually a faith healer and herbal doctor

Durga – goddess of death and destruction, and consort of *Shiva*

Dwarpala – guardian figure who keeps evil spirits at bay in temples

Gajah Mada – famous *Majapahit* prime minister who defeated the last great king of Bali and extended Majapahit power over the island

Galungan – great Balinese festival, an annual event in the 210 day Balinese *wuku* calendar

gamelan – traditional Balinese orchestra, with mostly percussion instruments like large xylophones and gongs

Ganesh – *Shiva's* elephant-headed son

gang – alley or footpath

Garuda – mythical man-bird creature, the vehicle of *Vishnu*, a modern symbol of Indonesia and the name of the national airline

gedong – shrine

gendong – street vendors who sell *jamu*, said to be a cure-all tonic

gili – small island (Lombok)

goa – cave; also spelt *gua*

gringsing – rare double *ikat* woven cloth (made only in the Bali Aga village of Tenganan)

gua – cave; also spelt *goa*

gunung – mountain

gunung api – 'fire mountain', ie volcano

gusti – polite title for members of the *Wesia* caste

Hanuman – monkey god who plays a major part in the *Ramayana*

harga biasa – standard price

harga turis – inflated price for tourists

homestay – small, family-run *losmen*

ibu – mother; also polite form of address to any older woman

Ida Bagus – honourable title for a male Brahman

iders-iders – long scrolls painted in the *wayang* style, used as temple decorations

ikat – cloth where a pattern is produced by dyeing the individual threads before weaving. Ikat is usually of the warp or the weft, although the rare double ikat technique is found in Tenganan; see *gringsing*.

Indra – king of the gods

jalak putih – local name for Bali starling

jalan – a road or street; see also *Jl*

jalan jalan – to walk around; an easy answer to *mau ke mana?* (where are you going?)

jamu – see *gendong*

jidur – large cylindrical drums played throughout Lombok

jimny – small jeep-like Suzuki vehicle; the usual type of rental car

Jl – Jalan; a road or street

jukung – see *prahu*

kabupaten – administrative districts (known as regencies during Dutch rule)

kain – a length of material wrapped tightly around the hips and waist, over a sarong

kaja – Balinese 'north' which is always towards the mountains; the most important shrines are always on the kaja side of a temple; see also *kelod*

kala – demonic face often seen over temple gateways; the kala's outstretched hands are to stop evil spirits from entering, although they are themselves evil spirits

kampung – village, neighbourhood

kantor – office

Kawi – classical Javanese, the language of poetry

kebaya – Chinese, long-sleeved blouse with low neckline and embroidered edges

Kebo Iwa – legendary giant credited with the creation of several of Bali's oldest stone monuments

Kecak – traditional Balinese dance, which tells a tale from the *Ramayana* about Prince Rama and Princess Siwi; does not have a *gamelan* accompaniment

kecamatan – subdistrict

kelod – opposite of *kaja*; the side of a temple oriented away from the mountains and towards the sea

kemban – woman's breast cloth

kepala desa – village head

kepeng – old Chinese coins with a hole in the centre; the everyday currency during the Dutch era, they can still be obtained quite readily from shops and antique dealers

ketupat – kind of sticky rice cooked in a banana leaf

kota – city

kretek – Indonesian clove cigarettes; a very familiar odour on Bali

kris – traditional dagger, often held to have spiritual or magical powers

Ksatriyasa – second Balinese caste

kulkul – hollow tree-trunk drum used to sound a warning or call meetings

labuhan – harbour; see also *pelabuhan*

lambung – long black sarongs worn by Sasak women; see also *sabuk*

langse – rectangular decorative hangings used in palaces or temples

Legong – classic Balinese dance, performed by young girls who are also known as Legong

leyak – evil spirit which can assume fantastic forms by the use of black magic

lontar – type of palm tree; traditional books were written on the dried leaves of lontar

losmen – small Balinese hotel, often family-run and similar in design to a traditional house (from the Dutch *'lodgement'*)

lumbung – rice barn with a round roof; an architectural symbol of Lombok

Mahabharata – one of the great Hindu holy books, the epic poem tells of the battle between the Pandavas and the Korawas

main ski – surfing

Majapahit – last great Hindu dynasty on Java; the Majapahit were pushed into Bali out of Java by the rise of Islamic power

mandi – Indonesian 'bath' consisting of a large water tank from which you ladle cold water over yourself

manusa yadnya – ceremonies which mark the various stages of Balinese life from before birth to after cremation

mapadik – marriage by request, as opposed to *ngrorod*

mekepung – traditional races involving water buffalo

meru – multi-roofed shrines in Balinese temples; the name comes from the Hindu holy mountain Mahameru

naga – mythical snake-like creature

nasi – cooked rice

ngrorod – marriage by elopement; a traditional 'heroic' way of getting married on Bali; see also *mapadik*

nusa – island; see also *pulau*

nyale – worm-like fish caught off Kuta Beach, Lombok; a special ceremony is held each year around February/March in honour of the first catch of the season

Nyepi – major annual festival in the Hindu *saka* calendar, this is a day of complete stillness after a night of chasing out evil spirits

nyunatang – circumcision

odalan – Balinese 'temple birthday' festival held in every temple annually (according to the *wuku* calendar, ie once every 210 days)

ojek – motorbike which carries paying pillion passengers

padi – growing rice plant; hence the English paddy field

padmasana – temple shrine resembling a vacant chair; a throne for the supreme god Sanghyang Widhi in the manifestation of Siwa Raditya

paduraksa – covered gateway to a temple

paibon – shrine in a state temple for the royal ancestors

pak – shortened form of *bapak* (father)

palinggihs – temple shrines consisting of a simple little throne; palinggihs are intended as resting places for the gods when they come down for festivals

pandanus – palm plant used in weaving mats etc

pande – blacksmiths; they are treated somewhat like a caste in their own right

pantai – beach

pantun – ancient Malay poetical verse in rhyming couplets

pasar – market

pasar malam – night market

pedanda – high priest

pekembar – umpire or referee in the traditional *Sasak* trial of strength known as *peresehan*

pelabuhan – harbour; see *labuhan*

Pelni – the national shipping line

Pendet – formal offering dance performed at temple festivals

penjor – long bamboo pole with decorated end, arched over the road or pathway during festivals or ceremonies

perbekel – government official in charge of a *desa* (village)

peresehan – one-to-one physical contest peculiar to Lombok in which two men fight each other armed with a small leather shield and a long rattan staff

Polda – Polisi Daerah; a regional police station

Polres – Polisi Resort; a main police precinct

prahu – traditional Indonesian boat with outriggers

prasada – shrine; see also *candi*

pratima – figure of a god used as a 'stand-in' for the actual god's presence during a ceremony

propinsi – province; Indonesia has 27 propinsi, of which Bali is one

puasa – to fast, or a fast

pulau – island; see also *nusa*

punggawa – chief, or commander

puputan – warrior's fight to the death; an honourable but suicidal option when faced with an unbeatable enemy

pura – temple

pura dalem – temple of the dead

pura desa – temple of the village for everyday functions

pura puseh – temple of the village founders or fathers, honouring the village's origins

pura subak – temple of the rice growers' association

puri – palace

puskesmas – community health centre

rajah – lord or prince

Raksa – Guardian figure who keeps evil spirits at bay in temples

Ramadan – Muslim month of fasting

Ramayana – one of the great Hindu holy books, stories from which form the keystone of many Balinese dances and tales

Rangda – widow-witch who represents evil in Balinese theatre and dance

rattan – hardy, pliable vine used for handcrafts, furniture and weapons

rebab – bowed lute

rijstaffel – Dutch influenced Indonesian meal; a sort of buffet of various rice dishes

RRI – Radio Republik Indonesia; Indonesia's national radio broadcaster

RSU or **RSUP** – Rumah Sakit Umum or Rumah Sakit Umum Propinsi; a public hospital or provincial public hospital

rumah makan – restaurant; literally, eating house

sabuk – 4m-long scarf that holds the *lambung* in place

sadkahyangan – most sacred temples or 'world sanctuaries'

saka – local Balinese calendar which is based on the lunar cycle; see also *wuku*

Sanghyang – trance dance in which the dancers impersonate a local village god

Sanghyang Widi – Balinese supreme being; this deity is never actually worshipped as such; one of the 'three in one' or lesser gods stands in

Sasak – native of Lombok; also the language

sawah – individual rice field; see also *subak*

selandong – traditional scarf

selat – strait

serambi – open veranda on a *bale tani*, the traditional Lombok family house

Shiva – the creator and destroyer; one of the three great Hindu gods

sirih – betel nut, chewed as a mild narcotic

songket – silver or gold-threaded cloth, hand woven using a floating weft technique

sorong serah – marriage ceremony

subak – village association that organises rice terraces and shares out water for irrigation; each *sawah* owner must be a member of the subak

Sudra – common caste to which the majority of Balinese belong

sungai – river

taksu – divine interpreter for the gods

tanjung – cape or point

tektekan – ceremonial procession

teluk – gulf or bay

transmigrasi – government programme of transmigration

Trisakti – 'three in one' or trinity of Hindu gods: *Brahma, Shiva* and *Vishnu*

tuak – palm wine

tugu – lord of the ground

TU – Telepon Umum; a public telephone

Vishnu – the preserver; one of the three great Hindu gods

wantilan – large *bale* pavilion used for meetings, performances and cockfights

waria – female impersonator, transvestite or transgendered; combination of the words *wanita* (woman; female) and *pria* (man; male); see also *banci*

waringin – banyan tree; this large, shady tree, found at many temples, has drooping branches which root to produce new trees

wartel – public telephone office; contraction of *warung telekomunikasi*

warung – food stall, an Indonesian equivalent to a combination corner shop and snack bar

wayang kulit – leather puppet used in shadow puppet plays

wayang wong – masked drama playing scenes from the *Ramayana*

Wektu Telu – religion peculiar to Lombok, which originated in Bayan and combines many tenets of Islam and aspects of other faiths

Wesia – military caste and most numerous of the Balinese noble castes

WIB – Waktu Indonesia Barat; West Indonesia Time

WIT – Waktu Indonesia Tengah; Central Indonesia Time

wihara – monastery

wuku – Balinese calendar made up of 10 different weeks, between one and 10 days long, all running concurrently; see also *saka*

yeh – water (Balinese); also river

FOOD
Menus

The following is a list of words in Bahasa Indonesia which may be useful when ordering in a restuarant:

asam manis – sweet and sour; for example, ikan asam manis (sweet and sour fish)

ayam – chicken; for example, *ayam goreng* (fried chicken)

babi – pork; since most Indonesians are Muslim, pork is rarely found elsewhere in the archipelago, but on Bali it's a popular delicacy

daftar makanan – food menu; *daftar minuman* is the drinks menu

daging – beef

dingin – cold

enak – delicious (also means 'comfortable')

garam – salt

gula – sugar

ikan – fish; there's a wide variety available on Bali

ikan belut – eel; another Balinese delicacy, kids catch them in the rice paddies at night

kaki lima – a food cart, often sitting by the side of the road

kare – curry; as in *kare udang* (curried prawns)

kentang – potato; *kentang goreng* are fried potatoes, also known as potato chips or French fries, and served in all tourist restaurants

kepiting – crab

kodok – frog; frogs' legs are very popular on Bali and frogs are caught in the rice paddies at night

krupuk – prawn crackers; they often accompany meals

makan – the verb 'to eat', so *makan pagi* (morning food) is breakfast; *makan siang* (afternoon food) is lunch; and *makan malam* (evening food) is dinner.

manis – sweet

mentega – butter

pahat – literally means 'bitter', but is used to indicate 'no sugar' in tea or coffee

panas – hot (temperature)

pasar malam – 'night market'; often a great place for interesting and cheap food stalls *(warungs)*

pedas – hot (spicy)

rumah makan – restaurant; literally 'eating house'

sambal – a hot, spicy chilli sauce served as an accompaniment with most meals

sayur – vegetable

soto – soup; usually fairly spicy

telur – egg

udang – prawn

udang karang – lobster; very popular on Bali and comparatively economical

warung – a small shop or stall, commonly serving food and acting as a general store

Balinese Dishes

The following is a list of some of the dishes you're most likely to find on Bali:

apam – delicious pancake filled with nuts and sprinkled with sugar

bakmi goreng – fried noodles

bakso ayam – chicken soup with noodles and meatballs; a street-stall standard

cap cai – usually pronounced 'chap chai'. This is a mix of fried vegetables, although it sometimes comes with meat as well.

es campur – ice with fruit salad; a warung standard

fu yung hai – a sort of sweet-and-sour omelette

gado gado – another very popular Indonesian dish of steamed bean sprouts, various vegetables and a spicy peanut sauce

lontong – rice steamed in a banana leaf

mie goreng – fried noodles, sometimes with vegetables, sometimes with meat; much the same story as nasi goreng

mie kuah – noodle soup

nasi campur – steamed rice topped with a little bit of everything – some vegetables, some meat, a bit of fish, and a *krupuk* (prawn cracker) or two. It's a good, sim-ple, filling meal and is always cheap.

nasi goreng – this is the most everyday of Indonesian dishes. Nasi goreng simply means fried *(goreng)* rice *(nasi)* – a basic nasi goreng may be little more than fried rice with a few scraps of vegetable to spice it up a bit. Fancier preparations of nasi goreng may include meat, and a 'special' (or *istime-wa*) nasi goreng usually has a fried egg on top. Nasi goreng can range from the bland to the very good.

nasi Padang – Padang food, from the Padang region of Sumatra, is popular all over Indonesia. It's usually served cold and consists of rice (once again) with a whole variety of side dishes. The dishes are laid out before you and your final bill is calculated by the number of empty dishes left when you've finished eating – this can mean, however, that dishes have been left out (unrefrigerated) all day. Nasi Padang is traditionally eaten with the fingers and it's also traditionally very hot – *pedas* (spicy) not *panas* (hot).

nasi putih – white rice, usually plain, and either boiled or steamed

opor ayam – chicken pieces cooked in coconut milk

pisang goreng – fried banana fritters; a popular streetside snack

pisang molen – deep-fried bananas

rijstaffel – Dutch for 'rice table'; Indonesian food with a Dutch interpretation, it consists of lots of individual dishes with rice. It's rather like a glorified nasi cam-pur or a less heated nasi Padang. These are normally found in upmarket hotels. Bring along a big appetite.

sate – one of the best known Indonesian dishes, sate are tiny kebabs of various types of meat served with a spicy peanut sauce. Street sate sellers carry their charcoal grills around with them and cook the sate on the spot.

Lombok Specialities

ayam Taliwang – this dish of fried or grilled chicken with chilli sauce is originally from Taliwang on Sumbawa, but it has almost become a Lombok speciality

kangkung – water convolvulus, the leaves are used as a green vegetable (like spinach in the west); you can see it growing in the river at Ampenan (in Mataram)

kelor – hot soup with kangkung and/or other vegetables

pelecing – a sauce made with chilli, trassi (fish paste), tomato, salt and bumbu

pelecing manuk – fried chicken with pelecing

sares – this dish is made from the pith of a banana tree stem, with coconut juice, garlic and *bumbu*, a hot spice; sometimes it's mixed with chicken or meat

sate pusut – a snack with a sausage-shaped mixture of grated coconut, meat, bumbu and brown sugar wrapped on to a sate stick; try it at the market

serebuk – a dish of grated coconut, sliced vegetable and kangkung

timun urap – sliced cucumber with grated coconut, onion and garlic

Fruit

Bali and Lombok are blessed with a staggering variety of fruit, including:

avocat – avocado enthusiasts may suffer from overkill on Bali – they're plentiful and cheap; Balinese regard them as a sweet fruit, and drink avocado juice mixed with sweetened condensed milk

blimbing – the 'starfruit' is a cool, crispy, watery tasting fruit – if you cut a slice you'll immediately see where the name comes from

durian – the most infamous tropical fruit, the durian is a large green fruit with a hard, spiky exterior. Cracking it open reveals a truly horrific stench. Hotels and airlines in Asia often ban durians, so it's hardly surprising that becoming a durian aficionado takes some time! One description of the durian compared it to eating a superb raspberry blancmange inside a revolting public toilet, but true believers learn to savour even the smell.

jambu – guava; the crispy, pink, pear-shaped ones are particularly popular

jeruk – the all-purpose term for citrus fruit. There is a wide variety available on Bali, and jeruk are chiefly grown in the central mountains. The main varieties include the huge *jeruk muntis* or *jerunga*, known in the west as the pomelo. It's larger than a grapefruit but with a very thick skin, a sweeter, more orange-like taste and segments that come apart very easily. Regular oranges are known as *jeruk manis* (sweet jeruk). The small tangerine-like oranges – which are often quite green – are *jeruk baras*. Lemons are *jeruk nipis*.

makiza – like a big yellow passionfruit

manggu – mango; cheap and delicious in season

mangosteen – one of the most famous of tropical fruits, the mangosteen is a small purple-brown fruit. The outer covering cracks open to reveal tasty pure-white segments with an indescribably fine flavour. Queen Victoria once offered a reward to anyone able to bring a mangosteen back to England which would still be edible on arrival.

nanas – pineapple

nangka – also known as jackfruit, this is an enormous yellow-green fruit that can weigh over 20 kg. Inside there are hundreds of individual bright-yellow segments with a distinctive taste and a slightly rubbery texture. As they ripen on the tree each nangka may be separately protected in a bag.

papaya or *paw paw* – these fruits are not that unusual in the west. It's actually a native of South America and was brought to the Philippines by the Spanish, and from there spread to other parts of South-East Asia.

pisang – bananas; the variety of pisang available on Bali is quite surprising

rambutan – a bright red fruit covered in soft, hairy spines; the name means 'hairy'. Break it open to reveal a delicious white fruit closely related to the lychee.

salak – found chiefly in Indonesia, the salak is immediately recognisable by its perfect brown 'snakeskin' covering. Peel it off to reveal segments that, in texture, are like a cross between an apple and a walnut but in taste are unique. Bali salaks are much nicer than any others.

sawo – looks like a potato, tastes like a pear

zurzat – also spelt 'sirsat', and known in the west as soursop. The warty green skin of the zurzat covers a thirst-quenching interior with a slightly lemonish, tart taste. You can peel it off or slice it into segsments. Zurzats are ripe when the skin has begun to lose its fresh green colouring and become darker and spotty. It should then feel slightly squishy rather than firm.

DRINKS

Popular Indonesian and Balinese drinks, both alcoholic and non-alcoholic, include:

air jeruk – lemon or orange juice

air minum – drinking water (*air* means water, and is very hard to pronounce); *air putih* (white water) and *air rebus* (boiled water) are also used.

arak – distilled rice brandy; one stage on from *brem*; it can have a real kick. It's usually homemade, although even the locally bottled brands look home produced. It makes quite a good mixed drink with 7-Up or Sprite. Mixed with lemonade or orange juice it's called an *arak attack*.

brem – rice wine; either home produced or the commercially bottled brand Bali Brem. It tastes a bit like sherry – an acquired taste but not bad after a few bottles!

es buah – more a dessert than a drink, es buah is a curious combination of crushed ice, condensed milk, shaved coconut, syrup, jelly and fruit. It can be delicious.

es juice – although you should be a little careful about ice and water, the Balinese make delicious fruit drinks which are generally safe to try. In particular, the ice-juice drinks are a real taste treat – just take one or two varieties of tropical fruit, add crushed ice and pass it all through a blender. You can produce mind-blowing combinations of orange, banana, mango, pineapple, jackfruit, zurzat or whatever else is available.

lassi – a refreshing yoghurt-based drink

stroop – cordial

susu – milk; not a very common drink in Indonesia, although you can get long-life milk in cartons; ask for 'ultrsa'

teh – tea; some people are not enthusiastic about Indonesian tea but if you don't need a strong, bend-the-teaspoon-style brew you'll probably find it's quite OK

tuak – palm beer, usually homemade; it's a white or pinkish colour, and almost slimy

LONELY PLANET

Phrasebooks

Lonely Planet phrasebooks are packed with essential words and phrases to help travellers communicate with the locals. With colour tabs for quick reference, an extensive vocabulary, and use of script, these handy pocket-sized language guides cover day-to-day travel situations.

- handy pocket-sized books
- easy to understand Pronunciation chapter
- clear & comprehensive Grammar chapter
- romanisation alongside script to allow ease of pronunciation
- script throughout so users can point to phrases for every situations
- full of cultural information and tips for the traveller

'...vital for a real DIY spirit and attitude in language learning'
– Backpacker

'the phrasebooks have good cultural backgrounders and offer solid advice for challenging situations in remote locations'
– San Francisco Examiner

Arabic (Egyptian) • Arabic (Moroccan) • Australia *(Australian English, Aboriginal and Torres Strait languages)* • Baltic States *(Estonian, Latvian, Lithuanian)* • Bengali • Brazilian • Burmese • Cantonese • Central Asia • Central Europe *(Czech, French, German, Hungarian, Italian, Slovak)* • Eastern Europe *(Bulgarian, Czech, Hungarian, Polish, Romanian, Slovak)* • Egyptian Arabic • Ethiopian (Amharic) • Fijian • French • German • Greek • Hill Tribes • Hindi/Urdu • Indonesian • Italian • Japanese • Korean • Lao • Malay • Mandarin • Mediterranean Europe *(Albanian, Croatian, Greek, Italian, Macedonian, Maltese, Serbian, Slovene)* • Mongolian • Nepali • Papua New Guinea • Pilipino (Tagalog) • Quechua • Russian • Scandinavian Europe *(Danish, Finnish, Icelandic, Norwegian, Swedish)* • South-East Asia *(Burmese, Indonesian, Khmer, Lao, Malay, Tagalog Pilipino, Thai, Vietnamese)* • Spanish (Castilian) *(also includes Catalan, Galician and Basque)* • Spanish (Latin American) • Sri Lanka • Swahili • Thai • Tibetan • Turkish • Ukrainian • USA *(US English, Vernacular Talk, Native American languages, Hawaiian)* • Vietnamese • Western Europe *(Basque, Catalan, Dutch, French, German, Greek, Irish)*

LONELY PLANET

Lonely Planet Journeys

JOURNEYS is a unique collection of travel writing – published by the company that understands travel better than anyone else. It is a series for anyone who has ever experienced – or dreamed of – the magical moment when they encountered a strange culture or saw a place for the first time. They are tales to read while you're planning a trip, while you're on the road or while you're in an armchair, in front of a fire.

These outstanding titles explore our planet through the eyes of a diverse group of international writers. JOURNEYS books catch the spirit of a place, illuminate a culture, recount a crazy adventure, or introduce a fascinating way of life. They always entertain, and always enrich the experience of travel.

ISLANDS IN THE CLOUDS
Travels in the Highlands of New Guinea
Isabella Tree

This is the fascinating account of a journey to the remote and beautiful Highlands of Papua New Guinea and Irian Jaya: one of the most extraordinary and dangerous regions on the planet. Tree travels with a PNG Highlander who introduces her to his intriguing and complex world, changing rapidly as it collides with twentieth-century technology. *Islands in the Clouds* is a thoughtful, moving book.

SEAN & DAVID'S LONG DRIVE
Sean Condon

Sean and David are young townies who have rarely strayed beyond city limits. One day, for no good reason, they set out to discover their homeland, and what follows is a wildly entertaining adventure that covers half of Australia.

'a hilariously detailed log of two burned out friends' – *Rolling Stone*

DRIVE THRU AMERICA
Sean Condon

If you've ever wanted to drive across the USA but couldn't find the time (or afford the gas), *Drive Thru America* is perfect for you. In his search for American myths and realities – along with comfort, cable TV and good, reasonably priced coffee – Sean Condon paints a hilarious road-portrait of the USA.

'entertaining and laugh-out-loud funny' – *Alex Wilber, Travel editor, Amazon.com*

BRIEF ENCOUNTERS
Stories of Love, Sex & Travel
edited by Michelle de Kretser

Love affairs on the road, passionate holiday flings, disastrous pick-ups, erotic encounters . . . In this seductive collection of stories, 22 authors from around the world write about travel romances. Combining fiction and reportage, *Brief Encounters* is must-have reading – for everyone who has dreamt of escape with that perfect stranger.

Includes stories by Pico Iyer, Mary Morris, Emily Perkins, Mona Simpson, Lisa St Aubin de Terán, Paul Theroux and Sara Wheeler.

LONELY PLANET

Lonely Planet Travel Atlases

Lonely Planet has long been famous for the number and quality of its guidebook maps. Now we've gone one step further and produced a handy companion series: Lonely Planet travel atlases – maps of a country produced in book form.

Unlike other maps, which look good but lead travellers astray, our travel atlases have been researched on the road by Lonely Planet's experienced team of writers. All details are carefully checked to ensure the atlas corresponds with the equivalent Lonely Planet guidebook.

- full-colour throughout
- maps researched and checked by Lonely Planet authors
- place names correspond with Lonely Planet guidebooks
- no confusing spelling differences
- legend and travelling information in English, French, German, Japanese and Spanish
- size: 230 x 160 mm

Available now: Chile & Easter Island ● Egypt ● India & Bangladesh ● Israel & the Palestinian Territories ● Jordan, Syria & Lebanon ● Kenya ● Laos ● Portugal ● South Africa, Lesotho & Swaziland ● Thailand ● Turkey ● Vietnam ● Zimbabwe, Botswana & Namibia

Lonely Planet TV Series & Videos

Lonely Planet travel guides have been brought to life on television screens around the world. Like our guides, the programmes are based on the joy of independent travel, and look honestly at some of the most exciting, picturesque and frustrating places in the world. Each show is presented by one of three travellers from Australia, England or the USA and combines an innovative mixture of video, Super-8 film, atmospheric soundscapes and original music.

Videos of each episode – containing additional footage not shown on television – are available from good book and video shops, but the availability of individual videos varies with regional screening schedules.

Video destinations include: Alaska ● American Rockies ● Australia – The South-East ● Baja California & the Copper Canyon ● Brazil ● Central Asia ● Chile & Easter Island ● Corsica, Sicily & Sardinia – The Mediterranean Islands ● East Africa (Tanzania & Zanzibar) ● Ecuador & the Galapagos Islands ● Greenland & Iceland ● Indonesia ● Israel & the Sinai Desert ● Jamaica ● Japan ● La Ruta Maya ● Morocco ● New York ● North India ● Pacific Islands (Fiji, Solomon Islands & Vanuatu) ● South India ● South West China ● Turkey ● Vietnam ● West Africa ● Zimbabwe, Botswana & Namibia

The Lonely Planet TV series is produced by: Pilot Productions
The Old Studio
18 Middle Row
London W10 5AT UK

LONELY PLANET

Guides by Region

Lonely Planet is known worldwide for publishing practical, reliable and no-nonsense travel information in our guides and on our web site. The Lonely Planet list covers just about every accessible part of the world. Currently there are nine series: travel guides, shoestring guides, walking guides, city guides, phrasebooks, audio packs, travel atlases, diving and snorkelling guides and travel literature.

AFRICA Africa – the South • Africa on a shoestring • Arabic (Egyptian) phrasebook • Arabic (Moroccan) phrasebook • Cairo • Cape Town • Central Africa • East Africa • Egypt • Egypt travel atlas • Ethiopian (Amharic) phrasebook • The Gambia & Senegal • Kenya • Kenya travel atlas • Malawi, Mozambique & Zambia • Morocco • North Africa • South Africa, Lesotho & Swaziland • South Africa, Lesotho & Swaziland travel atlas • Swahili phrasebook • Trekking in East Africa • Tunisia • West Africa • Zimbabwe, Botswana & Namibia • Zimbabwe, Botswana & Namibia travel atlas
Travel Literature: The Rainbird: A Central African Journey • Songs to an African Sunset: A Zimbabwean Story • Mali Blues: Traveling to an African Beat

AUSTRALIA & THE PACIFIC Australia • Australian phrasebook • Bushwalking in Australia • Bushwalking in Papua New Guinea • Fiji • Fijian phrasebook • Islands of Australia's Great Barrier Reef • Melbourne • Micronesia • New Caledonia • New South Wales & the ACT • New Zealand • Northern Territory • Outback Australia • Papua New Guinea • Papua New Guinea (Pidgin) phrasebook • Queensland • Rarotonga & the Cook Islands • Samoa • Solomon Islands • South Australia • Sydney • Tahiti & French Polynesia • Tasmania • Tonga • Tramping in New Zealand • Vanuatu • Victoria • Western Australia
Travel Literature: Islands in the Clouds • Sean & David's Long Drive

CENTRAL AMERICA & THE CARIBBEAN Bahamas and Turks & Caicos • Bermuda • Central America on a shoestring • Costa Rica • Cuba • Eastern Caribbean • Guatemala, Belize & Yucatán: La Ruta Maya • Jamaica • Mexico • Mexico City • Panama
Travel Literature: Green Dreams: Travels in Central America

EUROPE Amsterdam • Andalucia • Austria • Baltic States phrasebook • Berlin • Britain • Central Europe • Central Europe phrasebook • Czech & Slovak Republics • Denmark • Dublin • Eastern Europe • Eastern Europe phrasebook • Estonia, Latvia & Lithuania • Finland • France • French phrasebook • Germany • German phrasebook • Greece • Greek phrasebook • Hungary • Iceland, Greenland & the Faroe Islands • Ireland • Italian phrasebook • Italy • Lisbon • London • Mediterranean Europe • Mediterranean Europe phrasebook • Paris • Poland • Portugal • Portugal travel atlas • Prague • Romania & Moldova • Russia, Ukraine & Belarus • Russian phrasebook • Scandinavian & Baltic Europe • Scandinavian Europe phrasebook • Slovenia • Spain • Spanish phrasebook • St Petersburg • Switzerland • Trekking in Spain • Ukrainian phrasebook • Vienna • Walking in Britain • Walking in Italy • Walking in Switzerland • Western Europe • Western Europe phrasebook
Travel Literature: The Olive Grove: Travels in Greece

INDIAN SUBCONTINENT Bangladesh • Bengali phrasebook • Bhutan • Delhi • Goa • Hindi/Urdu phrasebook • India • India & Bangladesh travel atlas • Indian Himalaya • Karakoram Highway • Nepal • Nepali phrasebook • Pakistan • Rajasthan • South India • Sri Lanka • Sri Lanka phrasebook • Trekking in the Indian Himalaya • Trekking in the Karakoram & Hindukush • Trekking in the Nepal Himalaya
Travel Literature: In Rajasthan • Shopping for Buddhas

LONELY PLANET

Mail Order

Lonely Planet products are distributed worldwide. They are also available by mail order from Lonely Planet, so if you have difficulty finding a title please write to us. North and South American residents should write to 150 Linden St, Oakland CA 94607, USA; European and African residents should write to 10a Spring Place, London NW5 3BH; and residents of other countries to PO Box 617, Hawthorn, Victoria 3122, Australia.

ISLANDS OF THE INDIAN OCEAN Madagascar & Comoros • Maldives • Mauritius, Reúnion & Seychelles

MIDDLE EAST & CENTRAL ASIA Arab Gulf States • Central Asia • Central Asia phrasebook • Iran • Israel & the Palestinian Territories • Israel & the Palestinian Territories travel atlas • Istanbul • Jerusalem • Jordan & Syria • Jordan, Syria & Lebanon travel atlas • Lebanon • Middle East on a shoestring • Turkey • Turkish phrasebook • Turkey travel atlas • Yemen
Travel Literature: The Gates of Damascus • Kingdom of the Film Stars: Journey into Jordan

NORTH AMERICA Alaska • Backpacking in Alaska • Baja California • California & Nevada • Canada • Florida • Hawaii • Honolulu • Los Angeles • Miami • New England USA • New Orleans • New York City • New York, New Jersey & Pennsylvania • Pacific Northwest USA • Rocky Mountain States • San Francisco • Seattle • Southwest USA • USA phrasebook • Washington, DC & the Capital Region
Travel Literature: Drive Thru America

NORTH-EAST ASIA Beijing • Cantonese phrasebook • China • Hong Kong • Hong Kong, Macau & Guangzhou • Japan • Japanese phrasebook • Japanese audio pack • Korea • Korean phrasebook • Kyoto • Mandarin phrasebook • Mongolia • Mongolian phrasebook • North-East Asia on a shoestring • Seoul • South West China • Taiwan • Tibet • Tibet phrasebook • Tokyo
Travel Literature: Lost Japan

SOUTH AMERICA Argentina, Uruguay & Paraguay • Bolivia • Brazil • Brazilian phrasebook • Buenos Aires • Chile & Easter Island • Chile & Easter Island travel atlas • Colombia • Ecuador & the Galapagos Islands • Latin American (Spanish) phrasebook • Peru • Quechua phrasebook • Rio de Janeiro • South America on a shoestring • Trekking in the Patagonian Andes • Venezuela
Travel Literature: Full Circle: A South American Journey

SOUTH-EAST ASIA Bali & Lombok • Bangkok • Burmese phrasebook • Cambodia • Hill Tribes phrasebook • Ho Chi Minh City • Indonesia • Indonesian phrasebook • Indonesian audio pack • Jakarta • Java • Laos • Lao phrasebook • Laos travel atlas • Malay phrasebook • Malaysia, Singapore & Brunei • Myanmar (Burma) • Philippines • Pilipino (Tagalog) phrasebook • Singapore • South-East Asia on a shoestring • South-East Asia phrasebook • Thailand • Thailand's Islands & Beaches • Thailand travel atlas • Thai phrasebook • Thai audio pack • Vietnam • Vietnamese phrasebook • Vietnam travel atlas

ALSO AVAILABLE: Antarctica • Brief Encounters: Stories of Love, Sex & Travel • Chasing Rickshaws • Not the Only Planet: Travel Stories from Science Fiction • Travel with Children • Traveller's Tales

LONELY PLANET

Lonely Planet Online
www.lonelyplanet.com *or* AOL keyword: lp

Whether you've just begun planning your next trip, or you're chasing down specific info on currency regulations or visa requirements, check out Lonely Planet Online for up-to-the-minute travel information.

As well as mini guides to more than 250 destinations, you'll find maps, photos, travel news, health and visa updates, travel advisories, and discussion of the ecological and political issues you need to be aware of as you travel. You'll also find timely upgrades to popular guidebooks which you can print out and stick in the back of your book.

There's also an online travellers' forum where you can share your experience of life on the road, meet travel companions and ask other travellers for their recommendations and advice.

And of course we have a complete and up-to-date list of all Lonely Planet travel products including travel guides, diving and snorkelling guides, phrasebooks, atlases, travel literature and videos, and a simple online ordering facility if you can't find the book you want elsewhere.

Lonely Planet Diving & Snorkelling Guides

Known for indispensible guidebooks to destinations all over the world, Lonely Planet's Pisces Books are the most popular series of diving and snorkelling titles available.

There are three series: **Diving & Snorkelling Guides**, **Shipwreck Diving** series, and **Dive Into History**. Full colour throughout, the **Diving & Snorkelling Guides** combine quality photographs with detailed descriptions of the best dive sites for each location, giving divers a glimpse of what they can expect both on land and in water. The **Dive Into History** series is perfect for the adventure diver or armchair traveller. The **Shipwreck Diving** series provides all the details for exploring the most interesting wrecks in the Atlantic and Pacific oceans. The list also includes underwater nature and technical guides.

Index

Abbreviations

Text

Bold indicates maps.
Italics indicates boxed text.

Bold indicates maps.
Italics indicates boxed text.

Bold indicates maps.
Italics indicates boxed text.

Boxed Text

kamut
Apaka ~~tumut~~ Gilla?
j itgede = jeet gun dee

MAP LEGEND

BOUNDARIES

.... International
.... Provincial
.... Disputed

HYDROGRAPHY

.... Coastline
.... River, Creek
.... Lake
.... Intermittent Lake
.... Salt Lake
.... Canal
.... Spring, Rapids
.... Waterfalls
.... Swamp

○ CAPITAL	National Capital
◉ CAPITAL	Provincial Capital
● CITY	City
● Town	Town
● Village	Village
○	Point of Interest
■	Place to Stay
▲	Camping Ground
⌂	Caravan Park
⌂	Hut or Chalet
▼	Place to Eat
▣	Pub or Bar

ROUTES & TRANSPORT

.... Freeway
.... Highway
.... Major Road
.... Minor Road
.... Unsealed Road
.... City Freeway
.... City Highway
.... City Road
.... City Street, Lane

.... Pedestrian Mall
.... Tunnel
.... Train Route & Station
.... Metro & Station
.... Tramway
.... Cable Car or Chairlift
.... Walking Track
.... Walking Tour
.... Ferry Route

AREA FEATURES

.... Building
.... Park, Gardens
.... Cemetery
.... Market
.... Beach, Desert
.... Urban Area

MAP SYMBOLS

.... Airport
.... Archaeological Site
.... Bank
.... Beach, Surf Beach
.... Bird Sanctuary
.... Cave
.... Cathedral, Church
.... Cliff or Escarpment
.... Dive Site, Snorkelling
.... Embassy
.... Hospital
.... Lighthouse
.... Monument
.... Mosque

.... Mountain or Hill
.... Museum
.... Pass
.... Police Station
.... Post Office
.... Shopping Centre
.... Stately Home
.... Swimming Pool
.... Temple (Balinese)
.... Temple (Buddhist)
.... Temple (Hindu)
.... Temple (Other)
.... Tourist Information
.... Transport

Note: not all symbols displayed above appear in this book

LONELY PLANET OFFICES

Australia
PO Box 617, Hawthorn, Victoria 3122
☎ (03) 9819 1877 fax (03) 9819 6459
email: talk2us@lonelyplanet.com.au

USA
150 Linden St, Oakland, CA 94607
☎ (510) 893 8555 TOLL FREE: 800 275 8555
fax (510) 893 8572
email: info@lonelyplanet.com

UK
10a Spring Place, London, NW5 3BH
☎ (0171) 428 4800 fax (0171) 428 4828
email: go@lonelyplanet.co.uk

France
1 rue du Dahomey, 75011 Paris
☎ 01 55 25 33 00 fax 01 55 25 33 01
email: bip@lonelyplanet.fr
3615 lonelyplanet *(1,29 F TTC/min)*

**World Wide Web: www.lonelyplanet.com *or* AOL keyword: lp
Lonely Planet Images: lpi@lonelyplanet.com.au**